LANGUAGE TOPICS II

LANGUAGE TOPICS
Essays in honour of Michael Halliday

Edited by

ROSS STEELE and TERRY THREADGOLD

Volume II

JOHN BENJAMINS PUBLISHING COMPANY
AMSTERDAM/PHILADELPHIA

1987

The publication of this *Festschrift* to honour Michael Halliday was made possible by generous financial assistance from the APPLIED LINGUISTICS ASSOCIATION OF AUSTRALIA.

Library of Congress Cataloging in Publication Data

Language topics.

Includes bibliographies.
1. Language and languages. 2. Linguistics. 3. Halliday, M.A.K. (Michael Alexander Kirkwood), 1925-   . II. Steele, Ross. III. Threadgold, Terry.
P26.H29L36   1987   410   87-20848
ISBN 90 272 2042 5 (European)/1-55619-028-X (U.S.: set: alk. paper)
ISBN 90 272 2043 3 (European)/1-55619-029-8 (U.S.: v. 1: alk. paper)
ISBN 90 272 2044 1 (European)/1-55619-030-1 (U.S.: v. 2: alk. paper)

© Copyright 1987 - John Benjamins B.V.
No part of this book may be reproduced in any form, by print, photoprint, microfilm, or any other means, without written permission from the publisher.

Contents

VOLUME I

Contributors   xiii

Introduction   xix
Ross Steele

Comprehensive bibliography of books and articles by M.A.K. Halliday   xxiii

1. Starting Points

Sentence patterns and predicate classes   3
František Daneš

On two starting points of communication   23
Jan Firbas

The position of Czech linguistics in theme-focus research   47
Petr Sgall

J.R. Firth in retrospect: a view from the eighties   57
Eugénie J.A. Henderson

Daniel Jones' "classical" model of pronunciation training: an applied linguistic revaluation   69
John L.M. Trim

The Linguistic Sciences and Language Teaching revisited   79
Peter Strevens

2. Language Development

"Don't you get bored speaking only English?" — Expressions of metalinguistic awareness in a bilingual child   85
Michael Clyne

Toward practical theory: Halliday applied 105
Jerome C. Harste

Development of referential cohesion in a child's monologues 119
Katherine Nelson and Elena Levy

Exploring the textual properties of "proto-reading" 137
Christine C. Pappas

Before speaking: across cultures 163
John Regan, Zhao Shuming and Xiao-Ling Hong

Sharing makes sense: intersubjectivity and the making of an infant's meaning 177
Colwyn Trevarthen

The development of conversation 201
Gordon Wells and Mary Gutfreund

3. Sign, Context and Change

Today 229
Kenneth L. Pike

For Michael Halliday: *in hoc signo vinces*: sign design 231
Thomas A. Sebeok

George Herbert's *Love III* and its many mansions 233
R.J. Handscombe

The past and prejudice: toward de-mythologizing the English canon 245
Braj B. Kachru

Writing systems and language change in English 257
Angus McIntosh

On the major diseases of linguistics with some suggested cures and antidotes 269
Adam Makkai

"Breaking the Seal of Time": the pragmatics of poetics 281
Jacob L. Mey

The use of systemic linguistics in translation analysis and criticism 293
Peter Newmark

CONTENTS

Le graphémique et l'iconique dans le message — 305
Bernard Pottier

Order and entropy in natural language — 315
Andrew Schiller

Sign and signifex — 333
W.C. Watt

The practice and theory of translation — 347
Colin Yallop

4. Language Around the World

Grammatical relations, semantic roles and topic-comment structure in a New Guinea Highland language: Harway — 355
Bernard Comrie

Toward a bilingual dictionary of idioms: Hindi-English — 367
Yamuna Kachru

Mind your language: conscious and unconscious structuring in Swahili — 379
Joan Maw

Communicative functions of particles in Singapore English — 391
John Platt

Place-name study in Japan — 403
Seiji Shibata

Teaching English as a second language in India: focus on objectives — 417
Shivendra K. Verma

The impersonal verb construction in Australian languages — 425
Michael Walsh

Semantics and world view in languages of the Santa Cruz Archipelago, Solomon Islands — 439
Stephen A. Wurm

References — 453

VOLUME II

Contributors   xi

1. The Design of Language

Reproductive furniture and extinguished professors   3
Jean Aitchison

English intensifiers and their idiosyncrasies   15
D.J. Allerton

The tradition of structural analogy   33
John A. Anderson

Syspro: a computerized method for writing system networks and deriving selection expressions   45
Michael Cummings

Cultural, situational and modal labels in dictionaries of English   65
Arthur Delbridge

Morphological islands: constraint or preference?   71
Wolfgang U. Dressler

Some "dia-categories"   81
Jeffrey O. Ellis

English quantifiers from noun sources   95
Adrienne Lehrer

Two types of semantic widening and their relation to metaphor   107
Samuel R. Levin

The indefinite article and the numeral one   123
James P. Thorne

2. Text and Discourse

A comparison of process types in Poe and Melville   131
James D. Benson and William S. Greaves

Intonation and the grammar of speech   145
David Brazil

CONTENTS

Some preliminary evidence for phonetic adjustment strategies in communication difficulty — 161
John E. Clark, James F. Lubker and Sharon Hunnicutt

Evaluative text analysis — 181
Malcolm Coulthard

Gobbledegook: the tyranny of linguistic conceits — 191
Robert D. Eagleson

Text strategies: single, dual, multiple — 203
Nils Erik Enkvist

Finishing other's talk: some structural and pragmatic features of completion offers — 213
Allen D. Grimshaw

The textual basis of verbal inflections: the case of Yatzachi Zapotec — 237
Carol C. Mock

On the concepts of "style" and "register" in sociolinguistics — 261
Fred C.C. Peng

Social constraints on grammatical variables: tense choice in English — 281
Guenter Plum and Ann Cowling

Some phonological constraints on grammatical formations: examples from four languages — 307
R.H. Robins

Collocation: a progress report — 319
John McH. Sinclair

Linguistic analysis of real estate commission agreements in a civil law suit — 333
Roger W. Shuy

Antithesis: a study in clause combining and discourse structure — 359
Sandra A. Thompson and William C. Mann

3. Exploring Language as Social Semiotic

The hegemony of information — 385
Richard W. Bailey

Many sentences and difficult texts 401
Mackie J.-V. Blanton

Explaining moments of conflict in discourse 413
Christopher N. Candlin

Is there a literary language? 431
Ronald A. Carter

Coherence in language and culture 451
Benjamin N. Colby

Semiotics of document design 461
Mary Ann Eiler

Notes on critical linguistics 481
Roger Fowler

Grammar, society and the pronoun 493
Richard A. Hudson

The structure of situations and the analysis of text 507
Bernard A. Mohan

The place of socio-semiotics in contemporary thought 523
Gordon Bruce McKellar

Changing the subject 549
Terry Threadgold

4. An Interview with Michael Halliday 601
Paul J. Thibault

References 629

Contributors

JEAN AITCHISON
Department of Language Studies
London School of Economics
Houghton St.
Aldwych
London WC2A 2AE
U.K.

D.J. ALLERTON
Englisches Seminar der Universität Basel
Nadelberg 6
4051 Basel
Switzerland

JOHN A. ANDERSON
Department of English
University of Edinburgh
George Square
Edinburgh EH8 9JX
U.K.

RICHARD W. BAILEY
Department of English
University of Michigan
Ann Arbor MI 48109
U.S.A.

JAMES D. BENSON
English Department
Glendon College
2275 Bayview Avenue
Toronto Ont.
Canada M4N 3M6

MACKIE J.-V. BLANTON
Department of English
University of New Orleans
New Orleans LA 70148
U.S.A.

DAVID C. BRAZIL
Department of English
 Language & Literature
University of Birmingham
P.O. Box 363
Birmingham B15 2TT
U.K.

CHRISTOPHER N. CANDLIN
School of English & Linguistics
Macquarie University
North Ryde NSW 2113
Australia

RONALD A. CARTER
Department of English Studies
University of Nottingham
Nottingham NG7 2RD
U.K.

JOHN E. CLARK
School of English & Linguistics
Macquarie University
North Ryde NSW 2113
Australia

MICHAEL CLYNE
Centre for Migrant & Intercultural Studies
Monash University
Clayton, Vic. 3168
Australia

BENJAMIN N. COLBY
School of Social Sciences
University of California
Irvine CA 92717
U.S.A.

CONTRIBUTORS

BERNARD COMRIE
Department of Linguistics
University of Southern California
Los Angeles CA 90089
U.S.A.

MALCOLM COULTHARD
Department of English Language
& Literature
University of Birmingham
P.O. Box 363
Birmingham BI5 2TT
U.K.

ANN COWLING
Department of Linguistics
University of Sydney
Sydney NSW 2006
Australia

MICHAEL J. CUMMINGS
English Department
Glendon College
York University
2275 Bayview Avenue
Toronto Ont.
Canada M4N 3M6

FRANTIŠEK DANEŠ
Czechoslovak Academy of Sciences
Institute of the Czech Language
Velvarska 19
160 00 Praha 6
Czechoslovakia

ARTHUR DELBRIDGE
School of English & Linguistics
Macquarie University
North Ryde NSW 2113
Australia

WOLFGANG U. DRESSLER
Department of Linguistics
University of Vienna
Liechtensteinstrasse 46a
1090 Vienna
Austria

ROBERT D. EAGLESON
Department of English
University of Sydney
Sydney N.S.W. 2006
Australia

MARY ANN EILER
Department of Data Release Services
American Medical Association
535 North Dearborn Street
Chicago IL 60610
U.S.A

JEFFREY O. ELLIS
Formerly Reader in General Linguistics
University of Aston, Birmingham
4 Warrender Park Terrace
Edinburgh 9
U.K.

NILS E. ENKVIST
Department of English
Stiftelsens för Abo Akademi
Forskningsinstitut
Kaskisgatan 2C14
20700 Abo
Finland

JAN FIRBAS
Department of English
University of Brno
A. Nováka 1
602 00 Brno 2
Czechoslovakia

ROGER FOWLER
School of English & American Studies
University of East Anglia
Norwich NR4 7TJ
U.K.

WILLIAM S. GREAVES
English Department
Glendon College
2275 Bayview Avenue
Toronto Ont.
Canada M4N 3M68

CONTRIBUTORS

ALLEN D. GRIMSHAW
Department of Sociology
Indiana University
Bloomington IN 47401
U.S.A.

MARY GUTFREUND
Centre for the Study of Language and Communication
School of Education
University of Bristol
22 Berkeley Square
Bristol BS8 1HP
U.K.

RICHARD J. HANDSCOMBE
Department of English
Glendon College
York University
2275 Bayview Avenue
Toronto Ont.
Canada M4N 3M6

JEROME C. HARSTE
Language Education
Indiana University
Bloomington IN 47405
U.S.A.

EUGÉNIE J.A. HENDERSON
Department of Phonetics & Linguistics
School of Oriental and African Studies
University of London
Malet Street
London WC1E 7HP
U.K.

XIAO-LING HONG
Nanjing University
People's Republic of China

RICHARD A. HUDSON
Department of Phonetics & Linguistics
University College London
Gower Street
London WC1E 6BT
U.K.

SHARON HUNNICUT
Department of Speech Communication and Music Acoustics
Royal Institute of Technology
Stockholm
Sweden

BRAJ B. KACHRU
Department of Linguistics
University of Illinois
707 S. Mathews Avenue
Urbana IL 61801
U.S.A.

YAMUNA KACHRU
Department of Linguistics
University of Illinois
707 S. Mathews Avenue
Urbana IL 61801
U.S.A.

ADRIENNE LEHRER
Department of Linguistics
University of Arizona
Tucson AZ 85721
U.S.A.

SAMUEL R. LEVIN
English & Linguistics
Graduate Center
City University of New York
33 West 42nd Street
New York N.Y. 10036
U.S.A.

ELENA LEVY
Developmental Psychology
Graduate Center
City University of New York
33 West 42nd Street
New York NY 10036
U.S.A.

JAMES F. LUBKER
Department of Speech and Hearing
University of Vermont
Burlington VT 05405
U.S.A.

CONTRIBUTORS

ADAM MAKKAI
Linguistics Department
University of Illinois
P.O. Box 4348
Chicago IL 60680
U.S.A.

WILLIAM C. MANN
Information Sciences Institute
University of Southern California
4676 Admiralty Way
Marina del Rey CA 902 92
U.S.A.

JOAN MAW
School of Oriental & African Studies
University of London
Malet Street
London WCIE 7HP
U.K.

ANGUS McINTOSH
Gayre Institute for Medieval English &
  Scottish Dialectology
University of Edinburgh
2 Buccleuch Place
Edinburgh EH8 9LW
U.K.

GORDON BRUCE McKELLAR
Injury Research
Casa Colina Hospital for Rehabilitative
  Medicine
Pomona California
U.S.A.

JACOB L. MEY
Rasmus Rask Institute for Linguistics
Odense University
Campusvej 55
5230 Odense M
Denmark

CAROL C. MOCK
Department of English
Southwest Missouri State University
901 South National
Springfield MO 65804
U.S.A.

BERNARD A. MOHAN
Language Education
University of British Columbia
2125 Main Hall
Vancouver BC
Canada V6T 125

KATHERINE NELSON
Developmental Psychology
Graduate Center
City University of New York
33 West 42nd Street
New York NY 10036
U.S.A.

PETER NEWMARK
Department of Linguistic and
  International Studies
University of Surrey
Guildford GU2 5XH
U.K.

CHRISTINE C. PAPPAS
College of Education
University of Kentucky
Lexington KY 40506
U.S.A.

FRED C.C. PENG
Department of Linguistics
International Christian University
10-2, 3 Chome, Osawa
Mutaka Tokyo 181
Japan

KENNETH L. PIKE
Summer Institute of Linguistics
7500 W. Camp Wisdom Road
Dallas TX 75236
U.S.A.

JOHN PLATT
Department of Linguistics
Monash University
Clayton Vic. 3168
Australia

CONTRIBUTORS

GUENTER PLUM
Department of Linguistics
University of Sydney
Sydney N.S.W. 2006
Australia

BERNARD POTTIER
Department of Linguistics
Université de Paris-Sorbonne
1 rue Victor Cousin
75005 Paris
France

JOHN REGAN
Claremont Graduate School
Claremont CA 91711
U.S.A.

R.H. ROBINS
Department of Phonetics & Linguistics
School of Oriental and African Studies
University of London
Malet Street
London WC1E 7HP
U.K.

ANDREW SCHILLER
Linguistics Department
University of Illinois
Chicago IL 60680
U.S.A.

THOMAS A. SEBEOK
Research Center for Language
  and Semiotic Studies
P.O. Box 10
Indiana University
Bloomington IN 47402
U.S.A.

PETR SGALL
Department of Applied Mathematics
Faculty of Mathematics & Physics
Charles University
Malostranske n.25
118 00 Prague 1
Czechoslovakia

SEIJI SHIBATA
English Studies Program
Language Education Sector
Naruto Kyoiku National University
Takashima, Naruto-City
Tokushima 772
Japan

ROGER W. SHUY
Department of Linguistics
Georgetown University
Washington DC 20057
U.S.A.

JOHN McH. SINCLAIR
Department of English Language &
  Literature
University of Birmingham
P.O. Box 363
Birmingham B15 2TT
U.K.

ROSS STEELE (*Editor*)
Department of French Studies
University of Sydney
Sydney NSW 2006
Australia

PETER STREVENS
Bell Educational Trust
Red Cross Lane
Cambridge CB2 2QX
U.K.

PAUL J. THIBAULT
Department of Italian
University of Sydney
Sydney NSW 2006
Australia

SANDRA A. THOMPSON
Linguistics Program
South Hall 5607
University of California
Santa Barbara CA 93106
U.S.A.

CONTRIBUTORS

JAMES P. THORNE
Department of English Language
University of Edinburgh
George Square
Edinburgh EH9 9JZ
U.K.

TERRY THREADGOLD (*Editor*)
Department of English
University of Sydney
Sydney NSW 2006
Australia

COLWYN B. TREVARTHEN
Department of Psychology
University of Edinburgh
7 George Square
Edinburgh EH8 9JZ
U.K.

JOHN TRIM
Centre for Information on Language
  Teaching & Research
Regent's College
Regent's Park
London NWI 4NS
U.K.

SHIVENDRA K. VERMA
Central Institute of English
  & Foreign Languages
Hyderabad 500 007
India

MICHAEL WALSH
Department of Linguistics
University of Sydney
Sydney NSW 2006
Australia

W.C. WATT
School of Social Sciences
University of California
Irvine CA 92717
U.S.A.

GORDON WELLS
Department of Curriculum
Ontario Institute for Studies in Education
252 Bloor Street West
Toronto Ont.
Canada M5S 1V6

STEPHEN A. WURM
Department of Linguistics
Research School of Pacific Studies
Australian National University
Canberra ACT 2601
Australia

COLIN YALLOP
School of English & Linguistics
Macquarie University
North Ryde NSW 2113
Australia

ZHAO SHUMING
Nanjing University
People's Republic of China

1. The Design of Language

Reproductive furniture and extinguished professors

Jean Aitchison

1. Introduction

For at least a quarter of a century, a controversy has been bubbling between sociolinguists and psycholinguists. Are humans primarily like buses, which travel along regular routes? Or are they like taxis, which move about freely? Sociolinguists have taken the side of the buses. They stress the relative predictability of utterances, claiming that humans are governed by social conventions: most of the time, they select one out of several possible options within an existing framework (e.g. Halliday 1973). Psycholinguists, on the other hand, have tended to support the taxi viewpoint. Following Chomsky, they emphasize the creativity of language, and argue that humans perpetually create and comprehend novel and unpredictable utterances.

Of course, both sides recognize that the other is partially right. Sociolinguists agree that humans can cope with bizarre utterances, should the need arise. Psycholinguists accept that there are certain social situations in which preordained rituals must be adhered to. The question is one of emphasis. However, the problem is a serious one. It raises the important issue of the balance between memory and computation. Retrieving appropriate behaviour from a set of available options involves a powerful memory and minimizes on-line processing. Saying something entirely new requires considerable on the spot computation. So are humans primarily good at remembering, or at working things out? Anyone building a model of human behaviour needs to come to a decision about the trading relationship between these spheres.

This controversy is sometimes characterized purely as a sociolinguistic versus psycholinguistic issue. But this is an oversimplification. On closer examination, it pervades several areas of linguistics in one form or another. Within the field of psycholinguistics, a somewhat similar dispute grumbles on concerning the make-up of words. How are words represented in the mental lexicon? Are they stored disassembled into morphemes, or are they ready-made, able to be used without further glueing together? There is no *a priori* answer, unless one has some previous theory about the relationship between computation and memory. On the one hand, morphemes which can be assembled by means of a regular rule represent a lowered memory load, but demand considerable on-line computation. On the other hand, on-line computation is expensive in terms of processing time and energy, but is more economical on memory.

Linguists have traditionally preferred the first option, arguing that the lexicon should contain only items which cannot be derived via a rule: "The lexicon is really an appendix of the grammar, a list of basic irregularities" (Bloomfield 1933: 274). "Regular variations are not matters for the lexicon, which should contain only idiosyncratic items ... not predictable by a general rule" (Chomsky and Halle 1968: 12). There are, however, two problems with this reasoning. First, the messiness of the irregular/regular distinction. Second, the overall aim of most linguists.

Faced with the "commonsense" claim that the lexicon contains only irregular words, it turns out to be surprisingly difficult to divide words into those that behave regularly, and those that are irregular. Only the extreme cases are clearcut. Consider inflectional suffixes on verbs. At one end of the spectrum there are words such as *jump* which behave entirely predictably (*jumps*, *jumped*, *jumping*). At the other end are words such as *be* that are clearly irregular (*is*, *was*, *being*). But quite often rules apply to just one small clump of verbs. For example, are the past tenses *beat*, *cut*, *hit*, to be classified as irregular? Certainly they are irregular in the sense that you cannot blindly apply the usual *-ed*. But since the lack of an ending applies to a whole set of words, perhaps this is a rule, but a minor one. Indeed, English has at least eight different past tense types (Bybee & Slobin 1982), each one containing several verbs. Do people remember each form within each type entirely separately, or do they learn rules which apply to batches of verbs? And the same type of problem arises with derivational suffixes. Some seem to be consistent both in meaning and form, as with *-ness*, which forms abstract nouns such as *goodness*, *kindness*. Others seem to be regular in relation to a smallish clump of words: for example, *-ity* forms regular abstract nouns for a group of words whose stem ends in /l/ as in *mobility*, *stability*, but outside this group, the suffix is inconsistent, as in *celebrity*, *university*. It is therefore somewhat unclear as to what is meant by Bloomfield's glib talk of "basic irregularities" or Chomsky and Halle's "idiosyncratic items".

The second problem with the "commonsense" rule-oriented approach is that researchers differ in their purpose. The aim of most linguists is to describe the language in as simple a way as possible. This involves minimizing the number of items contained in any grammar, which accounts for the preference of linguists for rules over lists. But, until the memory/computation dispute is solved, there is no guarantee that the preference for rules has a sound psychological basis. Many rules might represent historical relics of word formation processes which are no longer relevant once the word has been formed. Arguably, "a linguist who could not devise a better system than is present in any speaker's brain ought to try another trade" (Householder 1966: 100).

This paper therefore tries to shed some light on this controversy in relation to the way in which humans deal with affixes, and in particular suffixes, both inflectional and derivational. This involves two issues, which are in theory separable, but are probably interlinked in practice:

  i. storage: how are polymorphemic words represented in the mental lexicon?
  ii. retrieval: how are polymorphemic words retrieved from the mental lexicon?

1.1. Storage of affixes and retrieval implications

Affix-storage might be done in various ways. There are three main alternatives, each of which has been defended in the psycholinguistic literature (Butterworth 1983; Jarvella & Meijers 1983; Cutler, Hawkins & Gilligan 1985). Consider the word *kindness*. Are its component morphemes detached, semi-detached, or attached?

  i. Detached: the basic unit is *kind*, and the suffix *-ness* is not directly attached in the primary lexical representation, but is possibly listed underneath as a sub-entry.
  ii. Semi-detached: the basic unit is *kind-ness*. The word is stored as a whole, but with its morphemic structure clearly marked.
  iii. Attached: the basic unit is *kindness*. No morphemic divisions are immediately noticeable, though there is a back-up store containing

morphological information which can be consulted if a morphemic division is required.

These three possibilities involve quite different retrieval procedures for words. If detachment represents the true state of affairs, then retrieval consists of assemblage. If semi-detachment is the correct option, then it is likely that some morphemes are more visible in storage than others. For example, stems might be more brightly lit than affixes, and retrieved first. Attachment implies that words are treated as wholes, in that their internal morphemic structure is irrelevant to retrieval.

As noted earlier, all of these options have been proposed in the psycholinguistic literature. The conflicting conclusions are partly due to the heterogeneous nature of the evidence on which they are based. The various investigations have used different methods (description and experimentation), have examined different processes (production and perception), and dealt with different modalities (speech and writing). In a complete treatment of the topic, each of these variables needs to be considered. In this paper, due to space restrictions, I shall be dealing with descriptive evidence concerning the production of spoken speech, though the results will hopefully shed light on the organization of the mental lexicon in general.

The evidence to be considered consists primarily of slips of the tongue, collected intermittently over several years. If, in the course of speech, suffixes and prefixes are wrongly selected, or added on in the wrong place, this would provide a *prima facie* case for on the spot assemblage. If, on the other hand, they are firmly attached to the stem, then words are likely to be treated as structural wholes for the purpose of retrieval.

2. Affix types

There is no reason, of course, for suffixes and prefixes to be treated similarly, or for all suffixes to behave in a unified fashion. Suffixes are traditionally split into two categories, inflectional and derivational. There are one or two borderline cases (e.g. comparative *-er*, *-est*, adverbial *-ly*), but in most cases in English, the distinction is reasonably clear. There are several criteria for distinguishing them (Aranoff 1976: 2), perhaps the commonest being to see which comes first: derivational suffixes can precede inflectional ones, but not vice versa. We get *immune + ize + d* (*immunized*), but not **immune + d + ize*. We get *immune + ize + ation + s* (*immunizations*), but not *immune + ize + s + ation. This observation suggests that inflectional suffixes are relatively easily detachable.

2.1. Inflectional affixes

The detachability of inflections is confirmed by several pieces of evidence. The first is variable usage: for example, teenagers in Reading, England, intermittently add a non-standard -s to verbs (Cheshire 1982), as in:

(1) We goes shopping on Saturdays.

And people tend to be inconsistent in their treatment of phrasal nouns: for example, *mothers-in-law* interchanges with *mother-in-laws*.

Slips of the tongue provide further evidence: every now and then inflections get added on in the wrong place. This sometimes occurs with phrasal verbs, where the inflection may get tagged on after the two sections, instead of in between, suggesting that the basic lexical entry comprises the whole phrase:

(2) Mavis wash upped the dishes.
(3) I'd forgot abouten that.

Cases of jargon aphasia also support the detachability of inflections, since some patients find it easy to inflect their own nonsense words (Buttworth 1983):

(4) I believe they're called flitters landocks.
(5) She wikses a zen from me.

These scattered fragments of evidence suggest that adding on suffixes in the course of speech is a possible, and perhaps normal procedure. They do not provide proof that inflectional endings are inevitably added on as speech is produced: they simply suggest that they quite often are.

2.2. Derivational suffixes

But what about derivational suffixes? How mobile are they? In order to discover this, I examined a collection of approximately 750 spontaneous speech errors in which one similar sounding word had been substituted for another, as in:

(6) The economy is going through a period of inflammation (inflation).
(7) I found the Far East quite erotic (exotic).

Such errors are often referred to as "malapropisms", from the fictional Mrs. Malaprop in Sheridan's play *The Rivals*, who frequently confused words such as *allegory* and *alligator*.

The aim of this investigation was to see to what extent malapropisms retained or lost derivational suffixes. The six most frequently occurring final sequences in the corpus were examined in detail. (Final sequences were dealt with, rather than "suffixes", because of the difficulty of establishing criteria for defining a suffix.) These were:

  i. *-ion* [ʃən] (58) e.g. *medication*.
  ii. *-al* [əτ] (39) e.g. *national*.
  iii. *-ent/-ant* [ənt] (29) e.g. *dependent*.
  iv. *-ic* [ɪk] (21) e.g. *erotic*
  v. *-ive* [ɪv] (19) e.g. *destructive*.
  vi. *-ate* [eɪt] (16) e.g. *emulate*.

The figure in brackets shows the number of times each was involved as an error, or target or both. When error and target matched, this was counted as one occurrence. A "target" is the word which a native speaker of English would judge the appropriate one, at which the perpetrator of the error is assumed to be aiming. *-ated* also qualified for inclusion, but was omitted because it was the only final sequence with two syllables, which might have affected its treatment.

Target maintenance for the final sequence was high (81%), and higher than would be predicted for the maintenance of the end of the word in malapropisms as a whole (Aitchison & Straf 1982). A well-documented finding in malapropisms is that the beginnings of words are preserved better than ends by adults (Fay & Cutler 1977), even though the difference is somewhat less for longer words (Aitchison & Straf 1982). However, this figure of 81% for maintenance of final sequences was higher even than the percentage of identical initial consonants (77%) in an overall group of malapropisms (Aitchison & Straf 1982). This suggests that the presence of a derivational suffix aids recall. A similar observation was made by Brown and McNeill (1966) in their famous "tip-of-the-tongue" experiment, who noted the beneficial effect of "chunked" suffixes.

However, it might be the case that some suffixes are easily retained and others not. It was therefore necessary to look at the figures for individual suffixes. Figures for the retention of each final sequence are shown in Table 1.

Table 1. Maintenance of final sequences

	Target	No. maintained	% Maintained
-ion	53	45	85
-al	29	25	86
-ant	25	18	72
-ic	18	18	100
-ate	15	11	73
-ive	13	7	54
	153	124	81

The high number of cases in which -ic was maintained, and the low number in which -ive was kept, suggests that it is necessary to look in detail at the instances where the final sequence was not retained. It turned out that, in the majority of cases, the alteration was part of a more extensive change which involved other segments as well. For example:

(8) A malicious (malignant) tumour.
(9) You need to fill in the relative (relevant) details.
(10) A mentally difficult (deficient) child.

In these examples, the overall meaning of the word seemed to have been influenced by another word with similar sound and meaning, in which the role of the suffix was not the crucial factor.

Out of the 29 cases in which the suffix was not retained, only 8 were possible examples of "pure suffix change" — cases in which the suffix alone was altered. These are listed below:

(11) Reproductive (reproduction) furniture.
(12) An itinerary (itinerant) glue-sniffer.
(13) An arduous (ardent) lover.
(14) He took an actual (active) part.
(15) It might be interesting to speculate (speculate).
(16) Children use proper deduceful (deductive) rules.
(17) I got it from an authoritarian (authoritative) source.
(18) The electric (electoral) roll.

In order to extend the data, and so understand the phenomenon involved, these 8 cases can be considered alongside the 10 possible instances of pure suffix change in which the final sequences examined provided the error, rather than the target:

(19) *It's a contential (contentious) matter.*
(20) *He's her possession (possessor).*
(21) *We need audial (auditory) and visual input.*
(22) *Topic and comic (comment).*
(23) *I need indulgement (indulgence).*
(24) *The speech production procession (process).*
(25) *An industrial (industrious) person.*
(26) *Can you interpretate (interpret) that?*
(27) *Her new house has a conservative (conservatory).*

An examination of these 18 errors shows that they cannot all be regarded as cases in which speakers have selected a stem, and then added on a wrong suffix. Perusal of their content and context, together with remarks made by those who made the error (where these were recorded) suggests that there were several other factors implicated, and that they involved phenomena widely found in speech errors as a whole.

The first reason is blending, when two words are combined into one, as in *sleast* (*slightest* + *least*). This accounted for one third of the total. It seems clearly to be the explanation in (21) *audial* (*auditory* + *visual*), (22) *comic* (*comment* + *topic*), (24) *procession* (*process* + *production*). It was also the most probable reason for (19) *contential*, where the speaker reported that she had hovered between *controversial* and *contentious*, and (15) *speculize*, where the speaker had apparently been on the verge of saying *surmise*. A blended sentence accounts for (20) *possession*, where the speaker said she had either meant *He's her possessor* or *She's his possession*. Blending might perhaps also be an explanation for (13) *arduous*, which could be a combination of *ardent* and *jealous*, and (26) *interpretate* (*interpret* + *interpretation*).

A second likely explanation is "derailment". Someone starts saying the target, but then stops paying attention, and gets derailed onto another, more common word which gets uttered more often than the target, as in:

(28) *The first half of the conference (concert).*

This is a possible explanation of (14) *actual* (*active*), (12) *itinerary* (*itinerant*), and (25) *industrial* (*industrious*).

A third possibility is that some wrong suffixes represent "classical malapropisms" or "errors of ignorance", cases in which the speaker has genuinely and permanently confused the word with another, and may have misperceived it at first hearing. (18) *electric* (*electoral*) and (27) *conservative* (*conservatory*) may come into this category.

A final reason is lapse of memory: the target word cannot be remembered, and a speaker then uses a back-up procedure always available to humans, the ability to create a new word by adding a productive suffix onto an existing word: this is possibly seen in (16) *deduceful* (*deductive*), and (23) *indulgement* (*indulgence*). Interestingly, *self-indulgement* (*self-indulgence*) comes into a list of words of this type examined by Cutler (1980).

If the explanations above are plausible for the words discussed, this leaves two only unexplained, (1) *reproductive* (*reproduction*), (17) *authoritarian* (*authoritative*). This small residue of apparently unmotivated "pure suffix changes" suggests that the phenomenon is probably non-existent. It therefore seems quite unlikely that humans routinely attach suffixes to words in the course of speech, even though as a back-up procedure, any word can be further analysed in order to create new words (Aranoff 1976).

We can now return to the three possibilities for the storage of polymorphemic words outlined earlier (derivational affixes detached, semi-detached or attached). Detachment now seems unlikely. But we still need to distinguish between the remaining two, semi-detachment and attachment.

The number of times in which the final syllable (consonant plus the final morpheme) was retained was sufficiently high to suggest that morphemic divisions are not particularly noticeable as words are picked for utterance. For example:

(29) *People have cyclonic (syphonic) toilets in America.*
(30) *A disruptive (destructive) child.*
(31) *I want to stipulate (stimulate) discussion.*

Syllables did not, however, outnumber morphemes as the final unit remembered: there was no clear preference between the two, a finding in line with that of Browman (1978). The overall impression, therefore, is that words are stored in a manner in which a chunk at the end of the word is prominent in storage, but that this chunk has no particular linguistic status. The semi-detachment possibility is therefore unlikely. The evidence suggests that words are maintained in the lexicon as structural wholes. Splitting words into morphemes is a back-up option which is available, but not part of the "front-line" lexical representation.

2.3. Prefixes

This general finding in relation to derivational suffixes is very similar to the conclusions reached concerning prefixes (Aitchison 1983-4). When the prefixes in the same corpus of data were examined, the overall number of prefixes maintained was high, and comparable to the figure for word-initial maintenance found in malapropisms as a whole. Apparently-prefixed words interchanged with unprefixed words ("apparently-prefixed" because criteria for prefix identification are somewhat unclear):

(32) *Those lovely blue flowers — concubines (columbines).*
(33) *A congregated (corrugated) iron roof.*

If words of this type were treated separately, as a category stored by stems, or with morphemic divisions marked, one would not expect this casual intermixing. On the other hand, this is exactly what one would expect if words are stored as wholes.

When the prefix was altered, other sections of the word were also changed in the majority of cases, as in:

(34) *He has a terrible speech predicament (impediment).*

There were relatively few examples of "pure prefix change", in which the initial sequence was altered, and the rest of the word remained the same, as in:

(35) *A most extinguished (distinguished) professor.*

When these were examined, within the context in which they had occurred wherever possible, they were seen to fall into several categories, the largest of which was blends:

(36) *The trains had been disrupted and dislayed* (*delayed + disrupted*).
(37) *At the moment of compact* (*impact + collision*).
(38) *I don't expose* (*expect + suppose*) *anyone will eat that.*

The analysis of prefixes, then, led to the same general conclusion as an examination of derivational suffixes, that words are stored primarily as structural wholes. Prefixes, however, showed additionally how important was the contribution of the rhythmic pattern of the word, indicating that the mental representation of words might be primarily in terms of metrical trees (Liberman & Prince 1977).

2.4. Prefixes and suffixes combined

In order to complete the picture, it is instructive to look at cases in which both a prefix and suffix were present in the target.

There were 70 cases in which one of the prefixes studied (Aitchison 1983-4) occurred with one of the suffixes discussed in this paper in the target, as in:

(39) *Look at the condescension (condensation) on the windows.*

Of these, 44 (63%) retained both prefix and suffix, but altered some portion of the stem, as in:

(40) *He's very competitive (combative).*

In 19 (27%) the prefix was changed, but not the suffix, as in:

(41) *Theory instruction (construction).*

In 7 (10%) the suffix was changed, but not the prefix, as in:

(42) *Reproductive (reproduction) furniture.*

In one example only were both prefix and suffix changed, though in this case parts of the stem were altered as well:

(43) *Mentally difficult (deficient).*

The tendency to retain both prefixes and suffixes is therefore strong. Words with prefixes and suffixes show the powerful "bathtub effect" (Aitchison 1987) seen in malapropisms and word searches in general — the tendency for the beginnings and ends of words to be remembered better than the middles, as if the word were a person lying in a bath with their head and feet more visible than the sections covered by the water. If stems were recalled first, then morphemes added, one would expect this phenomenon to be reversed, that is, middles would be retained, but beginnings and endings changed.

3. Conclusion

A study of prefixes and suffixes based on slips of the tongue suggests that inflectional suffixes, on the one hand, are often added in the course of speech. On the other hand, prefixes and derivational suffixes are already firmly attached, and polymorphemic words are retrieved from the mental lexicon as structural wholes. Morphemic divisions are available, perhaps as part of a linguistic "archive", and can be called up if required. But they are not part of the "front-line" lexical representation.

This leaves two questions. First, why have so many psychologists come to the opposite conclusion? Second, what light does all this shed on the bus versus taxi controversy outlined at the beginning of the paper?

A number of experimental psychologists have come to the opposite viewpoint for perhaps three reasons: first, the nature of many of their experiments has forced subjects to use the "back-up" options available to humans. Second, they have more often dealt with word recognition than production, and, if a word is not immediately recognized, morphemic decomposition may be a normal next step. Finally, many experiments have involved reading, and the segmentation of written words may involve morpheme-like chunks to a greater extent than spoken speech.

As far as the bus-taxi controversy is concerned, the evidence outlined here suggests that people try to be buses. They turn into taxis only if the bus-route is unsatisfactory. Humans start by using memory, and routine possibilities. If this proves inadequate, they turn to computation. More research is needed, in a number of other areas, to see if this finding is a truly general one.

English intensifiers and their idiosyncrasies

D.J. Allerton

Grammatical labelling, Michael Halliday (1985: 27) observes, is of two kinds, by class and by function; and in his work he carefully distinguishes class labels like VERB from function labels like PREDICATOR. The two types are, however, related: classes of items are set up on the basis of shared occurrence in a number of functions; and functions are partly recognized by particular constellations of classes, and partly by the semantic contribution of the elements within these constellations. We can allow for minor differences in the structural behaviour of elements by setting up subclasses of different degrees of "delicacy", to use the term favoured by Halliday (e.g. 1972(1969): 254). But just how different can elements be in their structural behaviour while still being recognized as members of the same class? For instance, the English word *ago* in *a week ago* (despite Quirk et al. 1985: 688-9) must be seen as a postposition (not an adverb like *previously*, which can stand alone, cf. *(a week) previously*), and as such must be compared to prepositions like *in* and *after*. But does this mean that we must set up a super-class of "adpositions" in English, to embrace prepositions and the postposition *ago*, or can we simply regard the latter as an exceptional kind of preposition? This would appear to be a relatively simple matter, but we meet a much more complex version of the same problem, with various semantic ramifications, when we consider English intensifiers.

Halliday (1985: 171) describes intensifiers under the heading of submodification, which suggests a partly semantic category, and he notes that this "may have the effect of disturbing the natural ordering of elements in the group". This is a significant problem. Consider the following noun phrases:

(1)   a. *a* **very** *difficult question*
      b. *a* **quite** *difficult question*

(2) a. **such** *a difficult question* (with the same meaning as (3))
    b. **quite** *a difficult question*
(3) **so** *difficult a question*
(4) *a difficult* **enough** *question*

Semantically all of the italicized intensifiers seem to have a similar function, that of indicating the degree of the adjectival quality (in this case, of *difficulty*). Syntactically the intensifier is always optional, but when it does occur in examples like these, it requires the presence of the adjective (except that *such* and *quite* can each occur without an adjective but with a different meaning). So in principle there is some justification for placing all of our words in the one class of intensifier. But then how do we explain the fact that they seem to occur in the four different structural patterns of (1), (2), (3) and (4), with *quite* appearing in both (1) and (2)?

A reasonable procedure would be to establish a central subclass as the norm, and then show how (and if possible why) the other subclasses have diverged from the norm. The syntactic class of intensifiers has, in many modern linguistic works, been separated off from the large traditional class of adverbs in recognition of the fact that some words (such as *very (good)*, *relatively (weak)*) occur exclusively or predominantly as modifiers of adjectives (and also of adjective-based adverbs) while others (such as *greatly (appreciate)*) seem to be specialized in the role of modifiers of the verb within the verb phrase. The label INTENSIFIER suggests a particular semantic type of adjective modifier, one which corresponds to adverbs of degree; and certainly this is the most common semantic type.

Unfortunately neither the syntactic nor the semantic basis for the intensifier class is really decisive. Syntactically it can be split off from the general class of adverbs because of its special characteristic of modifying adjectives, but if we compare the membership of the class with that of the class of verbal adverbials of degree, we find a substantial amount of overlap. Although there are a few purely adjectival degree modifiers like *very*, *too* and *relatively* and a few purely verbal ones like *greatly*, *too much* and probably *strongly*, there are dozens of dual purpose ones to set against these, for example *absolutely*, *entirely*, *hardly*, *mildly*, *partially*, *quite*, *rather*, *slightly*. Semantically, too, there are more similarities than differences between the two classes of modifier. Although the bulk of the intensifier class can be semantically classified as degree adverbials, there are minor types that refer to manner and aspect; and these three semantic types constitute the main subclasses of modifiers of lexical verbs. We can tabulate these types of modifier as follows:

	Modifiers of adjectives (INTENSIFIERS)	Modifiers of lexical verbs (VERBAL ADVERBIALS)
Degree	rather/very (*resentful*)	rather/greatly (*resent*)
Aspect	psychologically (*harmful*)	psychologically (*harm*)
Manner	openly (*hostile*)	openly (*oppose*)
Method/Instrument	—	(*close*) automatically

Of the intensifier subclasses, we shall concentrate on the degree type, but first we can note some examples of the others.

Aspect intensifiers can be exemplified further by *mentally (fit)*, *physically (fit)*, *temperamentally (unsound)*, *sexually (attractive)*, *medically (dead)* and *politically (unwise)*. They typically occur with adjectives which denote an assessment of good-quality, and refer to the field within which this assessment is valid. This means that they are quite similar to sentence adverbials of the viewpoint variety (Allerton & Cruttenden 1974: 8-9; cf. also the viewpoint subjuncts of Quirk et al. 1985: 566-569), and in fact the last two examples given above could equally be viewpoint adverbials; but while they are used as adjective modifiers within a noun phrase (e.g. *some politically unwise decisions*) they are unequivocally intensifiers.

Manner intensifiers can be further exemplified by *interestingly (different)*, *quietly (assertive)*, *strangely (cheerful)*, *cautiously (optimistic)*, *clearly (visible)* and *easily (accessible)*. In a sense they describe the manner in which the adjectival quality is displayed, but since they also describe a quality themselves, we can see them as adding a further, but less important, quality to the basic adjectival one: thus *interestingly different* means as much "different and also interesting" as "different in an interesting way". The last three examples in the above list are, however, slightly different, in that, although they express the manner of display of the adjectival quality, the manner in this adjectival context implies a particular degree of the adjectival quality: thus *cautiously optimistic* means something like "slightly optimistic", and *easily accessible* is close to "very accessible".

Like many semantic divisions, the one between manner and degree intensifiers therefore has an uncertain border area. This is not the only case of semantic lines being difficult to draw in this field. The example *sexually (attractive)*, which we classified above as an aspect intensifier, is not far from the manner type; and examples like *consistently (good)* and *continu-*

ally (absent), though, in a sense, of the degree type, might even form a further category of frequency intensifiers.

Using the label INTENSIFIER not only picks out adjectival modifiers as different, it also recognizes the central importance of the degree type amongst adjectival modifiers, compared with the situation amongst modifiers of lexical verbs, where the different semantic types are more equal in importance. Nevertheless intensifiers and verbal degree adverbials give as much an impression of two subclasses of a single class (like attributive and predicative adjectives) as of two separate classes (like nouns and adjectives). Indeed there seems to be greater similarity between adjective intensifiers and verbal adverbials than between the latter and adverbials of time and place, for instance.

Whatever the relationship between modifiers of adjectives and modifiers of lexical verbs, there is no harm in using the label INTENSIFIER for the first category, so long as we are clear that the semantic subclass of degree is the main subclass but not the only one. Moreover, the intensifiers we took as our starting-point (*very, quite, such, so*, etc.) as members of the degree subclass, are, like all degree words (cf. Bolinger 1972), subject to further classification according to the kind of grading involved. The notion of "gradability" is sometimes applied in a very general way with the suggestion that some adjectives are gradable and can therefore take degree intensifiers (and have a comparative form), while others are non-gradable. But this view is clearly an oversimplification, because, for instance, both *very* and *absolutely* express degree, and yet we find *very surprising, absolutely amazing* but hardly *?absolutely surprising, ?very amazing*. The need for a further semantic subclassification is clear.

Quirk et al. (1985: 445-446, 589f.) divide adjective and verb modifiers of degree into "amplifiers" (which "scale upwards") and "downtoners" (which "have a general lowering effect"). (They also refer to a third group, "emphasizers" (e.g. *really*), but they accept that these are difficult to distinguish from "focussing disjuncts" (1985: 447, 612f.); so it is best to put them on one side.) "Amplifiers" are subdivided into "maximizers" (e.g. *completely*) and "boosters" (e.g. *very*); and "downtoners" are divided into "approximators" (e.g. *almost*), "compromisers" (e.g. *more or less*), "diminishers" (e.g. *partly*) and minimizers" (e.g. *hardly*). Only "maximizers", "boosters", "diminishers" and "minimizers" are said to be limited to use with gradable adjectives (1985: 469). But this scheme is deficient in at least three respects: firstly, some "approximators" are not free to occur with all adjectives (cf. *?virtually large*, *?virtually rare* beside the natural *virtually adult*, *virtually unique*); secondly, *extremely* is wrongly placed with "maximizers" like *absolutely*, instead of with "boosters" like *very*; and thirdly, the "diminisher" includes intensifiers of apparently different semantic types, e.g. *slightly* compared with *partly*.

Let us consider an alternative semantic scheme for degree modifiers. We must begin by noting that the problem is complicated by the fact that a substantial number of adjectives are gradable in two (or even three) different ways, with the differences often correlating with a difference in the lexical meaning of the adjective, cf. *absolutely acceptable* with *very acceptable*. A further complication is that some degree intensifiers have a semantic component over and above their specification of degree, and this can place an additional restriction on their combination with adjectives: thus *slightly*, for instance, as well as indicating a low degree, usually refers to something undesirable or abnormal (except with comparative adjectives), cf. *?slightly kind*, *slightly unkind*; *?slightly similar*, *slightly different*. A final difficulty to be mentioned is the general semantic fluidity of words in this area.

If we set aside these complications, we can now sort degree intensifiers into three groups, each with its own kind of grading and with a relatively complex relationship to the semantic subclasses of adjectives. We need to distinguish the following subvarieties of degree intensifier:

1. SCALAR: These indicate parts of a mental scale of assessment of degree which ranges from immeasurably high down to zero. They represent prototypical gradability. They include *infinitely*, *extremely*, *very*, *pretty*, *rather*, *reasonably*, *fairly*, *somewhat*, *slightly*, *not specially*, *not very*, *not at all*. The order of this list is a rough order of rank, with an unintensified adjective appearing between *very* and *pretty*; boosters, moderators, diminishers and zeroizers might be distinguished. In addition the comparatives and superlatives *more* (or *-er*), *most* (or *-est*), *less* and *least* belong here, as also does *too*. These intensifiers occur with adjectives such as *big*, *small*, *bright*, *surprising*.

2. TELIC: These relate the actual degree of the adjectival quality to the degree required for a particular purpose, and place it above or below that mark, either by a wide margin or by a narrow margin. They include *easily*, *barely*, *only just*, *hardly*, *virtually*, *nearly*, *not quite*, *nowhere*. These intensifiers occur with adjectives such as *sufficient*, *cooked*, *afloat*, *fully-grown*.

3. ABSOLUTIVE: These emphasize that the degree of the adjectival qual-

ity is genuinely within the range required by the "superlative" type of adjective with which they occur. In other words the type of adjective used with them already represents the extreme end of a scale, and the intensifier emphasizes that the degree described really belongs there. The principal intensifiers in this subclass are *absolutely* and *utterly*, with *totally* and *entirely* as marginal members; typical superlative adjectives are *ridiculous*, *huge*, *scorching (hot)*, and *freezing (cold)*. (As Cruse 1986: chapter 4 points out, these adjectives occur naturally with an extreme high falling intonation.)

These three groups exclude Quirk *et al.*'s "emphasizers" (e.g. *really*), which can be treated as sentence adverbials of the validity-oriented type, like *superficially*, *generally*. Interestingly, *partly* can be put in this same class, whereas *partially* is a scalar degree intensifier.

Corresponding to our three degree intensifier classes we noted three adjective classes (which could also be called scalar, telic and absolutive). But the relationship between intensifier classes and adjective classes is not simply one-to-one. Many adjectives have a complex meaning *vis-à-vis* gradability and therefore co-occur with more than one class of degree intensifier. Thus as well as the three GRADABLE adjective classes we already have:

  (a) SCALAR, e.g. *big*, *bright*, *pretty*,
  (b) TELIC, e.g. *sufficient*, *cooked*, *perceptible*,
  (c) ABSOLUTIVE, e.g. *huge*, *scorching*, *gorgeous*

we need to distinguish further:

  (d) SCALAR-TELIC, e.g. *warm*, *late*, *noticeable*,
  (e) SCALAR-ABSOLUTIVE, e.g. *different*, *beautiful*,
  (f) TELIC-ABSOLUTIVE, e.g. *boiling (hot)*, *dead*, *possible*,
  (g) SCALAR-TELIC-ABSOLUTIVE, e.g. *dark*, *successful*, *acceptable*,

the latter four types co-occurring with the two or three correspondingly named degree intensifier classes. Thus, whereas *warm*, for instance, occurs with both *very* and *barely*, the purely scalar *bright* occurs only with *very*, and the purely telic *cooked* only with *barely*. Similarly while *beautiful* occurs with both *very* and *absolutely*, the purely scalar *pretty* occurs only with *very*, and the purely absolutive *gorgeous* only with *absolutely*. All of the above adjective subclasses are strictly sub-subclasses of the GRADABLE subclass, and stand apart from NON-GRADABLE adjectives like *dead, unmarried* and *wooden*, which at least in their primary meaning (cf. Kato 1986) do not occur with any degree intensifiers at all.

Before we begin a syntactic study of individual intensifiers, we need to consider a further possible role for intensifiers, that of modifying one of their own kind in a construction of the type ((INTENSIFIER) INTENSIFIER) ADJECTIVE. The most common type of this construction involves direct modification of the adjective with *more/-er*, *less* or *too*, each of which itself combines with scalar adjectives like *big* to produce an adjective complex which has a "differential" kind of meaning. A further intensifier can then be added to specify the "difference", e.g. *far more/less useful*, *marginally too big*. This would give us a further semantic class of intensifiers:

4. DIFFERENTIAL: These indicate the difference of degree between the item being described and some reference point. They include *far*, *much*, *a lot*, *marginally*, which are limited to differential adjective complexes (with *more/-er*, *less* or *too*), and *slightly* and *a bit*, which also occur with scalar adjectives, although even then they suggest a differential kind of meaning (cf. *a bit big* "a bit too big").

In the above list of differential intensifiers we could have included *too much*, *so much* and *how much(?/!)* beside *much*. Since *(too) much* can modify *too*, infinite recursion is, at least in principle, possible, cf. *(...) much too much too big*.

A further type of two-level intensifier construction is possible, but within the subclasses we already have. In particular, the postmodifying intensifier *enough* combines with a scalar adjective to give a telic adjective complex: thus *big enough* is comparable with *sufficient* and can be similarly intensified e.g. *easily/barely/nearly big enough*.

We can now summarize our classification of intensifiers and verbal adverbials in *Figure 1*. The obvious redundancy of this hierarchical classification would speak for a description in terms of syntactic features, not so much in a matrix format, which would involve almost equal redundancy, but rather with the format of a systemic description as a set of related options, as proposed by Halliday (1972(1969)). A further deficiency of this classification, which seems to be shared by most formats of description, is that it fails to differentiate major and minor (sub)classes; and yet, as we saw earlier, the degree type is the major subclass of intensifiers, and the scalar (sub)class is most characteristic within this. At this point, then, we can

```
MODIFIERS ──── INTENSIFIERS ──── DEGREE ──┬── SCALAR
OF ADJECTIVES                              ├── TELIC
AND VERBS                                  ├── ABSOLUTIVE
                                           └── DIFFERENTIAL

                                  ASPECT

                                  MANNER

              MODIFIERS
              OF LEXICAL ──────── DEGREE ──┬── SCALAR
              VERBS                        ├── TELIC
                                           ├── ABSOLUTIVE
                                           └── DIFFERENTIAL

                                  ASPECT

                                  MANNER

                                  METHOD/INSTRUMENT
```

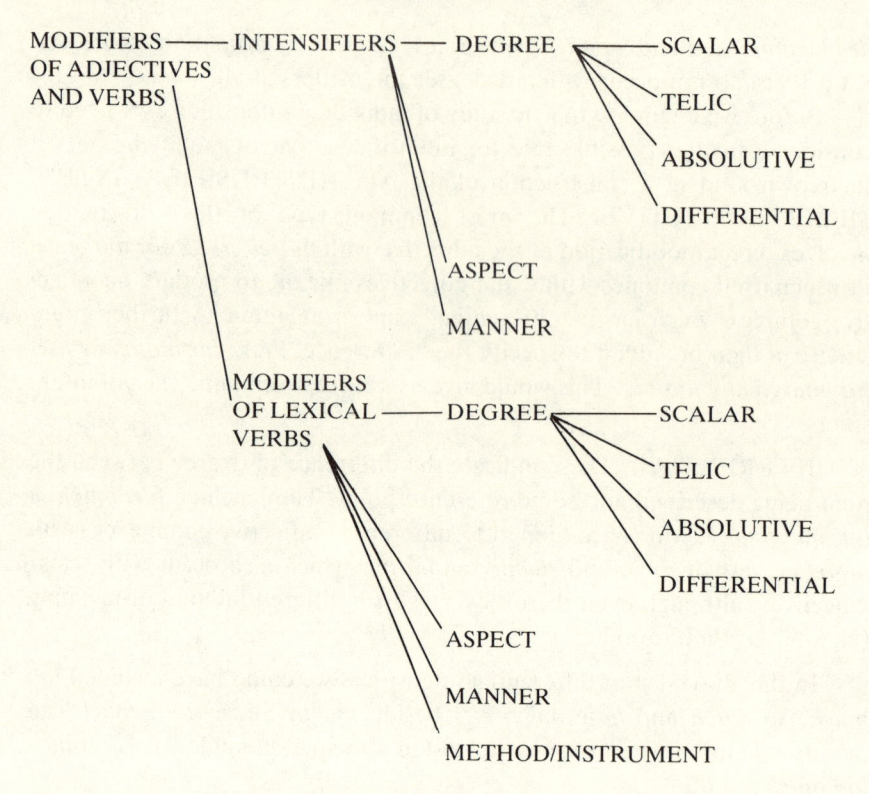

Figure 1.

return to our initial issue: why, within the prototypical scalar type of intensifier do we find *quite*, *such*, *so*, *too* and *enough* displaying such aberrant syntactic behaviour, as compared with the standard type represented by *very*?

Let us consider the syntactic status of a regular noun phrase that includes an intensifier, such as the ones we began with, viz.:

(1)   a.   *a very difficult question*

Syntactically it is an expanded version of a simple noun phrase consisting of determiner, adjective and noun, i.e. *a difficult question*. We can consider this to have the structure described in Allerton (1982: 23-24) of specifier (*a*) plus modifier (*difficult*) plus core/head (*question*), i.e. the noun *question* acts simultaneously as core to the specifier *a* and as head to the modifier *difficult*. In the phrase with the intensifier the modifier *very difficult* is complex with *difficult* as a head within it and *very* as a modifier. The appropriateness of Halliday's "submodifier" is clear. As a submodifier *very* has no direct relationship to its predecessor word *a*, and is only linked indirectly via the adjective and then via the noun; moreover, as a submodifier, *very* can only occur if an adjective is also present to act as its head. In these respects *very* is typical for the vast majority of intensifiers — in fact of all non-degree intensifiers and of most degree intensifiers.

But let us turn now to the status of *such*, as it occurs in the example we cited earlier:

(2) a. *such a difficult question*

A phrase like this is open to two slightly different interpretations, which we might refer to as the "exclamatory" and the "phoric" (Halliday and Hasan 1976: 33) readings, as illustrated by (5a) and (5b) respectively:

(5) a. *such a terrible error*(!), *such an unusual use*(!), *such a (stupid) fool*(!)
b. *such a/an (clerical) error [as that]*, *such a (medical) use [as the one described]*, *such an (electrical) engineer*

In the exclamatory use *such a* + ADJECTIVE + NOUN corresponds to *a so* + ADJECTIVE + *a* + NOUN, and, at least semantically, *such* is very close to *so*, both referring to the (high) degree of the adjectival quality. It is noteworthy that the same use of *such a* occurs with gradable nouns (Bolinger 1972: 58-90) such as *fool*, even when they occur without an adjective, but this is not possible with non-gradable nouns, e.g. *such an engineer(!). With the "phoric" interpretation, however, such a phrase is perfectly possible, as indicated in (5b); in fact, in this use, *such* has no special connection with an adjective, and may be regarded simply as a predeterminer which occurs only with the indefinite article, but is a variant of the post-determiner *such* in *no such error*, *many such errors*, etc.

It is the exclamatory *such* that interests us as an aberrant kind of determiner. In this use (as illustrated in (5a) *such* is dependent on the occurrence of an adjective or a noun with the adjectival quality of gradability (such as *fool, nuisance, intelligence, size*). In the exclamatory use *such* is also dependent, however, on the occurrence of an indefinite article, viz. generic *a* or zero, cf.:

(6) a. *such an expensive pen, such expensive pens, such expensive ink*

b. *such the expensive pen(s), *such any expensive ink, *any such expensive ink, *my such expensive ink

It is clear from (6a) and (b) that, as well as being limited to occurrence with the generic indefinite article, *such* is restricted to predeterminer position. These characteristics are also found in exclamatory *what*, cf.:

(7) a. *What an expensive pen! What expensive pens! What expensive ink!*
b. **What the expensive pen(s), *What this expensive ink! *What any expensive pen(s)!*
c. *What (expensive) pen? What (expensive) pens? What (expensive) ink?*

(The examples of (7c) show that interrogative *what* is a central determiner like *the*, *a*, *my*, etc. Exclamatory *what*, however, can also be used without an adjective, especially with a singular countable noun, e.g. *what a pen! (?)what pens! (?)what ink!* even when the noun is in no sense gradable. Exclamatory *what* therefore comes very close to being a predeterminer, although its principal role is probably still that of intensifying an adjective. Exclamatory *such*, too, as we have seen, has these predeterminer-like characteristics, and this is doubtless partly why these two marginal intensifiers have preserved their aberrant syntactic patterns.

Just as the marginality of exclamatory *what* is strengthened by its association with the central determiner *what*, so also the marginality of exclamatory *such* is reinforced by its association with "phoric" *such*. This other *such* occurs, as we saw in (5b) with any kind of noun, without an adjective being necessary. It can also occur with other determiners than generic indefinite articles, but then it appears as a predeterminer, e.g., *any such pen, two such pens, no such pens, some such pen.* (It will be noted that "phoric" *such* does not occur with *the*, but for semantic reasons; it is in complementary distribution with *same*, which occurs only WITH the definite article. Thus the predeterminer "phoric" *such* in *such a pen*, the postdeterminer "phoric" *such* in *any such pens* and the postdeterminer *same* in *the same pen* are fulfilling almost identical functions.)

A final point concerning *such* and *what* is their inability to occur as part of a predicative adjective phrase, cf.:

(8) a. *The pen was such expensive.*
b. *What expensive the ink was!*

although they can occur in predicative noun phrases:

(8) c. It was such an expensive pen.
    d. *What expensive ink it was.*

This suggests that perhaps *such* and *what* could be regarded as predeterminers with intensifier-like characteristics rather than the reverse.

Recalling another of our initial examples:

(2) b. *quite a difficult question*

we see that exclamatory *such* and *what* are not quite the only intensifiers to occur in predeterminer position, because *quite* occurs in this position, in addition to the standard position illustrated earlier with:

(1) b. *a quite difficult question*

The intensifier *rather* has the same two possibilities as *quite*. The question naturally arises for both of these intensifiers whether there is any difference in meaning between their occurrence in the standard (pre-adjectival) position and the special (predeterminer) position.

A first point to note is that, just like *such* and *what*, *quite* and *rather* are limited to occurrence with non-specific *a* and zero (except that *quite* also occurs as a quantifier modifier in *quite a few hours, quite some time*, etc.). Moreover, once again, like *such* and *what*, both intensifiers can occur with nouns without an adjective, e.g., *quite a pen! rather a fool!* but this time only a countable singular use is possible, and *rather* is further restricted to degree nouns (cf. **rather a pen!*). As the punctuation indicates, this use of *quite* and *rather* is exclamatory and emphatic in value, although it occurs in declarative as well as exclamatory sentences. Once again, therefore, it is tempting to see the use of the intensifiers in predeterminer position with adjectives as being "contaminated" by their use with nouns, and having therefore a more emphatic, perhaps even exclamatory, meaning.

In the case of *quite* there is a further complicating factor, its ambiguity. Consider the sentence:

(9) *The sisters were quite different.*

The ambiguity of (9) stems from the fact that *quite* has two different meanings, firstly "rather, somewhat" and secondly "absolutely, totally"; in other words, some occurrences of *quite* are SCALAR, and others are ABSOLUTIVE. Adjectives that have a scalar but no absolutive use, e.g. *good, funny, similar, pretty* require *quite* to be interpreted as "rather, somewhat", whereas those that have an absolutive but no scalar use, e.g. *excellent, ridiculous, identical, lovely* require *quite* to be interpreted as "absolutely". The adjective *different* (as well as *beautiful*) is a member of the mixed SCALAR-ABSOLUTIVE class and is therefore compatible with both values of *quite* — hence the ambiguity of (8).

The scalar *quite* and the absolutive *quite* have differing syntactic potentials. The examples in (10) demonstrate that while scalar *quite* favours predeterminer position, absolutive *quite* requires the normal pre-adjective position:

(10) a. i.*She's quite a good cook.*
 ii *(?)She's a quite good cook.*
 b. i.?*She's quite an excellent cook.*
 ii.*She's a quite excellent cook.*

It is thus scalar *quite* that takes up the theoretically marginal predeterminer position and, for this purpose, falls into the same class as *rather*, exclamatory *such* and exclamatory *what*, which could all replace scalar *quite* in (10a.i). The only further element which even partially resembles this little group is the complex intensifier *not ... very* (meaning "only moderately"), as exemplified in:

(11) *She's not a very good cook.* (OR: *She isn't a very good cook.*)

In this case *very* occurs in the normal intensifier position, and only *not* (or *n't*) precedes the determiner; but it would anyway in its natural position as negative particle.

This is perhaps the key to explaining the occurrence of intensifiers in our exceptional predeterminer position: they are all thereby maintaining a natural position they had and partially still have in some other function. Thus *not* is/was a negative particle; *such* and *what* are/were predeterminers; and *rather* and *quite*? They are/were verbal adverbials of degree, and in addition *rather* may also be related to a sentence adverbial. We can illustrate *rather* and *quite* as verbal degree modifiers with (12a):

(12) a. *She rather/quite attracted him*
 b. *She's rather/quite attractive.*
 c. *She's rather/quite an attractive woman.*

We can note that in (12a) *rather* and *quite* are modifiers of the lexical verb, but that in a sense they also modify the whole verb phrase (including *him*).

It is presumably therefore not a big step to allow them to modify a verb phrase consisting of BE with a predicative phrase or noun phrase, as in (12b) and (c), to allow them to follow rather than precede the reduced form of BE, which, at least phonologically, resembles an auxiliary (which would precede *rather* or *quite*, if inserted in (12a)).

A further function in the repertoire of *rather* is that of sentence adverbial (which occurs most commonly in final position) in the meaning of "to use a word that is more appropriate — in place of the tonic word", as in:

(13) a. *She's an* **attractive** *woman(,) rather.*
b. *She is — rather — an* **attractive** *woman.*

This can be compared with similar constructions in French with *plutôt* and in German with *eher*. In all cases it is a relatively small step from saying that the adjective is perhaps an appropriate word to saying that the adjectival is present to a moderate degree (only).

But the principal function of *rather* like that of *quite* is to act as a degree modifier within the verb phrase, especially in a predicative phrase after the verb BE. In fact, *rather* and *quite* are less common in predeterminer position with noun phrases in other positions, like subject, object, "object" of a preposition, etc., cf.:

(14) a. *?I had lunch with rather/quite an attractive woman today.*
b. *I had lunch with a rather/quite attractive woman today.*

The predeterminer position for *rather* and *quite* thus seems to be associated with predicative position. The same is true of our next small group of marginal intensifiers, *so*, *too*, *that* and *how*, which were represented by our initial example (3), which we can repeat as (15), showing the other intensifiers that follow this pattern:

(15) a. *so difficult a question*
b. *too difficult a question*
c. *that difficult a question*
d. *How difficult a question (did he give you)?*

Can we explain this aberrant pattern in a similar way?

Let us first note some of the characteristics of this pattern. The intensifier has again adopted a predeterminer position, but this time it has taken the adjective with it, so that the whole intensifier-adjective construction stands outside the basic noun phrase of article-plus-noun. Indeed the only alternative pattern for these intensifiers with a noun phrase is to postpone the whole intensifier-adjective construction as in (16); this is possible for the "submodifiers" *so*, *too* and *that*, providing that *so* and *too*, in their turn, are further submodified by a clause or non-finite clause, and that *that* is used anaphorically or exophorically, cf.:

(16) a. *(?)He asked me a question so difficult that we complained.*
       b. *(?)He asked us a question too difficult to be answered quickly.*
       c. *He asked us a question* **that** *difficult* **last** *year.*

(Of the above examples only (c) is natural in informal spoken English.) It is worth noting that this postponed use of the adjective phrase only allows a "phoric" scalar interpretation of the intensifier (hence the exclusion of *how*), whereas for the preposed pattern an exclamatory reading (as in (15)) is in principle always possible for *so*, *too* and *how*, and in the north of England it is possible for *that* as well.

A second important characteristic of the *so*-group is that they are even more limited in their co-occurrence with determiners than the other marginal groups that we have looked at. Preposed *such*, *what*, *rather* and *quite* had to occur with the indefinite article, but they could also occur with zero article with plural nouns and mass nouns. This possibility is more or less excluded for our present group, cf.:

(17) a. **He asked us so difficult questions.*
       b. **He asked us too difficult questions.*
       c. ?*He asked us that difficult questions.*
       d. **How difficult questions did he ask us?*

Such plural noun phrases are only marginally better with a postposed adjective phrase, as in (16); even the *that* of (16c) becomes rather unnatural in the plural.

This subclass of intensifiers, with its strong attachment to the article *a(n)*, is thus extremely limited in its occurrence with attributive adjectives in the noun phrase. In predicative position after BE, SEEM, BECOME, etc. these intensifiers are, however, just as natural as any, cf.:

(18) a. *The question he asked seemed so/too/that difficult.*
       b. *How difficult did the questions he asked seem?*

It is therefore tempting to think of modification of adjectives in predicative position as the natural or basic role for these and indeed most intensifiers, and to regard their occurrence with attribute adjectives in the noun phrase as peripheral not only in position (i.e. preposed or postposed rather than medial) but also in function. This generalization would not apply to *such* and *what*, which, as we noted earlier, are impossible with predicative adjectives, and are really as much predeterminers as intensifiers. The relationship between *so* and *such*, with their semantic equivalence in both "phoric" and "exclamatory" uses, is one that comes close to complementary distribution: *so* is basically a postdeterminer, but they compete with each other in the position we can describe as either attributive adjective premodifier or predeterminer.

Our final exceptional intensifier is *enough*, which we cited in the initial example:

(4)   *a difficult enough question*

This exemplifies the unique position of *enough* as a postmodifier of adjectives. How can this exceptional behaviour of *enough* be explained? Once again it may be useful to regard the occurrence of adjectives with *enough* in predicative position as being more basic, as in:

(19)   *The question was difficult enough.*

It seems natural to compare this use of *enough* with its occurrence as a verbal degree modifier, as in:

(20)   a.   *The question troubled us enough.*
       b.   **The question enough troubled us.*

Thus *enough* as a verbal adverbial is excluded from medial position, although it is perfectly natural for the majority of degree adverbials, cf.:

(21)   a.   *The question troubled us greatly/slightly/somewhat.*
       b.   *The question greatly/slightly/somewhat troubled us.*

The adverb *enough* thus prefers to act as a postmodifier; and even the determiner *enough* is occasionally found in postnominal position (cf. *cause enough* beside *enough cause*). It is not too surprising, then, to find *enough* as a postmodifier of adjectives.

Combinations of adjective-plus-*enough* are most common in predicative adjective phrases, as in (19). They also occur attributively within the noun phrase, but most commonly when the noun phrase in turn is in predicative position, as illustrated by Quirk *et al.*'s (1985: 421) (slightly adapted):

(22) a. *She's a brave enough student (to attempt the course).*
b. *She's brave enough a student.*
c. *She's a student brave enough *(to attempt the course).*

(22a) represents the expected pattern with the adjective-intensifier combination intervening between article and noun. But the two other patterns with an "external" adjective phrase are also possible, particularly in formal English. The preposed pattern of (22b) can occur when the *enough* has no complementation, but the postposed pattern of (22c) is only natural when there is complementation (with an infinitive or *that* clause). The existence of these two exceptional patterns, in both of which the adjectival combination with *enough* is external to the core noun phrase, gives the impression of a construction from elsewhere (i.e. from predicative position) being loosely attached.

The intensifier *enough* also has an interesting semantic property. It must be regarded as a scalar intensifier, because it combines with adjectives like *big, bright, pretty* (and not with *sufficient, cooked, perceptible* or with *huge, scorching, gorgeous*). But a combination of (scalar) adjective and *enough* seems to form a complex telic adjective phrase, which is then modifiable with telic intensifiers, e.g. *easily big enough, barely big enough, not quite big enough*. And telic adjectives as a group favour predicative over attributive position.

The predisposition of *enough* for predicative position is in striking contrast to the first subclass of idiosyncratic intensifiers we considered, viz. *such* and *what*, which are predeterminer-like and are in fact excluded from predicative position, cf.:

(23) a. **The question is such difficult.*
b. **What difficult the question is!*

Thus *enough* seems to be at the opposite end of a syntactic scale (or "cline") from *such* and *what*, with the central type (represented by *very* and *slightly*) in the middle.

The following table is an attempt to summarize our findings on exceptional intensifiers, and to show how they represent divergences from the central type, on the one hand towards predeterminers, and on the other towards adverbials (with I, A, D and N standing for Intensifier, Adjective, Determiner and Noun respectively, and NP and AP for Noun Phrase and Adjective Phrase respectively):

Table 1.

	Attributive NP			Predic.	Attributive NP	
	I+D+A+N	I+D+N	D+I+A+N	AP	I+A+D+N	D+A+I+N
such, what	+	+	−	−	−	−
quite, rather	+	+?	+	+	−	−
very, etc.	−	−	+	+	−	−
so, that, too, how	−	−	?	+	+	−
enough	−	−	+	+	−	+

(see also Bolinger 1972: 139)

The tradition of structural analogy

John A. Anderson

Linguistic structure, it is generally agreed, is not homogeneous. Representations of structure are assigned to different levels on the basis of their displaying different structural properties. Thus we recognise at least two different levels or sets of representations, whose components are constructed out of phonetically defined elements (i.e. constituting *phonological* levels) but which are distinguished by whether or not they embody *contrastivity*. On the basis of possession of contrastivity, *phonemic* representations constitute a level distinct from the *phonetic*. Along another dimension, we can distinguish among such representations on the basis of the domain with which they are most appropriately associated: commonly, a distinction is drawn between *word-level* phonological representations and *utterance-level* (or sentence-level). Both these distinctions are supported to the extent that their recognition and the introduction of further structure that this entails — viz. the expression of the relationship between different levels — facilitate the formulation of generalisations concerning the structure of language and languages.

Further sub-levels may be recognised on the same basis. To the extent, for instance, that the phonological structure of words is most appropriately built up in stages, we can recognise derivational sub-levels within that level. At the other end of the scale of differentiation lies the fundamental division among representations based on the character of the set of substantive elements, or *alphabet*, out of which they are constructed (Anderson 1982). All these representations belong to the "super-level" or *plane* of phonology characterised by an alphabet of phonetically defined elements. Syntactic representations are constructed out of a distinct alphabet defined in other terms and are thus assigned to a different plane.

This diversification of levels of representation is accompanied by a *modularisation* of the generalisations, or rules, which specify how representations are constructed and related. Again fundamental is the distinction between the "super-modules", or *components*, of phonology and syntax and the relationship between the two. My concern here is not with any specific articulation of modularity, although I have no doubt already implied particular divisions which are controversial. Instead, I am simply spelling out, rather abstractly, a characteristic shared by and explicitly formulated within a wide range of linguistic frameworks: the recognition of the modularity of linguistic generalisations and the corresponding differentiation into levels of the representation of linguistic structure.

Less commonly acknowledged in any explicit way is the need to constrain this diversificatory strategy within appropriate limits; modularisation of one principle of structure does not entail that a related one is also module-specific. Elsewhere (Anderson 1985 and forthcoming in *Lingua*; also Anderson & Durand 1986) I have argued for the appropriateness of a particular constraint called *structural analogy*. The structural analogy assumption (SAA) is defined as "minimise (or, more strongly, eliminate) differences between levels that do not follow from a difference in alphabet or from the nature of the relationship between the levels concerned".

Consider, for instance, the planar distinction between syntax and phonology. Rather typically, syntactic and phonological structures are expressed in superficially very different notations (cf. e.g. X' structures in syntax and metrical trees or grids or autosegmental associations in phonology). But it is less than clear that these differences reflect real (motivated) divergence in the structural properties that should be attributed to phonology and syntax. The SAA, in its strong form, requires that such implied differences be discarded if they are not consequent upon the difference in alphabet or upon the (say, interpretive) relation between phonology and syntax. *Dependency* analyses, on the other hand, embody a claim (imposed, other things being equal, by the SAA) that phonological and syntactic representations are constructed out of the same structural relations (of association, linear precedence and dependency): see again Anderson (1985), as well as Anderson and Jones (1974, 1977), Anderson *et al.* (1985), Anderson and Ewen (eds., 1980; in press), Durand (ed., 1986). The proper trading relation between modularity and the SAA is yet to be established; but any such transaction at least requires that both parties be actively present. My aim here is much more limited: what I attempt is a brief (and thus necessarily partial) historiographic sketch of strands — or maybe even loose threads — in the tradition of structural analogy. For the most part, I leave to the reader the evaluation — and, if this is positive, the pursuit — of its fruitfulness.

As far as I am aware, there has in modern times been little by way of explicit articulation of anything resembling the SAA since, or before, Hjelmslev's contention of an isomorphism between the two planes of expression and content:

> It turns out that the two sides (the planes) of a language have completely analogous categorical structure, a discovery that seems to us of far-reaching significance for an understanding of the structural principle of a language or in general of the "essence" of a semiotic. (1953: 101)

and Pike's (1967) insistence on the linguistic (and indeed cultural) universality of the *etic/emic* distinction and on the trimodal character of linguistic (and again non-linguistic cultural) structure.

Hjelmslev, however, fails to exemplify the claimed analogy in categorical structure between content and expression, principally because, in his terms, such an exemplification would anticipate, illegitimately, the results of the glossematic procedure to which his discussion is a preface. Siertsema (1965: 207-211) does attempt a reconstruction of part of the analogy that might be appropriate on the basis of descriptions offered by Hjelmslev himself (notably 1937, 1938, 1939). She summarises this in the table reproduced here as Figure 1:

Content plane (plerematic)			
Constitutents (pleremes)		Exponents (morphemes)	
Central const. (radical elements)	*Marginal const.* (derivational elements)	*Intense exp.* (noun morphemes: case comparison number gender article)	*Extense exp.* (verb morphemes: person voice stress aspect mood tense)
Expression plane (cenematic)			
Constituents (cenemes)		Exponents (prosodemes)	
Central const. (vowels)	*Marginal const.* (consonants)	*Intense exp.* (accents)	*Extense exp.* (modulations)

Figure 1.

"Exponents" (vs. "Constituents") are governable; "extense" (vs. "intense") exponents can characterise a complete utterance.

As Siertsema concedes, "there are some difficult points" of interpretation in the analyses presented by Hjelmslev. In the absence of a full glossematic treatment many of the "categorial" assignments remain uncertain. However, I suggest that the interest of the analogy strategy emerges rather clearly, precisely in the form of questions concerning the appropriateness of particular analogies. For instance, what predictions follow from the equation of "noun morphemes" (like case), on the content plane, with "accents", on that of expression? Hjelmslev (1939) suggests that "accent themes" (syllables) may display "accent declension", whereby the accent associated with a syllable varies according to the context. One might consider this to be manifested for example in the phenomenon of "iambic reversal" exhibited in *I saw Príncess Mary* vs. *I saw the Princéss*, and the like. But, apart from the fact that both nominal declension and "accent declension" are (apparently independent) typological variables, what further consequences are there of this particular analogy? I raise this as a question worthy to be pursued rather than necessarily as an expression of scepticism. Unfortunately, to my knowledge, there has been no systematic attempt to pursue the consequences of Hjelmslev's far-reaching inter-planar analogy assumption, which ignores even the differences of alphabet included in the characterisation of SAA suggested above, as well as the asymmetry between the two planes also assumed in my introductory remarks. But such a strong assumption, if pursued appropriately, promises to throw light on a wide range of phenomena, even in the process of its possible disconfirmation: where does the analogy break down?

A partial exception here is Togeby's (1951) work on the structure of French, which at least illustrates analogies merely alluded to in Hjelmslev's publications. Also, particular analogies are quite common in other work of this period and earlier: note especially Jakobson's analyses of case (1936) and tense (1932) in terms of the concept of "markedness" familiar from phonology. But the theoretical status of such analogies remains uncertain. Kuryłowicz (1948a, 1948b, 1949) deploys the inter-planar analogy assumption quite explicitly as a heuristic device, one that leads to a number of insightful analyses of linguistic structures, but again without giving it a theoretical status or exploring the consequences thereof. Here too belongs the Pikes' early work (e.g. 1947) on the "immediate constituents" of the syllable.

The clearest manifestation of analogy in Hjelmslev's own work lies in the status of the relations in terms of which the glossematic procedure is carried out, and in the distinction between "system" (paradigmaticity) and "process" (syntagmaticity) that (amongst other things) they induce. Hjelmslev (e.g. 1953: §11) distinguishes three kinds of "dependency" or "function": interdependences (where two terms are mutually presupposing), determinations (where one term presupposes another) and constellations (where two terms are merely compatible), the relation between process and system being one of determination. They structure both system and process in both planes and embody a claim that putative structural relations such as dependency, constituency, association and precedence, as well as derivationality or stratification, are reducible to (combinations of) these functions. I do not pursue such a claim here, but merely register therein an explicit adoption and specific articulation of the SAA.

Lamb (1966 etc.) develops a notation which expresses (certain combinations of) these relations, a notation which is trans-planar, in conformity with the SAA. But he also introduces a much greater degree of modularisation than is envisaged by Hjelmslev: up to six "strata", each of which introduces a distinct alphabet and thus represents a distinct plane (in the terms discussed above), and is involved in "commutation" relations with adjacent strata, again (in Hjelmslev's terms) introducing a distinction in plane. This, it seems to me, frustrated the development within stratificational theory of appropriate inter-planar analogies beyond the basic common structural principles embodied in the notation. Significantly, Lamb has since (1980) explicitly retreated to the Hjelmslevian two-plane position. I am indeed aware of no motivations for rejecting the essentials of this assumption. Linguistic description requires only two basic alphabets, both distributionally appropriate but both substantively based, one phonetically (phonetic features), the other "notionally" (word classes — cf. e.g. Lyons 1966).

Anderson (1985) suggests a distinctive, "inter-planar" status for *morphology*. It is a plane without its own alphabet and relates syntactic and phonological representations via structures which are purely relational. Lamb's (1966) "-eme" terminology generalises a common analogy, which recognises the appropriateness of according to each plane a *minimal contrastive segmental unit*: "phoneme", "morpheme", "lexeme" ... Now, this is misleading to the extent that it suggests an exact parallelism between phonology and morphology, given the distinction just made. But, if Anderson

(1985) is correct, then Lamb's recognition here of different basic units for the morphology ("morpheme") and syntax ("lexeme") is justified over the commoner "structuralist" assumption that the morpheme is the minimal segment of the syntax. Syntactic and morphological generalisations are distinct; and, whereas morpheme types (root, affix) are defined in purely relational terms, word classes introduce a substantive alphabet, notionally based. Again, this is not the place to confront this complex controversy, involving particularly the distinctiveness of morphology (but cf. Anderson 1980 for one account of part of the debate). Here I simply assert (but see again Anderson 1985 and forthcoming in *Lingua*) that more fruitful analogies with the phonology emerge from a word-based than from a morpheme-based syntax, as well as its rendering the distinctive structure of morphology more transparent.

Consider, however, with regard to the latter claim, in particular, the kinds of discrepancy that have arisen in the assignment of *heads* to morphological constructions: for some (it seems to me rather unsatisfactory) discussion see Zwicky (1985). Anderson (1980) suggests that since the root is the only obligatory part of a word, it is, in accordance with the characterisation of heads appropriate elsewhere, the head of the morphological construction associated with the word. However, Williams (1981) and others have argued that the head of a word is that element which determines the major category of the word, just as the head of a syntactic construction is the element which determines the category of the construction as a whole (as embodied in X' representations of syntactic structure). It is clear that adoption of both these criteria will lead to widespread conflict in the assignment of morphological heads: *goodness*, for example, will be assigned either the root or the category-determining affix as its head. But, I would suggest, the application of the second criterion is simply inappropriate with respect to morphological structure proper, which is unlabelled, provided (as anticipated above) one adopts the "word-and-paradigm" view advocated in recent years (to varying extents) by Robins (1949) and Matthews (1970, 1972, 1974), in particular, and adopted in Anderson (1984, 1985). On such a view, the rules of the morphology take the information provided by the syntax and lexicon concerning word class and morphological properties (number, tense, person, etc.) and subject the root to the particular morphological "processes" (affixation, root modification) determined by these and the morphological class (declension, etc.) of the root. Such a characterisation is appropriate both to inflectional and to derivational morphology, though in the case of the latter, typically a much larger array of morphological classes is necessary (given the range of processes associated with English abstract nouns such as the addition of -*ness*, -*ity*, etc.).

Morphological structure proper will then simply take the form of level (b) in part (ii) of Figure 2:

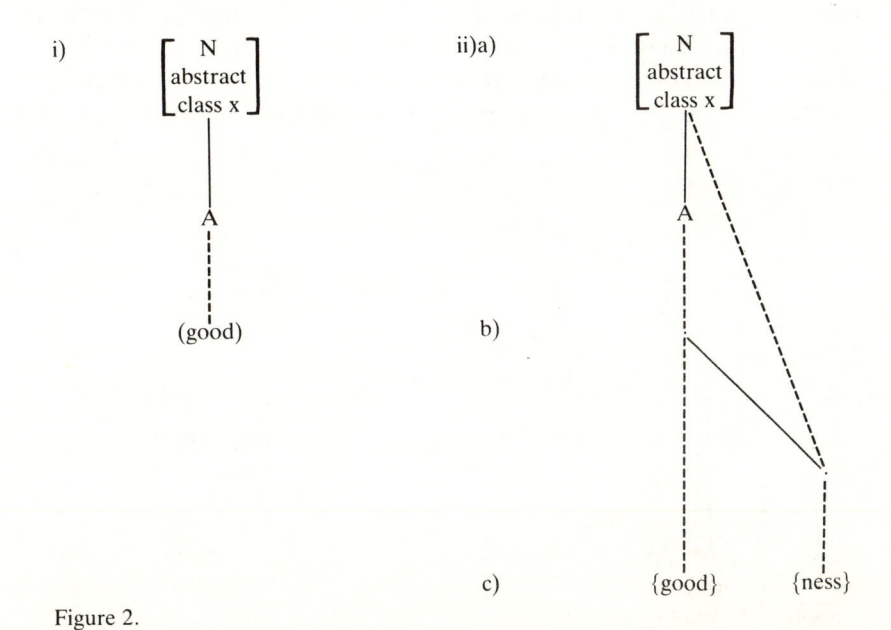

i) $\begin{bmatrix} N \\ \text{abstract} \\ \text{class x} \end{bmatrix}$

  |
  A
  ⋮
  ⋮
(good)

ii) a) $\begin{bmatrix} N \\ \text{abstract} \\ \text{class x} \end{bmatrix}$

b)

c) {good}   {ness}

Figure 2.

where (i) includes the relevant lexico-syntactic information, wherein the continuous lines indicate dependency and the discontinuous (non-immediate) association (cf. Anderson & Durand 1986); and the additional structure in (ii), notably the (adjunctive) dependency relation between root and affix expressed in (b), is assigned by the rules of the morphological component. The morphological structure of (b) introduces no new categorial information; the dependency stemma is unlabelled, and status as root or affix is determined by the dependency relation itself. Since morphemes, unlike words, are not assigned to syntactic categories (and it is inappropriate that they should be, in that they are not syntactic elements), the question of which morpheme in (b), for example, determines (as opposed to "signals") the major category of the word does not arise.

Thus phrases in the syntax are projections of words and their categories, irrespective of whether or not they are morphologically simplex (*pig*) or complex but unaffixed (*breathe*) or bear an affix which signals a change of major class (*piggish*) or not (*piglet*), as is consistent with the well-supported assumption that morphological elements do not participate in syntactic regularities. This is, indeed, a major objection to attempts to invoke an element "Tense" or "Infl" in the characterisation of syntactic structure (cf. Chomsky 1981; Anderson 1976: ch. 1). Only, too, on the basis of the exclusion of morphemes from the syntax can one effectively interpret the Pikean analogy of grammatical units like the clause or noun phrase and the syllable.

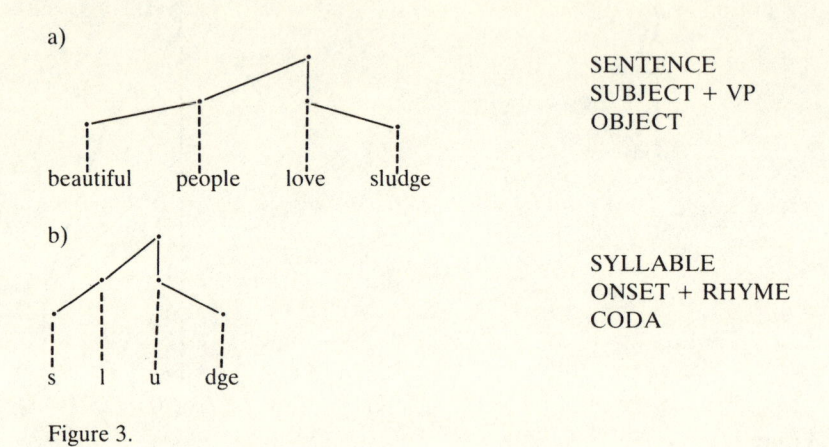

a)

beautiful people love sludge

SENTENCE
SUBJECT + VP
OBJECT

b)

s l u dge

SYLLABLE
ONSET + RHYME
CODA

Figure 3.

Whatever the appropriateness in detail of the analogy between English syntactic and suprasegmental phonological structure instantiated in Figure 3 (for an alternative proposal concerning the syntax see Anderson 1976: ch.4; for the phonology, Anderson 1986), provided it is more appropriate overall than the Hjelmslevian analogy of Figure 1, it is clear that the internal structure of *beautiful* is no more relevant to an evaluation of this than the internal structure of *dge* (in *sludge*: /dǝ/). Just as the internal relationships within the latter are irrelevant to the regularities governing clusters in English and to, for example, the measurement of syllable weight, so the morphological structure of *beautiful* is governed by quite different principles from those applicable to the phrase structure and word order of English sentences, and is irrelevant to their character.

In this respect, then, I am not in accord with the most radical "analogists" of recent times, Pike and Halliday. For them, the morpheme/ word distinction belongs to the "grammatical hierarchy" (Pike 1967) or "rank scale" (Halliday 1961) to which they also refer distinctions in syntactic constituency. In my opinion, it involves a distinction in level (or rather between level and inter-level). It seems to me that the common "structuralist" abolition of morphology detracts from the possibility of formulating the most appropriate analogies. On the other hand, the notion of a fixed *hierarchy* of units (as defended for the syntax in Halliday 1966), notwithstanding the possibility that units may be shifted down the hierarchy (Halliday) or either up or down (Pike), imposes a significant, analogous constraint on syntax and phonology. What is of interest here is the determination of the basis for (the restriction on the cardinality of the units of) the hierarchy and the explication of where the analogy breaks down (such as in the absence of (downward) "rank-shift" in the phonology). A discussion of this, involving in particular a suggestion that, within a dependency grammar, the hierarchy is limited in terms of the interactions of the restricted set of atomic (lexical) categories with the possible distinct dependency configurations that can be erected over strings of them, appears in Anderson (forthcoming) and, on the phonology, in Anderson (1986).

This is not the place, unfortunately, to explore the rich and detailed analogies developed within these two traditions: see again, for an explicit articulation of the analogy assumption, Pike (1967); and compare the syntactic descriptions provided at an early stage by Halliday (1961, 1967/68) with the phonology of Halliday (1967), for example — involving analogies of "scales" and "categories", many of which are parallel to those of the Pikean paradigm. In the case of the Hallidayan enterprise in particular, such an exploration would encounter uncertainties somewhat like those associated with an account, in this respect, of stratificational grammar: the degrees of diversification and analogy are left somewhat indeterminate in much later work (Halliday 1973; e.g. ch. 4, §6). Still less shall I attempt to dissect out the more fragmentary analogies of the tradition associated with Chomsky (e.g. the extension of the cycle from the phonology to the syntax, of "move-α" from syntax to "logical form". Let me merely register a degree of scepticism with respect to one aspect of Pike's proposals which relates to issues already raised above, namely the claimed trimodality of linguistic structure.

Pike (1967) recognises three "hierarchies": grammatical, phonological and lexical. From the start it has been clear that the notion of a "lexical hierarchy", analogous to the grammatical and phonological, is problematical, as one would predict on the basis of Hjelmslev's bi-planar assumption. This lack of analogy was emphasised by some consequences of the work of Crawford (1963), as is to some extent conceded by Pike (1976): the so-called "lexical hierarchy" was parasitic upon, not merely interpretive of the grammatical one. And this inter-dependence, at least, is maintained within more recent proposals for a "lexemic hierarchy" (Wise 1971) rather than (?) a "lexical" one. Thus Becker (1967), for instance, attributes to the tagmeme both "grammatical" and "lexemic" properties: a single element is, for example, said to be simultaneously "subject" ("grammatical") and "actor" ("lexemic"). This suggests that "lexemic" and "grammatical" structure are more intimately related to each other than either of them is to structure. If one accepts that grammatical functions are derivative of (are neutralisations or diversifications of) semantic structure (Anderson 1971, 1977), then "lexemic" and "grammatical" structure belong to the same plane. Even if one does not, the relationship between "lexemic" structure and "grammatical" is clearly of a more intimate character than the relationship of either to phonology. The Hjelmslevian (or Saussurean) bifurcation is inescapable.

More recently, after experiments with an integration of the hierarchies in a composite nine-cell unit (Pike 1974), four-cell grammatical and phonological tagmemes have been reinstated, along with a "referential" tagmeme (Pike & Pike 1977). Trimodality is maintained. But once again, as far as the interpretation of linguistic structure is concerned the referential hierarchy is clearly parasitic upon the grammatical (Pike & Pike 1977: ch. 12; 1983: §1.3.1.2). And, on the other hand, from the point of view of the referential hierarchy, different texts (and, by implication, different languages) can be regarded as providing alternative semiotic media for an extra-linguistic structure: "Grammar is the structure of the text as it is told (or written); reference is the structure of the events in history which the stream of speech (or writing) is referring to" (Pike & Pike 1983: 72). This formulation is quite in line with the Pikean conviction of the structural unity of language and culture; but it does, it seems to me, obscure the characterisation of what is properly linguistic, in particular the degree of stratification intrinsic to linguistic structure.

I end with a plea for explicit recognition and exploitation of the role of structural analogy in the study of language and for the directing of more attention to the determination of the trading relationship between (the consequences of) modularisation (or stratification) and analogy. I also wish to acknowledge the source of my awareness of the concept of structural analogy, as well as of much else in linguistics, in the teaching of Michael Halliday and his associates at Edinburgh in the early '60s. The work embodied in Anderson (1965), which argues for an extension of the Firthian notion of "prosody" to the syntax, is a possibly premature testimony to this indebtedness.

SYSPRO: a computerized method for writing system networks and deriving selection expressions

Michael Cummings[1]

1.1. A key factor in the development of "Systemic functional" linguistics in the mid-1960s from its "Scale-and-Category" origins was the recognition of the priority of the category "system" (Butler 1985: 40-46). Systems, in the Firthian sense of formal models for the paradigmatic aspect of language, had come to be seen as preconditions for structural realizations (Halliday 1966: 60-63). To represent systems diagrammatically a notation was devised which offered a limited logic for the description of paradigmatically arranged feature labels. Variations on the original notation since the 1960s have been minor, and good accounts of the basic notational devices can be found in numerous places (Halliday 1967: 37-38; Halliday & Martin, eds. 1981: 10-11, 56, 220; Butler 1986: 40-42; etc.).

1.2. A system is a set of exclusive choices or "terms". The condition on which the choices depend is an "entry condition". In systemic notation, systems combine to form system networks, such that a term in one system may be the entry condition for another system. Such systems are said to be related by dependency. Systems in a network may also be "simultaneous", i.e., possessing identical entry conditions. As well, systems may have "complex" entry conditions, consisting of terms from several logically prior systems. Such terms are alternatives in "disjunctive" complex entry conditions, or mutual in "conjunctive" complex entry conditions. The logical output of a network is its "selection expressions": all the distinct sets of combined choices which the network permits. Selection expressions too have a standard notation which has remained fairly constant (Berry 1975: 194; Halliday & Martin, eds. 1981: 11).

1.3. Systemic linguistics and its notation have formed the basis for a number of computational projects, especially those undertaken by Winograd (1972; cf. 1983: 272-356), and by Mann and Matthiessen (1983; cf. Mann 1984; Matthiessen 1984 and forthcoming). The application of system network notation to general problem-solving has led to the PASCAL program BARBARA (Grize 1981) which was designed to store and process system networks so that the user may check combinations of features against the network for logical validity (Bliss, Monk & Ogborn 1983: 201-202). However it appears that BARBARA is more useful for general problem-solving than for purely linguistic applications of systemic notation, and I have therefore attempted a program for the manipulation of system networks that would meet the particular needs of systemic linguists. I am indebted to the Bliss, Monk and Ogborn description of BARBARA, however, for inspiration and for a certain amount of terminology.

2.1. Under the name SYSPRO I have produced a package of modules written in PROLOG for the purpose of facilitating the use of systemic notation. The main module, *Network* (Appendix I), serves two basic purposes. It permits the user to input a system network, which is stored in a rule structure. It also outputs all selection expressions which are implied by the network. The need which is satisfied is the need of the linguist for deriving accurately a large number of complex selection expressions from a large and complex network. The second module, *Nets* (Appendix II), draws the stored network as a graphic on the output device. The need which is satisfied is the need of the user to view, in the standard notation, the network s/he has input.

2.2. PROLOG is generally understood to be one of the languages of choice for AI applications. For a general introduction to programming in PROLOG, cf. Clocksin and Mellish (1984). Some of the strategies used in the implementation of SYSPRO I owe to previous work with PROLOG in data retrieval and parsing systems (Baxter & Cummings 1983; Cummings & Regina 1985). The version of SYSPRO represented in Appendix I and II is specific to the dialect of MPROLOG, Version 1.5 (© 1984, Logicware, Inc., Toronto).[2]

3.1. The input procedure for *Network* is illustrated in Figures 1 and 2. In Figure 1 an elementary network is represented in systemic notation. This

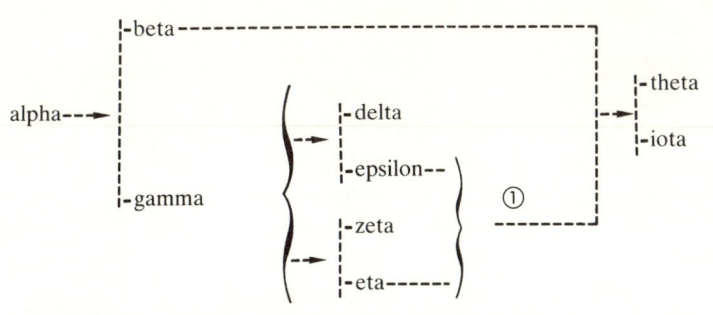

```
          |-beta--------------------------|
          |                               |       |-theta
alpha---->|                 (  |-delta  ) |------>|
          |                 (  |        ) |       |-iota
          |                 (  |-epsilon) ①
          |-gamma           }→ |          -------
                            (  |-zeta   )
                            (→ |        )
                            (  |-eta----)
```

Figure 1. Elementary network

network was designed only to show all of the notational devices that *Network* can handle. The label "alpha" is the entry condition for the first system. "Gamma" is the entry condition for a "brace" of simultaneous systems. The terms "theta" and "iota" belong to a system with a complex entry condition, which is either "beta" or the conjunction of "epsilon" and "eta". Arabic number "1" is introduced into the notation to designate the link between the conjunctive and disjunctive complex entry conditions.

3.2. Figure 2 is the log of the input dialogue for this network. To illustrate its simplicity, computer prompts have been italicized. After the usual PROLOG "?-" prompt, the user begins the input by typing "bar" (referring to the vertical lines which join terms). The computer's first question [Figure 2, line 2] asks whether the entry condition is single, disjunctive or conjunctive. Each subsequent question prompts for the entry condition label or for the term labels until the user concludes the system with the answer "no". The computer indicates that the first system is now complete and stored, and prompts for further entry. After s/he begins the next system [Figure 2, line 14], the user indicates a disjunctive complex entry condition with the response "or". The two entry conditions are input as "beta" and "link#1", for the system of choices "theta" and "iota".

3.3. The user begins to input the third system [Figure 2, line 31] by typing "bra" for "brace". Computer prompts now distinguish each bar after the brace, and the user has to indicate with a "no" when there are no more bars as well as no more choices in any bar. The last system input [Figure 2, line 54] caters to the designation of "link#1". This link is input as a pseudo-term in a pseudo-system. The entry condition for this system is designated

?- bar.

type? simple, or, and?
simple.

entry condition?
alpha.

1st choice?
beta.

another choice?
gamma.

another choice?
no.

system now recorded!

yes
?- bar.

type? simple, or, and?
or.

1st entry condition?
beta.

another entry condition?
link #1.

another entry condition?
no.

1st choice?
theta.

another choice?
iota.

another choice?
no.

system now recorded!

yes
?- bra.

type? simple, or, and?
simple.

entry condition?
gamma.

1st bar!

1st choice?
delta.

another choice?
epsilon.

another choice?
no.

2nd bar!

1st choice?
zeta.

another choice?
eta.

another choice?
no.

another bar?
no.

system now recorded!

yes
?- bar.

type? simple, or, and?
and.

1st entry condition?
epsilon.

another entry condition?
eta.

another entry condition?
no.

1st choice?
link #1.

another choice?
no.

system now recorded!

yes

Figure 2. Log of input session

conjunctive with the response "and". The conjunctive entry conditions are "epsilon" and "eta". The sole term is designated "link#1" and with this the whole network is now entered. Links in the form of pseudo-systems with only one term each correspond to the concept of the "gate" in the programming of the Nigel text generator (Mann & Matthiessen 1983: 5, 29-30, 62-63).

4.1. As noted, selection expressions in systemic notation have a traditional format. The whole expression is enclosed in braces. Dependencies are distinguished by colons, and simultaneities are enclosed by braces and distinguished by slants. Conjunctive entry conditions are labelled with ";l" and only one of the conditions shows the mutual dependency.

4.2. All of these features are replicated in the output of the *Network* module. The first part of Figure 3 shows that all the user need do to output all possible selection expressions is type the command "express". [Computer outputs in this and the following figures are no longer italicized.] Each resulting selection expression is numbered serially. The "theta" and "iota" choices when dependencies of "epsilon" and "eta" (in expressions #6 and #7) are shown after the last mutual condition. Since the designation of links is not part of traditional notation, "link#1" has been automatically excluded from the selection expressions, which have been appropriately reanalyzed. (But if the user wants to see the links in the selection expressions, s/he need only type in the switch "links_in" before deriving the expressions.)

4.3. Another facility which the program offers is a choice of initial entry condition for the selection expressions. In the "express" command, the user may designate the entry condition of some system in the network other than the earliest, for example, "express(gamma)". The program will derive selection expressions only for that subset of the stored network which begins with the designated entry condition.

5.1. The rules which represent the stored system network can be viewed with the command "showrules", as in the latter part of Figure 3. Each rule has a typical PROLOG structure. The name "rule" is predicated of two arguments. The first argument is the left-hand entry condition of some system, and the second argument is a right-hand term or set of terms of that

?- express.
1. {alpha: beta: theta}.
2. {alpha: beta: iota}.
3. {alpha: gamma: {delta/zeta}}.
4. {alpha: gamma: {delta/eta}}.
5. {alpha: gamma: {epsilon/zeta}}.
6. {alpha: gamma: {epsilon;I/eta;I: theta}}.
7. {alpha: gamma: {epsilon;I/eta;I: iota}}.

yes
?-showrules.

rule ([alpha], [beta]).
rule ([alpha], [gamma]).
rule ([beta], [theta]).
rule ([beta], [iota]).
rule ([link # 1], [theta]).
rule ([link # 1], [iota]).
rule ([gamma], [delta, zeta]).
rule ([gamma], [delta, eta]).
rule ([gamma], [epsilon, zeta]).
rule ([gamma], [epsilon, eta]).
rule ([epsilon, eta], [link # 1]).

yes
?-

Figure 3. Log of output session

system. Actually each argument is a set of one or more labels between square brackets, i.e., a PROLOG list structure (Clocksin & Mellish 1984: 41ff.). There is a rule for each dependency in the network. "Bar" systems are recorded with as many rules as there are dependent terms. Braces of systems are recorded with as many rules as there are combinations of simultaneous terms. Systems with single or disjunctive entry conditions show only a single label in the left-hand list. Systems with conjunctive entry conditions show all those entry conditions on the left. Bar systems show only single labels on the right but braces of systems show all the simultaneous choices in any one combination of terms in the right-hand list.

5.2. As we have seen, the *Network* module creates the rules and stores them in active memory as the product of the input dialogue. The program then interprets them to derive the selection expressions. *Network* will also store the rules in disk memory when the user types the command "save" and specifies a disk file name. This procedure simultaneously erases the rules from active memory to prepare for the next network to be input. The disk file can be restored to active memory at any time.

6.1. A limited amount of editing facility is built into the module. All the rules can be erased from active memory on the command "erase" if the user wishes to scrap the input without saving it to disk. In addition, the user can erase one rule or some selected fraction of the rules from active memory by using the PROLOG predicate "retractall". For example, the user may wish to eliminate from the network the connection between "beta" and the choice of terms "theta" and "iota". Inspection of the rules indicates that eliminating those with "beta" as the left-hand will effect this result. The user then types "retractall(rule([beta],X))" to erase just those two rules. A single new rule can be entered, perhaps to correct some misspelling, with "assert" as in "assert(rule([beta],[theta]))".

6.2. Some PROLOG interpreters include sophisticated editorial environments that permit interactive editing during a PROLOG session. MPROLOG, Version 1.5 (© 1984 Logicware, Inc., Toronto) offers just such an editing facility for rewriting rules or, if desired, even the program itself during the execution session (Logicware 1984b: 131-153).

7.1. The method of interpreting rules to produce selection expressions is achieved by a typical PROLOG strategy. A simple algorithm to represent all the selection expressions produced by the elementary network of Figure 1 is represented in Figure 4. This tree structure algorithm closely resembles

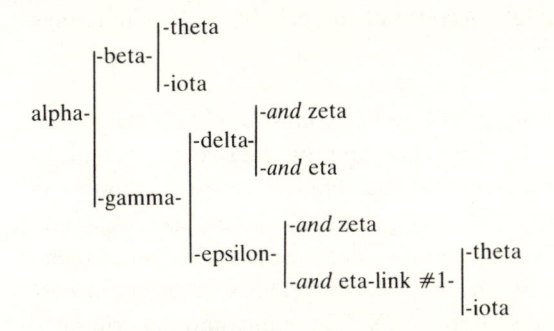

```
              |-theta
      |-beta-|
              |-iota
alpha-|                    |-and zeta
              |-delta-|
                           |-and eta
      |-gamma-|
                              |-and zeta
              |-epsilon-|                      |-theta
                              |-and eta-link #1-|
                                                |-iota
```

Figure 4. Tree algorithm for selection expressions

a "displayed" system network (cf. Fawcett forthcoming). Each selection expression can be read out of the tree from left to right and successively from top to bottom, just as one would read a system network.

7.2. The PROLOG clauses which interpret stored rules first determine which label occurs on the left-hand side of some rule and does not occur on the right-hand side of any rule. This is the initial entry condition for the whole network. The rules are then chained together, so that right-hand sides match left-hand sides in any succession of dependencies implied by those rules. As many chains can be formed from a given set of rules as there are selection expressions implicit in the network. Each chain comes to an end with the rule whose right-hand side yields a terminal label. At this point, the chain, in the form of a PROLOG list, is forwarded to output clauses which format the list in the proper notational conventions, and print it out.

7.3. As each selection expression is finished printing out, the program is made to backtrack (Clocksin & Mellish 1984: 58ff.). Each backtracking proceeds to the point where an alternative rule for a rule already selected in the chain may first be found. At this point, the program goes forward again on a new subchain until the next selection expression is printed out. As Figure 4 illustrates, the first chain will contain "alpha", "beta" and "theta". Backtracking will go as far as the original selection of the "beta"-"theta" rule. The alternative is the "beta"-"iota" rule, which reforms the end of the list to yield the next selection expression. The next backtracking is unable to find another left-hand "beta", so the backtracking continues until it turns up an alternative left-hand "alpha" rule, which initiates the third selection expression. (For a more complete account of the procedure cf. Cummings forthcoming).

8.1. Although the elementary network used as illustration contains only four real systems and nine labels, there is no limit on the size and complexity of networks which the *Network* module can handle, unless it is imposed by the hardware or by the PROLOG interpreter. However, size and complexity of networks does have obvious implications for user time and execution time. The entry dialogue for the elementary network takes about two and one-half minutes. On a shared VAX 750 minicomputer running MPROLOG, Version 1.5, the selection expressions are typically screened in about seven seconds of user time.

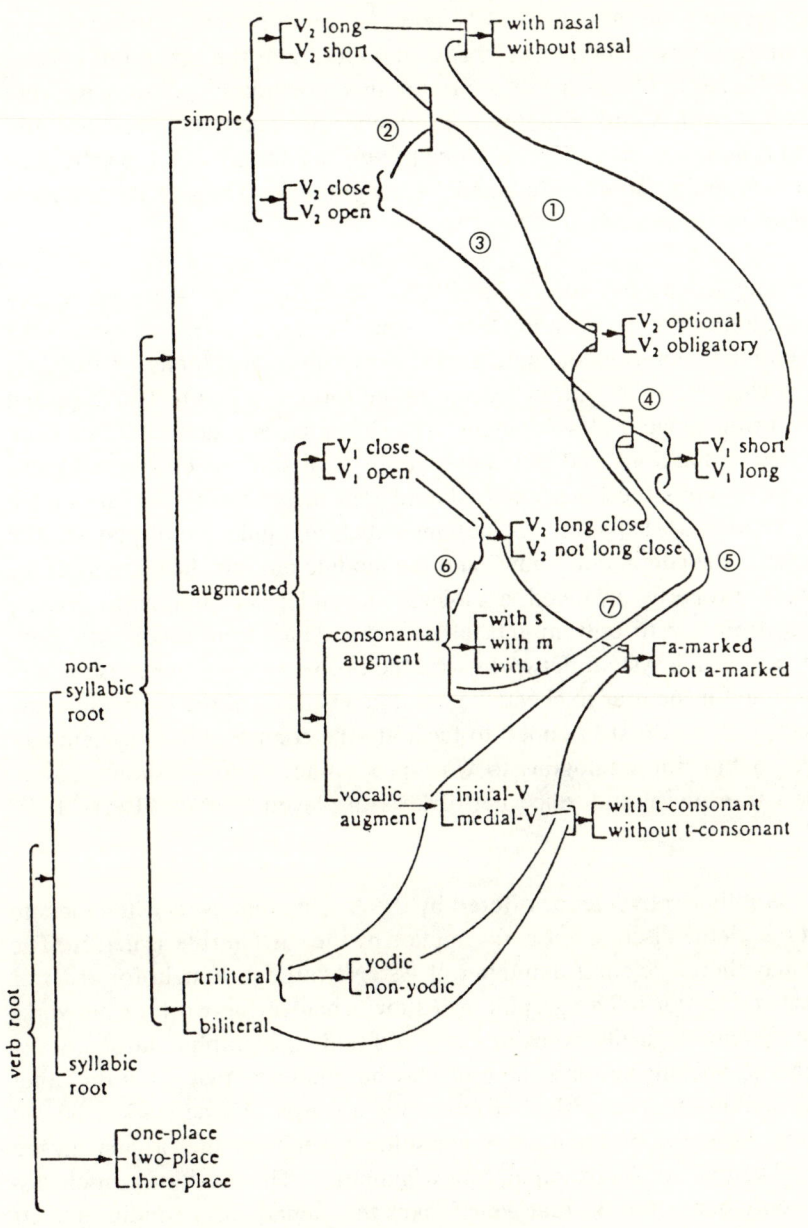

Figure 5. Network for Beja verbal root-morphemes

8.2. Figure 5, on the other hand, shows Hudson's network for Beja verbal root-morphemes, unedited except for numbering of the seven links (Hudson 1973: 527). The entry dialogue for this moderately complex network takes just over twenty minutes. The number of selection expressions produced is no fewer than 957. The same hardware and software typically print these out on the screen in just under forty minutes. (The actual cpu time is 23 minutes, 15 seconds.)

9.1. The second module in SYSPRO, called *Nets*, offers a graphic representation of the network implied by stored rules. The graphic mimics the conventional notation of system networks within the limits of ordinary screen characters. Its output resembles the format of Figure 1, except that in its current stage of development, *Nets* shows systems dependent on complex entry conditions as dependent on only the first of the entry conditions. That is, it omits the lines which should join these systems to subsequent entry conditions. However, all systems, labels and links are displayed. The user types the command "show" and the module outputs the systems of the network properly arranged as logical dependencies and appropriately spaced from top to bottom and left to right. Apart from solving the difficulty of drawing system networks with the proper spacing, *Nets* also makes it possible for the user to check the input in any stage of the entry dialogue. In fact, *Nets* was first intended to facilitate the composition of system networks, a function analogous to word-processing. Figure 6 shows a well-known transitivity and voice network as displayed by *Nets* (Berry 1975: 189).

9.2. Another convenience offered by the *Nets* module is its willingness to print out all the discrete networks implied by the current rule structure. The user may therefore enter a number of systems without thought for order or logical connections. The graphic will show whatever network or networks these systems logically constitute. In addition, the graphic automatically reduces to one any systems the user may have entered twice. On the other hand, should the user wish to display only a subset of a network, s/he can include the name of some entry condition other than the original in the "show" command, for example, "show(gamma)". The resulting graphic displays only one network, that which takes the named entry condition as its starting point.

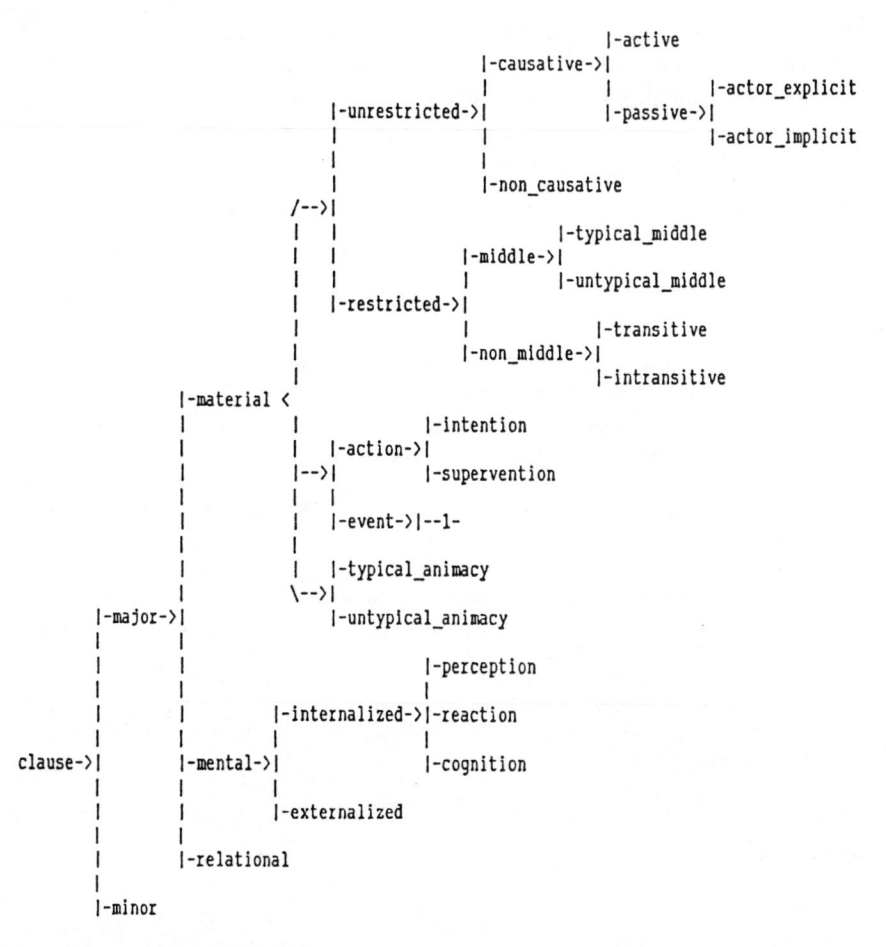

```
                                                    |-active
                                       |-causative->|
                                       |            |         |-actor_explicit
                           |-unrestricted->|        |-passive->|
                           |            |                     |-actor_implicit
                           |            |
                           |            |-non_causative
                       /-->|
                       |   |                        |-typical_middle
                       |   |            |-middle->|
                       |   |            |         |-untypical_middle
                       |   |-restricted->|
                       |            |               |-transitive
                       |            |-non_middle->|
                       |                            |-intransitive
           |-material <
           |           |              |-intention
           |           |   |-action->|
           |           |-->|          |-supervention
           |           |   |
           |           |   |-event->|--1-
           |           |
           |           |   |-typical_animacy
           |           \-->|
|-major->|             |-untypical_animacy
          |           |
          |           |                 |-perception
          |           |                 |
          |           |   |-internalized->|-reaction
          |           |   |                 |
clause->|             |-mental->|         |-cognition
          |           |   |
          |           |   |-externalized
          |           |
          |           |-relational
          |
          |-minor
```

Figure 6. Graphic display

9.3. The *Nets* program is another application of typical PROLOG strategy. Clauses which interpret the stored rules this time create a list of information units containing three cells. The first cell contains a vertical coordinate, the second a horizontal coordinate, and the third a label representing either an entry condition or a term. The order of the units in the list is the order of dependency in the network, a natural product of rule chaining. The horizontal coordinate is calculated simply from the length of previous labels, arrows and gaps. In general, the vertical coordinates in each system are left as uninstantiated variables until those of the dependent systems are calculated; they are then calculated by reverse instantiation. The list is then reformed by attaching to it a similarly formed list of vertical lines, and completely resorted to order by vertical and horizontal coordinates. Output clauses then write the label and line content of the cells on the screen as guided by the cell coordinates.[3]

Notes

1. An earlier version of this paper was read at the *13th International Systemic Workshop Conference*, University of Kent at Canterbury, England, July 16-18, 1986.

2. In MPROLOG, Version 1.5, a number of built-in predicates occur which are not shared by the widely known DEC-10 PROLOG nor by the generalized version described in Clocksin and Mellish (1984). The version of SYSPRO offered here is designed to run in the PDSS environment of MPROLOG, in both the VAX/VMS and the IBM-PC DOS compatible versions of the language (cf. Logicware 1984a).

3. The largest unsolved problem which the SYSPRO package represents is how to make it accessible to systemic linguists. Because of the variety, expense, and sometimes unavailability of computer software and hardware in the world, I wish that any interested systemic linguist would please send me any network for which s/he might like to receive a complete output of selection expressions. But SYSPRO is also a very short program, occupying just 22 blocks of disk space. It is therefore extremely portable, and I am happy to distribute the SYSPRO package on floppy disk for unlimited use, copying or modification to anyone who sends me a disk for that purpose.

Appendix

APPENDIX I

```
/*------NETWORK Version 1.0 by Michael Cummings------*/
/*------Copyright 1986 by Michael Cummings------*/
/*------Anyone wishing to use, copy or modify this program------*/
/*------may do so without need of explicit permission------*/

module network.

/*$eject*/
body.

operator(#,lr,502).
operator(ng,lr,500).
```

SYSPRO   57

/*-----Utility Predicates-----   */

member(A,[A|_]) .
member(A,[_|X]) :-
     member(A,X) .

append([],L,L).
append([X|L1],L2,[X|L3]) :-
     append(L1,L2,L3).

retractall(X) :-
     del_matching_statement(X), fail .
retractall(_) .

last(X,[X]).
last(X,[A|B]) :- last(X,B).
                                                                          */
/*-----Editing Predicates---

bar :-
     nl, mess99, nl, read_10(X), nl, bar(X), nl, nl, mess0, nl .
bra :-
     nl, mess99, nl, read_10(X), nl, bra(X), nl, nl, mess0, nl .

bar(simple) :-
     nl, mess1, nl, read_10(X), choice1(Y), choices(Z),
        member(A,[Y|Z]), assert(rule([X],[A])), fail .
bar(simple) .
bar(or) :-
     entry1(X), entries(Y), choice1(Z), choices(A),
        member(B,[X|Y]), member(C,[Z|A]), assert(rule([B],[C])),
        fail .
bar(or) .
bar(and) :-
     entry1(X), entries(Y), choice1(Z), choices(A),
        member(B,[Z|A]), assert(rule([X|Y],[B])), fail .
bar(and) .

bra(simple) :-
     nl, mess1, nl, read_10(X), bars(Y), arrange(Y,Z),
        assert(rule([X],Z)), fail .
bra(simple) .
bra(or) :-
     entry1(X), entries(Y), bars(Z), member(B,[X|Y]), arrange(Z,A),
        assert(rule([B],A)), fail .
bra(or) .
bra(and) :-
     entry1(X), entries(Y), bars(Z), arrange(Z,A),
        assert(rule([X|Y],A)), fail .
bra(and) .

```
bars([X,Y|Z]) :-
    firstbar(X), secbar(Y), morebars(Z), ! .

firstbar([Y|Z]) :-
    nl, nl, mess3, mess5, choice1(Y), choices(Z) .

secbar([Y|Z]) :-
    nl, nl, mess6, mess5, choice1(Y), choices(Z) .

morebars([[X|Y]|Z]) :-
    nl, nl, mess4, mess7, nl, inputs(_), choice1(X), choices(Y),
        morebars(Z) .
morebars([]) .

arrange([H|T],[A|B]) :-
    member(A,H), arrange(T,B) .
arrange([],[]) .

entry1(X) :-
    nl, mess3, mess1, nl, read_10(X), ! .

entries([X|Y]) :-
    nl, nl, mess4, mess1, nl, inputs(X), entries(Y), ! .
entries([]) :-
    ! .

choice1(Y) :-
    nl, nl, mess3, mess2, nl, read_10(Y), ! .

choices([X|Y]) :-
    nl, nl, mess4, mess2, nl, inputs(X), choices(Y), ! .
choices([]) :-
    ! .

inputs(X) :-
    read_10(X), dichot(X) .

dichot(no) :-
    !, fail .
dichot(_) .

erase :-
    retractall(rule(_,_)) .

mess99 :-
    write('type? simple,or,and?'), ! .

mess0 :-
    write('system now recorded!'), ! .

mess1 :-
    write('entry condition?'), ! .
```

```
mess2 :-
    write('choice?'), ! .

mess3 :-
    write('1st '), ! .

mess4 :-
    write('another '), ! .

mess5 :-
    write('bar!'), ! .

mess6 :-
    write('2nd '), ! .

mess7 :-
    write('bar?'), ! .

mess8 :-
    write('Name of save file?'), ! .

mess9 :-
    write('Name of restore file?'), ! .

/*----------------Output Predicates--------------                    */

express :-
    prime(X), express(X) .

express(X) :-
    nl,set_evaluation_limit(8333000),
    express(X,Y), Y\==[], decode(Y,Y1), moutput([X#Y1]), fail .
express(_) :-
    retractall(d(_)), assert(d(0)), retractall(pri(_)) .

express(X,Y) :-
    match(X,L,R), list_length(L,N), backing(X), or1(X,L,R,N,Y) .
express(X,_) :-
    backed(X), retractall(backed(X)), retractall(if(X)), !, fail .
express(_,[]) .

backed(_) :-
    fail .

or1(_,_,R,1,Y) :-
    express2(R,Y) .
or1(X,L,R,N,Y) :-
    N>1, assert(if(X)), express3(L,R,Y) .

express2([X|T],[X#Y|T1]) :-
    express(X,Y), express2(T,T1) .
express2([],[]) .
```

```
express3(L,[X|T],[X#Y|T1]) :-
    assemble(L), upflag(L), express(X,Y), express2(T,T1) .
express3(L,_,_) :-
    assemble(L), !, fail .
express3(_,_,[]) .

prime(P) :-
    rule(X,_), member(P,X), prime1(P), pflag(P) .

prime1(P) :-
    rule(_,Y), member(P,Y), !, fail .
prime1(_) .

pflag(X) :-
    pri(X), !, fail .
pflag(X) :-
    assert(pri(X)) .

pri(_) :- fail .

match(X,[X],R) :-
    rule([X],R) .
match(X,[H,Y|T],R) :-
    rule([H,Y|T],R), member(X,[H,Y|T]), test(X,[H,Y|T]) .

backing(_) .
backing(X) :-
    assert(backed(X)), fail .

test(_,L) :-
    assemble(L) .
test(X,_) :-
    not(if(X)) .

if(_) :-
    fail .

upflag(L) :-
    shift(L,L1), assert(flag(L1)), !, downflag(L1) .

shift([link#X|T],T1) :-
    find(X,LS,[]), flatten(LS,LSS), append(LSS,T,TX),
        shift(TX,T1) .
shift([H|T],[H|T1]) :-
    shift(T,T1) .
shift([],[]) .

find(X,LS,B) :-
    rule(L,R), member(link#X,R), test2(L,B,B1),
        append([L],[L1],LS), find(X,L1,B1) .
find(_,[],_) .
```

```
flatten([H1,H2|T],LSS) :-
    append(H1,H2,HX), flatten([HX|T],LSS) .
flatten([LSS],LSS) .

test2(L,B,_) :-
    member(L,B), !, fail .
test2(L,B,B1) :-
    append([L],B,B1) .

downflag(_) .
downflag(L1) :-
    del_matching_statement(flag(L1)), !, fail .

assemble([H|T]) :-
    if(H), assemble(T), ! .
assemble([]) .

links_in :-
    asserta((decode(X,X):-!)) .

links_out :-
    del_matching_statement((decode(X,X):-!)) .

clear :-
    retractall(backed(_)),
    retractall(if(_)),
    retractall(flag(_)),
    retractall(d(_)),
    assert(d(0)),
    retractall(pri(_)) .

/*-----Display Predicates-----                                        */

showrules :-
    nl, listing(rule/2) .

save :-
    nl, mess8, nl, read_10(X), nl, saving(X) .

saving(X) :-
    set_file_attributes("outfile",X),
    set_current_output("outfile"),
    ( rule(A,B), write(rule(A,B)), write('.'), nl, fail; succeed ),
    retractall(rule(Y,Z)), close_output("outfile"),
    set_current_output("output") .

restore :-
    nl, mess9, nl, read_10(X), restoring(X) .

restoring(X) :-
    [X] .
```

```
decode([link#_#[X#Y|TA]|T],Y1) :-
    append(TA,T,TZ), decode([X#Y|TZ],Y1), ! .
decode([link#_#[]|T],T1) :-
    decode(T,T1), ! .
decode([X#Y|T],[X#Y2|T1]) :-
    decode(Y,Y1), flag(X,Y1,Y2), decode(T,T1) .
decode([],[]) .

flag(X,Y1,'%'#Y1) :-
    flag(L), member(X,L), ! .
flag(X,Y1,Y1) .

flag(_) :-
    fail .

moutput([X#Y]) :-
    count, write('{ '), write(X), output1(Y), write(' }.'), nl,
      nl, ! .

output1('%'#[]) :-
    write(';I') .
output1('%'#[X#Y]) :-
    write(';I: '), write(X), output1(Y) .
output1('%'#[X#Y|T]) :-
    write(';I:'), write(' { '), write(X), output1(Y), output2(T) .
output1([X#Y]) :-
    write(': '), write(X), output1(Y) .
output1([X#Y|T]) :-
    write(': { '), write(X), output1(Y), output2(T) .
output1([]) .

output2([X#Y|T]) :-
    write(' / '), write(X), output1(Y), output2(T) .
output2([]) :-
    write(' } ') .

count :-
    d(X), Y is X+1, asserta(d(Y)), write(Y), write('. '), ! .

d(0) .


endmod /* network */  .
```

APPENDIX II

```
/*-----NETS Version 1.0 by Michael Cummings-----*/
/*-----Copyright 1986 by Michael Cummings-----*/
/*-----Anyone wishing to use, copy or modify this program-----*/
/*-----may do so without need of explicit permission-----*/
```

```
show :- prime(X),show(X),fail.
show :- retractall(pri(_)).

show(X) :- set_evaluation_limit(8333000),
      tree(1,I,V2,X,T,L),append(T,L,TL),
    sort(TL,TLs),nl,nl,screen(1,1,TLs),
      retractall(red(_)),retractall(orange(_)),!.

tree(N,V,V2,X,[V1/N/Xa|T],L) :- mr(X,Y),augm(N,Y,X,Xa),
    meas(Xa,N,N1),tree(N1,V,Vx,Y,T1,L1),tree1(N1,Vx,V2,X,T2,L2),
    append(T1,T2,T),lines(T1,T2,L3,V1),append(L1,L2,Lx),
    append(Lx,L3,L).
tree(N,V,Vx,link#X,[V/N/Xa|[]],[]) :- Vx is V+2,
    concatenate('--',X,Xx),concatenate(Xx,'-',Xa).
tree(N,V,Vx,X,[V/N/Xa|[]],[]) :- Vx is V+2,concatenate('-',X,Xa).

tree1(N,V,V2,X,T,L) :- mr(X,Y),
    tree(N,V,Vx,Y,T1,L1),tree1(N,Vx,V2,X,T2,L2),append(T1,T2,T),
    append(L1,L2,L).
tree1(_,V2,V2,_,[],[]).

mr('--',Y) :- left(X,N),!,rule([X|_],[H,I|T]),
      pick(N,1,[H,I|T],Y),oflag(Y).
mr(X,Y) :- rule([X|_],[Y]),rflag(Y).
mr(X,'--') :- rule([X|_],[H,I|T]),lflag(X,N),
    list_length([H,I|T],L),!,endbra(X,N,L).

rflag(Y) :- red(Y),!,fail.
rflag(Y) :- assert(red(Y)).

oflag(Y) :- orange(Y),!,fail.
oflag(Y) :- assert(orange(Y)).

lflag(X,N) :- left(X,N),Nx is N+1,asserta(left(X,Nx)).
left(_,0).

red(_) :- fail.
orange(_) :- fail.

pick(N,N,[H|T],H).
pick(N,Nx,[H|T],Y) :- Nxx is Nx+1,pick(N,Nxx,T,Y).

endbra(_,N,L) :- N<L.
endbra(X,_,_) :- retractall(left(X,_)),assert(left(_,0)),
      !,fail.

augm(_,link#_,link#X,Xa) :-
      concatenate('--',X,Xx),concatenate(Xx,'-',Xa).
augm(_,'--',link#X,Xa) :-
      concatenate('--',X,Xx),concatenate(Xx,'- < ',Xa).
augm(_,_,link#X,Xa) :-
      concatenate('--',X,Xx),concatenate(Xx,'->|',Xa).
```

```
augm(1,'--',X,Xa) :- concatenate(X,' < ',Xa).
augm(1,_,X,Xa) :- concatenate(X,'->|',Xa).
augm(_,link#_,'--','').
augm(_,_,'--',',-->|').
augm(_,'--',X,Xa) :-
      concatenate('-',X,Xx),concatenate(Xx,' < ',Xa).
augm(_,_,X,Xa) :-
      concatenate('-',X,Xx),concatenate(Xx,'->|',Xa).

meas(Xa,N,N1) :-
      string_length(Xa,L),N1 is N+L.

lines([Y/_/_|_],[],[],Y).
lines([Y/X/'-->|'|_],T2,[Y/X1/'/'|L],V) :-
     lines1(bra,X,Y,T2,X1,L,V).
lines([Y/X/''|_],T2,[Y/X1/'/'|L],V) :-
     lines1(bra,X,Y,T2,X1,L,V).
lines([Y/X/_|_],T2,[Y/X1/'|'|L],V) :-
     lines1(bar,X,Y,T2,X1,L,V).
lines1(Br,X,Y,T2,X1,L,V) :- bag_of(A/X/B,(member(A/X/B,T2)),Txs),
     last(Yz/_/_,Txs),X1 is X-1,
     V is Y+((Yz-Y)/2),Y1 is Y+1,lines2(Br,X1,Y1,V,Yz,L).
lines2(bra,X,Y,_,Y,[Y/X/'\'|[]]).
lines2(_,X,Y,_,Y,[Y/X/'|'|[]]).
lines2(Br,X,Y,Y,Yz,L) :- Y1 is Y+1,lines2(Br,X,Y1,1,Yz,L).
lines2(Br,X,Y,V,Yz,[Y/X/'|'|L]) :- Y1 is Y+1,lines2(Br,X,Y1,V,Yz,L).

screen(_,_,[]).
screen(Y,N,[Y/X/Z|T]) :-
    Nx is X-N, string_length(Z,L),N1 is X+L,inscribe(N1,Nx,Z),
    screen(Y,N1,T).
screen(Y,_,T) :-
    nl,Y1 is Y+1,screen(Y1,1,T).

inscribe(N1,Nx,Z) :-
    N1<132,tab(Nx),write(Z).
inscribe(_,_,_).
```

Cultural, situational and modal labels in dictionaries of English

Arthur Delbridge

When Dr Johnson acknowledged, in his *Plan*, the difficulty of deciding "between the equiponderant authorities of writers alike eminent for judgment and accuracy", he identified one of the lexicographer's perennial problems: how to judge that one usage is less appropriate (or less correct, or less elegant) than another, and then express this judgment in a dictionary. In spite of his difficulty, Johnson seemed not to hesitate to say of *banter* that it is "a barbarous word", that *keen* (as a verb) is "unauthorised", that *clever* is a "low word, scarcely ever used but in burlesque or conversation; and applied to anything a man likes, without a settled meaning". Later lexicographers have continued to use labels to express relationships between words and the general situational characteristics of their use while dictionary users have (as we know from their response to the labelling policy of *Webster's Third International*) expected to have their prejudices about particular words labelled accordingly in their favoured dictionaries. Labelling is necessary (so the common attitude runs) so that the language may be protected from change and decay, change typically implying change to the bad. The lexicographer has a duty to be authoritative, and to maintain right usage and discourage the wrong. This is the unprofessional attitude to the role of the lexicographer.

The contrasting professional attitude is captured by Robert Burchfield in his Preface to OEDSII:

> My colleagues and I ... do not personally approve of all the words and phrases that are recorded in this dictionary nor necessarily condone their use by others. Nevertheless, in our function as "marshallers" of words, we have set them down as objectively as possible to form a permanent record of the language of our time, the useful and the neutral, those that are

decorous and well-formed beside those that are controversial, tasteless, or worse.

However in OEDSIII, his attitude had changed. In the Preface to that volume he observes that:

> during the 1970s the markedly linguistic description of the post-war years was to some extent brought into question. Infelicities of language, whether in the spoken or the written word, were identified and assailed by a great many people who seemed to believe that the English language itself was in a period of decline.... One small legacy of these great debates is that here and there in the present volume, I have found myself adding my own opinions about the acceptability of certain words or meanings in educated use.

And in COD (1982), the label D indicates a disputed usage, while *Erroneous* with a capital E shows that in the editor's view the labelled usage is wrong.

Such labelling, showing particular relations between words and their use, is characteristic of monolingual dictionaries, written only for the well standardised languages of the world, for the use of those with native speaker competence, who wish either to consult an authoritative (that is, well-made) record, or to seek guidance on some aspect of usage they are uncertain or ignorant of. A typical motive for consulting the record is the wish to confirm what is the well-rooted, standard, prestigious word form current at the time of use. The lexicographical definition of the term *standard English* in *Webster's Third International* (sense 4) is "all words entered in a general English language dictionary that are not restricted by a label (as *slang*, *dial*, *obs*, *biol*, *Scot*)". Clearly the user needs to be able to interpret the labels that express the relations between words and their use.

However, in twentieth century monolingual English lexicography, the user is beset by two monstrous difficulties: one, uncertainty over the criteria by which labels are assigned in a particular dictionary and two, the lack of terminological consensus between dictionaries.

As to criteria, the user could expect to find suitable definitions either in Prefaces *or* in the dictionary entries for the words which serve as labels. Thus an OED reader interested in the meaning of *colloq.* as a label may seek out that listed sense of *Colloquial* which seems most appropriate, viz. definition 2:

> Of words, phrases, etc.: Belonging to common speech: characteristic of or proper to ordinary conversation, as distinguished from formal or elevated language. (The usual sense)

For *slang* as label, the reader may be drawn towards definition 1c of *Slang* as word:

> Language of a highly colloquial type, considered as below the level of standard educated speech, and consisting either of new words or of current words employed in some special sense.

These two definitions suggest a gamut of quality in which slang is at the bottom, and colloquial (unless it be "highly colloquial", in which case it is slang) has an intermediate position, with formal or elevated at the top.

If this structure seems clear to the dictionary user, it is nevertheless apparently difficult for the dictionary writer to apply it consistently. Let the articles on *pull* as noun, verb, and verb phrase in OEDSIII illustrate the point. It is easy to accept the label *colloq.* (chiefly *Austral.*) for *take a pull (at oneself)* in the sense of "pull oneself together". It is easy to accept that the noun *pull*, in the sense of "influence", should have been upgraded from *U.S. slang*, as it had been labelled in OED, to *colloq.* (chiefly *U.S.*) in OEDSIII. It is easy to accept the label *slang* for *pull* in the sexual sense of slang *lay*, as in "I'm not an easy pull". But it is harder to understand why *pull the other one, (it's got bells on it)* is unlabelled; or why *pull (or pull down) a wage* is labelled *colloq.* in 11f. but *slang* in 24f; or why *pull* in the sense of "pick up a partner (for sexual purposes)" is labelled *coarse slang*, even though *pull* for *lay* (as above) is only *slang*; or why *to pull (one's pud(ding) or wire)*, meaning "to masturbate", is only labelled *slang* while *pull off* (*Usu. refl.* "To cause (a person) to ejaculate by masturbation") gets the label *coarse slang*.

The criteria are not obviously linguistic; if they are moral, and make judgments on degrees of obscenity, some puzzlement over an apparent inconsistency in labelling is inevitable. The history of legal argumentation over obscenity shows how hard it is to get agreement among individuals.

As to the lack of terminological consensus between dictionaries, *Webster's Third International* enters no evidence of *pull*, either as verb or noun, in sexual senses, and the only sense of *pull* labelled *slang* is 7b. "to act or behave in the manner of (a Simon Legree)". It is hard to know whether the difference between the two dictionaries springs from their respective national cultures, or (more technically) simply from the degree of abridgement each editor observes.

Labelling is inevitably governed by editorial policy, though the most intensely argued prefatory statement on labelling may be of little help to the user, for it is well known that those who consult dictionaries usually pay little attention to editorial prefaces. The explosion of hostile criticism that greeted *Webster's Third International* at its first appearance showed that readers may be quietly aroused if a dictionary disappoints their expectations, especially on matters of policy. Gove decided to make no use of the label *colloquial*, which had been so widely used in the Second Edition, and to let the label *slang* alone carry information about informal usage. *Slang* meant "especially appropriate in contexts of extreme informality", though it was conceded that "there is no completely objective test for slang, especially in application to a word out of context" and that "no word is invariable slang". No mention is made, in Gove's definition, of slang as a style of language rather than a level of formality, nor of slang as rhetorical and connotative. The non-use of *colloquial* as a label dismisses the distinction between usages that are characteristically or appropriately either spoken or written. Yet no reader of modern fiction, or of feature articles in daily newspapers, can be confident that there are usages which belong exclusively to spoken English and could therefore merit the dictionary label *colloq.* in its modern sense. Editorial policy for many dictionaries insists on written evidence for usages that may then be labelled *colloq.*, thus suggesting that this label does not have a modal basis at all.

Labelling has become a can of worms, as Gove (1964: 357) recognised:

> This system has outgrown its usefulness. To put such labels on a dictionary definition is to fix the word beyond all allowance for variety.... This labelling system is effete, and no system of graduated demarcators has yet been devised to take its place.

If there were a system of graduated demarcators, it would need to be multidimensional and multi-valued. Even if it produced a set of terms for key points in a system ("formal spoken standard and formal spoken nonstandard, informal written standard and informal written nonstandard, through all possible combinations" as described by Allen 1964: 273), judgments made within the system would need to take into account not only the immediate verbal context of the utterance in its situation, but also the wider context of time and place. There is perhaps less difficulty with labels for time and place since, for so many varieties of English, there have been historical and socio-geographical studies which justify the allocation of labels like *obsolete*, *archaic*, *dialect*, *British*, *U.S.*, *South Australian* etc., as part of the lexicographical record. The chief difficulty with the other set, *slang, col-*

loquial, informal, vulgar, not in polite usage, erroneous, etc., is that even if for the lexicographer they are part of the record, for the user they serve as guidance.

If the guidance is taken not just from the label but from the editor's selection of a body of citational evidence, the individual user can make a more informed judgment. This is possible in the so-called "unabridged" dictionaries, with readers who will weigh the evidence for themselves. However, with smaller dictionaries of the sort usually available in homes and offices, a single label may be all there is for guidance, even though constraints on choice are multi-dimensional.

It was for this reason that the editors of *The Macquarie Dictionary* (which is "abridged" but not a learner's dictionary) chose only one from the set of difficult labels as a sign to the reader that the use of the labelled word may be subject to constraints of particular kinds, and that the reader may wish to consider whether the constraints really apply to the utterance that is the subject of inquiry. The label chosen was *colloquial*, and its definition suggests to the reader that both the right of choice and the responsibility for it rest with the individual. The definition reads:

> *colloquial* appropriate to or characteristic of conversational speech or writing in which the speaker or writer is under no particular constraint to choose standard, formal, conservative, deferential, polite, or grammatically unchallengeable words, but feels free to choose words as appropriate from the informal, slang, vulgar, or taboo elements of the lexicon.

Morphological islands: constraint or preference?

Wolfgang U. Dressler

Theoretical linguistics, especially in America, has often adopted the following research strategy:
1. A linguist transforms the most frequent or intuitively plausible state of affairs in a given problem area into an absolute constraint on the only state of affairs to be allowed. This, for example, is the way the principle of phonological biuniqueness originated in American structuralist phonematics.
2. When unexplainable counter-examples are found (e.g. Danish obstruent overlap), the constraint is either watered down or totally discarded.
3. As a consequence, generalizations on language-specific and cross-linguistic preferences are lost from sight.

This strategy has been criticized by Zwicky (1973), and in Dressler (1985a: 130, 136, 229, 304, 306, 308ff., 312, 373f., in press a). I have tried to show that a theory of universal preferences[1] does a better job than *ad-hoc* hypotheses of absolute universal constraints.

One such instance is the morphological island constraint[2] or lexical integrity hypothesis concerning the "inaccessibility of the elements of compounds to syntactic processes" (Allen 1978: 113). Claims are made that "potentially anaphoric elements in non-head position are never referential",[3] i.e. word formation rules create islands, or "No syntactic rule can refer to elements of morphological structure" (Anderson 1982) or "The syntax neither manipulates nor has access to the internal form of words" (Anderson in press). Thus (Sproat in press): *Drivers of trucks$_i$ fill them up with diesel* is possible but not **Truck$_i$- drivers fill them$_i$ up with diesel*.

This was understood many decades earlier by Bühler (1934: 340): "Das (Kompositum) verhält sich im Satzfeld im ganzen genauso wie ein Simplex;

alle syntaktischen Relikte in seinem Schoße sind wie verschluckt und bleiben unberührt".

However counter-examples have been found, and the question is now whether the hypothesis of morphological islandhood should be abandoned, further watered down or given a preference status. If we take up the last alternative, then we must at least respect the two following conditions: 1) the preference must be derived from higher-order principles. In Natural Morphology[4] these may be principles or extra-linguistic conditions which do not determine grammar, but grammatical preferences. 2) Further conditions or sub-preferences should be deduced which refine the probability of the preference being chosen by a language or not.

In agreement with explicit and implicit views held by linguists for a long time, Natural Morphology assumes the following functions[5] of morphology:

1. Word formation rules (of compounding or derivational morphology) have the function of forming new words (*enrichissement verbal*) — and new words, if accepted as neologisms, are stored as such in the lexicon.
2. Inflectional rules have the function of providing syntax with word-forms. It is to *them* that syntactic rules refer, not to the words on which the inflectional word-forms are based, nor to the base(s) of complex words. Thus there is no reason why bases of complex words should be accessible to syntactic rules.
3. Both word formation and inflectional rules have the function of motivating words or word-forms morphosemantically (and morphotactically) from their bases. Thus neither Natural Morphology nor psycholinguistics (see Stemberger & MacWhinney in press) have anything like internal bracket erasure (cf. Lexical Morphology). Consequently, internal parts of complex words may be semantically accessible.

We might therefore conclude that parts of words may be semantically, but not syntactically accessible. However, this conclusion is warranted only in a model where there is unidirectional flow of information from syntax down through inflectional morphology to the word formation component or up again in the reverse direction. But an interactional model such as Natural Morphology also allows other interactions among components (strata or modules) of grammar, although they are marked (less natural).[6] Therefore syntactic inaccessibility of parts of words is only a preference (Preference I).

The degree of accessibility depends on the following (sub)-preferences: the tighter bonded words are, the lower their internal accessibility (Preference II). Degree of bondedness correlates with the following scale of univerbation (Dressler 1981):

        juxtaposition — compounds — derivations.

Justapositions such as German *der Hohepriester* "the high priest", where both parts inflect (Gen. *des Hoh-en-priester-s*), have more properties of a noun-phrase than of a noun. As for the outputs of compounding vs. derivational word formation rules, compounds are clearly more descriptive (i.e. less tightly bonded) than derivatives.[7]

Thus we can predict:

Prediction I: Internal parts of derivatives should even be less accessible to syntactic rules than internal parts of compounds.

Since morphosemantically transparent words are more descriptive (and thus less tightly bonded) than morphosemantically opaque words, we can predict:

Prediction II: *ceteris paribus*, the more transparent a word is, the more accessible its internal parts should be. This prediction is well supported by psycholinguistic evidence (cf. Stemberger & MacWhinney in press). Both predictions should have effects in cross-linguistic preferences for accessibility.

However, accessibility is not only graded as to what is accessible, but also as to how it is accessible. Since natural (preferable) operations should be more general and productive (because of man's preference for more natural operations in processing, acquisition and diachronic change), we may predict:

Prediction III: Syntactic rules should refer in a more general and productive way to internal parts of units in the following order (if we take nominal elements):

        noun phrases — juxtapositions — compounds — derivatives

These predictions are borne out in German anaphoric coreference where there is no coreference to parts of derivations:

(1)   *Der Wagn$_i$+er   repariert ihn$_i$/sie$_i$*
       *The cart$_i$+right repairs   it$_i$/them$_i$ (sc. the cart$_i$/s$_i$)

As to compounds, I would like to elaborate on Rohrer's (1974) and Brekle's (1975) example:

(2) a. *Die Kinder gehen auf Ei+er$_i$ suche. Wenn sie sie$_i$/welche$_i$/ eines (von ihnen$_i$)/*es$_i$ finden, kommen sie zurück*
The children go on egg+s hunt. If they them$_i$/some$_i$/one$_i$ (of them)/ *it$_i$ find, come they back.
"The children go egg-hunting. If they find them/some/one/ *it, they come back."

b. *Die Kinder gehen auf Ei$_i$ suche. Wenn sie es$_i$/?eines$_i$/*sie$_i$/ *welche$_i$ finden, kommen sie zurück*
The children go on egg$_i$ hunt. If they it$_i$/?one$_i$/*them$_i$/*some$_i$ find, they come back.

Thus coreference to the internal element of the compound is possible; plural coreference to the plural *Ei-er* "egg-s" in (2a), singular coreference to the singular *Ei* "egg" in (2b). Coreference also holds for gender (German has morphological and syntactic gender differences only in the singular).

There is another type of coreference:

(3) *Ludwig ist ein Gepäck$_i$s träger. Oft trägt er ?es$_i$/*sie$_i$ mit Mühe.*
Ludwig is a luggage$_i$ carrier. Often carries he ?it$_i$/*them$_i$ with difficulty.

In this example *-s-* is an interfix (cf. Dressler & Merlini in press). Examples preceded by ? are more easily accepted by informants than those preceded by an asterisk*.

However, these two types of anaphoric coreference are a far cry from general anaphoric coreference to nouns as parts of noun-phrases. Important differences are:
1. They have a lower degree of acceptability.
2. The antecedent and the anaphoric pronouns must occur in two different, but adjacent clauses, i.e coreference is of a textual rather than of an intrasentential type.
3. The second part of the compound must be a deverbal action noun as in *-such-e* or a deverbal agent noun as in *-träg-er*; in many languages action and agent nouns inherit properties of their verbal base such as accusative complementation,[8] i.e. their complements may be treated more like complements of syntactic predicates than in any other type of compounds.
4. The verb governing the coreferent pronoun in the second sentence of

our examples must be identical with or syntactically and semantically very similar to the verb which underlies the action or agent noun. Thus this type of anaphoric coreference can be compared to coreference to parts of syntactic idioms (see Toman 1978), which are similar to compounds insofar as they are also lexically stored higher order units.

5. The compound *Ei+er suche* (2a) is a word-form-based compound (cf. Dressler in press a). Thus it has an internal inflectional suffix — such as number/case-forms of juxtapositions (from which these compounds have come) which has not yet become an interfix, i.e. a derivational linking element (cf. Dressler & Merlini in press).[9]

These German examples clearly fit all of the Predictions I-III.

Now let us look at Italian examples. Again we find anaphoric coreference only with a specific type of compounds:[10]

(4) a. *Luigi è un guarda boschi. Se li (Pl. m.)/*lo (Sg.m.) non sorveglia bene, non viene pagato.*
Luigi is a forests watch. If them/*it not watches well, he is not paid.
b. *Luigi è un guarda parco. Se lo/*li non sorveglia bene, ...*
Luigi is a park watch. If it/*them not watches well, ...
c. *Luigi è un guarda dighe. Se le (Pl.fem.)/*la (Sg.fem.) non sorveglia bene, ...*
Luigi is a dikes watch. . If them/*it ...
d. *Luigi è un guarda porta. Se la (Sg.fem.)/*le (Pl.fem.) ...*
Luigi is a door watch. If it/*them ...
e. *Luigi è un guarda porto. Se lo/*li ...*
Luigi is a harbour watch. If it/*them ...

(5) a. *Luigi è un porta bagagli. Spesso li/*lo porta con fatica.*
Luigi is a luggage carrier. Often them/*it carries with pain.
b. *Luigi è un porta bandiera. Spesso la/*le ...*
Luigi is a flag carrier. Often it/*them ...

(6) *Ecco il nuovo aspira polvere. Aspira bene, ma la (Sg.fem.) butta fuori (sc. la polvere).*
Here is the new dust duster (Sp.fem.). (It) sucks well, but it throws it out.

(7) *Luigi è un buon accalappia cani, ma poi li lascia andare/ma ne prende così pochi*

Luigi is a good dogs catcher, but then them (he) lets go/but of them he gets so few.

(8) *Questo è un buono lava vetri. Ma cí sputa sopra per lavarli.*
This is a good window-panes cleaner. But he spits over (them) for cleaning them.

(9) *È un bel porta monete. Ne contiene tante.*
(It) is a beautiful money (Pl.) carrier (purse). Of them it holds so many.

Again this type of anaphoric coreference has the following properties:

1. It has a lower degree of acceptability.
2. The antecedent and the anaphoric pronouns occur in different, but adjacent clauses.
3. The first part of the compound must be a verbal stem, and the compound must have the meaning of an agent (or instrument) noun.
4. The verb governing the coreferent pronoun must be identical or parallel.
5. The compound is word-form based, because the second part may be in the plural. Word-form-based compounds are less tightly bonded than stem- or word-based compounds.

According to Prediction II morphosemantically opaque compounds are less acceptable (impossible in German):

(10) Luigi è un mangia preti$_i$. Non li$_i$ ama per niente
Luigi is a priests eater (rabid anticlerical). (He) does not like *them*$_i$ at all.

(11) *Luigi è un rompi scatole$_i$. Le$_i$ rompe a tutti.*
Luigi is a boxes breaker (trouble maker). (He) breaks *them*$_i$ to all (persons).

Among these Italian compounds I found only one example of a double compound: *porta stuzzica denti* "tooth-pick-carrier" (lit. "carry pick teeth") formed from *portare* "to carry" and *stuzzica denti* "tooth pick". Now whereas Pl. *denti* (Sg. *dente*) seems to be accessible to our restricted type of anaphoric coreference in *stuzzica denti*, it is clearly inaccessible in *porta stuzzica denti*.

This difference is explainable: if compounding freezes a noun against anaphoric coreference, then double compounding (i.e. double embedding) must freeze it even more.

Sadock (1985: 416ff.) cited the case of Serbian anaphoric coreference to the base of a possessive adjective of the type (in translation):

(12) Those are *nasogo* ("of our" = Gen.Sg.) *nanowe* ("father$_i$-ly" = Nom.Pl. poss. adj.) shoes, he$_i$ has them forgotten.

Here the pronoun *he$_i$* corefers to the base of the possessive adjective *father$_i$-ly*. This situation, in fact, seems to hold for Slavic languages (Czech, Slovak, Slovenian, Serbo-Croatian) where the possessive adjective (with one specific suffix) has replaced the possessive genitive case and has thus been "inflectionalized". This can be seen from the semantic concord between the Gen. Sg. "of our" and the (base of the) Nom. Pl. of "fatherly".[11]

Despite the special nature of this occurrence, and the much smaller role compounding plays in Slavic than in German languages,[12] we may ask whether Prediction I holds true. Since no native speaker of Serbian was available, I tested Prediction I with the closely cognate language Czech (František Mareš, p.c.), where the following anaphoric coreference to the base of a compound seems to be possible in colloquial usage:

(13) *Jan je vlajk$_i$-o-nos. Často je$_i$. (Fem.Sg.Acc.) nosí s velkou námahou.*
John is (a) *flag$_i$*-carrier. Frequently *her$_i$* (vlajka = Fem.) carries with great strain.

Thus internal syntactic accessiblity within derivatives seems to imply it within compounds even in this case; the constraints seem to be similar to the German and Italian examples (1)-(9).

Lakoff and Ross (1972), Corum (1973), Browne (1974) and others have pointed to restricted possibilities of anaphoric coreference to bases of derivatives[13] in some American dialects:

(14) *McCarthy$_i$-ites are sad, because they voted for him$_i$ and he$_i$ lost.*

According to Prediction I there should also be restricted possibilities of anaphoric coreference to bases of compounds. And they do exist (according to my native informants, with varying inter-individual degrees of acceptability) as the following examples show:

(15) *Jack is a luxury$_i$ giver. He gives/presents them$_i$ well.*

(16) *Jack is a popular party$_i$ giver because he gives such good ones$_i$.*

(17) *Jack is a good story$_i$ teller, because he tells such good ones$_i$ (he tells them$_i$ very vividly).*

(18) *Jack was a well-known alms$_i$-giver, because he gave a lot of them$_i$.*

Without going into details, I want to underline a difference with the German (1)-(3) and Italian (4a)-(9) examples: the anaphoric pronouns do not agree in number with their antecedents.

Agglutinating languages generally have more morphosemantic transparency in word formation than inflecting ones, so that they should have anaphoric coreference to bases of complex word forms (Prediction II). And indeed Hungarian allows (according to Csaba Pléh, p.c.) English-type anaphoric coreference to bases of both derivatives and compounds:

(19) *Jó   törtenet-mond-ó, mert olyan   jó k-at   mond*
    Good story-tell-er,   because such   good — Pl. -Acc. tells
    "He is a good story$_i$teller because he tells such good ones$_i$.".

Incorporating languages have morphosemantically more transparent and less tightly bonded word formation processes than inflecting type word formation (e.g. English Latinate word formation). Therefore, according to Prediction II, we should expect incorporated nouns to be syntactically more accessible than, for example, nouns in Latinate English word formation or in German and Italian compounding discussed above. This is the case according to Sadock (1986; cf. Sadock 1985: 398f., 402, 410, 415 for agreement of incorporated nouns in West Greenlandic and Southern Tiwa). Whereas West Greenlandic has a derivational type of incorporation, Southern Tiwa also has a compounding type of incorporation. According to Predictions I and III there should be more accessibility of incorporated nouns in Southern Tiwa than in West Greenlandic, and this seems to be the case (J. Sadock, p.c.).

In this paper, I have deliberately concentrated on morphological aspects of islandhood and tried to show that languages differ greatly, but not unpredictably if we deduce universal predictions from the theory of Natural Morphology and add typological considerations.

Notes

1. Cf. also Plank 1981; Vennemann 1983. Preferences presuppose a non-discrete graduality, cf. Halliday's (1961: §10.6) notion of shading.

2. Originally formulated by Postal 1969; cf. Lakoff and Ross (1972), Corum (1973) and Browne (1974).
3. Selkirk (1982: 53) after Williams (1981), Botha (1981: 46, 1984: 9f.), Savini (1984: 96f.), Scalise (1984: 93), Sadock (1986), Sproat (1985: 326ff., in press); on Dakota and Tagalog clitics see Schwartz (1978).
4. See Mayerthaler (1981), Wurzel (1984), Dressler (1982, 1985a, 1985b, 1985c), Dressler, Mayerthaler, Panagl and Wurzel (in press); cf. the special issue of *Studia Gramatyczne 7* (1985): "Natural Approaches to Morphology".
5. I am happy to note this agreement with Halliday (1973) on grammar having a functional basis.
6. Cf. also Sadock (1985) with references.
7. See Stachowiak (1978); for support in language acquisition cf. Clark and Hecht (1982). Cf. the possibility of syntax-like coordination-reduction with compounds, but not derivative suffixations (Booij 1985; Toman 1985).
8. See Panagl (1976, 1980), Rosén (1983: 183, 195, 197) for Latin, Greek and other Indo-European languages; Sadock (1985: 421f.) for Japanese.
9. There are no relevant juxtapositions left over in German.
10. In these Italian compounds the verb precedes the noun (in the plural -*i*, -*e* or singular -*o*, -*a*, -*e*).
11. Examples from other Indo-European languages in Mittelberger (1966).
12. Cf. the contrastive analysis in Jeziorski (1983).
13. Acording to Lieber (1984: 197f., note 1), if I translate her note into my framework, anaphoric coreference is easier with bases of more transparent derivatives than with less transparent ones.

Some "dia-categories"

Jeffrey O. Ellis

In an unpublished paper (Ellis 1979) I introduced a term *diasystem* for use in comparative descriptive linguistics (especially of linguistic convergence areas) on the analogy of *diaphone* originated by D. Jones for the phonetics and phonology of the accents of single languages.[1] This analogy with Jones is in some respects strained and potentially misleading, but with Haugen's use of *diamorph*, *diaphone* and *dialinguistics*,[2] the analogy is closer. Rather than seek an alternative term, I propose in this paper to make explicit the differences, as well as the partial resemblances, between *diaphone* and *diasystem*, while elaborating and illustrating the diasystem concept and other related categories.

The comparison of grammatical systems as envisaged in Allen (1953: 90-95, also phonological systems, 95-99), Ellis (1966a: 51-52, 55-56, 103-105) and Levenston and Ellis (1964), embraces in effect larger or smaller sections of system networks (cf. Allen 1953: 92: "sub-systems ... total systems"). These have some terms in common (what might be referred to as "dia-classes") between two or more languages. The quantifications (Allen 1953: 90, 92-93; Ellis 1966a: 149-153; Levenston & Ellis 1964), which are basically of pairs of languages, represent an abstraction from the particular identifications. A more delicately focussed statement would separate out the common sections of a network, which might be termed "(grammatical) diasystems".

The term "diaphone" (or "diaphonic equivalence") is used for a phonological element common to, or underlying phonological or phonetic elements in different varieties of a language or in related or other languages, or related parts of different languages. A "diasystem" would not be exactly parallel to this. Firstly, though particularly useful in application to tongues (languages or varieties) that are in some genetic (including "borrowing") relationship, it would also be theoretically applicable like the Allen procedure (or Haugen's "diaphone") to *any* two or more languages. Secondly, it would differ in the categorial status of what is compared and in the kind of *tertium comparationis* for its identification (see Ellis 1966a: 33-39; cf. Allen 1953: 94-100 and Halliday 1957: 64-65; Ellis 1966a: 104-105, 114-115, 150).[3]

As used by its originator, Jones, "diaphone" referred not to comparison between tongues, nor dialects of a language, but to comparison between accents of a tongue.[4] Firth (1957: 1-2), in praising M. Kruszewski's conception of the phoneme (Albrow 1981: 10-11) speaks of "interlingual correspondences between sounds in related words in parallel morphological categories" *and* identifies this as being close to Jones' concept of the "diaphone".

"Interlingual" must be understood as comprising a range of kinds of possible pairs (or larger sets) of tongues, from say British and American English to members of a language family, or loans and their source like the Latin itself; even at its most expanded, "diaphone" (unlike phonological "diasystem" and "dia-class") depends on a place in the phonological realization of common formal items. (The realization chain will be taken up below as "dia-realizations".) Thus, for example, diaphones in the linguistic consciousness of English and Scandinavian speakers would have been part of the genesis of the mixed varieties of the Danelaw (Milroy 1984: 12, 27; cf. 11, 25).[5]

Moulton (1962: 15, 73, 77, 90) appears to think of "diaphone" as hyponymous to "phone" like "allophone" (i.e. as what Jones 1962: 30 terms "member of a diaphone" or "diaphonic variant") rather than (like "variphone", Jones 1962: ch. 28) as a "phoneme"-like derivation from *phon-* (Jones 1973: 190, 196). Haugen too (1954: 11ff.) uses "diaphone" for the individual partner, in his interlingual identifications of phonemes. (This might support a case for distinguishing non-Jones uses as "diaphon*eme*".)

Jones (see his list of "the chief diaphonic variants found in RP", 1958: xxxvi) does not seem to use "diaphone" for the alternation of phonemes in RP æ/ɑ, e.g. in "trans-", nor even as Trudgill (ed., 1984: 575) does for South-North "[a]/[ɑ]" realizations (pronunciations) of "the phoneme /æ/".[6]

For a more complex case like South æe, ɑ, ɑ:: North a, a, ɑ, (which subsumes "phoneme /æ/" "pronunciations") and South æ/ɑ "diaphone" or "diaphoneme", we may adapt Haugen's (interlingual) notation (1954: 12, e.g. (English-Norwegian) $_E/w>v/_N$ or $_N/u>ə/_E$) and formulate this equation as "$_S$/æ, ɑ>a/$_N$ or $_N$/a>æ, ɑ/$_S$; $_S$/ɑ>a, ɑ/$_N$ or $_N$/a, ɑ>ɑ/$_S$". There are thus two overlapping "compound" diaphones (in Haugen's 1954: 12 terms, diaphonic equivalences, in which one "diaphone" (diaphonic variant) is "compound"). The equation is formulated by Nixon (1976) as a "diasystem" in his quite different sense of "system", a diasystem being an array of overlapping compound diaphones.

Let us now consider grammatical diasystems. Where we speak of "variants" of diaphones, we should speak only of "instantiations" of grammatical diasystems, since here variance is only of place in the network, not an intrinsic variance (which would be internal shape of the system/section) as in the substance of diaphonic variants.

Allen's procedure of system comparison identifies "terms in systems" (and the remaining terms need not be of equal number). "Systems", without specification of place in networks, may be either the simple systems that are the building blocks of networks in systemic theory or, providing the plurality of "terms" that will give variety in the possible quantifications, larger sections of networks (Allen 1953: 92: "small systems ... large systems"). The larger sections are a less delicate system comprising the terms in the more delicate systems to which its own terms are the entry-points.

The "diasystem" procedure identifies *whole* systems (in the systemic theory sense) with *all* their terms (classes) effectively identical (dia-classes) — and, it follows, of equal number. Consequently, in practice, this procedure, in principle equally universal, is less likely than Allen's to be applicable to any set of languages irrespective of genetic affinity of their parts. The relation compared is not directly that between terms in a system (dia-classes), and the system containing them, but that between systems or other network-sections (diasystems) and larger network sections containing them, which may be termed "partial dia-networks", hereafter abbreviated to "dia-networks".

We may speak of a "*subsumptive* dia-network" where a network-section in one language subsumes the system (or larger section) in the other language. For example, the subsumptive dia-network "renarration" in Bulgarian (or Turkish) "contains" the Macedonian system "renarration" (Macedonian-Bulgarian-Turkish diasystem) as in Figure 1.[7]

The diagrammatic representation of a subsumptive dia-network is able to retain intact the relevant sections of the networks of both languages; other, non-subsumptive, dia-networks can be diagrammed only "one-way", retaining intact only the network-section of one of the two languages and

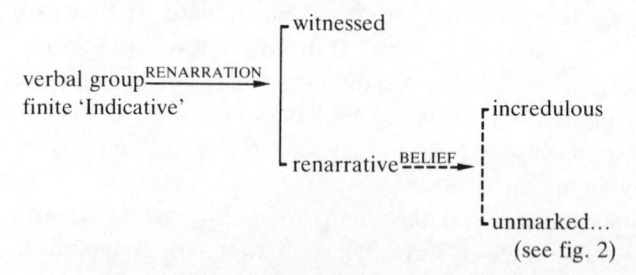

```
                              ┌─ witnessed
verbal group ──RENARRATION──→ │
finite 'Indicative'           │                    ┌─ incredulous
                              │                    ┊
                              └─ renarrative ──BELIEF──→
                                                   ┊
                                                   └─ unmarked...
                                                      (see fig. 2)
```

Figure 1. Bulgarian-Macedonian 'renarration' subsumptive dia-network
———— Macedonian-Bulgarian diasystem
------ Bulgarian

incorporating in it fragments of the other, thus losing some of the delicacy-ordering of the second as in Figure 2 where the Bulgarian system is intact.

In Figure 2, *assertive* represents an event not witnessed by the speaker (*renarrative* generally) but nonetheless asserted to be a fact. *Speaker* (as possible *witness*) is primarily a category relevant to conversation. The *renarration* system has different applications in different registers of the language (Andrejčin et al. 1947: 173ff., "in historical writing the assertive is used for conclusions"). According to some analyses (not followed here) the form here termed *assertive* realizes only a term in the tense system (perfect). We shall return to this under dia-realizations.

So far our examples of dia-network diagrams have been of pairs of languages (Macedonian, Bulgarian and Turkish yielding three pairs). While subsumptive dia-networks of more than two languages are possible, non-subsumptive dia-network diagrams of more than two languages are in gen-

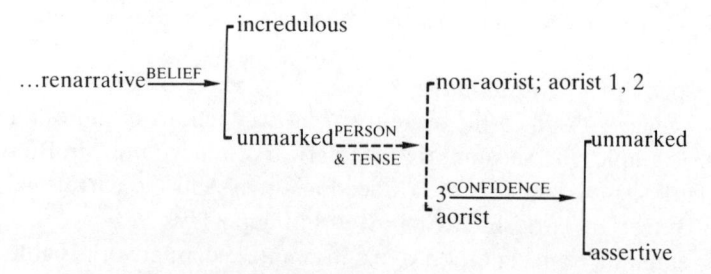

```
                          ┌─ incredulous
...renarrative ──BELIEF──→│
                          │                              ┌─ non-aorist; aorist 1, 2
                          └─ unmarked ──PERSON──→        │                       ┌─ unmarked
                                        & TENSE         │                       │
                                                         └─ 3 ──CONFIDENCE──→
                                                            aorist
                                                                                 └─ assertive
```

Figure 2. Bulgarian-Turkish 'belief' one-way dia-network
———— Bulgarian-Turkish diasystems
------ Bulgarian

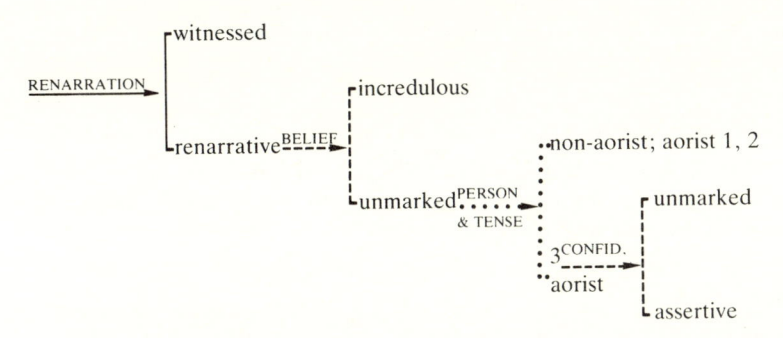

```
                    ┌─witnessed
RENARRATION ────────┤              ┌─incredulous
                    └─renarrative ──BELIEF──┤
                                            │         ..non-aorist; aorist 1, 2
                                            │        .                      ┌─unmarked
                                            └─unmarked──PERSON ────────────┤
                                                       & TENSE              │
                                                          .  3 CONFID.     │
                                                          .'aorist          │
                                                                            └─assertive
```

Figure 3. Bulgarian-Macedonian-Turkish 'renarration' one-way dia-network
────── Macedonian-Bulgarian-Turkish diasystem
------ Bulgarian-Turkish diasystems
······ Bulgarian

eral more difficult, but it is possible to construct a one-way diagram (with Bulgarian, and Macedonian, intact) of Macedonian, Bulgarian and Turkish *renarration* (as in Figure 3).

It should be noted that some possible diasystems are more significant than others. We have already mentioned the place of the system in the network. In addition, there is the question of its relative rarity (Halliday 1966: 178). Systems in two or more languages instantiating a diasystem could not be less "mutually exotic" (Halliday 1966: 177-178), but their degree of exoticness in relation to some or all other languages may affect the significance of the diasystem. For example, a simple binary system of number (Halliday 1966: 175) is technically a diasystem between all the languages in which it is instantiated, just as much as an admirative system of the verbal group would be (see below under dia-uses) but being so common it is not of the same significance. However, taken in the context of a given dia-network, some instances might still afford comparisons/contrastings worth making, as in the case of Bulgarian (or Macedonian) — Turkish singular::plural where the Turkish "singular" is number-unmarked and Bulgarian and Macedonian have a "second plural" form in some nouns used with numerals as is the Turkish "singular".

Associated with some of the applications of grammatical diasystems (and dia-classes) one could have "dia-uses" of terms (classes) in grammatical systems and of formal items. More generally these might be "dia-realizations" (including "dia-structures") at various stages in the chain of realization or exponence involved in comparing tongues in possible genetic relation, either as wholes or in part (e.g. calques),[8] including linguistic convergence areas.

We will use *morphological* of word-morphology, "*morphological*" of constituency at higher rank (Kress, ed. 1976: 65), including exponent items as well as structures — the "morphology" of compound lexical items or of "periphrastic" grammatical forms. Examples would be (clause) Balkan infinitive- replacement or (clause-complex) future tense involving infinitive-replacement.

Dia-realizations will extend over sections of greater or lesser extent of the realization chain in two or more languages (Ellis 1967: 42-44). The first stage (beginning at the semantic or deep end) is uses of grammatical classes or formal items, the relation between a class or item and a common use constituting a "dia-use".[9]

For example, Albanian has a system of the verb group distinguishing the "admirative" from the class "unmarked-for-admirativity".[10] The uses of the admirative comprise according to Fiedler (1966): the speaker's surprise (wonderment, etc.) at a fact or action; the speaker's or another's surprise at an utterance "regarded as unsatisfactory and repeated in the admirative"; one person's or general surprise at an utterance "the truth of which is not doubted but which is repeated in the admirative".[11] Used, for example, in North Geg epic folk poetry, this makes the presentation more vivid.

A dia-use of a similar form in older Romanian is interpreted by Mann (1977: 125, *păcătuit-am* (inverted perfect) "behold, I have sinned", cf. Sandfeld 1930: 149-151) as constituting a "mood ... peculiar to Albanian and Rumanian" (1977: 137), but this is not a dia*system* instantiated in the Standard Modern Romanian verb.

In Macedo-Bulgarian dialects we find the perfect forms that in some dialects and Standard Bulgarian and Standard Macedonian realize the renarrative terms in the renarration system. The auxiliary verb (here "be") is, in these cases, enclitic to the first element in the clause and used admiratively, for example Bulgarian *ti si imal novo palto!* "why, you've got a new coat!", Macedonian *ix, što si bil junak!* "oh, how fine you are!" (Sandfeld 1930: 119-120; cf. Schmaus 1966: 103 (Koneski 1965: 148-149): Macedonian *toj bil dobar čovek!*, Turkish *eyi adam imiş!* "what a good man!"

Since at least the second and third of Fiedler's Albanian uses of the admirative given above are "commentative" (like the renarrative) as well as "admirative",[12] Fiedler argues that the Albanian admirative form is derived (by inversion) from a perfect, "owing to the combination in the perfect meaning of different time-stages", and not, as for example, Jokl holds (Sandfeld 1930: 185), from the Geg future realized by "have" + infinitive (*me* + particle, e.g. *me ardhë*).

Thus it is possible to say that the renarrative (in Bulgarian and Macedonian — and Turkish) exhibits an "admirative" dia-use (Friedman 1979), while the admirative (in Albanian) exhibits a "renarrative" dia-use in Figure 3 above; for example Schmaus 1966: 117: (*Julius Caesar* III.2, transl. Fan Noli) *Në paska gen' ashtu* "If it were so as [Brutus says]"). This shows the usefulness of distinguishing between diasystems and dia-uses — while making explicit the criteria that identify the determining uses for the contextual-meaning name of system and classes (Ellis 1966c: 87-88).[13]

The next stage in the realization chain is the realization, "morphological", of grammatical classes by formal items or structures. For example, the Turkish, Bulgarian and Macedonian realizations of the renarrative instantiate dia-realizations in the following way:

The renarrative is realized by an originally perfect tense form. This is a dia-realization instantiated also, to the extent of a dia-use when the reference is past, in other languages, including Albanian (see above, and cf. Sadiku 1975), variets of Sanskrit and of Modern Persian, where, for example, it is not elaborated into a conjugational system. (The Bulgarian and Macedonian conjugational systems provide a renarrative in every tense, though there are fewer renarrative forms than witnessed ones. The present and imperfect tenses (and pairs of periphrastic tenses differentiated in the witnessed by present and imperfect of one component, most often an auxiliary verb), share their renarrative form.)

This originally perfect form is realized in the three languages by "be" (or zero) + past participle. In the Slavonic form yielding the *aorist* renarrative, this was so already before Turkish-Slavonic contact and since Turkish-Slavonic contact its tense distinctions are realized by ending-morphemes.

The structure of the Bulgarian and Macedonian grammatical calque of the Turkish comprises: the categories of past participle, ending -*l*(-), and tense (aorist::imperfect) of the participle stem, the item "be" (present tense), person and number of "be", and in Bulgarian presence or absence of the third person of "be", or "be" itelf may be in the renarrative. The category of -*l* participle with or without "be" provides the category of renarrative generally (and number and singular gender, absent in the Turkish participle); the aorist -*l* participle (in Macedonian, perfective aspect only, de

Bray 1951: 291, but cf. Lunt 1952: 92) corresponds to the Turkish plain *-miş*, while the new imperfect *-l* participle corresponds to *-yormuş* and other *-miş* forms with meanings of Bulgarian/Macedonian present and imperfect; the conjugation of "be" provides the person (and number) distinctions (including the absence of its third person in Macedonian, absence or presence in Bulgarian); and in standard Bulgarian the presence and absence of "be" in the third person aorist realizes the categories of assertive and non-assertive, corresponding to Turkish *-dir* and absence of *-dir* in all persons in the use of "be" generally,[14] while the renarrative of "be" (present/imperfect and aorist undifferentiated in this verb), *bil* (*săm* "am" etc.), + *-l* participle of the lexical verb realizes the category of "incredulous", Turkish *-miş imiş* (*im* "am" etc.).

The final stage of the realization chain relevant to comparison of form (as distinct from the step from phonology to phonic substance, the province of Jones-diaphones) is *phonological* realization of formal items and categories. The question of dia-realizations arises when genetic relation is at least possible (of languages (or varieties) or of items). For example, in the Turkish, Bulgarian and Macedonian phonological realizations of the category past participle, *-miş*, *-l(-)* and *-l(-)*, the Bulgarian and Macedonian

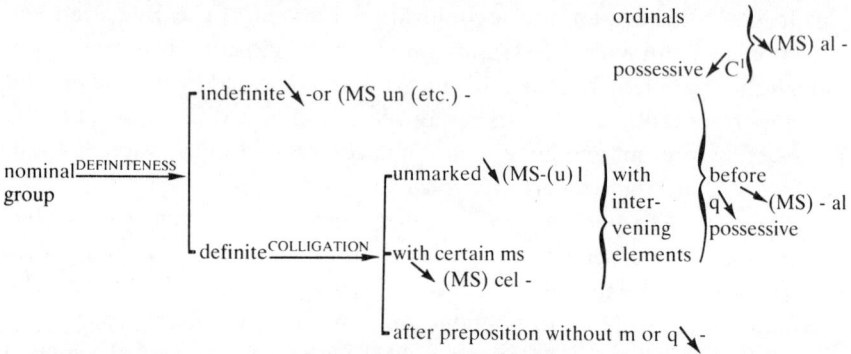

Figure 4. 'Definiteness' in Romanian nominal group
↘ = (is) realized by (↗ = realizing/realizes)
- = zero realization
MS = masculine singular
un (etc.): feminine o, plural unii, unele, partitive nişte
possessive = possessive use of genitive-dative or other expression of possession
C^1 = intensive complement in clause structure
m = modifier q = qualifier in group structure
group ... -(u)l: -u(l) is suffixed to noun or other initial element of group structure

SOME "DIA-CATEGORIES"

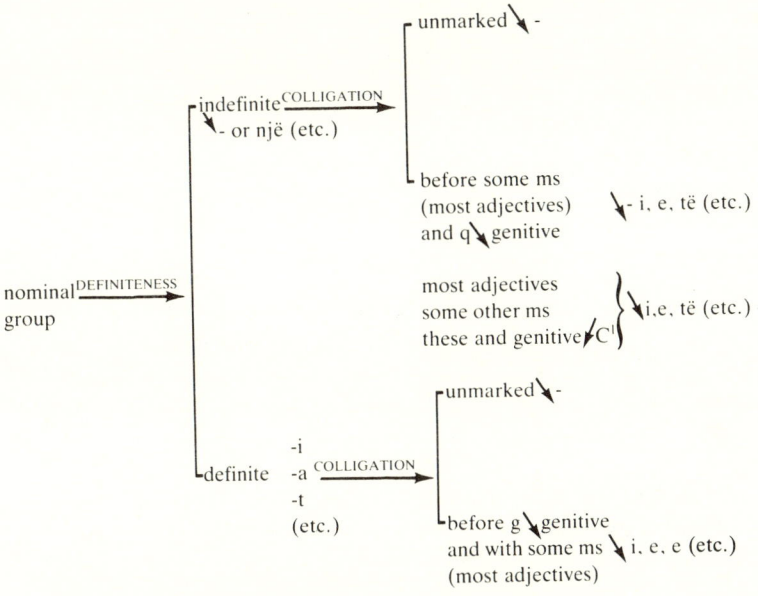

```
                              ┌─ unmarked ↘ -
                              │
           ┌─ indefinite ──COLLIGATION──►
           │   ↘ - or një (etc.)         │
           │                              └─ before some ms
           │                                 (most adjectives)   ↘ - i, e, të (etc.)
           │                                 and q ↘ genitive
nominal ──DEFINITENESS──►                    most adjectives
group                                        some other ms        } i, e, të (etc.) -
           │                                 these and genitive /C¹
           │                              ┌─ unmarked ↘ -
           │              -i             │
           └─ definite   -a ──COLLIGATION──►
                         -t              │
                         (etc.)          └─ before g ↘ genitive
                                            and with some ms  ↘ i, e, e (etc.)
                                            (most adjectives)
```

Figure 5. 'Definiteness' in Albanian nominal group
një (etc.): plural disa or ca
genitive = possessive use of noun etc. genitive-dative, genitive of certain words
-i, -a, -t; i, e, të; i, e, e: nominative singular masculine, feminine, plural
i, e, të; i, e, e: declinable particle, declining a little differently in the various uses or places; cognate (i, e) with latin *is*, Persian indeclinable *-i-*, Slavonic long adjective ending. (Also before m-derived nouns.)

instantiate a phonological dia-realization, as they do in the first person singular ("am") Bulgarian *săm*, Macedonian *sum* (beside Turkish *-im*), and so on.[15]

An example at group rank of dia-structures without phonological dia-realization of formal items is the dia-realization of "definiteness" in the Albanian and Romanian nominal group (cf. Stölting 1966; Gáldi 1966). The main facts of each language can be stated in modified network diagram form (see Figures 4 and 5).

There are on the face of it no dia-"systems" here, except the trivial initial "definiteness". However, let us write out some of the structures that realize the options (omitting recursive accumulations (hypotactic and paratactic), e.g. multiplications of modifiers or qualifiers, cf. Hetzer 1978: 165-169):

Romanian

un (etc.) (*m*) *noun* (*m*) (*al* (etc.) *possessive*)
noun-ul (etc.)
m-ul (etc.) *noun* } (*possessive*)/(... *al* (etc.) *possessive*)
C↙*al* (etc.) *possessive*
al (etc.) *ordinal noun* (...)
noun-ul (etc.) *al* (etc.) *ordinal* (...)
cel (etc.) *m noun* (...)
noun-ul (etc.) *cel* (etc.) *m* (...)
preposition noun

Albanian

një noun (...)
një noun i/e/të (etc.) *m* or *genitive*
(*një*) *i/e/të adjective noun* (nominative/accusative only)
C↙*i/e/ të adjective*
C↙*i/e/të genitive*
noun-i/a/t (etc.) (...)
noun-i/a/t i/e/e (etc.) *m* or *genitive*
i/e/e adjective-i/a/t noun (...)

To these can be added a dia-use with Romanian (most nouns) "definite" without suffixed article after preposition (except *cu* in most cases, "with") when without modifier or qualifier of some combinations of preposition and noun in Albanian (Hetzer 1978: 3, 105, 161).

Then, if we represent Romanian *-ul* (etc.), Albanian *-i/a/t* (etc.) by *-article*, Romanian *un*(-), Albanian *një* by "a", Romanian *al* (etc.) by *particle*$_{(1)}$ and *cel* (etc.) by *particle*$_{(2)}$, Albanian *i/e/të* (etc.) by *particle*$_{(indef.)}$ and *i/e/e* (etc.) by *particle*$_{(def.)}$, we find the following dia-structures:

"a" *noun* (...) (*particle*$_{(1)(indef.)}$ *possessiv/genitive*)
noun-article (...)
noun-article (... *particle*$_{(1)(def.)}$*possessive/genitive*)
C↙ *particle*$_{(1)(indef.)}$ *possessive/genitive*
noun-article particle$_{(1)(def.)}$ *ordinal*
noun-article particle$_{(2)(def.)}$ *m*
preposition noun

Examples of structures that do not instantiate dia-structures are Romanian *noun-article* (no particle) *possessive*, Albanian *noun-article particle*$_{(def.)}$ *genitive* uninterrupted.

To adapt a Romanian-Bulgarian-Macedonian example of Birnbaum's (1970: 83-84) of the genitive-dative "dia-syncretism" (in which "I give my son's teacher's book", "I give the book to my son's teacher" and "I give the teacher's book to my son" are all in Romanian: *Eu dau cartea profesorului fiului meu*) "a book of the teacher's" would be Romanian *o carte a profesorului*, Albanian *një libër të mësuesit*, while "the teacher's book" would be Albanian *librin e mësuesit*, and "to a teacher of my son's" would be Romanian *unui profesor al fiului meu* (or *de ai fiului meu*), Albanian *një mësuesi të birit tim*, while "to my son's teacher" would be Albanian *mësuesit të birit tim* (or *të tim biri*).

The possible disambiguation of this clause (with the definite nominal groups) that Birnbaum does adduce depends on clause structures that instantiate a dia-structure only in the most general sense, namely that in most Balkan languages, under particular conditions in the given language (or dialect), personal pronouns are used to anticipate direct and/or indirect object. In his example, Bulgarian has optionally a dative pronoun to anticipate indirect object in the second and third meanings of the clause:

Bulgarian: *Az (mu) davam knigata na učitelja na sina mi*,

and Macedonian has obligatorily an accusative pronoun to anticipate direct object in the first and both dative and accusative in the second and third:

Macedonian: *Jas [mu] ja davam knigata na nastavnikot na moj sin*.[16]

Albanian would have accusative pronoun *e* in the first if the article in *librin* had anaphoric reference (as well as cataphoric (eisphoric, Ellis 1971a: 369, 374-375) to *e mësuesit* ...), i.e. if the book had been mentioned earlier in the text — and could have been referred to by the pronoun alone; and similarly in the second and third could have *e* or dative *i* or *ia = i + e*.

Having sought to explore some possible aspects of dia-categories, we shall, in conclusion, make some brief comments on the place that dia-categories would have in linguistic studies generally:

1. Dia-categories as such are purely descriptive. Statements of their existence in given languages or varieties would not be statements of development (continuity and change between *états de langue*, genetic relation of tongues, linguistic borrowing, etc.). They would be part of the data for

arriving at statements of development, such as a statement of the origin of the Bulgarian (and Macedonian) renarrative in the Turkish system and in the realizational constraints of the "morphological" exponents available in the calquing language (Ellis 1952: 125, 1966a: 29, 1984: 92), which result in the greater complexity (asymmetry) of the Bulgarian network-section (Fig. 3 above).[17] A parallel "morphological" pattern between two languages (in a different historical relation) is afforded by the comparative asymmetry of Romanian definiteness (articulation and "particulation") in nominal group structure (Fig. 4 above) beside Albanian (Fig. 5 above), cf. Hetzer (1978: 104).

2. Dia-categories observable in given languages may on the other hand have nothing to do with any sort of genetic relation (even some that are significant "exotically"). Examples that can be referred to are some of the systems of verbs of "being" (Ellis 1971b (especially 29-31), 1984: 84, 92, 99, cf. 95-97), the dia-correlation in Akan and Welsh (Ellis 1978: 301-303) between the identifying "be" verb and informationally marked clause structure (highly "exotic" in the sense of rare though logically far from odd, Ellis 1978: 305), and apparently (despite Ellis 1966a: 131) the (partial) dia-relation in Turkish and Bulgarian between definiteness and case in the nominal group.

3. The notion of "dia-system" within systemic-functional grammar invites comment on "function", in the sense of the metafunctions of language.[18] The grouping of system networks in "functional components" of the grammar belongs in the description of each language and precedes the comparative identification of systems that may lead to the setting up of diasystems between languages. The relevance to dia-categories (even "dia-use") of the metafunctional aspect thus lies within the contextual data of the comparison process; the dia-categories themselves are formal, and there is (by definition) no question of speaking of *"dia-(meta)functions" or *"dia-functional components".

4. Instantiation of dia-categories[19] could be a possible formulation of formal relations between an "interlanguage", in either the general, computational, sense or the "learner's approximative system" sense (Ellis 1984: 92-93, 100-101), and one of the languages between which it mediates. An example could be Haugen's Norwegian-American bilingualism, insofar as the speaker-subjective concerns of his "diaphone" link up (through his "diamorph") with the linguistic borrowing applications of dia-categories.

5. Finally, we should note that (grammatical) dia*system* holds a central position among dia-categories (ranging from diaphone to "dia-use"), even in the (partial-)genetic linguistic applications of dia-description that bulk large in the field of its "practical" utilization and in which dia-*realization* is so important.[20]

Notes

1. The term *diasystem* (phonological) is used by Nixon (1976), in a quite different sense of *system*, reformulating the concept of diaphone in one sense.
2. Haugen (1954: 12 and 1979: 80) for *diamorph(ic)*; (1954: 11-19) for *diaphone*; (1979: 76) for *dialinguistics*: a term alternative to *bilingual description*, and Weinreich's (1953) *differential description*.
3. At the phonological level the phonological systems of systemic linguistics could similarly yield "phonological diasystems", in a different sense from Nixon's (1976).
4. Jones (1962: 204-205): "deviations from a type ... belonging to 'the same language' as that type", "deviating sounds ... belonging to separate languages or dialects and therefore not to be comprised in the diaphones of the language under consideration".
5. "Diaphone" in this paragraph is the "Jones-Firth diaphone", and not Haugen's speaker-subjective "diaphone" (1954: 12), Haugen's concern being with bilingualism (and second language teaching), not necessarily with related languages. His own reference to Jones (using "dialect" presumably in the more general American sense) leaves much unclarified (1954: 11-12): "The term 'diaphone' was used some years ago by Daniel Jones to refer to the sameness of phonemes in different dialects and can well be extended to refer to different languages as well".
6. Jones gives the alternatives in every dictionary entry concerned but cf. Jones (1962: 200-201, 1973: 201, n.24).
7. For network notation in general see Halliday (1967: 37-38; Kress, ed. 1976: 15); Halliday and Martin (eds. 1981: 10-12, also 74-98).
8. Calques or "loan-translations" (Weinreich 1963: 61-62) as most commonly understood are lexical calques, dia-realizations at the "morphological" stage (phonological dia-realizations being "outright transfer" loans (Weinreich 1963: 61-62). Syntactical calques are dia-structures or dia-uses. Grammatical calques other than syntactical calques are dia-realizations of grammatical items or of word-morphological structures, or "morphological" calques or dia-realizations.
9. On "uses" see Ellis (1966b: 114 and references there at n.84). Cf. McIntosh's (1966: 195) definition of (lexical) "use" (employing "class" and "group" in a non-technical sense): "a group of instances classed together because the meaning therein seems to require or justify a definition or paraphrase different from that of some other class". Cf. also ("M- and L-tense") Lyons (1977: 682), Levinson (1983: 77).
10. "Morphological" realizations include: unmarked *ka* "has", *ka pasur* "has had"; admirative *pas-ka, pas-ka pasur*, analysed as inversion of either future or perfect. Standard Mod-

ern Albanian appears to exhibit reduced occurrence of the marked term (see comments on registers and lexical verbs in Hetzer (1978: 96), Schmaus (1966: 104)), but the system still forms part of verb conjugation (Hetzer 1978: 95-96, 199ff.).

11. For example in Hoxha's 1960 exchange with Khrushchev, see Hetzer (1978: 92, 98, 255).

12. In some varieties (Schmaus 1966: 103) the non-inverted Albanian perfect too has, like perfect tenses in some non-Balkan languages, a "renarrative" use (Sanfeld 1930: 160), *ka ardhurë* (Standard Modern Albanian *ardhur*, Geg *ardhë*) "il est venu (à ce que j'apprends)".

13. Cf. Hetzer (1978: 95): "menyra habitore ... eine Verwunderung, wovon jedoch nicht auf das vollständige Anwendungsfeld dieser sprachlichen Form zu schliessen ist".

14. For this, including the differentiation of use in Turkish registers of zero and *-dir* for lexical "be" third person, see Lewis (1953: 33, 91-92, 1967: 97-98, 109, 139-141).

15. It may be worthwhile making explicit the relation between phonological dia-realization and diaphone. A diaphone (in any sense but Haugen's) abstracts from phonological realizations of common formal items; a phonological dia-realization *is* the realization of a given item or category. Unlike "morphological" dia-realization, any one phonological dia-realization (extra-linguistic considerations apart) is identifiable only along with others instantiated in the same language or varieties and together yielding the relevant diaphones (cf. Ellis 1966a: 81-82).

16. Koneski *et al.* (1966: 5) notes that Western dialects of Macedonian have anticipation of all indirect objects, of direct only if definite, while usage in Eastern dialects is less systematic, as in other Balkan languages except Albanian.

17. Other, extra-linguistic (sociolinguistic), parts of the data in this case include degrees of Turkish colonization of Bulgarian dialect-areas (Ellis 1952: 125).

18. The fullest treatment of the functional aspect of the grammar is Halliday (1985).

19. Cf. Asenova's "diasystème" (1977: 30), "une réalité vivante pour les sujets bilingues", which she says is more or less Pike's "hypersystem".

20. Acknowledgments and thanks are due to the Social Science Research Council for a Personal Research Grant in 1979-80 for Comparative Description of Balkan Languages.

English quantifiers from noun sources[1]

Adrienne Lehrer

Introduction

English has a set of constructions which are functionally similar to classifiers in classifier language. Such constructions are illustrated in (1).

(1) a. *a bunch of people*
         dozens of philosophers
         a number of people
         a bit of rice
         a lot of the money
     b. *a box of candy*
         cups of water
         a group of animals
         a row of peas

English is not usually considered a classifier language, which, as described by Greenberg (1972), Allan (1977a, 1977b), Denny (1976, 1979), Adams and Conklin (1973) and others, have a small, closed, paradigmatically-contrasting set of morphemes, and which are obligatory, at least in some constructions. However, the kinds of expressions illustrated in (1) above show that English has a way of providing functional equivalents of classifiers (Lehrer 1986). Although the expressions in (1a) and (1b) look syntactically alike, i.e. in both lists they seem to have the structure $_{NP}[(Det) N_1$ of $N_2]$, I will argue that they are in fact different. In particular, I will argue that in (1b) the first noun is an ordinary prototypical noun, while the expressions in (1a) have moved out of the noun class into the quantifier class.[2]

Developing explicit criteria for word and morpheme classification was a major concern of the American structuralist linguists (Fries 1952), but this interest was lost for almost a quarter of a century following *Syntactic Structures*, where word and morpheme classifications were based rather unreflectively along traditional lines. There was an interest during this time in showing that traditional parts of speech classifications failed to capture many parallel syntactic generalizations, for example stativity and dynamicity among verbs, adjectives, and nouns, and there was a small cottage industry, in which McCawley was active, devoted to showing that all sorts of things were verbs. Only in recent years have linguists returned to the traditional concern with *criteria* for classifications.

The purpose of classifying words into parts of speech within a language is to enable us to make general statements about the distribution of the members of the class instead of stating the distribution of each word individually. Thus we can say "determiners may be followed by nouns" instead of "*the* may be followed by *cat, dog, house, car*, etc." Anna Carlson writes (1978: 323):

> The question of exactly what justifies a syntactic category distinction is a difficult one, and one that is normally ... not satisfactorily answered. Elements that are said to form a category are claimed to be significantly like each other and significantly unlike the elements in other disjoint categories: how great a similarity or dissimilarity is left as a matter of judgment rather than explicit specification.

Items grouped together as belonging to one part of speech will usually have several morphological and/or syntactic properties in common. Sometimes words assigned to a class will lack one or more of these properties, and this exceptional information must be listed in the lexical entry. If, however, an item is assigned to a class when it lacks more than half of the properties found in the prototypical members, one can question the legitimacy of the membership of that item.

Another aspect of categorizing words, besides the distributional properties within a language, is that of making cross-language comparisons and generalizations. I follow Lyons (1966), in that applying labels, for example *noun, verb*, etc., depends on a notional criterion. We call a category "noun" if the core of items denote persona or things; it does not matter how many non-thing words may be in the class as well, provided they share (most of) the other morphological and syntactic properties.

Let us return to the expressions in (1) above. In deciding what part of speech they belong to, we can consider the following hypotheses:

(2) a. They are nouns (possibly a special subclass).
    b. They are quantifiers (possibly a special subclass).
    c. They form a separate part of speech.
    d. They do not belong to any part of speech.

Hypotheses (c) and (d) involve general theoretical issues and will be discussed later.

Criteria for nouns and quantifiers

Let us first look at the criteria for prototypical English common nouns:

(3) a. They have singular and plural forms. (Allan 1980 shows that the count-mass distinction is far more complex than a simple binary contrast, however.)
    b. They have genitive forms.
    c. They may be preceded by several classes of specifiers:
        i. Definite determiners (*the*, *this*, *that*, *these*) or genitive pronouns (*my*, *his*, *her*, etc.).
        ii. Quantifiers
            (The items in (i) and (ii) interact, so that not all combinations are possible.)
        iii. Adjectives (and other nouns)
    d. They (together with the modifiers and complements) serve as arguments to the predicate.
    e. They may be followed by prepositional phrases, participial phrases, and/or relative clauses.

Let us now consider the syntactic properties of quantifiers. Quantifiers are part of the noun specifier system, and they interact with determiners and numerals in complex ways. The semantic core of quantifiers is that they denote a quantity or amount, but when we look at the distribution of the English words with this meaning, we see that quantifiers are not a uniform class. Quirk *et al.* (1972) classify some quantifiers as predeterminers (*all, half, both*, plus multiples such as *double, twice*, etc.); others as determiners (*every, each, enough*), along with articles and possessive pronouns; others as ordinals (*first, second, last*); and others are put into a cardinal/quantifier class (*two, little, few*). Analyses can also be found in Jackendoff (1977) and Huddleston (1984). Huddleston does not even use the term "quantifier". What quantifiers have in common is the following:

(4) a. Quantifiers precede the head noun and any adjective or noun modifiers.
   b. Most quantifiers may be followed by a prepositional phrase, where *of* is the preposition and a definite determiner precedes the rest of the noun phrases.[3]

Beyond the rather weak generalizations in (a) and (b), distributional statements are limited to subclasses:

   c. *All* and *both* can directly precede the definite noun phrase: *all the men, both the men*.
   d. *All, both,* and *each*, may float rightward from the subject to precede AUX or follow the first AUX element: *The men all (both, each) left*.
   e. Some quantifiers occur with singular count nouns (*every, each*), others with mass nouns (*some, all, much, little*), others with plural nouns (*all, some, few, a few, many*).
   f. Some quantifiers may modify verbs: *much, a little, enough*, as in *I love you a little, but not too much*.

What part of speech does *Lot* belong to?

Let us return to the classifiers in (1) above to apply the criteria in (3) and (4). The items in (1b) *box, cup, row,* and *group* are clearly nouns. They occur in singular and plural constructions and can be preceded by adjectives:

(5) *Two large groups of furniture.*
    That cup of cream.
    Many heavy boxes of candy.
    Three even rows of peas.

Any restrictions on genitive forms are due to more general restrictions involving animacy and discourse factors on genitives with inanimate nouns (Riddle 1984).[4]

(6) *The group's decision*
    ?The box's size

Cup, box, group, etc. can occur freely as arguments of verbs. Prepositional phrases freely follow such words, but they are optional.

However, let us look at the items in (7), which include those in (1a):

(7) *a couple (of) books*
a lot of, lots of dogs
a bit of wheat
a good (great) deal of paper
oodles, scads, zillions of people
a dozen eggs; dozens of eggs
plenty of water
a hundred cats; hundreds of cats
a number of people
a large (small) amount of food
a bunch of people

One major way in which most of the expressions in (7) differ from quantifiers is that they require *of* before the NP. *A couple, a dozen, a hundred* (and higher units) do not take *of*, but their plurals do.

A second way in which the items in (6) differ from most quantifiers is that the second noun may follow the *of* without a determiner (although determiners are permitted):

(8) *A bit of (the) smoke*
Hundreds of (these) books
A lot of (his) money

Compare true quantifiers, where a definite determiner is needed:

(9) **Each of books*
*Some of water
*Many of people

The items in (7) look like nouns. They are preceded by the indefinite article (but so are some quantifiers, e.g. *a little* and *a few*) and they have plurals. But *a* cannot be replaced by a different determiner without destroying the quantifier meaning:

(10) **I bought the good deal of tobacco.*
*This lot of people came to the party.
*I asked your number of friends for advice.

Nor can plural forms of *number* and *lot* be preceded by a determiner:

(11) **My numbers of people came to the party.*
*The lots of cars bother me.

When the items in (7) are preceded by adjectives, the allowable adjectives are severely limited:

(12) *a whole (helluva) lot*
a little (tiny, good, *large) bit
a large (small, good, *bad) number[5]

When other adjectives are used, the quantifier meaning is destroyed; the meaning that emerges is that of the polysemous noun which serves as the historical source for these quantifier-like elements:

(13) He bought a tiny lot ("parcel of land").
*A tiny lot of people came to the party.
A large bit ("piece") of meat got caught in my throat.
*He bought a large bit of hamburger.
He got a bad deal.
*He had a bad deal of trouble.

Like quantifiers, the expressions above must be specified as to the co-occurrence restrictions for the countability of the following NP. *A bit*, *a good deal*, and *a small (large)* amount require a following mass noun:

(14) $A \begin{Bmatrix} bit \\ good\ deal \\ small\ amount \end{Bmatrix} of \begin{Bmatrix} water \\ cotton \\ *cars \\ *book \end{Bmatrix}$ [6]

A number requires a plural NP, as do expressions denoting plural quantities (*a dozen, dozens, a hundred, thousands*, etc.):

(15) $\begin{Bmatrix} A\ number \\ Oodles \\ Scads \\ Hundreds \end{Bmatrix} of \begin{Bmatrix} books \\ people \\ *salt \\ *cotton \end{Bmatrix}$

A lot and *lots* permit plural or mass nouns, as do *oodles* and *scads*:[7]

(16) $\begin{Bmatrix} A\ lot \\ Lots \\ Oodles \\ Scads \end{Bmatrix} of \begin{Bmatrix} water \\ cars \end{Bmatrix}$

Finally, like quantifiers that co-occur with mass nouns, the items in (7) that co-occur with mass nouns can be used to modify verb phrases:

(17) *I love you* $\begin{Bmatrix} \text{a lot, lots} \\ \text{a great deal} \\ \text{?oodles} \\ \text{?scads} \\ \text{*a number} \end{Bmatrix}$

A further observation has to do with *one(s)* substitution, a transformation discussed by Baker (1978) and Jackendoff (1977). *One* or *ones* may replace an identical noun phrase at the level of N̄ when it is lexically identical to the first N.

(18) a. *The corked quarts of wines and the capped ones of water are here.*
b. *Straight rows of beans and crooked ones of corn have been planted.*

Plural *ones* unlike singular *one* may not replace the entire NP. There must be some contrastive material.

(19) a. **He likes blue cars and I like ones (too).*
b. **He grows plants from California and I grow ones (too).*

What is interesting is that *one(s)* substitution may not apply to quantifier-like nouns, which shows that these expressions do not behave like regular nouns.

(20) a. **He has a large number of trees and I have a small one of bushes.*
b. **He makes a good deal of trouble and she a good one of help.*

Huddleston (1984: 238-239) says *a number*, *a lot*, and *a couple* are "number-transparent" (the head noun does not agree with the third person singular verb):

(21) $A \begin{Bmatrix} \text{number} \\ \text{lot} \\ \text{couple} \end{Bmatrix}$ *of people* $\begin{Bmatrix} \text{*is} \\ \text{are} \end{Bmatrix}$ *intelligent.*

However, if these expressions are treated as quantifier phrases which take plural nouns and not as the head of the NP, there is no mystery in the lack of match between *number* and the verb. *Number*, *lot*, and *couple* are not the heads; they are part of the specifier system.

Thus we see that the items listed in (7) are not prototypical nouns, but they share many properties of quantifiers. Before turning to the issue of justifying the existence of a quantifier class, the history of these words is sketched, since it provides part of the explanation for the behaviour of quantifiers.

The historical source of quantifiers

A. Carlson (1978) has traced the development of quantifiers in English. In Old English, those words that are the ancestors of Modern English quantifiers ("prequantifiers") had the same syntactic distribution and inflectional endings as adjectives. By the end of the sixteenth century, a new category of quantifiers emerged. In fact, at this time, the quantifiers formed a more homogeneous group than Modern English quantifiers (1978: 324).

After a new category has been formed, other items may move into it, including items that were never adjectives. I suggest that the expressions in (7) are moving into the quantifier class. *A number of*, *a lot of*, *lots of*, *a good deal of* and *a couple*[8] are quite firmly in the quantifier class. *A bunch* shows evidence of moving into the quantifier class. Not only is it being used with a general quantity meaning of "many", but it is often used with a following mass noun, and even in post verbal position. Someone said to me recently, "Thanks a bunch". The presence of *a few* in the quantifier class may facilitate the entrance of other expressions that begin with *a*. Number set classifiers (a term from Allan 1977a) like *dozen*, *hundred*, *million*, *zillion*, etc. have retained more of the properties of nouns and can be preceded by other quantifiers:

(22) $\begin{Bmatrix} Several \\ Many \end{Bmatrix}$ $\begin{Bmatrix} hundreds \\ zillions \\ dozens \end{Bmatrix}$ *of people*

In Old English "prequantifiers" and numbers were regularly followed by the genitive, which seems to have been replaced by *of* NP.[9]

Thus I conclude that expressions like those in (7), although they originated as nouns, have lost some of their noun-like properties and have acquired quantifier properties. I take this as evidence that there is indeed a quantifier class. These expressions must be treated as idioms, and they can be inserted into phrase markers wherever other quantifier expressions can be inserted. Thus *number* and *lot* would be entered in the lexicon as follows:

(23) *number*
1) QP   a   ($\begin{bmatrix} \text{adj} \\ \text{SIZE} \end{bmatrix}$)   number of $\begin{bmatrix} \text{N} \\ \text{Plural} \end{bmatrix}$

Meaning: "some" with analysis in terms of symbolic logic. The semantic overlap of *a small number* and *a few* and of *a large number* and *many* needs to be explored further.

2) Mathematical sense

(24) *lot*
1) QP   a   ($\begin{Bmatrix} \text{whole} \\ \text{helluva} \end{Bmatrix}$)   lot of $\begin{bmatrix} \text{N} \\ \text{Mass v.} \\ \text{Plural} \end{bmatrix}$

Meaning: "Multal". Further semantic specification: overlap in meaning with *much*, *many*, and analysis in terms of symbolic logic.

2) Other meanings, e.g. "parcel of land", "what one gets by chance", as in *draw lots*.

Quantifiers as a part of speech

Having assumed that there is a category of quantifier, I now wish to justify it. As we have seen, there is considerable diversity in the syntax of members of the class, enough to have led Culicover (1982: 90) to write, "it may be that quantifier is not a true syntactic category, simply a traditional informal one".

The two possibilities not yet considered are (1) that the items discussed above (*a number*), etc. do not belong to any part of speech, and (2) that they form a separate part of speech. If we can show that there is indeed a category of quantifier and that these items are members of it, then we have ruled out the possibility that they do not belong to any part of speech or that they form a new one. In fact, there would be no point in setting up a new category, since each item has a slightly different distribution from the others. But these differences are analogous to the differences found among the other quantifiers (*some*, *many*, etc.). In addition, the variation in subclasses is no greater than subclasses of verbs, nouns, or adjectives. Consider the following parallels:

1. That quantifiers are marked for taking singular or plural nouns is analogous to some nouns having no plural form (*equipment*) and others having only a plural form (*scissors*).

2. That most quantifiers are followed by *of*, but some are not (*every*) is analogous to some verbs taking direct objects (*hit the fence*) and others taking prepositional objects (*beware of the dog*).
3. That some quantifiers co-occur with determiners (*this many*) and others do not is analogous to verb subcategorization (e.g. some verbs take infinitival complements, whereas others do not). As mentioned earlier, the fact that other items appear to be behaving more and more like quantifiers suggests that there is a quantifier class that they are moving into.
4. That some quantifiers "float" to the end of the NP or that they can appear pre-verbally is analogous to the fact that some German prepositions such as *nach* and *laut*, can appear as postpositions as well. In addition, many grammarians have suggested that linear order should be separated from co-occurrence possibilities. If this view is accepted, then the fact that *all*, *each*, and *both* may occur preverbally, would not count against their inclusion in the quantifier class.
5. Finally, Jackendoff's specifier constraint (1977: 104) accounts for the fact that quantifiers are in paradigmatic contrast, in that if one occurs, others may not: "A NP specifier may contain at most one demonstrative, one quantifier, and one numeral".

Conclusion

We have seen that *a lot*, *a number*, and other items we have looked at have lost their noun properties and acquired those of quantifiers. In addition, I have tried to justify the existence of a quantifier class in English as a syntactic class, not simply as an informal notional one. (Cf. Lightfoot 1979.) Although the resulting class is messy, other studies also show that a similar lack of uniformity results when items change class. Maling (1983) finds that *like* and *worth* have changed from adjectives to prepositions, but they have not acquired all of the prototypical prepositional properties. Van der Auwera (1985: 175) argues that *that* has become a "highly pronominal relativizer", but it has not become fully pronominal because it has a non-pronominal origin.

In the case of quantifiers, if my analysis is correct, we have in English a syntactic class with members from at least two historical sources: adjectives and nouns. It is not surprising, therefore, that some of the members have retained remnants of their earlier category membership. For example *little* and *few* have retained some of their adjectival properties.[10] Since the newer items have come from and are coming from noun sources, many of them retain some of their noun properties as well.[11]

Notes

1. I wish to thank Barbara Hollenbach, Eliose Jelinek, Richard Oehrle and Johen van der Auwera for their helpful comments on earlier versions.
2. The idea that some NPs have moved into the quantifier class was first proposed in Akmajian and Lehrer (1976).
3. *Every* and the multiples are an exception to this rule.
   *Every of the men.
   *Twice of the men.
   Also a few post-nominal elements have been considered to be quantifiers, such as *galore* and *enough*.
4. In classifier expressions, genitives would be avoided because they would have to be added to the second noun, as in *the group of people's choice*, *the box of candy's cover*.
5. Other size words may appear.
6. Apparently some speakers find *amount of cars* acceptable.
7. There may be idiolect differences, so that for some speakers *oodles* and *scads* require plural nouns.
8. See Bolinger (1979) for observations on *a couple*.
9. See Allan (1977a), especially p.108 and p.117.
10. Among the quantifiers with an adjectival source, *little* and *few* and to a lesser degree *much* and *many* have retained some of their adjectival properties. Using Maling's criteria for adjective membership, we find the following:
    a. These four words can be preceded by adjective and adverb specifiers *very* and *too*.
    b. *Few* and *little* can be followed by *enough*: *few enough*, *little enough*; *?many enough*; **much enough*.
    c. These words are marginal or ungrammatical after *seem* and *consider*.
       *The books seem few, many.
       (Cf. *The books seem numerous*.)
       We consider your problems too $\begin{Bmatrix} ?many \\ few \\ numerous \end{Bmatrix}$ to bother with.
11. The lack of uniformity in quantifiers is mirrored also in the English AUX. Some members have retained their verbal properties (*have*, *be*, *do*), while others have lost them (the modals). In some syntactic analyses, items which never were verbs are included in AUX, for example *to* in many transformational accounts, and *better* in Oehrle (1984).

Two types of semantic widening and their relation to metaphor

Samuel R. Levin

Semantic widening is a process continually at work in the historical careers of lexical items. In this paper I wish to take up two types of widening that are not usually distinguished and describe the mechanisms that lie behind and give rise to them. We may call one of the types semantic *generalization* — applying this term in a manner somewhat different from its customary use — and I will refer to the other type as semantic *extension*. Both these varieties of semantic change have their origin in a widening of distributional privilege, but the respective effects of this widening differ from each other. Under generalization a new sense is added to a word's meaning, under extension a new concept falls within the meaning's range. Illustrating the two processes are the following sentences:

(1) His courage evaporated (generalization)
(2) The earth trembled (extension)

(In this and the following considerations I am assuming that at one time (2) as well as (1) required construal — that both were anomalous expressions, in that *evaporate* was once predicable only of liquid objects and *tremble* only of vital objects. Justification for this assumption will be provided below.) In processing (1) we interpret *evaporate* to mean something like "dematerialize" or "disappear". This sense generalizes the notion of evaporating and historically it is the sense that has been added to the meaning of *evaporate*. In processing (2) on the other hand no construal of *tremble* is required; historically, however, a new concept, that of the earth, has fallen within its range. We may thus say that *evaporate* has generalized its meaning, whereas *tremble* has extended its range.[1]

Synchronically, that the meaning of *evaporate* has undergone widening is suggested by the fact that its occurrence in a context like (1) prompts a (slight) sense of anomaly but, as we have seen, no comparable suggestion is made for *tremble* in (2). In order to show that *tremble* has indeed experienced semantic widening and that its type of widening is different from that experienced by *evaporate*, it is necessary to reconstruct the historical processes undergone by the two lexical items. This will be done below. First, however, some general comments on semantic widening are in order.

Trivial and nontrivial widening

The widening of a word's meaning originates in its advance into a new context. Although any such advance may be said to modify the meaning of a word, some such modifications are relatively trivial. This results from the fact that every word has a potential range of "normal" distribution not every part of which may at a given time have been utilized. Thus of some objects that are combustible it may not yet have been said that they burned. Given, however, that such an object — say a cherry pit — should be consumed by fire, it would be appropriate to say *The cherry pit burned*.[2] Contextual advance of this sort, in which the meaning of *burn* may be said to have been modified, can be regarded as simply the filling of a distributional gap and be ascribed to the notion "possible use". In such cases the semantic representation of the item — in particular, its selection restriction — is adequate as it stands to comprehend the new use. Nontrivial widening occurs when a word's advance is into contexts that do not fall within the "normal" range of the word's distribution. This is a way of saying that its selection restriction is transgressed. Of course, in a living language the notions of normal and preternormal lexical ranges are difficult if not impossible to define. Modifications that are in process of development will be manifested in usage but not reflected in the grammar. In order to grasp any such modification it would be necessary to compare successive stages of a language, focusing on processes that have already run their course. It might be thought that we are in a position to do this by comparing (a portion of) the contemporary grammar with (the corresponding portion of) an earlier grammar. But this is easier said than done. Even granting that a contemporary grammar might, by a comprehensive statement of selection restrictions, provide the information required for one term of the comparison, we are not in any such favourable position when it comes to stages of the language centuries earlier. Grammars of Old, Middle, and early modern English, if they deal with co-occurrence privileges at all, present this information in only the grossest terms. We have of course the evidence from the *Oxford English Dictionary*. In many cases, however, the OED will not provide the relevant information. But even if it should provide information that is relevant, we are not compelled to regard its testimony as definitive. Thus even though the OED gives among its earliest citations for *tremble* one in which it is predicated of the earth, I am assuming that its original (perhaps primordial) range was restricted to human or animal objects (where even its application to the latter may have been secondary).

Notice that it is immaterial whether we assume that *tremble* was originally predicated of humans (then of animals) and subsequently transferred to inanimates or whether we assume the opposite historical order. Everything that we may say about the distribution of *tremble* on one historical order will apply *mutatis mutandis* on the other (or any) order. The only question of substance is whether we are justified in assuming that a verb like *tremble* was originally predicated of a limited, homogeneous body of objects or whether it came on the lexical scene fully ramified as to its distributional range. There can be little doubt that the former assumption is the more likely. Certainly, in those cases where we are in a position to observe a word's being newly introduced into a language, its range is implicitly defined as that class of words of which its co-occurrent (in the sentence) is a member. Of course, where a word like *tremble* is concerned, we are making assumptions about developments that reach far back in time, and the evidence is not such as to bear out our claims. In fact, already in Classical Latin *tremere* is used of the earth, as well as of people. I continue to use *tremble* as my paradigm example of extension, rather than other forms whose careers bear out the process more obviously, in order to suggest the deep and pervasive nature of the phenomenon. Following, however, are a few cases where the development can be more clearly traced. The use of *harvest* as a verb applies in its earliest OED attestation (1400) to the gathering in of corn. The first citation of a non-grain application is from 1888, where a fortune is said to be harvested. A similar development may be traced in the use of *roast* as a verb, where it applies first to flesh (1297), then to chemical substances (1582), then to coffee beans (1724). As an example from more recent times, we may consider the intransitive verb *land* — from an original use restricted to ships (earliest attestation 1382), it has been extended now to apply to air-borne vehicles of various kinds. These examples represent a small sample of the number that could be adduced. What they would all show is that the distributional range of a form can be nontrivially widened and its meaning changed — in the sense that its semantic representation is modified.

Returning now to our first type, the advance of *evaporate* into the context represented in (1) also involves a nontrivial widening of its distribution with the result that its semantic representation was modified. We have been claiming, however, that there is a difference between these two types of change. In subsequent sections we shall try to reconstruct the historical processes that lie behind this difference.

Semantic representation

It is characteristic of semantic widening that (at least) in its first occurrence the resting sentence tends to be anomalous. It is therefore necessary to consider the question of semantic anomaly and develop a method for dealing with it. For this purpose we need a system of semantic representation; I will adopt the notation developed in Katz (1972). In this notation a typical reading for a noun is (in simplified form):

(3) *chair*; [+N,...]; (Furniture)(Portable)(Something with legs)... (Seat for one)

The reading (3) is "compressed". Quite apart from the ellipsis, which is introduced above simply to save space (for the full reading see Katz 1972: 40), the reading is compressed in that it is redundancy-free. Thus the marker "(Furniture)" entails "(Object)", "(Physical)", "(Nonliving)", and "(Artifact)". These redundant markers are omitted from the representation of lexical entries and are supplied by redundancy rules (see below) to form "expanded" readings, and it is upon the latter that the projection rules operate (Katz 1972: 45f.).

A typical reading for a verb (on one sense) would be something like:

(4) *run*; [+V,...]; ((Activity)(Physical)((Movement)(Forward)
$$[NP,S]$$
$$\underline{X}$$
(Characterized by springing steps))X)<(Human) $\overline{\mathrm{v}}$ (Animal)>

The readings for verbs contain semantic markers and a variable. Associated with the reading is a selection restriction in the form of a categorization of the variable. The segment above the variable specifies the syntactic environment (derivatively, the grammatical function) in which it (i.e. its value) must appear relative to the verb, and the segment below the variable enumerates the set of semantic markers with which the value of the variable must be compatible. Consider now the sentence (5):

(5) *The chair was running*

i.e. with the reading (3) as the value of X in (4). On the amalgamation of the two readings there is no duplication, hence satisfaction, of any of the markers in (3) by any of the markers making up the selection restriction in (4). However, as mentioned earlier, before the projection rules are applied to form derived readings it is necessary to expand all lexical representations. When this is done the reading (3) will contain the additional, redundant features "(Object)", "(Physical)", "(Nonliving)", and "(Artifact)". Even with the expanded reading, however, there is still no duplication (the duplication of "(Physical)" is an artifact of the notation and non-substantive).

If we examine the amalgamated markers in the projected reading for (5) we see that "(Human)" and "(Animal)" are compatible with "(Object)" and "(Physical)" and that they are incompatible, but only implicitly, with "(Nonliving)" and "(Artifact)". This suggests that non-duplication is insufficient as a criterion for anomaly, that something stronger should be sought. This stronger criterion can be obtained if the implicit incompatibility mentioned above is made explicit. And this can be done if redundant features are introduced not only for the readings of nouns but also for the selection restrictions in verbs. Thus both "(Human)" and "(Animal)" entail "(Living)" and "(Natural)". By adding the redundant features to the readings of verbs the implicit incompatibility is made explicit and, instead of mere non-duplication, we have incompatibility of markers as a criterion for anomaly.[3]

The difference between non-duplication and incompatibility as a criterion for anomaly has bearing on another question that is relevant in the present context. If the function of a semantic theory is simply to mark anomalous sentences as such, then non-duplication among amalgamated markers might be considered an adequate criterion. If, however, our goal is not merely to identify anomalous sentences but in addition to construe them, then incompatibility recommends itself. If the goal is construal it becomes important to ascertain not merely that the semantic markers of two items do not match, but to see positively in what respect their semantic representations are opposed to one another. For it is out of this opposition that the construal will need to be effected. Thus in the case of (5) any construal focused on the verb will be based upon the opposition between the markers "(Living)" and "(Nonliving)" (or perhaps "(Natural)" and "(Artifact)").

Some aspects of redundancy

The preceding discussion has implied a hierarchization of semantic features like that in Figure 1 below.

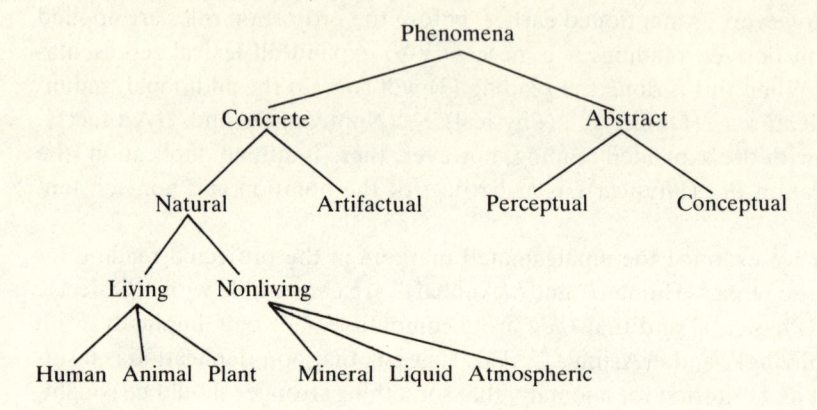

```
                        Phenomena
                       /         \
                Concrete           Abstract
                /     \            /       \
           Natural  Artifactual  Perceptual  Conceptual
           /    \
       Living  Nonliving
       /  |  \    |    \    \
   Human Animal Plant Mineral Liquid Atmospheric
```

Figure 1.[4]

Assuming the hierarchy in Figure 1, the following would be among the redundancy rules:

$\begin{Bmatrix} \text{(Human)} \\ \text{(Animal)} \\ \text{(Plant)} \end{Bmatrix}$ → (Living)

$\begin{Bmatrix} \text{(Mineral)} \\ \text{(Liquid)} \\ \text{(Atmospheric)} \end{Bmatrix}$ → (Nonliving)

$\begin{Bmatrix} \text{(Living)} \\ \text{(Nonliving)} \end{Bmatrix}$ → (Natural)

$\begin{Bmatrix} \text{(Natural)} \\ \text{(Artifactual)} \end{Bmatrix}$ → (Concrete)

$\begin{Bmatrix} \text{(Perceptual)} \\ \text{(Conceptual)} \end{Bmatrix}$ → (Abstract)

The redundancy rules are to be interpreted as follows: markers to the right of the arrow are positively entailed by those on the left. This applies equally for the readings of nouns and (the selection restrictions of) verbs. There is also a negative entailment, one, however, which holds only for nouns. Thus in the readings for nouns the markers within the braces are such that *on a given sense* the presence of one entails the exclusion of the others: viz. "(Human)" entails "-(Animal)" and "-(Plant)". This restriction does not apply to verbs, where more than one marker of the same level (hence appearing together within the braces) can appear as disjuncts in the selection restriction accompanying a given sense.

The asymmetry in question derives from the different naming functions performed by nouns and verbs: where nouns refer, verbs (and other predicates) have extension. An object of reference cannot be such that it incorporates contradictory or ontologically incompatible properties — nor can it be such as to embody incompatible properties at different times (and remain the same object). All this is of course not to say that the reference of nouns and hence their meanings may not change. Examples of nouns undergoing semantic widening (of both types) are a commonplace of historical semantics: thus *mill*, referring earlier to a machine or place for grinding meal, now used of a manufactory generally; *foot*, referring originally to a human appendage, used now in "foot of the chair", "foot of the mountain", etc. The result of these developments, however, is that the nouns simply refer to new referents.[5] And these new referents again have homogeneous properties. Neither before nor after the meaning change, therefore, can the reading of a noun contain incompatible semantic markers on the same sense. Thus the reading for *foot* will contain the markers "(Human)", "(Artifactual)", and "(Mineral)", but there is no contradiction or overlap among these markers, since each one will appear in a different sense of the reading.[6] The main point to emphasize in this discussion, however, is that it is because of the characteristic referential aspect in its naming function that the negative entailment among the semantic markers holds for nouns.[7]

Where verbs (and other predicates) are concerned, the situation is different. Nothing prevents a verb from having in its extension sets of objects which from the viewpoint of ontological characteristics and hence semantic markers are disparate. Thus animals and rivers run, living and nonliving objects move, natural and artifactual objects break, and so on. From this it follows that the selection restrictions in the readings of verbs may contain disjunctions of incompatible semantic markers and, where the historical process involved has been that of extension, these markers will pertain to the same sense.

Background

Let us return now to a consideration of the sentences (1) and (2) and attempt to reconstruct the historical processes through which they have passed and which lead to the different statuses that they presently enjoy.

At the stage before its context of use was widened the semantic representation of *evaporate* would have been somewhat as follows:

(6) *evaporate*; [+V, +--#]; ((Process)((Pass off)(As vapour))X)
   [NP,S]
   $\underline{X}$
   <(Liquid)>

On the basis of the reading (6) *evaporate* would be normally applied to subject nouns denoting liquids. The selection restriction in (6) entails that the noun of which *evaporate* is predicated denote something concrete. The expanded lexical entry for *evaporate* would thus entail (as redundant) the feature "(Concrete)" in its selection restriction. A sentence like (1) at its coinage would thus have been anomalous (deviant) in that the entailment "(Concrete)" of the selection restriction on *evaporate* would have contradicted, in the sense of being incompatible with, the inherent feature "(Abstract)" of *courage* (cf. also "His disappointment evaporated", "His hopes evaporated", etc.). At its coinage (1) would thus have required a construal which in some fashion resolved the opposition of the markers "(Concrete)" and "(Abstract)".

Let us now consider the case of *tremble* in (2). Before widening its semantic representation would have been somewhat as follows:

(7) *tremble*; [+V, +--#]; ((Activity)((Shake)(Involuntarily))X)
   [NP,S]
   $\underline{X}$
   <(Human) v (Animal)>[8]

A sentence like (2) at its coinage would have been anomalous in that the entailment "(Living)" of the selection restriction on *tremble* would contradict the redundant feature "(Nonliving)" of *earth* (cf. also "The building trembled", "The bridge trembled", etc.). At its coinage (2) would thus have required a construal which in some fashion resolved the opposition between the markers "(Living)" and "(Nonliving)".

Construal

Implicit in the preceding discussion has been the notion of feature transfer developed primarily in the work of Weinreich (1966) (employed earlier for restricted purposes by Katz & Postal 1964). Although such transfers may proceed in either direction, i.e. from verb to noun or the reverse, we are concerned in our examples with the shift of a feature from the reading of a noun into that of a verb since in the cases at hand it is the verb whose meaning has been modified (widened). Let us call that part of the reading consisting of the transferred feature and the feature in the host representation to which it is opposed the *Production Set* (*PS*), in that it is this part of the augmented reading which prompts and determines the mode of construal (see Levin 1977 where this construct is introduced). Thus for *evaporate* in (1) the reading at coinage, after transfer and adding of relevant redundancies, would be something like:

(8)   *evaporate*; [+V,+--#]; ((Process)((Pass off)(As vapour))X)
            [NP,S]
              $\underline{X}$
       <(Liquid)(Nonliving)...[(Concrete) (Abstract)]...>

where the *PS* is enclosed in square brackets, the transferred feature appearing to the right.

For *tremble* the augmented reading would become:

(9)   *tremble*; [+V, +--#]; ((Activity)((Shake)(Involuntarily))X)
            [NP,S]
              $\underline{X}$
       <(Human) v (Animal)...[(Living) (Nonliving)]...>

As the production sets stand above there is no indication of the manner in which their elements are related to each other. For our present purposes we need to introduce two such relations: *Disjunction* and *Conjunction* (these relations are discussed in Levin 1977 along with a third relation, that of *Displacement*). Thus between the members of a *PS* there will need to be (always) the sign of disjunction or that of conjunction. Depending on whether the members of the *PS* are disjuncts or conjuncts we have one or another mode of construal, each leading to a different type of semantic widening.

We assume that for the construal of (1) the members of the *PS* in (8) are to be regarded as disjoined, viz. [(Concrete) v (Abstract)].[9] In the face of a disjunction in the *PS* the construal moves to obtain a more generalized meaning of the verb, one that holds for phenomena of either type, in the present instance that are *either* concrete *or* abstract. This is achieved in the case of (8) by dropping the semantic marker "(Of vapour)" from the reading. We are thus left with a sense of *evaporate* in which it means simply to "pass off" or "disappear". When this additional sense of *evaporate* is registered in the lexicon, its reading becomes (10):

(10) a. *evaporate*; [+V, +--#]; ((Process)((Pass off)(As vapour))$\underset{X}{[NP,S]}$)<(Liquid)... (Concrete)...>;

b. ----- ; ((Process)(Pass off))$\underset{X}{[NP,S]}$)<...(Abstract)...>,

where (10b) is the new sense.

Historical reconstruction

Four historical stages may be distinguished in the preceding development. We assume first the stage (I) in which *evaporate* was not predicable of abstract objects. Stage (II) occurs at the moment of coinage, when a sentence like (1) was first uttered. At that stage (1) would have constituted a fresh metaphor and an *ad hoc* construal, one based on a disjunction of markers in the *PS*, would have been effected. At stage (III) the interpretation proceeds on the basis of a late or subsidiary rule in some component (semantic, perceptual, pragmatic) of the speaker's linguistic ability. At stage (IV) the lexical entry for *evaporate* is restructured into the form (10), the late or subsidiary rule being dropped. The current stage with respect to *evaporate* is either (III) or (IV) depending on the degree to which a construction like (1) is "faded" for a speaker. Here as in comparable cases the grammars (or total linguistic equipment) of individual speakers may vary as between (III) and (IV).

Turning now to the analysis of (2) we assume that the members of the *PS* in (9) are originally conjoined, viz. [(Living) & (Nonliving)]. A conjunction in the *PS* prompts a construal wherein the activity, process, or state represented by the verb is made consistent with predication of an object that jointly possesses the opposing features. This description of the process should not be understood as claiming that objects are taken to comprise contradictory properties; it is a matter, rather, of construing a word so that its meaning comprehends two opposing senses. In the present instance the meaning of *tremble* would be modified to mean the type of involuntary shaking that would be characteristic of an object that was both living and nonliving, the earth being conceived for the nonce as such an object. If this analysis seems strange or paradoxical, it may be pointed out that there is nothing unusual in construing a word as combining in its sense two contradictory semantic features. Suppose that instead of construing (2) on the assumption that it was the meaning of *tremble* that was modified (on its original use), we adopted the reverse interpretation, i.e. with *earth* as animated or personified (assuming thus that the feature "(Human)", and redundantly "(Living)", was transferred into its reading). We would then have a straightforward case of personification. That would mean of course that we would be regarding the earth as jointly living and nonliving (and *tremble* would then correspondingly have the meaning in question). In the personification of abstract concepts like virtue or freedom or of artifacts like knives and chairs we have comparable junctures. Thus where construal is concerned there is nothing exceptionable about speaking of a word's sense as combining two contradictory semantic features.

Where the verb is marked "(Human)", redundantly "(Living)", and the noun "(Nonliving)", the transfer N ← V yields personification. Let us refer to the transfer N → V in the same circumstances as "dispersonification", in the sense that restriction to co-occurrence with purely human (animate) subjects is momentarily suspended. Now when *tremble* is construed as meaning an involuntary shaking characteristic of an object that is jointly living and nonliving (thus as dispersonified), the earth must implicitly be regarded for the nonce as such an object, in other words as personified; this is so as to achieve parity between the verb *as construed* and the object it is predicated of.[10] Of course, depending on the direction of transfer and hence the focus of the construal, either personification or dispersonification is the primary process, and the respective concomitant process tends to go unnoticed. What leads us to overlook the concomitant construals is that as usages like (2) become naturalized, it is only the primary process that leaves a trail of semantic development; the concomitant process is viable only so long as the expression in question retains an air of anomaly and hence requires construal. Once the expression is naturalized the concomitant process is devitalized. What the preceding boils down to is that the words involved in the primary construal process undergo a historical change in their lexical representations, whereas those in the concomitant processes do not.

In the semantic development of *tremble* in (2) the same four stages may be distinguished as for *evaporate* (above). The difference lies in the mode of construal imposed at stage (II) and the subsequent development of the respective *PS*. In generalization, as for *evaporate* in (1), the members of the *PS* form a disjunction. On the continuing use of the expression the disjunction is dissolved with the result that an alternate reading is formed in which the transferred disjunct takes its place in the lexical representation alongside a new generalized sense, viz. (10b) (relabelled here as (11)):

$$[NP,S]$$
$$\underline{X}$$
(11) ((Process)((Pass off))X)<...(Abstract)...>

In extension, as for *tremble* in (2), the members of the *PS* form a conjunction. On the continuing use of the expression the conjunction is dissolved with the result only that the transferred conjunct takes its place alongside the original unchanged sense as an alternate selection restriction, viz. (12):

$$[NP,S]$$
$$\underline{X}$$
(12) ((Activity)((Shake)(Involuntarily))X)<(Human) v (Animal) v (Mineral)>

Thus in generalization a new sense (11) is added to the reading (6), resulting in the reading (10); in extension a new selection restriction is added to the original sense, yielding the reading (12) from (7).

Some aspects of disjunction and conjunction

The difference between generalization and extension has, as we have seen, been correlated with that between construal by disjunction and conjunction. If we look at the analysis that has been given *evaporate* in (1) and *tremble* in (2) we observe that the respective production sets comprise dissimilar combinations of features. In the analysis of (1) the *PS* contains the features "(Concrete)" and "(Abstract)", where "(Concrete)" was redundant on "(Liquid)" in the selection restriction of *evaporate* and "(Abstract)" was inherent in the reading of *courage*.[11] Inspection of Figure 1 shows that in order to arrive at this *PS* one passes from "(Liquid)" up the tree to "(Concrete)" for one term and then to arrive at the other term one goes to the top of the tree and down its other branch to "(Abstract)". A corollary of this distribution is that there is no single node (except trivially "(Phenomena)") that dominates both features. In the analysis of (2), on the other hand, the *PS* contains the features "(Living)" and "(Nonliving)" (redundant respectively on "(Human)" and "(Mineral)"), both these nodes being immediately dominated by "(Natural)".

These facts suggest that we might use some function of dominance or distance in the hierarchy of features to provide a structural correlate for the difference between construal by disjunction and conjunction. This hope is vain, however. First, as pointed out in note 4, it is likely that where construal is concerned there is no fixed hierarchy, that for different purposes different hierarchizations are implemented. Moreover, even given the hierarchy as presented in Figure 1, the facts pointed out above about the relation between the *PS* of (1) and that of (2) seem not to be significant. Thus cf.

(13) *The wind roared*

and

(14) *His talent languished*.

On the assumption in both cases that the construal is on the verb, we find in (13) that the *PS* associated with *roar* consists of the features "(Living)" and "(Nonliving)", "(Living)" from the selection restriction on *roar* and "(Nonliving)" transferred from *wind*. This is thus the same *PS* as we postulated for *tremble* in (2), which led, through conjunction, to the extension of its meaning. Yet in (13) the meaning of *roar* is generalized: we do not assume a special kind of roaring characteristic of the wind; we interpret (13) to mean that the wind produced some loud sound. If then the meaning of *roar* is generalized, the construal process was that of disjunction. In (14), on the other hand, the *PS* comprises the features "(Abstract)" and "(Concrete)", the latter feature from the selection restriction on *languish*, the former transferred from the reading for *talent*. This then is the same *PS* that we postulated for *evaporate* in (1), where the upshot, through disjunction, was semantic generalization. In (14) however, the process is one of extension: *talent* falls under the normal meaning of *languish*. The construal process was therefore that of conjunction.

From these considerations it can be seen that whether construal proceeds according to disjunction or conjunction cannot be a function of the features combined in the *PS*. The fact is that *a priori* an anomalous sentence can be construed either way; the dead and faded metaphors in the language provide ample evidence for this fact (see Levin 1977 for examples and discussion).

The one structural difference that emerges relates to the changes, after naturalization, that are effected on lexical representations consequent on the two types of construal. As was said at the beginning of this paper, under generalization a new sense is added to a word's meaning; under extension a new concept is added to a meaning's range. This is reflected in the revised lexical representations as the addition in the one case of a new sense and selection restriction, in the other simply of a new selection restriction.

Semantic widening and metaphor

It has been pointed out by a number of investigators that a theory of metaphor should incorporate a dimension that throws some light on the diachronic processes involved in their rise and fall (see e.g. Bickerton 1969: 50; Cohen & Margalit 1972: 722; Guenther 1975: 200). Although quite obviously the processes of generalization and extension discussed in this paper do not exhaust the types of semantic modification engendered by metaphoric construal, they seem fundamental. In connection with these processes two different construal mechanisms characterizing the advent of a metaphor have been described, and the subsequent diachronic developments which lead to the freezing of the metaphor have been sketched. Although the construal mechanisms for different types of metaphor may vary, it is probable that the diachronic developments experienced by these other types will follow the general course outlined in this paper.

Notes

1. Thus strictly speaking, only generalization instances semantic widening; extension instances rather distributional widening. Inasmuch however as both processes result in the expansion of semantic representations, it is not unreasonable to regard them both as types of semantic widening.

2. It makes little difference for the principle being discussed here whether the particular example cited is in fact novel.
3. Although Katz (1972) does not explicitly discuss redundancy relations for the markers in selection restrictions, introduction of such redundancies is a logical outgrowth of his views.
4. A number of comments are in order regarding the hierarchy in Figure 1. As constructed it incorporates no cross classification. Given the full array of semantic features, this condition could presumably not be maintained (see Chomsky 1965: 79ff.; and Katz 1972: 64ff. for some discussion). Figure 1 is misleading in another respect as well, in that it suggests there is a unique way to hierarchize semantic features. The fact is that for certain purposes a different hierarchization of the same set of features might be motivated. Consider a sentence like

   (i) *The engine screamed.*

This sentence is somewhat anomalous — it involves in fact a case of semantic generalization — in that *scream* "normally" or originally would require a human subject. *Engine* is marked "(Artifactual)". In order for the anomaly of (i) to be registered, it is necessary that a semantic opposition be developed out of the markers "(Artifactual)" and the selection restriction "(Human)" of *scream*. As the features are ranged in Figure 1 this opposition is developed by introducing the feature "(Natural)", redundant upon "(Human)", whereupon "(Natural)" stands opposed to "(Artifactual)", in this way marking the anomaly. If, however, the hierarchy, instead of being given as in Figure 1, were to be given in the form of Figure 2 below:

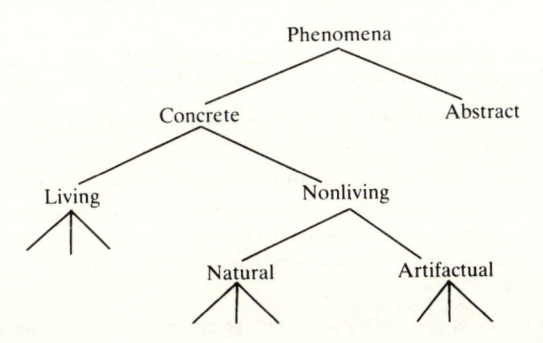

```
                    Phenomena
                   /         \
              Concrete       Abstract
             /       \
         Living    Nonliving
          /\       /       \
              Natural    Artifactual
               /\           /\
```

Figure 2.

then the opposition would develop as between the features "(Living)" and "(Nonliving)". There does not appear to be any *a priori* reason for preferring one or the other hierarchization. At the same time the selection of markers to appear in readings, particularly in selection restrictions, depends substantially on the hierarchization of semantic features that is implicitly or explicitly being employed. Moreover, if semantic analysis is carried out on a large scale, i.e. on large numbers of sentences, it is likely that more than one hierarchization will be motivated. In fact it is probably a principle of construal that semantic hierarchies will be (re)arranged *ad hoc* depending on the case at hand.

5. Not in all cases does semantic change in nouns involve a shift of reference. Where the change is of the types called amelioration or pejoration, for example, what is affected fun-

damentally is the meaning. Thus *marshall*, meaning formerly "tender of horses"; *gossip*, meaning formerly "close acquaintance". It might be thought that in such cases the reference also shifts as the meaning changes, but the shift involves only secondary attributes of the reference. The primary reference, to human beings in this case, remains unaffected. In widening (and narrowing) it is the primary reference which is shifted.

6. It would not be to the point to argue that the readings for verbs could be represented so that each disjunct of a selection restriction could be stated separately, and thus that verbs are no different in the relevant respect from nouns. What this argument would overlook is that under such a treatment the *sense* of the verb (that part of the representation indicating its meaning) would be the same for the two representations. Thus whether we represent the reading of a verb as:

   Verb; $((a_1)(a_2)...(a_n)) < R_1 \vee R_2 >$
   or as
   Verb; $((a_1)(a_2)...(a_n)) < R_1 >$
   $((a_1)(a_2)...(a_n)) < R_2 >$

   $((a_1)(a_2)...(a_n))$ (i.e. the sense) remains the same. In the case of homonymous nouns it is the senses that differ. Thus the different senses assigned to such nouns reflect the fact that there is more than one referent. On the other hand the different (disjunctive) selection restrictions on verbs simply reflect a wider range of application, the sense of the verb being unchanged. And this holds however we choose to represent the reading.

7. The distinction drawn in the preceding discussion between the different naming functions of nouns and verbs, and introduction of the referential character of nouns, is based on Thomason (1972: 212ff.), in which Thomason uses the "principle of referentiality" to explain the sortal characteristics of nouns as opposed to verbs. Thomason speaks rather of singular terms and predicates, but no difference of substance follows from the different terms used (in (1) and (2) the noun phrases may in fact be regarded as singular terms).

8. In order to simplify the notation I leave out of account the fact that plants can be said to tremble.

9. Disjunction as a relation in the *PS* is not to be confused with that relation as it obtains between the alternants in a selection restriction. A sufficient basis for their distinction is simply the fact that one is a relation between the members of a *PS*, the other not. It is also the case, however, that a disjunction in a selection restriction is exclusive, that in a *PS* in some sense inclusive.

10. In the more typical case of personification, although attention is as a rule not called to the fact, the verb is modified momentarily in a comparable fashion. Thus in *Virtue addressed her followers*, if we conceive of *virtue* as personified, then the sense of *address* is consequently modified so as to mean what *address* would mean when a personified abstraction is doing the addressing.

11. We might have assigned the feature "(Conceptual)" to *courage*, making "(Abstract)" redundant, but this would seem to make little difference for our present purposes.

The indefinite article and the numeral one

James P. Thorne

Perlmutter (1970) puts forward the hypothesis that *a(n)* is the unstressed form of the numeral *one*. As far as I know no one has demonstrated that the hypothesis is wrong. Since the issue is quite important — if Perlmutter is right then the category "indefinite article" can be dropped from the grammar — it is perhaps worth showing the reasons why it is.

Perlmutter's hypothesis rests upon two premises. The first is that sentences like (1) and (2) are synonymous:

(1) *I found a pen.*
(2) *I found one pen.*

The second is that *one* always takes stress and *a* never takes stress.[1] His conclusion, therefore, is that (1) and (2) are simply different phonological forms of the same surface structure; an optional rule mapping from surface structure to phonological form that produces the reduced form of the numeral *one* operating in (1) but not in (2).

Insofar as it might seem plausible to claim that sentences like (1) and (2) are synonymous it is because if sentence (2) is true, sentence (1) must be true and if sentence (2) is false, sentence (1) must be false. But the reverse is not necessarily the case. Whether or not sentence (2) follows from sentence (1) depends on how we interpret the expression *one pen*. *One pen* can be taken to mean *at least one pen* or *one and only one pen*. Sentence (2) is a consequence of sentence (1) only if sentence (2) is interpreted as *I have at least one pen*. Whether I have one, two, or a hundred pens I can in each case truthfully reply to the question *Do you have a pen?* by saying *I have a pen*. So it can be false that I have one and only one pen, but true that I have a pen. On the other hand if it is true that I have at least one pen then it must be true that I have a pen and false if it is false.

However, it would be a mistake to conclude from this that *a* means *at least one*. That two sentences are synonymous implies that they have the same truth conditions, but that they have the same truth conditions does not imply that they are synonymous.

Consider, for example, the two sentences

(3)   *Max has a wife.*
(4)   *Max has one wife.*

In a society in which monogamy is the rule, the effect of saying (4) is clearly very different from the effect of saying (3). This is so irrespective of whether (4) is interpreted as *Max has one and only one wife* or *Max has at least one wife*. But it would be difficult to see why this should be so in the second case if as well as having the same truth conditions as (3) it had also the same meaning. In fact, as sentences like (3) and (4) clearly show, expressions like *one wife* and *a wife* have different meanings. Noun phrases containing numerals designate sets. *One wife* designates either a set of wives with one and only one member or a set of wives with at least one member. *A wife* designates an individual belonging to the set *wife*. As a result anyone uttering (4) rather than (3) in a monogamous society is failing to uphold Grice's Co-operative Principle. More specifically, he is failing to comply with Grice's Second Maxim of Quantity: "Do not make your contribution more informative than is required". In speaking of a set and its cardinality, rather than of an individual, the speaker appears to invite the hearer to make the "conversational implicature" that Max could have any number of wives. As Grice says, the trouble with such overinformativeness is "that the hearer may be misled as a result of thinking that there is some particular point in the provision of the excess of information" (1975: 50).

To explain the difference in meaning between sentences (1) and (2) it is necessary to postulate different logical forms for them. The logical form for (1) is

(5) $(\exists x) (pen (x) \ \& \ I \ found \ (x))$

Using 1S for a set with at least one member and !1S for a set with only one member, the logical forms for sentence (2) are

(6) $(\exists x) (1Sx \ \& \ (\forall y) (y \in x \rightarrow pen(x) \ \& \ I \ found \ (x))$
(7) $(\exists x) (!1Sx \ \& \ (\forall y) (y \in x \rightarrow pen(x) \ \& \ I \ found \ (x))$

The fact that noun phrases containing numerals designate sets explains another difference between expressions like *one pen* and *a pen*. Despite the importance that he places on the evidence of stress Perlmutter fails to point out that noun phrases like *one pen* can be stressed in two different ways; either with equal stress on both words (*ońe pén*) or with relatively greater stress on the numeral (*ońe pèn*), and that this difference in stress correlates with a difference in meaning. Compare:

(8) *I found ońe pén on the table* (and two pencils).
(9) *I found ońe pèn on the table* (and the rest on the floor).

The latter (but not the former) can be paraphrased:

(10) *I found one of the pens on the table.*

That is to say, noun phrases containing a numeral can be used not only to designate sets but also subsets of previously mentioned sets. No such paraphrase is possible, of course, for (11):

(11) *I found a pen on the table.*

Notice also the clear difference in meaning between (12) and (13):

(12) *Only a dodo was left alive.*
(13) *Only ońe dòdo was left alive.*

From (12) it follows that the only individual left alive was a dodo. From (13) it follows that the number of dodos left alive was only one.

Perlmutter finds evidence for his hypothesis in sentences like:

(14) *There were five pens on the table not four pens.*
(15) *There were five pens on the table not one pen.*
(16) **There were five pens on the table not a pen.*

Perlmutter claims that all three sentences are contrastive structures with the focus, and hence contrastive stress, falling on the numerals, and that, therefore, sentence (16) is not well-formed at the level of phonological form because it has the wrong form of the numeral *one* — the form that cannot take ordinary stress, let alone contrastive stress. In the context of the explanation of the difference between *a* and *one* offered here it is at the level of logical, not phonological, form that sentence (16) is not well-formed. Since, if there are *five* pens on the table then there *is* a pen on the table, the sentence, as it stands, both implies and denies that there is a pen on the table.

Perlmutter acknowledges that there are two kinds of sentences that pose problems for his analysis. The first is a sentence like:

(17) *A boy is tall.*

Perlmutter claims that sentences like this are not well-formed phonologically and stipulates that for all sentences with surface structures of the type:

(18) [[Numeral N] [BE AP]]
    S NP   VP

the optional rule that maps *one* onto the reduced form *a* cannot apply. There are two problems with this account. The first is that it predicts that sentences like (19) are not well-formed, which is clearly not the case:

(19)   *A visit to the dentist is always alarming.*

The second is that in any case according to Perlmutter's hypothesis (17) should have the same meaning as (20) and this also is clearly not the case:

(20)   *One boy is tall.*

The important fact about sentences like (17) and (19) is that their most natural interpretation is as generic sentences. What makes sentence (17) anomalous is not that it is not well-formed but that it is difficult to think of a context in which it could be used, since anyone using it would appear to be asserting that being tall is a defining property of the set *boy*.

The second kind of sentence which Perlmutter sees as posing difficulties for his analysis is exemplified by (21):

(21)   *Max is one boy.*

Perlmutter claims that this sentence too is not well-formed phonologically, and stipulates that in the case of sentences with surface structures of the type:

(22) [[NP] [BE [Numeral N]]
    S   VP   NP

the rule that maps the numeral onto the reduced form must apply. This account runs into the same kind of difficulties as his account of sentence (14). First it predicts that sentences like (23) are not well-formed:

(23)   *Max is a boy you can always rely on.*

Second sentences like (24):

(24)   *Max is a boy.*

cannot be interpreted either as (25) or (26):

(25)   *Max is one and only one boy.*
(26)   *Max is at least one boy.*

All three sentences, (21), (25) and (26) are well-formed. Their anomalous character is a consequence of their all representing quite egregious violations of Grice's Second Maxim of Quantity.

Note

1. This is a consequence of the fact that *historically* the indefinite article develops from an unstressed form of the numeral *one*.

2. Text and Discourse

A comparison of process types in Poe and Melville

James D. Benson and William S. Greaves

In systemic linguistics, transitivity systems account for the way in which ideational, as opposed to interpersonal and textual meanings are represented in English clauses. Functionally, the clause consists of three components: the process, the participants in the process, and the circumstantial environment of the process. Halliday (1985) lists the following types of process: material, mental, relational, behavioural, verbal, and existential.

Material processes represent doings, or goal directed actions. For example, *reined* in *I reined my horse* is what the participant *I* does to the second participant, the *horse*. Some material processes have only one participant, involved more in a happening than a doing, for example *Usher*, in *Usher rose from the sofa*.

Mental processes include three types of sensing: perception, affection, and cognition. Perception involves the apprehension of data through the senses; affection involves emotional reactions such as liking and disliking; cognition is neither reactive nor sense based.[1] For example, *heard* in *Have I not heard her step upon the stair?* is the mental process of perception, *I* is the senser, and *her step upon the stair* is the phenomenon being processed; *dread* in *I dread the events of the future* is the mental process of affection, the participant *I* is the senser, and *the events of the future* is the phenomenon being processed; *knew* in *I really knew little of my friend* is the mental process of cognition, *I* is the senser, and *little of my friend* is the phenomenon being processed.

Relational processes are complex. An example of one major type, attribution, is *was* in *The room in which I found myself was very large and lofty*. *Very large and lofty* is an attribute of *the room in which I found myself*.

Behavioural processes account for the fact that some verbs represent actions which at the same time have a mental (or physiological) dimension.

An example is *looked* in *I looked upon the scene before me.*

Verbal processes include ways of saying, for example *murmured out* in *Usher, divining, perhaps, my thoughts, murmured out some few words.*

Finally, existential processes posit existence, for example *hung* in *Upon the wall there hung a shield of shining brass.*

Poe's *The Fall of the House of Usher* (*FHU*) and Melville's *Moby Dick* are radically different in the experiences they express, in the personality of their narrators, in style and in genre. *FHU* is a short story of psychological rather than physical action (although, of course, the house collapses at the end) which takes place in an interior setting. Usher lives primarily in a mental realm, suffering "a morbid acuteness of the senses", and even believes in the "sentience of all vegetable things". The narrator, as the story proceeds, is drawn into this life of sensation. *Moby Dick*, on the other hand, has none of the claustrophobia of *FHU*. It is an expansive novel of physical action (combined with the narrator's philosophical meditations), a whaling voyage which circumnavigates the globe. These differences might reasonably be expected to show a quite different distribution of process types in the two works, and, since the narrator plays an active role in both, the Subject *I* plus the Verb which it governs should reflect this difference.

Since finding *I* is a purely mechanical process, we decided to use the CLOC package developed by Alan Reed at the Computer-Centre in the University of Birmingham. CLOC, which is usually used in vocabulary studies, can provide the context (collocates) of any designated word (node). In this case, since our aim was grammatical rather than lexical, we designated *I* as the node, and CLOC searched our two texts, the whole of *FHU* and the first two and a half chapters of *Moby Dick*, locating all occurrences of *I* and noting the collocates within a span of four words before and after *I*. If any of the words within the span were on a list of function words they were rejected as collocates. If they collocated with *I* only once they were also rejected. Although the collocates were therefore selected on the basis of lexicality and frequency, the output was printed in context. For example, the pair *I* and *spoken* occurs three times as *I have already spoken*, *I have just spoken*, and *I have before spoken*. Some of the pairs included nouns, adjectives and adverbs as well as lexical verbs, but since CLOC gave the context in a concordance type citation, it was easy to identify the verbs and to differentiate between process types.

Context was also crucial in enabling us to distinguish different meanings when they were represented by the same orthographic forms, for example *see*, which can either be perception, as in *I see three people out there*, or cognition, as in *I see what you mean*. The following typical example of CLOC output gives general information about *I* in the text, lists *saw* as one of its collocates, and then cites all four cases. The first three are processes of cognition, whereas the last one is a process of perception:

node *I* occurs 165 times
collocate *saw* occurs 5 times
node-collocate pair occurs 4 times
762   of his family, and which made him what I now saw him — what he was. Such
1182 could but partially perceive his features, although I saw that his lips trembled as if he
1230 a sickly smile quivered about his lips; and I saw that he spoke in a low, hurried
1278 upon my sight — my brain reeled as I saw the mighty walls rushing asunder — there

In this way we identified 12 pairs of material processes (*I* + process type) in *FHU*: 2 *paused*, 2 *uplifted*, 2 *met*, 2 *taken*, 2 *read*, and 2 *speak*. There were 40 pairs of mental processes: 27 cognition (3 *know*/3 *knew*, 2 *considered*, 4 *learned*, 3 *thought*, 6 *found*, 1 *feel*/2 *felt*, and 3 *saw*); 13 perception (2 *perceive*/1 *perceived*, 2 *hear*/5 *heard*, 3 *felt*); and none of affection. There were 6 behavioural pairs (2 *gazed*, 2 *shuddered*, 2 *started*), and 10 verbal pairs (3 *said*, 2 *mention*, 3 *spoken*, 2 *tell*). There were no existential pairs. Relational pairs were not searched in this case, because forms of *to be* were present in the exclusion list. This yields a high proportion of mental processes to material processes, 58.8% vs. 17.6%. But in fact the weighting toward mental process is even greater.

According to Halliday (1985: 129), behavioural processes are "processes of consciousness represented as forms of behaviour". *Shuddered*, for example, in *because I shuddered knowing not why*, is a sensation which is manifested in outward behaviour, in this case a fear (affection) which has no cognitive basis. We may reasonably add the behavioural pairs, then, to the mental process pairs, giving a ratio of 67.7% to 17.6%.

In addition, other process types may be interpreted in a mental way. Two of the seemingly material processes, *paused* and *uplifted*, are part of a mental context. *I paused to think* means *I paused* for a cognitive reason; *I paused abruptly, and now with a feeling of wild amazement* means *I paused* in a perceptive manner. Similarly, *uplifted* in *when I again uplifted my eyes to the house itself, from its image in the pool, there grew in my mind a strange fancy* has a strong mental cast, which is not the case with the other occurrence: *I uplifted myself upon the pillows*. This leaves only 5 unambiguous material process pairs, or 7.4% of the whole. Finally, several of the verbal process pairs are located in this mental/behavioural environment. Here is one example: *"You must not — you shall not behold this!" said I, shudderingly, to Usher*.

The picture, then, in *FHU* is one of a narrator who processes experience primarily through the senses rather than performing goal directed actions, which is entirely compatible with the reader's impression of the overall effect of the story.

Moby Dick, on the other hand, shows a different distribution of process types. There were 19 material process pairs (2 *take*, 7 *go*, 2 *stood*, 2 *came*, 2 *spend*, 2 *sleep*, 2 *sail*). There were 30 mental process pairs: 28 of cognition (2 *know*, 3 *think*/10 *thought*, 3 *take*, 3 *mean*, 3 *tell*, 2 *find*/2 *found*); 2 of perception (2 *seen*); and none of affection. There were no relational or behavioural pairs, and 10 verbal pairs (7 *said*, 3 *told*). *Moby Dick* has nearly twice as many material process pairs as *FHU* (32.2% vs. 17.6%), fewer mental process pairs (50.8% vs. 58.8%), and fewer behavioural process pairs (0% vs. 8.8%). Moreover, none of the material process types have any of the mental or behavioural coloration found in the case of *paused* and *uplifted* in *FHU*. The 7 occurrences of *I + go* exist in an unambiguously material context: *that I ever go to sea; no, I never go to sea; do I ever go to sea; when I go to sea; I go as a simple sailor; again, I always go to sea*, and finally, *I always go to sea*.

Clearly, with twice as many material processes, the narration of *Moby Dick* is more action oriented than that of *FHU*. When it comes to mental processes, however, the difference is initially less obvious. A first person narrator, of course, is a sentient being, and an observer of that which he narrates. It is hardly surprising, therefore, to find that half the process types employed by Ishmael are mental. The kinds of mental process, however, are quite different, reflecting the natures of the two narrators. Ishmael, an active participant in the events around him, has a philosophical orientation. His mental processing is overwhelmingly cognitive: he *thinks, finds, takes, means, tells*, and *knows*. The narrator of *FHU* is much more passive, in several respects: he participates less materially in the world around him, and his mental activity, in addition to cognition, includes a significant number of simple perceptions. He not only *knows*, *considers*, *learns*, *thinks*, *finds*, *feels*, and *sees*, but also *feels*, *perceives*, and *hears*.

The frequency of mental process types in *FHU* shows that sensing is a prominent theme in the story. This forms a background against which other process types may be foregrounded in local environments. For example, the "Mad Trist", which the narrator reads aloud to Usher, emphasizes material processes. Ethelred *uplifted his mace upright, and with blows, made quickly room in the plankings of the door for his gauntleted hand; and now pulling therewith sturdily, he so cracked, ripped, and tore all asunder, that the noise of the dry and hollow-sounding wood alarumed and reverberated through the forest.* Here *uplifted*, *made*, *pulling*, *cracked*, *ripped*, *tore*, *alarumed*, and *reverberated* are not only actions, but increasingly violent and noisy ones, and they stand out sharply against the background of mental activity in the tale as a whole. The story within the story in fact prefigures the concluding "actions": Lady Madeline's appearance frightens Usher to death; she collapses on him (*bore him to the floor a corpse*), after which the house itself collapses.

We shall now indicate all the process types in the final paragraph of the story. There is a definite swerving away from mental processing here, in two ways: first, the narrator himself now acts, and second, although he continues to sense actions, he now presents them in a way which diminishes his subjectivity.

> From that chamber, and from that mansion, I fled [MATERIAL] aghast. The storm was [RELATIONAL: CIRCUMSTANTIAL: ATTRIBUTIVE] still abroad in all its wrath as I found [MENTAL: COGNITION] myself crossing [MATERIAL] the old causeway. Suddenly there shot [EXISTENTIAL (MATERIAL METAPHOR)] along the path a wild light, and I turned [MATERIAL] to see [MENTAL: PERCEPTION] whence a gleam so unusual could have issued [MATERIAL]; for the vast house and its shadows were [RELATIONAL: CIRCUMSTANTIAL: ATTRIBUTIVE] alone behind me. The radiance was [RELATIONAL: POSSESSIVE: ATTRIBUTIVE] that of the full, setting, and blood-red moon which now shone [MATERIAL] vividly through that once barely-discernible fissure of which I have before spoken [VERBAL] as extending [MATERIAL] from the roof of the building, in a zigzag direction, to the base. While I gazed [BEHAVIOURAL], this fissure rapidly widened [MATERIAL] — there came [EXISTENTIAL] a fierce breath of the whirlwind — the entire orb of the satellite burst [MATERIAL] at once upon my sight — my brain reeled [BEHAVIOURAL] as I saw [MENTAL: PERCEPTION] the mighty walls rushing [MATERIAL] asunder —

there was [EXISTENTIAL] a long tumultuous shouting sound like the voice of a thousand waters — and the deep and dank tarn at my feet closed [MATERIAL] sullenly and silently over the fragments of the "HOUSE OF USHER".

As he makes his escape, the narrator is still experiencing by the senses (as in *I turned to see whence a gleam so unusual could have issued*, and *I saw the mighty walls rushing asunder*), but the paragraph begins and ends with actions. At the beginning the narrator *fled*, but at the end the tarn *closed*, quite objectively and independently of the narrator's activity or mental processing. The effect of objectivity rather than subjectivity on the part of the narrator is emphasized by three relational clauses, which have circumstantial and possessive attributes: *the storm was still abroad in all its wrath* (circumstantial); *the vast house and its shadows were alone behind me* (circumstantial); and *the radiance was that of the full, setting, and blood-red moon* (possessive). There is a lingering subjectivity here, of course, since it is the narrator who is categorizing experience in these ways, but several existential process types emphasize that the events are occurring independently of the perceiving *I* altogether: *Suddenly there shot along the path a wild light*; *there came a fierce breath of the whirlwind*; *there was a long tumultuous shouting sound like the voice of a thousand waters*, instead of, for example, *Suddenly I saw along the path a wild light*; *I felt a fierce breath of the whirlwind*; *heard a long tumultuous shouting sound like the voice of a thousand waters*. Notice that the existential *there shot* is a grammatical metaphor in which the existence of the light is encoded as if it were an action. A similar grammatical metaphor is at work in *the entire orb of the satellite burst at once upon my sight*, in which *burst* is a material process representing an attack on the senses. This attack results in a particular psychological state (*my brain reeled as I saw the mighty walls rushing asunder*), but it is represented by an action, *reeled*, i.e. a behavioural process. Finally, the action of the last sentence differs from that of the first. The narrator was there, of course, the tarn was *at my feet*, but it is the tarn and not the narrator which participates in the action of the waters closing.

If in *FHU* the effect of a dominant background of sensing is to highlight action when it occurs, what is the effect of the dominant background of action in *Moby Dick*? In key passages in Melville's novel, one type of relational clause, the intensive identifying, confirms the solely cognitive thrust noted above which distinguishes Ishmael's mental processing from that of the narrator of *FHU*. *Moby Dick* is in fact a quest not only for the whale, but also for the whale's meaning, and identifying clauses are themselves meaning oriented.

There are two grammatical functions involved in such clauses: Identified and Identifier, and Token and Value. Halliday (1985: 115) explains the interrelation of these functions as follows:

> If we are looking at a photograph and ask "Which is Tom?", the answer is something like "Tom is the tall one". In this case, Tom is being identified by his form; we are told how he is to be recognized. But if we are discussing the children in the family, and someone says "Tom is the clever one", Tom is being identified by his function — in this instance, his standing or role in the group. Thus the relationship between "Tom" and "the tall one" is the reverse of that between "Tom" and "the clever one": in the former "Tom" is the meaning and "the tall one" is the outward sign, while in the latter "the clever one" is the meaning and "Tom" is the outward sign.

"Moby Dick" requires identification, but recognition as an outward sign is not an issue:

> For, it was not so much his uncommon bulk that so much distinguished him from other sperm whales, but as was elsewhere thrown out — a peculiar snow-white wrinkled forehead, and a high, pyramidical white hump. These were his prominent features; the tokens whereby, even in the limitless uncharted seas, he revealed his identity, at a long distance to those who knew him ("Moby Dick").

In other words, there is no need to identify the Value *Moby Dick* as a Token (as in *Moby Dick is the WHITE whale*), but there is every need to identify the Token *Moby Dick* as a Value — to understand his meaning.

Initially, Ahab does not get very far in understanding the meaning of Moby Dick. Ahab first speaks to the crew about the whale in "The Quarter Deck": *I see in him outrageous strength, with an inscrutable malice sinewing it. That inscrutable thing is chiefly what I hate*. Although he perceives its *outrageous strength* and understands that this is informed by *malice*, the cognitive process is frustrated. The *malice* is *inscrutable*, and what Ahab is left with is an understanding not of the whale but of his own mental process. His reaction to malice is hatred — not to the malice itself, but to his failure to understand it. The thematization in the equative clause (Halliday 1985: 42-43) singles out *that inscrutable thing* as the exclusive domain of his hatred.

In the chapter "Moby Dick", Ishmael explains what the white whale meant to Ahab by means of identifying clauses which move from Token to Value, in the direction of meaning. *Swam before him as* in *The White Whale swam before him as the monomaniac incarnation of all those malicious agencies which some deep men feel eating in them, till they are left living on with half a heart and half a lung* is a grammatal metaphor (Halliday 1985: 319-345) in which a material process is functioning as an identifying process. *The White Whale* is Identified/Token, and *the monomaniac incarnation of all those malicious agencies which ... half a lung* is Identifier/Value. Moby Dick swims before Ahab literally (material process), but also figuratively as meaning (identifying process). For Ahab the meaning of Moby Dick is that the whale is the embodiment of malice. This meaning is made explicit two sentences later:

> All that most maddens and torments; all that stirs up the lees of things; all truth with malice in it; all that cracks the sinews and cakes the brain; all the subtle demonisms of life and thought; all evil, to crazy Ahab, were visibly personified, and made practically assailable in Moby Dick.

To render this less unwieldy, we will reduce it to *evil is personified by Moby Dick*. This is clearly a passive construction. In the active *Moby Dick personifies evil*, *Moby Dick* is Identified/Token and *evil* is Identifier/Value. In the passive, the Subject is Value (Halliday 1985: 116), and this is the case here. So Ishmael identifies *Moby Dick* as meaning *evil* for Ahab. This is what is involved in his saying earlier that Moby Dick has the meaning of an "incarnation", something concrete and recognizable in the real world that can be acted upon by a person motivated by revenge:

> He piled upon the whale's white hump the sum of all the general rage and hate felt by his whole race from Adam down; and then, as if his chest had been a mortar, he burst his hot heart's shell upon it.

Ishmael, too, sees Moby Dick as a Token to be identified, but he approaches the problem of understanding quite differently from Ahab. In the chapter which follows, "The Whiteness of the Whale", Ishmael focuses not on the whale's *inscrutable malice*, but on its *whiteness*, and his affective reaction is fear not hatred. The predicated theme *It was the whiteness of the whale* in *It was the whiteness of the whale that above all things appalled me* gives *whiteness* tonic prominence and hence makes it new information. The chapter catalogues the positive and negative affective responses that whiteness occasions, and probes the causes for this effect. Near the end of the chapter, Ishmael states that we have not yet learned

> why, as we have seen it is at once the most meaning symbol of spiritual things, nay, the very veil of the Christian's Deity; and yet should be as it is, the intensifying agent in things the most appalling to mankind.

Here we have essentially two identifying clauses: *whiteness is ... the most meaning symbol of spiritual things, nay, the very veil of the Christian's Deity* and *whiteness is the intensifying agent in things the most appalling to mankind*. In both cases *whiteness* is Identified/Token (the outward sign). But the two Identifier/Values (meanings), *the most meaning symbol of spiritual things, nay, the very veil of the Christian's Deity* and *the intensifying agent in things the most appalling to mankind* are contradictory. In other words, the two meanings of *whiteness* are in conflict. The final paragraph offers further meanings of *whiteness*, and concludes: *And of all these things the Albino whale was the symbol*. *The Albino whale* is Identified/Token, and *the symbol of all these things* is Identifier/Value. In other words, for Ishmael the meaning of Moby Dick is that he is a symbol, which is why more than one meaning is possible, whereas for Ahab his meaning is that he is solely the embodiment of malice.

Essentially, Ishmael and Ahab have been trying to "decode" Moby Dick, and decoding is the theme of "The Doubloon", in which all the characters offer their readings of the coin which Ahab had earlier nailed to the mast as a reward for the one first to sight Moby Dick. Ahab is discovered contemplating the markings on the coin, *as though for the first time beginning to interpret for himself in some monomaniac way whatever significance might lurk in them*. Ishmael immediately comments on the imperative of pursuing meaning:

> And some certain significance lurks in all things, else all things are little worth, and the round world itself but an empty cipher, except to sell by the cartload, as they do hills about Boston, to fill up some morass in the Milky Way.

Most of the crew, although their readings are very different from each other, proceed straightfowardly, and treat the markings on the coin as Tokens to which they assign Values. The coin depicts a tower with three surrounding mountain peaks, a crowing cock, a flame, and the signs of the zodiac around the circumference.

For Starbuck, the three mountain peaks have a religious meaning: *A dark valley between three mighty heaven-abiding peaks, that almost seem the Trinity, in some faint earthly symbol*. Starbuck is a religious man, and so the Tokens *three mighty heaven-abiding peaks* are given the Value *the Trinity*. Stubb has no particular ideology, and so when looking at a different set of Tokens, the signs of the zodiac, uses an almanack as a code book producing Values *straight out of the book*. Flask, an unabashed materialist, disregards the signs, and takes the whole coin, quite literally, as a Token to be assigned a monetary Value: *It is worth sixteen dollars*. He then immediately converts the Value into a Token, which he evaluates in terms of what it will buy: *at two cents the cigar, that's 960 cigars*. The Manxman is superstitious. Having been taught *by the old witch in Copenhagen*, when he asks the question *And what's the horse-shoe sign?*, he unhesitatingly gives this Token its astrological Value: *The lion is the horse-shoe sign — the roaring and devouring lion*. By information focus *the lion* is Identified/ Token. Queequeg, coming as he does from a non-Western culture, has difficulty in understanding the coin, but attempts to assign the Token a Value all the same: *he don't know what to make of the doubloon; he takes it for an old button off some king's trousers*. Fedallah, a fire-worshipper, brings the coin into his religious context, but says nothing. He *only makes a sign to the sign and bows himself*. Pip, who is demented, merely comments on the behavioural processes of the group examining the coin: *I look, you look, he looks; we look, ye look, they look*. Instead of assigning a Value to the coin, Pip classifies the participants: *And I, you, and he; and we, ye, and they are all bats; and I'm a crow*. He, too, assigns the scene meaning. A prophet, he spells out the impending doom: *when aught's nailed to the mast, it's a sign that things grow desperate*.

Ahab, who actually speaks first in the text, presents a more complicated case. Concentrating exclusively on the tower, the crowing cock, and the flame, he utters a series of identifying clauses:

> The firm tower, that is Ahab; the volcano, that is Ahab; and the victorious fowl, that, too, is Ahab; all are Ahab; and this round gold is but the image of the rounder globe, which, like a magician's glass, to each and every man in turn but mirrors back his own mysterious self.

The ambiguity of these clauses is complex, as may be seen when the various possibilities are set out in tabular form. The entire paradigm of potential active and passive identifying meaning (cf. Halliday 1985: 126-127) is represented, but the clauses that Ahab did not actually speak are preceded by an asterisk. The full clause *the firm tower, that is Ahab* has been reduced to its essentials.

	POTENTIAL ACTIVE MEANING	POTENTIAL PASSIVE MEANING
unmarked focus	the tower is AHAB Id/Tk Ir/Vl the tower means Ahab	the tower is AHAB Id/Vl Ir/Tk the tower can be recognized in Ahab

	*Ahab is THE TOWER Id/Tk Ir/Vl Ahab means the tower	*Ahab is THE TOWER Id/Vl Ir/Tk Ahab can be recognized in the tower
marked focus	*AHAB is the tower Ir/Tk Id/Vl the tower can be recognized in Ahab	THE TOWER is Ahab Ir/Vl Id/Tk the tower, that's what Ahab means
	THE TOWER is Ahab Ir/Tk Id/Vl Ahab can be recognized in the tower	*AHAB is the tower Ir/Vl Id/Tk Ahab, that's what the tower means

Ahab is a *monomaniac*, and his self-preoccupation leads him to decode himself as much as the markings on the coin. The interpretations of the other crew members were all essentially active — the Subjects of the identifying clauses were Tokens, and this is the most obvious interpretation of *the tower is AHAB*; in the same way that Starbuck identified the mountain peaks as meaning *the Trinity*, Ahab identifies *the tower* as meaning *Ahab*. In the same way he could have said *the tower is the Captain*, *the tower is the leader*, or *the tower is the resolute one*. But the clause could also be passive, and in this case, Ahab is not saying that *the tower* "means" *Ahab*, but that *the tower* (as a Value) can be "recognized" as *Ahab*. The process must work something like this. Ahab stares at the coin and searches it for Value. The *tower* is understood to be a Value — similar to strength and determination, for example. Unlike the others, Ahab is not content to rest with this understanding. He wants to know where this Value can be found, and finds it in *Ahab*.

The active and passive meanings tend to go in and out of focus in analysis, because that is what they are doing in Ahab's mind. It is equally possible that Ahab is not asking about *the tower*, but about himself. Both answers to the question *Which/what is Ahab?* can have marked information focus in the context: *THE TOWER is Ahab*. If Ahab is Token, then he is saying that he can be understood as *the tower* (cf. *the tower* "means" *Ahab* above); if Ahab is Value, then he is saying that he can be recognized in *the tower* (cf. *the tower* can be "recognized" as *Ahab* above).

Like the others who follow him, Ahab finds a meaning (i.e. himself) in the coin. Unlike the others, he seems to violate the context by asking what he himself means, and it turns out that he means *the tower*. At the same time, he seems to recognize himself. This possibility arises because the coin is also a mirror, in which he sees himself (i.e. his strength) reflected. So Ahab looks at the real tower and sees a meaning, but he also seems to be looking in a mirror and not seeing the real tower at all — only a picture of himself. In the first case he is imposing a meaning on the coin in a way that is not different in kind from that of the other crew members who decode the coin. In the second case he is doing something radically different, in fact losing touch with "reality". This interpretation holds for the other clauses in the series: *the volcano, that is Ahab; and the victorious fowl, that, too, is Ahab; all are Ahab.* The final clause in the series explicitly makes the coin a mirror: *this round gold is but the image of the rounder globe, which, like a magician's glass, to each and every man in turn but mirrors back his own mysterious self.* [T]*his round gold* is Identified/Token, and *but the image of the rounder globe, which, like a magician's glass, to each and every man in turn but mirrors back his own mysterious self* is Identifier/Value. This is clearly Narcissism. Ahab recognizes only himself when he looks at the symbols, but in understanding the coin — and the world — as a mirror, he shows that he understands to some extent what is happening.

Although the interpretations are all different and conflicting, the interpreters are all certain of their interpretations. Does this mean that Melville feels that the meanings are so chaotic that no ultimate certainty is possible? The answer lies with Ishmael, who is the only one who does not offer an identifying interpretation of the coin. What he does do is to contextualize it, telling us where it came from, who made it, and what it looks like. It is in fact, a Token with a Value richly symbolic:

> Now these noble golden coins of South America are as medals of the sun and tropic token-pieces. Here palms, alpacas, and volcanoes; sun's disks and stars; ecliptics, horns-of-plenty, and rich banners waving, are in luxuriant profusion stamped; so that the precious gold seems almost to derive an added preciousness and enhancing glories, by passing through those fancy mints, so Spanishly poetic.

Of all these things, that is to say, the coin is the symbol. For Ishmael, the meaning of the doubloon, like the meaning of the Albino Whale, is that it is a symbol with a plurality of Values, and that any single interpretation of it is narrow and limiting.

Note

1. See Halliday (1985: 108-112) for a full discussion of the grammatical criteria used in distinguishing mental processes from material processes and the different types of mental processes.

Intonation and the grammar of speech

David Brazil

In *Intonation and Grammar in British English* (Halliday 1967), stress is properly placed on the need to bring these two aspects of linguistic organisation into a single focus. The author's position is stated with characteristic clarity: all formal oppositions in a language are either lexical or grammatical, and since intonation is not lexically differentiating in English it must be grammatically differentiating. His proposal is that, once the meaningfully opposed variables we call "intonation" have been identified, they should be integrated into the grammar as exponents of grammatical systems in just the same way as are the non-intonational oppositions which realise other systems. The present state of the grammar, and the possibility of building intonationally-realised systems into it, will set the upper limit to just how much of the intonation of naturally occurring speech can be accounted for; but the assumption is that a progressively more delicate grammar will progressively take in more and more of it.

This view is in marked contrast to that which sees intonational meaning as some kind of "attitudinal" addition, superimposed upon a lexico-grammatical signal, and presumably deriving its communicative significance from some independent meaning system. The notion of a "parallel channel" model that all this seems to suggest receives support from statistical investigations (Crystal 1969). Data-based studies show positive correlation between the extent of the units we devise to describe grammar and the extent of those we devise to describe intonation, but the correlation is never total. A possible interpretation of these results would be that the speaker's decisions with respect to the two postulated modes of meaning are made on the basis of two different sets of principles, with perhaps a third (so far undescribed) factor being responsible for the partial coincidence. Another would be that either one description or both fails to reflect the considerations that underlie the decision making; and that coincidence is only partial because the categories we are comparing are derived from two mutually incompatible assumptions about what is being described.

Neither of these possibilities can easily be explored within the frameworks provided by currently available linguistic theories. In this paper, I suggest that if we want to relate intonation satisfactorily to other linguistic resources, we shall have to do so within models which differ radically from any of those that current practice takes as starting points.

In *An Introduction to Functional Grammar* (1985: xxiii), Halliday writes: "Traditionally, grammar has always been a grammar of written language: and it has always been a product grammar". "Product" is here used for one term of the Hjelmslevian pair, process/product. Halliday continues: "A process/product distinction is a relevant one for linguistics because it corresponds to that between our experience of speech and our experience of writing: writing exists whereas speech happens". The distinction is made in order to define more clearly the aims of the text-explicating description that Halliday is presenting. Since the text is self-evidently a product, he excludes from consideration those factors which a process-orientated approach would need to take into account. But intonation is, in a fairly inescapable way, a feature of spoken language. I have argued (Brazil 1985) that its significance is most satisfactorily grasped if it is seen as a feature of the occurrence of speech as a *happening*, rather than of the existence of language as a *text*. The possibility suggests itself that, by following through the logic of the "discourse approach" to intonation, and seeking to examine other linguistic phenomena from a similar perspective, we might make a useful start on developing a process grammar of speech.

As Halliday says, this is an enterprise that involves "going back to the beginning". The kind of conceptual leap required can best be appreciated if we enumerate some of the facts that such a grammar will need to take into account:

1. Speech is characteristically used in pursuit of a *purpose*. While a product grammar may concern itself with specimen sentences, either found in data or invented expressly to be contemplated and analysed, people who are involved in the process of producing speech usually perceive of it as having some non-exemplificatory function in the conduct of human affairs.
2. Speech is *interactive*. The word is often used to indicate the observable participation of two parties. It is used here to mean, rather, that a

speaker always pursues his/her purpose with respect to a second party, whose own separate perspective on the existing situation is always taken into account. If we informally count among possible purposes those of "telling" and "asking", speakers invariably "tell someone" or "ask someone"; and in offering to do either they proceed on the basis of the best assessment that they can manage of who knows what. Starting with a view of discourse as a jointly constructed object, even if it happens to a "monologue", is very different from starting with the assumption that it reflects a single person's intuitions about what is, and what is not, well-formed.

3. Speakers and hearers assume *sensible and co-operative behaviour*. It is taken for granted that the speaker's purpose will be recognised by the hearer, and that the latter will seek to recognise it, and then behave in a similarly co-operative way if and when (s)he becomes speaker. If I say *I saw John in town*, I assume that my hearer will be both able and willing to meet me half way in determining which of the many possible Johns is intended. Moreover, I expect him/her to know that I am telling him/her something, whereas if I say *You saw John in town* I shall probably expect him/her to know that I am asking him/her something. The assumed understanding that makes this possible, that either party is more likely to know what (s)he saw than anyone else, is sufficiently generally recognised for a third party to feel fairly confident that (s)he knows what is going on; but in an example like *John was in town*, we need access to the special understanding on which all conversation builds in order to know whether the speaker is telling or asking. In approaching the telling/asking distinction in this way, we are clearly not giving the normal priority to considerations of grammatical mood. More generally, we can say that both participants are set to apprehend the *usefulness* of a stretch of speech rather than its correctness, usefulness being taken to mean its potential for furthering whatever conversational business is in hand.

4. Talk takes place in *real time*. All the kinds of constituency analysis grammarians deal in can be applied only to a finished (and therefore already-existing-as-a-product) object. The concept of sentencehood includes the concept of completeness. But the facts of piecemeal encoding and piecemeal decoding are not to be denied. The discontinuity or interruption of "grammatically informed" expectations has often been regarded as "performance error", but since speech *is* per-

formance, we need now to focus upon the moment-by-moment usefulness of successive increments in the unfolding discourse. The grammar will be expressed not in terms of constituents but in terms of *states*; the fact that a Markovian model cannot accommodate the rules for the generation of sentence-like products (Chomsky 1957) is no reason for assuming that it cannot work for a process grammar.
5. Speakers are set to exploit the *here-and-now values* of the linguistic choices they make. Intonational evidence can best be interpreted if we recognise that speakers proceed on the basis of what value an element has, for both parties, to the immediate and often unique set of discourse conditions it occurs in. The case of "John" above is not special: it merely illustrates particularly clearly the general truth that oppositions, equivalences and other relationships between elements are subject to continuous negotiation and renegotiation, so that a concept of *existential value* has to be substituted for the largely taken-for-granted notion of meaning derived from a publicly available semantic system.

To begin to develop the kind of description outlined above, I shall return to the (admittedly invented!) remark *I saw John in town*. It is not difficult to imagine a context for a conversational fragment like:

Speaker A: *I saw John in town.*
Speaker B: *Oh.*

where B is evidently satisfied of the conversational adequacy of A's utterance: (s)he regards it as telling him/her something relevant to his/her present informational needs. We will say that the state precipitated at the end of A's utterance is a state of *adequacy*.

However in another situation, what is told may be regarded by both parties as being merely preliminary to what the present situation demands. There may be a continuation, like:

Speaker A: *I saw John in town. He's going back to the States.*
Speaker B: *Oh.*

The fact of having seen John is not in itself newsworthy. Although saying it may be said to constitute a "telling", it has no pretensions to conversational adequacy. Although *I saw John yesterday* precipitates a state of *progression* (some conversational headway having been made), a further progressive increment, at least, is needed before a state of adequacy results.

Finally, notice that even the achievement of a progressive state depends upon some part of the increment having a *proclaiming* tone. With only *referring* tones, as for instance

//r i SAW john in *TOWN*//

whatever information is present is introduced as something already understood. It is specifically labelled as *not* intended to change the existing informational status quo: that is to say as *not* constituting a progressive increment. Often it will be heard as presaging a further increment which *will* be progressive:

//r i SAW john in *TOWN*//p but he DIDn't see *ME*//.

If there are further increments with referring tones, these will merely postpone fulfilment of the speaker's assumed commitment to say something progressive eventually:

//r i SAW john in *TOWN*//r WHILE i was *SHOP*ping//r i TRIED to attract his at*TEN*tion//...//p but he was BUSy buying *ON*ions//

We will say that each of the increments with referring tone in this example is *useful*, but not progressive.

The relationship between the three types of state we have distinguished can be represented as in Figure 1.

What determines whether a particular *progressive* increment precipitates a state of *adequacy*? The decisive factor seems to be simply the partic-

States of

USEFULNESS   PROGRESSION   ADEQUACY

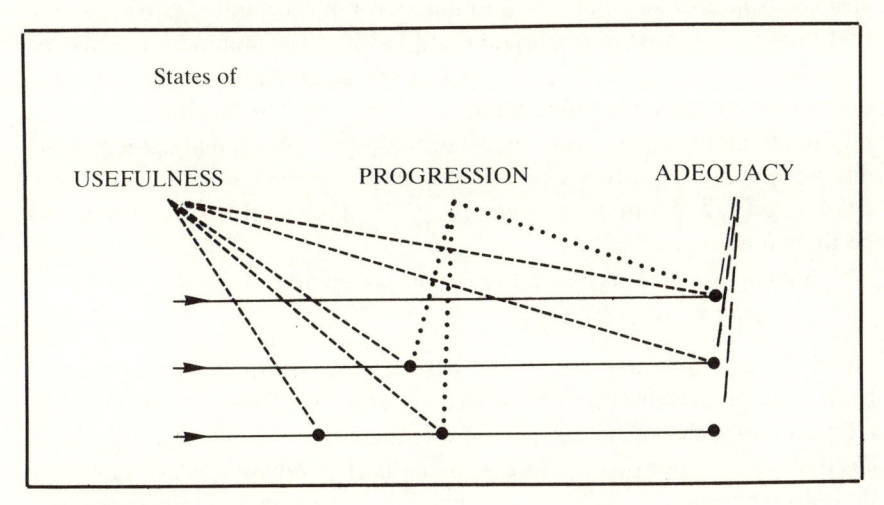

Figure 1.

ipants' shared understanding of what, in the given set of conversational circumstances, will be sufficient justification for the utterance. (Occasional rejoinders like *So what*? show that speakers and hearers sometimes have different perceptions about what will be adequate.) We shall expect no formal indication either of adequacy or of lack of it. The question of whether a particular *useful* increment is offered as one intended to constitute *progression*, on the other hand, is determined by intonation. A *useful* increment can be provisionally defined as the least stretch of speech which, given appropriate intonation and appropriate discourse conditions, will precipitate a state of adequacy.

What are the minimum requirements for usefulness? One of these is implicit in Figure 1: it must constitute *at least one complete tone unit*. No stretch of speech will be heard as a possible candidate for adequacy if it has the "incomplete" implications that attach to discontinued tone units. But there are also minimal requirements involving what, in a product analysis, would be regarded as grammatical categories.

An increment which satisfies the intonational requirement for usefulness is //p i *SAW*//. But in none of the conversational settings we have so far visualised would this constitute a progressive increment: nothing could be said to have been "told". It would need a further (possibly referring) increment before any obvious conversational need could be said to be satisfied: for example, //p i *SAW*//r john in *TOWN*// (= "Your suggestion that his absence from this meeting is due to illness is not acceptable"). We can say that the speaker, having embarked upon *I saw* ... is committed, because of sensibleness/co-operativeness considerations, to go on until (s)he has produced something that is situationally interpretable. Just how far it is necessary to go after subject-verb ... in order to do this will depend upon present discourse conditions. It is easy to imagine circumstances in which: *I saw John in town*; *I saw John* and even *I saw* (= "I'm not that stupid!") would be the minimum requirement.

A complication is introduced in an utterance like

//p i SAW *JOHN*//p in *TOWN*//.

Here, the first tone unit seems likely to be regarded by both speaker and hearer as a progressive element — it constitutes a situationally interpretable telling — though not necessarily an adequate one. The increment, //p in *TOWN*// is a further progression — an additional telling — which may well be judged necessary to achieve adequacy. It is common practice in product grammars to give priority to a similarity between

//p i SAW john in *TOWN*//

and

//p i SAW *JOHN*//p in *TOWN*//

by attaching the same sentence-constituent or clause-constituent label like "adverbial" or "adjunct" to the last element in both. Differences are then treated as differences of relationship between constituents in the postulated larger structure. The expectation that everything will be a constituent of some potentially free-standing unit results in *in town* being attached to what precedes it in either case. An increment approach need have no such expectation. The present line of argument leads us to recognise, at the initial stage of the analysis, two distinct types of increment:

(i) *Free increments* like *I saw John in town* and *I saw John*, which, given appropriate intonation and discourse conditions, are alone sufficient to constitute adequacy;

(ii) *Bound increments* like *in town* (as it occurs in the second of our two examples) which can be progressive only if they occur with a free increment.

Having made this distinction, we can now state a simple provisional rule for the chaining of free and bound increments: after any occurrence of either type of increment, there is a binary choice of either type. This rule will cover all cases where adverbials or adjuncts seem to be "moved" to the beginning of the sentence or clause. (Note that the concept of "moveable" constituents is necessarily a feature of a product grammar.) Importantly, too, it is a Markovian rule.

What of the internal organisation of *free* increments? A problem we have to confront here concerns terminology. Since all the available labels apply to the categories of a product grammar (categories which are ultimately constituents or sub-constituents of the postulated product "sentence"), we risk being misled by adopting them for the consecutively occurring parts of an increment. In looking at the grammatical requirements of the free increment, we will keep, for convenience, traditional labels like Subject, Verb, Object and Adverbial; but their use will need modification as the analysis develops.

The free increments we have considered so far have sequences of elements as follows: S V; S V O; and S V O A. Obviously, we are dealing here with facts that are usually dealt with by postulating different classes of verb (transitive/ intransitive, etc.). But such classification depends on our observing how the verbs pattern in already-existing structures. The consideration we are at present foregrounding is a quite different one. The unity of the free element is thought of as deriving from *the commitment a speaker enters into by initiating it*. Quite simply, (s)he incurs an obligation to go on until (s)he has produced a useful increment, an obligation which only an appropriate sequence of elements will discharge. Difficulties in making the traditionally-required decisions about whether a particular verb does or does not "predict" an object or an adverbial can, in fact, be related to common-sense uncertainty about what sets of discourse conditions are likely and what are not.

Two conditions seem to distinguish the free increment:

(i) All the component parts of the situationally required sequence are realised. This is best appreciated by observing the treatment of existentially non-selective items. In general, speakers may either omit these or realise them non-prominently, as in:

Which heart did you play?
//p the *QUEEN*// or //p the *QUEEN* of hearts//

Where the item is part of the sequence needed for a free increment, omission is *not* an option:

How do you know it was John?
//p i *SAW* him//
How did the typewriter get on top of that cupboard?
//p *JOHN* put it there//

Each of the non-prominent items in these responses is fully predictable in the way that *hearts* is predictable, yet the places they occupy in the expected sequence have to be filled. This requirement for completeness with respect to its parts enables us to distinguish the free increment from the bound increment, the latter being characterised by an observable *deficiency* with respect to one or more of them (e.g. *in town*).

(ii) The expected elements always occur in the same order. This seems at first sight to be contradicted by the facts. The ordering SP(O) (A) which is exemplified by the examples we have used so far is regarded in a general way in product grammars as in some sense an "unmarked" ordering, but great interest seems to attach to the significance of changing it. It has already been said that the concept of a "change" in order is not one that can be accommodated in a description which takes the linear generation of speech as a central fact. There are obvious advantages for a Markovian approach in giving conceptual precedence to the expectation that the order of elements will always be the same. The question we have to ask is whether apparent variations in that order are a direct result of adopting a product perspective, and whether, by following through the logic of a process model, we may find other ways of accounting for cases where the ordering seems to be broken.

In asking this question, we are stepping outside the tidy area in which we can work from pre-fabricated examples. The provisional template that such an exercise provides us with needs to be tested against a great amount of naturally occurring data. Progress has been made so far by using examples which bring along with them, so to speak, fairly obvious indications of likely discourse settings. Working in the real world involves us in recovering relevant features of the environment as best we can from the data, and being always ready to admit ignorance where this is necessary. And in an evolving descriptive method, there are considerable problems in finding a coherent means of exposition. All that is attempted in what follows is an examination of some of the discrepancies between what has been sketched out above and certain representative "found" examples. What modifications do we need to make to this excessively simple model to enable it to accommodate reality?

(1) //r in *MOST* cases//p we can SEE the solution im*MED*iately//

This is an example of a bound increment preceding a free one so there is no question of its being "out-of-place" in the structure of the latter. It could equally well follow. Indeed, in the context in which it actually occurred,

> //p it DOESn't really present a *PROB*lem//r in *MOST* cases//p we can SEE the solution im*MED*iately//,

there is no reason for saying that it "belongs to" the second free increment rather than to the first. Arguably, only the need to apply sentence-derived punctuation conventions forces us to make this kind of decision at all.

(2) //p i *DON'T*//r on the *WHOLE*//p *LIKE* it//
(3) //r the deCISion to a*BAN*don it//p was ap*PLAU*Ded//

Although these would be given quite different analyses by current sentence grammars, they can both be regarded as instances of *suspension*. In common-sense terms, a grammar which seeks to describe processes must allow for the times when a speaker, having committed him/herself to produce a free increment, breaks off in the middle, suspending completion temporarily but retaining his/her original obligation. The preceding sentence, in fact, exemplifies this: "A speaker (having ... increment) breaks off in the middle". It is the defining feature of suspension that the commitment to complete remains in force after the completion of the interpolated increment. (Note that this definition results in our taking in very many more cases than would usually be referred to as "parentheses" or "asides".) The free increments in (2) an(3), *I don't like it* and *The decision was applauded* comprise sequences which follow the expected ordering: S V O and S V respectively.

What is interpolated is a bound increment in each case, and they exemplify two kinds of deficiency. Both begin with elements other than the expected S. In (2) there is only an A. In (3) the S and the finite element of the V are missing. Breaking into the expected sequence somewhere later than its putative beginning, they then both continue to the situationally appropriate end. The possibility of describing the result in Markovian terms remains.

One major difference between this kind of analysis and a product oriented one is exemplified in the treatment of //r the deCISion to a*BAN*don it// in (3). No distinction is here made between this and //r the deCISion//r to a*BAN*don it//... because this is a distinction that is fully accounted for by showing how the intonation organises the utterance into useful increments. If it is presented as a single tone unit, it has a value which grammars have sought to capture by saying that *the decision to abandon it* is the "subject". Presented as two tone units, it can be taken as meaning something like *the decision — and what was decided, of course, was to abandon it —*, an interpretation which seems to demand a different syntactic explanation. A general requirement for a process grammar is that it should avoid treating as syntactic, existential distinctions which are fully accounted for intonationally or otherwise. We are concerned primarily with describing the rules for the sequencing of elements, the part of the encoding process that is not affected by prevailing discourse conditions. Accounting for the interpretations placed upon the resulting sequences involves observations which have only existential validity, and this must be kept separate.

(4) //r+ LAWyers should *SEEK*//p to as*SIST* people//
(5) //p we must re*MEM*ber//r+ MOST de*CIS*ions//p are TAKen by of*FIC*ials//
(6) //r we are con*CERN*ed//p with ad*MIN*istering the *SYS*tem//

All these are examples of *extension*. In (4), an utterance which ended with *seek* would not generally be thought to constitute a useful increment. Completion may be made with a nominal element, for example *Lawyers should seek solutions* or, as in (4), with a sequence of one of the standard patterns. In this case it is a subject-less non-finite Ø V O sequence. In (5) it is an S V A sequence. In the terms we have adopted so far, we can say that by not producing the expected nominal after *seek* or *remember*, the speaker extends his/her commitment (and hence what will count as a useful increment) to the end of whatever new sequence (s)he enters upon. (6) exhibits the same kind of extension-by-substitution after the preposition *with*. In each of these cases, a simple, left-to-right analysis can be made where each element is predictable on the basis of the state precipitated by the preceding one.

(7) //r they FOUND the address they were *LOOK*ing for//p in *TIME*//
(8) //r+ the deCISions the officials *TAKE*//p are based on ex*PER*ience//
(9) //r the *STAFF*//r who are CAREfully *TRAINED*//p SEE things *DIF*ferently//

These illustrate another way of extending the useful increment which can be accommodated in a finite state description. After the nominal *address* in (7), the speaker begins a new sequence SV(O) (A) but omits the nominal which would substitute for *address*; we get neither ... *they were looking for the address* nor ... *they were looking for it*. In (8) it is *decisions*, the notional 0 after *take*, that has zero realisation. (9) is slightly different in that the nominal in question is the S of the interpolated sequence. If the V is finite, the S plays a crucial part in indicating where in the predictable sequence we have got to, and what the next options are, and must therefore be realised with a non-selective (and therefore non-prominent) *who*. Not surprisingly, though, similar cases occur where the break-in to the new sequence is made with a non-finite V, for example *My decision to follow surprised him*.

All the examples (7), (8) and (9) involve suspension, so the question of where the first useful increment ends is determined by whatever commitment the speaker is deemed to have entered into at the beginning. When something similar happens after a nominal which is final in a predicted sequence, intonation and the shared expectations of speaker and hearer become crucial in deciding what is happening.

(10) //p they MADE a decision which pleased *EV*eryone//
(11) //p they MADE a de*CIS*ion//p which pleased *EV*eryone//

In (10), the organisation into tone units signifies that the whole utterance is required to achieve usefulness, and the choice of proclaiming tone signifies progression. In (11), this same state is reached after *decision*: the remainder precipitates a further progressive state at *everyone*. A consequence of this is that the here-and-now value of the second increment may be either *The decision pleased everyone* or *The fact that they made a decision pleased everyone*, depending on the shared understanding of what the exact purpose of the discourse was at this point. But the concept of adequacy has also to be taken into account if we are to make a correct analysis of our intuitions about the relation between the two increments. It could easily happen that the assertion *They made a decision* though progressive, was not adequate. If we feel that there is some kind of "dependency" relationship between the two consecutive parts, it could well be because, in the sort of context we automatically assume for an utterance like this, the second progressive increment is necessary to achieve adequacy. To provide a principled explanation of the various "meanings" of examples like these — and grammarians have spent much time in trying to do so — we need to take account of how the states of *usefulness*, *progression* and *adequacy* differ.

(12) //p it's *RAIN*ing//
(13) //p it's a PITY he can't *COME*//
(14) Speaker A: //p he's NOT *HERE*//
      Speaker B: //p it's a *PITy*//

The use of *it* in cases like these resembles the use of *who* in (9). They are both non-prominent, because non-selective. We can say, indeed, that in the given environment they could never be selective: there is simply no existential choice available. Just as *who* fills the S slot when there is a sequencing requirement that it should be filled, but there is no choice of referent, so *it* supplies a similar need when there is no choice (12) or when the choice has not yet been made (13). In the latter case, the patent inadequacy of saying that something is a pity, without saying what, means that adequacy cannot be achieved until the second (SV) increment is completed. And since potential adequacy is a requirement of usefulness, *It's a pity* cannot be deemed useful. This is borne out in the possible utterance

//p it's a *PITY*//p he CAN'T *COME*//

where the first tone unit has all the intonational requirements for progression, but where — unless some special discourse conditions have been previously set up, as in (14), it hardly would be said to amount to a "telling".

A matter of considerable interest is the possible interpolated *that* in examples like *It's a pity that he can't come*. There are similar possibilities in (5) and (7). This item resembles *it* and *who* in (9) and (13), in that it occurs non-prominently at a point where no existential selection could ever be in question. It differs, however, in two respects: nothing significant seems to be changed if it is omitted; and it plays no part in the sequencing rules we are seeking to establish. Is it possible to regard it as being in some sense extra to the grammar which defines all the things a user can do with language, and to relate to this the fact that it seems to fall outside the sequencing rules that such a grammar comprises? The hypothesis enables us to deal with very many instances including

(15)   //p he WENT *IN*//p and TOOK his *HAT* off//
(16)   //p it was *RAIN*ing//p but he deCIDed to *GO*//

In (15), two successive free sequences, *He went in*, *He took his hat off*, would, if uttered in the same set of discourse conditions, have the same communicative value. It is the absence of an S before *took* that makes the second tone unit a bound sequence. If we change the example to *He went in (and) the boy took his hat off*, the optional nature of the *and* becomes clear. What is not yet clear is why it ceases to be optional when it is related to deficiency.

Product grammars commonly see *and* and *but* as being systematically opposed. Taking the present view, it is possible to say that *but* in (16) also has non-selective status like *and* in (15). We can always paraphrase *but* as "and + we-are-agreed-in-expecting-things-to-be-otherwise". Shared expectation is taken by speakers to be already negotiated. Hence, *It was raining and he decided to go* would, if uttered in those circumstances which alone would justify the *but* in (16), have exactly the same communicative value. Again we can say that, provided the conditions of co-operative understanding presupposed by the mechanisms of process grammar actually exist, then users would not be prevented from doing anything if *and* and *but* were not available. (Being able to do everything a language can do is, of course, quite different from being able to produce — or recognise — all the "sentences" that are possible in the language.)

Why, then, does the language make them available at all? Possibly because speakers (and more especially writers) must sometimes allow for the possibility that the assumed meshing of minds does not exist. There is nothing new in the suggestion that the language, as it is manifested in writing, is "overbuilt" for the needs of the speaker, but there is a problem in applying this notion to our present preoccupation. The effects of literacy and of a literature-based culture, to say nothing of the self-conscious attention to language by generations of prescriptive grammarians, have been to introduce much of the redundancy of writing into speech: the mechanisms we are seeking to describe may well be overlaid in practice by language forms which cannot be accounted for in terms of the operation of those mechanisms. *And* and *but* are only two of the items that seem to occur characteristically without prominence to make explicit background understandings which are assumed to be already implicit in the prevailing discourse conditions. To put it another way, they play no part in the purpose-oriented processes we have been describing. The state precipitated is always the same, whether the items are included or not. It is therefore not surprising that they operate extraneously with respect to the sequences that facilitate the pursuit of communicative purpose.

It is not possible, in this short paper, to begin to develop the kind of expository framework that would bring these various observations into an economical and revealing statement. Nor, indeed, has the work been done which would determine what had to be included in the statement. We have looked at only some of the issues that arise when we try to apply a simple formula to naturally-occurring data. Further progress will require a large-scale analysis of a spoken corpus, intonation transcripts of which are available.

Experience shows that adjusting to the quite different style of analysis that processes require creates considerable conceptual difficulties for anyone trained in product analysis (as we all are). It is reasonable to ask what profit would follow from "making a fresh start". Relating grammar to intonation in a unified model will seem to many a fairly poor reward for the effort involved. But Firth's view that the study of conversation will provide "the key to a better understanding of what language is and how it works" (1935) is still worthy of respect. In particular, we might expect that a study of the minimal rule systems that speakers and hearers must operate, in order to engage in purposeful interactive discourse, will give us a clearer idea of what they must be presumed to "know" about their language than an approach which simply links the competence of the speaker/hearer with the ability to identify completed, uncontextualised, and written sentences.

Some preliminary evidence for phonetic adjustment strategies in communication difficulty

John E. Clark, James F. Lubker and Sharon Hunnicutt

Introduction

One of the long term objectives of experimental phonetics has been to understand the physical properties of the speech signal and to establish quantitative relationships between these properties and the linguistic information they encode.

Most of this effort has been directed at segmental string encoding and the more linguistic aspects of suprasegmentals. In many instances, investigations have focused on simple syllabic sequences, words, or sentences, articulated in quiet and highly controlled laboratory conditions. The experimental literature abounds with investigations in which subjects have been required to utter extremely unlikely sequences such as /h pa:p t/. The argument in favour of this sort of methodology, viz. that it provides reasonably rigorous experimental control, is quite understandable given that even from data collected under these conditions, there is much unexplained variability to be observed in its physical properties. The argument against this methodology is that it is too divorced from real language. Perhaps, however, there should be little cause for surprise that this sort of approach has formed the basis for evolving objectives and their associated methodologies in speech production research. It seems common in the history of science for a discipline to proceed from atomistic through to more holistic studies.

Increasingly, linguists have become concerned to account for the general ecology of language. In one aspect of this, Lindblom (1983a) has argued that there is a principle of economy in articulation, that we do not normally utilise the limits of "phonetic space" and that we may hyper-or hypo-articulate if we so choose. This underexploitation of phonetic capability in realising phonological structure is seen as part of a potential "cost benefit conspiracy" in which the speaker produces the level of linguistic performance he or she judges to be appropriate for any given communicative context. More specifically, Lindblom (1983b) has advanced the notion of a "distinctiveness principle" as part of his teleological view of speech processes, with particular reference to phonological structure.

If this viewpoint is a valid one, then it implies that speakers have the ability to make intuitive use of the phonetic strategies required for realising the phonological relationships needed in any given communicative context. It also suggests that it should be possible to construct experiments designed to expose the ways in which speakers make use of this intuitive knowledge. Such experiments are likely to be the converse of the classical approach to studying speech production, in that they will encourage variability, rather than attempt to constrain it. One hopeful outcome of such experiments is that they may in some measure penetrate the normal opacity of our high-level articulatory planning.

There are also some very strong practical reasons for investigations of this kind. Not least of these is the need to develop an understanding of the ways speakers are likely to use their phonetic resources in dealing with automatic speech recognition devices which fail to accept an initial unmarked spoken input. Information of this kind has practical importance for establishing reliable telecommunications procedures, particularly in areas such as aviation and shipping where a high degree of safety is involved and where operations are often conducted over transmission systems with very poor signal to noise ratios. It is also important, for educational and rehabilitative purposes, that there be a better understanding of the intuitive phonetic strategies used by normal speakers in spoken interaction with the hearing impaired community.

Speech production research has not at this time focused a great deal of attention on investigating this type of context-motivated adjustment of articulatory performance. There is, however, some evidence from Lieberman (1963) and Hunnicutt (1985) that speakers may intuitively fine-tune their production intelligibility in some form of "trade off" between phonological load and the information provided by the available high level linguistic context. Some general evidence that speakers can fine-tune their production to enhance intelligibility is found in investigations by Tolhurst (1954) and Chen et al. (1983), and in exploratory work conducted since this present study by Lindblom and Lindgren (1986).

The value of research in this area to the hearing-impaired community alone, is evident from complementary work by Picheny *et al.* (1985, 1986) who have demonstrated both the superior intelligibility of so-called "clear" speech to hearing-impaired listeners, and corresponding differences in some of its acoustic features when compared to "conversational" speech. Hearing aid and impairment researchers have a strong interest in the outcome of research in the area; Gordon-Salant (1986), and Revoile *et al.* (1986a, 1986b) have explored in various ways the question of how phonetically relevant features of speech signals might be processed to enhance the cues they provide to phonological structure for the hearing impaired in future generation hearing aids.

However, there is not a great deal of detailed information on the intuitive phonetic responses of speakers to the effects of controlled manipulation of communication environment difficulty. The investigation described here is a pilot study to explore the possibility of obtaining such information.

The experiment

Two American English speaking subjects (S.S. and T.R.) were asked to read a list of sentences which included pairs of sentences of the form "I said X not Y", where X and Y were CVC minimal pair words. The sentences were:

> *I said heart not hut. / I said hut not heart.*
> *I said pen not pan. / I said pan not pen.*
> *I said park not bark. / I said bark not park.*

These sentences were intended to provide minimal contextual information which might relieve any functional load on the phonological contrast between X and Y.

The experiment had two parts. In the first part, the speakers were asked to read the sentences four times in random order from flash cards in a quiet sound treated room. This is the classic "open loop" data gathering experiment of the kind commonly done in phonetics. It was open loop in the sense that the speaker had no communication goal in the form of a listener with whom to interact. The only goal was the obvious one of reading the sentences with normal, or unmarked, articulatory effort.

In the second part, the speakers were fitted with headphones presenting noise at +85dB having a long term spectrum approximating that for adult speech mixed with their own side-tone at +6dB S/N. They were told that their objective was to communicate with a listener also wearing headphones who sat facing them outside the sound treated room through a double glazed window. The noisy headphone signal was explained as being exactly that which the listener was also hearing, and that this aspect of the experiment was concerned with testing noisy communication channels. In actuality, the listener had a noise free signal to listen to. It was explained that the listener was required to identify the test sentences (although not told how) and that he would sign by putting his hand to his ear if he wished the sentence to be repeated. The listener appeared to write down something each time a sentence was spoken. Although the request for repeats was designed to seem quite random to the speaker, they were in fact structured to ensure that the complete "X not Y" test ensemble listed here was repeated by the speaker, since a significant number of irrelevant sentences were also included to distract the subject from the purpose of the investigation. The sentences were read eight times in four randomised counterbalanced sets.

All the speech was recorded to professional standards using a high quality microphone at a fixed distance of 20cm from the speaker's lips. Prior to, and following each recording session, a calibration test tone was recorded to allow the measurement of relative speech levels on the tape.

The general hypothesis underlying this experiment was that if speakers do fine-tune their production in response to perceived contextual demands, then there should be observable changes in speech characteristics between the first and the second parts of the experiment described above, particularly in those instances where the speaker perceived a lack of initial success in communication and was required to repeat a sentence. Moreover, such changes might be expected to contribute to enhancing the necessary phonological contrasts occurring between the minimal pair X and Y words.

Data analysis

The data was divided into three conditions. Condition 1 was quiet reading, condition 2 was the first reading in noise, and condition 3 was the listener-requested repeated reading. Three aspects of the data were considered. The sentences as a whole, the general suprasegmental properties of the keywords, and the acoustic cues of the minimal pair segments in the keywords.

Sentence level

The objective of analysis at this level was to quantify differences in production strategies motivated by the three experimental conditions as expressed by changes in overall articulatory settings.

i. *Long term spectrum*

The speech was first analysed for overall energy distribution trends using a software 10 channel filterbank analyser in which each filter had a 500Hz bandpass. The object in taking this measure was to quantify any long

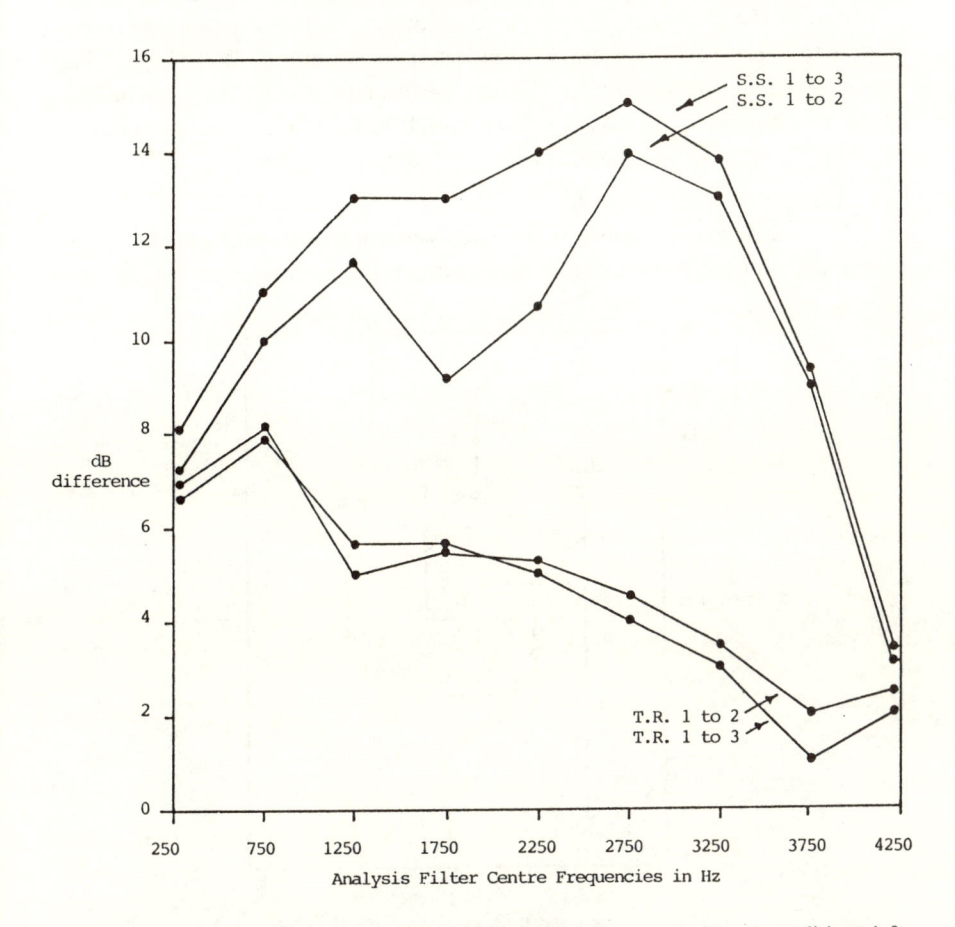

Figure 1. Long term spectral energy distribution differences between conditions 1 & 2 and conditions 1 & 3.

term spectral changes in vocal tract settings which might affect phonatory quality. Figure 1 shows the relative intensity differences between conditions 1 & 2, and 1 & 3 in the long term speech spectrum. The frequency axis values are the centre frequencies of the filterbank analyser. In the case of subject S.S., there is a striking increase in energy in the speech spectrum up to 3.25KHz, and thereafter a declining difference. Subject T.R. shows less overall change from condition 1 to 2 & 3, with a much lower frequency maximum difference at 750Hz. S.S. also exhibits an appreciable difference between conditions 2 & 3.

Part of the change in the energy distribution in the long term spectrum is due to increased respiratory force used in conditions 2 & 3, but the greater part of the change in energy distribution seems likely to be the result of changes in laryngeal setting which have produced much greater high frequency energy for vocal tract resonance excitation.

ii. *Average sentence intensity*

The mean r.m.s. intensity for each sentence was measured using an integration time constant of 20mSec, with the data corrected for silences

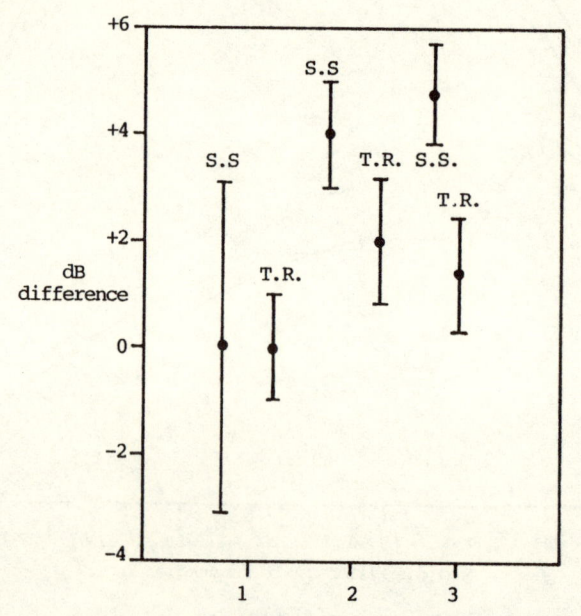

Figure 2. Mean intensity of sentences across conditions 1, 2 & 3 relative to condition 1.

within the sentences by means of a threshold detection system. Figure 2 shows the relative mean intensities and 95% confidence intervals of all the sentences in conditions 1, 2 & 3, taking condition 1 as the 0dB reference for both speakers. There are appreciable differences between condition 1 and conditions 2 & 3 for both speakers. S.S. shows the greatest absolute difference, but also exhibits the greatest variability in condition 1. There is little to distinguish between conditions 2 & 3 both within or between speakers.

iii. *Mean pitch*

The mean pitch for each sentence as expressed in fundamental frequency (Fo) was measured using a microcomputer-controlled analogue pitch and intensity meter, developed in the Speech Hearing and Language Research Centre (S.H.L.R.C.) at Macquarie University, which samples the smoothed pitch every 10mSec. This measure gives an estimate of the basic Fo setting for each speaker. Figure 3 shows the mean pitch and 95% confidence intervals over all sentences in conditions 1, 2 & 3. Both speakers show large increases in Fo setting, with the most striking change occurring in S.S., whose mean Fo shifted almost an octave upwards. S.S. shows a weak tendency to slightly higher pitch in condition 3 than in condition 2.

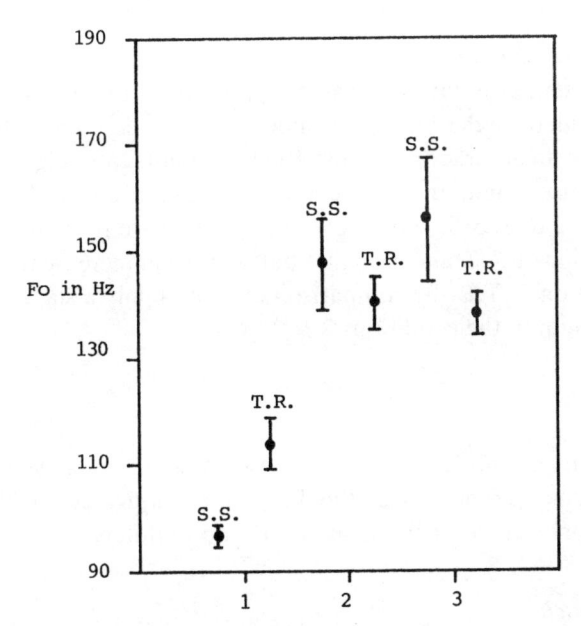

Figure 3. Mean fundamental frequency of sentences across conditions 1, 2 & 3.

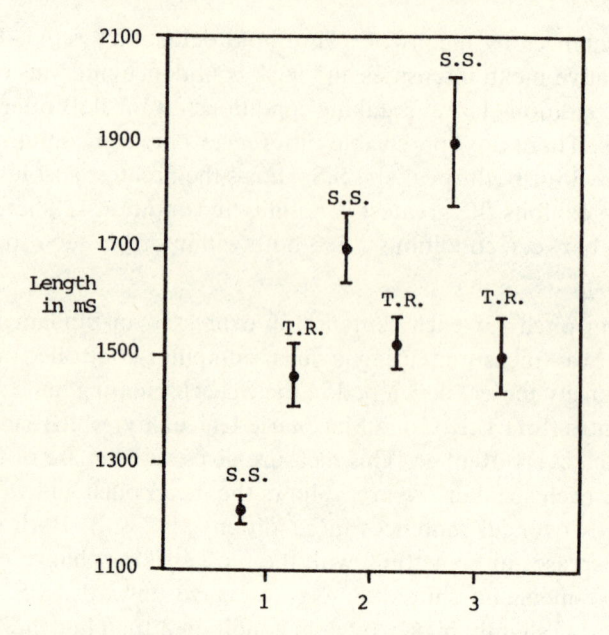

Figure 4. Mean length of sentences across conditions 1, 2 & 3.

iv. *Mean sentence duration*

The mean sentence duration was measured from the overall intensity envelope (provided by the pitch and intensity meter described above) for each sentence to an accuracy set by the 10mSec sample rate. Figure 4 shows the mean sentence length and 95% confidence intervals over all sentences in conditions 1, 2 & 3. S.S. shows a very large increase in sentence length between conditions 1 & 2, and a smaller but significant increase from condition 2 to condition 3. T.R. by comparison exhibited only a slight tendency to increased length in the conditions 2 & 3.

Word level

The objective of this level of analysis was to determine any changes in the suprasegmental properties of the keywords, motivated by the three experimental conditions, which might contribute to differences in sentence prosody.

i. *Keyword pitch*

Using the equipment described for the sentence level, the mean pitch

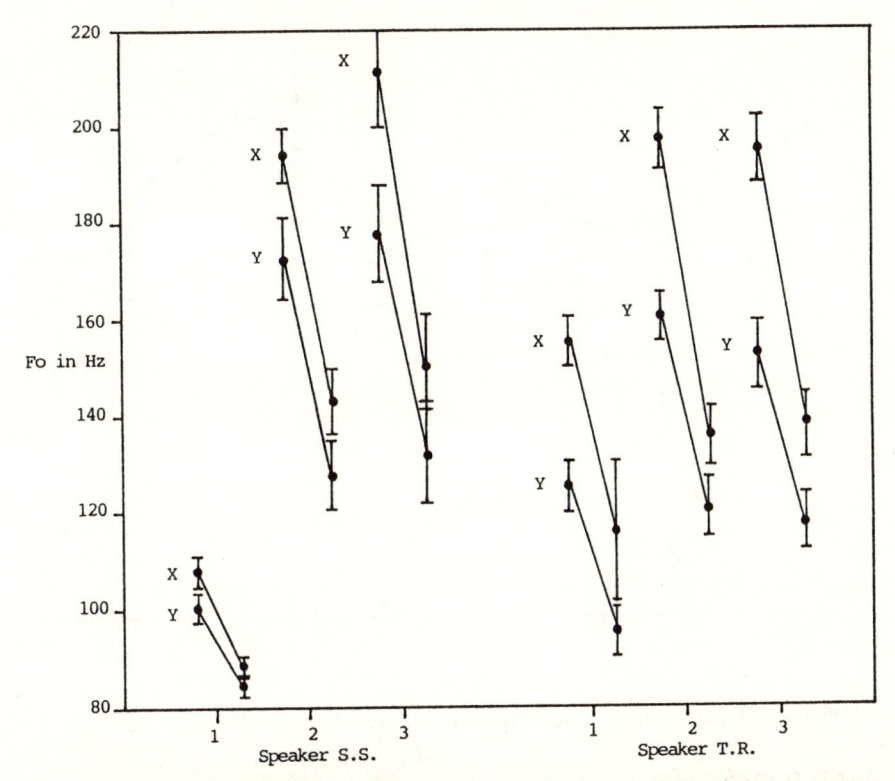

Figure 5. Mean fundamental frequency of X & Y keywords across conditions 1, 2 & 3.

of the X and Y keywords was measured and, for each keyword, an estimate of maximum and minimum pitch was obtained. Figure 5 shows the mean Fo values and 95% confidence intervals for the X and Y keywords in conditions 1, 2 & 3. For both speakers there is an overall increase in Fo between condition 1 and conditions 2 & 3 plus an increased range of Fo movement. In both these respects S.S. shows a greater change from condition 1 to conditions 2 & 3 than T.R. Both speakers show higher overall Fo and greater Fo range on the "X" words than the "Y" words. S.S. shows the most marked increase in overall Fo and Fo range. Comparison of the word level Fo and intensity data suggest that the Fo behaviour is dominated by laryngeal rather than respiratory force control.

ii. *Keyword length*

The length of the X and Y keywords was measured using the

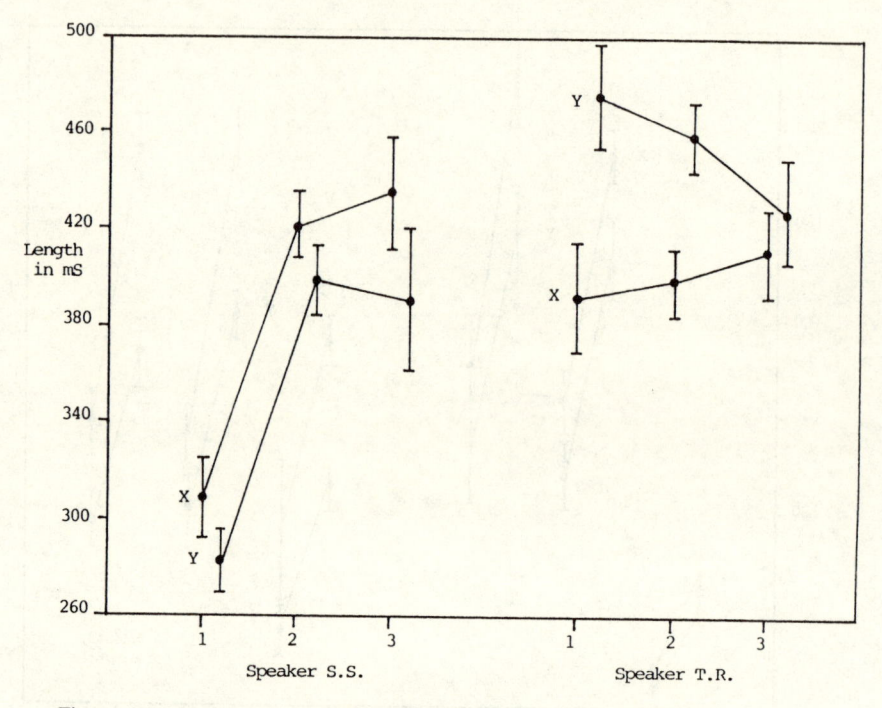

Figure 6. Mean length of X & Y keywords across conditions 1, 2 & 3.

S.H.L.R.C. computer speech editing system. Figure 6 shows the mean word length values between the three conditions. Only S.S. shows an increase in word length between condition 1 and conditions 2 & 3. T.R. actually shows a declining duration trend for Y keywords, and informal observation suggests that this is partly due to rather idiosyncratic lengthening of the final consonants of the keywords, particularly during condition 1. The effect was most marked on the sentence final "Y" words. S.S. by comparison exhibits word level durational data that is consistent with the overall pattern of the "X" word being the more strongly articulated.

iii. *Keyword intensity*

The intensities of the X and Y keywords were measured using the S.H.L.R.C. computer speech editing system by placing markers at the start and finish of each word and computing the r.m.s. intensity over the whole word. Figure 7 shows the mean intensities and 95% confidence intervals on a scale relative to each speaker only for conditions 1, 2 & 3. Both speakers

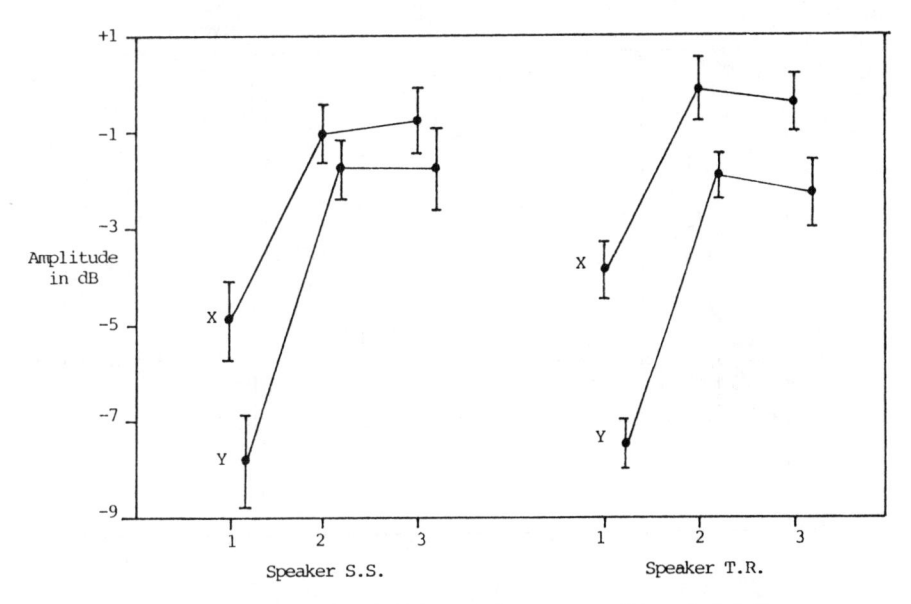

Figure 7. Mean intensity of X & Y keywords across conditions 1, 2 & 3.

show marked increases in word intensity from condition 1 to conditions 2 & 3, and greater intensity on the "X" than the "Y" keyword. There is nothing to distinguish conditions 2 & 3. In relative terms, T.R. exhibits a greater change in word level intensity between condition 1 and the remaining conditions than at sentence level, suggesting some syntactic selectivity. The overall increase in intensity for both speakers probably largely reflects the greater overall articulatory effort observed in sentence level intensity, but a clear syntactic position difference is also evident.

Segmental level

Acoustic parameters providing primary cues to three of the word initial minimal pairs in the keywords were examined. The pairs were: /p-/ vs /b-/ in "park" and "bark"; /e/ vs /ae/ in "pen" and "pan"; /ʌ/ vs /a/ in "hut" and "heart".

i. */p/ versus /b/ in "park" and "bark"*

Voice onset time and r.m.s. intensity were taken as the primary cues for this voicing distinction. They were measured on the time domain

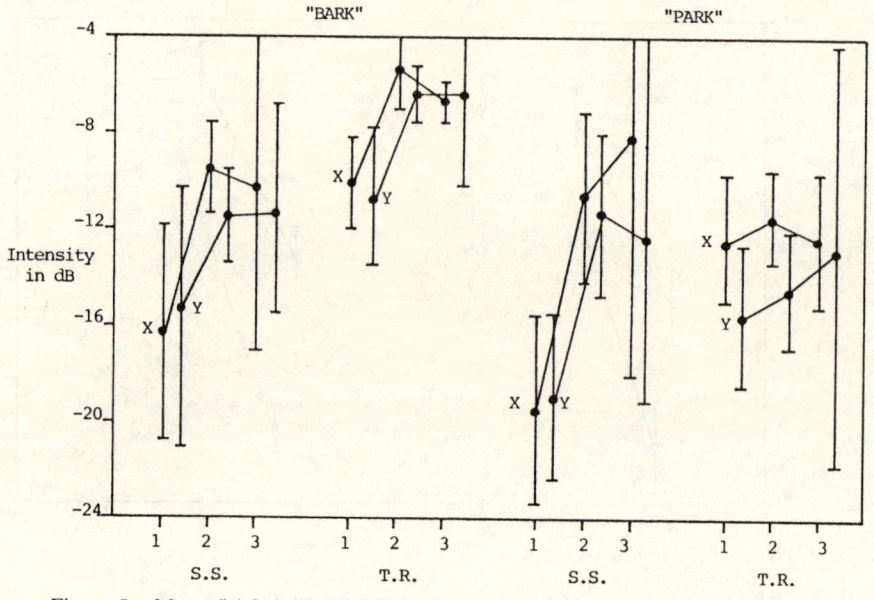

Figure 8a. Mean /b/ & /p/ VOT intensity in X & Y keywords across conditions 1, 2 & 3.

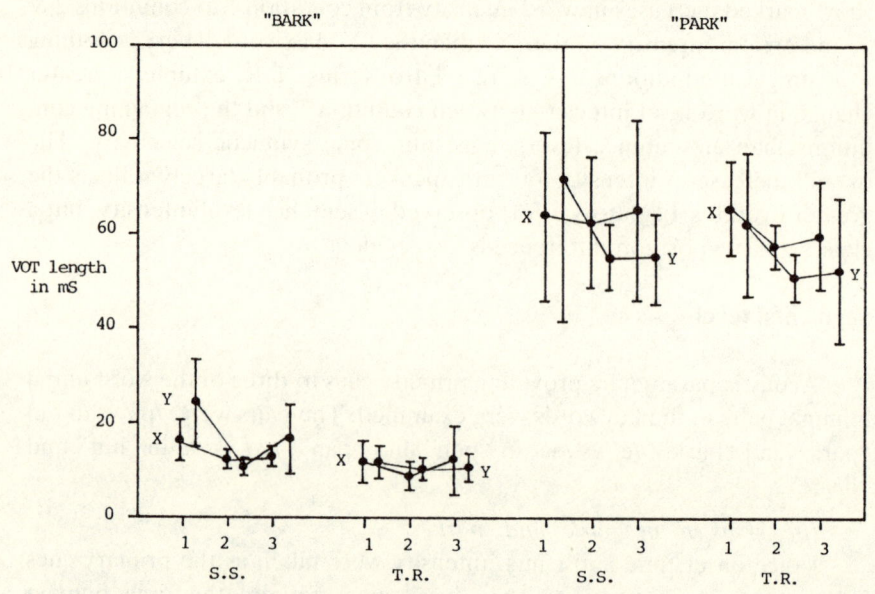

Figure 8b. Mean /b/ & /p/ VOT intensity in X & Y keywords aross conditions 1, 2 & 3.

waveform of the test token from the point of occlusion release to the start of the first complete pitch period using the computer speech editing system referred to earlier. The data in Figures 8a and 8b shows means and 95% confidence intervals for VOT intensity and length respectively. The variability shown by the intensity data is so great that it is unlikely to be contributing significantly to the realisation of the voicing contrast. The VOT durations data shows no evidence of significant enhancement of contrast across the conditions. There is a very weak trend to greater VOT length in conditions 2 & 3 for "X" compared to "Y" sentences.

ii. /e/ versus /ae/ in "pen" and "pan"

Formant frequencies and vowel nucleus durations were taken as the primary cues determining this contrast. The F1, F2, and F3 values for these vowels were measured using standard FFT and LPC autocorrelation techniques with a 51.2mSec Hamming weighted sample window centred on the vowel target. The durations of the vowel nuclei were also measured using the computer speech editing system described earlier. Figures 9a and 9b show the formant values plotted in their conventional F1/F2 and F2/F3 planes for X and Y keywords respectively, and Figure 9c shows the nucleus durations. The formant data shows that both speakers tend to produce progressively more peripheral vowel quality in conditions 2 & 3 compared to condition 1. The effect is more marked in speaker S.S. than T.R. These more peripheral vowel qualities appear to enhance contrast between the two vowel types to some extent. The peripheral shift in vowel quality from conditions 1 to 3 is also more marked in "X" position words.

The durational differences are clearly important to both speakers in establishing contrast between these vowels, which is to be expected given their relatively similar formant patterns. However, they do not show any real tendency to enhanced contrast between conditions 2 & 3 in terms of either changes in their absolute length differences or the ratios between their lengths.

iii. /ʌ/ versus /a/ in "hut" and "heart"

These two vowels are also distinguished by formant frequency patterns and nucleus durations, with the addition of a strong rhotic quality in /a/ which is manifested acoustically as a very low value of F3 compared to nonrhotic vowels. These vowels were subjected to the same analysis as the vowels in (ii). Figures 9a and 9b show their formant values plotted with those of /e/ and /ae/, and Figure 10 shows their nucleus durations in conditions 1, 2

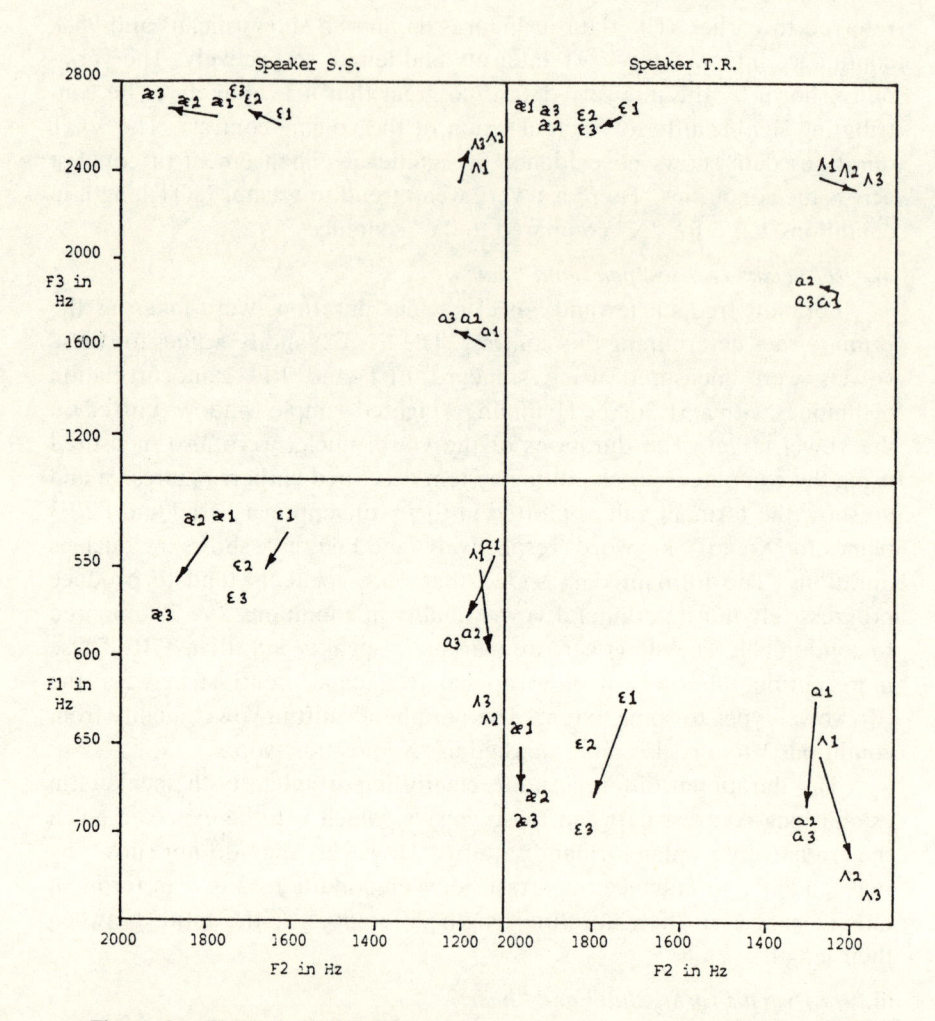

Figure 9a. F1/F2 & F2/F3 plane formant plots for the vowel targets in the X keywords "pen, pan, heart, hut".

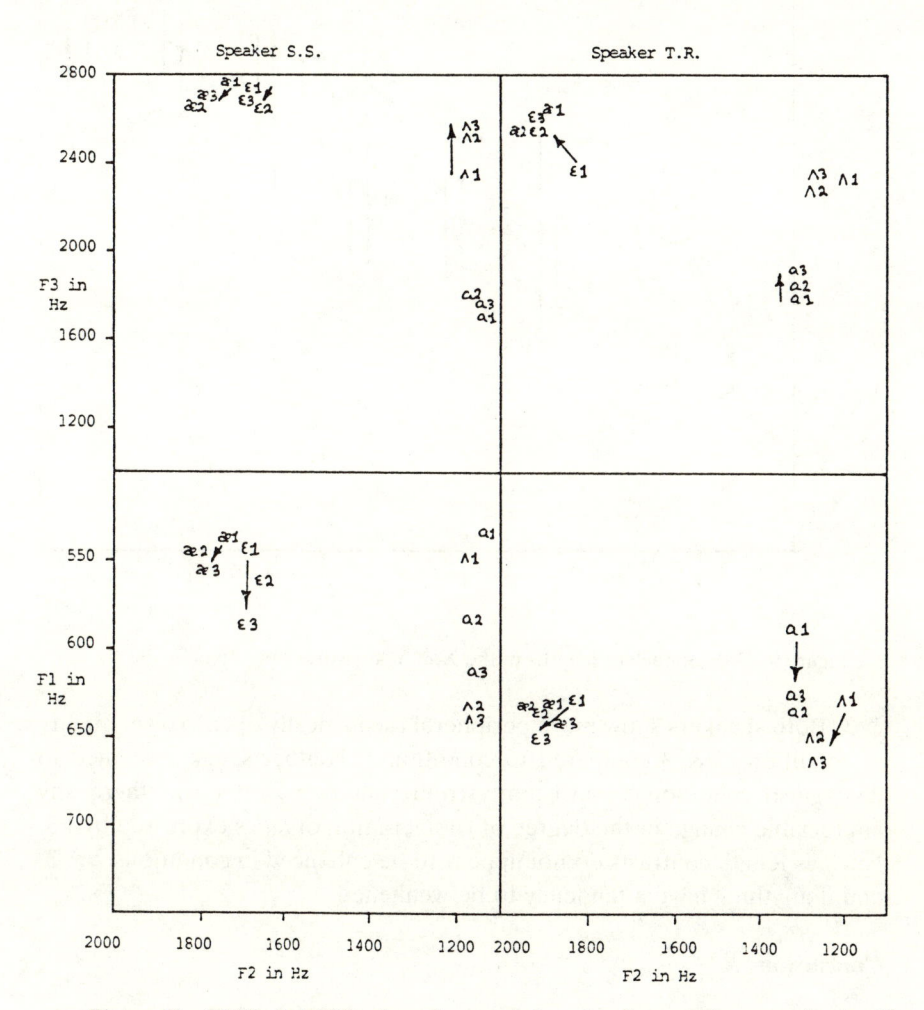

Figure 9b. F1/F2 & F2/F3 plane formant plots for the vowel targets in the Y keywords "pen, pan, heart, hut".

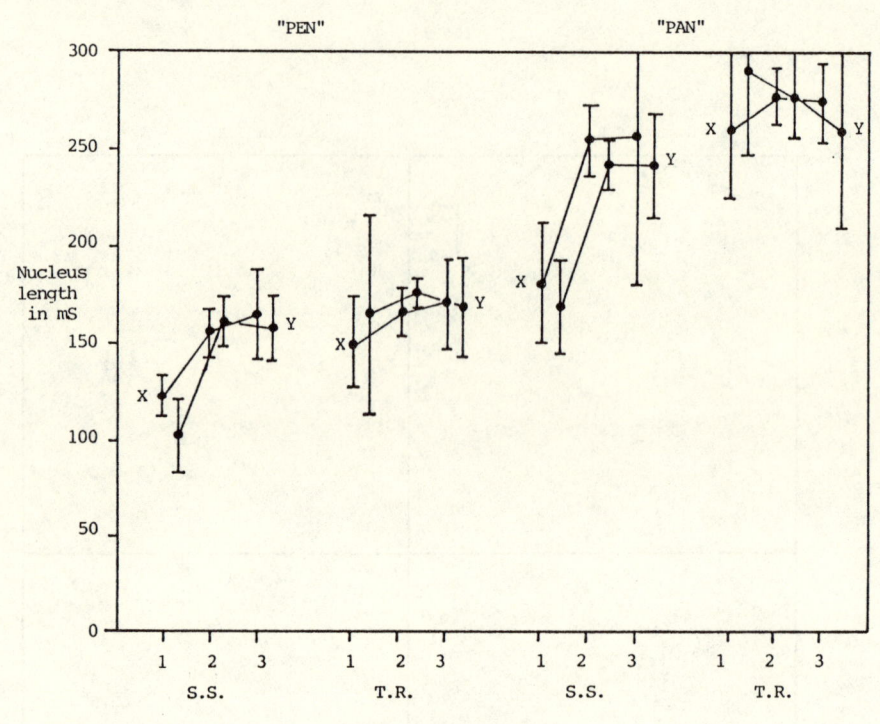

Figure 9c. Vowel nucleus lengths in the X & Y keywords "pen, pan".

& 3. Both speakers show more peripheral (acoustically open) vowel quality in conditions 2 & 3 compared to condition 1. Neither speaker seemed to distinguish condition 3 consistently from condition 2, nor was there any appreciable change in the degree of rhotacisation of /a/ as expressed by F3. Nucleus length contrasts do not appear to be enhanced in conditions 2 & 3, and if anything have a tendency to be weakened.

Conclusion

The aim of this preliminary investigation was to examine some of the ways in which speakers might fine-tune their production strategies in response to an apparent deterioration of their general communication environment, and to a perceived reduced success in communicating with a single listener. The basic hypothesis initially focused the experiment on the question of segmental contrasts, and the possibility that the speakers might

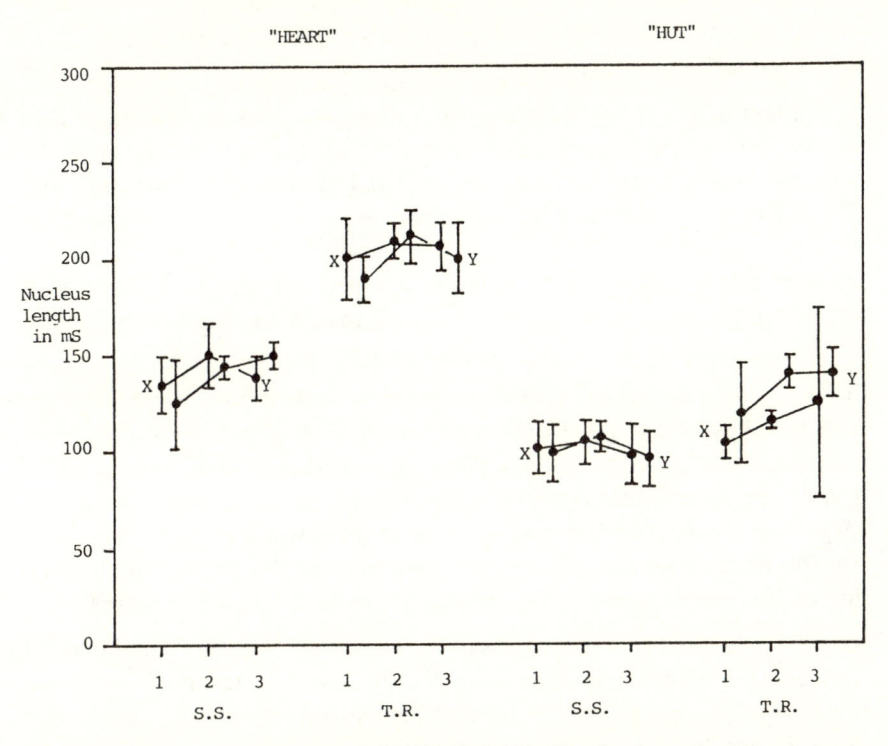

Figure 10. Vowel nucleus lengths in the X & Y keywords "heart, hut".

produce measurably enhanced cues to these contrasts in an environment of perceived communication difficulty, when compared with one of no perceived difficulty. However it would seem that the suprasegmental aspects may well be more significant. In our experiment there was only a small number of speakers and a limited amount of data. It was evident that of the two speakers, S.S. responded more positively in his attempts to compensate for the deterioration in the communication environment. Thus in appraising the data the additional variable of speaker motivation must be taken into account. Moreover, there are more natural ways of producing a perceived deterioration in the communication environment itself. Against this background, the following tentative conclusions are offered:

i. Both speakers made appreciable overall adjustments to their basic settings of respiratory force as expressed by increased overall speech intensity, and of laryngeal adjustment as expressed by long term spectral energy distribution in response to a communication context which was perceived to have become more difficult.

ii. Speaker S.S. made somewhat greater changes to these base settings than speaker T.R. In the case of overall intensity, S.S. began from a less forceful base, and reached a similar intensity level to T.R. under the "difficult" conditions 2 & 3. In the case of long term spectrum, S.S. made very considerable laryngeal setting changes to produce greatly increased spectral energy between 1KHz and 3KHz. It may be assumed that this increase was an attempt to compensate for the effects of the masking noise introduced into the speaker's perceived communication path in conditions 2 & 3.

iii. Both speakers made substantial changes to their basic pitch settings, with S.S. having the greater absolute increase. It is noteworthy that the basic pitch settings of the two speakers are quite similar in conditions 2 & 3, despite their very different long term spectral energy distributions. This suggests quite independent management of these two aspects of phonatory control. At least part of the shift to higher pitch settings is also likely to be due to the increased respiratory driving forces used by both speakers.

iv. S.S. attempted to enhance overall sentence intelligibility and keyword contrast by progressively increasing overall sentence duration. Although there is no appropriate data analysis to demonstrate the effect, some of this duration resulted from marked pauses within the sentences of the form "I said X ... not Y". This strategy was clearly intended to allow the listener more time to process and identify the X and Y keywords.

v. Both speakers attempted to enhance keyword contrast by increasing their stress levels as expressed by the range of pitch movement over the words. The effect is more marked for S.S. than T.R., and is supplemented by increased word intensity. S.S. also showed a marked increase in word duration which is not seen in T.R.'s data at either sentence or word level. Additionally, there is a clear stress bias favouring "X" words in the data from both speakers suggesting an intuitive syntactically and/or semantically motivated component to their contrast enhancement strategy. Indeed, to the extent that the motive is semantic, the stress in the "X" words might be explained by the primary importance of this being the word held up in distinction to the "Y" word (i.e. "Y" is not the word). The effects of stress are also reflected to some degree in the more peripheral vowel quality data.

vi. The segmental data does not show strong evidence of segmental contrast enhancement in the cues for which data has been obtained. As noted in (v), conditions 2 & 3 show more peripheral vowel quality of the kind expected with increased word stress, but do not show any very appreciable accompanying increase in vowel quality distance that might result in enhanced phonological contrast. The stop consonant voicing contrast shows no appreciable enhancement of any kind.

vii. Overall, the most marked fine-tuning of the speech production was in its suprasegmental dimensions of voice quality and prosody. This is in broad agreement with the findings of Picheny *et al.* (1986), although some of the effects observed in the present study appear to be somewhat stronger, perhaps due to the more demanding communication context in which the speech of the present study was elicited. The lack of any marked segmentally motivated fine-tuning suggests that either speakers lack the well developed intuitions about segmental contrast enhancement strategies which are apparent at the suprasegmental level; or that the speech production process itself does not allow for major adjustment at the segmental level. This is in some contrast to the findings of Chen *et al.* (1983), Lindblom and Lindgren (1986) and Picheny (1986), and is in part a question of interpretation of data. Changes in vowel quality and in segmental durations while related to segmental structure, are in many instances arguably a consequence of prosodic adjustments. There is clearly the need for further investigation of the relationship between the acoustic consequences of segmental and prosodically-motivated adjustments in conversational versus "clear" or intelligibility-motivated speech.

We may speculate that if this latter assertion is true, it may argue for a strong component of preprogramming in the strategy of motor control at least within a larger articulatory unit of the span of a syllable or greater; and that the skilled motor behaviour used to realise segmental structure within such a unit normally operates somewhere near a contrastively optimal level in fully stressed syllables. Since speakers obviously do exhibit a degree of articulatory headroom, perhaps this is most strongly related to the control of suprasegmental structure. If further investigations were to show that it is only ever possible to observe weaker effects at the segmental level, it may suggest that the internal spectral and temporal relationships within syllable level units are not amenable to much further enhancement once fully stressed articulation is reached. None of this really argues against Lindblom's basic concept of economy, only that his "cost benefit conspiracy" notion may operate most powerfully in units above the segment. Thus it may be that in enhancing contrast, a speaker's best strategy is to capitalise on his or her degree of freedom in manipulating prosody within an appropriate syntactic context. This may give the listeners more time to listen, increase the demand on their attention because of increased stress, and perhaps provide indirect enhancement of segmental intelligibility by virtue of the wider pitch excursions accompanying the stress.[1]

Note

1. The authors would like to thank the technical staffs in the Phonetics Laboratory at Stockholm University, and the Speech Hearing and Language Research Centre at Macquarie University for their support in the experimental aspects of this research. Particular thanks are due to Rich Schulman in Stockholm, and to Sarah Robertson and especially Peter Koob at Macquarie. We are also grateful to Bjorn Lindblom for stimulating discussions preceding the experimental work and for helpful comments arising from his own research. Finally, it is a particular pleasure to thank Michael Halliday for making some of his customarily acute and valuable observations at a preliminary seminar presentation of material from this study.

Evaluative text analysis

Malcolm Coulthard

> The higher level of achievement is a contribution to the *evaluation* of the text.
> (*Halliday* 1985: xv)

Introduction

The past thirty years have seen fascinating and lively debate about the nature and boundaries of linguistics, but one tenet has remained unchallenged: that linguistics is concerned solely with making descriptive and not prescriptive statements. It is agreed that linguistics can properly concern itself with evaluating alternative grammars but not with evaluating the comparative communicative success of two alternative sentences generated by a given grammar — despite the fact that pure and applied linguists in their role as teachers are daily involved informally in doing just that, telling students how to improve their linguistic skills.

There were, of course, in the late sixties and early seventies, important sociolinguistic reasons for emphasising the validity of difference and denying the inherent inferiority of minority dialects. However, this battle has long since been won, following research into working class English in London by Bernstein, Halliday and Hasan, into West-Indian English in Birmingham by Wight and Sinclair and into Black English in New York by Labov. Now the advances in descriptive linguistics of the last generation should give us the confidence to reintroduce evaluation, to admit what we have always secretly acknowledged, that some texts and some writers are better than others, and to try to account not simply for difference and how existing texts mean, but also for quality and why one textualisation might mean more or better than an alternative.

While proposing this new area of investigation I can as yet offer neither "discovery procedures" nor any "categories" and my only methodology is a study of breakdowns. Just as studies of aphasia and slips of the tongue have provided fruitful evidence for hypotheses about how language is organised in the brain, so I propose to examine badly written text in order to work towards an account of successful communication. The text I will focus on is taken from a pamphlet *Holidays and Travel for Diabetics*, published in 1977 by the British Diabetic Association and brought to me, by a woman who worked in a diabetes clinic, because it was "too difficult" and her patients "couldn't understand it".

I propose to examine the first 13 sentences of the text, up to the end of the first section entitled *Food*, but I have included the next section on *Drink* in order to show how the text continues. Before reading my commentary, I would like you to read the text once and then to make a note of what you have understood and retained and what you consider to be the overall message and tone of the text.

Holidays and Travel for Diabetics
(1) The well-controlled diabetic can enjoy travelling and holidays abroad as much as anyone else, but he must go well prepared.

Food
(2) Most diabetics think that food will be a problem when travelling. (3) However, food in any country consists of the same basic ingredients. (4) Potatoes, rice and other starchy vegetables or cereals, and products containing flour and/or sugar are the main source of carbohydrates. (5) Bread, in whatever form, has 15 Grams of carbohydrate to the ounce. (6) Rice and pasta (macaroni, spaghetti, ravioli, etc.) are used instead of potatoes in many countries. (7) Before travelling you should buy the 10-Gram Exchange List, available from the British Diabetic Association. (8) 10-Gram portions of unfamiliar foods can then be weighed until you learn to judge them at a glance. (9) Protein foods are easily recognisable (meat, fish, eggs and poultry), and fats consist of butter, margarine, cooking fats and olive oil. (10) Overweight diabetics should cut fats to a minimum as they are very high in Calories or Joules. (11) A basic knowledge of cooking helps you to assess any dish so it is always worthwhile to study a cookery book. (12) Sweets and puddings should be avoided, but fresh fruit and plain ice cream or cheese and biscuits are easily calculated substitutes. (13) As "starters" tomato juice, hors d'oeuvres and clear soup are all low in carbohydrates and Calories or Joules.

* * * * *

Drink
(14) All spirits are free of sugar and dry wine or sherry contains so little sugar that moderate amounts can be taken. (15) All beers, sweet cider,

sweet wines and liqueurs (except diabetic preparations) contain some sugar. (16) Alcohol should be avoided by the overweight diabetic as it is high in Calories or Joules. (17) Fruit drinks and minerals usually contain high quantities of sugar, but Coca Cola is known to have 20 grams carbohydrate to the 6-ounce (150ml) bottle — a useful form of "topping up" when swimming, dancing, etc. (18) Four ounces (100ml) of fresh orange juice contains 10 grams carbohydrate. (19) Tea and coffee are, of course, free, but avoid Turkish coffee which is often served sweetened.

* * * * *

I shall discuss the text under the headings "ideational", "interpersonal" and "textual". However, the approach will be somewhat different from that in the illustrative Appendix 1 of Halliday's *Functional Grammar* (1985) because I am interested not only in how the text means but also in the fact that it is just one of a series of possible textualisations of the message.

Ideational analysis

We have long been accustomed to thinking of "ideational" in terms of clauses but have no real way of approaching the ideational content of a whole text except as a collection of the ideational contents of the constituent clauses. This, however, is not useful or even possible for my purposes because what I am interested in exploring is the possible textualisations of the ideational, of which the one we have here is merely one sample realisation. Looking at the communication process from the composer/writer's point of view, we can see the ideational as pre-textual. However, unless one focuses on oneself, which is a flattering redefinition of the label "ideal speaker/hearer", the only access one has to the writer's ideational is through his/her text(ualisation). Thus, at this stage it is heuristically very useful to begin from an actual text, derive the ideational and then propose alternative and preferable textualisations. My task here, while not easy, is considerably simplified because the "text" is a mere thirteen lines from a much longer text, though a justifiable isolable unit because the lines comprise a section marked as such by the writer.

We have no automatic or standard or even agreed procedures for going from text to ideational content, but I must stress that the general points I am trying to make do not, in fact, depend on the "correctness" of my ideational analysis. What we need initially is a summary of the ideational content and I suggest that the message the author wants to put across and the message the diabetic/reader wants to read is:

(1) Food abroad need not be a problem for the well-controlled diabetic.

This is, as we know, no more than a summary. For reasons we will now consider, (1) could not be a possible textualisation of the ideational content for the intended audience. Let us compare (1) with (2) and (3):

(2) Jesus Saves. (outside a church)
(3) Smoking can seriously damage your health. (on a cigarette packet)

Each of these texts depends on an enormous amount of unstated information, argument and deduction; and in this form can only function as a *reminder* which requires the reader to supply the underlying information or as an *ex cathedra* statement whose truth depends on the authority of the author. Obviously the decision about how much and what of any ideation is to be textualised depends on audience and purpose (see *Interpersonal analysis*, below), but we can, irrespective of audience, begin to unpackage the summary ideation into some of its component parts. (1) could be decomposed into:

(1a) Food abroad consists at one level of analysis, like food at home, of combinations of fats, proteins and carbohydrates.
(1b) A well-controlled diabetic has solved the problem of analysing food and balancing his diet at home.
(1c) Therefore the problem is one of bringing already acquired skills to bear on unfamiliar food.

This is not simply a first attempt at an expansion but an attempt at a first expansion. One could go on indefinitely expanding, but the only useful expansions are audience-oriented. Thus, at the next level, I would need to decide whether my expansion was for diabetics or non-diabetics; and if for diabetics, whether it was for those who had just learned of their diabetes or for those who were already well-controlled, and so on. At this point it becomes useful to discuss interpersonal factors.

Interpersonal analysis

It is the "interpersonal", or sense of audience, which allows us as writers to keep the ideational within manageable limits and it is the ideational/interpersonal interface which causes most difficulties for writers of all ages and abilities. Without a clear sense of audience, it is impossible to make the right selections from the ideational. (It is, of course, an irony that we frequently complain about the quality of students' writing but too often put them in the impossible situation of having to write essays and examination answers aimed not at a real known person but at an imagined construct, the ideal marker, who is at once intelligent and generally well informed but fortuitously ignorant of the central topic of the assessed work.)

Since Halliday and Hasan's *Cohesion in English* (1976), we have been very conscious of the many ways in which texts are organised by means of, and analysable into "given" and "new". (This textualisation feature will be considered in *Textual analysis*, below.) However, what is less recognised is that any writer is faced with two major interpersonal decisions: firstly, what can (s)he assume his/her intended audience (should) know and secondly, what of what they know is it useful or necessary to repeat. Thus, not only is there textually "given" and "new", there is also *ideationally* "given" and "new". Indeed, one of the significant contributions of Brazil (1985) was to demonstrate that speakers have available, in the intonation system in the proclaiming/referring tone choice, an option for marking items as ideationally given or new. There is no comparable option for the writer but this is not to say that (s)he cannot lexicalise the distinction. In fact, I have just noticed that my use of "we have been very conscious" and "less recognised" at the beginning of this paragraph are markers of ideational given and new: it is for this reason that, while texts are created for a particular audience, once they exist, they paradoxically define their own audience.

It thus becomes important to ask why the ideationally given is re-presented. When we look at the diabetes text we can see that most of the content of sentences 4, 9, 10, 12 and 13 is ideationally given for the intended audience and the function of textualising is to reassure. Because the examples of fats, carbohydrates and proteins for "food in any country" are the same as the ones the reader already knows, it should be evident that there is no problem. However, the text itself doesn't make this communicative strategy overt to the reader: the comparison between "home" and "abroad" is not lexicalised. More obscure is the function of the thrice repeated phrase *Calories or Joules* in sentences 10, 13 and 16. *Joules* must be assumed to be ideationally given as it is not glossed, so the phrase must be there as a reminder that Joules is an alternative measure. However, in the context of travel abroad, one might have expected a reminder that Joules tend to be used in Europe where Calories are used in England and, more importantly, that Calories and Joules like Fahrenheit and Centigrade, while measuring the same phenomenon, use different scales; indeed one might even have expected a sample conversion scale.

If we now move from the interpersonal/ideational interface to the purely interpersonal, the writer here has to decide what "tone" to adopt — a problem we are perhaps more conscious of in letters but one which pervades all written texts. One of the strangest decisions in this text is the pronoun choice *he* in sentence 1, *he must go well prepared*, which implies that the text will be *about* rather than addressed *to* diabetics.

At the interpersonal/textual interface there are other important decisions to make. It is a truism that newspapers aimed at different audiences have markedly different lexical, grammatical and suprasentential choices because different audiences have different preferences for the balance of text and illustration. All such audience-related decisions must precede the textualisation. Significantly, this textualisation avoids illustrations, diagrams and tables, which some of my students proposed as components of a better alternative textualisation.

All texts depend on interaction with their readers and relative success or failure depends on what the reader takes away. This text could have been more reader-sensitive not simply in the ways I have outlined above, but also in having a user-friendly organisation of the ideational. One strong candidate for such a structure is the Problem-Solution structure which could have organised the ideational as follows:

Problem or Question	*Solution or Answer*
Will food be a problem?	No, because food is essentially the same in all countries; but recognition might be a problem.
How will I recognise the food?	Ordinary food will be recognisable just like food at home but there may be problems with unfamiliar dishes and with quantities.
How can I cope with this?	(i) a cookery book will give you an idea of what local dishes contain. (ii) the *10 Gram Exchange List* will help you with quantities.
What if I still have problems?	You can use the avoidance strategies that you already use to choose reliable food.

Evaluation: therefore food will not be a problem.

Textual analysis

Textualising the ideational presents other difficulties. Firstly, *sequencing*: information and ideas are rarely best represented linearly; as Johns (1980) demonstrates, on many occasions one requires a two- or even multi-dimensional representation but to textualise is inescapably to impose a linearity. Secondly, *signalling*: as Winter and Hoey have long ago demonstrated, the placing of clauses together in a text in itself creates relationships between the clauses; but a secondary writer's decision is whether to signal these relationships by lexical realisation. If (s)he chooses not to, (s)he allows the possibility of ambiguity or misunderstanding. I have long wondered whether sequence in the following wall-text is simply inevitable linearity or in fact an intended realisation of a consequence relation:

NO CRUISE
NO SS20

The problem with all text analysis and commentary is that it is very text-consuming and runs the risk of failing on the interpersonal level by either boring the readers or losing them in the fine detail. However, I can at this point see no other way of textualising my ideation than by commenting on sentences individually. What I want to show is some of the ways in which this textualisation creates difficulties that alternative textualisations don't have.

Sentence (1) is obviously a textualised summary of the message but it is a flawed one, given the basic reassuring aim of the text, as we can see by comparing it with (1a).

(1)   The well-controlled diabetic can enjoy travelling and holidays abroad as much as anyone else, but he must go well prepared.

(1a) The well-prepared diabetic will enjoy travelling and holidays abroad just like/as much as anyone else.

(1) has a modality problem: *can* on its own would raise some doubts; when combined with the second clause it produces a sentence with marked uncertainty. *But* here has a crucial role because it is the textual realisation of the interpersonal "this may surprise you", as Winter (personal communication) points out. We can see this clearly in his pair of examples, where the *and/but* choice is audience dependent:

Theirs was an arranged marriage *and* they were very happy.
Theirs was an arranged marriage *but* they were very happy.

It is for this reason that the *but* clause in (1) with its implication "you won't have thought of this" sounds like a warning and makes the whole sentence sound discouraging, unlike (1a) which recombines the ideational into an unambiguous reassurance which then needs to be expanded and justified.

Sentences (2) and (3) jointly realise what we recognise as a "strawman" argument, a false assertion followed by a denial and justification or explanation of the denial. It is possible to guess at the writer's reason for choosing this structure. Interpersonally (s)he is hoping to begin with an assumed reader worry and to dispel it by pointing out that it is not a foolish worry because many other diabetics share it. However, again, the textualisation is less than successful. Firstly, sentence (2), unlike the preceding one, has no modal uncertainty, but rather presents itself as fact. While trained linguists and sophisticated readers know that "think" is a typical signal of a writer's withdrawing his/her endorsement or averral from a proposition so that (s)he can later evaluate it (Tadros 1985), for the less sophisticated and target readers of this text the structure looks very like:

Eight out of ten film stars use LUX.
Most people think that Mrs Thatcher should resign.

where majorities and what they think are used as support or validation. The writer could have achieved his/her interpersonal aim without being ideationally misleading, by overtly signalling the ureliability of his/her assertion, either through an initial *although* or *despite the fact that* or by marking his/her interpersonal strategy through: *like most diabetics you may think* which simultaneously personalises the message, recognises the potential worry of the reader and indicates its unreliability.

Sentence (3), as the second part of the rhetorical structure, has different problems. There is the *however* to signal the denial of the previous assertion, but the denial itself is never realised, while the justification, though realised, is never signalled as a justification. One might have expected one of the following options:

(3a) *However/in fact* they are wrong *because* food in any country ...
(3b) *However/in fact* food in any country ... *so* they are wrong.

It is not insignificant that a major problem in student essays is a lack of signalling.

The ideational decision taken at the end of sentence (3) is to expand the hyponym *ingredients* into *carbohydrates*, *proteins* and *fats* and then to exemplify these in order to demonstrate the truth of the assertion that they are, indeed, the same in all countries. At this point two writer decisions create more confusion for the reader. The first problem comes from the sequence in which (s)he chooses to exemplify the ingredients. Whereas at first sight there is no reason for the writer not to begin with carbohydrates, once (s)he decides that (s)he wants to say much more about them than about fats and proteins, his/her decision to discuss them first means that (s)he obscures his/her "Hyponym → Sub-category → Example" pattern by inserting four sentences, (5)-(8), between (4) about carbohydrates and (9) about fats and proteins. This first sequencing decision obscures the pattern, the second destroys it completely. Consider the following pattern where each category is followed by examples:

Hyponym	*Sub-category*	*Example*
ingredients	⎧ carbohydrates	potatoes, rice and other starchy ....
	⎨ protein foods	meat, fish, eggs and poultry
	⎩ fats	butter, margarine, cooking fats, olive oil

The author chooses this sequence in sentence (9) but in (4) the examples were given before they were categorised as carbohydrates. If this were an isolated sentence, there might be no reason to prefer examples followed by categorisation to category followed by examples. However, this is not an isolated sentence and its position and meaning in this text require *carbohydrates* as theme and not rheme.

In other texts, a reader might have coped with this theme/rheme inversion more easily but in this text the idiosyncratic choice of *ingredients* as the hyponym for carbohydrates, fats and proteins allows the string "potatoes ... sugar" to appear to be the real list of sub-categories. A similar observation could probably be made about the thematic organisation of sentence (6): it is difficult to see why the writer feels it necessary to give us the information about rice and pasta being used instead of potatoes, unless we see it as an answer to a potential reader question: "What will I eat instead of potatoes?".

Conclusion

As my aim is not to analyse the text *per se*, I think that by now I have written enough to make clear the aims and methods of this approach. I have tried to provide a framework for future and more systematic research into the process of textualisation: research into ways of deriving ideational content from texts and ways of expanding ideations prior to textualisation; research into the interpersonal options and more and less successful strategies for blending ideationally new and old; and research into text macro-structures and their relative communicative success.

Eventually we will have a sounder basis on which to write a rhetoric of text, but even now my own work with students suggests that a lot can be taught about the process and techniques of writing by focusing on badly written texts and, in the light of analysis, attempting to rewrite them. For those who teach non-native speakers, it is as well for everyone to be aware that the task is not simply one of teaching students to read but rather of teaching them to read imperfectly (and often badly) written text.

Gobbledegook: the tyranny of linguistic conceits

Robert D. Eagleson

In order to examine some of the characteristics of official and legal documents, let us look at the opening paragraph of a chapter in the *CE(RR) Act Handbook*[1] of the Australian Public Service:

PART III — MEDICAL FITNESS
Chapter 1 — Management of invalidity cases

Potential invalidity cases to be handled quickly
1 1.1 It is essential that departments handle as quickly as
2 possible any case where it appears that the health of an
3 officer or employee is impairing, in other than a temporary
4 manner, his ability to perform his duties. This is essential
5 both so that staff are kept informed of where they stand
6 and of likely action in respect of their cases, and so that,
7 as far as possible, situations are avoided where a staff
8 member's paid sick leave credits expire before a final
9 decision is made about redeployment to another position, or
10 retirement. In this connection it should be noted that the
11 Common Rule re Sick Leave (Public Service Arbitrator's
12 Determination No. 119 of 1951) provides that the maximum
13 period allowable with pay in respect of any continuous absence
14 through illness is 52 weeks, unless War Service Sick Leave and
15 Compensation Leave are granted. The 52 week period may be
16 extended by up to 6 months in compensation cases and/or
17 by the period of War Service Sick Leave. It should also be
18 noted that a Permanent Head should not backdate the retirement
19 to a date earlier than that on which the Commonwealth Medical
20 Officer certified that the officer or employee was unfit for
21 his duties. Thus any delays by the department in handling
22 these cases could lead to the officer or employee concerned
23 being without either salary or pension for a period. In
24 exceptional circumstances, for example, where an officer or

> 25 employee has been disadvantaged by maladministration, a
> 26 department may seek the agreement of the Board's local
> 27 Regional Director if the Permanent Head proposes to set a
> 28 retirement date preceding the date of the Medical Officer's
> 29 certification that the staff member was permanently unfit.

We notice at once a strong flavour of the language of legislation. It is perhaps specially obvious in the qualification *in other than a temporary manner* (lines 3-4), which consistently occurs in this chapter whenever the clause *the health of an officer is impaired* and its equivalents appear. Many government documents, of course, arise as a result of legislation and in order to put legislation into effect. The writers try to imitate or at least keep close to this legislative language. This happens partly because of a misplaced respect for this language and their mistaken belief that it is appropriate for manuals of regulations. It is also a style that accords with their excessive caution. Not only do they dot every *i* but they feel obliged to include superfluous ones. In this paragraph, for example, the qualification is unnecessary: the chapter title and the internal heading declare unequivocally that invalidity is the subject and hence exclude temporary illness. There can be no possibility of misinterpretation, but the combination of respect for legal language on the one hand and caution on the other cannot be resisted: the writers find themselves straining after a style which they do not master and which may be unfamiliar to their readers.

Moreover, these unnecessary insertions flowing from the quasi-legalistic character of the language complicate the task of the reader. In this case, for instance, the adjunct *in other than a temporary manner* separates the predicator from its object and so creates a discontinuity which, research has shown, militates against comprehension.

Other characteristics of language produce a similar result in this text: the constant recourse to the passive voice, for example *are kept*, *are avoided*, *is made*, and the concentration of nominalisations such as *redeployment*, *retirement* and *certification*. Awkward, convoluted sentence patterns, of which the final sentence is a good illustration, also contribute to increasing the reader's task unnecessarily and undermine the patent design of the paragraph. Promptness of action is essential but little is done to speed the reader's comprehension of the regulations.

Another characteristic which hinders a ready grasp of the content is poor organisation, a serious flaw which too often goes unrecognised. The paragraph begins with an exhortation to prompt action, only to turn aside at sentence 3 (line 10) to comment on Determination No. 119, but then to return in sentence 6 (line 21) to the need for punctuality and the danger of delay, before sentence 7 (line 23), the final one, extends a matter raised in sentence 5 (line 17). While all the issues which are taken up in the paragraph have connections with each other, this disjointedness in organisation continually forces the reader to change directions and frustrates his/her expectations.

Time and time again this characteristic mars official documents. It is a common fault, for example, in traditional versions of insurance policies. Benefits available to the client are described in three or four places. Conditions, exclusions, obligations are similarly scattered through the policy. What makes the present text such a useful illustration is that it exhibits this regular deficiency in organisation within the ambit of a single paragraph. We cannot say that the object is to mislead or to conceal information. The whole intention of the *CE(RR) Act Handbook* is to ensure that departments administer the regulations correctly. The writers, who work within the Public Service Board, want to prevent personnel officers in the various departments making mistakes and creating problems which staff in the Public Service Board, and perhaps the writers themselves, will have to solve. Their arrangement of the material, however, makes it difficult for the reader to absorb the material smoothly in a gradual logical progression.

Efforts to rewrite a standard lease for commercial premises in New South Wales revealed another common but unfortunate characteristic of legal documents. The nature of this imperfection becomes clear in clause 14 of the original version:

> The tenant agrees ...
> 14. (a) To indemnify and save harmless the landlord his employees licensees and agents from and against all or any actions, suits, claims and demands by or on behalf of any person or corporation whatsoever in respect of any accidental death or accidental bodily injury or accidental damage to property which may arise directly or indirectly out of his business at the demised premises or out of the occupation or use by him his employees or agents of the demised premises and such other parts of the building as they may be permitted to use under this lease.
>
> (b) The landlord shall not be liable for any damages he or any employee agent licensee or visitor of his may suffer by reason of any injury to any person or damage to any property or equipment that may be at any time in the building arising from fire or from the overflow of water supply or rain water which may leak into the building or issue or

flow from any part of the building or arising from any defect in the gas electric or water connections or any fittings or appliances used in connection therewith.

(c) That if his employees agents licensees or visitors shall use the lifts or escalators in the building such use shall be gratuitous only and not of right and the landlord shall not be liable for an accident which may happen in connection with the said lifts or escalators whether through the negligence of any servants or employees of the landlord or any other person or through any defect in the said lifts or escalators or anything used or connected therewith or otherwise nor for the said lifts or escalators ceasing to run at any time for any cause whatsoever.

(d) To pay the costs of repairing and making good any damage to the premises or to any other parts of the building caused by overflow of water resulting from neglect by him or his employees or visitors and to indemnify the landlord against all claims for damage thereby caused. All repairs shall be carried out by a builder approved by the landlord.

The sub-clauses (a)-(d) have been added over time and somewhat carelessly as the break in the parallelism between them reveals, with (a) and (d) being introduced with the infinitive particle *to*, (b) with the definite article *the*, and (c) with the conjunction *that*. In effect, as conditions have changed or loopholes been uncovered, there has been a progressive accumulation of detail. Sub-clause (a) is the original and basic item; sub-clause (b) emerged after incidents involving fire and water damage; sub-clause (c) was added once lifts and escalators were introduced; and sub-clause (d) catches up an oversight in (b). The result is a cumbersome statement of indemnity rambling over numerous sub-clauses, which obliges the reader to wade through masses of particulars to discover whether the lease applies in a specific situation. This process of progressive accumulation needs to be reversed with the specification of principles replacing the listing of detail, with generalisation substituting for aggregation.

Along with this accumulative approach to official documents goes a tendency to treat them in a patchwork fashion. As a result an unevenness marks the way the various sections of a document are handled, as the *Teachers (Non-Government Schools and Pre-Schools) State Award* illustrates. During the period 1975-81, the Award underwent a number of amendments as conditions of service changed. Extracts from the 1975 and 1981 Award show the changes which occurred for teachers progressing from the status of two-year to three-year certificated assistants:

(1) *1975 Award*
(d) A two-years trained assistant other than one specified in paragraphs (b)

and (c) above, who has completed satisfactorily three ninths of a degree course or three units of study, or two units of study and one ninth of a degree course, shall be deemed to be three-years trained and, upon satisfying requirements shall be paid a double increment with retention of normal incremental date and shall be entitled to progress by normal increments to the top of the incremental scale.

(e) A two-years trained assistant who obtains three-years trained status by attending the training course conducted by the Sydney Teachers' College and obtains the Certificate in Teaching the Deaf shall receive one additional increment with retention of normal incremental date.

(2) *1981 Award*

(d) A 2 years' trained assistant other than one specified in paragraphs (b) and (c) above who has completed satisfactorily 3/9th of a degree course or 3 units of study or 2 units of study and 1/9th of a degree course or 1 unit of study and 2/9th of a degree course shall be deemed to be 3 years' trained. Upon satisfying the above requirements such assistants shall progress to that step on the incremental scale achieved through normal incremental progression by a 3 years' trained assistant who enters the teaching service as such and who has the same years of service as the 2 years' trained assistant and shall thereafter be accorded the same incremental progression as the said 3 years' trained assistant who entered the service as such.

(e) A 2 years' trained assistant who obtains 3 years' trained status by attending the training course conducted by the Sydney Teachers' College and obtains the Certificate in Teaching the Deaf shall receive one additional increment with retention of normal incremental date.

Meanwhile the conditions for teachers moving from the status of conditionally certificated to certificated assistants remained the same, namely:

(3) *1975 & 1981 Awards*

(a) (i) If a Conditionally Certificated Assistant with two-years training or three-years training satisfies in his first year of service the requirements specified for the award of a Teachers' Certificate, the salary of such assistant shall be adjusted to the rates prescribed in the Certificated Assistants' Scale immediately above the rate being received after completing 12 months' satisfactory service on the first year rate of the appropriate scale.

(ii) If a Conditionally Certificated Assistant with two-years' training or three-years' training satisfies other than in his first year of service the requirements specified for the award of a Teachers' Certificate, the salary of such assistant shall be adjusted to the rate prescribed in the Certificated Assistants' scale immediately above the rate being received with effect on and from the first day of the month succeeding the date on which such requirements were satisfied; provided that where the latter date and normal incremental date are the same, the

adjustment shall be to the rate prescribed by such scale next but one above the rate being received. Such assistants shall thereafter be eligible for subsequent progression in accordance with such scale on his or her normal incremental date.
(b) The salary of a Conditionally Certificated Assistant with two-years' training or three-years' training who have been in receipt of the 4th or 5th year rate of salary respectively for 12 months or more at the time of satisfying the requirements specified for the award of a Teachers' Certificate, shall be adjusted to the rate prescribed by the Certificated Assistants' scale next but one above the rate being received. In such case, the assistant's future incremental date is to be the anniversary of the date of transfer to the Certificated Assistants' scale.

Seemingly the drafters of the Award concentrated on modifying the pertinent sections under review, for example extract (2) (d), and did not take care to ensure that the conditions for the various categories were all brought into line at the same time. As the extracts show, a number of discrepancies crept into the Award as a result, specifically with reference to the payment of increments, with the conditionally certificated assistants apparently receiving more generous treatment than the certificated ones because their retention of the normal incremental date is explicitly safeguarded in (3) but is lost in (2) (d), though retained in (2) (e). In merging material from other clauses in the 1975 Award into a new clause (2) (d) the drafters of the 1981 Award untidily omitted any reference to the normal incremental date. By the end of the year the parties to the Award were in dispute, with the deficiency in drafting procedure, rather than any intent to deceive, being the real cause. To underscore this last observation and to be fair, it was the employer who was wanting to apply the more generous interpretation for the benefit of the employees.

To change to another tack, very frequently official documents show little awareness of their real audience. A good illustration is the wording which the Publications Section of the Human Rights Commission devised for a leaflet which was designed to reduce discrimination in the selling or renting of property:

> Racial discrimination is practised by various real estate agents, property owners and landlords in a number of parts of Australia. It is an important community problem, and a direct cause of considerable personal distress.
> As a *real estate agent* (or an employee of a real estate agency), as a *landlord*, as a person dealing in property or housing, or as a person managing accommodation (such as a motel or caravan park), it is important for you to know about the *Racial Discrimination Act 1975.*

This leaflet was being prepared for distribution to real estate agents and landlords. Its wording was hardly such as to win their support. Yet there are substantial explanations for such a result. The Publications Section is not responsible for the formulation of policy, and hence is writing on behalf of someone else. It is moreover often removed from extensive contact with the real audience for a leaflet. As a consequence, it is very easy to slip into concentrating on the concerns of the organisation — in this case the restraining of racist estate agents — and to overlook the sensitivities of the majority of estate agents, who have not practised discrimination. But members of the public are not aware of these background conditions to the preparation of the publication: all they would have perceived, if it had been released in this form, would have been the gratuitously accusatory flavour of the leaflet.

The effect of these background conditions is not always insulting though it may be no less disconcerting. Consider, for example, the introduction to a leaflet on pensions which the Department of Social Security distributes:

> *This leaflet is only a general guide. It was up to date in March 1984.*
> *If you want to know more about age pension ask at any Social Security office.*
> *Our addresses and telephone numbers are in the telephone book.*
> *Our staff will be pleased to help you.*

There is no doubt that citizens need to be given these warnings and offers, but such details are hardly their first concern when they pick up the leaflet. On the contrary, they are more likely to want to know what benefits are available and whether they are eligible for these benefits. The Department, however, has approached the venture with its own interests in view and concerned to protect itself and not be accused of misrepresentation. A different strategy for presenting the material is needed, otherwise readers might well discard the leaflet and turn elsewhere for advice. Again it must be emphasised, it was not the Department's intention to disconcert readers and it has tried to use fairly straightforward language. Here discrepancy between intention and achievement arises not from design but from misunderstanding, which has led to faulty execution.

In addition to this misconception of the writer's task, there is another factor which operates to put the audience's needs at a discount. This is a fear to move away from legal language in case the departure exposes the organisation to dishonesty. The Taxation Department, for example, frames its final notice in these terms:

> PURSUANT TO THE PROVISIONS OF THE INCOME TAX ASSESSMENT ACT 1936 AS AMENDED, I HEREBY REQUIRE YOU TO FURNISH TO ME AT MY OFFICE, AT THE ABOVEMENTIONED ADDRESS, WITHIN FOURTEEN DAYS OF THE DATE HEREOF, A RETURN IN WRITING ON THE APPROPRIATE FORM, DULY SIGNED BY YOU SETTING FORTH A FULL AND COMPLETE STATEMENT OF ALL INCOME DERIVED FROM ALL SOURCES WHETHER IN AUSTRALIA OR OUT OF AUSTRALIA DURING THE YEAR(S) ENDED 30 JUNE ... FAILURE TO COMPLY WITH THE REQUIREMENTS OF THIS NOTICE MAY RESULT IN LEGAL PROCEEDINGS BEING INSTITUTED WITHOUT FURTHER NOTICE.
>
> XYZ
Deputy Commissioner of Taxation
and Delegate to the Commissioner

During an exercise in a workshop on Plain English, members of the departmental section concerned with this notice joined enthusiastically with others in proposing alternatives to remove the cant in it. Just as a new version was emerging they began to draw back, expressing the fear that the new wording may not be as legally watertight and binding as the established version.

Such a reaction does not spring just from craven fear. Nor is it for purely selfish motives that others are hesitant to change. Many lawyers, for example, are afraid to move far from traditional terminology for fear of prejudicing the rights of their clients. They persist with language which has been accepted in courts before and hence will hold up if challenged, rather than risk their clients' cases with words of untested effect.

While this "better safe than sorry" policy may be sound business practice, it locks us into awkward language and means that there can rarely be substantial change. As a result, documents become increasingly incomprehensible as the years pass. Moreover this policy has the force of discouraging us from questioning whether the administration of government and law really requires language to be distorted as it is in officialese and legalese.

Sometimes the acceptance of gobbledegook is virtually mindless. *Plain*

English[2] records an incident in Great Britain in which Ilford councillors questioned the meaning of the following by-law which had already been passed by the council's Highway Committee and the Home Office:

> Provided that the by-law shall not apply to any person riding a bicycle or tricycle otherwise than to the obstruction or danger of any person lawfully using such footpath if the person riding has lawful authority so to do.
> *Plain English* (1979: 1:10)

The Deputy Borough Solicitor admitted, "I was hoping that no member would raise it and ask for its meaning. The person who worded it left the council a week ago." The community has been so brainwashed about the precision and nicety of legal language, so defeated in its efforts to comprehend such language, that it is in danger of yielding to anything that even resembles legal language, humbly accepting that the cause of any incomprehension lies in the community's own inadequacy.

This British episode may be an extreme example but it is true that many put excessive trust in legalistic language, failing to recognise that it is not as perfect as they imagine, that it can, indeed, be a snare. On several occasions in converting insurance policies and financial statements to Plain English, I have come across sections in which the traditional wording did not express what was intended and in fact exposed the companies to possible heavy claims. The obscurity of the wording, however, concealed these flaws from the staff until endeavours to determine the content in preparation for a Plain English version detected them. Fortunately no clients became aware of them. Equally mesmerised by the gobbledegook, they too were prepared to accept the interpretations being placed on the wording by the staff.

What we are contending with here is a seemingly universal cankerworm. All too many have become unthinkingly enamoured of inflated language. Unless a publication is couched in it, somehow it does not seem important enough. We have the evidence from Bardell (1978) and Turk's (1978) experiments in which they asked scientists to react to two versions of a report on the same scientific experiment. While the scientists found the passage with the plainer style more interesting, more precise, more dynamic, stimulating and objective, giving the impression of a more competent scientist with greater consideration for his readers, nonetheless they voted that the other style seemed more appropriate for scientific writing. There is an irrationality in this behaviour, but the scientists' assessment of the current situation is sadly accurate. We may prefer one style, but we burden ourselves with another because we feel we should adopt its mode of expression. Schwartz's investigations (1984) confirm Bardell and Turk's results. Further evidence is often provided by postgraduate as well as undergraduate students when they fall into the trap of exaggerated writing which they defend on the ground that academic writing needs such flourishes if readers are to be impressed with the value of the ideas. Executives reveal the same fanciful and whimsical notions as they change "go" to "proceed", "ask about" to "seek advice as to", "school" to "educational institution" in the writing of their subordinates. Robert Gordon's verse is bitingly true:

> If you write English
> Plain enough
> Nobody wants
> To read your stuff;
> But jargon, redundancy,
> Bluff and cant
> Are guarantees
> Of a federal grant.
>   (Source unknown)

Two central observations flow from these considerations. First we have to lead the community to adjudge Plain English to be not a simplified or even a rewritten version of officialese but instead a better version of language. Indeed we must see it as the true and responsible version. A lot of official and legal English is unquestionably bad English. Rather than being rewritten, it should be discarded entirely. Plain English is using a different variety of English: it is not just a rewording for the benefit of the simple-minded.

By the same token, we should not present Plain English as an innovation, an invention of this decade which all have to set about learning. It has always existed and we are already familiar with it, as we regularly use it when we seek to explain official and legal documents written in gobbledegook. Indeed it is easy to demonstrate that many of these documents started out in a plain style only to undergo a process of linguistic inflation. A neat case in point is a paragraph which appeared in the chapter on housing loans in the 1981-82 annual report of the Aboriginal Development Commission:

> Consistent with the provisions of the Act, the Commission gives equal consideration to joint applicants where one partner is non-Aboriginal. The

children of mixed marriages are regarded as Aboriginal and benefit from the provision of a stable environment.

This paragraph had originally begun more simply:

> The Commission gives equal consideration to joint applicants where one partner is non-aboriginal.

But as it passed up the hierarchy, one addition after another was made until the original intent to record was smothered by the desire to impress. In the end, the important principle set out more clearly in the original version was obscured by these accretions. We need to sharpen the recognition that Plain English is a component of the language and that in referential discourse it can be left to stand on its own.

However, if we are going to expect officials and lawyers to change, we must go further than advocating the merits of Plain English. We must devise procedures to give these writers protection as they abandon terminology which has the support of precedence. There must be a means, such as a legislative committee, through which Plain English variants can have acceptance in law.

Secondly there is a real need for balance in our approach to the current situation in which gobbledegook is rife. No doubt some use language to confuse and mislead, and some may even resort to the complication of legalese to earn more. But we cannot regard these reasons as the only ones, or even the major ones. Far more serious and widespread are false linguistic values, subservience to legal language, over-caution, remoteness from and insensitivity to audience, and inept use of language. Above all we need to recognise that we have reached a position where language is, in a sense, in control. It is not the case that one group is manipulating it to exercise power over another group. On the contrary, both the producer and the recipient are equally enslaved: writers producing such language with considerable strain are enslaved because they believe they should, not because they greatly relish such language or because it clarifies their thoughts for them; and the writers no less than the readers are enslaved because they too are bemuddled by the obfuscation of the passages they have produced.

Today, writers as well as readers suffer under the tyranny of linguistic conceits and whims. We do not simply have the manipulation of language *to* control, but the dread state of language *in* control. We will only overthrow this tyranny when we acknowledge the snare and encumbrance it has become for official and legal writers as well as for the community at large.

Only then might we be prepared to restore the status and recognise the social responsibility of a plainer form of English.

Notes

1. The *Commonwealth Employees (Redeployment and Retirement) Act Handbook* (1982) printed by the Australian Government Publishing Service.
2. *Plain English* is the publication of the Plain English Campaign in the United Kingdom.

Text strategies: single, dual, multiple

Nils Erik Enkvist

Introduction

The term "strategy" has become commonplace in linguistics, but it has been more often used than stringently defined. The purpose of this paper is to try to trace some avenues towards the definition of "strategy"; to apply this definition more specifically to guiding principles of text production that might be called "text strategies"; and to suggest a text-typological dimension in terms of single-strategy texts, dual-strategy texts, and multiple-strategy texts. Needless to say, I am dealing with global problems of decision theory, text theory, text typology and text analysis and description: my offering will therefore consist of suggestive hints rather than the kind of exhaustive discussion that would readily fill a bookshelf and perhaps a library.

Definitions

To define the term "strategy" we must place it within a model of decision-making. Its classic military sense is:

(1) art of so moving or disposing troops or ships or aircraft as to impose upon the enemy the place & time & conditions for fighting preferred by oneself. *(Concise Oxford Dictionary,* s.v. strategy.)

In the military art, strategy leads on to tactics:

(2) art of disposing military or naval or air forces ... in actual contact with enemy; (pl.) procedure calculated to gain some end ... *(Ibid.,* s.v. tactics.)

Strategies, then, involve big decisions and large-scale dispositions, whereas the actual carrying-out of the operations is a matter of tactics. Another way of defining strategies is to say that they involve an adjustment of goals to resources or vice versa. If the resources prove inadequate to achieve a certain goal, either the strategy must limit the goal or increase the resources. The actual employment of resources would then be a matter of tactics.

Where the precise boundary between strategy and tactics runs is a question even the military do not like to press too hard. To decide on strategies one must know one's tactical resources. And to optimize their tactics, commanders in the field are likely to need some understanding of the strategic purpose of their operations. As we shall see, similar considerations can be applied to the distinction between text strategies and their syntactic realizations, *mutatis mutandis*: what military tactics is to strategy, syntax (including lexis) is to text strategy.

Decisions are made in a decision space, a multidimensional space whose dimensions are set by factors that affect the decision. Whenever a person is faced with more than one alternative action, he must make a decision and choose between the available alternatives. If he knows the consequences of each alternative, his decision can be called determinate. If he can estimate the probabilities of different possible consequences of the alternative, his decision can be called statistical. And if he must guess, without having a chance of estimating the consequences, the decision might be labelled as stochastic.

A person will notice that he must make a decision when he is faced with a choice of actions. I said "notice", which is literally true, in the everyday sense, only when the need for choice is conscious. In the production of discourse, however, many decisions are made automatically: some may involve a conscious phase and a more automatic realization phase; others may be wholly conscious. We know that the internalization of syntactic rules has largely been a process below the level of consciousness: we "know", and use, syntactic rules that we are incapable of verbalizing (unless we happen to be linguists, and even then many of our internalized rules will resist simple description). Such syntactic rules, and no doubt many others even at the level of discoursal macrostructure, will be applied automatically and unconsciously. But there may be situations where a speaker or writer stops to ponder: he may try putting various words into a sentence, judging their effect; he may cut up a long sentence into several short ones, or combine several short sentences into a long one, and so forth. Apart from the decisions that are normally made automatically, and the decisions that are normally made deliberately, there is a large body of decision types which can involve different degrees of consciousness and deliberation, depending on the person, his skills at communicating and level of training, the situation (including the time at his disposal), his level of ambition, and a number of situational factors that vary from task to task.

Still we may assume that automatic decisions and deliberate decisions are based on much the same mechanism. When making decisions, we have a goal; and when making decisions, we must make an inventory of the factors that affect them. We then refer these factors to the goal: we consider what we want to do and achieve, and then try to assess the importance of each decision-affecting factor in the light of this goal. Let me illustrate this with a simple example, a couplet by Crabbe from *The Borough* (IV. 78):

(3) To Learning's second seats we now proceed,
    Where humming students gilded primers read;

Let us assume that Crabbe's purpose was to write a poem in rhymed iambic pentameter couplets. If we also assume that Crabbe would have liked to minimize poetic license by retaining whenever possible the canonical word-order patterns of English, we can see that he was faced with a decision between two conflicting decision factors. The ordinary, canonical word-order pattern that dominates in everyday English speech would require the arrangement:

(4) We now proceed to Learning's second seats,
    Where humming students read gilded primers;

But such a canonical word-order pattern would destroy the rhyme and, in places, the scansion as well. Crabbe's purpose made him regard rhyme and metre as more important than canonical word order: metricity won the struggle, and SVX had to yield to SXV.

In the light of such an example, we can now define a strategy, and more specifically a text strategy, as a goal-determined weighting of decision-affecting factors. Crabbe wanted to write a rhyming poem in iambic pentameter couplets, and to achieve this goal he gave more weight to a syntactic pattern producing rhymes than to the canonical, common (and "prosaic") word-order arrangement of Modern English. If we go on to model what I have so far called decision-affecting factors as parameters, we can rephrase our definition:

(5) A text strategy is a goal-oriented weighting of decision parameters.

A parameter is a variable which varies within a certain range, and whose values can be used to classify the unit involved under a certain heading in a taxonomy. Such a definition seems to fit our decision-affecting factors nicely. A parameter, then, has a value and a weight. Crabbe gave the metricity parameter the value of rhyming iambic pentameter and a weight greater than that of the word-order parameter set at canonical word order.

According to this view, then, texts arise as results of decisions, which involve strategies consisting of goal-oriented weightings of parameters, some of whose effects conflict and some of whose effects conspire towards the same result. The genesis of discourse is thus a compromise, the result of a battle between forces some of which conflict and some of which conspire: figuratively speaking, a text is like a battlefield after the battle (cf. Enkvist 1985, forthcoming a and b). So far the model of text production as conflict and conspiracy has a strong metaphoric element: to what extent it might be possible, and worthwhile, to simulate a discourse production with an actual algorithmic model involving parameter conflict and conspiracy is an open question. But in text description and typology, at least in some relatively simple instances, parametric approaches can be used to advantage (Thürmer and Thürmer 1985).

The text-strategic principle

In many texts, there is an obvious major text-strategic principle which dominates the arrangement of the text. Thus a chronicle is a list of events arranged in chronological order, and thus a temporal-dominated text. A guidebook is arranged by place and by sight, and is thus locative-dominated; but within the divisions of text signalled by shift of place or of sight, a guidebook can provide information of different kinds, for instance in the form of chronologically arranged narrative. A biography has unity of hero and is thus fundamentally an agent-dominated text, but at the same time the text is also temporal if the hero's actions are related in temporally explicit (though not necessarily chronological) order; and a biography may of course also contain guidebook-like descriptions of places that were important to the person being written about and our grasp of his/her life. We might therefore try to make a distinction between single-strategy texts, that is, texts — or perhaps rather passages — dominated by one definite strategy; dual-strategy texts, in which the text or the passage is a blend of two strategies; and multiple-strategy texts, in which the text or passage is a blend of several strategies.

Such a line of argument leads to a number of problems. One is the question of the span of the strategy. A brief passage may follow one single strategy, but a long text — a biography for instance — is likely to blend strategies. Thus we should remember that our classification of a piece of discourse will depend on how much of that discourse we are looking at. If we find a temporal-dominated passage in a long text we have no justification whatever for labelling the entire text as being temporal-dominated. To be meaningful, a classification of discourse in terms of single, dual, and multiple strategies must explicitly state the spans of these various strategies. Presumably most long texts will be found to be multiple in their strategies. The tensions arising from dual and multiple strategies can of course also be viewed in Bakhtinian terms (Bakhtin 1981).

Another problem is the all-pervasiveness of time and temporality, in text strategies as in life. We have been born into time; we are doomed to live and to die in time, and also to produce discourse in time. Discourse is linear and the dimension of its linearity is time. Therefore all text strategies are in a sense temporal, and the only text type that can make use of a truly single strategy is a chronicle. Spatial relations can of course also be translated into temporal ones, as in

(6) The team had lined up for a photograph. From left to right we see Smith, Jones, Brown, McCormack ...

In the text these names come one after the other (from left to right, as it happens, in our script, but from right to left in Hebrew), but the order stands for their spatial order in the picture. Similarly, social and other kinds of order may be reflected in discourse linearity: why do we say *ladies and gentlemen*, for instance, instead of **gentlemen and ladies*?

Such examples can be labelled as instances of experiential iconicity (Enkvist 1981) because in them the text becomes a picture, an icon, of the world. Just as people who hear or read a text start out by assuming that the text must make sense, and exert themselves to interpret it by giving it coherence, so people who decode a text start out by assuming that the text is iconic. For instance:

(7) a. John and Mary got married and had a baby.

does not mean the same as

(7) b. John and Mary had a baby and got married.

because we assume that the order of the text reflects the order of events in the world.

Two text categories

Some cookery-books, like the *Alice B. Toklas Cook Book*, contain sentences of the type:

(8) a. In a huge copper pan put quantities of granulated sugar, moisten with cream, turn constantly ... (Toklas 1961: 164)
b. In a generously buttered fireproof dish, place a thin sprinkling of 4 finely chopped shallots (*Ibid*: 176)

A count of topicalized locatives bound by valency bonds to verbs such as *put*, in the Brown and LOB corpora, shows that such topicalizations are rare. I should like to interpret them as instances of experiential iconicity, which is of course practical in operational instructions. The quoted sentences are cookery-book-writer's shorthand for

(8) a'. First take a huge copper pan. Then put into it quantities of granulated sugar ...
b'. First take a fireproof dish and butter it generously. Then place in it a sprinkling of 4 finely chopped shallots ...

Here *4 finely chopped shallots* is also derivable from an underlying sentence, or predication: *take 4 shallots and chop them fine*. If I am right, Alice B. Toklas faced a conflict between experiential iconicity which helped her to concentrate the text, and the syntactic inertia which likes to keep locatives within the verb phrase when they are valency-tied to verbs such as *put*. (Note that *put* takes an obligatory locative, and implies place: if you put something, you must put it somewhere.) In a cookery book, the importance of experiential iconicity, and the weight of the experiential-iconicity parameter, were sufficient to break the valency bonds linking *put* and its locative, or at least to stretch them, so that the locative could be fronted.

Guidebooks are another text category whose strategy is conspicuously reflected in adverbial replacement, specifically by a fronting of locatives. For instance:

(9) Parallel with the Via dei Dipinti, on the W., is the wide Cardo Maximus, with arcaded shops, which runs from the Tiber to the Forum and thence to the Porta Laurentina. To the W. of this street and likewise parallel is the narrow Via Tecta, on the brick walls of which have been affixed many of the best preserved inscriptions found in the ruins. The Via Tecta runs beside a grain warehouse called the Piccolo Mercato; some of its rooms have been restored and four of them are used as an Antiquarium for objects of minor interest from the excavations. In the S. wall of the warehouse have been incorporated several layers of the tufa blocks of the primitive city walls.

(Muirhead 1956: 324-325, on Ostia)

The structure *locative + verb + subject NP* is very common in guidebooks. It reflects the strategy of first guiding the readers to a certain definite place and position, and then telling them what they are supposed to see. Also each fronted locative marks a section of the text, a text unit corresponding to a stop-or-stage- on-the-route and its sights. In (9), there are four stops or stages, namely the Cardo Maximus, the Via Tecta, its inscriptions, and the South wall of the warehouse, each of which is heralded by a fronted locative. The passage between two fronted locatives is likely to explicate the sights seen from the position defined in the first of these two locatives.

The pervasiveness of time is revealed by the fact that the locative strategy of the guidebook is inextricably interwoven with a temporal strategy which presents the sights in a temporal order. And the order of presenting sights obviously coincides with the order in which the tourist is expected to contemplate these sights. As students of literary narrative have shown in detail (Genette 1972), temporal strategies may be of great complexity. Here it must suffice to note that the relations between place and time in a guidebook tend to be related in a simple and consistent fashion (sights being presented in the order in which they should be seen), and that a guidebook is thus an example of a dual-strategy text rather than of a single-strategy one.

Text strategies and rhetoric

There are many links between my argument and classic arguments in rhetoric. Matters that I have linked with text strategies overlap with those traditionally discussed in connection with paragraph structure, with *topica*, or the *topoi* one can take up in connection with specific types of subjects, and with text typology. Relations between clauses and sentences can be reinterpreted as exponents of strategies at interclausal and intersentential levels; relations between text units similarly expose linking strategies at the relevant level. Thus, relations between "paragraphs", whatever a "paragraph" may be, indicate strategies of linking "paragraphs" to each other.

If I am merely restating matters well known to us, in some cases since ancient times, what is the use of rephrasing all this information in terms of text strategies? I believe there is some virtue in trying to view such matters as integral parts, not only of relatively abstract rhetorical patterns or of detailed nitty-gritty syntax, but in the fresh perspective of text theory and text modelling. Familiar objects may increase in interest if we succeed in viewing them from a fresh angle.

Text strategies and systemic functions

Text strategies can be defined and grouped in various ways. In homage to Michael Halliday, I shall try to do so in terms of systemic functions:

1. Text strategies in an *ideational* perspective appear as patterns of *topoi*, of ideas and materials for textualization and patterns through which different types of ideas can be linked to each other (in terms of before-and-after, cause-and-effect, and so on). We are here concerned with the logical strategies of texts. The term "ideational" could perhaps also be applied to text production as a cognitive operation of the kind that can be modelled with the aid of a cognitive network. In a cognitive network a text strategy can be illustrated, and even determined, in terms of (a) the point of entry where the text-producer enters into the network, and (b) the path followed through the network. In other words, we visualize a speaker/writer as going into the knowledge store at a specified point, and then choosing a path through the store, picking up items for textualization as (s)he goes on. (The information picked up need of course not be presented in the order in which it was collected: the order of the surface text can be affected by strategies at the textual and interpersonal levels.)

There is also a third way in which we can see text strategies in an ideational light. Information theory tells us that information consists of the elimination of uncertainties. We eliminate uncertainties by choosing one of several alternatives (for instance, one of the alternatives within a systems network). The text strategy then determines the order in which uncertainties are eliminated, presumably by optimizing it through considerations of textualization and interpersonal interaction.

2. Textualization — as related to Halliday's *textual* component — can be modelled in terms of the grouping, conjunction, and embedding of "text atoms" of some kind (cf. "kernel sentences", Chomsky 1957; Ohmann 1964; Sigurd 1974, 1977; Källgren 1979; Longacre 1983; and the "text base" in van Dijk & Kintsch 1983). In such text models ("Predication-based" we might call them if we choose to define "text atoms" as predications) the text strategy turns out to be the programme which steers the textualization of text atoms.

In intertextual terms we might see text strategies as macrostructural principles of text organization, most concretely in instances where the text is rigidly tied to a conventional, pre-existing pattern. I have used the term "template text" for texts whose macrostructure is set in advance and where the text producer, so to say, enters new data into pre-existing gaps, as when filling a hotel-registration card or an income-tax return. These are extreme instances of template texts; but we could say that there is a scale running from such rigidly pre-set template texts to texts with unlimited strategic freedom, many text types falling on the scale between extremes. This approach to intertextuality, as a factor determining text strategies, thus has to do with textual conventions.

3. The purpose of text strategies as part of the *interpersonal* component is to optimize the interaction between communication partners, partly in terms of ideation (for instance, estimating realistically the receptor's previous knowledge and capacity of processing text and information under the prevailing conditions, reckoning with noise and other disturbances, etc.); partly in terms of linguistic processing (through choosing syntactic structures that do not unnecessarily increase the processing load); and partly in terms of co-operation: Gricean maxims, politeness and face, turn-taking conventions, and other matters loosely grouped under the blanket term "pragmatics" (Levinson 1983). Ideational and textual strategies are of course ultimately formed to satisfy requirements set by interaction and thus fall within the interpersonal component. Here the components do not relate like slices of a pie but rather like Russian dolls or Chinese boxes.

Finishing other's talk: some structural and pragmatic features of completion offers

Allen D. Grimshaw

Lee: ... and then tr- check on *another* one. check *who* was *acting* chairman when they received the: (Pause)
Sherm: an appointment?
Lee: an appointment.

1. Introduction

I am a sociologist, not a linguist. My interest in discourse is less in how it is put together structurally than in what its producer-users manage to socially accomplish with it — and how.[1] My own work on language in use has focused on the examination of social accomplishment in talk; that work has been deeply informed by what Michael Halliday has told us about production and interpretation of socially meaningful utterances in contexts of situation and of text.

During the summer of 1973 I attended a course on "Textual cohesion" taught by Halliday at the Summer Linguistic Institute of the Linguistic Society of America held in Ann Arbor. In that course, which was based on work Halliday and Hasan had been doing on the topic (published in 1976), I learned a good deal both about what holds texts together and about how the same words can do very different "work" when differently "located" in text and when produced with varying prosodic features. I also learned a good deal about Halliday's fondness for Lewis Carroll and Alice. Most importantly for present purposes, however, from listening and talking to Halliday whenever I could, I gained a sense of the multiplicities of ends served by single utterances and of means available for same ends — and of how these multiplicities could be retrieved by dogged stripping away of the laminations of meaning in text. In some ways, Halliday sensitized me to nuances of text as Goffman did for those of interaction. Along with others such as Cicourel, Gumperz, Hymes and Labov, he taught me to "take talk seriously".

What follows reflects, I hope, my learning of some of Halliday's lessons. I have spent much time since then analyzing a fragment of text from a single, naturally occurring conversation (a doctoral dissertation defence); a text which Halliday and others have also studied (Grimshaw forthcoming; Grimshaw *et al.* forthcoming). While I was interested in such social interactional features of the discourse as the *processes* involved in evaluation, in conflict and in communicative nonsuccess, I became intrigued by the phenomenon of participant completion of utterances initiated by fellow interactants. While there are not enough instances in the text to permit a full description of their lingusitic structure, textual placement and pragmatic (i.e. in Halliday's terms, instrumental and regulatory) employ, they appear in sufficient numbers to permit some principled speculation about these several dimensions. While there has been some previous work on the topic (Jefferson 1973; Sacks 1967), I consider mine a very preliminary effort.

This paper is divided into two parts. In the first, I will essay an essentially deductive taxonomy of analytic dimensions of the phenomenon. In the second, I present truncated analyses of two instances from the dissertation defence corpus. One final introductory comment, a qualifier. There are a number of kinds of completions which routinely and ritually occur in everyday life. Among such are, for example, athletic and political chants and slogans constituted by elicitations and responses (BEAT/PURDUE!; SIEG/HEIL!) and responsive readings or their oral equivalents ("There is but one God" / "and Allah is his name!"). Similar conventional completions occur in conversation. While both group and individual manifestations of such elicited completions accomplish social ends such as solidarity enhancement and/or signalling of membership, I will not have the space to deal with them here.

2. A taxonomy of dimensions[2]

A look at the example displayed at the beginning of this paper identifies some of the many variable features of completion offers. It is evident that: (1) the completion provided is elicited/solicited; (2) it is "on topic";

(3) it probably does not provide new information (since it appears to be in a form much like that of "test" questions); (4) it is apparently accepted by the speaker who had had the floor and for whom the completion is provided. (More specifically, by the speaker who had permitted limited entry/ conditional access for the completion within her "turn space" (Lerner)). If I provide some contextual information, i.e. that the exchange occurred during the course of a dispute over whether there had been past gender discrimination in an academic department, at least some readers might conclude that the pause indicated a certain reluctance to provide the completion sought. That same information might permit further inferences about the ends (goals) of the two participants in their ongoing dispute and, for example, that the completion was made openly and not as an "aside" to an audience.

Other completions offered in the corpus of the dissertation defence and those which we hear in the course of our everyday interaction vary on these dimensions and on others. In the following discussion I can comment only briefly on six defining dimensions of what, filled out, would constitute a partial outline for a taxonomy of completion offers. They are, with no order of priority of importance implied: (1) contexts of situation; (2) interactional features; (3) $ends_1$ (goals); (4) $ends_2$ (outcomes); (5) sequential features; (6) act characteristics (in Hymes' 1974 sense). I realize that these dimensions are neither exhaustive nor mutually exclusive. As will be seen, I have little to say either about contexts of text or syntactic characterizations; these matters and others would have to be included in any full description. Finally, readers will be able to think of both exceptions and amplifications to characterizations made in what follows; I take refuge in the fact that the phenomenon can only be sketched in the space available.

2.1. *Contexts of situation*

At least three aspects of context of situation might be expected to influence whether completions will be offered and, if they are, whether they will be seen as appropriate: topic, setting, and participant attributes which include the character of relationships among participants. While such features of topic as symmetry or asymmetry of knowledge or of interest of participants will doubtless influence frequencies of completion offers, it is difficult to think of a topic which is intrinsically exempt from the phenomenon *independently of characteristics of setting and of participants*. If I do not make/proffer completions during the course of a discussion of astronomical phenomena or of St. Stefan of Perm, it is because I believe I have nothing *to* offer. If I do not provide some possible completions during a bitter domestic dispute between close friends, it is probably because I do not want to *risk* making an offer.[3]

It is fairly easy to identify likely constraints of setting and of participant attributes and relationships. I have observed that, *ceteris paribus*, completions are less frequently proffered during sermons, lectures and Presidential press conferences than in cocktail party conversations, faculty meetings and "table talk". Such differences are not, of course, independent of the status differences between principal speakers and their audiences. I would argue that there probably are direct effects of the physical scene (thus, completion offers are even less likely in large lecture halls where speakers are on elevated platforms than in ordinary classrooms, and offers are less likely to come from members of larger audiences than smaller) and of "seriousness" or "formality" (Presidents may receive unwanted completion offers when they give political speeches ("heckling"), comics and late night show hosts get offers from their audiences and even the most distinguished of speakers may be treated with less respect when they speak before their peers). There are, moreover, some churches where completion and other offers are expected. The principle, however it requires qualification and specification, will hold for this speech phenomenon as it does for others.

Again, I expect that considerations of relations of power and affect among interlocutors and importance or "utility"[4] of completion offerers' interactional ends will act as critical constraints on appearance of the phenomenon just as they do in all talk. While I have a hunch that persons of greater or equal power within a relationship are more likely than those with lesser power to make offers and that offers are more likely amongst those sharing positive than negative affect, I cannot demonstrate this. It is impossible to list participant attributes that have to be taken into account; it is not easy to separate participant effects from those of interactional features, ends (goals, not outcomes), etc. Consider the following:

Presidential aides will not offer "open" completions to their bosses when the latter are on public display; they are expected, however, to provide information so their bosses won't appear uninformed. Teachers offer completions to students; graduate students are more likely than undergraduates to offer completions to teachers; all students can provide solicited completions — in such contexts completion slots may be used as "test" questions. Some couples do "routines" in which they finish one anothers' utterances. There are, moreover, considerations of tact and politeness regarding speaker attributes: it is usually considered appropriate to offer completions to adults learning a new language or to neophytes talking about an unfamiliar topic but it would be considered impolite for an adult to offer a completion for a stutterer who appears to be "groping" for a word.[5]

More generally, there are questions of the participant status of offerer, i.e. hearers with different "footings" with different "ratified or non-ratified" participant status (Goffman 1981) variously have rights or *obligations* to offer completions — or may be proscribed from making such offers except under extraordinary circumstances.

There are further complications; those listed hopefully suggest some as yet unexplored richnesses.

2.2. Some "interactional" features

Some completions are directly solicited by speakers using question formats, for example *What's his name* ...? or, as in the stereotype of language-learners, *How do you say* ...? Some are elicited by provision of slots, as seems to have been the case in the example at the beginning of this paper. Still others are offered without any obvious invitation by current speaker; in some instances it seems that hearers seize upon opportunities unintended by floor-holders. Each of these three types (solicited, elicited, unsolicited) may be more or less spontaneous or considered. Further complexities are added by the fact that some "unsolicited" offers are apparently "involuntary" (and sometimes regretted, hence our notion of "blurts"). While unsolicited completions are usually "freely offered" even if occasionally regretted, some are provided only reluctantly; reluctance is often a feature of responses to elicitations and solicitations — and not only those, like the example, which are in some sort of "test" format.

As will be seen when I discuss ends$_1$ (2.3), completions can be either collaborative (i.e. cooperative, or directed toward "helping" speaker) or competitive, or even hostile. Completions may also be collaborative in the sense that two or more hearers *jointly* provide a completion, whether serially or simultaneously (in chorus or in counter-point, etc., see also 2.5 on sequencing). I have heard one speaker provide a first name, a second a surname and still a third a location. Hearers may offer contradictory completions — with the accuracy of each's offer becoming a side-topic and a consequent basis for alienation from interaction (Goffman 1967) of those offering them — or the focus of meta-discussion by all parties to the interaction.

Offers may also vary in the degree to which they are overtly "contributed" to the speaker and the latter's ongoing talk. Responses to solicitations and elicitations are clearly in the form of appropriate contributions; their content may cause them to be viewed otherwise. Unsolicited offers may be seen as interruptions or as otherwise disruptive. They are sometimes made as "asides"; such asides can vary considerably in "blatancy". It will not always be clear to speaker or to other participants whether all, or only some, are intended to hear. This can become quite complicated when offerings are made very softly; perhaps so softly that their very production can be denied if challenged.

2.3. $Ends_1$

As has already been implied, completion offers may vary very considerably in the degree to which they are intendedly helpful — and to whom. They may be intendedly humorous; humour can be used to provide tension release, to embarrass a cointeractant, to enhance one's own status as a participant. A completion offerer may focus on speaker as recipient; (s)he may intend an offering for the entire group or for one or some other hearers. An offering may be aimed at some immediate interactional goal; it could be used to "set up" some private agenda, possibly "further down the line" in the ongoing, possibly even for some later encounter. It may be used to pursue different interactional goals with different participants — or multiple goals with same participants.

2.4. $Ends_2$

Outcomes are, of course, equally diverse. Completions may be unheard (by speakers in whose turns they are inserted, or by some or even all other cointeractants), they may be heard but *apparently* ignored (again by some, or all, participants) or simply disattended as the stream of interaction rushes ahead, they may be apparently ignored but later become the focus of comment or extended talk, there may be delayed "uptake" for all or some participants.[6] They may be accepted, with varying degrees of gratitude, appreciation and/or enthusiasm — and varying sincerity in overt response. They may be rejected; rejection may take the form of correction, denial, attack or other challenge; as already noted, they may simply be truly or putatively unheard or ignored. They may be interactionally helpful in several intended ways just suggested; they may be interactionally helpful in ways *not* intended. They may be harmoniously integrated into the ongoing, they may be assimilated, but with some difficulty, they may be disruptive. They may be harmoniously integrated — but at the cost of deflection of the ongoing from critical agenda concerns. They may cause participants to lose "proper involvement" (Goffman 1967). Recipients may, in short, experience and display (or not) the full range of emotional responses — and associated behaviours. "Misfires" are an ever-present risk.

2.5. Sequential features

Offers vary in placement and in timing. Those which are essentially responses would ordinarily be expected to appear at turn-transition junctures (Sacks, Schegloff & Jefferson 1974) i.e. immediately following a current speaker's utterance *or* as insertions in speaker pauses. This will be the case whether an invitation is an open one or whether a preferred respondent is designated. Eager offerers may, however, not wait for a turn-transition, and may interrupt or overlap current speaker.[7] Unsolicited offers can also be inserted in pauses, but in pauses which are not intended by current speaker as turn-transition junctures; they will also appear as interruptions and/or overlaps. Respondents other than designated next-speakers may exploit pauses to produce completions before the designated takes the floor; this may be particularly likely when a designated is either reluctant or wishes to formulate an optimally appropriate offer. Some completions, moreover, may be delayed while the offerer engages either in searching behaviour or in consideration of appropriateness and may not be offered until after a conversation has moved away from the venue appropriate for a completion offer. Indeed, it is sometimes the case that, as participants in a conversation, we will recover a "solicited" completion after the conversants have dispersed.

Similar and additional considerations will be seen to be involved in joint (collaborative) or simultaneous offers.

2.6. Act characteristics (cf. Hymes 1974)

Completions vary in content, length, form and inferential status. With regard to content, they can be on or off topic and informative or vacuous (to varying degree). Assessment of both topicality and informativeness can often be difficult, of course. The ambiguities of talk can be employed as a resource to use apparent topicality to shift topics — and the actually informative can be so subtly expressed as to elude both cointeractants and analysts who may not share knowledge. The difficulties of disambiguation (Grimshaw 1987; forthcoming, Chapter 2) can be very considerable; I cannot review them here.

Completions may be no more than vocalizations or syllables; they are often single words or short phrases; they can be sentences. In some instances they may be elaborated into full turns, with offerers gaining the floor to tell narratives or make "speeches". Offers can, of course, be employed as devices to obtain the floor; my concern here is with those where floor rights are not at issue.

While the corpus on which I draw for illustrations is a limited one, there is no reason to expect that variations in form of completions will be any less diverse than those of any other talk. They differ in syntactic complexity, in subtlety of semantic expression and in prosodic features. They differ in register (i.e. formal or colloquial), in "footing" (i.e. with offerer as animator, author or principal in Goffman's (1981) senses), and in type and degree of "bracketing" (see, again, Goffman 1981). These differences are signalled by variations in syntax, lexical selection and prosodic features. These same features, along with paralinguistic and kinesic accompaniments (e.g. smiles, grins, winks, furrowed brows, etc.) are further employed to signal differences in "key" (Hymes 1974; see also Goffman 1974) i.e. the offering's serious or humorous and sincere or mocking nature.

Finally (for purposes of this truncated overview), offered completions vary in the amount of inferential work which may be required to incorporate them meaningfully into the ongoing talk. Some will reflect speaker's (at least intended) subscription to Grice's (1975) Cooperative Principle; some will require no more than conventional (for either cointeractants or for their culture or sub-culture more generally) implicature; some will require quite considerable inferential work. Speakers may make errors, either in production or in their assessments of cointeractants' communicative competence. Hearers may not possess necessary skills for interpretation-as-intended or may have lapses in "proper involvement" (Goffman 1967). Analysts may either fail to recognize the necessity for implicature and/or disambiguation or may have the requisite resources. Each of these varieties of "communicative nonsuccess" occurs within the small corpus of completions offered in the text from which the following examples are drawn. Figure 1 summarizes the preliminary taxonomy I have developed for my exploration of the phenomenon of completion offers.

Context of situation constraints on completion offers:
    setting, scene and topic (Hymes' [1974] "act situation");
    participant (including audience) attributes, relationships;
    participant "ratification" status and "footing" (Goffman 1974).

Interactional features:
    elicited-solicited-offered
        (spontaneous-considered, freely or reluctantly offered);
    collaborative-competitive;
    individual-joint
        (if joint, same, similar or different);
    overt (blatant?)-covert (asides).

End$_1$ (goal, purpose):
    contributory to event purpose-otherwise;
    interactionally helpful-otherwise
        (e.g., helpful, hostile, humorous, etc.).

End$_2$ (outcome):
    unheard-spuriously unheard-heard but putatively ignored-accepted-accepted
        with corrections-challenged (attacked, corrected, denied, rejected);
    no, immediate, delayed "uptake";
    contributory to agenda-otherwise;
    harmoniously integrated-interactionally disruptive;
    recipient (and audience) reactions, e.g., amusement, anger, disgruntlement,
        embarrassment, gratitude, etc.

Sequential features:
    instantaneous-delayed;
    pause insertion-interruption-overlap;
    if joint, simultaneous-serial.

Act characteristics
    length: vocalization, syllable, word, sentence, longer;
    content: on-off topic informative-vacuous;
    form: grammatical, prosodic, kinesic, registral, key;
    inferential status, i.e., implicature required or not.

Figure 1. Some features of completion offers: An exploratory taxonomy

3. Two illustrative cases[8]

The two instances I employ for illustration of some variation in completion offers are all drawn from the text of a single event — a doctoral dissertation defence; while there *is* topic variation, the setting and scene are thereby "held constant". The principals in the two cases are the same, i.e. the chair and another member of the dissertation committee; their audience consists of the two additional members. Both examples occur during the course of the *in camera* evaluation session; the "theme" in both examples is construction of a consensual evaluation and assessment of the candidate's "prospects".

Readers would find the defence similar to others in most particulars (Grimshaw forthcoming). The four committee members are all full professors; three are males, the "outside" member is female — as is the absent candidate.

The method employed in my fuller analysis is an adaptation of Labov and Fanshel's (1977) "comprehensive discourse analysis"; limitations of space will constrain me to present only abbreviated analyses here. I proceed by first providing brief synoptic summaries of the textual and interactional contexts and display of the actual text (edited for easier reading) and then sketching the outlines of analyses.

3.1. Case one: The committee's response

The first case is one of third-party intervention, apparently intended to be helpful and, to some extent, apparently successful.

3.1.1 Synopsis

The talk of interest occurs during the *in camera* evaluation session. Adam had started the session by asking James for his reactions and James had responded by saying, among other things, *I would certainly be in favour of ... passing her*. He says some positive things, he also lists a number of complaints. One complaint is about the length of the dissertation (a motif throughout the defence), and Adam responds by telling an anecdote about a paper of his which grew to unmanageable length. Adam then turns to James and addresses him with (1); the fuller analysis reveals that he is attempting to get James to make a more refined (and positive) evaluation:

(1) Adam: so *you* say *pass*:
(2) James: oh, yeah. =
(3) Adam: = ... is *that* a: ..., that's a *neutral* term.
(4) (1.5 second pause)
(5) James: I'm not sure.
(6) Adam: I mean (1.0)
       I mean is

(7) Sherm: we don't we don't need, no ...
what are you *looking* for. Adam.
(8) Adam: *Well*, I'm I'm, I, I, I, just — I *guess* I have in the back of my mind, that I want to *be*, able to *convey*, *some* sense, of how:, the committee's response.
(9) Sherm: Oh, the committee's *response* to the enterprise as a whole.
(10) Pat: hm =

James then responds with what is essentially a recapitulation of his earlier evaluation, i.e. the jointly formulated characterization of what is "needed" elicits a response but it is not the response Adam wanted.

The utterances of concern are Adam's (8) and Sherm's (9); limitations of space will permit me to do no more than note some particularly interesting features abstracted from the more complete analysis.

3.1.2. Some act characteristics

While some of the dysfluencies in Adam's (8) doubtless reflect competition for floor space, they continue after Sherm has stopped speaking; it does not appear that Adam has clearly in mind what he wants to say. *Well* is often used as a temporizing and delaying feature as well as a floor-holding device and the speech which immediately follows it is marked by a very considerable repetition and apparent reluctance[9] or inability to come to a point. *Guess* and *some* are used as qualifying disclaimers. The last part of the utterance is also marked by repetitions, but is more fluent (smooth?) than the beginning. Adam's utterance is rich in formulaic expressions (see Fillmore forthcoming for an extended treatment of formulaic discourse in this segment of the defence). To state that a thought (or doubt, or whatever) is at "the back of one's mind" is to distance it somewhat and treat it as not a pressing issue. Conventional usage suggests, however, that it may be a litotes, i.e. that users of the expression actually consider the issue to which they refer as one which should *not* be overlooked (and which they think is in some danger of being so). *Convey* is conventionally employed, at least by some academics, as a euphemistic substitute for more direct "tell". In delicate matters of this sort, *convey* may also signal a kind of distancing from the possibly bald act of telling someone "bad news". Finally, it has been suggested that *convey* may be intended to remind Adam's companions of his official liaison role, in a counter to the implied accusation that he is taking too personal a role. *The committee's response* is another formulaic convention which, like *back of my mind*, *convey*, and *some sense of* is employed to distance participants from an act and, possibly, to obscure actual intentions and probable or likely effects.

Adam has been oriented to Sherm through his prior utterance (7), gradually moving forward to a "flight" position; he settles slightly as he finishes this speech. His face has a somewhat "quizzical" expression. He engages in substantial movement during this exchange, for example, sliding back in his chair while keeping his upper body forward, shifting his weight from one buttock to the other, even lifting his body from the chair using his arms on the chair arms for leverage. He shows considerable hand and arm movement. The overall impression is that of what Scheflen (1973) characterized as "aggressive defending", or even challenging.

Sherm's delivery, in contrast, is unhesitant and matter of fact. The *Oh*, which is somewhat shortened, is that of comprehension following bewilderment or uncertainty, i.e. *the light has dawned*. *Whole* is partly "swallowed". *The enterprise* and *the enterprise as a whole* are both used by sociologists (and other academics) to refer to projects of more than ordinary moment (and sometimes to their discipline, as in "the sociological enterprise"). The stress on *response* is modest; I cannot explain why it is placed there rather than on *committee's*.

Sherm nods his head affirmatively before he begins speaking (i.e. as Adam is uttering the formulaic *convey*, *some sense*). His utterance is accompanied by modest emphatic punctuation with his left hand. He raises his right forefinger and touches his ear. As he finishes, he nods affirmatively once again (somewhat more vigorously) and points toward James — though he does not orient toward him.

As will be seen, some implicature is required for interpretation of the collaboratively completed utterance; both the implicit addressee (James) and the other audience member (Pat) apparently accomplished the necessary inferential work without difficulty.

3.1.3. *Sequential and interactional features*

From the first point at which Sherm's (9) joins and overlaps with Adam's (8), their production is contrapuntal; the last part is actually more like a "round". It sounds very much like the following, with minimal actual overlap of 0, 1, and 2, and almost total overlap of the last two phrases:

```
        0          1 2        3                       4
   some sense/   /of/of how:   /the committee's response
                 /oh/   /the committee's/response to the enterprise as a whole.
```

Much talk, of course, exhibits this contrapuntal character. This case seems to me to be particularly interesting, however, because it displays collaborative construction of a completion by "offerer" and "recipient" in which both draw on shared knowledge of formulae but in which each part of the formula employed is validated by the recipient as it is produced. It seems as if Adam knows that there is some better way of trying to get James to provide a more refined evaluation than that he has been trying, that he casts around looking for help, that he starts by using the formulaic *convey some sense*, seizes upon Sherm's tentative beginning of another formula (i.e. *committee's response*, etc.) and that the two complete their formulation through a process of mutual "coaching" or "prompting".

3.1.4. Ends (goals, purposes) and ends (outcomes)

Whatever it was that Adam was attempting to accomplish in his exchange with James in lines (1)-(6) (I argue in forthcoming, Chapter 5 that he was seeking a more positive evaluation of the dissertation than James had provided), he was not being successful. It is evident from Sherm's question (7) to Adam that he was no less uncertain than James as to the end sought by Adam; it seems reasonable to infer that his entry into the ongoing was to obtain clarification of Adam's oblique talk so that the business of the committee might move forward.

Sherm's initial intervention was successful at least to the extent that it encouraged Adam to attempt to reformulate his request to James for a more elaborated (and/or more positive) evaluation of the dissertation. Adam continued to have difficulties, however, and Sherm continued to try to help, this time through his collaborative completion, with Adam himself, of the latter's clarified — though still oblique — request. Despite its continuing obscurity (which I have discussed elsewhere, *loc. cit.*) the reformulation *is* successful, as evidenced by both Pat's (10) confirmatory vocalization and James' restatement of his position (not shown). Thus, the completion contributed to the major agenda of the event, even though it did not succeed in eliciting the kind of evaluation sought by Adam. It was, moreover, harmoniously integrated; while neither the recipient nor Sherm's audience (James and Pat) acknowledged Sherm's contribution, neither did any of the three reject it as in any way inappropriate.

3.2. Case two: Older but smarter

The second case occurs as a pause insertion (in a minimal pause, not at a recognizable floor re-allocation juncture) and is *apparently* not intended to be taken seriously (see discussion below). It is neither accepted by current speaker nor acknowledged by other ratified participants.

3.2.1. Synopsis

In the immediately preceding talk Sherm has, in the course of presenting his own generally very favourable evaluation, remarked on the necessity that Lee (the candidate) being older, it would be critically important for her to complete quickly and publish at least *one piece* from her project *just to give her ... confidence* =. Following an elaboration by Sherm of his reasons for his position, Adam begins a response with his (31):

(31) Adam: Well, I can tell you what her view on *that* is.
            and *that*
(32) Sherm: what.
(31) Adam: is, .h I'm *older*, and therefore I'm in a *worse* competitive position, and I? and I've *really* got to produce.
(33) Sherm: but I'm *smarter* = (laughs) *yeah*. (said very softly)
(31) Adam: *and* I'm going to.
(33) Sherm: yeah. (said very softly)

3.2.2. Some act characteristics

Adam's voice is fairly loud, his pitch is low and his tempo is slow (though without hesitancy). The style of his utterance is portentous and lecture-like (what is sometimes called "plonking"). While the tempo is slow, the utterance is made with assurance. The *well* is used as a backwards referencing conjunction: it is the beginning of a volunteered comment — not of a reluctant response, i.e. it is the *well* of "let me tell you" and not that of "if you insist on an answer ..." The first *that* is anaphoric, referring back to Sherm's immediately prior (27) with its expressed concern about Lee; the second exophorically refers to a "view" of Lee which is located in the historical-ethnographic context of situation and not in the text. Both instances of repetition are associated with interruptions. Lerner notes that two formats are regularly used to project "compound turn units" like that Adam attempts, i.e. (1) contrast stress (I'm *older*) and, (2) parenthetical insertion into the projected contrast (*and therefore* ...).

The position attributed to Lee is stated in the form of a quotation. It is clear that the initial pronoun in Adam's utterance and those in the "quoted" material are not co-referential. At the same time, the "quote" itself is not claimed to be of an actual utterance, or even of one that Lee might possibly have made; it is, rather, suggested as something that Lee has "thought" to herself and formulated verbally to Adam in some less direct manner. Lerner makes the interesting suggestion that when a quote format is in force it is easier for other participants to enter into a turn space because of a "relaxation of the right to speak one's own turn to completion, since the talk in the turn is on another's behalf and not on one's own behalf". (I discuss the phenomenological status of topic and report in these utterances in forthcoming, Chapter 9.)

When Sherm begins his second interruption/overlap with his contrastive *but I'm smarter* in (33), Adam raises his voice and completes his characterization by speaking "over" the remaining overlapping portion of Sherm's utterance. He also raises his head slightly and raises and then lowers his eyebrows; he could be said to look "surprised". He then begins to use both head and eyebrow movements for emphasis until he completes his own utterance.

Sherm's first three words in (33) are said briskly, quite loudly, on falling intonation. The laugh is loud (boisterous) and sounds "pleased". The two *yeah*s, which are separated by pauses from the end of the laugh and from each other, follow Adam's *produce* and *going to*. They are very quiet. Sherm uses a quote attributed to Lee in the same manner which Adam is doing, namely, not as something that Lee actually did or might say but rather as reflecting what she has probably thought to herself and verbally conveyed in a less direct way. Within the "thought process" attributed to Lee, *but* serves as a discourse marker contrasting Lee's situation with that of other faculty who, while competitively advantaged because they are younger are less smart than Lee. It is not clear, however, whether the *but* should be labelled as adversative or contrastive (in the sense of these terms employed by Halliday and Hasan 1976). It is clearly contrastive in that the comparative *smarter* follows, with an implied contrast to others at Lee's career stage. It is also adversative, however, in that the clear implication is that Lee can succeed "in spite of" her disadvantages since she *is* smarter. It is not clear, further, that the usage can easily be assigned to either the external or internal classes identified by Halliday and Hasan, since the utterance does refer to a presupposed expression in Adam's utterance but is simultaneously a speaker-hearer, interactive, exchange.

Sherm has been "listening" to Adam. He begins to smile before he actually starts speaking (in anticipation of saying something humorous? in personal enjoyment of something he then decides to share?). His hands have been clasped in front of the lower part of his face. As he begins speaking, Sherm tilts his head back, turns up his lips, unclasps his hands and moves them downwards and out from his body. As he speaks, his body and extremities are in motion; he leans forward, uncrosses his legs, lifts his foot. As he laughs, he raises himself off his chair, shifts back and straightens up — simultaneously moving his feet up and down. In short, his hearty laugh has a full kinesic accompaniment. He continues "smiling" and "settling" well into the talk following. In sum, the kinesic record shows Sherm as thoroughly enjoying his own utterance. There are no visible signs of temporary "sobriety" during the times in which the two *yeah*s are uttered.

3.2.3. Sequential and interactional features

As I have noted, Sherm's completion offer is "squeezed into" Adam's talk at a juncture not intended for such use. While Adam contests Sherm's floor claim by raising his own voice and while he does display kinesic behaviours conventionally associated with "surprise", he does not make any verbal response. Complaint about the "interruption", acceptance or rejection of Sherm's "hypothesis" and other kinds of utterances would all "fit" but none are made. He simply "plows on" with his attribution of a position to Lee, neither accepting nor rejecting Sherm's offer. It seems reasonable to speculate, however, that his nonacknowledgement (as contrasted to explicit and open denial) of Sherm's offered attribution does, in fact, constitute a denial that Lee would make the claim that Sherm suggests she might.

While Sherm's (32) is clearly in the form of a request for information (the lack of question intonation notwithstanding), it seems to me that its actual function is to validate Adam's claim to the floor and to encourage Adam to provide the answer which is, indeed, forthcoming. Adam is, in fact, already launching into elaboration of the position which he attributes to Lee. It is reasonable to conclude that Adam's offer was rhetorical and that he fully intended to provide his answer whether asked or not. Sherm is not through. Having asked Adam what Lee's view is, and having let Adam continue with a formulation of Lee's view of the problem, Sherm once again offers an utterance completion. It is not, in this instance, successful, and Sherm completes his utterance by confirming Adam's simultaneously produced and overlapping answer to the latter's formulation of Lee's problem.

Sherm's offered completion to Adam's ongoing (31) is not accepted; it is essentially ignored. It is topically and syntactically appropriate in that it offers new information which identifies a possible solution to Lee's age-engendered disadvantage and in that Sherm inserts it, as a syntactically appropriate subordinate clause, at the very place where Adam himself produces such a clause. This topical relevance and grammaticality demonstrate that Sherm has been attending to Adam and following the latter's developing argument; it is not sufficient to get his offered completion accepted.

The fact of nonacceptance raises two questions: (1) Is there some reason why *any* proffered completion would have been rejected, i.e. was this an interactionally inappropriate juncture for such an offer to be tendered — and if so, why? (2) If *some* completion would have been accepted, what would have been accepted, what would it have looked like? I think that the answer to these questions is that most completions would have been rejected and that the only ones which would have been accepted would have looked much like Adam's own completion and would have to have had very similar illocutionary force (i.e. to have made the point that Lee knew she had to *produce* and was *going to*). One thing is clear, namely, Adam was not prepared to treat the matter lightly. Nor does he, as he might have done, pick up and reinforce in a serious manner Sherm's characterization of Lee as being a potentially successful competitor because she is *smarter*.

3.2.4. Ends (goals, purposes) and ends (outcomes)

There are substantial problems in interpreting the interactional significance of Sherm's utterance. Among possible interpretations of Sherm's "intent" are the following: (1) simple anticipation of Adam's probable completion; (2) ironic anticipation of Adam's possible completion, (a) for humorous purposes, (b) for purposes of tension reduction; (3) self (and other) reference, namely, *we* are older but smart — and it has worked for us; (4) assertion that Lee is indeed *smarter*. While it is not possible to adjudicate authoritatively amongst these and other possible interpretations of Sherm's intentions, examination of the contexts of text and of situation makes particularly plausible an inference that Sherm seized upon an opportunity too attractive to ignore — and offered his completion for the joint ends of displaying his cleverness, of reducing tension, and of reminding Adam not to be too serious. It is difficult to believe that he intended his contribution to be taken as a serious contribution to the agenda; both his laughter and his subsequent confirmation of Adam's "competing" completion at the end of his own utterance belie such an interpretation.

Whatever Sherm's intentions, the outcome is clear. Neither Adam nor Sherm's other interlocutors openly acknowledges Sherm's offer. Adam apparently hears it; his own utterance manifests temporary disarray as he recycles a fragment (*and I*). He treats the offer as if it were no more relevant to what he is saying than the "noise" which might result from an involuntary sneeze or the sound of a backfire from a passing car. The offer is, in sum, neither accepted as a contribution nor integrated *nor* treated as disruptive. That this characterization is probably correct is not analytically adequate, either for conversation analysts or for students of interactional accomplishment in talk. The former want to know whether and how such an outcome is systematic (i.e. "rule-governed"). The latter want to know what other interactional moves might have the same outcomes; and in what contexts (situational and textual) different outcomes might have followed for-all-intents-and-purposes "same" interactional moves. Answers to both questions will require investigation of many more instances of the phenomenon.

Finally, Lerner correctly observes that sneezes and backfires have social effects and are fit to the social organization of ongoing interaction. So too was Sherm's offering. It may be the case, moreover, that Sherm's action had long- term effects on the social organization of relations among participants in the immediate event under investigation; this cannot, of course, be demonstrated with the evidence at hand. More importantly, no such effects can be located in the text of the defence.

3.2.5. *Reasonableness and temporality*

Some interesting questions surface when we expand our interest in this event to include a look at implications of notions of *reasonableness* and *temporality*. If the notion of adjacency-pairs is extended to include the possibility of ellipsed or implicit questions as first-pair parts (an extension which will probably not be acceptable to many conversational analysts), then Sherm's (33) can be heard as a second pair-part reasonably adjacent to Adam's (31) (up to the overlap) as first pair-part (Schegloff & Sacks 1973; Sacks, Schegloff & Jefferson 1974). It can be heard as reasonable on at least two grounds, namely, (1) it fits comfortably as a possible-plausible answer into a slot reserved for an answer to a question such as, "How might a person who is older and in a poor competitive position overcome those disadvantages?" and (2) it is consonant with a view shared by at least Adam and Sherm that Lee is, indeed, *smarter* (than some unspecified set of others).

The question here is, in what sense does/can a "reasonable" answer reflect communicative nonsuccess (Grimshaw 1980; 1982; forthcoming, Chapters 8-9), and what variety? Is it possible to answer reasonably *and nonaccidentally* without some understanding?

Attention to the timing of Sherm's (33) and of equivalent offerings in similar exchanges reveals additional complicating dimensions for analysis and interpretation. I have just claimed that Sherm's utterance can be interpreted as a reasonable second pair-part to that portion of Adam's (31) which had been completed when Sherm spoke; the record shows it is not what Adam had planned. If Sherm had permitted Adam to finish, he could then have offered/provided a slightly different (33), which would still have been an appropriate second pair-part to Adam's (31) *and* have manifested understanding of Adam's full illocutionary intent, namely, something like, "And since? I'm smarter. I can". Such an offering could have been made either at the end of Adam's (31) in a new speaker turn, or even after *produce*. Sherm's contribution might then have supplemented Adam's in some quite complex ways. First, it would have contributed to a joint characterization of Lee as both committed to the hard work necessary for productivity and possessed of the competence ("smartness") to do so. As the talk occurs, it is possible to read Sherm's version as meaning that Lee believes that her intellectual capabilities alone will help her overcome her disadvantages; an interpretation supported by Sherm's use of the adversative *but*. Adam, in contrast, takes Lee's high competence as given and focuses on her recognition of requirements and commitment to meeting them. Second, Sherm, by extending Adam's use of comparatives (*older, worse*) with his *but ... smarter*, attributes to Lee a conflict orientation of contest with specifiable others who are younger and in better competitive positions. Adam, in contrast, switches from a comparative frame to an emphasis on maximum individual effort in terms of some impersonal standard, attributing to Lee a competitive orientation. Thus, while both the overall characterizations which emerged are deemed as positive by at least some academics, namely, Sherm's that Lee is competent, confident (maybe even arrogant) and aggressive and Adam's that she is competent, highly motivated and self-driven, they *are* different. If Sherm had made even a very similar utterance (e.g. that suggested above) *slightly later*, the jointly constructed characterization would have been much closer to that of Adam's (31) alone.

It is conceivable, but unlikely in my view, that Sherm fully understood what Adam had and was going to say in the remainder of his (31) and intended his (33) as a contrastive, qualifying or elaborative remark. Since Sherm's talk elsewhere in the text reveals an evaluation close to Adam's *and* since his offering had, at least in part, a humorous intent, such an interpretation is not persuasive. We must ask then, in what sense can it be said that Sherm did or did not understand Adam? If Adam's (31) was an instance of communicative nonsuccess, of what variety was it? Should judgment about communicative success or nonsuccess be made about responses to utterances which have not been completed? If Sherm is at fault what was his defeasibility (*loc. cit.*)? What is the relation of failures to follow turn-taking rules and those of sequencing as sources of communicative nonsuccess to other varieties of nonsuccess? Sherm's response is, finally, reasonable — can nonsuccess be said to have occurred at all? What, then, must be done to make the exchange analytically interpretable?

3.2.6. *Humour, tension-release and interactional responsibility*

Sherm's (33) is reasonable (in the sense outlined above) in content. It is also acceptably (though not optimally) placed. It does not appear to have been intended to be taken fully seriously. I use the modifier because I am not saying that the content of his utterance should be ignored because of its form; there is a question as to what degree of seriousness was intended. I do not think, for example, that Sherm would have risked the pleasure of "having some fun", if he had thought he might be putting the candidate at risk. At the same time, he used a variety of topic exploitation to change a serious discussion, at least in part and at least momentarily, into a humorous one. I don't think it can be argued that he did not see his contribution as a humorous one; his timing, voice quality and his own following laughter and his kinesic behaviours all document the intendedly humorous status of his utterance.

There are, however, imponderables, among them Sherm's probable interactional intent. Was he attempting to defuse what he perceived as mounting tension over a prospective evaluative outcome? Was he signalling to Adam that the latter should not take himself too seriously? Speak for Lee? Get into potentially problematic areas? Was he simply unable to resist the temptation to "score" with the opportunity with which Adam had provided him? There are other questions, even less amenable to principled documented answers. To what extent is the exchange simply a recapitulation and play upon clichés of academic thought and discourse and formulaic expressions about careers (much of Adam's utterance is formulaic) with

Sherm playing upon academic preoccupation with smartness? Is it possible that Adam's beginning has reminded Sherm of the aphorism, "too soon old — too late smart"? (Such questions as this last raise deeper problems about, for example, cognitive "triggers" in completion offers, which cannot be considered here.)

The above considerations, and others could be adduced, lead me to the conjecture that while we cannot determine whether Sherm in some way understood all or part of the referential content of Adam's ongoing, we can conclude that he understood Adam's illocutionary intent (to make a serious positive comment about Lee's future behaviour, and so on) and chose to act as if he had not (i.e. he chose to Misunderstand (see *loc. cit.* for an explanation of my use of upper case here) Adam's illocutionary intent). This is a variety of Misunderstanding which is *related* to "taking things literally", that is, declining to treat conventions as such, or refusing to employ invited implicatures; it also differs from those cases. It differs in that Adam's utterance is neither a convention nor in any obviously intended way a violation of Grice's maxims. Sherm, instead of taking the "not-intended-to-be-treated-seriously" seriously, has taken the "intended-to-be-treated-seriously" unseriously. This conclusion strongly implies a need for distinguishing between understanding the referential content of locutions and understanding their illocutionary point or intent: while someone may mishear by not understanding either content or intent or both, Misunderstanding requires that intent be understood and that understanding be denied and can include understanding and denial of referential content.

This last distinction permits us to say that Sherm has Misunderstood even though we cannot determine whether or not he understood Adam's completed or projected referential content. The distinction can be schematically summarized in the following simple diagram:

	REFERENTIAL CONTENT	ILLOCUTIONARY POINT (INTENT)
UNDERSTANDING	+	+
MISHEARING	+/−	+/− (one must be negative)
MISUNDERSTANDING	+/−	−

Left unanswered is the question of whether Sherm correctly anticipated the likely referential content of Adam's further projected utterance; the question is moot for present purposes.

In my more extended treatments of this exchange (Grimshaw forthcoming), I identify additional questions and directions for research (particularly with regard to Adam's own, insistent, completion). I believe, however, that the truncated discussion in this paper demonstrates the interactional complexity and the potential theoretical relevance of such offers and other instances of displayed understanding.

In conclusion, the two cases presented here show how the interaction of "act characteristics", "ends" and "results" make some completions more and others less significant for the accomplishment of immediate and longer-range agendas of participants. I hope that readers will find the slot I have provided sufficiently challenging that they will provide completions.

Notes

1. My interest in talk is in how it is so employed by its users as to facilitate accomplishment of their interactional agendas, i.e. to "get things done" or "attain goals" through what they say, and how. Conversational analysts, in contrast, believe that a prior task must be "local explanations" which can be documented from the actual text, arguing that "only after the systematics are well described can some gain be made by looking at the uses some sort of organization is put to". Conversation analysis (CA) researchers will be critical of my analysis because, in their view, "There is not a clear distinction made between an initial intuitive sense of the materials and the analysis of the showably-oriented-to-features and their systematic relationships which produce the social world as a comprehensible and intuitively accessible occasion — as well as (though secondarily) an object for analysts". I am most grateful to Gene Lerner (from whose personal communication the quotes above are abstracted) for providing me with a critical, instructive and provocative reading of an earlier version of this paper. He is now completing a dissertation which employs a CA perspective in investigation of a considerably larger body of materials in a considerably more systematic way. I have referenced a number of his comments and suggestions in what follows; he is in no way responsible for either my misuse of what he has said or for my failure to subscribe to a CA perspective in my own analysis. I *do* believe that my work represents more speculation and that at least some of my inferences are validated by reference to features of the ethnographic-historical (situational) and textual contexts. At this juncture in the development of sociological study of discourse there is, I believe, room for both our enterprises.

2. Lerner does not believe that my taxonomy is useful. He writes: "Enumerating theoretically derived parameters offered as explanatory of some describable phenomenon is an endless task. The 'defining dimensions' or rather 'constitution of the situation' — since we are dealing with actual happenings on particular occasions — must be found in the *conduct of the interaction* by and for the parties". I do not disagree. We differ, however, in our views of what constitutes relevant "conduct". He would apparently limit that domain to recorded behaviour of actual happenings on particular occasions; I include other behaviours of participants which are known from the historical-ethnographic record and

from text more remote from a "particular occasion". Analysts and participants are continually challenged by the necessity of *disambiguating* conduct; I have described elsewhere (1987; forthcoming, Chapter 2) how I understand disambiguation to be done.

3. As will be seen below, I might nonetheless make completion offers in the course of such discussions or such disputes. Such offers would presumably be topic independent in the sense that they would be humorously intended to reduce tension and/or perhaps employed in efforts to initiate topic shifts. In the case of disputes I might feel constrained to provide solicited completions.

4. "Utility" combines considerations of salience of an end for an actor *and* the actor's perception of likely "costs" to both her/himself and the cointeractant(s) from whom provision of the end is sought. See Grimshaw (1980, 1981 or forthcoming).

5. Lerner nicely observes that, "the non-entry into a stutterer's 'groping' won't necessarily be a matter of politeness, but a participant's analysis that what is happening is not a search for a word". Such an analysis probably is made; I suspect that not "helping" despite experienced tension is a matter of consideration for the speaker. Indeed, children are sometimes explicitly instructed not to make such offers — just as they are told not to remark on other infirmities.

6. Each of these outcomes represents a variety of "communicative nonsuccess". See Grimshaw (1980; 1982; and forthcoming, Chapters 8-9).

7. As Lerner observes, it is the placement of such offers which permits them to be identified by participants (and analysts) *as* eager. In his view, "the issue is not that they can be spotted as eager, but what systematic provides a means to do recognizable eagerness!" His point is well taken.

8. The original version of my paper included discussion of a third instance involving the same committee member and the candidate which occurred during the course of a dispute over the latter's charges of past sex discrimination. To shorten my paper, I agreed to drop the third example. I will be pleased to provide copies of it to interested readers.

9. Such an interpretation is documented in Grimshaw (forthcoming, Chapter 5). The delicacies of negotiations over evaluation of the candidate's performance are treated at length in this monograph.

The textual basis of verbal inflections: the case of Yatzachi Zapotec

Carol C. Mock

Introduction

Before text linguistics became popular, many linguists used to assume that the reason a particular morpheme was appropriate to use in particular contexts was that it had a more or less specific meaning apart from the contexts in which it was used. But the importance of texts is finally being recognized, and J.R. Firth's dictum that "meaning is use in context" has been put in more modern terms: discourse is what determines the meaning of linguistic items. Hopper and Thompson (1980) argue for the importance of *narrative* discourse as the defining context for the cluster of semantic parameters that characterize transitivity: the number of participants in a sentence, kinesis, aspect, punctuality, volitionality, polarity, mode, agency, affectedness and individuation of the object of a transitive sentence. All of these relate to the traditional notion of transitivity in some way; as Hopper and Thompson point out in the preface to their 1982 collection, "Decisions as to how to present events and situations with respect to the people and things involved in them are decisions affecting the transitivity of a clause in actual language use" (1982: xii). Hopper and Thompson (1984) make the further claim that even the familiar categories "noun" and "verb" are imposed on words only variably, to the extent that the items happen to function in particular discourse contexts either to identify something as an entity that can be manipulated (i.e. as a noun), and to affirm or deny the occurrence of an event or the existence of a relation (i.e. as a verb).

If we take seriously the claims that Hopper and Thompson make about the discourse basis of grammatical categories (the idea that the formal meaning of structural elements and grammatical categories is controlled by the pragmatic functions they fulfill), systemic linguists must re-examine their understanding of how grammatical semantics are organized. Systemic functional grammar has long claimed that the formal meaning of grammatical categories is based on their relational status as options within systems at particular ranks: choices giving formal shape to more general socio-semantic options from a higher level of organization. If, however, the discourse functions of individual morphemes directly determine their formal, grammatical meaning, it becomes a serious theoretical question whether morphemes also realize choices at particular places within grammatical system networks. That is, in what sense if any can we say that grammatical categories are meaningful as distinctive choices? Or that grammar is organized in terms of a limited number of paradigmatic options?

One way to approach the issue is to analyze texts to see whether the grammatical categories that we have taken to be a single set of choices are actually opposed to each other *in the same sorts of context*. I mean "same context" both in syntactic and discourse-functional terms: for example, an independent clause (a syntactic matter) as narrative event (a textual function); or a syntactically dependent clause used as background information. Narrative texts have been studied in enough detail that by now we have a handle on their discourse structure. If we find that two supposedly opposed grammatical options do *not* both occur in roughly identical discourse contexts, but serve instead as formal signals to *define* such contexts as different from chunks of discourse having other communicative purposes, then we have misanalyzed the relations between them by assuming they belong to a single system. For example, unless both perfective and imperfective aspects occasionally turn up in the *same* kinds of discourse contexts, e.g. both as plot moves or both in similarly backgrounded material, the apparent opposition may be only an artifact of analysis, a false contrast resulting from comparing forms that belong in complementary contexts.

In this regard, an attractive part of grammar to investigate is the inflection of verbs for mode and aspect. Such categories lend themselves to textual analysis. For one thing, it is relatively easy to know when we have found an instance of the formal item we are seeking; and for another, inflected verbs are frequent enough in most texts (except laundry lists and inventories) so that normal patterns of occurrence can be compared with rarer cases. A study of the use of mode and aspect in narrative texts should demonstrate whether they are in fact grammatically contrastive, or whether they are controlled by the heightened or reduced transitivity of different portions of the text. An analysis of their discourse roles also constitutes a test of Hopper and Thompson's claim that verbal mode and aspect contribute to the degree of transitivity of individual sentences and to the foregrounding of major events against a backdrop of subsidiary information (for a similar test in another language, see Kalmár 1982). In this paper, I consider the relation between textual functions and modal/aspectual inflections in a language that has only four morphemes for mode and aspect (and no tenses at all), the variety of Zapotec spoken in the town of Yatzachi in the Sierra de Juárez northeast of the city of Oaxaca, Mexico.[1] My textual data comes from Inez Butler's *Gramática Zapoteca de Yatzachi el Bajo* (Mexico, D.F.: Instituto Lingüístico de Verano, 1980), a detailed grammar packed with carefully identified data. Three texts have been taken as a data base (with a total of 309 finite clauses): Butler 1980: 33ff.; 1980: 48ff.; and 1980: 283ff.

According to Hopper and Thompson (1980), the semantic transitivity parameters combine more or less freely in such a way that individual sentences can be characterized on a cline from most highly transitive to least transitive (but see Tsunoda 1985 for combinatorial restrictions among the parameters). Furthermore, high-transitivity characteristics are preferentially selected for the main events of a narrative, in the cognitive-pragmatic process called "foregrounding" (1980: 255). Although a great deal of information about the nature of foregrounding in narrative texts has been accumulating (e.g. Jones and Longacre 1979), it remains to be verified whether foregrounding, the textual prominence of particular clauses, is accomplished by means of the same mechanisms in genres other than narrative.

Verbal mode and aspect are said to be among the grammatical features that manifest transitivity, although their connection with narrative foregrounding is most directly obvious. With reference to mode in particular, many languages make a grammatical distinction between "realis" and "irrealis" mode — the contrast between real and merely possible events — and take realis as the more highly transitive mode, for the simple reason that it makes more sense to report things that really happen. Within aspectual systems, perfective aspect ranks higher on the transitivity scale than does imperfective aspect; we normally find it more useful to report events as complete wholes rather than as on-going processes, especially in the main line of narrative texts. In the course of this study, I have found that the verbal inflections of Yatzachi Zapotec do support the Hopper-

Thompson transitivity hypothesis in its general outlines, but that text-formation processes are complex enough that mode and aspect are not completely determined by the discourse contexts in which they occur. Thus, although a particular mode or aspect is the *unmarked* choice in a given discourse context, certain other modal or aspectual choices are also possible as highly effective alternatives, in the same context. The theory of markedness plays an important role in the matter, challenging us to refine our insights about grammatical categories beyond a simple formalization of their paradigmatic relations into system networks.

Analytical procedures

My approach to the question of the relation between discourse function and verbal inflections has been to analyze the finite clauses of the three narrative texts quantitatively from three complementary perspectives: according to their textual function, according to the presence of particular transitivity parameters in each clause and the cooccurrences among them, and according to how well the transitivity parameters correspond to the textual function of each clause. Finite clauses in Yatzachi Zapotec are identifiable as those with surface-grammatical subjects whose verbs are inflected for mode and aspect. They include not only independent main clauses, but also clauses embedded as nominal modifiers (relative clauses) and as noun phrases (nominalizations). Restricting the data in this way yields the bulk of relevant data on mode and aspect in Yatzachi Zapotec, for infinitives and other deverbal forms are rare.

In the first analysis of the data, I classified each finite clause in terms of the functional contribution it made to the development of the story, using the following set of functional categories: in-sequence moves in the plot, scene-setters, direct quotations, quotation-framing devices, and comments the narrator made "on the side", directly to the audience. Ultimately, in order to test the transitivity hypothesis with minimal complications, I merged these finely detailed functional categories into three more general ones: plot-moves, direct conversation, and background material.

Background material, however, is so nonspecific as a functional category that it might be useful to establish notional subdivisions within it. On the basis of my observations alone, the major subtypes of background in these Zapotec stories would seem to include the expression of intentions and results, the setting and shifting of temporal frames for the narrative action (including introductory remarks), and identifying participants and props by means of their qualities, actions, or locations, usually in a relative clause.

After making the functional classification, I tabulated all the grammaticized transitivity parameters used in each clause. For Yatzachi Zapotec these are polarity, verbal inflections for mode and aspect, the number of overt or clearly recoverable participants (agents and objects) and the syntactic status of each clause as independent or dependent. Individuation and affectedness of verbal objects could not be investigated adequately because so few clauses in the texts had objects at all. Finally I cross-classified all these data to see whether they supported the transitivity hypothesis, that is, whether the high-transitivity signals identified in the second procedure occurred as plot-moves more frequently than they did in backgrounded or conversational discourse. Finding that they did so, I then asked the question systemic linguists need to answer: given the discourse basis of grammar, is there any room left for a real choice among modes and aspects, or are verbal inflections completely in harmony with the general foreground/background structure of the narratives? Note that the first step of the analysis was basically non-structural, being oriented to the narrative development of the texts: the finite clauses were compared at this stage for the sole purpose of seeing how they were used in the stories. Some such separation between formal and pragmatic analysis is essential if we are to avoid circular reasoning.

Before looking in detail at the results, let us consider the grammatical systems which would appear to underlie Yatzachi Zapotec mode and aspect. First of all, there are two grammatically signalled verbal modes, realis and irrealis. Irrealis mode, more commonly called "potential aspect" by Zapotecanist scholars, is used mainly to refer to future plans and unfulfilled past intentions, to make polite commands, and in verbal complements after verbs of obligation and desire. Such functions are modal rather than aspectual; but as Wallace (1982) points out, normal usage in any language blurs the clear boundaries we postulate for grammatical categories. Irrealis mode is marked by a prefix, while realis mode has no overt marker. In realis mode, one or another aspectual prefix fills the same morphological position that is filled by a modal prefix in irrealis mode:

(1)   a.   *n- aquə* "is, was"
               STAT-be
               (STAT = stative aspect)

b. *go-quə* "was, used to be"
   PERF-be
   (PERF = perfective aspect)
c. *g- aquə* "could be"
   IRR-be
   (IRR = irrealis mode)

Within realis mode, Yatzachi Zapotec verbs take one of three aspects, perfective, called "completive aspect" by Zapotecanists because of its normally telic focus,[2] continuative, and stative. In terms of their perfectivity, the last two are subcategories of imperfective aspect; see the system network fragment below.

Because there is no perfect aspect morpheme in Yatzachi Zapotec, the stative often assumes a perfect interpretation, as predicted by aspect theorists such as Friedrich (1974) and Givón (1982). In particular, the stative inflection of motion verbs is sometimes equivalent to an English or Spanish perfect (e.g. "has gone", "has come"). It is difficult to think of "have gone" as imperfective, despite my analysis of the stative as a subcategory of imperfective, without taking into account the "topography" of motion verbs in Zapotecan and Mixtecan languages: "having gone (but not returned)" is only half of the concept of going on a journey, and is thus incomplete or imperfective; cf. Butler (1980: 301-310) for this interpretation in Yatzachi Zapotec, Kuiper and Merrifield (1975) for the phenomenon in Diuxi Mixtec, Speck and Pickett (1976) for Texmelucan Zapotec, Pickett (1976) for Istmus Zapotec.

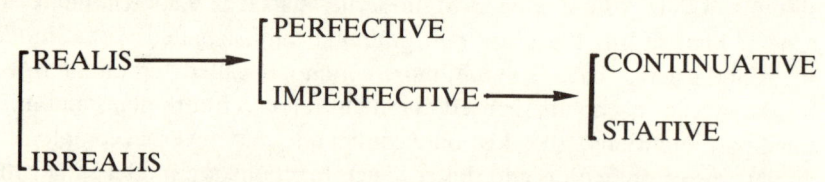

```
                  ┌ PERFECTIVE
┌ REALIS ────────►│                              ┌ CONTINUATIVE
│                 └ IMPERFECTIVE ────────────────►│
│                                                 └ STATIVE
└ IRREALIS
```

The realization of the mode and aspect options is morphologically complex, having a number of separate shapes that result from phonological and morphological processes. Rather than listing all the forms, I refer the interested reader to Butler's grammar and present only a sample allomorph for each selection expression:

[irrealis] *g-*   [realis : perfective] *gw-*
                   [realis : imperfective : continuative] *ch-*
                   [realis : imperfective : stative] *n-*

(Realis mode and imperfective aspect have no morphemic realization independent of the subaspects continuative or stative.)

Correlations among the parameters of transitivity

The quantitative data accumulated in this study support the Hopper-Thompson notion of transitivity in two ways. For one thing, the various high-transitivity parameters tend to cooccur within the same clauses even without an obligatory grammatical rule that they should do so; secondly, these same features occur most frequently in the pieces of text classified on non-structural grounds as plot moves. Note that these data provide a more general type of evidence for the transitivity hypothesis than what is presented in Hopper and Thompson (1980) where they point to *obligatory* pairing of transitivity features in the morphosyntax or semantics of a clause. Here the cooccurrences are statistical rather than absolute. Tables 1 through 4 summarize the correlations among the grammaticized transitivity features, showing their tendency to cluster together in a single clause. (Text 2 has been omitted from Table 4 because its aspect profile is skewed by a preponderance of dialogue.)

Let us look at some of the details:

A. More than 82% of all finite clauses have realis mode, and all but 3% of realis mode clauses are also affirmative (Table 1). Looking at this fact from the other side, we can say that irrealis mode is strongly associated with negative polarity: a full 1/4 of irrealis clauses are also negative, whereas only 3% of realis clauses are. Thus there exists a positive correlation between two low-transitivity features, negative polarity and irrealis mode.

B. One part of the numerical data runs contrary to the predicted association among high-transitivity features. Clauses in realis mode, which Hopper and Thompson claim are higher on the transitivity scale than clauses in irrealis mode, do not cooccur with two participants, an agent (A) and a patient (O), as often as they do with only one participant (A or S): two-thirds of all finite clauses had only one participant, and more than half of them were also realis (Table 2). Upon closer study, these skewed proportions prove to be the result of including conversational sections of the texts in the calculations. Dialogue has the lowest proportion of clauses in realis mode (only 70%) and the highest proportion of two-participant clauses

Table 1. Relative frequencies of mode and polarity features in finite clauses

	Realis	Irrealis	n
Affirmative	.80	.13	295
Negative	.025	.045	22
n =	262	55	317

Table 2. Relative frequencies of mode and participant features in finite clauses

	Realis	Irrealis	n
Two participants	.24	.09	104
One participant	.58	.09	213
n =	262	55	317

Table 3. Relative frequencies of polarity and participant features in finite clauses

	Affirmative	Negative	n
Two participants	.32	.01	104
One participant	.61	.06	213
n =	295	22	317

Table 4. Relative frequencies of participant and aspect features in finite clauses

	Perfective	Imperfective	n
Two participants	.185	.095	44
One participant	.34	.38	113
n =	82	75	157

(40%). There appears to be a simple pragmatic reason behind this distribution: the interpersonal exchanges of conversational sections of these narratives are most frequently commands and expressions of the speaker's intentions, both of which normally select irrealis mode in Yatzachi Zapotec; and commands often ask the interlocutor to act upon something, in a two-participant clause.

Interestingly, in Butler's detailed description of uses for irrealis mode (pp. 30-33), almost half of the separate functions she identifies have to do with intentions or commands, and more than a third of all uses specified are tied to concurrent use of negatives. Irrealis mode, as a semantic "area", encompasses both purposes and negations, and there is surely another pragmatic link between negation and the interpersonal metafunction; for why do we bother to assert that something is *not* so, except to clear up someone's misconceptions about what *is* so or to wriggle out from under accusations? That is, in direct dialogue, negation is equivalent to both denial of truth value and contradiction of another person's point of view, and is often linked to the assertion of an alternative reality.

C. Although it has not been possible to make a meaningful quantitative study of the correlation between polarity and aspect in realis mode, there being only eight instances of negative realis clauses, polarity does show a weak tendency to correlate with another transitivity parameter, the number of clause particants (Table 3): affirmative polarity occurs in a larger proportion of two-participant clauses than in the more numerous one-participant clauses. Put another way, there are more than four times as many negative clauses having only one participant than negative clauses with two (2 negatives in 104 two- participant clauses, 20 negatives in 213 one-participant clauses).

D. Cross-classification of the parameters of aspect and the number of participants also turned up a positive association between perfective aspect and the presence of two participants (Table 4): of all two-participant realis clauses in Texts 1 and 3, 66% (or 29) took perfective aspect, whereas only 47% of the more numerous one-participant clauses did. Perfective clauses are twice as likely to have two participants, both an agent and an object, than are imperfective clauses in these texts.

To summarize these correlations, we can say that the formal parameters of affirmative polarity, realis mode, perfective aspect and two participants in the clause, which Hopper and Thompson list among other signals of high transitivity, do in fact occur together in Yatzachi Zapotec texts, supporting one another in a quantifiable way. The significance of this fact will become clearer when we consider the way these grammatical factors correlate with the discourse functions — plot moves, background information and conversation.

Syntactic independence and the transitivity hypothesis

But first let us look at a factor which Hopper and Thompson (1980) did not list: the syntactic independence of a clause. It is reasonable to suspect that syntactic independence plays a role in the pragmatic process of foregrounding; that is, that highly transitive, foregrounded material is more likely to turn up in independent clauses than in clauses that have either been rankshifted or pushed down hypotactically. This may be so because the main communicative thrust of a narrative (assertion of the sequencing of events) is often elaborated upon by descriptions and explanatory comments made on the side. In English, for example, hypotaxis is a common way of indicating that a comment is considered to be non-essential information (e.g. "However you look at it, the problem demands a solution."; compare the stronger interpersonal effect of a paratactic version: "You can look at it any way you want, but the problem still demands a solution"). Holding syntactic independence constant and taking the five grammaticized transitivity parameters of Yatzachi Zapotec as free variables, I find that high-transitivity features are more likely to occur in independent clauses than in dependent ones. As shown by the statistics in Table 5, realis mode, perfective aspect, imperfective-continuative aspect, and two-participant verbs are all

Table 5. Correlations between transitivity parameters and syntactic independence

	Affirmative	Realis	Perfective	Continuative	2-Particip.
Clause type:					
Independent (n = 217)	92%	87%	73%	54%	35%
Dependent (n = 100)	95%	73%	55%	21%	29%
n =	295	262	214	153	104

more common in *in*dependent clauses; the exception to this tendency is affirmative polarity, which is virtually ubiquitous in both types of clause:

Realis mode occurs in 87% of all independent clauses, but in only 73% of the dependent ones. Within realis mode, perfective aspect shows a weak positive correlation with syntactic independence: almost 3/4 of the independent realis clauses take perfective aspect, as compared to only 55% of the dependent clauses. Within imperfective aspect, the subcategory of continuative correlates strongly with syntactic independence: in independent clauses, 54% of the imperfectives are continuative, but in the dependent clauses only 21% are; that is, only 1/5 of the imperfective verbs in dependent clauses are continuative rather than stative. Interpreting this in terms of its ideational meaning, we can say that imperfective aspects normally turn up in the dependent clauses to indicate either enduring qualities or particular locations (both of which take stative aspect), rather than to express that an event is either habitually true or currently in progress (two of the functions of continuative aspect).

Overtly transitive verbs are not common in these texts. Of all the finite clauses, only 1/3 had two participants (that is, both an object *and* an Agent, Actor or Perceiver), or a clearly recoverable direct object distinct from the other participant. There is but a weak correlation in these data between number of participants and syntactic independence, the tendency following the same pattern as the other correlations (transitive verbs turning up more often in independent clauses than in dependent ones): 35% of the independent clauses had two participants, as opposed to 29% of the dependent ones.

Thus it is clear that syntactic independence is a structural fact that correlates positively with the parameters listed in Hopper and Thompson (1980). Unlike the parameters they propose, however, it is not something that makes much sense within the confines of an individual clause. Rather, like foregrounding itself, it is primarily a relation among sentences. Whether or not there are other transitivity parameters, as well, which cluster in quantitatively identifiable ways with the ones we have considered, remains a question for future research.

Mode, aspect and text structure

Let us turn now to the crux of the matter, to how completely these formal parameters match up with the discourse functions Hopper and

Table 6. Correlations between semantic transitivity and textual function

	Plot moves	Background	Quotations
Kinetic event	95%	40%	61%
Punctual event	87%	29%	52%
Volitional agent	81%	49%	53%
n =	95	125	97

Thompson claim to be their foundation. In this section, I describe the distribution of mode and aspect in relation to the discourse structure of the texts, and identify the types of context in which *choices* of mode and aspect are possible, noting the meaning of each modal and aspectual option in various contexts and taking into consideration the role of system-based markedness.

Tables 6 and 7 summarize the distribution of the transitivity parameters, both semantic and grammaticized, according to their textual functions as plot move, background information, or dialogue. It is strikingly clear from the quantified data that the features identified by Hopper and Thompson as highly transitive (whether grammaticized or not) are more characteristic of plot moves than of background material, while the conversational data lie somewhere in between. Table 6 shows that the occurrences of kinesis, punctuality and volitionality, which are not grammaticized choices in Yatzachi Zapotec, are not as extreme as those of the grammaticized features in Table 7; but even so, these three features are consistently more likely to turn up in plot moves than in dialogue or background material. Kinetic and punctual events are most common in plot moves, as are volitional agents: 95% of all plot-move clauses have kinetic verbs, 87% of them express punctual events, and 81% have volitional agents.

Table 7 shows the textual distribution of the transitivity parameters that are integral parts of Zapotec grammar. Some of the correlations between these grammaticized features and the structure of narrative texts are categorical in nature: there are no negatives and no irrealis verbs in plot move clauses, and virtually all the plot moves also take perfective aspect.[3] Negatives turn up only in two pragmatic contexts, indirect quotations (two-thirds of all occurrences of negative morphemes), where they function to contradict a preceding assertion or to form negative commands, and in backgrounded evaluations in which the narrator comments upon the plot or

Table 7. Correlations between grammaticized transitivity and texutal function

	Plot moves	Background	Quotations
Affirmative	100%	96%	88%
Realis	100%	88%	70%
Realis perfective	96%	22%	2%
Independent clause	80%	42%	84%
Two participants	34%	17%	40%
n =	95	125	97

the participants.

Unexpectedly, only 80% of the plot moves were realized as independent clauses, which raises the question of how to analyze reported events that in the real world would seem to advance the narrative, but which are buried syntactically in various sorts of subordinate constructions. Upon investigating the problem in detail, I found that one major cause for such subordination is the temporal "chunking" of the text; almost all the subordinated plot moves follow directly after independent clauses which serve to reset the temporal or situational frame of the narrative by announcing a new circumstance. Example (2) uses a grammatically independent clause to tell what the attendant activities were during which a significant plot move, meeting a demon, took place:

(2) *Na' lažə'ə   -bo' lo'o yixə'ə-nə'   ch-   otob -bo' burr*
    and STAT/walk-3 in brush-DEF CONT-collect-3 burro
    bžin' ca',
    mule PL
    [catə' b-   ežag-bo' to xayid   golə]
    when PERF- find-3   one leather-clad old (Text 1, lines 6-7)
    "He was walking around in the brush getting the burros and mules together *when he came upon a demon-man*"
    (STAT = stative aspect, 3 = third-person pronoun, DEF = definite article, CONT = continuative aspect, PL = plural, PERF = perfective aspect.)
    (Text 1, lines 6-7)

There are three other unusual phenomena in the text structure that deserve comment. One is that Yatzachi Zapotec narratives sometimes accomplish the backgrounding of "old" or out-of-sequence events simply by means of a choice of aspect, in contexts where in written English, at least, we tend to subordinate the less important information:

(3) na' jə- ya'aqu-e' jseš lbajo -n' ba-
and PERF/go- return-3 Yatzachi el Bajo-DEF already-
zjən- aqu-e' bia ca'
STAT/PL- be-3 animal DEF/PL

"They went back to Yatzachi el Bajo [after they had turned into those animals]."

or "They went back ... as those animals." Literally, "They went back to Yatzachi el Bajo — already they have turned into those animals."

(Text 3, lines 9-10)

Secondly, the verbs in clauses that introduce or terminate direct quotations are unlike normal plot-move verbs in taking continuative aspect rather than perfective (e.g. "He says: 'I am not strong'"); in effect they are background devices for framing the dialogue material, despite the possibility of analyzing the quotations as syntactic direct objects of the quotation-framing clauses. This sort of phenomenon has been noted in many languages (Partee 1973; Munro 1982). A third point concerns directly quoted conversational chunks of the text: they are the freest, least constrained pieces of the discourse, as shown by the middle-range statistical values of both the grammaticized and the purely semantic parameters of transitivity. Anything goes, and text analysts would do well to keep dialogue separate from other kinds of text in their quantitative investigations.

The findings of Table 7 make it clear that not all the grammaticized oppositions that characterize transitivity are actively opposed to one another in the narrative context of plot moves; irrealis mode and negative polarity, in particular, are absent. This is hardly surprising, for by definition each event in a story is asserted to be something that *did* take place. If we maintain for the sake of argument that in some other functional context there is a grammatical choice between realis and irrealis mode, we cannot say thereby that the opposition is merely neutralized in narrative contexts; the meaning of [realis] is the only one that makes sense here, whereas when a grammatical distinction is neutralized, both choices are equally meaningful, as Halliday makes clear in his discussion in "Syntax and the Consumer" (1964) of a grammatical neutralization between agentive and instrumental prepositional phrases in English.

So we must look in some functional context other than in plot moves for evidence that realis and irrealis are opposed as a grammatical system in Yatzachi Zapotec. In these data there are two places where a genuine modal choice appears: in direct quotations and in backgrounded clauses. As we have seen in Tables 6 and 7, the conversational parts of the texts have a markedly free distribution of mode and aspect, as well as of the other transitivity features. This is not surprising, because dialogue is more strongly interpersonal than either plot moves or background information; and in these Zapotec texts, the conversational segments serve primarily to express psychological states and mental processes, rather than to advance the plot line. In Text 1, direct quotations most often signal either the intentions of the speaker or commands to the addressee; Text 3 has only a few direct quotations, and in Text 2 the dialogue is a repetitive series of factual claims and counterclaims of the pattern "How strong you are, X!", "No, I'm not strong, Y is stronger. Y does thus and so to me." (In such a dialogue the imperfective aspects [continuative] and [stative] inevitably predominate). The most straightforward examples of the opposition of realis and irrealis mode can be found in conversations, as in example (4):

(4) a. *bito   n-   ac-a' nada'   gual*
       NEG STAT-be-1 1/EMPH   strong   (Text 2, line 35)
       "*I* am not strong."
       (NEG = negative, EMPH = emphasis marker)
   b. *bi   g-   aquə-š   -a' nda'   gual*
      NEG IRR-be -ATT-1 1/EMPH strong   (Text 2, line 30)
      "*I* cannot be (called) strong!"
      (ATT = attenuative marker)

In example (4b), irrealis mode signals the impossibility of an imagined condition ("It isn't psosible that I could be really strong"), whereas (4a) demonstrates that denials can be made in realis mode ("I simply am not strong").

Modal choices are apparent in backgrounded material as well. Example (5) illustrates the use of [realis : stative] and [irrealis] in relative clauses; (6) demonstrates the modal opposition in adverbial complements:

(5) a. *benə'   ca'   [ba-   zjən-   žaš]*
       person PL/DEF already STAT/PL-be LOC
                                         (Text 3, line 37)
       "the people [who] are/were already there"
       (LOC = locative)

b. *be'e -n   [ə- selə' xayid   -ən']*
      person-DEF IRR-send demon-man-DEF

   (Text 1, lines 43-44)

   "the person [whom] the cowboy would send."

(6) a. *...par j-   eyežo'o-n   to   latja de'e de...*
       so that PERF/go -enter -3/INAN one place that
       STAT/lie   (Text 3, line 51)

   "... so that it entered a place that lay ..."

   (INAN = inanimate pronoun)

   b. *...par g-   ao   xayid   -ən'*
       so that IRR-eat demon-man-DEF (Text 1, line 37)

   "... so that the demon-man may eat"

In the relative clauses of (5), the choice between realis and irrealis is virtually the choice between an already realized event and one that is only an intention. Relative clauses are realis when they serve to identify the participant or the prop they modify (5a); they are irrealis to identify a possible future event in which the participant may be involved, as in (5b). Somewhat similarly, the major difference between result and purpose clauses is the choice of mode, as shown in (6).

There is one other context that yields a contrast of mode: the complements of mental process clauses. Such complements require one mode or the other in a way consistent with the "intentional" quality of the main clause verb: irrealis is chosen in clauses which act as complements to verbs of desire (7), but realis mode is used in those which are neutral as to intention (8):

(7) *ja'aquən ch-   aclažo'-o [g-   on -a' le']*
    how/much CONT-want -2   IRR- give-1 2   (Text 1, line 22)

    "How much do you want me to give you?"

    (CONT = continuative)

(8) *ch-   güia-bo' [mbalaz n-   aquə liž   -e'e-nə']*
    CONT-see -3   elegant STAT-be house-his-the

    (Text 1, lines 19-20)

    "He sees that his house is elegant."

Thus we can see that there is a truly distinctive opposition of mode in Yatzachi Zapotec, but it does not show up in the highly transitive context of plot moves, where realis mode is part of what defines a narrative event. Modal choices show up instead in the freer contexts of dialogue and backgrounded material. As a system, mode is obviously an important paradigmatic choice in conversational contexts and in most types of backgrounded clauses, where it signals the difference between expressing intentions and possibilities, and reporting actual events. But it functions at such a high level within the speech event that it amounts to a decision about whether to relate facts (via realis mode), or to speculate about possibilities (via irrealis mode). The fact that only realis mode appears in plot moves surely does not mean that mode is semantically irrelevant in that context, but rather that its relevance is part of the overall transitivity bundle signalling the foregrounded or highlighted nature of the plot line.

The normal, unmarked choice of mode is realis, both in narrative and conversational contexts. The irrealis category is a marked option not only statistically, but also in the cognitive sense that it signals a shift into the intangible world of possibilities, and in a formal systemic sense as well, in that no aspect options are available within irrealis mode,[4] whereas there *are* choices of aspect in realis mode: perfective versus imperfective, and stative versus continuative.

Having seen that a real choice between realis and irrealis mode is possible in some, but not all, discourse contexts, let us look at how aspect features are distributed among the major discourse functions. It turns out that there is just barely a viable choice of aspect in foregrounded narrative clauses, perfective aspect clearly being the unmarked choice for events that advance the story. In this context the meaning of perfective is generally telic, emphasizing the end or completion of the event; but it also can function to signal the entrance into a state, as in (9), where the senser, a bird, began to feel cold; or the attempt to do something (with an added directional morpheme), as in (10):

(9) gw-   zolao ch-   eyag-əb
    PERF-begin CONT-cold-3/ANIM   (Text 2, line 8)
    "He (an animal) began to feel cold."
    (ANIM = animal)

(10) le'e gw-   šįwtinte j-   eso'   yi' gwzi'o -nə' lao
     then PERF-thunder PERF/go-enter fire lightning-DEF in
     campnary-ən'
     belfry   -DEF

"Then it thundered [and] the lightning tried to hit (literally, went-enter) the belfry." (Text 3, lines 48-49)

Thus the perfective feature is the dominant aspect used in plot moves.

The selection expression [imperfective : continuative] turned up in only one sequence of plot moves, in which the events were violent and graphic — a matter of eagles stealing children, dropping them in a cave and returning to eat them later (11). The use of an imperfective aspect in that context gave the crisis an iterative meaning: it kept happening again and again. Interestingly enough, this reiteration slowed down the momentum of the story to such an extent that the following clause was one of the temporal reframing constructions of the type illustrated in (2) above. To get the plot moving forward again, it was apparently necessary to reset the clock:

(11) ca'   zjən-   aqu-e' bsia   da'o-nə'   ch-   j- esi' -e   no
     thus STAT/PL-be -3 eagles big   -the CONT-go-take-3 some
     bidao' che benə'   ca'...
     children of people DEF/PL
     "So the big eagles were there and they kept going and taking some of the people's children ..."
     na'   ch-   eyo'a-b le -bo'   ch-   jə-   yedeb-əb to
     and CONT-carry-3 PN-3/CHILD CONT-go- put in -3 one
     lo'o   yech...
     inside hole
     "And they kept carrying them away and putting them inside a hole ..."
     na'   ch-   j- eye-   dao-b   bida'o -nə'
     and CONT-go-return-eat -3 children-DEF
     "And they kept going back there to eat the children."
     ca' ba-   ch-   ac che benə' lao' yez   ca'   [catə'
     thus already-CONT-be for people of   town DEF/PL when
     gw-   so'o-n   -e' xbab...]
     PERF-PL- make-3 thought
     "So it was for the people of those towns when they decided ..."
     (Text 3, lines 10-15)

The choice of [imperfective : continuative] in the plot moves of (11) is so unusual that although it *can* be said to be paradigmatically opposed to perfective aspect in such a context, its occurrence is startling; it appears to be an attention-grabbing stylistic device. It is best interpreted as a highly marked aspect here, for it is just barely capable of advancing the narrative. But in background clauses, imperfectives are the most frequent aspect choices, forcing [perfective] to carry a correspondingly heavy load of information. Example (12a) illustrates an unmarked imperfective — stative aspect — in a background clause (interestingly enough, a clause whose backgrounding is signalled *only* by the selection of an imperfective, inasmuch as other potential signals of backgrounding are lacking); (12b) uses the marked perfective in virtually the same context, for a much narrower aspectual concept:

(12) a. *to   -e' ba-   n-   aqu-e' bez -ən'*
         one -3 already STAT- be -3 lion -DEF
     "One of them already is/has become the lion."
     (Text 3, lines 21-22)
   b. *ben'   [go-   quə bež-ən]*
      person/DEF PERF-be lion-DEF
      "The person [who] had been the lion (but no longer was)"
      (Text 3, line 31)

In these two examples, the choice between stative (imperfective) and perfective with the verb "be" conveys the difference between simple predication of a participant's identity (with a stative imperfective) and its predication as having *ceased to be* his current identity (by means of perfective). The perfective is used in this type of background clause 25% of the time, for out-of-sequence reporting in a "past-within-past" temporal frame.[5]

To find a functioning context for the opposition between the two imperfective aspects (stative and continuative), again we have to look at directly quoted conversation or background material, because both of the imperfective aspects are so rare in plot-move contexts. In direct quotations and background material, continuative aspect is used to report ephemeral desires (7 above) and sensations (8 and 9 above), and temporary conditions or activities, as with the first verb of (13) and the second verb of (2).

(13) *castigon' ch-   ac-o' n-   ac-o' rier   ni*
      suffering CONT-be-2 STAT-be-2 muleteer here
      "You are unhappy being a muleteer like this" or "You are suffering as a muleteer here."
      (Text 1, lines 8-9)

Stative aspect is used with the copula to report enduring conditions, as in the second occurrence of the verb *ac (aqu)* "be" in (13),[6] with semantically punctual verbs for perfect continuative reference as in (14), and with locative verbs as in (15b) or the first verb of (2).

(14) *benə' ca'   [zjə-   žiague'i yež -ən']*
     person PL/DEF STAT/PL-destroy town-DEF
     "the people who have been destroying the town"
     (Text 3, line 34)

(15) a. *n-   aquə-ch   biz-ən'   gual*
        STAT-be -COMP   cat-DEF   strong
        "The cat is stronger."
        (COMP = comparative) (Text 2, line 36)
    b. *gual -əch   to   ze'e zo   -n*
        strong-COMP one wall STAT/stand-3/INAN
        "A wall is stronger."
        (INAN = inanimate) (Text 2, lines 25-26)
    c. *gual -əch   be'e -nə'*
        strong-COMP wind-DEF
        "The wind is stronger."
        (Text 2, lines 21-22)

All together, the two imperfectives occur in 66% of the backgrounded clauses (or a full 75% of realis background clauses), and in 67% of direct quotations (96% of realis dialogue). Stative clearly predominates in backgrounded data, occurring in 96% of imperfective relative clauses and in 78% of all background imperfectives (n=65); but usage is more evenly divided in the conversational data: 41% stative, 59% continuative (n=80). These figures may in fact be slightly imbalanced because of the structure of the extensive dialogues in Text 2. If data from Text 2 is excluded, the proportion of conversational imperfectives is reversed, but still without a clear preponderance of one aspect: 58% stative versus 42% continuative (n=12). The relative frequency of imperfectives in backgrounded clauses remains roughly the same if Text 2 is omitted: 74% stative and 26% continuative (n=42). Not only is stative more frequent in the textual tabulations, but it also is deletable with only a minor shift in meaning, as illustrated in example (15c) above.

The basic semantic difference between stative and continuative is a distinction between long-term versus temporary relevance for what is reported. The patterns in which each aspect occurs suggest that the markedness of this system is not context-sensitive; stative is the unmarked choice for long-term relevance, and continuative, the marked option for temporary relevance, in both dialogue and background material. (Note that continuative was found in one series of plot moves (11), but stative has not turned up in that context at all. Imperfective itself is the marked option there.)

Conclusion

This study has demonstrated that in narrative texts realis mode and perfective aspect are closely associated with other parameters of high transitivity as defined by Hopper and Thompson (1980), and that they give prominence to the main events within the story line. The study also supports the old adage, "You can tell a person by the company he keeps", in the sense that the full semantic range of each modal and aspectual morpheme can be found only in the contexts where they are the unmarked options. In such contexts they cooccur with other grammatico-semantic features which support their distinctiveness. At the same time, however, the processes of text formation are complex enough that mode and aspect are not fully predetermined by the general discourse context in which they occur, at least when such contexts are broadly defined as plot moves, dialogue, and background material. This has been shown in two ways: first, mode and aspect inflections can signal the narrative structure of portions of a text without much help from other highlighting devices. Thus we have occasionally found plot moves signalled in large part by the use of the perfective aspect, even in syntactically dependent clauses; and sometimes the presence of stative aspect in the first of two neighbouring independent clauses is itself sufficient to signal that the first event is merely background information. Secondly, there are certain limited functional contexts in which major discourse choices about "what to say" coincide closely with a distinctive choice between irrealis and realis mode, or between one verbal aspect and another within realis mode. Thus both realis and irrealis modes are found in dependent clauses, signalling the choice between result and purpose; both perfective and imperfective aspects occur in relative clauses, where they constitute a direct grammatico-semantic choice; and both stative and continuative imperfectives turn up in dialogue portions of the texts, with continuative signalling a marked temporary relevance for the verb as opposed to the long-term relevance that stative aspect expresses.

The semantic distinctiveness of mode and aspect inflections has therefore been demonstrated as something both tied to and yet not entirely dependent upon the discourse structure of narrative texts. It is therefore justifiable to maintain, as systemic linguists often do, that grammatical systems are significant components of a model of grammar, provided they are carefully situated within the appropriate contexts of discourse. We must also add the proviso that not all grammatical morphemes are active members of a truly viable grammatical system in any and all discourse contexts. That is, there are contexts in which what can be a real choice among alternative meanings in other situations becomes merely a required part of a "bundle" of structural signals which together constitute the real choices, for example, the concurrent choice of several high-transitivity parameters, including realis mode and perfective aspect, for the single communicative purpose of advancing a narrative through its sequence of separate events. With this in mind, the theory of grammatical markedness must be seen to be context- dependent in many cases, in the sense that what is an unmarked choice in one discourse context is definitely a marked selection in other discourse contexts.[7] Thus perfective aspect is the unmarked choice in clauses which move the story along, but the marked choice in relative clauses that give background information about participants. Inasmuch as the markedness of one option or another is part of its meaning, the discourse functions of mode and aspect — and presumably of other grammatical systems as well — contribute to their formal distinctiveness in a nontrivial way. The importance of discourse cannot be discounted when grammatical systems are being investigated.

Notes

1. My thanks are due to Inez Butler for her careful correction of the language examples in the article. Yatzachi Zapotec is an attractive language for me to investigate not only because of the limited number of mode and aspect categories in its grammatical inventory and the accessibility of textual data, but also because I have worked for several years on a related language, Isthmus Zapotec (cf. Mock 1983a, 1983b, 1983c, 1984a, 1984b).

2. The category labels "potential aspect" and "completive aspect" have gained a certain uniformity of use in the Zapotecanist literature through the predominance in the Zapotec region of linguists from the Mexico branch of the Summer Institute of Linguistics. On the other hand, the terms I prefer to use, "realis mode" and "perfective aspect" respectively, are more widely current in aspect literature; cf. Comrie (1976), Friedrich (1974), Givón (1982), Timberlake (1982), Wallace (1982). For the use of aspect terminology in Zapotec languages, see the work of SIL linguists: Pickett (1955, 1967), Briggs (1961), Lyman (1964), Butler (1976), Marks (1980).

3. Quotations are framed by the clauses that introduce them and/or signal their conclusion. This framing is taken to be a special subtype of background material, despite the superficial "embedding" of the quoted dialogues as syntactic direct objects of the quotation clauses. There are two reasons behind this analysis: the aspect marking of the superordinate, "quotative" verb is not what one normally finds for plot-move verbs, being continuative rather than perfective; and the quotation frame is often repeated at the end of the quoted material.

4. Certain other Zapotecan languages *do* have aspect distinctions within irrealis mode: e.g. Isthmus Zapotec (cf. Pickett 1955, 1967) and Mitla Zapotec (Briggs 1961).

5. Other examples of this "pluperfect" usage in rankshifted perfective clauses are to be found in Text 1, lines 5 and 55, and in Text 3, line 3. In Text 3, lines 34-35 contain an out-of-sequence use of stative aspect in an analogous relative clause.

6. The semantic distinction that in English is lexicalized as a choice between the verbs "be" and "become" is carried by choices of mode and aspect in Yatzachi Zapotec, the verbal root being the same morpheme:

    go-quə   "became, came to be." The telic meaning of perfective here signals completed entry into the state or relation of "being" (= "becoming").

    n-aquə   "is, was, has been." Choice of [stative] aspect is atelic, for long-term conditions or relations.

    ch-aquə   "is or was temporarily." [Continuative] aspect narrows the temporal focus of the verb to in-progress or iterative meanings.

    g-aquə   "may be, may become." [Irrealis] mode neutralizes the distinction between "being" and "becoming".

7. If discourse genres are to be accounted for by system networks on a separate stratum, the *markedness* of grammatical options will be predetermined by discourse selections, even when no particular grammatical feature is preselected in an absolute fashion.

On the concepts of "style" and "register" in sociolinguistics

Fred C.C. Peng

Introduction

In sociolinguistics, the concepts of "style" and "register" have been in vogue for quite some time, although "style" was not new because it had already been used in literary criticism. However, they have been employed in various ways because no uniform usage is in practice. In some cases "style" and "register" are used as interchangeable terms because there has been no clear-cut distinction between the two concepts; in other cases, "register" is used according to the definition proposed by British scholars to account for something that could not be handled by the concept of "style" alone in sociolinguistics. Because this ambiguity can be misleading, I shall attempt in this paper to explore the relationship between these two concepts in order to account for language behaviour that is the subject-matter of sociolinguistics.

To do so requires some preliminary thinking of what language behaviour is. We must cease to consider language as merely a code for the simple reason that, in sociolinguistics, language is best thought of as a language or languages (Peng 1986a: 13) in so far as it is an institution rather than a system; that is, there are two aspects to each language, the dynamic aspect in which case the language concerned is an institution, and the static aspect in which case the language concerned is a self-contained system without recourse to language users and the context of situation where it is used. I shall be concerned with both because "style" is related to the static aspect and "register" to the dynamic one.

"Style"

One definition of "style" involves wording or sentence constructions which are of importance in writing and concern the editor of a journal or may include punctuation and other technical work when the editor does the copy-editing of a manuscript or when a writer submits his/her manuscript (cf. a "Style Sheet"). However, this is not what I mean here by "style". In order to explain what I mean by it, let me now quote Gleason (1965) and Joos (1962) to see what they had to say about style in the sixties, when the TG paradigm ran rampant. They classify style into five categories which are recapitulated below:

	Joos (1962)	*Gleason (1965)*
(1)	Frozen Style	Oratorical Key
(2)	Formal Style	Deliberative Key
(3)	Consultative Style	Consultative Key
(4)	Casual Style	Casual Key
(5)	Intimate Style	Intimate Key

These classifications, though not identical, are similar. I shall therefore use the definition offered by Gleason (1965 :428) to explain my position: "Style is the patterning of choices made within the options presented by the convention of the language and of the literary form".

I presume what he means by "patterning of choices" here is the selection from among available variations, a selection that is culturally patterned (or favoured); the availability of such variations is, thus, said to be based on the convention of the language and of the literary form. Viewed in this fashion, then, his idea may be represented by the following diagram:

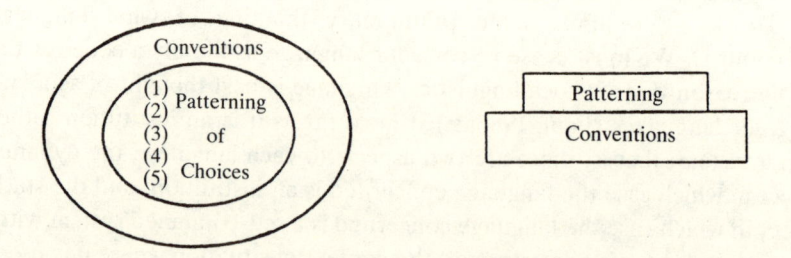

Figure 1. The Two-layer Schematic Representation of *Style* in terms of Gleason's Definition

Style defined as such has four aspects: (1) diction, (2) the stylistic implications of a word, (3) the stylistic implications of grammatical constructions, and (4) phonological differences. I shall now add my comments to these four aspects with illustrations.

The first aspect implies that the selection of variations is done through the choices of synonyms. But I must hasten to point out that synonyms are in name only because it is impossible in any language to have two words meaning exactly the same thing. Put differently, if a language had complete synonyms, then it would be meaningless to talk abut "style" which, as the term implies, means subtle differences in the shades of meaning between and among so-called synonyms; in other words, if there is such a thing called "style", it means that complete synonyms do not exist. It is because of this dictum that I believe the value of transformations in the TG paradigm is nill on the ground that even the same thing may have different meanings on account of style when placed in different sentences, such as active and passive sentences. The following is an example from English but could easily be replaced by another one in a different language.

Usually *big* and *large* are considered synonyms. Therefore, *I have a big suitcase* and *I have a large suitcase* are, at the level of diction, two stylistically different variants expressing the "same meaning", although no TG linguist would speak of one being the "transform" of the other. But when *big* and *large* are placed in a different linguistic context, say, *He is a ---- man*, the difference in meaning of the two adjectives emerges right away: *He is a big man* is now ambiguous but *He is a large man* is not, although stylistically speaking *big* and *large* may still be considered adequate, at the level of diction, because of the shades of subtle meaning displaced by the choice of one word against the other.

I shall illustrate the "stylistic implications of a word" with an actual example in the context of situation. In Japan, there used to be a Saturday TV program (Channel 8, TBS, Tokyo) called *Panchi De Deito* ("A Date by a Punch"). There were two hosts who introduced as guests a young man and a young woman looking for a possible date with each other after the program. The couple were separated by a curtain on a stage but the audience could see both of them. After a series of introductions initiated by each host and the couple's self-descriptions cued by the host, each side's host would peek through a window in the middle of the curtain to see what the other side's young guest looked like, while at the same time cracking a joke about what he saw. The couple were then allowed to meet each other for the first time on stage and to ask questions. After the get-acquainted encounter was over, the hosts would ask the couple to each push a button that was connected to one half of an electric panel which had the shape of a heart. If both pushed the light-on switch, then the panel would be lit with a perfect heart-shape; but if both or one of the couple failed to push the button(s), then the panel would not be lit or only half lit. Usually, it was the young man who pushed the light-on button resulting in only one half of the heart lit. At that moment, the hosts would ask the young woman who failed to push the button why she did not push it. The often heard answer was: *Chotto ne* (lit. "just a little"). In that case, of course, the young couple would not be dating, because one partner refused to accept the date. *Chotto ne* illustrates Gleason's second aspect. The young lady, by answering the question "Why didn't you push the button?" with *Chotto ne* and nothing more, left the decision of whether it meant "just a little disappointed (and, therefore, I didn't push the button)" or "I was greatly disappointed (and, therefore, did not push the button)" to the audience and the young man. It is this implication of a choice between two variable meanings — a dictionary meaning and a euphemistic meaning of otherwise a direct refusal — that is stylistically significant.

What the third aspect, the "stylistic implications of grammatical constructions", means is whether or not there can be grammatically different constructions that have the *same* meaning. If complete synonyms do not exist, it automatically follows that there are no such things as different constructions having the same meaning. In other words, the differences in grammatical constructions reflect the differences in their meaning, no matter how subtle or implicit the differences in meaning may be. It is such subtle or implicit differences that are of stylistic value. Thus, what TG linguists have said in the past about transforms and their underlying constructions is, stylistically speaking, nonsensical, because every time there is a stylistic change to a grammatical construction, a change in meaning has automatically taken place. Consider the following examples from translations of the *Book of Mark* from the Bible:

> And going on a little further, he saw James the son of Zebedee and John his brother, who were in their boat mending the nets (Mark 1:19) RSV (1952)

> When he had gone a little further, he saw James, son of Zebedee and his brother John in a boat, preparing their nets (Mark 1:19) NIV (1978)

Differences in the grammatical constructions can be observed, notably *And going on ...* and the relative clause in the RSV vs. the subordinate clause *When he had gone ...* and the splitting of *in a boat* from the verb phrase of *preparing their nets* without a relative clause in the NIV.

The implications of such grammatical differences are not only indicative of the importance of stylistic differences but also suggestive of the existence of social change that leads to the preference of one style over the other. The following is the same passage from two other translations that are farther apart in time:

> And when he had gone a little further there, he saw James the son of Zebedee and John his brother, who were in the ship mending their nets. KJV (1611)

> A little farther up the beach, he saw Zebedee's sons, James and John, in a boat mending their nets. LB (1971)

Observe that if the difference in diction (*ship* vs. *boat*) is ignored, the grammatical constructions in the use of the relative (*who*) clause are the same in the RSV and the KJV, while the use of verb phrases involving the participles (*preparing* vs. *mending*) are very much alike in the NIV and the LB, even though there is a time difference of more than 350 years between the KJV and the LB but only 26 years between the RSV and the NIV. Stylistic preference in terms of grammatical constructions may in some way reflect the social conventions prevalent at the time when the choice is made for a particular translation. Stylistic preferences due to change in the social conventions may be undertaken at the expense of the original meaning, as can be seen in the avoidance of sexist words in English. In 1983, when the Revisionist Standard Version of the Bible was published, *lord* and *king* were regarded as sexist words and changed to *sovereign*; likewise, *Jesus* was no longer *son of God* but *child of God* and *the Father* became *Father and Mother*. While the difference in meaning of *son of God* and *child of God* may be tolerable, the change from *the Father* to *Father and Mother* is simply an alteration of the original meaning in the Greek.

The last aspect of Gleason's definition of style is the phonological aspect. The effects of alliteration and rhyming in poetry have often been studied. I am of the opinion that spoken English may display this aspect more vividly than written English, e.g. *because* being said as *'cause* and *afraid* as *'fraid*. This trend is true of all languages in which there is a writing system. In Japanese, *sorede* ("therefore") often comes out as *soide, no da*

Table 1. Criteria and their features for indentifying styles

Style \ Criteria	Group size	Characteristic Devices	Advance Planning
(1)	A fairly large group whose members cannot meet face-to-face; they are unknown to one another; if met, they are to remain social strangers; often the hearers (or audience) are invisible to the speaker (or author) when it is used for print through mass media; otherwise, they are a crowd as in the case of declamation.	Elaborate rhetorical devices are employed; sentences are intricately related; to do well requires high skill; folklore regards it (mistakenly) as the ideal of all language.	Its structure is planned over still longer spans; it is used exclusively by specialists.
(2)	A small group whose members are split into one manic speaker and a set of catatonic hearers; a social group (or committee) of seven or more whose members are divided into active and chair-warming persons; it may be used in speaking to medium or large groups; it may also be used in speaking to a single hearer; conversations between strangers begin in formal style.	Sentence structures are more complex and varied than in consultative; run-on constructions are less frequent; the vocabulary is more extensive and includes a number of words that are avoided as "too fancy" for consultative speech; full-name address; some effort to avoid repetition of the major words; use of synonyms or near-synonyms is necessitated; anacoluthon is common with some speakers; the leading code-label is 'may'; the grammar tolerates no ellipsis cultivates elaborateness; the semantics is fussy; the defining features: (i)	The speaker must plan ahead, framing whole sentences before they are delivered; the formal has a captive audience, and is under obligation to provide a plan for the whole sentence before he begins uttering it, and outline of the paragraph before introducing it, and a delimitation of field for his whole discourse before he embarks on it; exempt from interruption, the text organizes itself into paragraphs; the paragraphs are linked explicitly; intelligent persons do not attempt it but instead have the text all composed and written out at

Table 1. Continued

Style \ Criteria	Background Information	Feedback and Response	Phonology
(1)	Background information may be given but not required.	The reader or hearer is not permitted to cross-question the author.	It is defined by the absence of authoritative intonation in the text.
(2)	Formal style is designed to inform; background information is woven into the text in complex sentences;	Participation drops out; this is forced whenever the group has grown too large; the insertions then may overlap, causing semantic confusion, or each listener must space his insertions out beyond the logical limit of 30 s.; the feedback of response encouragment characteristic of consultative is not possible; the speaker is left on his own to maintain the pace of delivery; he can no longer proceed freely, adjusting momentarily to the observed response; beyond its code-labels, the formal style is strictly determined by the absence of participation;	The pronunciation is explicit to the point of clattering there is usually a sharp break clearly marked in the intonation: this usually is reinforced by special hesitation signals, *er*.

Table 1. Continued

Style/Criteria	Group size	Characteristic Devices	Advance Planning
		detachment and (ii) cohesion; to speak in deliberative key is a difficult art to learn.	leisure; exressive anacoluthon is often an indication that the speaker is having difficulty oraganizing his sentence structure far enough in advance.
(3)	It is the usual form of speech in small groups except among close friends; consultative style is our norm for coming to terms with strangers; the minimum size is a dyad; it is used particularly between chance acquaintances.	It is the one type of language which is required of every speaker; it is used in most orally conducted everyday business; fluency problem must be met; the rupture of consultative is marked either by formal leave-taking or by casual leave-taking; adjournment of consultation is marked by consultative leave-taking, e.g., 'I might not be back for a while'; it is common to change constructions almost imperceptibly in the middle of sentences in ways that suggest, on careful examination, that the speaker has lost tract of what he started to say; occasionally, the shift is abrupt enough to be quite noticeable; patterns of clause connection are generally simple; and is used heavily; on is a general duty preposition; good consultative style produces cooperation without the integration, profiting from	Consultative speakers never plan more than the current phrase, and are allowed only a limited number of attempts to return to their muttons before abandoning them; a consultative conversation is not planned more than a few words in advance, nor is much thought given to clear connection of that is being said with what has preceded; usually, any stretch of six or seven words is consistent within itself structurally; the difficulty appears only when longer sequences are considered — sequences beyond the span of structural attention of either the speaker or the hearer.

"STYLE" AND "REGISTER" IN SOCIOLINGUISTICS

Table 1. Continued

Style / Criteria	Background Information	Feedback and Response	Phonology
		the absence infects the speaker also; he may speak as if he were not present; few children have any command of deliberative speech when they enter school,	
(3)	The speaker supplies background information; he does not assume that he will be understood without it; consultative style states a public sort of informateion as fast as it is needed; where there happens to be no public information for a while, a consultative conversation is broken off or adjourned: public information is essential to consultative style.	The addressee participates continuously; most often the dyadic members talk alternately, though one may hold the floor for a very long period; neither, however, is inactive; while one is speaking, at intervals the other gives short responses, mostly drawn from a stmall inventory of standard signals; these are a basic part of the system, essential to its operation; among them are: *yes, no, uhhuh, N'n, Mmm, That's right, I think so*; consultative code-labels include the standard list ofl istener's insertions *yes, yeah, unhuhn, that's right, oh, I see, yes, I know*, and a very few others, plus the 'well' that is used to reserve the roles between listener and speaker the speaker listens for these FEEDBACK SIGNALS as indications of how much is getting across and what the reactions are;	Normal pronunciation; no particular ways to utter conversation.

Table 1. Continued

Style/Criteria	Group size	Characteristic Devices	Advance Planning
		the lack of it; if the hearer wishes to change roles, he may break in by saying: *Well*; the speaker may invite the change of roles by using the same word with a different intonation perhaps best known in writing as: *Well?*	
(4)	Treating the listener as a stranger is hard work in the long run; therefore, we sooner or later try to form a social group with him; casual style is or friends, acquaintances, insiders; so, the smallest group size is a dyad; addressed to a stranger, it serves to make him an insider simply by treating him as an insider; when people have well-established relationships with each other and the situation is informal, they are likely to shift to *casual key*; good casual style integrates disparate personalities into a social group which is greater than the sum of its parts, for now the personalities complement each other instead of clashing.	On the positive side, we have two devices which do the same job directly: (i) ellipsis and (ii) slang, the two defining features of casual style; positively, casual key is characterized by the use of *slang*; this is a prime indication of in-group relationship; ellipsis (omission) makes most of the differences between casual grammar and consultative grammar; casual English requires a shorter form, say, 'I believe I can find one' if not the still more elliptical 'Believe I can find one'; all the weak words of English can be omitted at the beginning of a casual sentence: 'Been a good thing if...' for 'It would have been a good thing if...' and similarly' (A) friend of mine...' or '(The) coffee's	Advance planning seems not needed, because slang and elliptical utterances are employed more or less instantaneously.

Table 1. Continued

Style Criteria	Background Information	Feedback and Response	Phonology
(4)		he adjusts his rate and manner of delivery on the basis of this information; he slows down — not in rate of words per minutes, so much as ideas per minute — when he senses that the hearer is having difficulty, and he speeds up when the hearer signals impatience	
	Negatively, there is absence of background information; casual key implies a complete rapport and mutual interest; the background information so freely inserted into consultative conversation is not needed — indeed, it is carefully avoided, since to give it would imply a lack of confidence that the hearer shares all pertinent assumption; casual style takes a public sort of information for granted; i.e., it never informs; when there is no public information for a while, a casual conversation (among men) lapses into silence and kidding.	Since casual key implies a complete rapport and mutual interest, feedback and listener's response are not needed; the use of slang is another indication that feedback and are unnecessary, because the dyadic members will talk alternately with slang to maintain in-group relationship; there is no reliance on listeners' participation; this is not rudeness; it pays the addressee the compliment of suppsoing that he will understand without those aids.	Some ellipsis is only phonological: 'Can I help you?' is casual.

Table 1. Continued

Style / Criteria	Group size	Characteristic Devices	Advance Planning
		cold'; those most often involved are articles, pronouns, auxiliaries, and *be*: *Car broke down. Got a match? Anybody home?* such expressions are a highly diagnostic feature of the casual key; they will generally by interpreted as signaling informality; owever, most speakers are not aware either of the phenomenon or of its significance; that is, they do not know what it is about an utterance that gives them the impression of informality; they simply sense it somehow.	
(5)	At the other extreme, the INTIMATE KEY is a completely private language developed within families or between very close friends; since it is not used in public, it is of little concern to the schools; normally the intimate group is a pair.	The systematic features of intimate style are two, just as in the others: (i) extraction, e.g., *Ready, Engh, Cold* and (ii) jargon; both are stable, once the intimate group has been formed; extraction is not ellipsis; an elliptical sentence still has wording, grammar, and intonation; intimate extraction employs only part of this triplet; intimate style tolerates nothing of the system of any other style: no slang, no ellipsis, and on; any item of an intimate code the the folklore calls 'slang' is not slang but jargon — it is not ephemeral, but part of the permanent code of this group.	No advance planning is necessary for extraction and jargon.

Table 1. Continued

Style / Criteria	Background Information	Feedback and Response	Phonology
(5)	Now in intimate style, the role (played by public information) is not merely weakened; rather, it is positively abolished: intimate speech excludes public information; definition: an intimate utterance pointedly avoids giving the addressee information from outside of the speaker's skin; it tolerates no background information.	Intimacy does not tolerate the slang imputation that the addressee needs to be told that she is an insider (because she is more than an insider); hence, no need for feedback, though extracted responses are in order.	No sentence intonation is employed; however, word-level intonation still exists.

("it is") as *nda*, and *ore no uchi* ("my home") as *orenchi*. (For a detailed discussion of such phonological effects in spoken Japanese, see Peng 1981: 161-200).

By comparing the explanations of style by Joos and Gleason, I have subjectively establised six criteria. The contents of their five classifications (see above, p. 262) are mapped onto these six criteria in Table 1.

The six criteria observable in Table 1 are by no means directly applicable to sociolinguistics because they were not intended by Joos and Gleason for sociolinguistics and there are two factors mixed together in them: (1) the code itself and (2) the context of situation in which the code is used. If the concept of style is to be of functional use in sociolinguistics, the two factors must be separated, at least conceptually, so that "style" can be distinguished from "register" later. I believe the "confusion" or interchangeability of style and register is due to a great extent to the mixing of the code (or the classification of it) and the context of situation in which language behaviour using the code takes place. I therefore propose that, of the six criteria, the first ("Group Size") be separated from the rest so that only the code can be properly classified in reference to the five remaining criteria. In this sense, the code being considered does not belong to De Saussure's *langue* but rather to his *parole*. In De Saussure's view, sentences, utter-

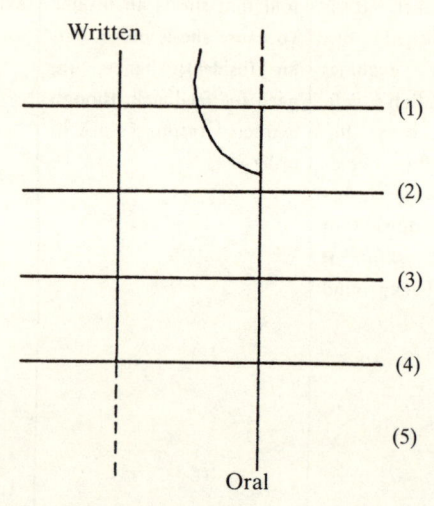

Figure 2. Proto-type of the twofold classification of styles in terms of the linguistic code alone.

ances, or even paragraphs, fall outside the domain of *langue* (Sampson 1980). But the linguistic code under consideration is not necessarily limited to written materials; rather, it must include spoken materials, so that languages like Ainu which have no extant writing systems can also be subject to stylistic classification analysis. Figure 2 presents my conception of the schematic representation of the dual classification of style in terms of the linguistic code. When a language has had a tradition of a writing system, both written and spoken materials are included; but if a language under consideration has yet to develop a writing system, only its spoken materials are represented.

On the "Oral" line, the dotted section means recitation of written materials, such as poems or scripture lessons and texts; on the "Written" line the dotted section implies the potential appearance of verbatim spoken (often private) materials in writing, as in the case of dialogues and expletive expressions reported in an interview or a novel. The extended "Oral" line is intended to illustrate only those styles of the languages which have not had any writing system. My classification of five styles, in keeping with Joos and Gleason, is: (1) Elaborate, (2) Deliberative, (3) Consultative, (4) Casual, and (5) Intimate.

"Register"

"Style", for me, is a structural concept which pertains to the linguistic code itself; "register" is a functional concept. The five (structural) styles I have proposed do not take into account the context of situation mixed in Joos and Gleason's criteria. A theoretical discussion of context of situation and register is presented in Peng (1986b: 91-106). Can context of situation be matched with the five styles I have proposed?

My own inclination is that the context of situation also has types which can be identified quite distinctly, such as wedding ceremony, funeral, graduation ceremony, party, etc. Thus, when one meets a stranger at a bar, that context of situation will not be the same as a dinner banquet at a wedding where the same person also meets a stranger. The linguistic code employed in those two distinct contexts of situation will not follow the same style, i.e. correlations exist between the code used and the context of situation in which it is used. However, I hasten to add that if the correlations are strictly one-to-one and that if there are no exceptions to the one-to-one correlations, then the separation of the linguistic code from the context of situation advocated above would not be as sociolinguistically significant. The truth of the matter is that very often one style is not always necessarily used in the right type of context of situation; each of the five styles is not fixed permanently to a particular type of the context of situation. People can make mistakes about the use of an approprate style in a given context of situation or they may even intentionally manipulate the styles in such a way that a wrong style is deliberately used in a given context of situation, for instance, uttering four-letter words, on an extremely formal occasion such as a wedding ceremony or a church service.

I suggest that the various types of the context of situation can be classified on a scale of gradations as I have done for the styles discussed above, by using "Group Size" which was deleted then. Group size, of course, can range from one person (in the case of a dyadic interaction) to several (in the case of a committee) or even to hundreds and thousands of people (as in a political rally). The context of situation in dyadic interaction will be rather distinct from the context of situation, when the group size is made up of hundreds of people. The context of situation with a larger group size can be regarded as "higher" on the scale than the context of situation with a small group size; the former is probably more "formal" than the latter. However, group size alone is not the determinant for deciding on the formation of such a scale of gradations. Other determinants can be: the relationships between the speaker and the hearer in a dyad (e.g. members of a family or total strangers); the place or physical setting where the interaction takes place (e.g. in a living room or in bed); the topic selected (e.g. intended for an election campaign or for a speech at a wedding banquet to bless the newly-weds); and the relative differences in social status and class. Undoubtedly, there may be others but these four in addition to group size will suffice because even if more are added the result will not be altered. Let me propose the following scale: (1) Frozen, (2) Formal, (3) Average, (4) Informal, and (5) Private.

The *frozen* context of situation is one where not everybody or anybody can conduct a speech act. For instance, in Japan, the ceremony held at the Imperial Palace (on New Year's Day or some other occasion such as the Culture Day when the Emperor decorates distinguished scholars with the Order of the Rising Sun) constitutes a frozen context of situation, because ordinary people such as the people in the street cannot attend.

In contrast, the *formal* context of situation is one where ordinary people can take part in all sorts of speech acts, e.g. at funerals, weddings, graduation ceremonies, etc. The frozen and the formal contexts of situation have one thing in common: both last only for a relatively short period of time. These contexts of situation are only infrequently encountered, e.g. few people (if any) would attend a funeral or wedding every day.

By comparison, the *average* context of situation is encountered daily and even rather frequently within each day more or less as a routine. Such frequent encounters, however, invariably give rise to a problem: whereas the two contexts of situation just mentioned have a clear-cut segmentable beginning and ending (e.g. a wedding ceremony), the average context of situation is so frequently encountered that it is difficult to tell when it begins and ends. For instance, when an office worker goes to work, (s)he meets fellow co-workers, superiors, and/or subordinates in order to conduct the routine work within an eight-hour working period. Does it constitute one context of situation (say, from morning when (s)he leaves the house to evening when (s)he comes home) or is it a series of (average) contexts of situation that are concatenated? Either way there exists a methodological problem. I shall take a daily routine to be a concatenated series of average contexts of situation (unless it is interrupted by one of the two contexts of situation already described). How to segment the concatenation into discrete contexts of situation remains a problem.

The *informal* context of situation also seems to fall into the domain of daily activities but the "atmosphere" is different. The chief characteristics are: (1) instead of the working place, it pertains for the most part to a bar, a public restaurant, or a train ride, or even a "gossip" place in the courtyard of an apartment complex (called *Danchi* in Japanese) where housewives living there can gather to socialize among themselves; (2) the group size tends to be small, ranging from a dyad, to half a dozen or more; but (3) invariably their interaction takes place in the presence of by-standers who are considered "outsiders" or simply ignored by them. For instance, in a bar where a company employee and his friend happen to be drinking after work, other customers in the same bar do not count as interactants although they are part of this informal context of situation.

The *private* context of situation has the following characteristics: the interlocutors are always a dyad and tend to be in a quiet or secluded place; if someone else happens to be around, their voices are kept low or the other person is simply ignored.

The concept of register lies in the correlations between the five types of context of situation and the five types of style:

(Fr)	FROZEN	-	ELABORATE	(El)
(Fo)	FORMAL	-	DELIBERATIVE	(De)
(Av)	AVERAGE	-	CONSULTATIVE	(Co)
(In)	INFORMAL	-	CASUAL	(Ca)
(Pr)	PRIVATE	-	INTIMATE	(In)

Figure 3. Registers illustrated by the correlations of gradations of styles and gradations of the context of situation

A register thus means each of the 25 correlations between the two scales of gradations, but of the twenty five correlations only five are one-to-one (straight) correlations. I shall call such correlations *Appropriate Registers*, and the remaining twenty correlations *Inappropriate Registers*. For instance, while the Fr-El correlation or In-Ca correlation is an appropriate register, Fr-De or Pr-Ca is an inappropriate register. All appropriate registers occur in every society but not all inappropriate registers are conceivable in any given society. An inappropriate register, when employed, does not necessarily mean "ungrammatical" or "unacceptable", it simply implies that it is improper to what is expected of the interlocutor(s) and that the consequences may be grave, the gravity being in proportion to the "distance" of deviation from the expected appropriate register as perceived by the interlocutor(s). For example, when a scholar is summoned by the Japanese Emperor to the Imperial Palace, what is expected of him is the use of the elaborate style, if he says anything at all, in order to have the appropriate (Fr-El) register in the interaction with the Emperor. It is unlikely that on such an occasion the extremely inappropriate (Fr-In) register will be used by either the Emperor or the scholar. Sometimes a wrong register is used not due so much to the wrong choice of style from the gradations as to the wrong choice of a word (owing to a memory malfunction or a slip of the tongue) in one of the four aspects proposed by Gleason and discussed above. A vivid example is the mistake President Reagan made in 1986 when, proposing a toast at a formal banquet to Prince Charles and Princess Diana, he called Prince Charles "Prince David" two or three times. Whether this "mistaken" register did any harm to the visit of the Royal couple to the United States is hard to evaluate; but the impact on the participating VIPs and the millions of TV viewers that night was negatively great. A more detrimental case would be Mr. Nakasone's recent remark about the intelligence of the American people being lower because of the Blacks and Hispanics and other minority groups in the United States, a highly inappropriate register that cost him an apology to the US Government and the American people.

Conclusion

In this paper, I have attempted to delineate the concepts of "style" and "register" in sociolinguistics. I believe that the two concepts, though related, can now be said to constitute two distinct theoretical constructs: "style" is a structural notion, a term that indicates the existence of variations in the linguistic code which can be classified into a scale of gradation comprising five types, whereas "register" is a functional notion dependent on contexts of situation that can also be classified into a similar scale of gradation comprising five types. The concept of the context of situation owes its origin to distinguished British scholarship beginning with Malinowski, through Firth, and now to Halliday whose insights into language functions have made my work in linguistics very rewarding and to whom this paper is dedicated.

Social constraints on grammatical variables: tense choice in English

Guenter Plum and Ann Cowling

1. Introduction

In this paper[1] we will explore the issue of grammatical variability within a framework that brings together Labovian variation theory and Hallidayan systemic- functional grammar. Our concern is to test the general theoretical assumption of systemic-functional grammar that the realisations of the linguistic system in text are conditioned by the context of their production (Halliday 1971/1973: 116; 1977: 206-207). A quantitative study of the two grammatical variables *tense* and *recursion*, which together account for the selection of tense in the English verbal group (Halliday 1976, 1985), has been carried out in order to investigate the various conditioning factors which may be implicated in the choice of tense. The data[2] is drawn from a clearly delimitable section of sociolinguistic interviews conducted with 24 speakers of Australian English, the total sample numbering 4,436 verbal groups.

Although the idea that language is in some sense probabilistic is not new, it is largely due to Labov's pioneering work in urban dialectology that the concept of probability has become respectable again in language studies (see Sankoff 1978 for a review of the history of probability in linguistics). The task involved in the "probabilisation" of grammar is in principle no different from that identified by Sankoff for variation theory in general when he says (1978: 236) that "variation theory is in large part the study of to what extent these probabilities are intrinsic to language as a system, and how extrinsic considerations impinge". However, so far the variables investigated by variationists have generally been phonological, morphophonemic and morpho-syntactic or morpho-lexical but rarely "purely" syntactic, to use a typology of the linguistic variable suggested by Romaine (1981: 15).

When the investigation of grammatical variables of a purely syntactic kind within a variationist framework has been undertaken, the objective has generally been to study language development, be it of L1 (Labov & Labov 1977) or L2 (Klein & Dittmar 1979). Any investigation of grammatical variation *per se*, especially if it involves the investigation of any non-linguistic or external (contextual/social) constraint operating on the variable in question, appears to raise an issue from which variationists have generally retreated, viz. the issue that grammatical variation may in effect be synonymous with semantic variation which then demands explanation in terms other than those of style or social dialect.[3] The inclination to consider grammatical variation as meaningful choice only in the context of language development, and to consider such variation in other contexts as "stylistic" variation akin to phonological variation, is certainly one reason for the general lack of variationist studies of purely syntactic variation, and the subsequent failure to extend to syntactic variables the probabilistic models so successfully developed for the modelling of largely non-syntactic variables. The disinclination to deal with grammatical variation is bound up with a particular view of language and society, reflected in a view of linguistics as a "social" linguistics which is characterised by (and limited to) "the use of data from the speech community to solve problems of linguistic theory" (Labov 1966: v).

The strongest exposition of this attitude to grammatical variation is found in Weiner and Labov (1983) (= Labov & Weiner 1977), an investigation of the choice of passive in English which is explicitly designed to counter a position ascribed by the authors to Bernstein (1971) concerning differences in the use of the passive between middle-class and working-class speakers (but cf. Atkinson 1985, esp. Chapter 6). A recent reiteration of the orthodox variationist position on this issue is found in Sankoff (1986) who considers that "distinctions in referential value or grammatical function among different surface forms can be neutralized in discourse" (p.17), basing this view on "the study of syntactic variation within a framework similar to that of phonological variation" (p.16). It is our contention that a view of meaning which is appropriate to the study of phonological variation continues to influence the conceptualisation of syntactic variation in such a way as to prevent an appreciation of its social significance (but see section 6 below).

The lack of interest in grammatical variation in the variationist paradigm may also be explained in terms of a particular linguistic, rather than social-linguistic, theory, viz. generative grammar, the largely syntagmatically focused grammar which provides the framework for most variation studies. As a general consequence, any investigation of the constraints operating on grammatical variables is likely to suffer from an inability to integrate information on the conditioning of one grammatical variable with the conditioning of some other grammatical variable to provide a coherent theoretical account. "The fact that grammatical structures incorporate choice as a basic building block "and" that they accept probabilization in a very natural way, mathematically speaking" (Sankoff 1978: 235) has of course been true for any grammar since De Saussure, but the focus of generative grammar on structure makes it somewhat less than conducive to a probabilistic modelling of grammar.

Halliday's work contrasts with the variationist position in respect of both the approach to social facts and the type of grammar used to model language. The difference is in some sense captured by the appellation "systemic-functional linguistics". Halliday considers his functional linguistics a "sociological" linguistics in the sense of Firth (1935/1957: 27) (cf. Halliday 1974/1978: 35), since his model of language and its determining semiotic environment incorporates theories of social structure and process (Halliday 1978: 108ff.). And the type of grammar preferred by Halliday is one which is ideally suited to modelling conditioning of any kind, be it by linguistic or by social facts, viz. a grammar which is paradigmatically focused, one which models grammatical choices rather than grammatical structures. It is this kind of grammar for which probabilisation is a natural development.

Systemic grammar gives primacy to choice and treats structure as derivable from the choices made via realisation rules. Choices are modelled in "systems", a system being defined as a set of mutually exclusive options with an entry condition, i.e. with a specification of the conditions under which the choices are available. Systems in turn are modelled in "networks" or systems of systems. Choices or options are potentially part of a single comprehensive network which is synonymous with the grammar of a language.

Since the probabilisation of grammar can only be achieved on the basis of observed frequencies of occurrence of grammatical categories (the choices/options or "systemic features") in actual language, a model of language is needed which can relate the potential of the language system to its actualisation. Systemic grammar follows Hjelmslev (1947) and his conceptualisation of language as system/process, where the dialectical relationship between system and process (or text) accounts for the fact that the frequencies observed in text both reflect the system (at a given point in time) as well as shape the system (over time).

A second dialectic relationship, following Whorf (1956), is held to obtain between system/process on the one hand and the contexts of culture/situation within which both system and process "function", i.e. within which they have developed, are maintained and will inevitably change. The functional or contextual side of the grammar is derived from the theory of context developed by Firth and his students, based on Malinowski (1923; 1935), and commonly known as "register" theory (Firth 1950; Halliday, Macintosh & Strevens 1964). Against the background of mutually determining or dialectically related categories of a functional model of language, contextual meanings (not formal conceptual meanings), including meaning choices of the kind usually investigated in variation studies such as casual/formal style, speaker's sex, age, etc., are considered to stand in a relationship to their realisations in language which is in some sense "deterministic". A meaning — be it a choice of "being male", of "acting casually", or "talking" (rather than writing) "about the weekend" (rather than about linguistics), of "narrating" (rather than describing or constructing an argument) and an infinite number of other choices in some "most delicate" system of such choices, all of which are made simultaneously in the generation of text — determines, within a specifiable range of possibilities, its own linguistic realisations.

However, it is evident that choices in contextual meanings cannot stand in a one-to-one relationship to choices at the different strata of the linguistic system because of the different nature, size and total number of the categories at both contextual and linguistic levels. It must therefore be held that the nature of the realisational relationship between context and language is one of greater or lesser likelihood, i.e. that the relationship is probabilistic (Halliday 1977: 206-207; Martin 1984). The hypothesis that (contextual) meanings are realised probabilistically is thus concerned with the relationship between language and its context: it seeks to capture what determines the realisation of the linguistic system in process or text.

2. Description of the corpus

The corpus data is taken from sociolinguistic interviews conducted for

Table 1. Social stratification of interviewees in corpus

class	adult male	adult female	teenager male	teenager female	total
MC	2	2	2	2	8
UWC	2	2	2	2	8
LWC	2	2	2	2	8
total	6	6	6	6	24

the Sydney Social Dialect Survey. A large number of sociolinguistic interviews were conducted in this survey, from which 24 interviews with native speakers of Australian English were selected with the aim of obtaining a balanced stratified sample. The role of the interviewer *vis-à-vis* the interviewees was held constant although the identity of the interviewer was not. But although there was a total of six interviewers involved, the variation in terms of their social characteristics was considerably less than that of the interviewees (cf. Table 3, Appendix 3). A breakdown of the social characteristics of interviewees is given in Table 1.

The section of the interview analysed for this study concerned the games the interviewees used to play at primary school age. This section was selected largely on the grounds of its easy delimitability within the ongoing interaction of the interview, the games section beginning with the interviewer's first question on the games topic and ending with the interviewer's switch to a different topic.

Interviewees were asked what games they used to play as well as how they played these games at that time. The "games" section is characterised by a variable degree of interaction between interviewer and interviewee. It ranges from the "dependently" produced text typically associated with an interview, i.e. a text where the interviewer asks, prods, and helps in various ways and the interviewee gives generally brief answers, to the text produced "independently" by the interviewee insofar as (s)he tells a story, gives a description, argues a point of view etc. in an extended, essentially non-interactional turn.

Clearly, in a study concerned with the choice of tense in text, the form of the questions asked to elicit the passage studied is of considerable importance. However, since the dialect survey was not designed for the kind of contrastive text analysis undertaken here, it has to be accepted that the eliciting moves followed by the interviewers in the 24 interviews were not held constant, and therefore perhaps are not strictly comparable. We therefore have to contend with the fact that speakers were variously, and often within the same interview, asked to "recount" or to "state", i.e. to choose between telling "what we played" vs. "what was played", and between "how we played some game" vs. "how some game was, or is, played". By the same token, it needs to be stressed that all interviewees had the opportunity to make the same choices, irrespective of how the questions were phrased. (See Appendix 1 for three texts which are typical of the major strategies taken by speakers in answering the interview question.)

3. The grammatical variables: tense and recursion

The analysis of tense in the corpus is based on the interpretation of tense in the English verbal group by Halliday (1976, 1985). In a rather simplified version, we might consider the choice of tense a conjoint choice in two systems, viz. *tense* and *recursion*, the entry condition being *finiteness*. The system *tense* itself, however, is a system with the choice of tense "proper" versus modality. At the next level of delicacy, the system *tense* distinguishes the further choices between past, present and future.

The system *recursion* consists of the choices "stop" vs. "go", i.e. of the choice to select a second time in the system *tense* from among past, present and future vs. the choice to stop making further tense selections. The choice of modal is only available once, i.e. at the place for the primary choice of tense or at α. The total number of choices is five, numbered by the Greek letters α, β, γ, δ, and ϵ. The English tense system is viewed as one that "adopts the first chosen point of time relative to the moment of speaking as the reference point for a further choice of time relative to the last reference point", and recursion is the device used to achieve this "regressive referencing", also referred to as "serial modification" by Halliday (1985: 177).

A very simplified network of the choices for tense and modality, with recursion serving as the simple but powerful device for building up the very complex verbal groups of English, is presented in Figure 1.

The network in Figure 1 is to be read as follows: for primary tense, i.e. at α, choose between tense or modality, and if tense has been chosen, go on to choose between past, present and future; simultaneously choose between stop and go at α; if go has been chosen, i.e. the choice has been made to

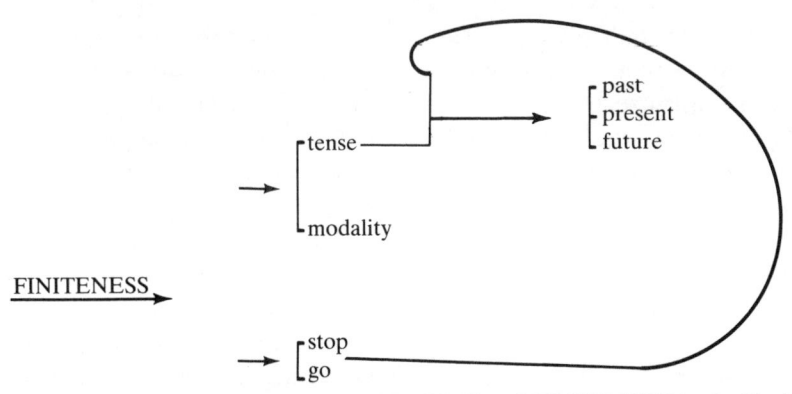

Figure 1. Systems of TENSE/MODALITY and RECURSION in the English verbal group

"go around" again, choose at β for tense only, i.e. between past, present and future, modality only being possible at α. Certain restrictions or "stop rules" (Halliday 1976: 155) apply to the possible combinations but since these will not affect the analysis of the corpus and the interpretation of the results they have not been incorporated in the network.

The following examples illustrate the systemic choices:

tense at α	*... at β*	*... at γ*	
[present/stop]			plays
[present/go:	past/stop]		has played
[present/go:	past/go:	future/stop]	has been going to play
modality at α	*tense at β*	*... at γ*	
[modal/stop]			may play
[modal/go:	past/stop]		may have played
modal/go:	past/go:	future/stop]	may have been going to play

If the choice at α is tense, then there are 36 possible combinations for finite tense choice; if the choice at α is modality, however, then there are only 12 possible combinations.[4]

The linguistic variables investigated in this study are (i) the system *finiteness* with its variants tense and modality at primary delicacy; (ii) the system *tense* with its variants past, present and future at the next level in delicacy; (iii) the system *recursion* with its variants stop and go in respect of both tense and modality. All the choices made in the corpus among the variants of these variables were coded at α, β, γ, etc. (see section 4 below).

It is obvious that a linguistic variable, defined by its position in a system of choices, is irreconcilable with the concept of a linguistic variable as having potentially two or more variants "which mean the same thing". While a model of language based on the notion of choice, as in systemic grammar, may operate with a notion of the "functional equivalence" of variants (cf. Lavandera 1978), it must rule out the requirement that variants be "truth-conditionally equivalent". The latter concept is heavily relied on by Labov (1978) in his defence of the concept of style shifting, although the concept is neither unassailable in Labov's practice of it (Romaine 1981) nor is it essential for an explanation of the kind of solidarity behaviour studied by Labov.

The three variables investigated here are of interest for two reasons: (i) the choices between tense and modality, and between past/present/future, on the one hand and stop/go, i.e. recursion, on the other hand represent independent choices, although made simultaneously, and therefore are potentially realisations of different meanings; (ii) one choice, viz. that between stop/go in recursion, would appear to be an abstract choice in the sense of Weiner and Labov (1983) and therefore, according to their argument, unlikely to be socially conditioned; whereas the other two choices, viz. those between tense and modality at α on the one hand and for a particular tense at α, β, etc. on the other hand would appear to be examples of surface variation (again in the sense of Weiner and Labov). But whereas the latter choices, especially the choice of a particular tense, must be expected to be contextually conditioned in some way, there seem to be no grounds for expecting tense in particular to be specifically socially conditioned (Sankoff & Labov 1979: 213).

4. Results

The investigation of external conditioning is concerned with the choices made among the variants of our grammatical variables at α only. Specifically, we will be investigating the choice of stop (rather than go) in the system *recursion*, of tense (rather than modality) in the system *finiteness*, and of past (rather than present) in the system *tense*. Table 2 gives the results for individual speakers. The decision to investigate one variant rather than the other in a two-term system is of no consequence since the results for one are the converse of the results of the other. The external

Table 2. Distribution of TENSE/MODALITY and RECURSION in corpus

speaker #	sex	age	class	α T/M total	β total	γ total	M total	α T total	α past	α pres	α fut	β past	β pres	β fut	γ pres
1	male	adult	LWC	21	0	0	0	21	2	19	0	0	0	0	16
2	male	adult	LWC	45	10	0	2	43	20	23	0	7	2	1	0
3	male	adult	UWC	374	16	0	152	222	209	13	0	3	13	0	0
4	male	adult	UWC	74	6	0	18	56	48	8	0	4	2	0	0
5	male	adult	MC	81	2	0	39	42	29	13	0	2	0	0	0
6	male	adult	MC	181	12	0	33	148	122	26	0	8	3	1	0
7	male	teen	LWC	213	5	0	35	178	28	150	0	3	2	0	0
8	male	teen	LWC	186	6	0	41	145	53	91	1	1	5	0	0
9	male	teen	UWC	247	5	0	49	198	143	54	1	2	3	0	0
10	male	teen	UWC	297	10	0	99	198	49	145	4	6	4	0	0
11	male	teen	MC	280	6	0	39	241	152	87	2	3	3	0	0
12	male	teen	MC	203	7	0	40	163	83	80	0	5	2	0	0
13	fem	adult	LWC	138	11	2	39	99	57	42	0	8	3	0	2
14	fem	adult	LWC	223	21	0	46	177	55	118	4	13	8	0	0
15	fem	adult	UWC	144	11	0	37	107	78	29	0	8	3	0	0
16	fem	adult	UWC	224	24	0	63	161	119	41	1	15	9	0	0
17	fem	adult	MC	135	8	0	20	115	63	52	0	0	8	0	0
18	fem	adult	MC	194	27	1	37	157	118	39	0	10	16	1	1
19	fem	teen	LWC	164	12	0	29	135	58	77	0	6	6	1	0
20	fem	teen	LWC	114	9	0	21	93	33	59	51	6	3	0	0
21	fem	teen	UWC	196	2	0	101	95	64	31	0	1	1	0	0
22	fem	teen	UWC	370	24	0	84	286	79	194	13	7	12	5	0
23	fem	teen	MC	179	0	0	43	136	121	15	0	0	0	0	0
24	fem	teen	MC	153	4	0	75	78	64	14	0	2	2	0	0
Total:				4,436	238	3	1,142	3,294	1,847	1,420	27	120	110	8	3
Average:				184.8	9.917	0.125	47.58	137.3	76.96	59.17	1.125	5	4.583	0.333	0.125
Minimum:				21	0	0	0	21	2	8	0	0	0	0	0
Maximum:				374	27	2	152	286	209	194	13	15	16	5	2
Standard Deviation:				89.01	7.587	0.448	34.06	66.17	48.61	50.00	2.787	4.032	4.303	1.049	0.448

conditioning factors investigated are sex, age and class.

There are two reasons for not pursuing the investigation in respect of choices made beyond α. There simply is not sufficient data for such an investigation on account of the very strong skew in the system *recursion*. Since the total number of finite verbal groups, finiteness serving as the entry condition to the system offering the choices between tense/modality and recursion, is 4436, the number of likely choices at β and at γ decreases rapidly to nearly zero in accordance with the probability for choosing between stop and go. In this corpus, a choice for β was made in only 238 verbal groups, and a choice for γ in just three. Secondly the statistical assumptions which have to be met for an investigation of successive choices in the same as well as in successive verbal groups, were not met here (see also sections 4.5/6).

The data was analysed using GLIM, a statistical package widely used in both the social and physical sciences, which is able to fit a variety of linear models to both categorical and numeric data. We fitted a logit model to the data, the same model used in Sankoff's VARBRUL program (Sankoff & Labov 1979). The results obtained using these programs are equivalent. (GLIM parameter estimates can be transformed to give VARBRUL parameter estimates, and vice versa.)[5]

Owing to the sampling technique used and the small size of the sample, the results should be understood as applying only to this sample. We do not mean to imply that they hold for all speakers of Australian English.

4.1. Recursion: stop vs. go

The chosen model is

$$\log\left(\frac{p}{1-p}\right) = \text{mean} + \text{age} + \text{sex}$$

This means that the choice of recursion at α, i.e. the choice of stop rather than go, depends on the speaker's age and sex. The effect of class is not statistically significant nor is the interaction between age and sex.

The following parameter estimates were obtained:

mean	2.759
adult	0
teenager	0.8186
male	0
female	-0.4887

Because the parameter estimate for teenagers is larger than that for adults, we conclude that teenagers choose stop at α more frequently than adults. Similarly, since the parameter estimate for males is larger than that for females we conclude that males choose stop at α more frequently than females.

GLIM fits estimated values for each cell and calculates standardised residual values. An examination of the residuals shows that the model does not predict well for teenage females. For this group we find that there is significant variation with class.

4.2. Finiteness: tense vs. modality

The best model that adequately describes the data is

$$\log\left(\frac{p}{1-p}\right) = \text{mean} + \text{class}$$

This means that the choice of tense at α, i.e. the choice of tense rather than modality depends on the speaker's class. The effects of age and sex are not statistically significant nor are any interactions.

The following parameter estimates were obtained:

mean	1.431
LWC	0
UWC	-0.6453
MC	-0.2332

Looking at the parameter estimates for class we see that the largest is for LWC, followed by that for MC, and then by that for UWC. Thus LWC choose tense the most, followed by MC, then UWC. Put the other way around, LWC speakers choose modality the least, MC speakers choose modality more frequently, and UWC speakers choose modality the most.

The residuals show that the fitted model does not predict well when the ratio of tense/total number of choices at α is low.

4.3. Tense: past vs. present tense

The selected model is

$$\log\left(\frac{p}{1-p}\right) = \text{mean} + \text{age} + \text{class}$$

This means that the choice of tense, i.e. the choice of past rather than present tense, varies according to the speaker's age and class. The effect of sex is not statistically significant nor are any interactions.

The following parameter estimates were obtained:

mean	1.436
adult	0
teenager	-0.9228
MC	0
UWC	-0.3924
LWC	-1.462

Following the same method of interpretation, we conclude (i) that teenagers choose past tense less frequently than adults; (ii) that LWC speakers choose past tense less frequently than UWC speakers, and that both LWC and UWC speakers choose past tense less frequently than MC speakers.

Examination of the residuals shows that this model does not predict well when the ratio of past/total number of occurrences is either very high or very low.

4.4. *Correlation between tense choices of interactants*

The possibility that the interviewer's grammatical choices constrain the grammatical choices made by the interviewee appears to be particularly strong in the case of the choice of tense (specifically past vs. present tense), but rather less so for the choice between tense and modality and least for the choice of recursion. A choice of past over present tense is much more likely to be maintained over a number of clauses as the realisation of some particular orientation towards past-time events than a choice of modality over tense or one of stop over go.

In order to investigate the possibility of the interviewer being ultimately responsible for the interviewee's grammatical choices in respect of tense at α, the Spearman rank correlation coefficient was calculated between the choices made by interviewer and respective interviewee (see Table 3). It was found to be 0.449 (P value = 0.0157). In other words, there is a significant dependence between the choices made by interviewer and interviewee.

However, this correlation does not establish the direction of the dependency, i.e. the statistical procedure used does not establish whether it is the interviewer or the interviewee whose choices of past or present lead the interactant to follow suit. In fact, an examination of some texts provides very clear evidence that an interviewee's persistent choice of present tense in response to repeated past tense questions, observations, etc. by the inter-

Table 3. Interviewees vs. interviewers choice of TENSE at α

#	sex	age	class	sex	class	total no	past no	past %	pres no	pres %	total no	past no	past %	pres no	pres %
								past : present interviewees					tense at α interviewers		
1	male	adult	LWC	fem	MC	21	2	9.5	19	90.5	12	8	66.7	4	33.3
2	male	adult	LWC	male	MC	43	20	46.5	23	53.5	13	10	76.9	3	23.1
3	male	adult	UWC	fem	MC	222	209	94.1	13	5.9	5	5	100.0	0	0.0
4	male	adult	UWC	male	MC	56	48	85.7	8	14.3	40	39	97.5	1	2.5
5	male	adult	MC	male	MC	42	29	69.0	13	31.0	11	10	90.9	1	9.1
6	male	adult	MC	fem	MC	148	122	82.4	26	17.6	19	17	90.0	2	10.
7	male	teen	LWC	male	MC	178	28	15.7	150	84.3	64	53	82.8	11	17.2
8	male	teen	LWC	fem	MC	144	53	36.8	91	63.2	44	29	65.9	15	34.1
9	male	teen	UWC	fem	MC	197	143	72.6	54	27.4	28	28	100.0	0	0.0
10	male	teen	UWC	male	WC	194	49	25.3	145	74.7	39	20	51.3	19	48.7
11	male	teen	MC	fem	MC	239	152	63.6	87	36.4	29	22	75.9	7	24.1
12	male	teen	MC	fem	MC	163	83	50.9	80	80	49.1	29	75.9	7	24.1
13	fem	adult	LWC	fem	MC	99	57	57.6	42	42.4	31	25	80.6	6	19.4
14	fem	adult	LWC	male	WC	173	55	31.8	118	68.2	57	47	28.5	10	17.5
15	fem	adult	UWC	fem	MC	107	78	72.9	29	27.1	33	32	97.0	1	3.0
16	fem	adult	UWC	fem	MC	160	119	74.4	41	25.6	26	21	80.8	5	19.2
17	fem	adult	MC	fem	MC	115	63	54.8	52	45.2	38	31	81.6	7	18.4
18	fem	adult	MC	fem	MC	157	118	75.2	39	24.8	18	18	100.0	0	0.0
19	fem	teen	LWC	male	WC	135	58	43.0	77	57.0	72	62	86.1	10	13.9
20	fem	teen	LWC	male	WC	92	33	35.9	59	64.1	46	34	73.9	12	26.1
21	fem	teen	UWC	fem	MC	95	64	67.4	31	32.6	30	24	80.0	6	20.0
22	fem	teen	UWC	fem	MC	273	79	28.9	194	71.1	43	39	90.7	4	9.3
23	fem	teen	MC	fem	MC	136	121	89.0	15	11.0	36	24	66.7	12	33.3
24	fem	teen	MC	fem	MC	78	64	82.1	14	17.9	40	31	77.5	9	22.5
				Total:		3,267	1,847		1,420		803	651		152	
				Average:		136.1	77.0	56.9	59.2	43.1	33.46	27.1	82.1	6.33	17.9
				Minimum:		21	2	9.5	8	5.9	5	5	51.3	0	0.0
				Maximum:		273	290	94.1	194	90.5	72	62	100.0	19	48.7
				Standard Deviation:		64.50	48.6	24.2	50.0	24.2	16.50	13.9	12.4	5.13	12.4

viewer will eventually lead to the interviewer switching to the interviewee's dominant tense choice. Table 3 shows that for the interviewer the choice of past tense predominates over present tense in every interview as well as having an overall incidence which is almost four times that of present tense. We may conclude from this clear propensity for a past tense choice on the part of the interviewer that as far as the non-congruent choice of present tense by interviewees is concerned, it is the interviewee who leads and not the interviewer.

4.5. The variability of the data

The statistical analysis used allowed for the different speakers' different probabilities of choice in a system. Nevertheless, the data was found to be more variable than predicted by the logit models. This variation was greatest for the choice of past vs. present tense and smallest in the case of stop vs. go (as indicated by the scaled deviance in the respective saturated models). Three possible explanations are offered for this which, although expressed as statistical properties, are essentially linguistic and sociological in nature.

Firstly, successive choices are not statistically independent. The model used assumes that each choice is statistically independent of previous choices. It seems highly likely that this assumption is not correct for this data. For example, if in a sequence of clauses past was chosen in the first clause, this will affect the probability of choice in the second clause so that the probability of choosing past is now higher than it was previously. On intuitive grounds, we might expect this dependency to be greatest for the choice of past vs. present and least for the choice of stop vs. go, the same order as was found for lack of fit of the models. Thus it appears that further investigation of the syntagmatic change in probabilities is warranted, as well as studies in paradigmatic probabilities.

Secondly, the assumption of constant probability for each speaker may be incorrect because the speaker may behave linguistically variably in the segment of the sociolinguistic interview chosen as the speaker's contribution to the total corpus. Although that segment, i.e. the "text" constituted by the discussion of primary school age games, is constant with respect to its subject matter and also to the social relationship between interviewee and interviewer, the organisation of the text itself is likely to vary. An extended turn by the interviewee obviously has a different internal organisation compared with a stretch of text which consists of a sequence of brief exchanges between interviewer and interviewee. Expressed in terms of the register theory that is part of Halliday's contextual model of language, there are likely to be changes in the textual organisation or "mode" of the interview segment, while its "field" and "tenor" are likely to be held constant. (See Horvath 1985 for a study which explores these differences in text, and which is both variationist and systemic.)

Moreover, an extended turn may take any number of forms, for example, the generic structure of a narrative text will differ from that of a descriptive, procedural or expository text and so on. Such differences go far beyond differences between casual and formal context; the latter may be quite irrelevant to such textual "rhetorical" differences, or to the differences between the texts' genres. A theory of text would seek to account for contextual factors in a much more differentiated fashion than by simply assigning a stretch of text to categories such as casual and formal, or even to delimit a text by reference to topic alone (cf. Martin & Rothery 1981; Halliday & Hasan 1985).

Thirdly, the lack of fit may be due to the gross social categories used, for example age could have been fitted as a numeric variable and class could have been expressed as a number of different factors such as income, housing, education etc. However, such refinements of social indices have generally been found not to be needed in sociolinguistic studies focusing on phonological variables. In fact, it has generally been found that quite gross social categories are sufficient in order to demonstrate associations between them and linguistic variables which are socially sensitive, i.e. "sociolinguistic variables". Whether such robustness of social-linguistic association can also be expected for grammatical variables needs to be established empirically (cf. Sankoff 1986: 2, who appears to assert this to the point of expecting group behaviour to be reliably exemplified in a single individual). Given the lack of quantitative studies of grammatical variables, it seems more important to develop further a theory of context by focusing on text rather than a refinement of the social categories with which a given grammatical variable may be associated.

4.6. Internal conditioning

In this study we have only investigated external conditioning. We regard the question of internal conditioning as perhaps more interesting but as a matter requiring a greater depth of study. The question of variation between individuals arises here in that unless it can be shown that such variation is not significant, data cannot be aggregated. In this data, there was considerable variation between individuals even after controlling for the effects of sex, age and class. We suggest that a corpus of data from one speaker be used in initial investigations of internal conditioning. The likelihood of significant syntagmatic variation (see section 4.5 above) also needs to be taken into account in an investigation of internal conditioning.

5. Interpretation of results

The interpretation of the results for the three grammatical variables quantified in this study presents a major problem in that we do not know how to integrate the results for recursion with those for tense/modality and past/present for two reasons. Firstly, the conditioning factors found to account for the variation in individual speakers' choice for recursion (age and sex) differ from those found to be significant for tense/modality (class) and past/present (age and class) in so far as that while the latter two have the factor "class" in common, recursion and past/present share the factor "age". But while the age factor in respect of tense choice can probably be explained as the result of speakers' temporal distance from the experiences talked about (adults favouring past tense while teenagers favour present tense), no such explanation can be offered for recursion (adults favouring "go" while teenagers favour "stop").

Secondly, considering the conditioning factors for recursion on their own, the factors age and sex could lead us to speculate along some of the lines pursued fruitfully in many sociolinguistic studies and perhaps propose explanations in terms of the "development" of recursion (since adults choose repeatedly for tense more often than teenagers) and/or the use of "prestige" forms (since females choose repeatedly for tense more often than males). But in the absence of any independent evidence that recursion is learned rather late (the teenage speakers are already between 14 and 17 years of age!) or that recursion is indeed "prestigious" (despite the fact that most of the repeated tense choices result in nothing more complex than an $\alpha\hat{\ }\beta$ structure!), we prefer not to pursue this line of enquiry. What we can conclude, however, is that the ever more delicate temporal referencing achieved by means of recursion is at least for this corpus shown to be socially conditioned. Recursion might be an "abstract" grammatical variable in some everyday sense but this does not appear to rule out its being socially sensitive.

Turning to the conditioning factors found to account for the variation between the choice for tense/modality (class) and past/present (age and class), we will proceed on the assumption that the conditioning of the choice of tense by age can indeed be explained by reference to the speakers' temporal distance from their experience of the games played. This is not unreasonable since at least some of the games played at primary school age are still being played by the teenagers at the time of their talking about them in the interview, most notably games which are also "sports", e.g. cricket and football. In what follows then, we will seek to give an interpretation of the conditioning of the choices between tense/modality and past/present tense by "class".

Let us restate the salient pattern of variation in respect of these choices by focusing on class:

tense/modality:
UWC speakers favour modality while LWC speakers favour tense.

past/present tense:
MC speakers favour past while LWC speakers favour present tense.

Since the choice of modality in the corpus is largely one concerned with making a choice in a system of "modalisation" rather than "modulation", i.e. with epistemic rather than deontic modality, and within the system of modalisation with "usuality" rather than "probability" (see Halliday 1985: 332ff.), it is reasonable to advance an interpretation which integrates the choices made between tense and modality on the one hand with those made between past and present on the other.

The corpus texts range from being essentially narrative in kind to being descriptive, and they often change between these types within the one text. The boundary between types is not easily drawn. Some of the texts are narrative-like in a most conventional way, particularly those told predominantly in the past tense; others are less obviously so, particularly those which are predominantly told in the present tense but also those which chose modality for their primary "tense" choice.

It is possible that typologically those texts which are not realised predominantly by past tense may still be considered narratives, specifically "generic narratives", and need not necessarily be considered descriptions (cf. Longacre 1976: 208 for the suggestion of a "deep structure narrative" cast in the form of a "surface structure procedural discourse" realised by present tense rather than the more congruent past). Such an interpretation should be uncontroversial for those texts which favour modality. Here it will only be assumed that a predominant choice of tense, be it past or present, as well as a choice of modality, may realise texts which lie on some continuum ranging from narrative to description. It should be pointed out that the present tense in the corpus texts is almost always a "generic" present tense and not a "historical" present tense. Rather than having the function of relating a succession of past events in the present tense, the "generic" or "timeless" present tense in the corpus texts is used to make statements of general validity (see Wolfson 1979; Schiffren 1981 on the function of the historical present tense).

If we now bring together Halliday's interpretation of modality, specifically of "usuality" in modalisation, and the choices favoured by the speakers belonging to different social class groups, we find that the three "values" of modality postulated by Halliday, viz. High, Median and Low, also apply to the grammatical choices made:

LWC choose the meaning "always"   realised by present   = High
UWC choose the meaning "usually"   realised by modality = Median
MC   choose the meaning "sometimes"   realised by past   = Low

Speakers choose to mean differently in their accounts of the past and this is shown clearly by the grammatical choices they make to realise their meanings. But what motivates the choices made by speakers belonging to different social classes in response to the same questions in the same context?

Starting from the contextual end of a functional model of language rather than from the formal grammatical choices that constitute our texts, we will turn for a possible answer to Bernstein's much misunderstood notions of "code" and some of his related ideas on the Whorfian notion of "fashions of speaking" and on communications systems. Bernstein sees the urban (British) LWC speaker as operating within "closed communications systems" that are realised by "socio-centric utterances" while the MC speaker is said to operate within an "open system" realised by "ego-centric utterances". Bernstein characterises closed systems as stressing the "particularistic" nature of meaning choices, thereby limiting their accessibility to members of the speaker's cultural group. On the other hand, open systems are considered by Bernstein to stress the "universalistic" nature of meanings, thereby making them accessible to all, regardless of group membership.

Such a view of the meaning choices associated with different social groups, a view formulated within a sociological model concerned with the maintenance and transmission of cultural patterns, makes it possible to consider the LWC speaker's consistent favouring of present tense choices as a reflection of an assumption that his/her meanings are accessible to the interactant via the interactant's quasi-membership of the group. If so, then one should expect some differences in behaviour depending on the class of the interactant, a hypothesis not borne out by this study and one which only further research can test (see Table 2 for a comparison of the class membership of interactants).

However, it is more likely that the LWC speaker interprets the demands of the situation in such a way that (s)he attempts to *create* the conditions under which a closed communications system can function. In effect, this would amount to the spontaneous creation of a subgroup whose members are the speaker and the interactant, i.e. interviewee and interviewer. We would argue that the LWC speaker interprets the demands of the interview situation, and especially the demand for a recalling, i.e. a recounting and explaining, of games played in primary school days, as a prompt to "share" with the interviewer his/her experience in a way which is symmetrical. (S)he can quite reasonably assume a cultural sharing of a child's experience of the games played at primary school age, and build on this by relating his/her particular experiences. This is done by including the hearer as someone of an "as you-and-I know" category. It is in this sense that we offer an interpretation in terms of the speaker's "modalisation" of the linguistic choices: events and states, and their grammatical realisations as processes, are asserted to be "always" valid.

The MC speaker, on the other hand, is typically more concerned with distancing him/herself from his/her meanings, and thus by abstracting these meanings (s)he attempts to make them universally available. The favoured use of the past tense as the one more congruent with the past-time experiences related in the interview would appear to achieve the effect of a more "objective", if not "objectified", account. Whereas events assume a generalised quality in the accounts of the LWC speaker, they are individuated and unique in the accounts of the MC speaker: they are asserted to be "sometimes" valid.

Intermediate between LWC and MC speakers in a hierarchy of class are the UWC speakers whose "modalisation" of meanings is also intermediate in that they choose to assert "usualness" for the past-time experiences recounted. In some ways such a choice appears to be the most grammatically congruent one by combining the MC speaker's choice of individuation with the LWC speaker's choice of general validity: "this is what I/we usually did" rather than "this is what I/you always do" (LWC) or "this is what I sometimes/once did" (MC). The UWC speakers occupy in every sense a "mid" position.

6. Conclusion

The results of this study of tense, and of recursion in respect of tense, bear out the insights gained in other quantificational studies, that the same speakers may group differently in respect of different linguistic variables. In this study, the major and also most clearly interpretable differences of association between a grammatical variable and social constraints pertain to the choice of past vs. present tense and its conditioning by social class.

The variable linguistic behaviour, found in this study to be associated with social class, cannot be equated with features of a social dialect in the way in which variationist studies have generally interpreted such differences between groups as being merely "different ways of saying the same thing", involving the neutralisation of the differences between different forms, i.e. variants of some grammatical variable, as suggested by Sankoff (1986). Instead, such variable behaviour is here interpreted to be the manifestation of the differential interpretation of the demands of the same context of situation by different groups with respect to some given linguistic variable, or as differences in a group's "sociolinguistic coding orientation" (cf. Halliday in Halliday & Hasan 1985: 41ff.). Such an interpretation is also implied by Labov (1972: 396), who suggests that "evaluation" and "syntactic elaboration" in narrative show evidence of a middle-class "over-development" which is dysfunctional relative to a working-class vernacular. We would therefore appear to be justified in concluding that the social conditioning of grammatical variation is an issue which demands further empirical investigation and that it cannot be accounted for *a priori*, i.e. dismissed, in terms of what is deemed to be "abstract" and "surface" variation respectively.

Appendix

1. Three (partial) Texts

(i) *Exemplification of choice of past over present*

Q: Let's start with talking about games. What kind of games did you play?
R: What kind of games would I ... I used to play hockey, yes, hockey, yes, hockey, field hockey, ice hockey, not ice hockey ... no, field hockey. That's about it, I think. No, that was the only really organised sport. I used to play rounders at school. Do you know rounders? That's a soft- it's sort of with a tennis ball, it's like softball, what's called softball, I think. But with a tennis ball instead of one of those rather fancy sort of things. You probably used a cricket bat actually, or a stick ... yes, that was the sort of thing, but that was it virtually. We used to play a bit of cricket but not — not anything — not really organised.
Q: What about chasings. Did you ever play that?
R: Oh yes, yes. I've got a wonderful story about chasings. I got ah ... There was this — we used to have wonderful games of chasings, of course, and there was this verandah that was out of bounds, you see, and in my excitement I was up on the verandah and across and the teacher caught me, and blow me down, five minutes later I did exactly the same thing. I of course got punished for that. He sort of said, "Come with me".
Q: Did you have special ways of chasings? What were the rules of chasings?
R: Oh, just if you tagged somebody, of course, they had to chase you. We used to have a wonderful game of chasings at my home. My home was a rather rambling sort of a place. It had a very big backyard and my father was a builder at this stage. Of course, there was timber and things around the place and there was also a very big shed, so we used to have a very elaborate sort of a route round this place ... that you could follow all sorts of tracks through it, so, if you were being chased by a foreigner, you could outwit them. Completely. And a lot of it used to include going across the galvanised iron roofs which were of course ... That was very much frowned on because if you trod on the bit that wasn't supported, you put a dent in the roof and it leaked forever after.
Q: Did you ever play something called ....

(ii) *Exemplification of choice of modal over tense*

Q: Can you go back to when you were nine or ten and remember some of the games that you used to play?
R: Yes, we played a game — nine and ten we used to play a lot of handball, used to play a lot of ah ... what were they? Well, we played cricket, we played football. When it was football, we played nothing else but football. Cricket, it was cricket every day, that was the standard thing we played all the time .... And I must tell you this tale. Where I lived was an area where there was a huge big brick pit and that was full of water and it was something like nearly ... oh it took, well, talking feet, it was about nearly two hundred yards across that brick pit and it had no bottom; it was virtually — it was hundreds of feet deep. But in the summer we were there every day; we lived on that brick

pit. And there were signs all round it; it had a fence around it. It was a huge thing and we called it the mill pond, and we made canoes and we made barges, we made everything, but basically we all wanted to swim in it, and we swam in it and we'd swim down, we'd go down twenty feet through reeds and we all swam in the nude and at that stage of our life we were — . We all started going there at the age of eleven and there ....
.... It was the most fascinating swimming hole because it was a hundred and fifty, you know, two hundred yards wide — it was a tremendous area and we all swam in it. We were there, you know, literally dozens of us in it every day. We'd run — hurry home from school and say to Mum we were going up the park and you'd go straight down to the mill pond, and then we'd have a game of pushing in and we'd push in and push in and fight, and then when it was, you know, when you didn't do that, you could catch little fish in there, it was full of small carp fish, and bring them home. That was another game we played. Then we could go over to the sand hill which was by the Australian golf links, which was another fascinating place. It's all filled in today but they were huge, big —. Well, they excavated out the sand, Hooker Rex used to take the sand out of there, and there were big ponds there, and we'd go over and we'd have another game. We'd look for frogs and we'd spend the whole Saturday morning with all our dogs — about twelve of us would go over and we'd all take our dogs and every household had two dogs ....

(iii) *Exemplification of choice of present over past*

Q: What I want to ask you about is some of the games you used to like to play when you were in primary school. What were some of the games that were popular at school?
R: Oh one called "roll the ball". And you got a square cricket net, and you serve the ball, and the idea is to hit a person with the ball without before and the last one gets a chance ... like you have to hit round, and if you hit it out of the square on the full you're out, and if it hits you anywhere except on your hand you're out, too. And you use a tennis ball, and if someone hits it in the air and you catch it they're out, and a chance is when you win the whole game, that you're the only person left, and the next time you get out you stay in because you've won the last game.
Q: How did kids get out?
R: Oh when it hits their body except for their hand.
Q: Is it a bit like brandings?
R: yeah except in a little confined area.
Q: And how many kids played?
R: Oh as many ... about twelve.
Q: And they all got in the cricket nets?
R: Yeah.
Q: So you crowded in?
R: Oh no, not really. Everyone's moving around so you don't — like there wouldn't ever — they have — they fit pretty well ... Most of the time kids get out pretty quickly so there's left about eight for the first — might be only about three minutes. The first four bat pretty quick.
Q: What about the person who's in? Where does he stand?
R: Oh like you can hit — everyone's in kind of thing. And you got to hit the ball with

your hand. And everyone can hit, and if you get hit you're out with the ball.
Q: What's that called?
R: Roller ball. ....

2. Coding procedures for verbal groups

(I) Instances of ellipsis have been included provided there was some residue of the verbal group which permitted a non-arbitrary coding for tense:

(1) -Have you seen Tom?
(1a) -Yes, I *have*. i.e. "I have seen him"
(1b) -Yes. i.e. "I saw him yesterday"
         or "I have seen him"

Type (1a) permits the "filling-in" of the verbal group and a non-arbitrary coding for tense while type (1b) does not. Both tense choices in (1b) are possible, and the change in tense *vis-à-vis* the question (1) is in fact quite common. Response type (1b) has therefore not been inclued in the analysis.

(II) Coordinate verbal groups have been scored for each instance of a main verb, with tense choice being assigned by reference to the presupposed verbal operators, whether modal or non-modal:

(2) We'*d go* and *play* and *have* a great time.

(III) Sequent tenses, though limited in choice, nevertheless exhibit some degree of choice and have therefore been included:

(3a) If you *had* this colour, you *could pass*.
                              were able to pass.
(3b) If you *have* this colour, you *can pass*.
                              will be able to pass.

(IV) Identical morphological series with two distinct meanings:

(4a) *have to* run   "must" (obligation)
     have got to run
     got to run
(4b) *have* marbles   "own" (possession)
     have got marbles
     got marbles

All three forms in either series have been treated as a single present tense choice at α. (Of course, *got* in the sense of "received" is distinguished from the above, and it may enter into a number of choices, e.g. *got* "past", *have got* "past in present", *will have got* "past in future", etc.)

(V) Two verbal groups in the one clause:

(5a) you *are supposed to grab*   "present; passive"
(5b) there *were* missiles *shooting*   "past"
(5c) you *had* marbles *lined up*   "past"

Verbs in "phase" have only been analysed in respect of the tense choice for the first verb; in examples (5a-c) all choices are at α only.

(VI) The following categories of verbal groups have been excluded:
  (i) finite ellipsis which is not recoverable from a preceding utterance, e.g.
      (6) the school *called* De La Salle
  (ii) unanalysable verbal groups (not involving correction), e.g.
      (7) anybody could have been could have had a anything happened then
  (iii) tags (only the verbal group in the matrix sentence is included)
  (iv) rhymes
      (8) he loves me, he loves me not, etc.
  (v) textual Adjuncts
      (9) that is
  (vi) corrections, false starts
  (vii) interpersonal Adjuncts
      (10a) (you) see   (10b) if you like
      (10c) I suppose   (10d) I (don't) think
      (10e) as I say   (10f) I mean
      (10g) I (don't) know   (10h) blow me down
      (10i) just say   (10j) as you said
      (10k) I reckon   (10l) that's right
      (10m) what was it? (when not directed at interlocutor)

Types (10 l,m) usually occur as a speaker's comment on his or her own thoughts or utterances.

A number of type (10) Adjuncts may be either interpersonal or experiential; if the latter then they have been included in the analysis, e.g.

   (11a) I dunno, it was from some somewhere I know 'cause they were ...

In (11a) the first instance of *know* has been analysed as interpersonal and the second as experiential, so only the first instance has been excluded from the analysis. The following examples have been treated similarly:

   (12a) I think it was then that ...   (excluded)
   (12b) I can't think of the rules of that one.   (included)

   (13a) I remember one boy had to ...   (excluded)
   (13b) I remember one variation of that ...   (included)

Because some of these types are rather formulaic in the corpus texts it was decided to include only the first five tokens although they were judged to be experiential. The following types come in this category:

   (14a) I (don't) know
   (14b) I (don't/can't) think
   (14c) I (don't/can't) remember/recall
   (14d) I'm (not) sure

(VII) Due to the task of recalling games played, and of reconstructing the rules of these games, speakers made heavy use of two contrasting pairs of verbal groups, depending on tense choice:

"past time reference"
(15a) *used to* throw   (modal)
      had to throw   (past tense)

"present time reference"
(16a) *must* throw   (modal)
      have to throw   (present tense)

The incidence of these types varied greatly in the texts, and it might have been defensible to view their occurrence in a similar light to the formulaic *I (don't) remember*, the sometimes experiential verbal group with an at times extraordinarily high frequency of occurrence, and therefore also limit its inclusion in the analysis in some way. However, it was felt that because of the interesting choices available to the speaker here, i.e. both for tense and modality unlike for the formulaic experiential types, all occurrences should be included.

Notes

1. Several of the issues discussed here, making use of some of the same data, were raised in a paper by G. Plum entitled "Quantification of text and context" given at the Annual Conference of the Australian Linguistics Society, Canberra (August 1981). While he is thus largely responsible for the linguistic interpretation, the reexamination and reinterpretation of the data presented here was made possible by A. Cowling's work and statistical expertise.

2. The data used in this paper is taken from sociolingusitic interviews collected for the Sydney Social Dialect Survey under the direction of Dr Barbara Horvath (Horvath 1985). We wish to thank Dr Horvath for making the transcriptions of the interviews available to us.

3. Cf. the response by Labov (1978) to the demand by Lavandera (1978) for an extension of variation studies "above and beyond phonology" which would "involve a conceptual leap" contrary to the opinion expressed by G. Sankoff (1973), i.e. which would consider grammatical variation as a potential carrier of semantic difference; also see the response by Romaine (1981) to both Labov and Lavandera.

4. For a complete paradigm of finite tense choices as well as a discussion of the stop rules, see Halliday (1976, 1985). For an account of the coding procedures followed in the coding of the corpus see Appendix 2.

5. For more details on the statistical theory and on model fitting, see Fienberg (1978) and Baker and Nelder (1978).

Some phonological constraints on grammatical formations: examples from four languages

R.H. Robins

Introduction

In general, phonology has been kept out of grammar (in its older meaning) or syntax (in its modern definition). The structuralists, working "upwards" in their analyses, made it a point of principle to complete the phonemic analysis in every detail before passing on to the identification and classification of morphs and morphemes and their distribution in relation to each other in higher order units and structures. Several subsequent theoreticians have reversed this ordering in their descriptive statements, treating phonological and phonetic statements as the latest stages in their presentation of their languages. This procedure is shown in such terms as *exponency* (Firth 1957: 15; Halliday 1961: 241-292) and *phonological rules*, whose input is the final output of the surface structure rules of the syntactic component (Chomsky & Halle 1968: 14; Chomsky & Laznik 1977: 428), and in the two lower strata of phonemic and phonetic realization in stratificational linguistics (Lamb 1966: 20; Palmer 1958).

Of course phonological factors determine much of the allomorphy in a language, as in the obvious cases of the English regular noun plural forms, /kæts/, /dɔgz/, and /hɔ:siz/, and the regular verb past tenses, /snift/, /bri:ðd/, and /snɔ:tid/. But phonological factors are not expected actually to determine the extent or the operation of a meaningful grammatical rule. This assumption was formally set out as the *Principle of phonology-free syntax* (*PPFS*) and defended by Zwicky (1969: 453): "No strictly syntactic or 'morphological' rule must be ordered within the phonological component". There has been some subsequent discussion on this (Plank 1984; Posner 1985; Zwicky 1985), mostly turning on ways in which rules of exponency or morphophonemics can be framed to avoid admitting the suspension of such rules as those of grammatical concord under certain phonological conditions. Thus instead of treating Spanish forms like *el agua* ("the water") and French *mon, ton,* and *son* before feminine nouns beginning with a vowel (*mon amie* "my lady friend", etc.) as a phonologically conditioned case of non-agreement, the forms *el, mon, ton,* and *son,* are analysed as "phonologically conditioned allomorphs" (Zwicky 1969: 434), which happen to be phonetically identical with their masculine counterparts.

Such allomorphy, in which there is no detectable semantic or syntactic distinction, is not of concern here. Nor are such variations as are found in English adjectives between inflected comparatives (and superlatives) and those formed with *more* (and *most*). Certainly the choice is in the main phonologically determined; monosyllabic adjectives generally use the inflected forms, *harder* and *smoother* being preferable to *more hard* and *more smooth* (in the same sense), while **difficulter* and **eruditer* are unacceptable, and Lewis Carroll's *curiouser and curiouser* was deliberately deviant. Between *harder* and *more difficult* there is no identifiable difference in meaning as far as the comparative degree is concerned, and all English adjectives whose positive meaning permits it can form comparatives and superlatives in one or the other way (some disyllabic adjectives have both forms in free variation, *pleasanter* and *more pleasant,* and it is semantics, not phonology, that excludes **uniquer* and **more unique*). Likewise the formation of inflected verbs from English adjectives (*blacken, redden, lighten, darken,* etc.) is confined to adjectives ending in a plosive or fricative consonant; there is no **greenen, *yellowen, *palen,* etc. and some adjectives ending in a plosive are also excluded, there being no **pinken,* for example. But here again we have in all cases alternative forms, with transitive or intransitive meanings, which can be used in place of the non-existent derived forms or as semantically indistinguishable alternatives to them: *make* (*paint, colour,* etc.) *black, pink, red, green,* and so on, and *become* (*turn, grow,* etc.) *pale, dim, bright, dark,* etc.

These types of phonologically determined restrictions are discussed extensively in Zwicky (1969) and in the subsequent writings which flowed from it; but they are excluded from further consideration in this paper. The functional differences between the inflected and the periphrastic forms in English mentioned above are ordinarily undetectable or virtually nil, except at an extremely high level of "delicacy" (in Halliday's technical usage) or in poetic diction where the requirements of rhyme and metre must be met; and the linguistic analysis of poetry is a separate and specialized subcomponent of linguistic analysis, albeit an important one.

Further, we are not here concerned with restrictions, which may certainly have semantic consequences, but which are lexically, not phonologically, conditioned (i.e. restrictions that apply to individual words as separate lexical items). Examples appear in all languages. Latin, for example, has no simple past tense formed from *quatio* ("to shake"); yet presumably the only readily available substitute *concussi*, from *concutio* ("to shake or agitate violently"), retains its basic intensification, so that, for example, *Zephyrus folia leviter quatit* ("the west wind lightly shakes the leaves") would be acceptable, but the past tense substitution in ?**Zephyrus folia leviter folia concussit* ("the west wind lightly shook violently the leaves") would scarcely be. In English, for many speakers, including the present writer, certain verbs, such as *forgo* and *abide* (*by*), have no very acceptable past tense. *The chairman usually forgoes his right to a casting vote* and *the chairman did not forgo his right* are acceptable, but *the chairman forwent his right* is, at least, rather awkward. Similarly there is nothing odd about *the Russians did not abide by the Black Sea Clauses of the Treaty of Paris after 1870*, but *the Russians abided by the Black Sea Clauses up to 1870* is a bit strange, and *abode by* would be quite impossible in such a sentence.

In this paper it is our intention to look at some examples of specific restraints on the use of certain syntactic constructions and morphological forms, primarily or wholly controlled by the phonological composition or cumulative length of some of the words concerned, but which also have an identifiable effect, semantic or stylistic, on the expressive resources of the language such as are otherwise available to it. We shall examine in turn cases in classical Latin, classical Greek, English, and Yurok (an American-Indian language of northern California).

Our interest here is the examination in these four languages of what would appear to be formations and constructions bearing observable connotations of style or register or even sometimes of cognitive meanings, which nevertheless are only available for use under certain phonological conditions. In some cases these conditions may operate along scales rather than with strict cut-off points, but at either end of such scales the operation of the rule is quite plain.

Classical Latin

In classical Latin the rule often called "gerundive attraction" is well known and is part of the formal teaching of Latin grammar. From Latin verb stems a verbal noun, the gerund, can be regularly formed: *amare* ("to love"), *amandum* ("(the state or act of) loving"), *monere* ("to advise"), *monendum* ("(the act of) advising"), and the gerunds of transitive verbs retain their transitivity. These verbal nouns inflected as neuter singular nouns of the second declension, and they could be used in regular nominal constructions, e.g. Juvenal 3.233, *aeger moritur vigilando* ("he dies, sick with keeping watch"), *ad bene vivendum* ("in order to live well"), *ars scribendi* ("the art of writing").

Priscian (Keil 1855: 409-413) compares the Latin gerund with the Greek infinitive. But whereas the Greek infinitive distinguished several tenses as well as the three voices, active, middle, and passive, the Latin gerund was found in one voice only, the active, and carried no morphological distinction of tenses, the meanings of which had to be supplied by the context in which the gerund was used. Though it was a verbal noun, sharing aspects of nominal and verbal syntax as well as nominal morphology, Priscian surely reflected native intuitions when he described it as nominal rather than verbal, *magis nomen quam verbum* (410); and probably for this reason the construction of a direct noun object with a transitive gerund was avoided, though it was not impossible, and examples of it are found. Priscian refers to this type of construction as rare, *rarus huiuscemodi constructionis usus* (410), and it was avoided particularly by the authors of the classical age.[1]

The corresponding construction of the noun with the gerundive, a verbal adjective passive in meaning, *amandus* ("lovable, to be loved"), etc., was preferred. Thus Priscian (410) translates the Greek *tou anagnōnai Bergilion charin agrupnō* ("I stay awake for the sake of reading Vergil"), by *legendi Virgilii causa vigilo*, rather than by *legendi Virgilium causa vigilo*. The difference in the constructions comes out more clearly if a feminine noun is made the transitive object: *legendi Sappho causa* ("for the sake of reading Sappho") as compared with *legendae Sapphos causa* ("(lit.) for the sake of Sappho to be read") where the verbal adjective is in gender concord as well as case concord with the underlying object noun. This conversion, or transformation, of a nominal gerund construction into an adjectival gerundive construction is traditionally known as the "gerundive attraction".

However, when genitive plurals of nouns of the first and second declensions in *-arum* and *-orum*, and consequently genitive plurals of gerundives, which were formed with the same endings, would be involved, causing rhyming sequences *-arum -arum* or *-orum -orum*, gerundive attraction was avoided for the most part. Classical Latin kept itself free of rhyme in poetry as in prose, and the penultimate long vowels of these genitive plural forms would have borne the word stress and reinforced the rhyme effect. So instead of such sequences as *castrorum oppugnandorum causa* ("in order to attack the camp"), we tend to retain the untransformed gerund plus object construction *castra oppugnandi causa*.[2] Occasionally a non-agreeing construction of plural noun with singular gerundive was used, e.g. Cicero, *Philippics* 5.3: *facultas agrorum suis latronibus condonandi* ("the opportunity of giving lands to his brigands").

All this is traditionally referred to as "euphony", but it appears that to some extent the practice of authors varied in making their choice between the syntactic dislike of oververbalizing the gerund and the phonetic dislike of prominent rhyme sequences, but the general tendency is quite clear, and where a long sequence of genitive plural rhymes would be generated the construction would certainly have been avoided; while such a sentence as *Adranus urbium Graeciae antiquae visendarum causa Athenas profectus est* ("(the Emperor) Hadrian set out for Athens in order to visit the cities of ancient Greece") would be quite acceptable, the syntactically equivalent sentence **Caesar castrorum magnorum Helvetiorum oppugnandorum causa aciem instruxit* ("Caesar drew up his battle line in order to attack the large camp of the Helvetii") would certainly be rejected.[3]

This is a clear case in which phonological factors either inhibit or prevent the operation of a syntactic transformation, designed to avoid an apparently awkward syntactic construction, obviously not rendered any less awkward just because the alternative was felt, phonologically, to be even worse.

Classical Greek

In classical Greek of the fourth century B.C., Goodwin (1912: 14) draws attention to the distinctive meaning of the periphrastic form of the passive pluperfect (past participle with imperfect indicative of *einai* "to be"), as it was used by Demosthenes (*On the crown* 18.23): *oute gar ēn presbeia pros oudena apestalmenē tote tōn Hellēnōn* ("for there was then no embassy out on a mission to any of the Greeks") (*ēn ... apestalmenē*, "was in a state of having been despatched"). The non-periphrastic pluperfect form *apestalto* would have borne a different meaning: "no embassy had then been sent out".

However, if instead of *presbeia* ("embassy") a singular collective noun, the plural *presbeis* ("ambassadors") had been used, the semantic distinction just described would be unavailable with the verb *apostellō* ("to send out") because as a verb with a consonant-final stem only the periphrastic form of the third person plural of the perfect and pluperfect would be possible (thus *luō*, stem *lu-*, "to release", *leluntai*, "they have been released", *lelunto*, "they had been released", beside *lelumenoi eisin/ēsan*, "they are/were in a state of having been released"; but there were no such forms as **apestalntai*, **apestalnto* (stem *stal-*).

Where both forms are possible there are several examples of their contrastive use: Homer, *Iliad* 16.225 *entha de hoi depas eske tetugmenon* ("and there was his goblet, well fashioned"); *Odyssey* 20.365-6: *eisi moi ophthalmoi te kai ouata kai podes amphō/kai noos en stēthessi tetugmenos* ("I have (lit. there are for me) eyes and ears and two feet and a mind well formed in my breast"); Thucydides 4.31.2: *eruma autothi ēn palaiōn lithōn logadēn pepoiēmenon* ("there was a defensive position there of old stones carefully constructed"). In all these examples the copula and the participles retain their own meanings.

In Homeric Greek and in the Ionic dialect of Herodotus, and occasionally in fifth century Attic as late as Thucydides, non-periphrasic third person plural forms of the perfect and the pluperfect were available with consonant-final stems through the realization of the Indo-European **-ntai*, **-nto* as *-atai* and *-ato*, respectively; this vocalic realization was quite common in Homer even with vowel final stems, e.g. *Iliad* 2.90 *pepotēatai* ("they have flown") (stem *potē-*). There are some cases where the two forms are juxtaposed in contrast with each other: thus Herodotus 7.65, *estalmenoi men ... ēsan houtōs Indoi, prosetetachato de sustrateuomenoi Pharnazathrēi* ("the Indians were (in a state of having been) equipped in this way, but they had been assigned as fellow-soldiers to Pharnazathres"): Thucydides 4.31.2-32.1, *hōde ... die tetachato; ... houtō men tetagmenoi ēsan. hoi de Athēnaioi tous ... prōtous phulakas euthus diaphtheirousin* ("they had been stationed in this way ... Thus were they (in a state of having been) drawn up. But the Athenians immediately destroyed (lit. destroy, historic present) the foremost guards").

Inscriptional and other evidence shows that these non-periphrastic forms disappeared in Attic Greek after 400 B.C., though such forms from vowel-final verb stems continued in regular use (e.g. Polybius 1.58.9). What this amounts to is that after 400 B.C. a semantic contrast available within the passive verb system disappeared in classical Attic Greek with one phonologically definable set of verbs, the consonant-final stem verbs, when the third person plural, perfect or pluperfect was involved, while it continued in use in another set, the vowel final stem verbs. This has nothing to do with semantically distinguishable sets; the two types of verb stems are entirely arbitrary as far as their lexical meanings are concerned. It is simply a case of certain phonotactic rules foreclosing a contrast in meaning in one set of verbs while leaving it in operation in another set.

English

In current English there is a regular and frequently used possibility of syntactic variation, which leaves the cognitive meaning of a sentence untouched but carries distinct connotations or overtones of style or register appropriate to different contexts. This is referred to as "preposition stranding", or in traditional terms "ending a sentence with a preposition", usually by postposing it to the NP that it governs. This variation in word order, discussed briefly in Zwicky (1969), was formerly condemned in the schoolroom, just because of the colloquial style that it indicated, but it is in many contexts entirely acceptable, and with some prepositions it is the only order possible.

Compare these two cognitively and factually equivalent sentences (said by a guide conducting a group of visitors): *We are now passing the school to which the Princess of Wales sends Prince William*, and (in personal conversation) *That's the school (that) Princess Di sends her Bill to*. Of course the order of preposition and noun phrase could be changed in each case perfectly acceptably, but there would be a slight incongruity of style between the context and the vocabulary chosen on the one hand and the syntactic form on the other.

"Ending a sentence with a preposition" is a familiar mark of informality, and this is evidenced in the teaching remark made in the schoolroom "A preposition is the wrong word to end a sentence with". But some prepositions in some constructions can only be used in this way, and such expressions usually carry a trace of colloquiality or dismissiveness. James

Mill is reported (Russell 1946: 801) to have said on his first reading of the work of Immanuel Kant "I see well enough what poor Kant would be at". *ptmb*I see at what poor Kant would be* would have been impossible; but Mill's choice of language, leaving aside the adjective *poor*, is scarcely compatible with a favourable estimate of Kantian thinking. In today's English, *I could never see what Marcuse with his notion of "repressive tolerance" was* {*driving at* / *up to*} has similar implications. **up to what he was* or (in the metaphorical sense) *at what he was driving* are both unacceptable, but the use of either obligatorily postposed prepositional construction in the sentence just quoted serves to cast doubt on the worthwhileness of pursuing Marcuse's work any further. By contrast the sentence *I still find it hard to grasp the empirical data and the theoretical basis on which Einstein erected his general theory of relativity*, where the preposition *on* precedes the relative clause, suggests that it is the speaker's incapacity, and not any doubt about the seriousness of Einstein's thought, that is being indicated.

Where a preposition can occupy both a final and a non-final position, only the latter is fully compatible with a deliberately elevated or dignified style: "It is for us, the living, rather to be dedicated here ... to the great task remaining before us — that from these honoured dead we take increased devotion to that cause for which they gave the last full measure of devotion ..." (Lincoln's *Gettysburg Address*). Abraham Lincoln could hardly have said on such an occasion "increased devotion to that cause which they gave the last full measure of devotion for".

However, as we saw in earlier examples, one may choose to strand a preposition after its NP to achieve a deliberately "undignified" informal impression. But if we lengthen the NP sufficiently there comes a point, no doubt personally and situationally variable, where, despite the colloquial form of the sentence, preposition stranding is impossible. The following sentence in formal style is entirely acceptable: *We are now passing the school to which the Princess of Wales sends Prince William, the future King William V, a king expected to be on the Throne of England well into the second half of the twenty first century*. But we could not say something like **Here's the school (that) Di sends her boy, likely to be the King, alive and kicking, till 2060 at least, to*. More acceptably, perhaps, the preposition *to* could be put after *boy*, with the rest of the sentence following in a loose apposition, but such a splitting of the extended NP would still be rather awkward.

Irrespective of the style of the utterance, preposition stranding is here excluded by the spoken length of the NP, and length is a phonological feature. This is different from a strict syntactic restriction, like the well known prohibition on the extraction of an NP from a clause dominated by an NP, which operates independently of both style and length; e.g.

> How many young ladies do you believe *the story (that) the leader of the Workers Revolutionary Party distressed with his unwanted amatory advances?
> How many girls do you believe *the story (that) he pestered?

Both these sentences are equally acceptable without *the story* and equally unacceptable with these two words in the place indicated.

In the stylistically variable placing of prepositions English is unlike the Romance languages, among others, in which such a sentence form, at least in the standard varieties, is impossible.[4] But German permits, indeed it requires, a somewhat similar stranding of a "separable" prepositional prefix, which may be placed at a considerable distance from the verb to which, in a different tense, it would be prefixed, e.g. Humboldt 1836: 113: *So nehmen auch in den einfachen, abgeleiteten Wörtern die Nebenlaute in richtig organisierten Sprachen einen kleineren, obgleich sehr bedeutsamen Raum ein*, so also in simple derived words the secondary sound units take on a smaller though a very significant place in properly structured languages; but in the perfect tense we would have *so auch in den einfachen, abgeleiteten Wörtern haben die Nebenlaute ... Raum eingenommen*. Unlike the English usage, such lengthy constructions (*Rahmenkonstruktionen*) are a mark of a formal rather than of an informal style.

What we see in the English examples that we have been considering is that a shift in the relative order of a preposition and the NP that it governs, carrying recognized stylistic implications, is effectively excluded from acceptable use when the NP reaches a certain length, irrespective of other syntactic, stylistic, or contextual features. Length in spoken discourse is a matter of phonology, not of syntax nor of lexicon.

Yurok

The Yurok examples that we shall be examining in this context involve a rather different grammatical process, one which at least in traditional terms would be considered as lying wholly within the compass of morphology.

Two separate synchronic processes are found operative in Yurok verbs, bringing with them a semantic modification of the meaning of the verb base under the general heading of frequentative or iterative. The first process is the infixation of *-eg-*, and its less common phonologically determined allomorphs *-ɟg-* and *-eʔg-*, between the initial consonant or consonant cluster and the first vowel of the verb base.[5] This process of infixation can in principle be applied to any verb. Thus:

> *la:yek'*, "I pass; *lega:yek'*, "I pass regularly"
> *łkyork^w ek'*, "I watch"; *łkyegork^w ek'*, "I am a regular spectator"
> *kɟtkɟk'*, "I fish for trout"; *kɟgɟtkɟr'*, "I often fish for trout"
> *nepiʔmoh*, "we eat"; *negepiʔmoh*, "we always eat"
> *ʔoʔroyeʔw*, "he is in debt"; *ʔeʔgoʔroyeʔw*, "he is always in debt"
> *tewomeł* (non-suffixed verb), "to be glad"; *tegewomeł*, "to be of a happy disposition"

The exact meanings of these infixed forms vary according to context and usage and have given rise to some idiomatic expressions, e.g. *lega:y-*, "to use the same track every time" (*la:y-*, "to pass"); *pegiʔiyeʔmoh*, "lots of us were gathering mussels" (*piʔiy-*, "to gather mussels"); *kegoʔmoy-*, "to be an interpreter" (*koʔmoy-*, "to hear"; *kegoʔmoy-* can also be used just to mean "to hear a lot").

The second process involves *ablaut* or a change of the first vowel from *e* or *ɟ* to *u:* before *k^w*, *k'^w*, *w*, and *ʔw*, and to *i:* in all other phonological environments; only short vowels are found with this *ablaut* in my own field notes, but Berman (1982: 210) provides one example of an ablauted long *ɟ:*. The basic meaning associated with this process is also frequentative, but individual verb forms take on several more marked or specialised functions. Thus:

> *nek-*, "to put"; *ni:kuʔ*, "it is regularly put (there)"
> *leko:t-*, "to stab"; *li:ko:t-*, "to go around stabbing people, to be a 'bravo'"
> *newoy-*, "to be seen"; *nu:wiʔ*, "it is to be seen" (of a static object such as a prominent rock)
> *pewom-*, "to cook"; *ku pu:womin* (attributive form) "the (professional) cook"
> *tɟgɟw* (non-suffixed verb), "to settle a dispute"; *ti:gɟw*, "to be at peace"

Ablaut formation differs from infixation in two respects: (1) It is lexically restricted, and not, as is *-eg-*, generally available to all verbs.

(2) Those verbs to which it does apply are a lexical subset of an already phonologically limited set, namely those whose first vowel is *i* or *ɹ* (and *ɹ:*). And it must be emphasized that this phonologically defined set of verbs has no concomitant syntactic or semantic correlations. Thus *new-*, "to see", can take *ablaut*, but not, for example, *nowkʷ-*, "to care for"; *leko:t-*, "to stab", can *ablaut*, but not *la:y-*, "to pass".

However, *ablaut* can operate as a secondary process on verbs already infixed, which necessarily have *e* or *ɹ* as their first vowel, though, again, such doubly frequentative forms are lexically restricted. The following examples illustrate this formation:

cwin (non-suffixed verb), "to talk"; *cwegin*; *ku wonoyeʔik ʔo cwi:gin*, "(the Christian) God (one who talks a great deal in the sky)"
kemoloc-, "to envy"; *kegemoloc-*; *ki:gemoloc-*, "to be jealous by nature"
meɬʔen, "to beg"; *megeɬʔen*; *mi:geɬʔen*, "to go around begging, to be a beggar"

Further examples may be found in Robins (1958: 84-85).

It might be argued that, since potentially any and every verb can be infixed with *-eg-*, *ablaut* is not, in effect, phonologically restricted in its availability. This, however, assumes that semantically the *-eg-* infix becomes meaningless when its vowel is ablauted. This seems unlikely, since the *-eg-* infixed forms are used, frequentatively, without the *ablaut*, and their ablauted forms usually take on a specific meaning of their own, in addition to the lexical meaning of the verb base and the already frequentative meaning of the infix. But on the other hand, among those verbs admitting *ablaut*, the ones that have *e* or *ɹ*(:) as their first vowel can accept the process immediately.

It seems obvious that a meaning-changing derivational process, lexically restricted to a limited number of verbs, is further phonologically constrained, in that it can only operate directly on verbs whose base form is of a certain phonological structure or to those that have already undergone a prior process of derivation, itself independently meaning-changing.

Conclusion

In their different ways, it does appear that in the languages we have examined there are clear cases where syntactically and semantically distinctive formations may be arbitrarily constrained or restricted by the phonological composition of the words involved. Of course this does not happen extensively, nor does it operate more than peripherally. No language could tolerate much phonological resistance to its communicative requirements. But it may well be found that such restraints are found in other languages than those discussed here, thus showing just one more facet of the fascinating interplay of the constituents of human speech.

Notes

1. Cf. Hofmann (1965: 373) *im allgemeinen archaisch und nachklassisch*.

2. Cf. Hofmann (1965: 373) *die schwerfällige Genitivendung -orum zu vermeiden*.

3. It is interesting to observe that when Cicero does once (*Orator* 68), doubtless for some special effect, collocate three genitive plurals in a gerundival phrase, he suffixes the middle one with *-que*, and, which by the shift of the word stress destroys the rhyme: *licentiam ... faciendorum iungendorumque verborum* ("the freedom to form and to concatenate words").

4. Sentences have been quoted from some varieties of colloquial French with a stranded preposition in final position: from a soldier's letter (Frei 1929: 187), *la jeune fille qu'il doit se marier avec*; Guiraud (1966: 41) has a similar example: *l'homme qu'elle est venue avec*, and the sequence *le gars qui j'ai voté pour* is attested in the colloquial French of Quebec (Bouchard 1982: 224).

5. All Yurok words begin with at least one consonant; for details of the morphology see Robins (1958: 80-85).

Collocation: a progress report

John McH. Sinclair

Introduction

This paper is a contribution to the extended discussion of the nature of lexis, and its relation to grammar (Butler 1985). The relation of lexis to semantics is also touched on, but not developed. It is a discussion that began for the present writer in sessions with Firth, whose concepts of collocation and colligation are central (Firth 1951). Colligation never took off at all, and collocation was accepted as an insight, celebrated in one or two papers, but was singularly unproductive as a springboard for new descriptions.

Michael Halliday was one of the principal celebrants, and lexis was neatly fitted into his first full scale model, as "most delicate grammar" (Halliday 1961, 1966). At this time, the advent of computers made it possible in principle to study lexis, and Halliday inspired and encouraged the study (Sinclair 1966). Hence it is appropriate to offer a progress report on this occasion, in gratitude.

Two models of interpretation

It is contended here that in order to explain the way in which meaning arises from language text, we have to advance two different principles of interpretation. One is not enough. No single principle has been advanced which accounts for the evidence in a satisfactory way.

The two principles are:
(1) *The open choice principle*: This is a way of seeing language text as the result of a very large number of complex choices. At each point where a unit is completed (a word or a phrase or a clause), a large range of

choice opens up, and the only restraint is grammaticalness.

This is probably the normal way of seeing and describing language. It is often called a "slot-and-filler" model, envisaging text as a series of slots which have to be filled from a lexicon which satisfies local restraints. At each slot, virtually any word can occur. Since language is believed to operate simultaneously on several levels, there is a very complex pattern of choices in progress at any moment, but the underlying principle is simple enough.

Any segmental approach to description is of this type; any which deals with progressive choices; any tree structure shows it clearly: the nodes on the tree are the choice points. Virtually all grammars are constructed on the open choice principle.

(2) *The idiom principle*: It is clear that words do not occur at random in a text, and that the open choice principle does not provide substantial enough restraints. We would not produce normal text simply by operating the open choice principle.

To some extent, the nature of the world around us is reflected in the organisation of language and contributes to the unrandomness. Things which occur physically together have a stronger chance of being mentioned together; also concepts in the same philosophical area, and the results of exercising a number of organising features such as contrasts or series. But even allowing for these, there are many ways of saying things, many choices within language that have little or nothing to do with the world outside.

There are sets of linguistic choices which come under the heading of register, and which can be seen as large scale conditioning choices. Once a register choice is made, and these are normally social choices, then all the slot-by-slot choices are massively reduced in scope or even, in some cases, preempted.

Allowing for register as well, there is still far too much opportunity for choice in the model, and the principle of idiom is put forward to account for the restraints that are not captured by the open choice model.

The principle of idiom is that a language user has available to him or her a large number of semi-preconstructed phrases that constitute single choices, even though they might appear to be analysable into segments. To some extent, this may reflect the recurrence of similar situations in human affairs; it may illustrate a natural tendency to economy of effort; or it may be motivated in part by the exigencies of real-time conversation. However it arises, it has been relegated to an inferior position in most current linguistics, because it does not fit the open-choice model.

At its simplest, the principle of idiom can be seen in the apparently simultaneous choice of two words, e.g. *of course*. This phrase operates effectively as a single word, and the word space, which is structurally bogus, may disappear in time, as we see in *maybe, anyway* and *another*.

Where there is no variation in the phrase, we are dealing with a fairly trivial mismatch between the writing system and the grammar. The *of* in *of course* is not the preposition *of* that is found in grammar books. The preposition *of* is normally found after the noun head of a nominal group, or in a quantifier like *a pint of* .... In an open-choice model, *of* can be followed by any nominal group. Similarly, *course* is not the countable noun that dictionaries mention; its meaning is not a property of the word, but of the phrase, and as a countable noun in the singular it would have to be preceded by a determiner to be grammatical.

It would be reasonable to add phrases like *of course* to the list of compounds, like *cupboard*, whose elements have lost their semantic identity, and make allowance for the intrusive wordspace. The same treatment could be given to hundreds of similar phrases — any occasion where one decision leads to more than one word in text. Idioms, proverbs, clichés, technical terms, jargon expressions, phrasal verbs and the like could all be covered by a fairly simple statement.

However, the principle of idiom is far more pervasive and elusive than we have allowed so far. It has been noted by many writers on language but its importance has been largely neglected. Some examples follow:

(a) Many phrases have an indeterminate extent. As an example, consider *set eyes on*. This seems to attract a pronoun subject, and either *never* or a temporal conjunction like *the moment, the first time*, and the word *had* as an auxiliary to *set*. How much of this is integral to the phrase?

(b) Many phrases allow internal lexical variation. For example, there seems to be little to choose between *in some cases* and *in some instances*; or *set X on fire* or *set fire to X*.

(c) Many phrases allow internal syntactic variation. Consider the phrase *it's not in his nature to* .... The word *it* is part of the phrase, and the verb *is*, though this verb can vary to *was* and perhaps can include modals. *Not* can be replaced by any "broad" negative, including *hardly, scarcely*, etc. *In* is fixed, but *his* can be replaced by any possessive pronoun and perhaps by some names with *'s. Nature* is fixed.

(d) Many phrases allow some variation in word order. Continuing the last example, we can postulate *to recriminate is not in his nature*, or *it is not in the nature of an academic to* ....

(e) Many uses of words and phrases attract other words in strong collocation; for example *hard work*, *hard luck*, *hard facts*, *hard evidence*.

(f) Many uses of words and phrases show a tendency to co-occur with certain grammatical choices. For example the phrasal verb *set about*, in its meaning of something like "inaugurate", is closely associated with a following verb in the *-ing* form, e.g. *set about leaving*. What is more, the verb is usually transitive, e.g. *set about testing it*. Very often *set* will be preceded by *to* and quite often *how* will be two or three words to the left. In general, grammatical categories like negative, pronoun, adverbial will be found in co-occurrence patterns.

(g) Many uses of words and phrases show a tendency to occur in a certain semantic environment. Continuing the discussion of *set about*, it is distinguished by an environment of trying or attempting, suggesting that there is a problem to be solved. We do not set about something simple, like opening a door, unless it is stuck or locked etc. Further, *set about* is characteristically used to describe a secondary goal; in order to achieve X, we set about doing Y.

The overwhelming nature of this evidence leads us to elevate the principle of idiom from being a rather minor feature, compared with grammar, to being at least as important as grammar in the explanation of how meaning arises in text. Support comes unexpectedly from a different quarter.

In the course of the COBUILD project at the University of Birmingham to study lexicography based on analysing long texts, a number of problems arose, not all of which had been anticipated:

(a) The "meanings" of very frequent, so-called grammatical words are a headache in any lexicography, but the problem they typify fits in with some of the newer difficulties.

(b) Some "meanings" of frequent words seem to have very little meaning at all, e.g. *take* in *take a look at this*; *situation*, in the phrase *ongoing meaningful situations* made famous in the U.K. by the satirical magazine *Private Eye*.

(c) The commonest meanings of the commonest words are not the meanings supplied by introspection; e.g. the meaning of *back* as "the posterior part of the human, extending from the neck to the appendix" (*Collins English Dictionary* (*CED*) 1979 sense 1) is not a very common meaning. Not until sense 46, the second adverbial sense, do we come to "in, to or towards the original starting point, place or condition".

I cite *CED* because I think it is a good dictionary, not a bad one. I think most speakers of English would agree with *CED*'s ordering of senses, whatever the evidence from frequency. What is disquieting is the lack of good reason for the enormous discrepancy between the sense to which our intuitions give priority, and the most frequent one.

(d) The commonest meanings of many less common words are not those supplied by introspection. The first sense offered in *CED* for *pursue* is "to follow (a fugitive etc.) in order to capture or overtake", yet by far the commonest meaning is the fifth sense "to apply oneself to (one's studies, hobbies, interests etc.)".

From this evidence we can put forward some tentative generalisations:

(1) There is a broad general tendency for frequent words, or frequent senses of words, to have less of a clear and independent meaning than less frequent words or senses. These meanings are difficult to identify and explain, and with the very frequent words we are reduced to talking about uses rather than meanings. The tendency can be seen as a progressive delexicalisation.

(2) This dependency of meaning correlates with the operation of the idiom principle to make fewer and larger choices. The evidence of collocation supports the point. If the words collocate significantly, then to the extent of that significance their presence is the result of a single choice.

(3) The "core" meaning of a word — the one that first comes to mind for most people — will not normally be a delexical one. A likely hypothesis is that the "core" meaning is the most frequent independent sense. This hypothesis would have to be extensively tested, but if it proved to hold good then it would help to explain the discrepancy referred to above between the most frequent sense and what intuition suggests is the most important or central one.

(4) Most normal text is made up of the occurrence of frequent words, and of the frequent senses of less frequent words. Hence normal text is largely delexicalised, and appears to be formed by exercise of the idiom principle, with occasional switching to the open choice principle.

(5) Just as it is misleading and unrevealing to subject *of course* to grammatical analysis, it is also unhelpful to attempt to analyse any portion of text which appears to be constructed on the idiom principle.

The last point contains an implication that a description must indicate how users know which way to interpret each portion of an utterance. The boundaries between stretches constructed on different principles will not normally be clear-cut, and not all stretches carry as much evidence as *of course* does to suggest that it is not constructed by the normal rules of grammar.

It should be recognised that the two models of language that are in use are incompatible with each other. There is no shading of one into another; the switch from one model to the other will be sharp. The models are diametrically opposed.

The last two points taken together suggest one reason why language text is often indeterminate in its interpretation and hence very flexible in use. If the "switch points" between two modes of interpretation are not always explicitly signalled, and the two modes offer sharply contrasting ways of interpreting the data, then it is quite likely that an utterance will not be interpreted in exactly the same way in which it was constructed. Also two listeners, or two readers, will not interpret in precisely the same way.

For normal texts we can put forward the proposal that the first mode to be applied is the idiom principle since most of the text will be interpretable by this principle. Whenever there is good reason, the interpretive process switches to the open choice principle, and quickly back again. Lexical choices which are unexpected in their environment will presumably occasion a switch; choices which, if grammatically interpreted, would be unusual are an affirmation of the operation of the idiom principle.

Some texts may be composed in a tradition which makes greater than normal use of the open choice principle; legal statements for example. Some poems may contrast the two principles of interpretation. But these are specialised genres that require additional practice in understanding.

It thus appears that a model of language which divides grammar and lexis, and which uses the grammar to provide a string of lexical choice points, is a secondary model. It cannot be relinquished because a text still has many switch points where it will come into play. It has an abstract relevance, in the sense that much of a text shows a *potential* for being analysed as the result of open choices, but the other principle, the idiom principle, dominates. It could be imagined as an analytic process which goes on in principle all the time, but whose results are only intermittently called for.

This view of how the two principles are deployed in interpretation can be used to make predictions about the way people behave, and the accuracy of the predictions can be used as a measure of the accuracy of the model. Areas of relevant study include the transitional probabilities of words, the prevalent notion of "chunking", the occurrence of hesitations etc. and the placement of boundaries, and the behaviour of subjects trying to guess the next word in a mystery text.

Collocation

The above is the framework within which I would like to consider the role of collocation. Collocation, as has been mentioned, illustrates the idiom principle. On some occasions, words appear to be chosen in pairs or groups and these are not necessarily adjacent.

One aspect of collocation has been of enduring interest. When two words of different frequencies collocate significantly, the collocation has a different value in the description of each of the two words. If word A is twice as frequent as word B, then each time they occur together has twice the importance for B than it does for A. This is because that particular event accounts for twice the proportion of the occurrence of B than of A.

So when we count up all the occurrences of A with B, and evaluate them, one figure is recorded in the profile of A, and another figure double the size, is recorded in the profile of B.

By entering the same set of events twice, once as the collocation of A with B and again as the collocation of B with A, we incur the strictures of Benson, Brainerd and Greaves (1985) who say "There are two problems here: double counting of nodes and double counting of collocates. The parts now add up to considerably more than the whole, which makes computation under any statistical model inaccurate".

I would like to consider separately the two types of collocation instanced above. Let us use the term "node" for the word that is being studied, and the term "collocate" for any word that occurs in the specified environment of a node. Each successive word in a text is thus both node and collocate, though never at the same time.

When A is node and B is collocate, I shall call this *downward* collocation — collocation of A with a less frequent word (B). When B is node and

A is collocate, I shall call this *upward* collocation. The whole of a given word list may be treated in this way.

There appears to be a systematic difference between upward and downward collocation. Upward collocation of course is the weaker pattern in statistical terms, and the words tend to be elements of grammatical frames, or superordinates. Downward collocation by contrast gives us a semantic analysis of a word.

Collocation of *back*

Let us illustrate collocational patterns, in a provisional way, with the word *back*. I shall make no attempt to differentiate separate senses, but will put the collocates into *ad hoc* groups.

No standard of statistical significance is claimed at present because many typical collocations are of such low frequency compared with the overall length of a text. Because of the low frequency of the vast majority of words, almost any repeated collocation is a most unlikely event, but because the set of texts is so large, unlikely events of this kind may still be the result of chance factors.

But no speaker of English would doubt the importance of these patterns. One recognises them immediately, because they are features of the organisation of texts; often subliminal, they cannot be reliably retrieved by introspection.

In distinguishing upward and downward collocation I have made a buffer area of ±15% of the frequency of the node word. So if a word occurs 1000 times, then when it is a node, collocates are grouped into: (a) upward collocates — those whose own occurrence is over 1150; (b) neutral collocates — between 850 and 1150; (c) downward collocates — less than 850.

Neutral collocates are added on an *ad hoc* basis to upward or downward groups, and are given round brackets. Since this has to be a summary account of a very large set of data, I have removed some items which seem to be of little general significance. These include personal names, contracted forms like *I'll*, and word forms whose co-occurrence with *back* is infrequent and carries no conviction of any general significance. Of the last category, the form *anger* only occurs in the title of the play *Look Back in Anger*.

The nouns and verbs listed below as collocating with *back* are representative only. Given the uncertainty at the limits of statistical significance, it could be more misleading to include doubtful contenders. Thus while *get*, *go* and *bring* are unlikely to be challenged, *beach*, *box* and *bus* are much less convincing when the actual instances are examined.

The qualification for an instance being scrutinised is co-occurrence within four words of *back*, on either side. Early evidence (Jones & Sinclair 1974) suggested that this was a reasonable limit. No account is taken of syntax, punctuation, change of speaker or anything other than the word-forms themselves.

No doubt the studies which succeed this one will sharpen up the picture considerably. For example, the evidence of *back* suggests that few intuitively interesting collocations cross a punctuation mark. But it would be unwise to generalise from the pattern of one word, particularly such an unusual one as *back*. Future studies may also find that tagged and parsed texts are helpful in various ways. For the moment, it is salutary to draw attention to the strength of patterning which emerges from the rawest of unprocessed data.

In pushing us forward into new kinds of observation of language, the computer is simultaneously pulling us back to some very basic facts that are often ignored in linguistics. The set of four choices, a,b,c,k, from the alphabet, arranged in the sequence b,a,c,k, with nothing in between them, i.e. *back*, is an important linguistic event in its own right, long before it is ascribed a word-class or a meaning. It is difficult for users of English to notice this, but it is the computer's starting point.

Upward collocates: *back*

Prepositions/adverbs/conjunctions: at, (down), from, into, now, on, then, to, up, when
Pronouns : he, him, me, she, them, we
Possessive pronouns : her, his, my, (your)
Verb : get, (go), got

The meaning of *back* as "return" could attract expressions of time and place; *after* and *where* are also prominent. The presence of four subject pronouns may have a more general explanation than anything to do with *back*, but the absence of *you* and *I* from the list may be worth pursuing. Possessive pronouns suggest the anatomical sense of *back* and would explain why *they* and *their* do not figure prominently. The two verbs *get* and *go* are superordinates of a large number of verbs of motion, many of which will be found in the downward collocates.

I have selected a few examples of these words to show the way in which the basic syntax of *back* is established:

> It really was like being back *at* school.
> He drives back *down* to the terrace.
> When our parents came back *from* Paris
> I followed him back *into* the wood.
> A hefty slap *on* the back

> *He* turned back to the bookshelf
> When can I have *him* back home, doctor?
> *She* went back to her typing
> It would be nice to have *them* back
> *We* went back to the bungalow

> She has gone back to *her* parents
> He went back into *his* office
> I ran back to *my* cabin
> Go back to *your* dormitory at once

> Now I must *get* back to work
> They *go* back to the same nest

Downward collocates: *back*

Verbs:	arrive, bring etc., climbed, come etc., cut etc., dates etc., drew etc., drove etc., fall etc., flew, flung, handed, hold etc., jerked, lay etc., leaned etc., looked, looking etc., pay, pulled etc., pushed etc., put, ran, rocking, rolled, rush, sank, sat etc., sent etc., shouted, snapped, stared, stepped, steps etc., stood, threw, traced, turned etc., walked etc., waved
Prepositions:	along, behind, onto, past, toward, towards
Adverbs:	again, forth, further, slowly, straight
Adjective:	normal
Nouns:	camp, flat, garden, home, hotel, office, road, streets, village, yard
	bed, chair, couch, door, sofa, wall, window
	feet, forehead, hair, hand, head, neck, shoulder
	car, seat

mind, sleep
kitchen, living room, porch, room

The word class groupings above are based on frequency with *back*; many words actually occur in more than one word class. Verbs are given in their most frequent form. Note the preponderance of past tense verbs, reflecting the temporal meaning of *back*.

The prepositions and adverbs suggest some typical phrases with *back*, and the nouns are largely those of direction, physical space and human anatomy.

A few typical examples follow:

Verbs:
You *arrive* back on the Thursday
May *bring* it back into fashion
We *climbed* back up on the stepladder
They had *come* back to England
She never *cut* back on flowers
It possibly *dates* back to the war
The bearer *drew* back in fear
We *drove* back to Cambridge
You can *fall* back on something definite
I *flew* back home in a light aircraft
He *flung* back the drapes joyously.
Don't try to *hold* her back.
She *lay* back in the darkness
He *leaned* back in his chair.
He *looked* back at her, and their eyes met
Pay me back for all you took from me
Pulled back the bedclothes and climbed into bed
I *pushed* back my chair and made to rise.
Shall I *put* it back in the box for you
I *rolled* back onto the grass
She *sat* back and crossed her legs
Edward was *sent* back to school
He *shouted* back
The girl *stared* back
They *started* walking back to Fifth Avenue
He *stepped* back and said ...
He then *stood* back for a minute

	The woman *threw* her head back
	These could be *traced* back to the early sixties
	He *turned* back to the bookshelf
	She *walked* back to the bus stop
	We *waved* back like anything
Prepositions:	Hands held *behind* his back
	Walked back *toward* the house
Adverbs:	Later we came back *again*
	Rock us gently back and *forth*
	If you look *further* back in my files
	The *straight* back to his cabin
	He went *slowly* back to his book
Adjective:	Things would soon get back to *normal*
Nouns:	I crawled back to *camp*
	I'll drive you back to your *flat*
	Not a bit like his back *garden*
	He turned and went back *home*
	We had to go back to the *hotel*
	You've just got back from the *office*
	Set back from the *road*
	The back *streets* of Glasgow
	All the way back to the *village*
	On his *way* back to the apartment
	Without even a back *yard*
	Go back to *bed*
	He leaned back in his *chair*
	Stepping outside the back *door*
	A man standing by the back *wall*
	Tom went back to the *window*
	Britain would be back on its *feet*
	He brushed back his *hair*
	With the back of his *hand*
	She put her *head* back against the seat
	The hairs on the back of my *neck*
	He gestured back over his *shoulder*
	They got back into the *car*
	There was some beer on the back *seat*
	In the back of his *mind*

Then we go back to *sleep* again
You must come back to the *kitchen*
She went back into the *living room*
Beside me here on the back *porch*
He came back into the *room*

Conclusion

All the evidence points to an underlying rigidity of phraseology, despite a rich superficial variation. Hardly any collocates occur more than once in more than two patterns. The phraseology is frequently discriminatory in terms of sense; for example there are almost as many instances of *flat on her back* as *back to her flat*. Some, like *arrive*, seem characteristic of the spoken language, some, like *hotel*, show the wisdom of allowing a nine-word span for collocation.

Early predictions of lexical structure were suitably cautious; there was no reason to believe that the patterns of lexis should map on to semantic structures. For one thing, lexis was syntagmatic and semantics was paradigmatic; for another, lexis was limited to evidence of physical co-occurrence whereas semantics was intuitive and associative.

The early results given here are characteristic of present evidence; there is a great deal of overlap with semantics, and very little reason to posit an independent semantics for the purpose of text description.

Linguistic analysis of real estate commission agreements in a civil law suit

Roger W. Shuy

1. Introduction

The use of linguistic analysis to assist in the resolution of legal cases is not a new phenomenon. The exercise of the law is accomplished by means of language, spoken and written, which is subject to the same analytical routines as language in any other setting of life.

What follows is a linguistic analysis of the three Commission Agreements which concern the case of *Roy Green v. Aldena Coastal Properties, Inc.*[1] The first document relates to a Lease dated October 31, 1975. The second relates to Supplemental Lease Agreement No. 1, dated March 8, 1976. The third relates to Lease Agreement No. GS-04B-15540, dated October 6, 1976.

This analysis clearly demonstrates that there is no evidence in the language used by the signers of these three documents that the intended meaning of the property referenced by these documents was any other property than that which was clearly specified as Exhibit A "together with the entire water frontage bordering the property described herein" (in documents No. 1 and No. 2) or simply as Exhibit A (in document No. 3). Furthermore, this analysis clearly demonstrates that there is no evidence in the language used by the signers of these documents that the intended meaning of *lease, leases* or any other words used to refer to *lease* or *leases* was associated with any property except that property clearly defined in these three documents. Finally, this analysis demonstrates that if the intention of the signers of these documents was to provide an exclusive agreement to the Broker for commission on all property held currently and in the future by the Owner and leased to GSA, the signers did not insert such information in the crucial parts of the texts where, by the conventions of the English language, it could be expected to appear.

Since the dispute in this case concerns the extent of clarity or ambiguity in these three Commission Agreements, linguistic analysis should contribute toward solution of this dispute. Depending on the nature of the data to be analyzed and the problem to be addressed, analysis of written or spoken language can be carried out at many levels: phonological (the sound system), morphological (the way words are put together), grammatical (the study of grammatical inflections as well as usage), syntactic (the way words are fitted together to make phrases, clauses or sentences), or discourse (the way sentences are fitted together to make larger units, from paragraphs to entire written discourses).

In this particular case, syntax and discourse analyses are the most appropriate levels to select for establishing the clarity or ambiguity of the discourse used. Three types of discourse analysis have been used: *Referencing Analysis*, *Topic-Comment Analysis* and *Contrastive Analysis*.

By *Referencing Analysis*, we mean the study of anaphora; how clearly defined references are referred to by subsequent less defined references (a syntactic analysis). Referencing is traditionally understood to mean how a writer uses certain words to refer to previously used words. A common way of doing this is with pronouns. For example, in the sentence, "Mr. Jones purchased some property so that he could construct a building on it", the pronoun *he* references Mr. Jones. Linguists refer to this referencing system as anaphora. *He*, in this sentence, is the anaphoric reference to Mr. Jones. There are other referencing systems in English as well. The most commonly used one in the three Commission Agreements analyzed here is that of noun (or nominal) referencing. That is, once a noun such as *property* or *lease* is introduced and defined, all following uses of the words *property* or *lease* refer to the same property or lease unless a new definition is introduced. This clearly established principle of the English language syntax is very important in this dispute, as will become evident in the analysis.

Topic-Comment Analysis entails the study of the processes involved in topic introduction, maintenance, changing, and recycling (a discourse analysis). The English language principles of discourse are similar to those of syntax, only at a larger level.

A topic of discussion, in writing or speech, is considered to be continuous until clearly marked to the contrary by topic shift or change. A topic is considered to be maintained as long as such clearly marked topic change is

not introdeuced. To reintroduce or recycle a previously introduced topic, one must clearly indicate, through language, the clearly defined recycled topic. Linguists who analyze discourse speak of four kinds of topics:
  a. *substantive topics*: topics which specify the basic agenda or propositions of the discourse.
  b. *corollary topics*: topics which are a consequence of the substantive topics. They deal with the details, methods or plans which grow out of the substantive propositions.
  c. *transitional topics*: topics which are found primarily in conversational discourse or informal writing and include small talk, personal affairs, anecdotes, etc. They provide small, interruptive interludes between substantive and/or corollary topics.
  d. *ostensible topics*: topics which are found primarily in conversational discourse or informal writing. They serve as the announced or professed reasons for the discourse but actually serve only as a cover for the substantive topics.

In the three Commission Agreements analyzed here, only substantive and corollary topics can be expected to occur. That is, topics about property and leases serve as the substantive topics and the specifics about time, manner, amount, persons involved, etc., serve as the corollary topics. The clearly established principles of topic introduction, maintenance, changing and recycling are very important in this dispute, as our analysis will show.

Contrastive Analysis involves the comparison of one language system with another for similarities and differences. In this case, since the dispute hinges on the clarity or ambiguity of what was said or what was not said, the contrast is between what was said and what could have been said to support the contention of the opposite viewpoint. This analysis is important in this dispute because it points out clearly where language could have been used to present the position that the documents provide an exclusive agreement to the Broker for commissions on all property held currently and in the future by the Owner and leased to GSA.

2. Referencing analysis

Since the issue in conflict concerns the question of whether-or-not certain property is subject to commission by Mr. Green, language referencing to property is a critical factor.

2.1. Commission Agreement No. 1

The preamble to the October 2, 1975 Commission Agreement defines the property in question as that which is referenced by Exhibit A, "together with the entire water frontage bordering the property described herein". Following the rules of English language referencing, subsequent references to "property" or "said property" will be understood to refer to the property described in Exhibit A "together with the entire water frontage bordering the property described herein". Again, following the rules of English language referencing, any new meanings intended by the writers or signers of this agreement must be newly designated. English referencing (technically called anaphora) works as a chaining sequence as follows: Defined reference → Anaphoric reference → Anaphoric reference, etc. If an intervening referent is introduced or if the writer's intention is to alter the meaning of the defined reference, such activity must be marked by new definitions. Otherwise, it is the accepted convention of English to understand that anaphoric references are to the original marked definition.

Paragraph eight of Commission Agreement No. 1 clearly illustrates a change in the marked or defined reference to property. With specific reference to the name, Waterford Plaza, at 343 Dunstan Avenue, this paragraph marks a new property reference chain. This was necessary since the burden of this paragraph is to exclude Waterford Plaza, at 343 Dunstan Avenue, as commissionable to Mr. Green. Thus the chaining sequence has been broken, as follows:

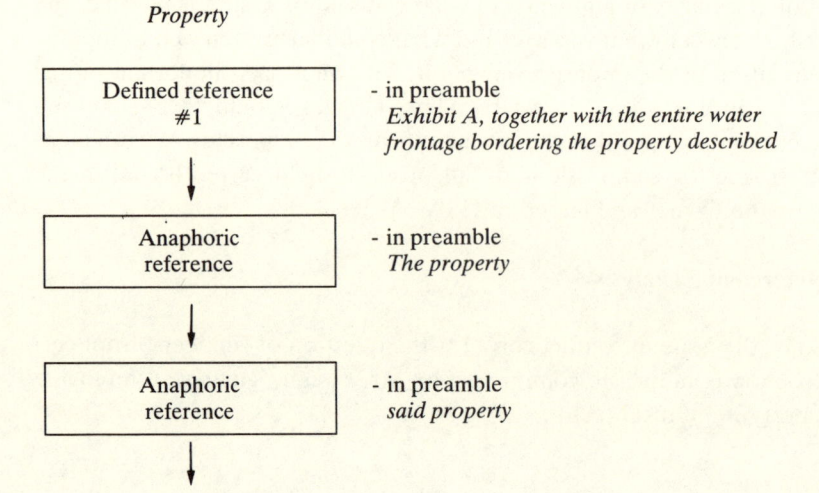

Property

Defined reference #1	- in preamble *Exhibit A, together with the entire water frontage bordering the property described*
↓	
Anaphoric reference	- in preamble *The property*
↓	
Anaphoric reference	- in preamble *said property*
↓	

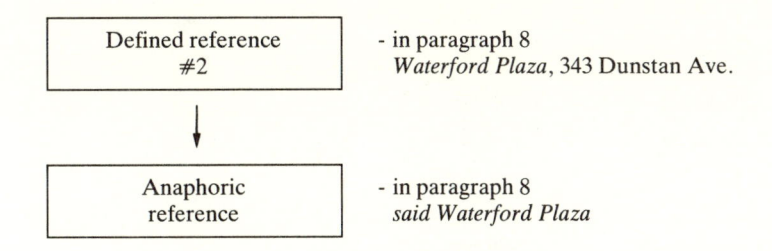

```
┌─────────────────────┐
│  Defined reference  │     - in paragraph 8
│         #2          │       *Waterford Plaza*, 343 Dunstan Ave.
└──────────┬──────────┘
           ↓
┌─────────────────────┐
│     Anaphoric       │     - in paragraph 8
│     reference       │       *said Waterford Plaza*
└─────────────────────┘
```

In that the conventions of English language anaphora specify that a referencing chain is broken by the introduction of a new defined reference, all references to property in paragraph eight refer to Waterford Plaza, 343 Dunstan Avenue and to no other property. This means that the words "... in the event any further or future lease or leases are entered into between OWNER-LESSOR and lessee" refer to only the property designated as Waterford Plaza, 343 Dunstan Avenue. The meaning of this paragraph is that this building is excepted from commission to the broker unless a separate written instrument is executed.

In addition to anaphoric referencing related to property, these documents contain what can be called anaphora within anaphora. That is, within the unbroken anaphoric chaining sequences, sub-references exist. Because of the relationship between property and leases, references to *lease* or *leases* within a chaining sequence can be clearly identified by that chaining sequence. Thus the defined reference to *a Lease* dated the 2nd day of October 1975 is followed by anaphoric references to that lease, as follows:

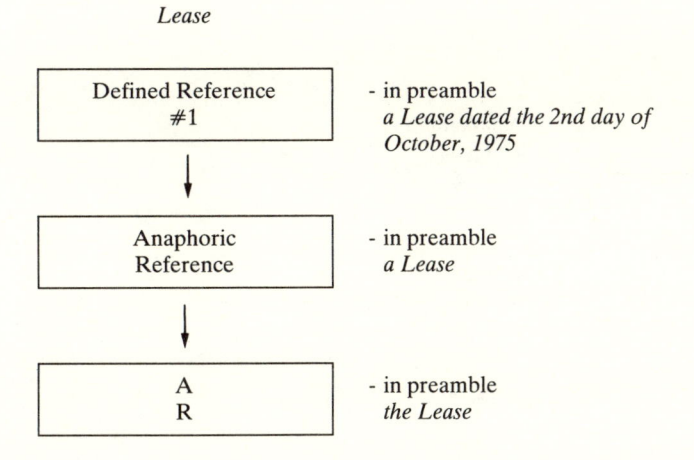

Lease

```
┌─────────────────────┐
│ Defined Reference   │     - in preamble
│        #1           │       *a Lease dated the 2nd day of*
│                     │       *October, 1975*
└──────────┬──────────┘
           ↓
┌─────────────────────┐
│     Anaphoric       │     - in preamble
│     Reference       │       *a Lease*
└──────────┬──────────┘
           ↓
┌─────────────────────┐
│         A           │     - in preamble
│         R           │       *the Lease*
└─────────────────────┘
```

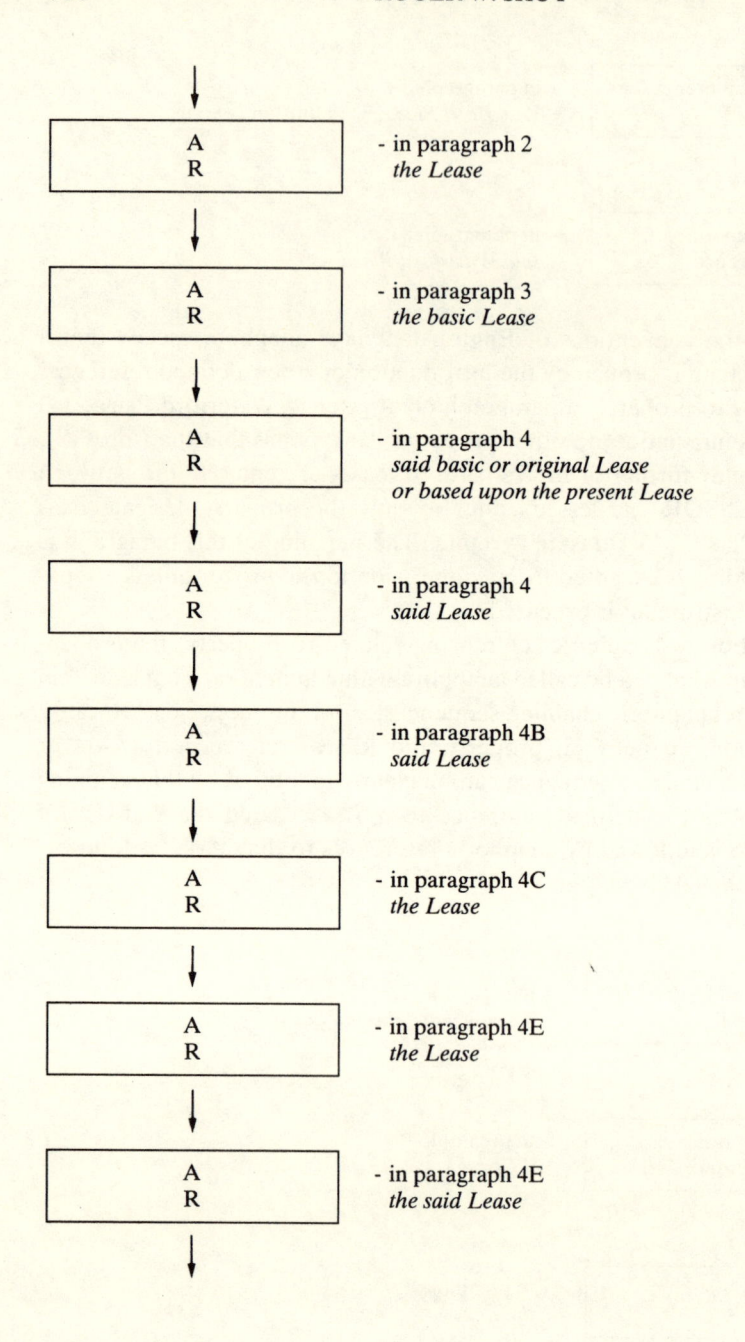

```
   ↓
┌─────────┐
│   A     │   - in paragraph 2
│   R     │     *the Lease*
└─────────┘
   ↓
┌─────────┐
│   A     │   - in paragraph 3
│   R     │     *the basic Lease*
└─────────┘
   ↓
┌─────────┐
│   A     │   - in paragraph 4
│   R     │     *said basic or original Lease*
└─────────┘     *or based upon the present Lease*
   ↓
┌─────────┐
│   A     │   - in paragraph 4
│   R     │     *said Lease*
└─────────┘
   ↓
┌─────────┐
│   A     │   - in paragraph 4B
│   R     │     *said Lease*
└─────────┘
   ↓
┌─────────┐
│   A     │   - in paragraph 4C
│   R     │     *the Lease*
└─────────┘
   ↓
┌─────────┐
│   A     │   - in paragraph 4E
│   R     │     *the Lease*
└─────────┘
   ↓
┌─────────┐
│   A     │   - in paragraph 4E
│   R     │     *the said Lease*
└─────────┘
   ↓
```

```
┌─────────────────┐         - in paragraph 4E
│      A          │           the Lease above described
│      R          │
└─────────────────┘
         │
         ▼
┌─────────────────┐         - in paragraph 8
│ Defined Reference│          any further or future lease or Leases
│      #2         │
└─────────────────┘
```

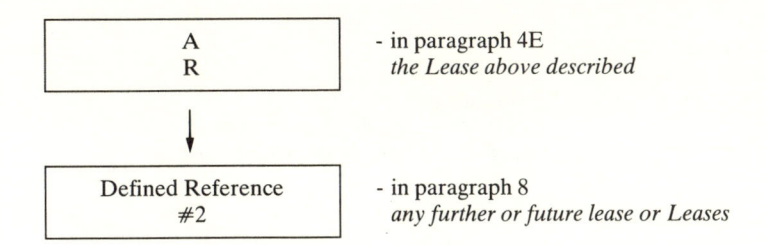

This chaining sequence indicates clearly that all references to *Lease* refer to Defined Reference No. 1 (*a Lease dated the 2nd day of October, 1975*) except for the last reference in paragraph eight, which breaks the chaining sequence by defining a new lease referent. Evidence of this anaphoric specificity can be found in two sources:

(1) The structure of the lexicon. *A* lease is used in the English language as a first reference (e.g., *A* man came today. *The* man fixed the refrigerator. But not, *The* man came today. *A* man fixed the refrigerator.) The use of the article, *the*, assumes clear referencing. The use of the article, *a*, introduces a new referent.

(2) The structure of the capitalization system. All references to the specific October 2 lease are in capital letters. This is not the case for the second defined reference.

The significance of this anaphoric referencing to property and to lease for property is as follows. It shows clearly that in Commission Agreement No. 1, all references to property up to paragraph eight are to the property defined as Exhibit A, "together with the entire water frontage bordering the property described herein" and all references to leases up to paragraph eight are to leases related only to that property. It also shows clearly that in paragraph eight, a newly defined property reference is Waterford Plaza, 343 Dunstan Avenue and all references to leases in paragraph eight are to further or future lease or leases relating only to that property.

2.2. *Commission Agreement No. 2*

The second Commission Agreement, dated March 3, 1976, also begins with a clearly defined reference to the property under discussion as specified in Exhibit A, "together with the entire water frontage bordering the property described herein". The reference chaining system is as follows:

Property

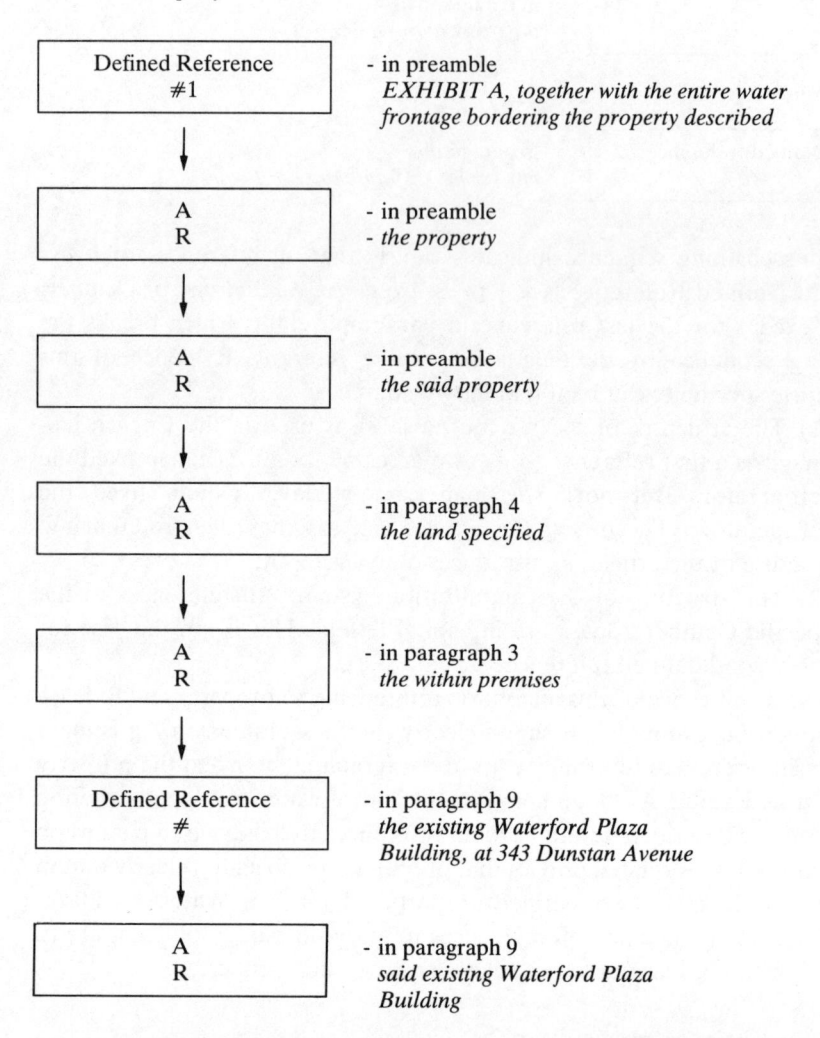

```
┌─────────────────────┐
│  Defined Reference  │   - in preamble
│         #1          │     EXHIBIT A, together with the entire water
└─────────────────────┘     frontage bordering the property described
           │
           ▼
┌─────────────────────┐
│          A          │   - in preamble
│          R          │   - the property
└─────────────────────┘
           │
           ▼
┌─────────────────────┐
│          A          │   - in preamble
│          R          │     the said property
└─────────────────────┘
           │
           ▼
┌─────────────────────┐
│          A          │   - in paragraph 4
│          R          │     the land specified
└─────────────────────┘
           │
           ▼
┌─────────────────────┐
│          A          │   - in paragraph 3
│          R          │     the within premises
└─────────────────────┘
           │
           ▼
┌─────────────────────┐
│  Defined Reference  │   - in paragraph 9
│          #          │     the existing Waterford Plaza
└─────────────────────┘     Building, at 343 Dunstan Avenue
           │
           ▼
┌─────────────────────┐
│          A          │   - in paragraph 9
│          R          │     said existing Waterford Plaza
└─────────────────────┘     Building
```

Paragraph nine in the second Commission Agreement, like paragraph eight of the first Commission Agreement, specifies a change in the defined referent to property, marking a new property reference chain. This marking exempts Mr. Green from commission for procuring any tenant for that property "not related to the U.S. Customs Service in that specified property".

REAL ESTATE COMMISSION AGREEMENTS 341

In addition to anaphoric referencing related to property, this document also contains anaphora within anaphora. Again, the references to *lease* or *leases* can be clearly identified within the property references chaining. This chaining is as follows:

Lease(s)

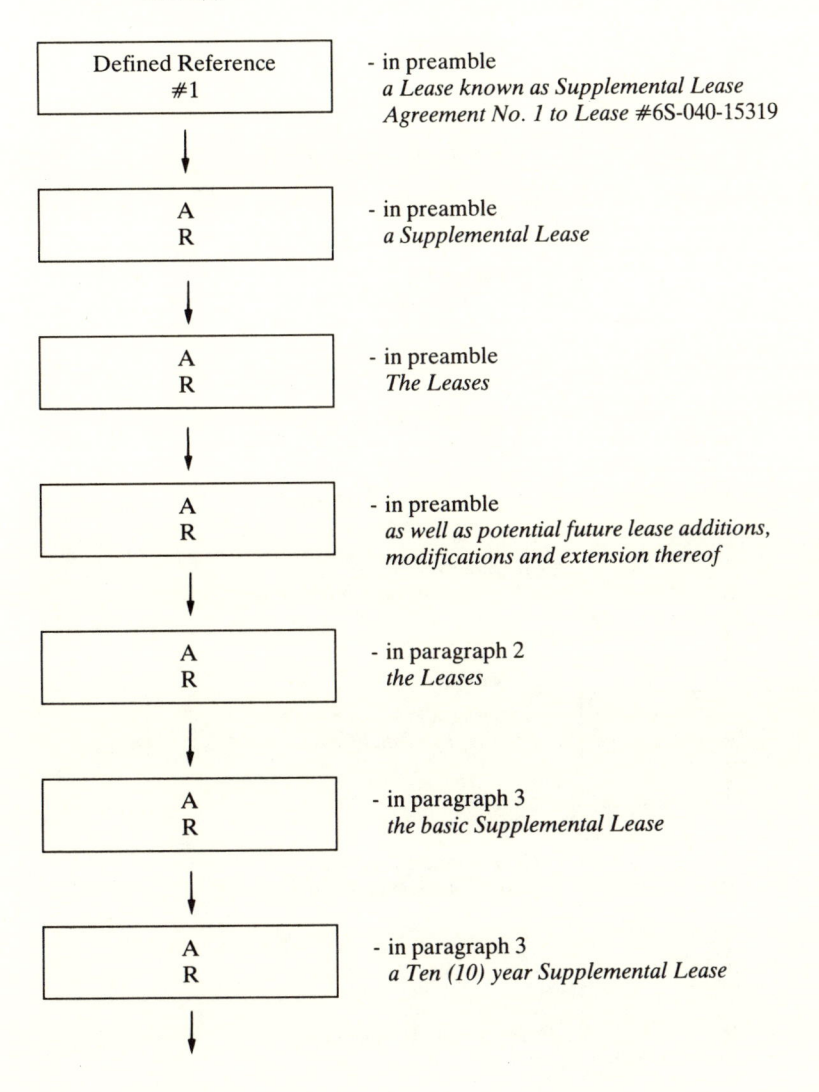

```
┌─────────────────────┐
│ Defined Reference   │   - in preamble
│        #1           │     a Lease known as Supplemental Lease
└─────────────────────┘     Agreement No. 1 to Lease #6S-040-15319
          │
          ▼
┌─────────────────────┐
│          A          │   - in preamble
│          R          │     a Supplemental Lease
└─────────────────────┘
          │
          ▼
┌─────────────────────┐
│          A          │   - in preamble
│          R          │     The Leases
└─────────────────────┘
          │
          ▼
┌─────────────────────┐
│          A          │   - in preamble
│          R          │     as well as potential future lease additions,
└─────────────────────┘     modifications and extension thereof
          │
          ▼
┌─────────────────────┐
│          A          │   - in paragraph 2
│          R          │     the Leases
└─────────────────────┘
          │
          ▼
┌─────────────────────┐
│          A          │   - in paragraph 3
│          R          │     the basic Supplemental Lease
└─────────────────────┘
          │
          ▼
┌─────────────────────┐
│          A          │   - in paragraph 3
│          R          │     a Ten (10) year Supplemental Lease
└─────────────────────┘
          │
          ▼
```

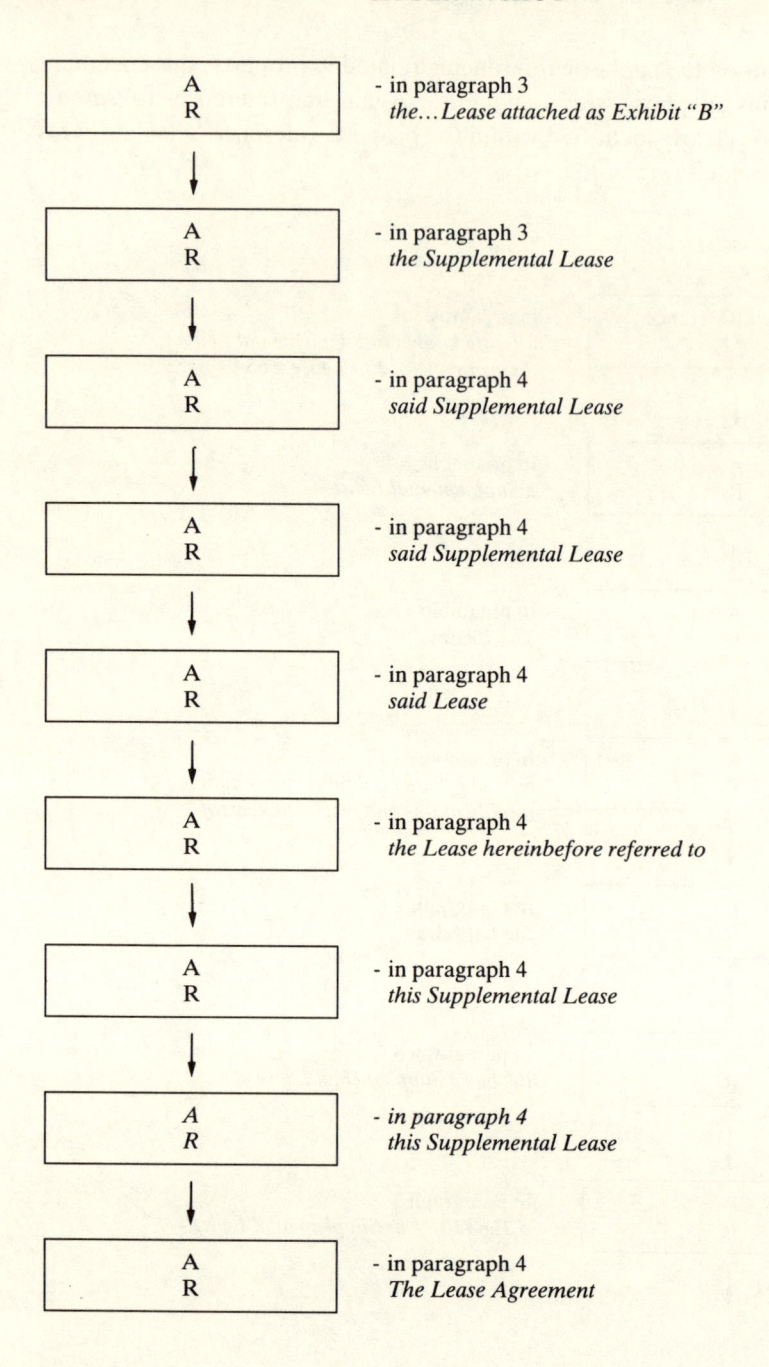

A R	- in paragraph 3 *the…Lease attached as Exhibit "B"*
↓	
A R	- in paragraph 3 *the Supplemental Lease*
↓	
A R	- in paragraph 4 *said Supplemental Lease*
↓	
A R	- in paragraph 4 *said Supplemental Lease*
↓	
A R	- in paragraph 4 *said Lease*
↓	
A R	- in paragraph 4 *the Lease hereinbefore referred to*
↓	
A R	- in paragraph 4 *this Supplemental Lease*
↓	
A *R*	- *in paragraph 4* *this Supplemental Lease*
↓	
A R	- in paragraph 4 *The Lease Agreement*

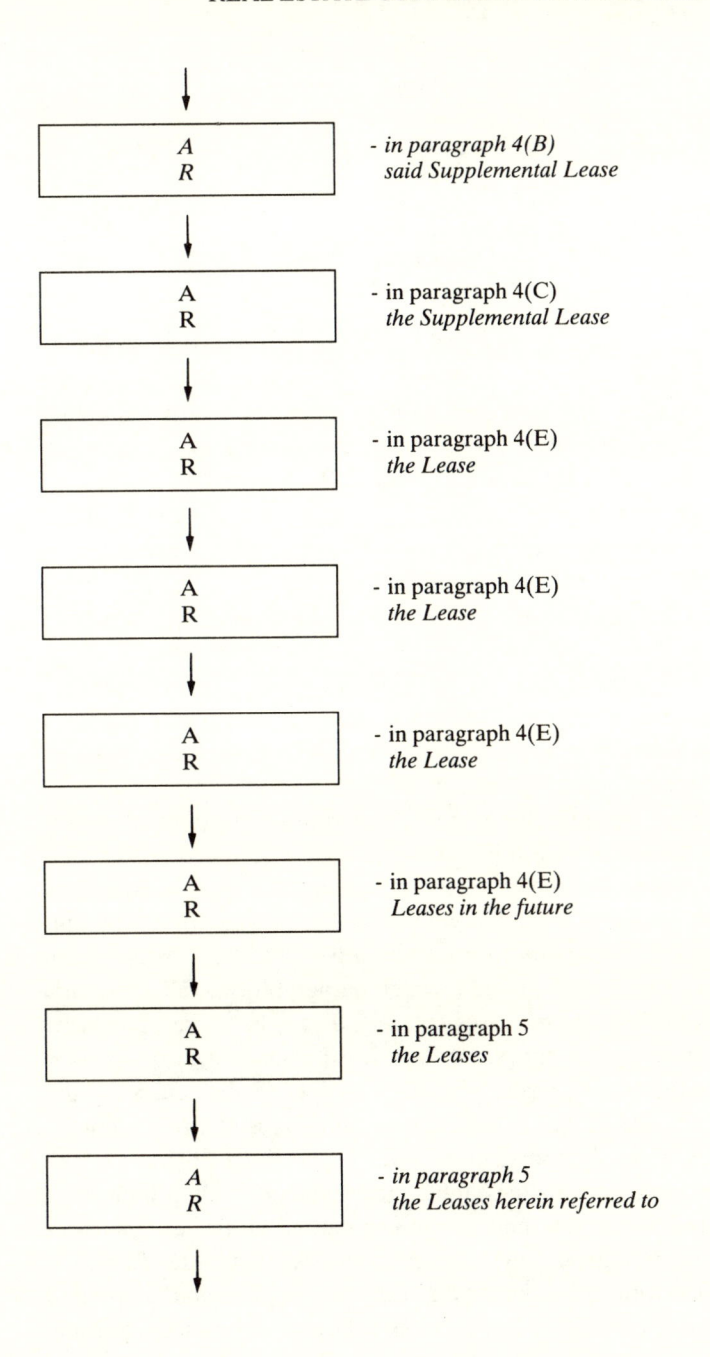

REAL ESTATE COMMISSION AGREEMENTS 343

```
    ↓
┌─────────┐
│    A    │   - in paragraph 4(B)
│    R    │     said Supplemental Lease
└─────────┘
    ↓
┌─────────┐
│    A    │   - in paragraph 4(C)
│    R    │     the Supplemental Lease
└─────────┘
    ↓
┌─────────┐
│    A    │   - in paragraph 4(E)
│    R    │     the Lease
└─────────┘
    ↓
┌─────────┐
│    A    │   - in paragraph 4(E)
│    R    │     the Lease
└─────────┘
    ↓
┌─────────┐
│    A    │   - in paragraph 4(E)
│    R    │     the Lease
└─────────┘
    ↓
┌─────────┐
│    A    │   - in paragraph 4(E)
│    R    │     Leases in the future
└─────────┘
    ↓
┌─────────┐
│    A    │   - in paragraph 5
│    R    │     the Leases
└─────────┘
    ↓
┌─────────┐
│    A    │   - in paragraph 5
│    R    │     the Leases herein referred to
└─────────┘
    ↓
```

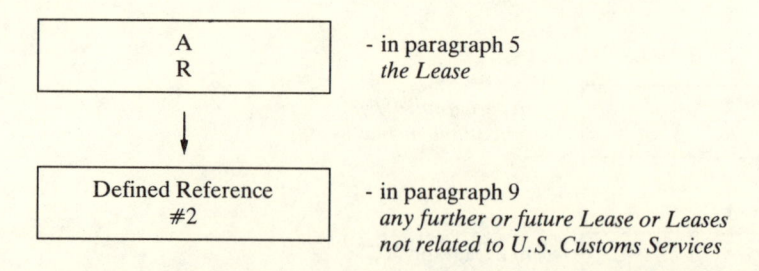

```
┌─────────────────┐
│       A         │      - in paragraph 5
│       R         │        the Lease
└─────────────────┘
         │
         ▼
┌─────────────────┐
│ Defined Reference│     - in paragraph 9
│       #2        │       any further or future Lease or Leases
└─────────────────┘       not related to U.S. Customs Services
```

This chaining sequence is essentially the same as the one indicated in Commission Agreement No. 1, with minor exceptions. In Commission Agreement No. 2, since this Agreement must encompass a supplementary lease as well as the original lease, referencing to *lease* or *leases* is differentiated. Nevertheless, all references to Defined Reference No. 1 Lease(s) are to the property defined in Exhibit A, "with the entire water frontage bordering the property described herein". The reference to *the Leases* (plural) first in the preamble and repeated in paragraph two, 4(E) and 5 (twice) evidences recognition of the fact that, contrary to Commission Agreement No. 1, this second Agreement must take into account the original lease and the supplementary lease. Both *Lease* and *Leases*, however, fall within the anaphoric chaining sequence which relates to the property described clearly as defined by Exhibit A, "with the entire water frontage bordering the property described herein".

Another way to visualize the lease referencing to the defined Reference for this property is shown in Figure 1.

This visualization of the referencing sequence makes clear the anaphora to *lease(s)* in this second Commission Agreement. In the preamble, clear reference is first given to both Lease No. 1 and the Supplementary Lease. Then, from the preamble through paragraph two, all anaphoric references are to both of these leases (plural). Then, in paragraph three, the referencing picks up the supplementary lease again. Since it is necessary, if not obligatory for the sake of clarity, to specifically reidentify the anaphoric reference once it has been diverted (in this case by first identifying both leases individually and then by referring to them together in the plural), it is then necessary to reestablish here their individual identity if individual identity is to be referenced. Thus in paragraph three, this document clearly specifies that it now references the Supplemental Lease by referring to it as the *basic Supplemental Lease*, the *Supplemental Lease* and the *Lease attached as Exhibit B*. The thirteen following references carefully

REAL ESTATE COMMISSION AGREEMENTS

```
                    ┌──────────┐   ─ Exhibit A, with the entire water frontage
                    │ Property │     bordering the property described
                    └────┬─────┘
           ┌─────────────┴─────────────┐
           ▼                           ▼
    ┌──────────┐              ┌───────────────┐
    │ Lease #1 │              │ Supplementary │
    └────┬─────┘              │    Lease      │
         │                    └───────┬───────┘
         ▼                            ▼
  ┌──────────────┐  ─ in preamble   ┌──────────────┐  ─ in preamble
  │Defined Reference│  Lease #65-   │Defined Reference│   a Supplementary Lease
  │    # 1a      │   04B-15319      │    #1b       │
  └──────┬───────┘                  └──────┬───────┘
         │                                 ▼
         │                         ┌───────────────┐  ─ preamble
         │                         │ A Supplemental│
         │                         │    Lease      │
         │                         └──────┬────────┘
         └────────────┐      ┌────────────┘
                      ▼      ▼
                  ┌────────────┐   preamble
                  │ The Leases │
                  └──────┬─────┘
                         ▼
                  ┌────────────┐
                  │  potential │
                  │future lease│   preamble
                  │addition mod.│
                  └──────┬─────┘
                         ▼
                  ┌────────────┐   para. 2
                  │ The Leases │
                  └──────┬─────┘
                         │
                         │          ┌──────────────────┐  para. 3
                         │          │  The basic       │
                         │          │Supplemental Lease│
                         │          └────────┬─────────┘
                         │                   ▼
                         │          ┌──────────────────┐  para. 3
                         │          │  Supplemental    │
                         │          │     Lease        │
                         │          └────────┬─────────┘
                         │                   ▼
                         │          ┌──────────────────┐  para. 3
                         │          │ herein attached as│
                         │          │     Exhibit B    │
                         │          └────────┬─────────┘
                         │                   ▼
                         │          ┌ ─ ─ ─ ─ ─ ─ ─ ─ ┐
                         │            All following       13 references
                         │          │ references up   │   from para. 3
                         │            to paragraph 4(E)   to 4(E)
                         │          └ ─ ─ ─ ─ ─ ─ ─ ─ ┘
                         ▼
                  ┌────────────┐   para. 4(E)
                  │ Leases in  │
                  │ the future │
                  └──────┬─────┘
                         ▼
                  ┌────────────┐   para. 5
                  │ The Leases │
                  └──────┬─────┘
                         ▼
                  ┌────────────┐   para. 5
                  │The Lease herein│
                  │  referred to   │
                  └──────┬─────┘
                         ▼
              *   ┌────────────┐   = such a lease para. 5
                  │ The Lease  │
                  └──────┬─────┘
                         ▼
                  ┌────────────┐   para. 9
                  │Future Leases│
                  └────────────┘
```

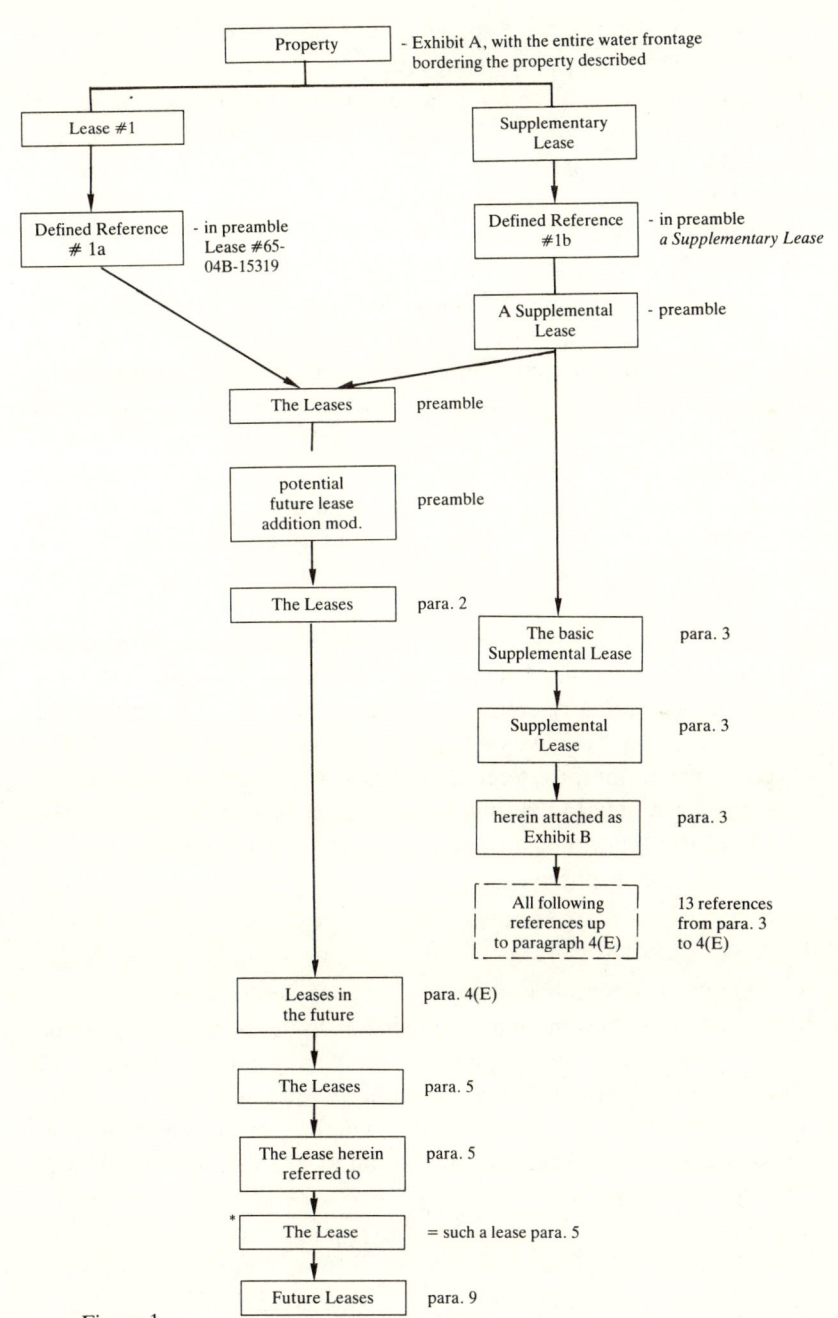

Figure 1.

and clearly reference only the Supplemental Lease either by specific reference to *Supplemental Lease* or chained anaphora (*said Lease* or the *Lease*) which, by the rules of English language anaphora, clearly specify the Supplemental Lease. Finally from paragraph 4(E) to the end of this document, all references to *Lease* are plural, referencing clearly the combination of both Lease No. 1 and the Supplemental Lease.

The significance of this anaphoric referencing to property and lease for property in the second document is as follows. It shows clearly that in Commission Agreement No. 2, all references to property up to paragraph nine are to the property defined as Exhibit A, "together with the entire water frontage bordering the property described herein" and that all reference to lease or leases up to paragraph nine are lease or leases relating only to that property. It also shows clearly that in paragraph nine, a newly defined property reference is the existing Waterford Plaza Building at 343 Dunstan Avenue and that all references to further or future lease or leases to that property, not related to the U.S. Customs Services, are not commissionable to Mr. Green unless a separate written instrument is executed toward that end.

It should be further mentioned here that there is, in Commission Agreement No. 2, one other reference to future leases (paragraph 4E). It is clear from the anaphoric reference in this document that this reference to "Leases in the future" is governed, under anaphoric rules of the English language, by the property reference to which it relates, in this case, the property reference only to that which is described in Exhibit A, "together with the entire water frontage bordering the property described herein", and not to any other property.

2.3. *Commission Agreement No. 3*

The anaphoric referencing sequence in Commission Agreement No. 3, signed August 31, 1976 is in many ways similar to the previous two Agreements. Again, in order to understand the referencing in this document, it is first necessary to clearly determine the property references.

This document also begins with a clearly defined reference to the property under discussion as specified in Exhibit A, further identified as 55 N.W. 8th Street, as follows:

REAL ESTATE COMMISSION AGREEMENTS   347

Property

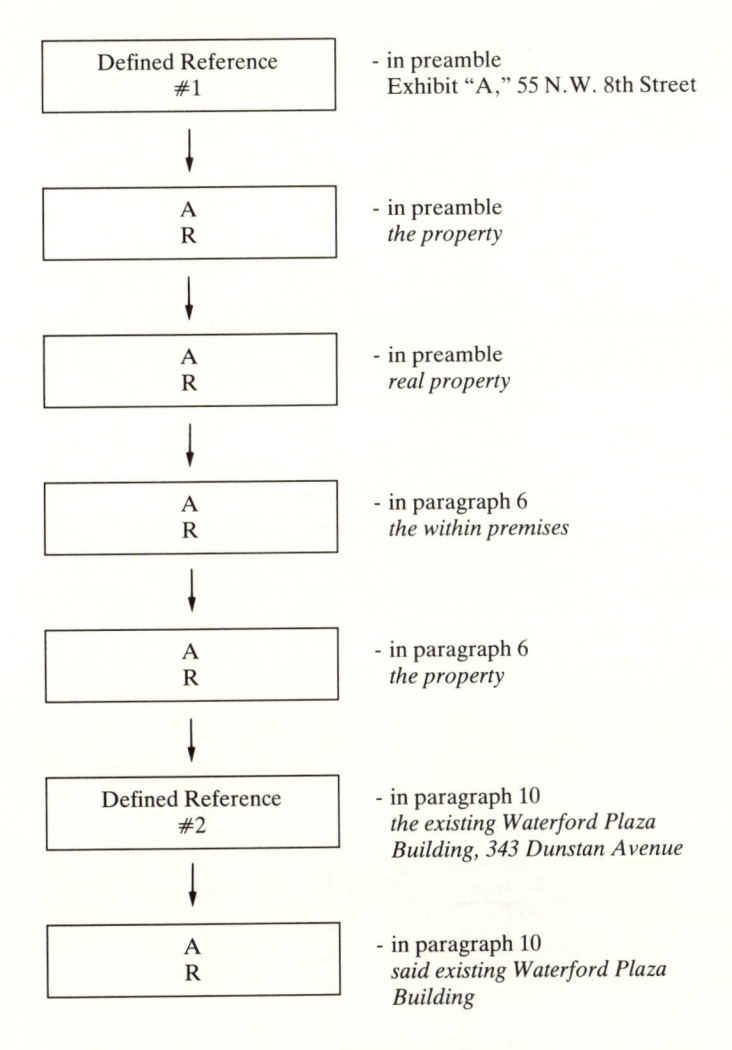

```
┌─────────────────┐
│ Defined Reference│   - in preamble
│       #1        │   Exhibit "A," 55 N.W. 8th Street
└────────┬────────┘
         ↓
┌─────────────────┐
│       A         │   - in preamble
│       R         │   *the property*
└────────┬────────┘
         ↓
┌─────────────────┐
│       A         │   - in preamble
│       R         │   *real property*
└────────┬────────┘
         ↓
┌─────────────────┐
│       A         │   - in paragraph 6
│       R         │   *the within premises*
└────────┬────────┘
         ↓
┌─────────────────┐
│       A         │   - in paragraph 6
│       R         │   *the property*
└────────┬────────┘
         ↓
┌─────────────────┐
│ Defined Reference│   - in paragraph 10
│       #2        │   *the existing Waterford Plaza
└────────┬────────┘   Building, 343 Dunstan Avenue*
         ↓
┌─────────────────┐
│       A         │   - in paragraph 10
│       R         │   *said existing Waterford Plaza
└─────────────────┘   Building*
```

Paragraph ten in Commission Agreement No. 3, like paragraph eight of Commission Agreement No. 1 and paragraph nine of Commission Agreement No. 2, specifies a change in the defined referent to property, marking a new property reference chain. Again, this marking exempts Mr. Green from commission for procuring any tenant for that property "... not related to the U.S. Customs Service".

In addition to anaphoric referencing related to property, this document also contains anaphora within anaphora. Again, the reference to *lease* or *leases* can be clearly identified within the property reference chaining. This chaining is as follows:

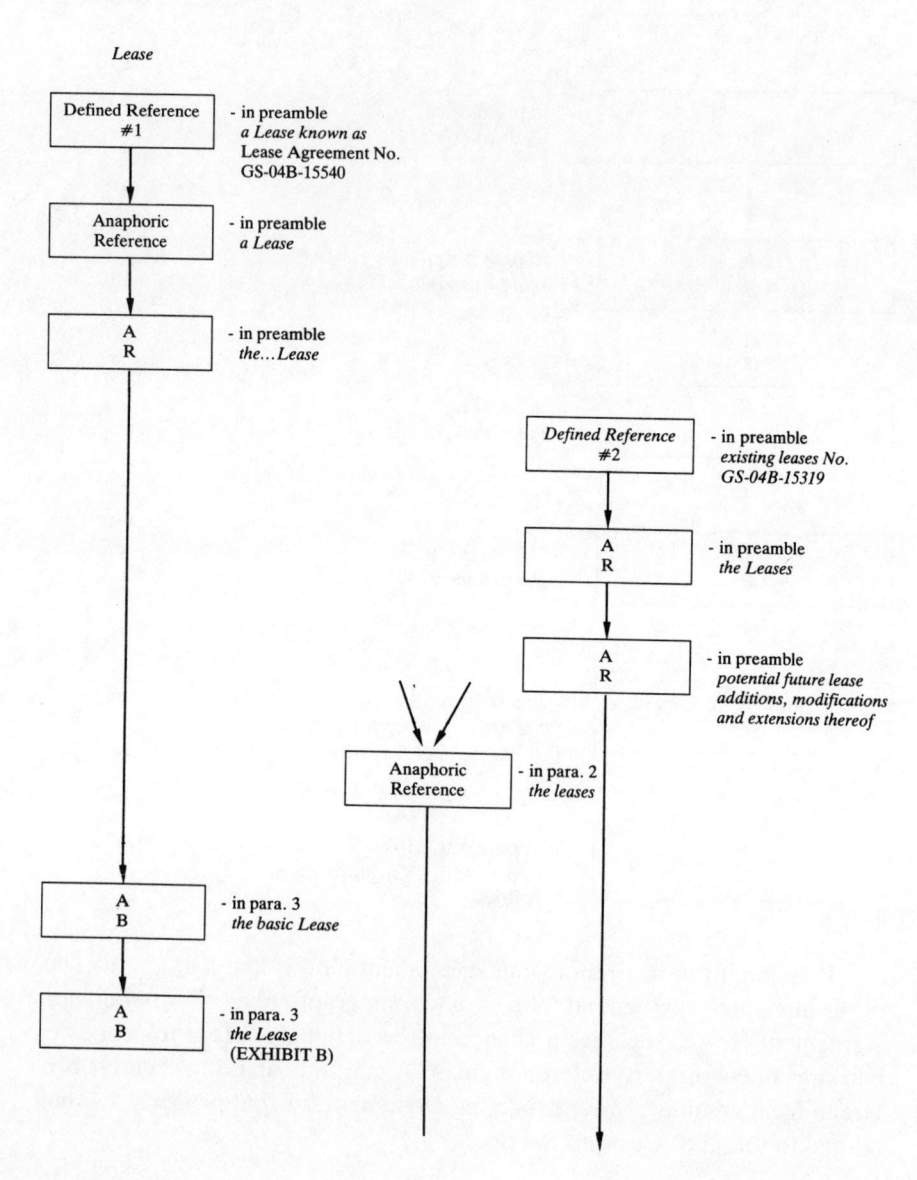

Lease

```
┌──────────────────┐    - in preamble
│ Defined Reference│      a Lease known as
│       #1         │      Lease Agreement No.
└────────┬─────────┘      GS-04B-15540
         ↓
┌──────────────────┐    - in preamble
│   Anaphoric      │      a Lease
│   Reference      │
└────────┬─────────┘
         ↓
┌──────────────────┐    - in preamble
│       A          │      the...Lease
│       R          │
└────────┬─────────┘
         │
         │                    ┌──────────────────┐    - in preamble
         │                    │ Defined Reference│      existing leases No.
         │                    │       #2         │      GS-04B-15319
         │                    └────────┬─────────┘
         │                             ↓
         │                    ┌──────────────────┐    - in preamble
         │                    │       A          │      the Leases
         │                    │       R          │
         │                    └────────┬─────────┘
         │                             ↓
         │                    ┌──────────────────┐    - in preamble
         │                    │       A          │      potential future lease
         │                    │       R          │      additions, modifications
         │                    └────────┬─────────┘      and extensions thereof
         │                             │
         │         ↘         ↙         │
         │          ┌──────────────────┐  - in para. 2
         │          │   Anaphoric      │    the leases
         │          │   Reference      │
         │          └────────┬─────────┘
         ↓                   │
┌──────────────────┐         │         - in para. 3
│       A          │         │           the basic Lease
│       B          │         │
└────────┬─────────┘         │
         ↓                   │
┌──────────────────┐         │         - in para. 3
│       A          │         │           the Lease
│       B          │         │           (EXHIBIT B)
└────────┬─────────┘         │
         ↓                   ↓
```

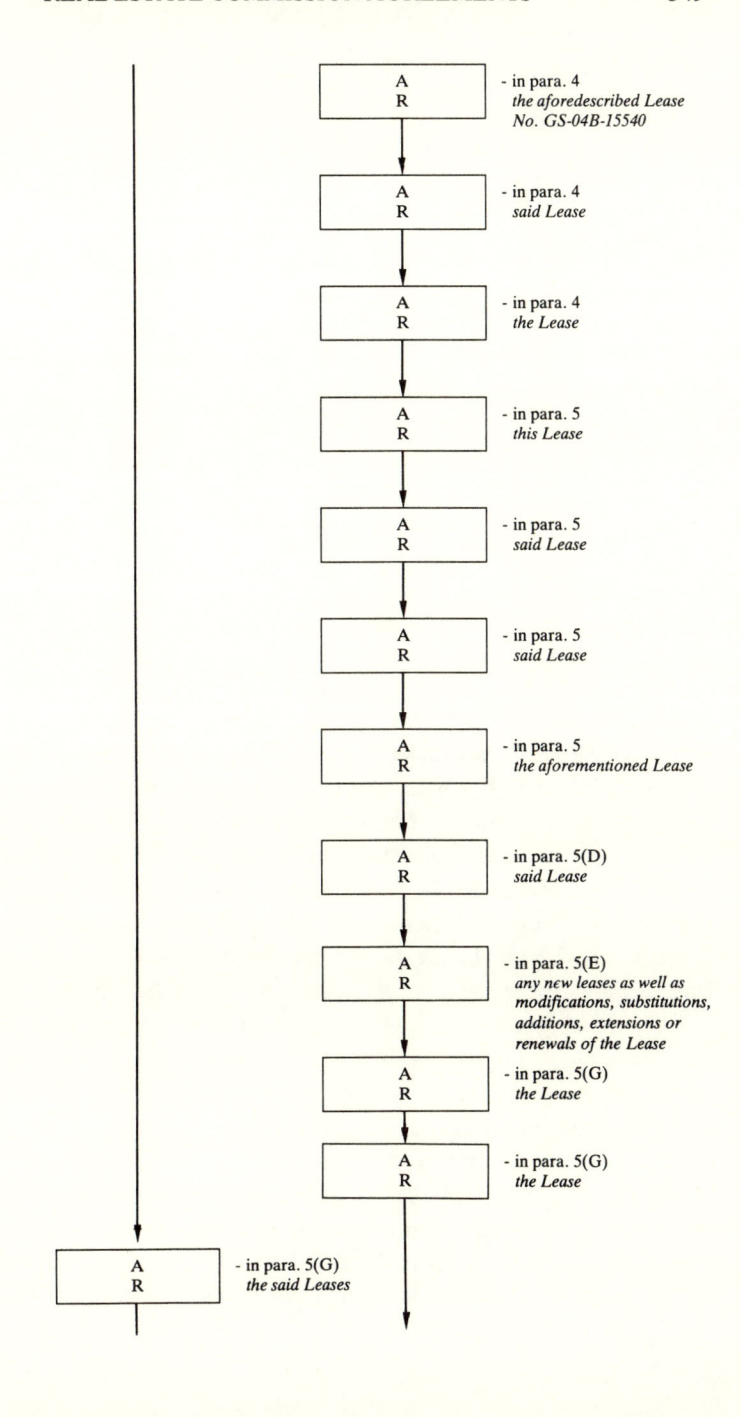

REAL ESTATE COMMISSION AGREEMENTS 349

```
A
R    - in para. 4
     the aforedescribed Lease
     No. GS-04B-15540

A
R    - in para. 4
     said Lease

A
R    - in para. 4
     the Lease

A
R    - in para. 5
     this Lease

A
R    - in para. 5
     said Lease

A
R    - in para. 5
     said Lease

A
R    - in para. 5
     the aforementioned Lease

A
R    - in para. 5(D)
     said Lease

A
R    - in para. 5(E)
     any new leases as well as
     modifications, substitutions,
     additions, extensions or
     renewals of the Lease

A
R    - in para. 5(G)
     the Lease

A
R    - in para. 5(G)
     the Lease

A
R    - in para. 5(G)
     the said Leases
```

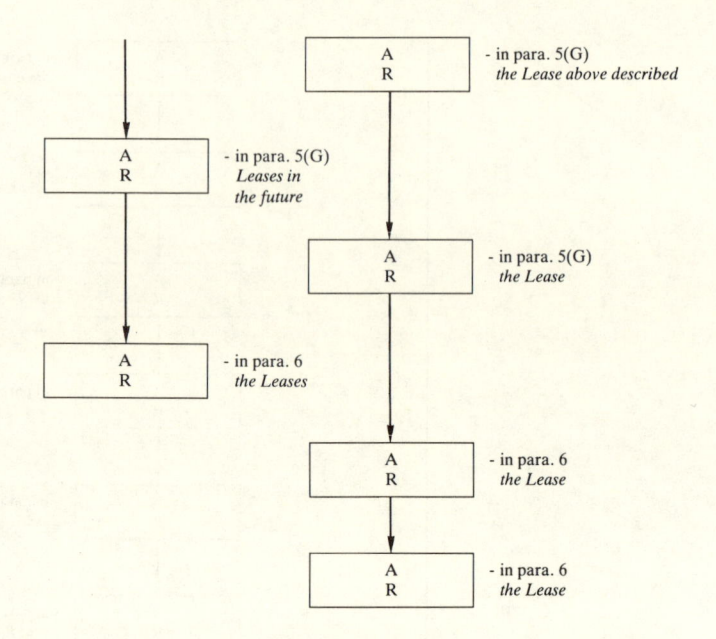

```
                                    A         - in para. 5(G)
                                    R         the Lease above described


         A              - in para. 5(G)
         R              Leases in
                        the future

                                    A         - in para. 5(G)
                                    R         the Lease


         A              - in para. 6
         R              the Leases

                                    A         - in para. 6
                                    R         the Lease


                                    A         - in para. 6
                                    R         the Lease
```

This reference chaining is different from that of the preceding Commission Agreements in that anaphoric references are made to two separate leases individually, and, on four occasions to both leases together (in paragraphs 2, 5(G) and 6). After the first combined reference to both Defined Reference No. 1 and Defined Reference No. 2 (in paragraph 2) both Defined References are clearly reestablished by specific language (in paragraph 3). The words which reestablish the topic as Defined Reference No. 1 are *The basic Lease*. When the reference shifts to Defined Reference No. 2, the words specifically reestablish the reference as Defined Reference No. 2 by reading, *the aforementioned Lease No. GS-04B-15540*.

The combined reference to both Defined Reference No. 1 and Defined Reference No. 2 in paragraph 5(B) is less specific but is clearly marked by the plural, *Leases*. Again when the reference shifts back to Defined Reference No. 2 alone, the language is specific, *the Lease above described* (paragraph 5(G)). The language then switches to combined references to both Defined References immediately by using the word, *Leases*, the plural form and then back to the second lease by reference to *The Lease* (paragraph 5G). The last switch to combined Defined References is in paragraph six *the Leases* with an immediate return to the second lease (*the Lease*) in the same paragraph.

A third Defined Reference is identified in paragraph ten, as follows:

| Defined Reference No. 3 | — in paragraph 10 *further or future Lease or Leases not related to the U.S. Customs Service* |

This defined reference has no subsequent anaphoric references but must be set off as a separate defined reference since it refers to a new and specific property 343 Dunstan Avenue from that of the rest of the document. As in the other documents, this reference to *Lease* is defined by the property to which it refers.

The significance of this referencing and anaphoric referencing to property and lease for property in the third document is as follows. It shows that in Commission Agreement No. 3, all references to property up to paragraph ten are to the property defined in Exhibit A and that all references to lease or leases up to paragraph ten relate only to that property. It also shows clearly that in paragraph ten a newly defined property reference is the existing Waterford Plaza Building, 343 Dunstan Avenue and that all references to further or future Lease or Leases to that property, not relating to the U.S. Customs Service, are not commissionable to Mr. Green unless a separate written instrument is executed toward that end.

It should be further mentioned here that there is, in Commission Agreement No. 3, one other reference to new leases (paragraph 5E). It is clear from the anaphoric reference in this document that this reference to "any new leases" is governed, under anaphoric rules of the English language, by the property reference to which it relates, in this case, Defined Reference No. 2 (in the preamble, *existing leases No. GH-04B-15319*, and thereafter by anaphoric referencing as outlined above) and not to any other property.

3. Topic-comment analysis

It has been shown that the rules of English anaphora obtain in determining specific references to property and specific references to leases which relate to that property. The three Commission Agreements analyzed here are specific and clear in their anaphoric references by the rules of English syntax. There are, in all cases, structural clues such as plural markers, article determination (*a* vs. *the*) or specific terms used primarily by the legal profession (such as *said* property) to produce unambiguous referencing in these documents. Our analysis, based on the anaphoric rules of English, has been largely a syntactic analysis.

Discourse analysis, however, offers further support for this syntactic analysis. Topic-comment analysis on written and spoken discourse has rules quite parallel to the syntactic rules of anaphora. To introduce a topic, one has to clearly identify or mark the substance of that topic. Likewise, once that topic has been changed to another topic, it is necessary to clearly mark or specify its reintroduction or recycling. For example, if one were writing about a specific piece of clearly identified property and then were to change the topic to another piece of property, it would be necessary to clearly mark this change of topic. Then, if one wished to recycle discussion about the first piece of property, it would be necessary to clearly mark, through topic identification, this return to the original topic. As such, topic-comment analysis of discourse follows the same general rules as those of anaphoric referencing. That is, the topic, once established, is expected to be unified and consistent unless or until clearly marked to the contrary. Such an analysis of the three Commission Agreements yields exactly the same results as the Referencing Analysis.

3.1. Commission Agreement No. 1

There are, in legal documents such as these, two types of topics:
a. *substantive topics*: topics which are the substantive reason for the existence of the documents.
b. *corollary topics*: topics which serve the substantive topics by specifying how they will be accomplished (manner, conditions, amount of payment, etc.).

The substantive topic of this document is the relationship of certain property to a lease. The primary aspect is the property since a lease is meaningless without clear identification with the property it prescribes. Thus, it is first necessary to identify the property before one specifies any lease related to it. The corollary topics are those which implement and provide procedures, conditions and details for the substantive topic of property-lease relationship.

Topic-comment analysis of Commission Agreement No. 1 is as follows:

Substantive topic: *Comment*:

> Specific
> Property
> +
> Specific
> Lease

Exhibit A

Corollary topics:
- (1) Preamble is true
- (2) Mr. Green is sole broker — for the lease between Owner and GSA
- (3) Time and amount of Lease — 10 years, $177,540 per year
- (4) Commission — 10% of said basic Lease + details of payment
- (5) Notification — where and how
- (6) Enforcement possibilities — enforcing party reimbursed if successful
- (7) Binding nature — heirs, successors, etc.
- (8) Exceptions to substantive topic — Waterford Plaza

The significance of this analysis is that there is only one substantive topic of which all other topics are corollary. If there are any claims that changes were made in the substantive topic, such changes are unmarked in the structure of this discourse event and cannot be supported.

3.2. Commission Agreement No. 2

The substantive topic of this document is also the relationship of certain property to a lease.

Substantive topic: *Comment*:

> Specific
> Property
> +
> Specific
> Lease

- Exhibit A, together with entire water frontage, bordering the property described herein
- Supplemental Lease

Corollary topics:

(1) Preamble is true
(2) Mr. Green is sole broker — of leases between Broker and GSA
(3) Time and amount — 10 years, $222,588.00 per year + additional rental or compensation
(4) Commission — 10% Supplemental Lease + any additional benefits. Parking space + other details
(5) Event of sale or condemnation — commission details
(6) Notification procedure — addresses
(7) Enforcement possibilities — enforcing party reimbursed if successful
(8) Binding nature — heirs, successors
(9) Exception to substantive topic — Waterford Plaza Building

As for Commission Agreement No. 1, the significance of this analysis is that there is only one substantive topic of which all other topics are corollary.

3.3. *Commission Agreement No. 3*

The substantive topic of this document is the relationship of certain property to two leases.

Substantive topic:

Specific Property + Specific Leases

Comment:
- Exhibit
- Lease Agreement No. GS-04B-15540 and GS-04B-15319

Corollary topics:

(1) Preamble is true
(2) Mr. Green is sole broker — of the Leases between Owner and GSA
(3) Time and amount — 10 years, $271,576 per year
(4) Options to renew — additional two 5-year periods

(5)	Commission	- 10% this Lease + other compensation
(6)	Event of sale or condemnation	- 10% commission, details
(7)	Notification procedure	- addresses
(8)	Enforcement possibilities	- enforcing party reimbursed if successful
(9)	Binding nature	
(10)	Exceptions to substantive topic	- Waterford Plaza Building

Again, this analysis shows that there is only one substantive topic of which all other topics are corollary. If claims are made that there are changes in the meaning of the substantive topic, such claims are not supported by the structure of this discourse event. The rules of topic maintenance are clearly honoured here. No newly marked substantive topic (property + lease) is evidenced.

4. Contrastive analysis

Contrastive analysis is a procedure used by scientists of all disciplines to determine the unique structure of substances or events by displaying in juxtaposition like things from unlike things. The type of contrastive analysis performed on the three Commission Agreements is a contrastive analysis of what the documents say with what they do *not* say, in relation to the dispute (i.e. *what is said vs. what is not said*).

If it were the intention of the signers of these Commission Agreements to provide an exclusive agreement to the Broker for commissions on all property owned currently and in the future by the Owner and leased to GSA (this, of course, does not even address the issue of whether the lessor in question is GSA, Customs Service or any other federal department), there would be clear indications of that intention in these documents. From the previous analysis of referencing and topic-comment, it is clear that such indicators do not exist. If they *were* to exist, one might expect to find them, however, in such places as this contrastive analysis points out.

4.1. Initial substantive topic identification

Commission Agreement No. 1
The clearest place for the signers of these documents to have indicated

that their intention was to provide an exclusive agreement between the Lessor and the Owner for a right to commissions on all property owned currently or in the future by the Owner would be property identification and referencing, primarily in references to property which is not specifically subject to exclusion from commission by the Broker.

In the first Commission Agreement, a golden opportunity for such a statement would have been in the preamble where the Defined Reference to the property is made:

What It Says	*What It Does Not Say*
the property more specifically set forth in Exhibit A attached hereto and made a part hereof and together with the entire water frontage bordering the property described herein	the property more specifically set forth in Exhibit A attached hereto and made a part hereof and all other property currently owned by the OWNER-LESSOR or purchased at any future date in any other location and leased to the GSA

Commission Agreements No. 2 and No. 3

Exactly the same statements could have been made in the second and third documents. Since all subsequent references to property are structurally explicit anaphoric references to Exhibit A, "together with the entire water frontage bordering the property described herein" (the second document) or simply Exhibit A (the third document), the possibility that what was intended by the signers was for all currently owned or future purchased property by the Owner is totally unfounded by the language of these documents.

4.2. Anaphoric reference identification

Another possibility to support the prosecution's claim is that even though the initial, substantive topic reference to the property under discussion (in each of the three preambles) was to the property described in Exhibit A, a later reference or later references to property actually opened the door to a broader definition of property. If this were the case, the following words would have been required:

Commission Agreement No. 1

What It Says	*What It Does Not Say*
in preamble: the property	this property and all other currently or future owned property

in preamble:
    said property

said property and all other currently or future owned property

Commission Agreement No. 2

What It Says   *What It Does Not Say*

in preamble:
    the property

this property and all other currently or future owned property

in preamble:
    the said property

the said property and all other currently or future owned property

in paragraph 4:
    the land specified

the land specified here and all other currently or future owned property

in paragraph 5:
    the within premises

the within premises and all other currently or future owned premises

Commission Agreement No. 3

What It Says   *What It Does Not Say*

in preamble:
    the property

this property and all other currently or future owned property

in preamble:
    real property

real property in this case and all currently or future owned property

in paragraph 6:
    the within premises

the within premises and all other currently or future owned premises

in paragraph 6:
    the property

this property and all other currently or future owned property

    As is evident from the documents themselves, there is no indication either in the initial substantive topic reference nor in any subsequent anaphoric reference, that the signers of these three documents intended the meaning of *property* to include, at any time, any property than that which was specified as Exhibit A "together with the entire water frontage bordering the property described herein" (in documents No. 1 and No. 2) or simply as Exhibit A (in document No. 3). No language evidence is present to indicate, furthermore, that any subsequent anaphoric reference to the original Defined Reference was present or was intended. I wish to be perfectly clear about this. I do not claim that there was no intention on the part of the signers not to include all currently or future owned property of the Owner for the Broker's commission; only that there is no evidence of such intention in the actual language or structure of the written discourse, as determined by the principles of the structure of the language in which these documents were written.

5. Conclusion

Disputes in legal issues often revolve around the wording, syntax or structure of language. There are many tools available to linguists for analyzing documents. In the case of these Commission Agreements, the three analytical routines selected (anaphora, topic analysis and contrastive analysis) were chosen because they are most appropriate for addressing this legal issue. The problem, in short, determines the analytical routines to be used. Our analysis, which also demonstrates that even the jargon ridden and complex language of law and business is capable of being untangled, was instrumental in settling the dispute.

Note

1. All references to specific people, organizations and places have been changed to protect the anonymity of the participants.

Antithesis: a study in clause combining and discourse structure

Sandra A. Thompson and William C. Mann

1. Introduction

Current research at the USC Information Sciences Institute (ISI) is aimed at designing computer programs with some of the capabilities of authors. This effort has involved a study of the nature of text as a medium of communication. Phenomena of clause-combining in text, described in terms of interclausal relations, have received some attention in the discourse literature (see, for example, Beekman and Callow 1974; Beekman, et al. 1981; Chafe 1984; Ford and Thompson 1985; Grimes 1975; Halliday and Hasan 1976; Hobbs 1979; Jordan 1984; Longacre 1976; Longacre and Thompson 1985; Mann and Thompson 1985; Mann and Thompson 1986; Mithun 1984; Thompson 1985a; Thompson 1985b; Winter 1982).

We believe that the same relations which are useful in describing clause combining also prevail between larger portions of text. In this paper we show that a description which posits the same relations at clausal and larger scales makes it possible to explain some features of clause presentation and gain insight into larger-scale text structure.

The paper first presents an informal description of a theory, called Rhetorical Structure Theory (RST), in which the same sorts of relations that characterize clause combining operate at higher levels of text structure. It then considers in closer detail one text relation as it is found in edited texts in written English. This is the text relation we call Antithesis. Antithesis is then exemplified using natural texts, which enables us to examine specific benefits of using the same descriptions for clausal and larger portions.

2. The descriptive framework: a brief overview of rhetorical structure theory

Rhetorical Structure Theory is a theory of text organization. It describes the kinds of parts a text can have, how they can be arranged, and how parts can be connected to form a whole text.[1]

Relationships between parts of a coherent text are crucial to making the text function as a single unit. Writers use a small set of general, highly recurrent relations to structure most expository text. We have given these relations names such as Cause, Solutionhood, Motivation, and Antithesis, comparable to the names with which the linguists cited above describe interclausal relations.

Consider, for example, the following short text, which has been divided into Units prior to analysis.[2] This text, an internal memo from the librarian at Information Sciences Institute (ISI), contains a relation of Motivation:

1. Some extra copies of the Spring 1984 issue of AI Magazine are available in the library.
2. This issue includes a "Research in Progress" report on AI research at ISI.

In Unit 1, the librarian implicitly offers to give away copies of the magazine. Unit 2 describes a particular report in the magazine. In addition to the content expressed by each of these two Units, another *implicit, relational* proposition arises from their standing in a Motivation relation, namely that Unit 2 provides *motivation* for taking up the offer conveyed by Unit 1. This relational proposition is, roughly, that the report's reference to ISI research plausibly motivates obtaining a copy of the magazine. It is this implicit relational proposition of Motivation that makes the text cohere as a text.[3] Relations between parts of a text can take several forms, but one form predominates in expository texts. That is the Nucleus — Satellite form, in which the nuclear portion realizes the primary goals of the writer and the satellite provides supplementary material. We will focus on the nucleus-satellite form.

RST can be used to demonstrate that texts are organized hierarchically. Text spans, the groups into which the text is arranged, are represented in RST by Rhetorical Structure Schemas. Each RS Schema indicates how a particular portion of text structure is functionally decomposed into other spans, which at the finest level of decomposition are single Units.

RS Schemas of the nucleus-satellite form are defined entirely by identifying a set of relations, almost always just a single relation, which relate pairs of spans of text in a coordinated way. Each Schema is represented by a diagram in which a vertical line indicates the nucleus part and one or more dependent branches indicate that the other part is ancillary. RS Schemas thus typically consist of a core and an ancillary portion — a nucleus and a satellite, as in Figure 1.

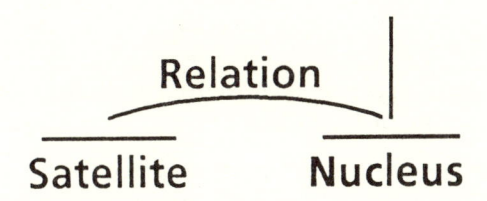

Figure 1. The simplest Generic schema

In the "AI Magazine" text, the nucleus is the first part (Unit 1), and the satellite, which provides the motivation, is the second part (Unit 2). We can diagram this text schematically as in Figure 2.

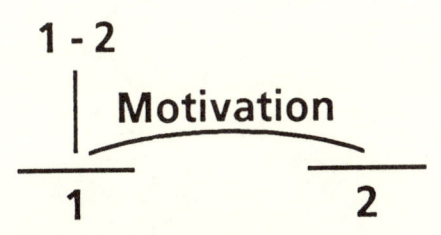

Figure 2. RST analysis of "AI Magazine" text

Let us examine several other brief examples. First, the beginning of an advertisement for a Los Angeles tanning salon:

1. We all know about February warm spells and the beginnings of great tans — all to be ruined by rain and fog March through June!
2. But now (finally!) we have a solution to that dilemma...

This text extract embodies the relation of Solutionhood.[4] A problem is presented, expressing a need which is then fulfilled by a solution. Figure 3 is a diagram of the tanning ad extract. The purpose of the ad is found in

Unit 2, the announcement of a Solution to the Problem posed in Unit 1.

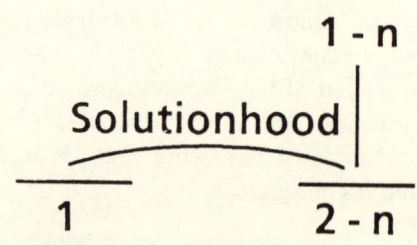

```
                        1 - n
                          |
           Solutionhood   |
          ⌒⌒⌒⌒⌒⌒⌒⌒⌒⌒
          _____           _____
            1              2 - n
```
Figure 3. RST analysis of "Tanning" text extract

Next is a slightly longer text, an item from the bulletin of the Academic Senate of the University of California:

1. The Academic Council has endorsed a request to establish a committee which will give retired faculty members a voice in the systemwide Academic Senate, particularly as regards retirement matters.
2. Faculty members remain Senate members after retirement,
3. but no systemwide Senate committee represents emeriti at the present time.
4. Discussions are underway about the form the emeriti committee should take.

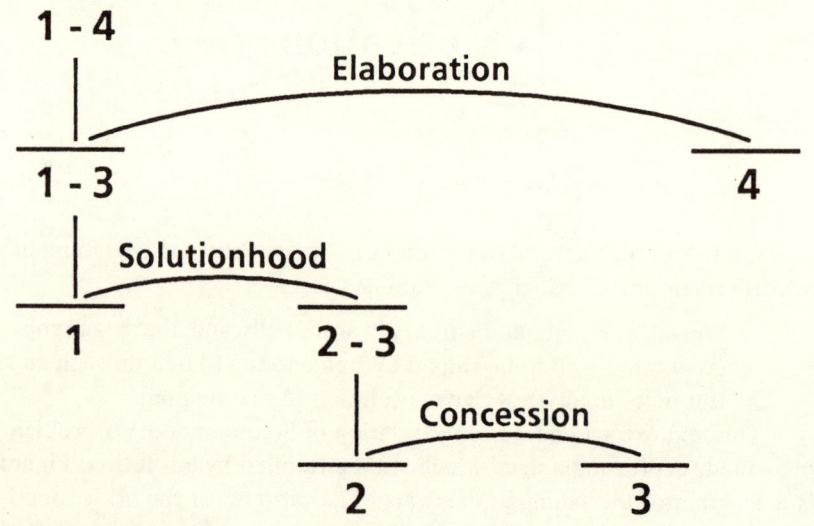

```
  1 - 4
    |
    |           Elaboration
    |      ⌒⌒⌒⌒⌒⌒⌒⌒⌒⌒⌒⌒⌒⌒⌒⌒
  _____                          _____
  1 - 3                            4
    |
    |   Solutionhood
    |  ⌒⌒⌒⌒⌒⌒⌒⌒
  _____        _____
    1          2 - 3
                 |
                 |   Concession
                 |  ⌒⌒⌒⌒⌒⌒⌒⌒
               _____        _____
                 2            3
```
Figure 4. RST analysis of "Emeriti Committee" text

This text illustrates three relations, as diagrammed in Figure 4. The RST analysis of this text makes several claims about its structure:

1. The Nuclear Unit of the entire text can be determined by starting at the top of the RST diagram and following only nuclear (vertical) lines down to the terminal node. There is a strong tendency for the Nuclear Unit to represent the central purpose of the text. In this text the Nuclear Unit is Unit 1; this matches our judgment that the announcement in Unit 1 is the central message that the writer of this text wants to convey.
2. Units 2-3 are in a Solutionhood relation with Unit 1. Units 2-3 pose a problem, the lack of representation for emeriti, to which Unit 1, announcing the formation of the new committee, is the (partial) solution.
3. But Units 2 and 3 themselves manifest a relation between them, which we call Concession. This relation holds when a writer chooses to strengthen a point by affirming that point in the face of a potentially opposing point.
4. Finally, Unit 4 is in an Elaboration relation with the rest of the text. The Elaboration relation is particularly versatile; it supplements the nuclear portion with various kinds of detail, including relationships of:
    *set: member
    *abstraction: instance
    *whole: part
    *process: step
    *object: attribute

Since Unit 4 discusses an *attribute* of the committee, namely its form, it satisfies the definition of Elaboration.

As a final example, consider this text, from The Linguistic Reporter, 1971:

1. The University Press of Kentucky has announced the establishment of the Kentucky Foreign Language Conference Award to be given annually for the best manuscript dealing with some aspect of foreign language and/or literature.
2. The Award, $500 and acceptance of the manuscript for publication, is offered in conjunction with the Kentucky Foreign Language Conference.

3. The deadline for submission of manuscripts for the 1972 Award is December 1, 1971.
4. For further information, write Kentucky Foreign Language Conference Award, The University Press of Kentucky, 104 Lafferty Hall, Lexington, Kentucky, 40506.

This text makes an offer. The first part, (Units 1-2), and the second part, (Units 3-4), are connected by a relation of Enablement. That is, Units 3-4 jointly provide information enabling the reader to comply with the offer expressed in 1-2. Unit 2, in turn, can be analyzed as an Elaboration of Unit 1, since it provides a further attribute of the award.

Accordingly, we can describe these relations by invoking two RS Schemas, one containing the Enablement relation and the other the Elaboration relation. Units 3 and 4, then, are Enablement satellites.

This text can be schematically diagrammed as in Figure 5.

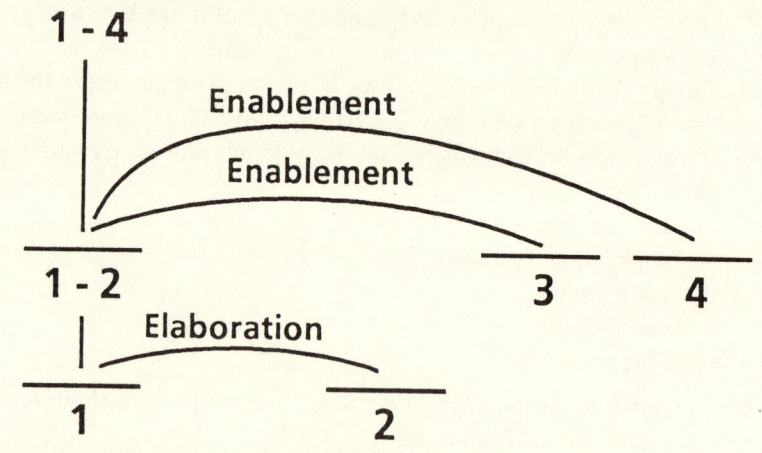

Figure 5. RST analysis of "Kentucky Award" text

With these examples, we have illustrated, though by no means exhaustively presented, the basic design of Rhetorical Structure Theory as a device for analyzing texts.[5]

To round out our discussion of the Schemas and the relations which they represent, we note that:

1. The definition of RS Schemas allows the schema elements to be arranged in any order and still be an instance of that Schema.

Although schemas do not encode the order of segments, in our diagrams we have generally ordered the segments in the same order as their text spans occur in the text.
2. As we have seen, for example in Figure 5, analyzed just above, we allow for multiple satellites within one schema.
3. Multi-nuclear schemas also appear occasionally, though they are not nearly as frequent in our data base as nucleus-satellite schemas. We will not discuss them further in this paper; for more discussion see Mann and Thompson (1987).

The definition scheme will be illustrated in detail for the Antithesis relation below.

In addition to Motivation, we have already mentioned relations of Solutionhood, Elaboration, Concession, and Enablement. Other relations which we have found to be useful in the analysis of texts include Antithesis, Evidence, Circumstance, Concession, and Reason.

This concludes our overview of the descriptive apparatus. We now pursue the goal set forth in Section 1, to demonstrate, by discussing the Antithesis relation in some detail, that clause combining is a special case of the hierarchical organization of texts.

3. The antithesis relation

Before defining the Antithesis relation, we need to introduce the concept of Positive regard.

Writers pursue different goals with different texts and text spans. Some are intended to persuade, i.e., to create belief. Others are intended to create approval or interest. Still others are intended to create desire to act. These are all varieties of positive regard. In analyzing any one text span and decomposing it into parts, we use a single primary notion of positive regard — belief, approval, or desire to act — with the choice depending on the analyst's perception of the writer's intent.

In analyzing the structure of a text, we recognize that a particular text span can be further analyzed as a pair of spans, Nucleus and Satellite, related by the Antithesis relation, provided that the five defining conditions that follow are satisfied.

1. Nucleus and Satellite are in contrast. (Two items are in contrast if they are

>   a. perceived as being the same in many respects,
>   b. perceived as differing in a few respects, and
>   c. compared with respect to one or more of these differences.)
> 2. One cannot have positive regard for both Nucleus and Satellite because of an incompatibility that arises from the contrast.[6]
> 3. The writer has positive regard for the nucleus. Thus the nucleus is the "antithesis" span, and the satellite is the "thesis" span.
> 4. The writer intends that the reader have positive regard for the nucleus.
> 5. Understanding the satellite, and the incompatibility between the satellite and the nucleus, tends to increase the reader's positive regard for the nucleus.

As an illustration of the Antithesis relation, consider the last two clauses of a letter to the editor of *The Christian Science Monitor*. The writer of this letter has been deploring US foreign policy.

> 1. By setting the best example possible of a thriving, generous, democratic state, with room for each of its people to pursue his highest sense of right,
> 2. by doing unto others as we would have them do unto us,
> 3. how much more we could do for our world.
> 4. *Rather than winning them with our arms,*
> 5. *we'd win them by our example, and their desire to follow it.*

Units 4 and 5 are in an Antithesis relation:

> 1. Nucleus and Satellite are in contrast, since *winning them with our arms* involves adversary relationships and to *win them by our example* involves amicable relationships.
> 2. One cannot have positive regard for both Nucleus and Satellite because of an incompatibility that arises from the contrast; one cannot compatibly intend both seeking approval and attacking.
> 3. The writer has positive regard for the nucleus, for planning *to win them by our example*.
> 4. The writer intends that the reader have positive regard for the nucleus, for *win(ning) them by our example*.
> 5. Understanding that the satellite *winning them with our arms* is violent, and therefore negative in this context, and that the nucleus *win them by our example* differs by being non-violent, and therefore positive, increases the attractiveness of the nucleus.

The definition given above thus applies to the *Monitor* letter extract.

Now we will take up three more substantial texts as a basis for evaluating the function of the *Antithesis* relation.

3.1. Sample text I — Common Cause plea

Our first text is a letter of persuasion urging members of California Common Cause, the California chapter of the national citizens' lobby, to vote against CCC endorsement of the Nuclear Freeze Initiative, then on the upcoming California ballot:[7]

1. I don't believe that endorsing the Nuclear Freeze Initiative is the right step for California Common Cause.
2. Tempting as it may be,
3. we shouldn't embrace every popular issue that comes along.
4. When we do so
5. we use precious, limited resources
6. where other players with superior resources are already doing an adequate job.
7. Rather, I think we will be stronger and more effective
8. if we stick to those issues of governmental structure and process, broadly defined, that have formed the core of our agenda for years.
9. Open government, campaign finance reform, and fighting the influence of special interests and big money, these are our kinds of issues.
10. Let's be clear:
11. I personally favor the initiative and ardently support disarmament negotiations to reduce the risk of war.
12. But I don't think endorsing a specific nuclear freeze proposal is appropriate for CCC.
13. We should limit our involvement in defense and weaponry to matters of process, such as exposing the weapons industry's influence on the political process.
14. Therefore, I urge you to vote against a CCC endorsement of the nuclear freeze initiative.

(signed) Michael Asimow, California Common Cause Vice-Chair and UCLA Law Professor

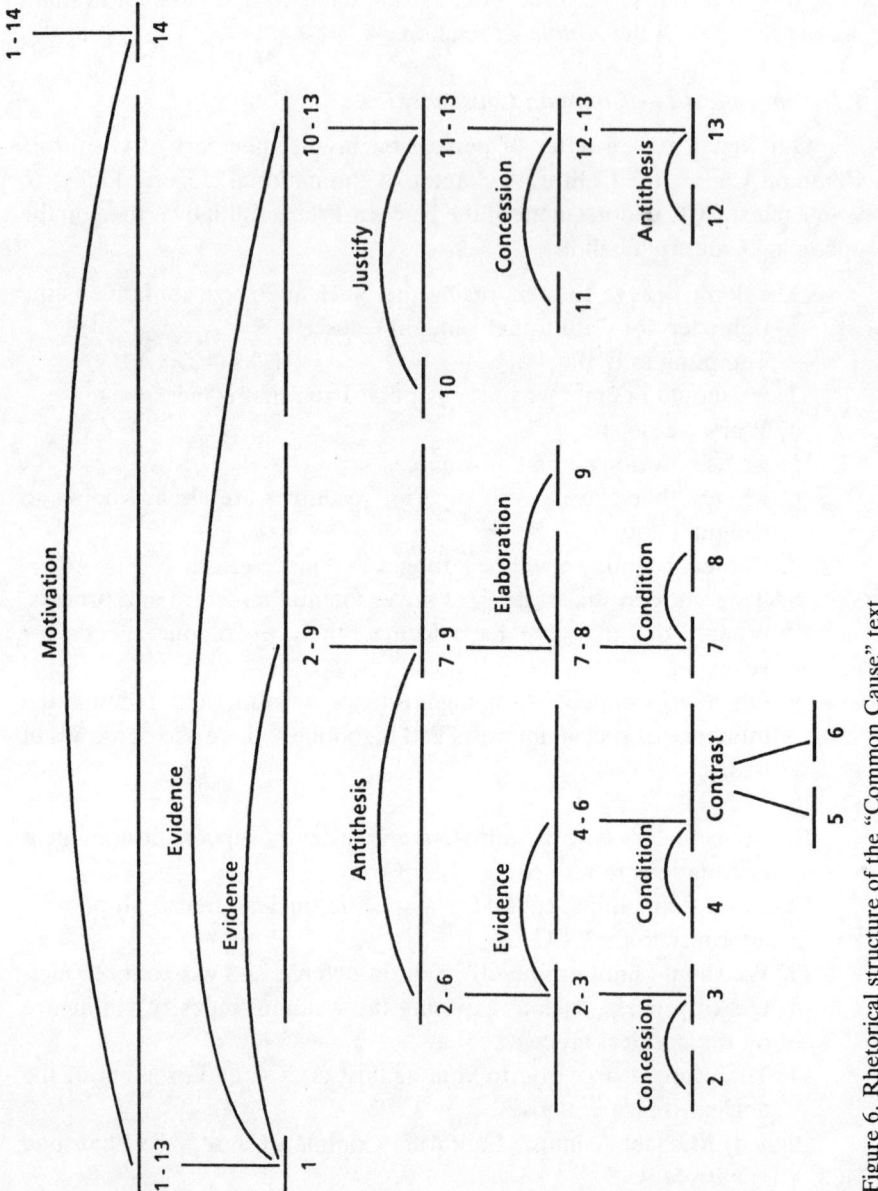

Figure 6. Rhetorical structure of the "Common Cause" text

CLAUSE COMBINING AND DISCOURSE STRUCTURE 369

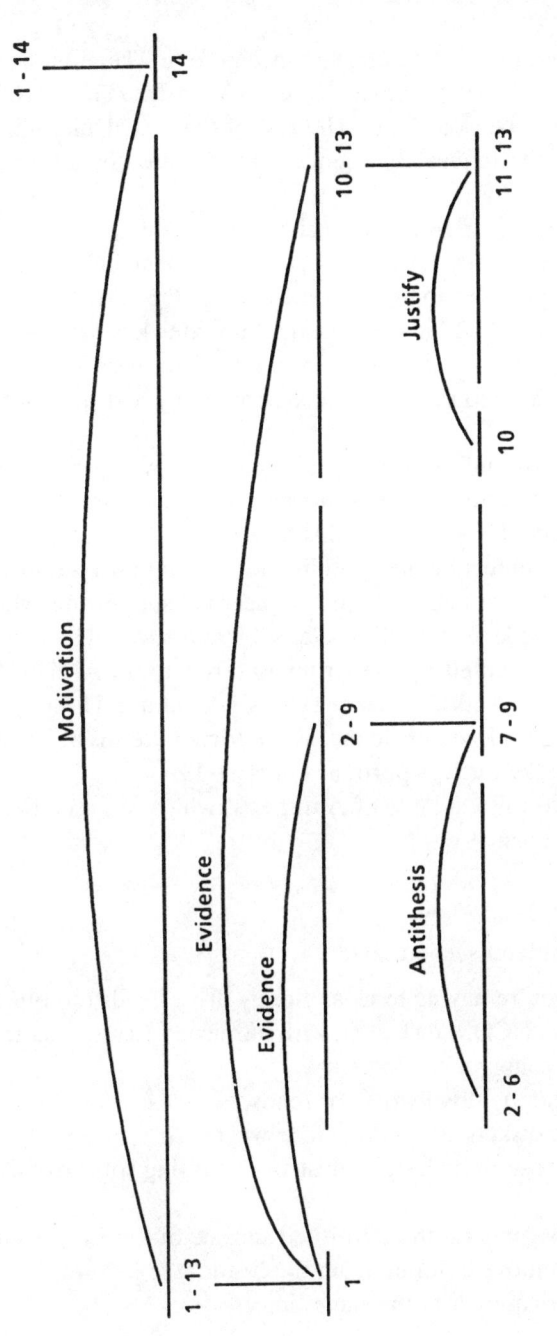

Figure 7. Top three levels of the RST analysis of the "Common Cause" text

The RST analysis of this text appears in Figure 6. The analysis shows that the entire text can be described in terms of a MOTIVATION RS Schema. Unit 14 is the Nuclear Unit. The rest of the text, Units 1-13, provides motivation for the request and hence is represented by a Motivation satellite.

RST predicts that Unit 14 is the nucleus of the entire text, since the top-most RS Schema directly terminates only by nuclear linkages to Unit 14. Indeed, Unit 14 provides the central message of the text. However, as we have seen with the "AI Magazine" text, the writer has provided additional text to ensure the success of his request, since bare requests and directives are more likely to succeed if accompanied by text that motivates the reader to comply.

We will not go through the entire analysis, but will just sketch the claims for the gross structure that this analysis makes. Figure 7 shows the top three levels of the RST analysis of this text.

Another major subsection lies within the Motivation section of the text: Unit 1 is presented as a claim, with two pieces of supporting evidence, represented by two Evidence satellites, Units 2-9 and 10-13. The first piece of evidence is then presented by the writer in terms of an ANTITHESIS Schema with a nuclear Antithesis span (Units 7-9) and a Thesis satellite (Units 2-6). The second piece of evidence is put forth in terms of a justification satellite (10) for the nuclear portion, Units 11-13.

We will return to this example of Antithesis, which relates a five-Unit span to a three-Unit span.

3.2. Sample text II — Syncom ad

Let us now consider a second text.[8]

1. What if you're having to clean floppy drive heads too often?
2. Ask for SYNCOM diskettes, with burnished Ectype coating and dust-absorbing jacket liners.
3. As your floppy drive writes or reads,
4. a Syncom diskette is working four ways
5. to keep loose particles and dust from causing soft errors, dropouts.
6. Cleaning agents on the burnished surface of the Ectype coating actually remove build-up from the head,
7. while lubricating it at the same time.

8. A carbon additive drains away static electricity
9. before it can attract dust or lint.
10. Strong binders hold the signal-carrying oxides tightly within the coating.
11A. And the non-woven jacket liner,
12. more than just wiping the surface,
(11B.) provides thousands of tiny pockets to keep what it collects.[9]
13. To see which Syncom diskette will replace the ones you're using now,
14. send for our free "Flexi-Finder" selection guide and the name of the supplier nearest you.

The RST analysis of this text appears in Figure 8. Again, we will not discuss each part of the RST analysis in detail, but will simply outline its description of the overall structure of this text.

Starting at the top, we see a Solutionhood relation between Unit 1 and the rest of the text. That is, the entire text after the "What if" question is offered as a solution to the problem of having to clean floppy drive heads too often.

In the Solution portion of the text — the stretch of text consisting of Units 2-14 of the text — we see a MOTIVATION-ENABLEMENT Schema with a nucleus (Unit 2) and two satellites. One is for the Motivation relation (Units 3-12), and the other is for the Enablement relation (Units 13-14). Within the Motivation portion (Units 3-12), we find an ELABORATION RS Schema with a nucleus and an Elaboration portion. This Elaboration portion of the text consists of four pieces of information, which correspond to the "four ways" that your Syncom diskette is working to keep loose particles and dust from causing mischief.

An Antithesis relation appears in this text between Units 11 and 12:

11A. And the non-woven jacket liner,
12. more than just wiping the surface,
(11B.) provides thousands of tiny pockets to keep what it collects.

The writer does not view the Thesis span, expressed in Unit 12, with positive regard — that the jacket liner *only* wipes the surface — (signalled by *just* in Unit 12.) The writer clearly does view the Antithesis span (the two parts of Unit 11) with positive regard, that the jacket liner *also* provides pockets to keep what it collects.

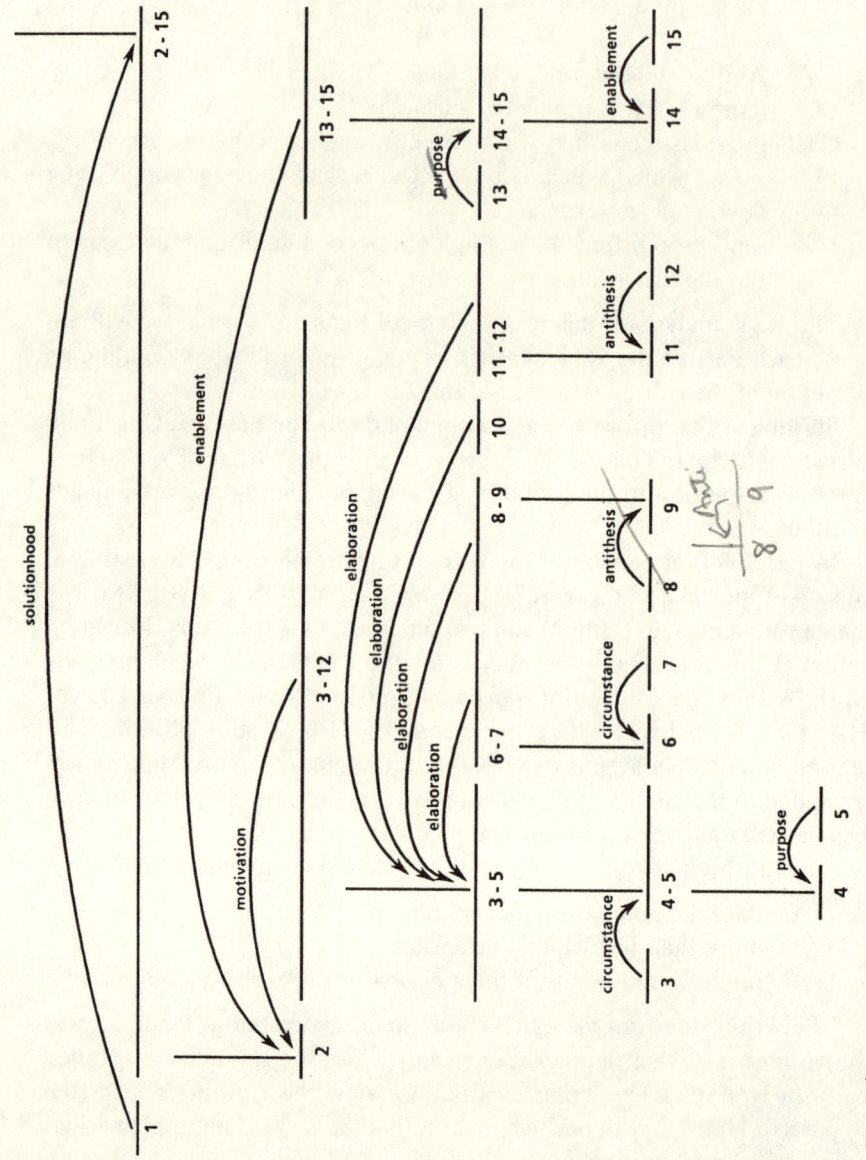

Figure 8. RST analysis of the "Syncom" text

3.3. Sample text III — a personal letter

We have seen several examples of the Antithesis relation holding between a pair of adjacent clauses. The italicized Units 4-5 in this excerpt from a personal letter comprise another. The writer has announced that thumb surgery will be necessary and is giving the background story, which involves hereditary arthritis:

1. Thumbs began to be troublesome about 4 months ago
2. and I made an appointment with the best hand surgeon in the Valley
3. to see if my working activities were the problem.
4. *Using thumbs is not the problem*
5. *but heredity is*
6. and the end result is no use of thumbs
7. if I don't do something now.

In Unit 4, the writer offers the thesis that the use of thumbs at work might be the problem, and she signals lack of positive regard for this thesis by the use of the negative; belief is the kind of positive regard involved in this case. In Unit 5, she offers the Antithesis, which she does regard positively, that heredity is causing the problem. Units 1-7 of this letter can be rhetorically represented as follows, then, with 1 serving as statement of the problem solved in 2-3 and 1-3 serving as statement of the problem solved in 4-5.

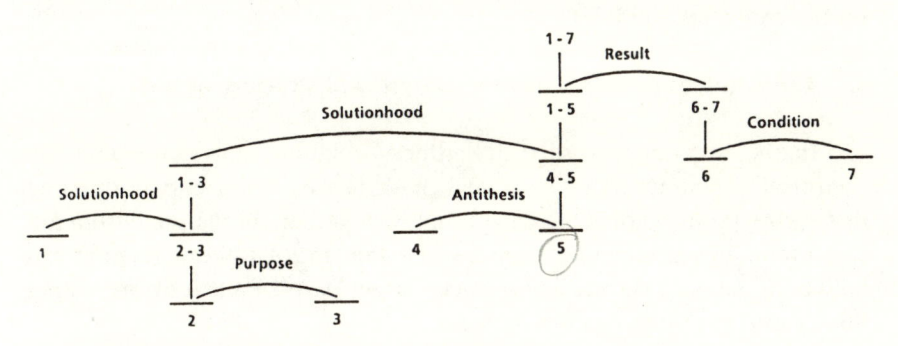

Figure 9. RST analysis of "Thumb Heredity" text

As these examples suggest, the Antithesis relation can take many different forms. In each case, the statement of the Thesis span allows an inference of lack of positive regard, but the range of syntactic options used to convey this lack of positive regard is broad. For example, the Thesis span might be introduced by a conjunction such as *rather or instead of*, as in the foreign policy letter discussed above. In other instances, the Thesis span might contain a "hedge" word indicating lack of positive regard. Figure 10 lists these and other syntactic options that occur in our data, without attempting to taxonomize them.

---

1. Rather than THESIS, ANTITHESIS.
2. Instead of THESIS, ANTITHESIS.
3. THESIS [... tempted ...]. However, ANTITHESIS
4. THESIS [... too many ...]. ANTITHESIS
5. THESIS [... some ...]. Yet ANTITHESIS.
6. THESIS [... might have ...]. ANTITHESIS.
7. THESIS [... purported ...]. ANTITHESIS.
8. Not THESIS, but ANTITHESIS.
9. ANTITHESIS, not THESIS.
10. ANTITHESIS <part a>, more than THESIS, ANTITHESIS <part b>.
11. ANTITHESIS without THESIS.

Figure 10. List of types of syntactic coding for the Antithesis relation

The study of text relations in general, as we would expect, reveals no one-to-one mapping of function into form. Figure 10 shows the Antithesis relation to be typical in this respect. Although Figure 10 does not show it, the Antithesis relation can also occur without any signal such as *Rather*; several examples will follow.

4. The Antithesis relation and the hierarchical structure of texts

In this section, we use the Antithesis relation as evidence that the rhetorical organization of texts is well-characterized by a theory postulating that the relations binding the parts of a text together are the same from top to bottom. In particular we demonstrate that the Antithesis relation can hold both between clauses and between larger parts of a text by presenting three cases and three types of evidence.

4.1. The Antithesis relation at both higher and lower levels of the same text

The Antithesis relation strongly supports our claim that relations at the lowest levels of text structure, i.e., interclausal relations, are best viewed as special cases of relations among higher levels of text structure: our sample texts contain several instances of the Antithesis relation, some of which relate multi-clausal text spans and some of which relate just a pair of Units or even clauses.

This relation figures prominently in the Common Cause text, as Figure 6 shows. The entire first piece of evidence for the central claim of the text, namely that endorsement of the nuclear freeze initiative is wrong for California Common Cause, is expressed in the form of an Antithesis argument (Units 2-9). That is, the to-be-rejected Thesis portion of this argument (comprising Units 2-6) is the idea that CCC should embrace every popular issue that comes along. The Antithesis span (comprising Units 7-9) is that CCC will be stronger and more effective if it sticks to its traditional issues.

The Antithesis relation appears again in this text, relating Unit 12 to 13:

12. But I don't think endorsing a specific nuclear freeze proposal is appropriate for CCC.
13. We should limit our involvement in defense and weaponry to matters of process, such as exposing the weapons industry's influence on the political process.

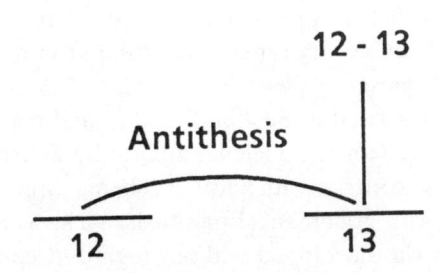

Figure 11. Units 12-13 of the Common Cause text analysis

Here the Thesis text span, conveying the idea that CCC might endorse the nuclear freeze initiative, is expressed by a single Unit (12), while the Antithesis text span, conveying the idea that CCC should limit its defense involvement, is also expressed by a single Unit (13). In this text, we see a single RS Schema, namely the ANTITHESIS RS Schema, instantiated once for relating higher-level text spans and once for relating Units at the clause level.

4.2. The Antithesis relation and grammatical hypotaxis

Turning to the Syncom Text, we see from Figure 12 that the ANTITHESIS Schema represents the relationship between Units 12 and 11, as discussed above in Section 3.2:

11A. And the non-woven jacket liner,
12.   more than just wiping the surface,
(11B.) provides thousands of tiny pockets to keep what it collects.

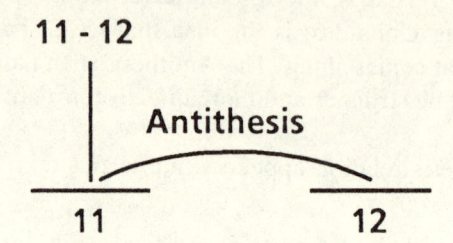

Figure 12. Units 11-12 of the Syncom text analysis

Something interesting appears in this instantiation of the ANTITHESIS Schema: The Thesis span, Unit 12, is expressed by a hypotactic "subordinate" clause.[10] This suggests that not only do the same functional relationships that tie stretches of text together also tie Units to each other, but also that these very same relationships can relate a hypotactic clause to its "main" clause.

In fact, the texts discussed in Section 2 and 3, and many other texts, reveal strong correlations between nucleus-satellite RS Schemas and grammatical hypotaxis. These contrast with another schema form, the multi-nuclear, which correlates with grammatical parataxis.[11] This is an unexpected benefit of RST, which was developed without regard to considerations of the grammar of clause combining.

In the case of the Antithesis relation, our data confirm this general finding in many examples in which the *satellite Thesis* is a hypotactic clause, such as the one in the *Monitor* letter about U.S. foreign policy:

4. Rather than winning them with our arms,
5. we'd win them by our example, and their desire to follow it.

However, we have found no cases in which the nucleus Antithesis is a hypotactic clause.

4.3. An Antithesis conjunction connecting spans larger than single units

Analysis of the Common Cause text also shows the unity of interclausal relations and relations between larger organizational entities. Consider this portion of the text:

2. Tempting as it may be,
3. we shouldn't embrace every popular issue that comes along.
4. When we do so
5. we use precious, limited resources
6. where other players with superior resources are already doing an adequate job.
7. *Rather*, I think we will be stronger and more effective
8. if we stick to those issues of governmental structure and process, broadly defined, that have formed the core of our agenda for years.
9. Open government, campaign finance reform, and fighting the influence of special interests and big money, these are our kinds of issues.

Unit 7 begins with the conjunction *Rather*, a contrastive conjunction which in this case signals the relation of Antithesis. Note that this conjunction does *not* signal that Unit 7 is the Antithesis span for the immediately preceding clause Unit 6. In fact, as Figure 7 shows, *Rather* in Unit 7 relates Units 2-6, as the Thesis span, to Units 7-9 as the Antithesis span. That is, it relates the situation of "embracing every popular issue that comes along" to the incompatible situation of "stick[ing] to ... our agenda..."; neither of the elements that make the situations incompatible is expressed in the clauses adjacent to *Rather*.

In this situation, an antithesis conjunction links not two adjacent Units, but two much more extensive spans of text. This fact supports our claim that the Antithesis relation reveals that the same kinds of rhetorical organization that relates pairs of single clauses can relate portions of text at higher levels as well.

Our data base contains a number of similar instances. Consider this excerpt from a personal letter about the Bay to Breakers footrace in San Francisco:

1. At one-third of the distance into the race I was tempted to give up
2. since I heard that the race had already been won.
3. *However*, I persisted

4. and came in somewhere between twenty and thirty thousandth.

This excerpt is diagrammed in Figure 13:

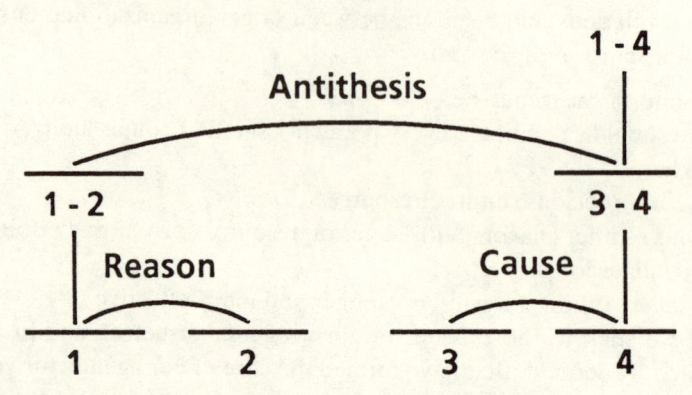

Figure 13. RST analysis of "Bay to Breakers" text extract

Again, we see a contrastive conjunction, *However*, joining as Thesis span and Antithesis span not just the Units on either side of it, but rather the span including Units 1-2 to the span including Units 3-4.

The same point can be made for instances of the Antithesis relation that do not involve an explicit contrastive conjunction.[12] For example, consider this excerpt from the end of an advertisement for The Sports Connection's tanning salon:

   1. Unlike most Suntan Salons we will not be charging a membership fee on top of session fees.
   2. A membership at The Sports Connection is a membership at the "Tanning Connection"
   3. and only $15 per session will be charged.

In this excerpt, the Antithesis span is clearly Unit 1, but the Thesis span is not Unit 2. It is the clause combination consisting of Units 2-3, as shown in Figure 14.

A final example of an unsignalled Antithesis relation between spans of text larger than single Units comes from a newspaper column called "Tennis Tips":

   1. Too many players hit an acceptable shot,
   2. then stand around admiring it
   3. and wind up losing the point.

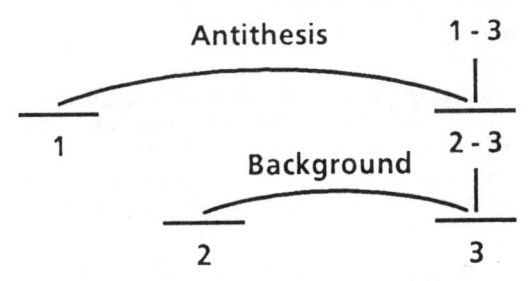

Figure 14. RST analysis of second "Tanning" text extract

4. There is no time in an action game like tennis to applaud yourself and still get in position for the next shot.
5. And you always have to assume there will be a next shot.

Figure 15 shows the rhetorical structure for this excerpt. Units 1-3 express the Thesis span, while Units 4-5 express the Antithesis span, for which the writer obviously has positive regard. Once again, although no explicit conjunction links the two parts of the Antithesis relation, the two parts themselves are larger than single Units.

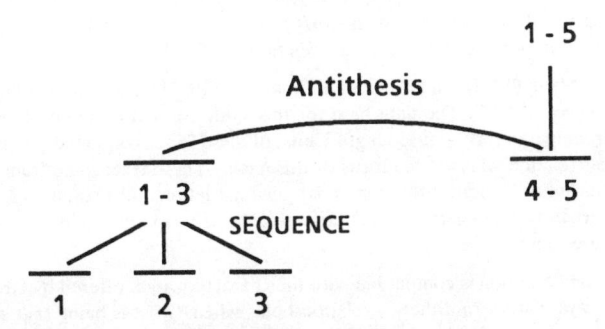

Figure 15. RST analysis of "Tennis Tips" text extract

5. Conclusion

We consider the function of the Antithesis relation to be strong support for the claim that the relationships underlying the grammar of clause combining are the same as those governing the way texts in general are organized. Clauses combine according to the same types of functional relationships that are central to overall text organization.

Acknowledgments

We are pleased to acknowledge the input of Barbara Fox, Cecilia Ford, and Christian Matthiessen in the development of this approach to the study of texts. We are grateful to the Netherlands Institute for Advanced Study for fellowship support for S. Thompson during the preparation of this paper. This research was sponsored in part by National Science Foundation grant IST-8408726, and in part by AFOSR contract FQ8671-84-01007; the opinions in this report are solely those of the authors.

Notes

1. For brief descriptions of RST, see Mann (1984) and Mann and Thompson (1985, 1987).
2. The size of the Units is not a theoretical matter; it varies with the needs of the analyst. For the purposes of this paper, Units are roughly equivalent to clauses, except that relative clauses and complement clauses are considered parts of the Unit in which their governing item appears, not as independent Units.
3. Discussion of such relations as discourse structuring devices can be found in Beekman and Callow (1974); Beekman et al. (1981); Crothers (1979); Grimes (1975); Hobbs and Evans (1980); Longacre (1976, 1983); Mann (1984); Mann and Thompson (1985, 1987); Matthiessen and Thompson (1986), and Meyer (1982).
4. This is similar to "Response" in Grimes (1975). See also Jordan (1984) for discussion of "Solution" as an important text-structuring relation.
5. See especially Mann (1984), and Mann and Thompson (1987) for discussion of other uses and consequences of RST. The data base for this study consists of about 75 short texts containing from two to forty clause-length Units; of these 75, 20 contained occurrences of the Antithesis relation which is the focus of this paper. These texts come from a variety of sources, including: administrative memos, personal letters, advertisements, editorial notices in journals and newsletters, book jacket blurbs, letters to the editor, news articles, travel brochures, and recipes.
6. This part of the definition is compatible with the characterization offered by Greenbaum (1969), who says that an "antithetic" relation holds when "what is being said is in complete opposition to what has been said before" (pp. 36-37).
7. Quoted (with permission) from The Insider, California Common Cause state newsletter, 2.1, July, 1982. This text was the "con" part of a "pro" and "con" pair of letters on this issue. For further discussion of the discourse relations in this text, see Mann (1984) and Mann and Thompson (1985, 1986)
8. June, 1982, BYTE magazine; Copyright c 1982 Byte Publications, Inc. Used with permission of Byte Publications, Inc. This was a half-page ad which included a picture and several different typefaces. While one could easily argue that these features are also relevant to the message conveyed by the text, we have not considered them essential to the organizational structure of this text. For extensive discussion of the discourse relations in this text, see Mann and Thompson (1985).

9. Our analysis of this purpose clause as part of Unit 11 rather than as a separate Unit derives from our judgment that *to keep what it collects* is an infinitival relative clause on the head noun *pockets* rather than a purpose clause for the predicate *provides thousands of tiny pockets*, since it is the pockets that keep what the liner collects, not the liner itself. Our overall point, however, is not affected if the alternative analysis is adopted.

10. See Halliday (1985) and, following him, Matthiessen and Thompson (1986) for a discussion of the necessity of distinguishing among "subordinate" clauses, the types *hypotaxis* and *embedding*.

11. See Matthiessen and Thompson (1986) for further discussion of hypotaxis in these terms.

12. See Mann and Thompson (1986) for discussion of the pervasiveness of unsignalled relations.

3. Exploring Language as Social Semiotic

The hegemony of information

Richard W. Bailey

From the beginning of his influential career in the study of language, Michael Halliday has consistently asserted the reciprocal relation between sign systems and the social life of the community in which they are embedded. In one formulation of this principle, he has written: "Since reality is a social construct, it can be constructed only through an exchange of meanings. Hence meanings can be seen as constitutive of reality. This, at least, is the natural conclusion for the present era, when the exchange of information tends to replace the exchange of goods-and-services as the primary mode of social action" (Halliday 1978: 191). In her further elaboration of this idea, Terry Threadgold (1986: 44) has pointed out that "acts of communication are forms of social discourse which maintain and regulate social activities and define status and power relations".

These important ideas — language as social action, communication as the domain of status and power relations — form the subject of this paper on the history of information exchange through literacy.[1] As Halliday has often done, I direct these observations particularly to teachers who, supported by political structures dedicated to the free exchange of information, can foster social conventions in which more and more people can effectively participate in the exchange of ideas. As I will show, this exchange is constrained by social circumstances that have profound implications for the conduct of our communication.

Many have speculated that the demand for information is, in economic terms, indefinitely elastic: the more information available, the more will be consumed. Information, broadly defined, is usually regarded as available to all. In the United States "freedom of information" legislation asserts the right of citizens to gain access to government documents and records, and the smallest village libraries are linked through a network that allows patrons to obtain publications not in the local collection. Even where information is not so freely available, systems of education are predicated on the idea that anyone who is literate can become proficient in the technology of information and, therefore, can participate in the economy of information wealth.

Certainly the economic view of information flow has much to commend it, and it has been plausibly argued that by 1990, half the American workforce — fifty-five million people — will be engaged in information employment (Strassmann 1983: 117).[2] Such predictions often assert that information workers provide the primary source of national wealth in societies like our own, supported, of course, by agricultural and industrial enterprises in secondary roles. And very often these estimates are accompanied by the presumption that the global economy will eventually come to resemble that of post-industrial societies. Without denying that information is an important economic resource, we need to examine these assumptions and predictions to see if they provide a reasonable basis for understanding the economic structure of the uses of information. Having done so, we should be in a position to speculate about the individual and social consequences of changes in the information economy.

As scholars and teachers confronting the undoubted evolution in literacy now underway, we need to examine fundamental issues: How did information come to be regarded as a commodity subject to economic forces? In the future, who will have access to information and who will control that access? What are the economic trends that shape the value of information and of literacy? And what are the consequences of the information economy for teaching and learning?

The insatiable greediness of writing and printing

The notion of creating new information and making it available at increasingly rapid rates for financial gain is one that arose in European societies following the introduction of moveable-type printing. Before that time, information was regarded as unchanging, and the technology involved in transmitting it was weighted toward its preservation through painstaking literal copying of existing information or modest extending of it through commentary and annotation. Most of those who wrote in the monastic scriptoria copied rather than composed documents; the ancient tradition of enumerating each alphabetic character in the Bible ensured accurate copies of the text. Talmudic scholars (like most of their Christian counterparts) elaborated their commentaries within the strictest canons of literal interpretation. Writing and reading were thus largely devoted to conservation; information was stored for future use rather than applied to immediate occasions and then discarded. In fact, one of the objections to cheap paper books was that they were not as enduring as manuscript books written on parchment. What good was a book that would last only two-hundred years in comparison with one that would last for a thousand? (Clanchy 1983: 7-22).

In medieval times (as in many cultures today), most information was conveyed through face-to-face communication. By what now seem to us prodigious acts of memory, complex and elaborated ideas were transmitted orally. Young people learned mnemonic systems that were aimed at precisely the same goals pursued by present-day designers of information retrieval systems: accuracy of recollection, speed of access, and aptness to the immediate task. Unaided by machinery, persons thus educated were able to recapitulate and transmit to the next generation the organized information they had memorized. Though it is certainly true that new information was produced when such oral systems predominated, even that was usually elaboration of old ideas, and nearly all information was organized to be recapitulated through literal recall.

Beginning at the end of the fifteenth century, the printing press and mass production of books made for important changes but not ones that had an immediate and transforming effect on the technology of information transfer. People continued to think about the new technology in old-fashioned ways. One representative view was expressed by John Jones in 1566 who prefaced his inventory of human diseases by complaining of the "superfluous plenty" of books for the medical practitioner. So many had been published, he thought, "that books seem rather to want readers than readers books.... I doubt not but many good men doth both perceive and inwardly bewail this insatiable greediness of writing and printing, which to say the truth, for my part, I do as much lament as any man else may do besides" (John Jones 1566: A.viii).[3] Such misgivings did not prevent Jones from publishing his book, of course, but his presumption that the availability of information had outstripped the need for it was more than the conceit of an author wishing to profess modesty in bringing his book to the attention of the learned world. He and many of his contemporaries continued to believe that virtually all information was already known; the task they faced was to improve its accuracy by correcting the mistakes of earlier writers or to compile information from disparate sources for the convenience of readers.[4] For them, information continued to seem freely available, the common property of all who by privilege of birth or opportunity had managed to become literate. An exclusively private right to one's ideas and expressions did not emerge (nor did the word for the violation of that right, *plagiarism*) until the seventeenth century.

Discovery, evolving ideas, and mass consumption of information accompanied the spread of literacy through increased opportunities for schooling at the end of the sixteenth century. Even so, many literate men (for women were systematically denied opportunities to become literate) probably shared the view of information expressed by the "countryman" in Nicholas Breton's imaginary dialogue published in 1618:

> This is all we go to school for: to read common prayers at church and set down common prices at markets, write a letter and make a bond, set down the day of our births, our marriage day, and make our wills when we are sick for the disposing of our goods when we are dead. These are the chief matters that we meddle with and we find enough to trouble our heads withal.[5]

As this view shows, literacy had become more common, but the information economy had yet to come to be. Breton's rustic, of course, relies upon information workers — authors and publishers of liturgies, messengers to carry letters, registrars to organize and store bonds and wills, and lawyers to litigate disputes concerning them. But these workers were perceived as providing services that were unrelated to each other in any significant way and tangential to the sources of real wealth — agriculture, manufacture, and trade.[6]

The idea of information as part of an economic system is a distinctly modern one, and the perception that users of information are "consumers" is even more recent. Or perhaps it would be more accurate to say that this new sense of information has replaced the older term for a similar idea expressed by the word *intelligence*. The earliest English uses of *intelligence* describe mental capacity, but in the Renaissance *intelligence* could also be used for information having particular value — "military intelligence" or similar news from which people could gain an advantage over others. But intelligence as valued information was not quantified and hence not clearly defined as an economic commodity. The perception of information consisting of *bits* or *bundles* or *chunks* — each with a measurable value — emerges only in our century as a part of statistical theory applied to the capacity of transmission networks such as the telephone and eventually to the very sophisticated notions of information efficiency that are at the heart of artificial intelligence systems and computers.[7] Once information was viewed as quantifiable, it could be packaged, distributed, and consumed. Jones's metaphor — the greediness of writing and printing — was drawn from human appetites, but only in our century has the metaphor become literal and the production of information been conceived as parallel to processing raw materials or consumer goods.

It is both tempting and easy to see in the consumerization of information some sort of revolutionary change that affects the basic sources of wealth and the habits of those who make use of information. Yet many workers who comprise the American information economy are engaged in traditional tasks: assembly-line employees constructing machinery by which information is processed and service-workers maintaining that machinery; managers engaged in decision-making through information transfer; professionals who retrieve, combine, and disseminate information as part of quite familiar roles ranging from medical care to teaching to architectural design to adjudicating disputes in the legal system. The information economy, in part at least, is merely a new perspective from which to view conventional economic enterprises.

What has changed, however, is the increasing pressure for productivity and the growing specialization of roles within the bureaucracies that make use of information. Relatively simple skills and practices traditionally learned in childhood — use of paper and pencil, searches for information in reference books, dissemination of information through low-technology channels such as the postal service, messenger systems, and bookstores — are now competitively unproductive and hence expensive as salary and benefit rates have risen. High-technology makes for greater efficiency, but at a social cost in the increased training required for significant participation in information transfer systems. The structure of this economy has been rationalized, and the hierarchy of value in information itself is paralleled by a hierarchy of power in access and control. Literacy, the skill that is fundamental to the information system, has thus been differentiated into levels with distinctly different opportunities and rewards.

What is now occurring in the information revolution has a parallel in the social consequences of the first technical and industrial revolution. Selective breeding of farm animals, a scientific breakthrough, turned agriculture toward capital intensive patterns; the consequent enclosure of the common grazing lands forced small farmers into the cities. Cottage spinners and weavers were similarly uprooted by the mechanization of cotton and woollen production. In the same way, the common property implied by free information and general literacy is now being transformed by forces that extend private ownership and restricted access to information wealth and technical literacy.

Access to literacy as social power

A popular contemporary view holds that literacy is the "technology of the intellect" (Goody 1986: 4), and since virtually all who engage in discussions of that view are literate, it is no surprise that the connection between literacy and intellect is widely accepted. The introduction of literacy and measures to make literacy more "efficient" are perceived as liberating, and literacy programs are applauded because they promise to provide opportunities and grant power to the newly literate. Such programs give access, in other words, to a technology that is regarded as essential to intellectual work by individuals and fundamental to the political organization of modern societies.

Closer examination of the consequences of literacy provides a more ambiguous view of the social transformation involved. While individuals may benefit from greater literacy, they almost inevitably do so at a social cost to others in the community. From ancient times, the most precious skills of literacy have been the valued property of an elite class. Scribes occupied an important role in ancient Israel and in the Egypt of the Pharaohs, and documentary evidence from both cultures testifies to the hegemony of power established and maintained by those who had mastered the techniques of literacy. In the words of an Egyptian scribe:

> Put writing in your heart that you may protect yourself from hard labor of any kind and be a magistrate of high repute. The scribe is released from manual tasks; it is he who commands....Do you not hold the scribe's palette? That is what makes the difference between you and the man who handles an oar. (Goody & Watt 1968: 37)[8]

These information workers could evade the rigours of physical toil and maintain themselves when famine or warfare took their toll of those whose talents occupied a less favoured place in the community. Such scribes established themselves as a privileged caste, and, through restricting the opportunities by which others might master the mystery of literacy, conveyed the skills and social position of their rank from one generation to the next.[9]

Many scholars who have written about the history of literacy have presumed that the ability to read and write is intrinsically liberating and that those who have acquired literacy are in a position to think and reason that is far superior to those who have not achieved it. Empirical evidence for that opinion is, however, distinctly lacking. In fact, literacy may better be seen only as a vehicle for intellectual activity and social progress rather than as a source for them.[10] Far from being a causal factor in social progress, literacy is at best an enabling one in societies where the activities encoded in written form are privileged and valued. From the individual perspective, literacy may promote different modes of thought; from the social perspective, it does not of itself revolutionize the structure of power and the sources of wealth in the community.

In contrast to the usual view of the significance of literacy as a technology is the position articulated by Claude Lévi-Strauss: "The primary function of written communication is to facilitate slavery" (1974: 299). In European societies, he notes, compulsory education arose in connection with the extension of military service and of proletarianization. In support of his scepticism about the intrinsic value of writing, Lévi-Strauss tells of an encounter with the Nambikwara in the Amazon basin: during his fieldwork with these people, he found that a chief began to mimic his note-taking and thus to display literacy to his people as a way of asserting a special bond with the gift-giving Europeans. That display was a leap from the proximate goal of reading and writing — information storage and retrieval — to the ultimate end of social control:

> It has not been a question of acquiring knowledge, of remembering or understanding, but rather of increasing the authority and prestige of one individual — or function — at the expense of others. A native still living in the Stone Age had guessed that this great means toward understanding ... could be made to serve other purposes. (Lévi-Strauss 1974: 298)

What the chief had accomplished was to skip the gruelling labour of becoming literate and to move directly to a position of superior authority and control as a consequence of his "literacy".

As contemporary societies are now organized, the lack of literacy is a virtual guarantee that the illiterate will be remote from the sources of power and authority. The possession of literacy, on the other hand, is not necessarily a passport to full participation in the important affairs of a community. Hence Paulo Freire's assertion that "the very decision to teach people to read and write is a political act" (1980: 27). Literacy does not, as he well understands, inevitably lead to liberation and political consciousness. It may, in fact, have precisely the opposite effect.

For all their success, however, literacy campaigns face the challenge of an exploding world population and the more and more demanding prerequisites for effective participation in information wealth. From 1970 to 1990, the proportion of illiterates is expected to decline from 32.5% to 25.7% of the world's population; the absolute numbers of illiterates will, however, increase from 742 to 884 million in that twenty-year span. These estimates suggest that ten nations will then have more than one million illiterates in the 15- to 19-year age group: Afghanistan, Bangladesh, Ethiopia, India, Indonesia, Morocco, Nepal, Nigeria, Pakistan and Sudan. These countries thus face staggering difficulties as they attempt to take part in the prosperity that information is presumed to provide. (See UNESCO 1980: 14-15; My T. Vu 1983; Sandell 1982).

Mass literacy is not only a recent development in history — effective and compulsory education has been in place for little more than a century in most industrialized nations — it is also widely associated with revolutionary democracies and socialist nations (Hoyles 1977). While literacy has been especially fostered by protestant Christianity and by Islam (because of their emphasis on personal study of holy scriptures), it is an even more important component of political systems that seek to engage the widest possible participation in the decisions of government. Perhaps the most important accomplishment of the twentieth century is this spread of literacy and the consequent expansion of the world population potentially equipped to take part in the economy of information. Paradoxically, the number of illiterates is growing greater at the same time that educational systems and literacy campaigns are attracting greater investment.

Poor nations have more illiterates than rich ones, and within a country, illiteracy increases with the distance from the sources of wealth. Worldwide, women are in an especially disadvantaged position; estimates for 1980 suggest that 35% of women are illiterate compared to 23% of men. As has long been recognized, illiterate women are less likely than literate ones to participate in family planning programs (and thus to free themselves for economically-rewarded employment) and less likely to make efforts to free themselves from traditionally subordinated roles. Efforts on behalf of women's emancipation through literacy have been made, of course, but there is little reason to think that the proportionate gap between the literacy rates for women and men will change by the end of this century (Bailey 1983: 30-44).

Definitions of literacy tend to obscure the significance of the problem since they are often based on the ability to write one's name or to decode only the most elementary texts. Literacy of that limited kind provides little access to social power and has minimal economic value. A large number of those regarded as literates are thus not in a position to profit from their skill. Since 1962, UNESCO has emphasized that literacy must be defined in terms of the varying demands of different communities, and literates are seen as those whose skill allows them "to engage in all those activities in which literacy is required for effective functioning". Thus literacy surveys have come to acknowledge a class of "neo-illiterates" who may have lost the literacy achieved in primary schooling or who have never reached the threshold of skill "required for effective functioning". With the constant elevation of that threshold, the numbers of people who are effectively illiterate will continue to increase *both* as a proportion of the world's population and in absolute numbers.

Is there any reason to expect that the huge numbers of illiterates will continue to accept passively their exclusion from what is now regarded as the main source of wealth and prosperity: information? Developed nations, especially those in the West, consume a hugely disproportionate share of the world's resources. Their hegemony in manufacture and trade has long been dominant; their control of the information wealth of the world has newly come to the attention of the information dependent and deprived. Proponents of a "New World Information Order" — whereby nations poor in information resources exercise control over the "news" that the information rich nations report — have been accused of assaulting basic human rights to the freedom of information. The dominant economic powers now acknowledge that vendor nations should have some control over their natural resources and agricultural exports. But countries poor in information technology have yet to persuade the global community that information should be subject to similar export and price controls. Entrepreneurs who profit from news-gathering and news-distributing enterprises face a contradiction that they have been unable to conceal. They argue that the information resources — the source of their wealth — are freely available to all (and hence immune from "trade restrictions"); at the same time, they treat commerce in information as an oligopoly by controlling access to it (see the McBride Report 1980).

The economic specialization of literacy

In terms of the global economy of information, however, the illiterates of the present and future are not only those who live at the margins of power and wealth as do many women, the citizens of the poorest nations and people at the bottom of the social hierarchy. They also include persons who fulfil roles that in the past have been rewarded by secure employment and middling incomes. The increasing costs of salaries and benefits have moved the preoccupation with productivity from the manual worker to the clerical worker and, now, to managers, technologists, teachers, and a whole range of employees whose skill with information has hitherto guaranteed some measure of prosperity. Developing trends in the field of artificial intelligence support so-called "expert systems" in which decision-making and task-completion are rationalized and automated. Today's headlines emphasize manufacturing, materials-handling systems, programmed machinery. Computer-controlled assembly lines have allowed highly efficient factories to produce goods with a human staff consisting only of maintenance workers and their managers. Tomorrow's headlines, as a consequence of the information economy, will report the parallel displacement of white-collar workers in a wide range of fields. And technical unemployment produced by the electronic revolution is not likely to be balanced by equivalent growth in the information industries (Porat 1978: 8).

The educational system in Europe and North America has responded to these changes by narrowing the scope of teaching in the direction of job-specific skills. Life-long learning, a concept with much to commend it, presumes the continued narrowing of specialization in the workplace and the expectation that public institutions will assume the training responsibilities formerly conducted by firms in the private sector, both for entry-level employment and for the constant re-training that the new technology demands. The continually returning student in such programs is likely to attain a series of highly specific literacies in information. There is less and less attention given by the schools and colleges to the breadth of education that such persons will achieve. The long-term result is likely to be a community that is collectively much more literate than the one of which we are now a part. Yet individuals within it may be significantly less broadly literate than in the past.

On a global scale, the peasantry and the urban proletariat have occasionally been roused to revolution by doctrines emphasizing greater personal freedom and increased collective prosperity. Citizens of Third World nations may continue their passive acceptance of subsistence agriculture, natural resource extraction, and cyclical poverty, but members of the present middle classes may not so willingly resign themselves to technical displacement as they are compelled to seek employment in economies that have fewer and fewer opportunities for engaging and rewarding work. The specialization of literacy leads to greater rationalization of economic enterprises and further social constraints even for the privileged. The threshold of illiteracy continues to rise and, even in the most prosperous Western societies, the resources invested in education are not adequate to train large numbers of citizens in the new and more complex skills demanded by information technology (Coombs 1985). Thus the control of information will become an increasingly contentious issue, not only across the gulf between the prosperous and the poor but also between the diminishing number of persons who exercise authority and monopolize wealth through information and those who are displaced by the revolution brought about by electronic literacy. Without some alternative to the emerging differentiation of literacy, we will be obliged to accept as inevitable the fact now acknowledged by UNESCO: "The notion of literacy varies from country to country" (UNESCO 1980: 16). Within countries, it will vary more and more from individual to individual.

The production and consumption of information

Over the past generation, more and more information has been made accessible but the growth in the availability of information has not been accompanied by an equal increase in its consumption. A study by the late Ithiel de Sola Pool produced the following result:

> By compiling data on trends in the circulation and in the use of 17 public media of communications, we found that from 1960 to 1977, words made available to Americans (over the age of 10) through these media grew at the rate of 8.9 percent per year, or more than double the 3.7 percent growth rate for the gross domestic product in constant dollars. However, the words *actually attended to* from those media grew at just 2.9 percent per year. Per capita consumption of words from those media (allowing for population growth) grew at but 1.2 percent per year. (1983: 609; my emphasis)

These findings demonstrate that the increased availability of information has not been accompanied by an equal increase in its consumption. Information, in other words, is not a commodity fairly characterized in economic terms as elastic. Our impression that we are bathed in an ever-increasing flow of words is certainly correct; it is also true that our indifference to many of these words has also grown more profound.

The relative positions in the media marketplace have changed dramatically in the last quarter century. Virtually every medium using print declined in popularity. In 1960, American adults were estimated to have read from print an average of 11,000 words per day; by 1977, reading had fallen to 8,500 words per day.[11] In part, this change reflects a shift in preference, but one that also follows economic laws: newspapers, magazines, books, and mail either stayed at the same cost per word transmitted or became more expensive (as measured in constant dollars). The electronic media, on the other hand, increased in popularity and decreased correspondingly in unit cost: radio, directly transmitted television, cable television, data communication, facsimile and telex transmissions all became cheaper and more prevalent modes of communication.

Among the most significant trends of those Pool identified is the tendency for the mass media to grow at slower rates than the media devoted to point-to-point communication.[12] Point-to-point media include the telephone and data communications systems, first-class mail, telex, and facsimile. These have all become more cost effective for both producers and consumers as they have increased their market share. Within the mass media, the "customization" of information toward more narrowly focused audiences has long been apparent to magazine and book publishers as "general circulation" materials have diminished in popularity while publications and programming directed to special interests (through satellite and cable television systems especially) have come to occupy a larger and larger share of material selected by an increasingly discriminating audience.

What these trends suggest is that the patterns of consumption in the information market have changed. With the possibility of selecting specialized information, audiences have become more particular about the information that they access and use (whether for entertainment or as part of their employment). But once again, economic factors come into play. The most specialized information is the least freely available. Data bases for which users individually pay threaten to supplant such resources as free public libraries for which costs are distributed through the community as a whole. Point-to-point communications systems involve costly hardware and transmission networks that levy charges against their users. Cable television systems (including, of course, ones providing teletext capabilities)[13] are supported through access fees. Books and magazines are increasingly expensive and thus are available to those with correspondingly high levels of discretionary income. From a national perspective, all of these systems require a considerable investment in the information infrastructure: telecommunications equipment, substantial investments in programming and publishing activities, and a gross national product that will support education to a level permitting access to the information the systems contain.

The rise of information monopolies

The economic consequences of these developments have been governed by the ethics of capitalist economies. The organizations that dominate the information economy are the diminishing number of large, transnational corporations which engulf their competitors and aim to control the marketplace and increase profits.[14] "Privatization" of information wealth, begun in the Renaissance, continues at an increasingly rapid pace. The asymmetrical flow of information across national boundaries has grown through the technology of remote sensing[15] as well as through more conventional means, and those nations (and individuals) subject to the curiosity of these firms find to their dismay — or never discover — that they have yielded economically valuable information. With the new technology, even public information becomes proprietary and thus available only to those who are able to pay for it. The technical superiority of these organizations and their command of resources places them in a position to dominate the information marketplace whatever the future may bring in new information systems. Greater availability of communications apparatus (whether in developed or in less developed nations) can only increase their domination of the information economy and their control over the form and content of the information that is offered. Thus we face another paradox. As more and more information is acquired and organized, so access to it becomes less and less freely and generally available.

The challenge to a global society

The present state of affairs can thus be briefly summarized: the more specialized the information, the more likely it is to have greater economic value. And the most efficient technology by which persons gain access to that specialized information is the most costly, both in the charges imposed for its use and in the investment required in education, machinery, and maintenance for access to it. As a result, the number of people who effectively command the literacy of information technology has diminished and is likely to decline at a more and more rapid rate, leaving the computer literate (and those with the power to buy their services) in positions of control.[16] What share of information wealth will the rest of the world's population command? Without some radical transformation in the trends now apparent, the answer would seem to be very little. The hegemony of information now being consolidated in post-industrial societies will come more and more to constrain the information available, the technology by which value is added to it, and the access to power and authority that information enables.

Evolving literacy, therefore, will surely parallel evolving stratification of economic functions and the distribution of wealth. In such a world, democratic ideals will be difficult to maintain. If there is a solution to this problem, it will be found by increasing access and investment in technology.[17] Scholars and teachers will not be isolated from these economic consequences. Our work and the organizations that employ us will be inevitably and irresistably transformed by emerging measures of "productivity". However much we treasure our own conventional literacy and our traditional information skills, we will be compelled either to adapt to the new economy or to submit to further erosion of our own social and economic position.

Whether we retain some measure of control over the literacy skills we value most will depend upon our understanding of our place in the global information economy, our analysis of what is most valuable in our ideals and our work, and our recognition that the problem we face in the emerging literacy of information has profound consequences for ourselves and for our successors. Literacy, as I have shown, has long been enmeshed with economic and political issues: like it or not, as teachers and scholars we are now obliged to consider our work in those terms if the best that we believe about literacy is to prevail.

Notes

1. For comments on earlier versions of this paper, I am glad to thank Barbara Couture whose observations on the "contextual semiotic" of written discourse (Couture 1986: 69-92) offer a bridge between the macro-trends discussed here and textual instantiation.

2. Estimates like Straussman's are subject to much dispute and controversy. The primary study of the information economy in the 1970s produced this conclusion: "It remains to be seen whether the information work force increases at the pace of the 40s and 50s ever again. I rather doubt it. Resurgence in the information occupations is likely only if new types of information industries are launched by entrepreneurs — information utilities, search services, storage and retrieval, computer-based diagnostics of everything from cars to hearts, facsimile and electronic mail transmission services, specialized microcomputer programming, and so on. But as of this decade (N.B.: the 1970s), the private and public bureaucracies are glutted with information workers. No more can be easily absorbed". (Mark Uri Porat 1977: 134).

3. I have modernized the spelling of this quotation.

4. There are many examples of such compilations of existing lore; one that remains in print and is still widely read is Richard Hakluyt's *Principal Navigations, Voyages, Traffiques and Discoveries of the English Nation* (1589-1590).

5. Nicholas Breton, *The Court and the Country* as quoted in Cressy (1980: 11)

6. Needless to say, the belief is still alive that producers of tangible goods are the mainstay of the economy. Popular prejudice against bureaucrats, lawyers, and professors (all of them information workers) continues to flourish.

7. See Richard W. Bailey (1976) for a discussion of information theory applied to poetic structure.

8. Quoted from V. Gordon Childe, *Man Makes Himself* (London: Watts & Co., 1936), p.211.

9. China was an exception in that plebians could acquire literacy and join the privileged class; they probably seldom did so. See Max Weber (1958: 416-420).

10. What makes this question difficult, of course, is that literacy is not an independent variable in developed societies. Given the huge investment in literacy training, we are likely to assume that literacy is universally a causal factor of economic prosperity and intellectual activity without questioning that assumption. The best study of literacy in a culture where literacy and illiteracy coexist in relative social equilibrium produced this conclusion:

> Vai script literacy does not fulfill the expectations of those social scientists who consider literacy a prime mover in social change. It has not set off a dramatic modernizing sequence; it has not been accompanied by rapid developments in technology, art, and science; it has not led to the growth of new intellectual disciplines. (Scribner & Cole 1981: 239).

11. Pool was unable to measure the undoubted increase in internal written communications in corporations and other large bureaucracies; he estimates that 90 percent of such written communications are directed to other workers in these organizations.

12. The onset of this trend appears in 1972; from 1972 to 1977, mass media increased at 2 percent per year while the point-to-point media increased 6 percent per year.

13. *Teletext* (first used in print in 1975 and subsequently faced with competition from the synonyms *viewdata* (1975) and *videotext* (1980) is the generic name for information retrieval systems using home television sets to allow users access to centralized data bases.

14. Satellite Business Systems is typical of conglomeration in the information sector. Designed to "manage much of the rapidly expanding data transmission requirements of corporate business", it is a joint venture of IBM, Comsat, and Aetna Life and Casualty Company (see Schiller 1981: 41).
15. I have in mind here the use of earth satellites as an aid to economic forecasting and the identification of unexploited natural resources.
16. In this respect I share the anxiety of Anthony Adams of Cambridge University: "I remain convinced that the way computer education is going in our society there is a real danger of our producing a computer educated elite, perhaps the Party of 1984, with the rest of us reduced to the status of proles" (Adams 1985: 17). There is, as I argue below, an alternative to this result, but it is an expensive and transforming one.
17. Such a solution was already discerned by Marc Uri Porat in the study cited above:

> The bureaucracies offer employment to millions of workers. However, it is the inefficiency of expanding private and public bureaucracies that induces a rise in prices, resulting in lost jobs. As more and more information workers join the ranks of the 'nonproductive', more and more noninformation jobs in agriculture, manufacturing, and services are lost since the economy cannot sustain them. The solution is *not* to dispense with the unneeded information workers, as they would merely join the ranks of the unemployed. The solution is to help them become more productive, hence generating employment and output in all sectors of the economy. And, to bring the paradox a full circle, the most likely source of increased productivity in the secondary sector is computer and communication technology — precisely the instruments that encouraged the growth of bureaucracies in the first place, and precisely the instruments that have been blamed with automation-induced unemployment (Marc Uri Porat 1977: 183).

Many sentences and difficult texts

Mackie J.-V. Blanton

Language, text, and human consciousness

All cognition is, in the final analysis, a matter of language. Ordinary language and the "fresh" language of art, science, literature and philosophy which relate to the ongoing story of human endeavours, indeed, amount to many sentences. We conceive, debate, share and experience these possible models of reality by and through the ordinary and fresh language of speech and writing. All language in this sense is an explicit and at times undisclosed psychology, and a description of the relevant grammar of a language, therefore, is always a description of human consciousness.

Moreover, because of the historicity of human consciousness, because of the public and private tensions driving the creativity of human consciousness, because of the inevitable evolution of language wherever it is used, the texts of art, science, literature and philosophy actually constitute the complex textuality of the fabric of human language. A true examination of meaning and signification, then, is an examination of the relevant grammar of ordinary and fresh language.

How can linguists foreground this issue and its difficulty? In fact, can we? What are the public and private tensions that provide the impulse to continue our difficult task of analysis? There is little, if any, confidence in linguistics, outside the discipline itself, among scholars in literary studies. Witness, for example, the pronunciamentos regarding linguistics found in the formidable erudition of intellectual historians such as George Steiner (1976: 90-91):

> The complexity and delicacy of the material of literature are such that neither formal logic nor linguistics has contributed more than the obvious to our understanding of a literary work.... Almost invariably, ... (the apparatus of linguistics) ... is often awesome, but the insights obtained are

usually jejune and in reach of the most obvious critical reading. Neither the linguist nor the phonetician has the historical awareness, the familiarity with formal and biographical context, the training of tactile sensibility, that mark the competent critic. They lack what Coleridge called the required "speculative instruments".

Steiner's observations, however, are not one-sided. He despairs also of the direction taken by many current literary analysts. Thus, having noted earlier in *Extraterritorial* that literary criticism and literary history have today become "minor arts" of ontological derivativeness, offering, instead of critical analysis, criticisms of criticism (pp. 88-89), he declares that "a responsible collaboration with linguistics may prove the best hope" (p. 92). Steiner's *Extraterritorial*, in fact, suggests throughout its discussion that we privilege textual difficulty when we study *language truth*: when we study how truth is made by the author of a given text to sound true and to what extent truth, by the reader, is recreated to be felt as true. Moreover, language truth entails various kinds of truth. Hence, to understand the various truths in the world that we come to know as literary truth, scientific truth, artistic truth, philosophical truth, we study textual difficulty. We study, with a sure and untroubled cross-referencing knowledge of clinical and social psychology, cultural anthropology, history and geopolitics, the interaction of syntax and genre:

> Once it is in a condition of literature, language behaves exponentially. It is at every point more than itself.... All language ... stands in an active, ultimately creative relationship to reality. In literature, that relationship is energized and complicated to the highest possible degree. A major poem discovers hitherto unlived life-forms and, quite literally, releases hitherto inert forms of perception. (Steiner, 1976: 90)

Other scholars, however, doubt the ultimate assistance of linguistic explanation to literary theory. Harold Bloom (1979: 9) asserts that:

> [w]ords will not interpret themselves, and common rules for interpreting words will never exist.... Linguistic explanations doubtless achieve a happy intensity of technicality, but language is not in itself a privileged mode of explanation. Certainly the critic seeking *the* Shelley should be reminded that Shelley's poems *are* language, but the reminder will not be an indefinite nourishment to any reader.... There is always and only bias, inclination, pre-judgment, swerve; only and always the verbal agon for freedom ... by words lying against time.

Although we can find in Bloom's insistence a denial of the adequacy of linguistic method for literary analysis, we also find in it more than a hint of a *language truth* of the sort asserted by Steiner: at the very heart of the interplay between syntax and genre there is only interpretation, the privileged mode of explanation. The text generates interpretation and is engendered by it. Language, once it is in a condition of literature, releases new forms of perception, freeing an initial text from fixed meaning, privileging and liberating the identity of the reader. For every reader armed with the required speculative instruments, i.e. with an inclination for the energies of language, there is a new text released to language and to literature, and perhaps to the forwarding norms of science and philosophy.

At the beginning of all acts of reading is, pre-existentially, the unopened text. Each interpretation of a single work engenders a different text. There is, then, no single text, in the sense of an autonomous work related to its author. What there is is the verbal, self-assembling struggle for freedom, through interpretation, between the author-in-the-reader and the work under interpretation. Hence, there is no single "written work" free from the oral elements of dialogue that we also know as inner speech. It is speech that ultimately drives writing. In this sense, there is only the latently oral text seeking to surface in spoken and written language, the text in us as interpreters who generate into existence a new text whose life rests on our talking about it, analyzing it, writing about it.

The text is us. The analyst of language and text, like any reader of the world and of a text, creates the world by analyzing and naming it, not so much to create a proprietary, preemptive truth, but to defer and thus seemingly outlast death; hence, as Bloom said above, to lie against time.

Thus, for Steiner's language animal, his *zoon phonanta*:

> [t]he unvoiced or internal components of speech span a wide arc: ... from the subliminal flotsam of word or sentence-fragments ... to the highly-defined, focused and realized articulacy of the silent recitation of a learned text or of the taut analytic moves in a disciplined act of meditation.

This seems only reasonable: a book or a piece of language of any definable length, spoken or written, comes into being after an act of disclosed or undisclosed meditation of some undefinable stretch of time. Therefore:

> [q]uantitatively, there is every reason to believe that we speak inside and to ourselves more than we speak outward and to anyone else. Qualitatively, these manifest modes of self-address may enact absolutely primary and indispensable functions of identity; they test and verify our *being there*. (Steiner 1976: 65)

Well might we wonder what this has to do with linguistic method. If we accept not as challengeable, but as influentially challenging insights, Bloom's and Steiner's erudition on language and human consciousness, the lesson we come away with is that we now have a way of talking about our subject matter: in Hartman's (1985) words, in a way that is "more overtly and philosophically conscious than before".

If we are prepared to accept that there is no "text" as an empirical entity which always remains the same from one moment to the next, then we are mobilized, without methodological guarantees, to an untroubled, analytic freedom. If we are unwilling to accept this, we are stuck with schematic analyses in which we can always be sure that the ambiguous tenor of evidence and the variousness of language itself will be such as to allow no categorical or comprehensive or conclusive formulation of *the total location of language*. Ontological interpretation is legitimate for a linguistic methodology, but language data in a condition of literature will preclude our narrating our observations in grammars which make statements of the sort that claim that "sentence (3a) may be paraphrased by (3b), or more naturally, by (3c); and (4a) does not occur in normal English speech, unlike (4b)".

Given the specific requirements of syntax and genre, the problem lies not in choosing from among various accounts or diagrams or schemas that work, but in finding just one theory of the reader's reach and willingness to interpret a text that meets the empirical demands of the relevant grammar of that text. The concept of the relevant grammar of a text rests on a notion of human interpretation. "Normal spoken English", or any language normally spoken, is a subset of *the grammar of text and interpretation*. The grammar of text and interpretation constitutes the total location of language.

The rich decidability of language

How is a page of literature to be read, and what orders of meaning can we draw from it? We can trace language to an original inner voice, as Steiner suggests; or, in a functionalist-semiotic perspective on language, we could see any expression of language, written or spoken, as a making of language, an internal and external designing, shaping, and putting together of language to serve some purpose.

Although we are in a somewhat different territory from literary theory when we speak of the linguistic analysis of literary texts, I agree with Eagleton (1983) quoting Roland Barthes, that literature as object and literary criticism as method have no distinguishable, delimitable stability; literature, quite simply, is definable as "what gets taught" (p. 197). Because "what gets taught is continually reread and hence continually changing, the canon of literary truth or literary diction is continually in dispute, for canons do not survive, across intellectual generations, from one anthology to the next. Literature, Eagleton argues, is not a "distinct bounded object of knowledge" (p. 205) with unique invariant properties. Consequently, literary theory has no stable properties for analysis and, as an effective project, is itself indistinguishable "from philosophy, linguistics, psychology, cultural and sociological thought" (p. 204). Thus Eagleton argues that to be a theorist of language is to be a theorist of the rhetoric of discourse: and the horizon of rhetoric "is nothing less than the field of discursive practices in society as a whole ... as forms of power and performance" (p. 205). Language, where philosophical, literary or scientific, is *not* an illusion and provides the clues to mastering "in some disinterested spirit the underlying sign-systems which generate" literary works (p. 214).

Facts, values, reasons, criteria are not independent of interpretive history. They are its products. The worlds we see, value, espouse are the consequences of discourse. Our beliefs and conventions are historically contingent; thus, we ought not to hold to them with an absoluteness that molds us. As we read the world, reading our own human discourse, so do we read texts. The world is a text, the text a world.

Facing a text, the reader is inscribed in the text. Facing a reader, the text inscribes the reader into it. The text absolves the identity of the initiating author and evolves the identity of the author-in-the-reader. The relation of a reading of the present moment to a reading of another moment is not directed by the author. It is an indirect relation. A major question for us to wonder about is what kind of restructuring occurs between successive readings.

If reorganization during the act of writing can take place, it is reasonable for us to assume that restructuring during reading takes place, thereby always approximating, but deferring, a final text. Of course, if there is no final text, there is also no initial text. There are only initiating texts, texts within texts, and chains of texts. This raises two questions: what is the nature of rereading that allows for a restructuring of interpretation along a chain of texts? And in what way does such a restructuring account for the interplay of syntax and genre? These are pragmatic questions.

The true data of text linguistics, then, are the processes through which human reading and interpretation generate texts. The *something* within the language of a text which suggests to us the nature of a text, during a given reading or a given period of readings, is not the grammaticality of the text but rather the willingness of the reader to see a paraphrasable world of a given nature in this text. Hence, the surfacing structure of language, as textuality demonstrates, is a relation of abstractions layered there in a text to be semanticized and pragmaticized by a reader. Texts along a chain of texts, therefore, are human efforts to actualize the semantics of all of human consciousness as manifested through the act of reading the world. Text linguistics, then, in studying difficult texts, studies a text as a transformation in the system of human consciousness. When we study the textual factors governing the surfacing structures of a text which motivate a reader to interpret naturally, what we have, in Riffaterre's words, "in effect, is a reader who keeps reading":

> [When a natural reader] keeps reading and rereading, ... he discovers relations with other texts. He then reaches the level of intertextual reading and becomes capable of integrating his culture, whether personal or national, into his reading. All these stages are subject to rules that are constant and affect all speakers of a language. Thus anybody is capable of reading properly, without the benefit of formal training. Of course, not everybody is capable of explaining, or even becoming aware of, the procedures he instinctively follows. (Riffaterre 1985: 114)

Conceptual aims in a study of difficult texts

The goal of science is not solely the solving of empirical problems, but also of conceptual ones (Laudan 1984). The conceptual foundations of the sciences and the theory of scientific methodology go hand in hand; otherwise, it is useless to appraise and validate, epistemically and pragmatically, scientific theories in general. For example, implicit in some approaches to the linguistic analysis of literary texts is the general principle of the hierarchization or quantification of prose and poetic styles. These linguistic approaches suggest the independence of the interpretive, textual, semantic, and syntactic aspects of language. However some linguists emphasize the syntactic aspect to the detriment of the interpretive, semantic and textual aspects. Linguistic analysis, then, responds to the laws of its own structure rather than giving a handle to formal thought. As Granger (1983: 7) notes:

> It seems that the logical analysis of language is ordinarily pursued in a perspective so purely syntactical that it cannot but lead to an exacerbated formalism, and consequently it fails to respond to [the more foundational problem] of the articulation of *logos* and of the concrete world.

Comments of the same type were made more than a decade ago by Stanley E. Fish (1972). Fish's observations, reprinted in Freeman (ed., 1981: 53-78), question the linguist's general tendency to subordinate interpretation to description, treating interpretation as if it were a function of the description of the language of the text. The consequence of this kind of linguist's approach is problematic because genre and interpretation are neglected or appear to be reducible to syntax and, ultimately, to any currently touted theory of grammatical categories. In general, the linguist does not account at all for genres or for the sets of chains of interpretations which constitute genres. The linguist's attempts at literary interpretation amount to being no more than personal expressions of values. Agreeing with Fish, Kolln (1986: 110) observes:

> [The linguist's] penchant for assigning value judgments to linguistic phenomena can only strengthen the skepticism that literary scholars feel when confronted with the apparatus of quantification that stylistics so often depends on.

Analysis, whether literary or linguistic, neither equates with nor exhausts the total being of literature. As Steiner (1978: 4) says for music, meaning it for literature as well, our task should be to "locate the energies which can transmute the fabric of human consciousness" in listener and performer, reader and author. Literature *means* despite there being no way to paraphrase the grammaticality of a literary text into the immensity of its interpreted meaning. In literature, being, meaning, and interpretation are inextricable.

In general, linguists have tended to ask the wrong question first, wondering first *how* a text means rather than *what* a text means. In a linguistic analysis of literary texts, description should follow from interpretation, not interpretation from linguistic description.

> The future belongs perhaps to those who will know how to formulate the modalities of the usage of symbolic thought, and of language in particular, into concepts without getting lost, as we too often do conceptually, in the open labyrinth of its forms. In any case, [inspired progress] ... in the positive sciences of man ... [will undoubtedly be] in preparing the ground for the conceptual expression of the relations between logic and reason, in fur-

nishing the proper instruments to define clearly, in our behavior, the trace of the rational. (Granger 1983: 193)

Text, reading, and interpretation

Interpretation dwells in texts and emerges as texts, rendering the existence of texts inseparable from each other. Because the whole is greater than the sum of its parts, there is so much more than the syntax of a text and so much more in an interpreted text than the physical text open for interpretation. The question of *how* a text means, i.e. the schematic scanning of a text for its syntactic categories, belongs to the ontologically secondary slice of investigation. The question of *what* a text means is primary, continuing in the phenomenological sphere of inquiry. Texts are created and enacted. When we study created and enacted texts, we learn what the language itself has to tell us by looking for an interpretation of what a text has to say. A linguistic analysis of text must describe the textual, interpretive, and grammatical factors through which the thought emerges. A book or poem or document of any sort, giving rise to different interpretations over time, will give rise to different corresponding texts and, therefore, to different corresponding factors, textual, interpretive, and grammatical.

Literature is an extension of human consciousness, as well as a practice in limitations. At the outset, the words of literature are secret and hold secrets: through their relationships to each other, they admit of many different interpretations. A text contains all the truths that a reader has been able to find there, and all the truth which a reader has not found there, or not yet, though it still remains there to be found. There is no "foreclosure of the text", as Barthes (1975: 15) has taught us. The text is the ground for creative, generative interpretation.

The important theoretical concern here, of course, entails what constitutes "true meaning" (i.e. "all the truth that a reader has been able to find in a text") and "creative, generative interpretation". Creative interpretation is a self- reflexive learning process by which persons, in reading the world, come to understand their relationship with aspects, features, or properties of the world, or with those of some particular world experience. We can never remove the need, unconscious or conscious, of language users and makers to read and know their world. If we could, we would be removing a fundamental learning process, i.e. creative interpretation, which is automatic to human beings, however developmentally slight in any one individual, and sufficient for being sentient and necessary for being human. *True meaning* is all that a species can come to know about itself incrementally over time.

Deductive work in linguistics, then, need not be initially *only* language centred, and begin *only* by focusing first on grammatical issues of syntax and semantics before moving out into context-sensitive, pragmatic, interpretive concerns. After all, linguists cannot categorize "etic" material until they have interpreted it, noticed its functions and relations to other categories, renoticed it, and interpreted it again. For everyone, then, interpretation of the world is prior to categorizing it. And reading it is prior to interpreting it. Context-sensitive, pragmatic, and interpretive concerns engender the need to make and use a semantics, lexicon, and syntax. Representational form depends on the structure and function of the human need to relate to a universe of discourse and texts. Hence, within a linguistic spectrum, future solutions are likely to come from an integration of linguists' modelling languages and the ways people organize and process the world. True meaning consists of sets and networks of human procedures and operations that culminate in a choice of whether or not a reading and its interpretation, and *not* a sentence, are true: true to function, form, intention, knowledge, and the boundaries of self, i.e. interests, capability, ability (imagination, curiosity, and memory).

On the face of it, it would appear that linguistics ought to leave well enough alone and leave literature alone, and be content to be an interpretationless science of algorithms, networks, strata, or components, all of which could, at best, suggest values (perhaps) but not the variance and invariance of true meaning. On the face of it, it might be better for linguists simply to see that language is already out there, to be observed in various ways by linguists of any persuasion; and literature, then, would just be one of language's several ways to manifest itself, a way that others (literary reviewers, historians, and theorists) of a persuasion of a different sort can best handle. A division of labour might be more genuine and honest. However, the activity from the other side of the division is uniquely challenging to linguistics. In literature we find language forms being fulfilled that the observed categories and rules of linguists had neither realized nor predicted. Pieces of literature circumvent prediction as they appear, introducing into the world of experience new forms and new meaning.

It appears to be a matter of where one believes the basic categories to be found — in language or in literature; or whether one thinks that there are basic categories in the first place; or whether one contends that a division of data into language and literature is an empirically and rationally feasible one. The true case may not be that creators of literature make use of what speakers of the world have at their disposal from birth. What may be the case is that speakers throughout the world in having language forms at their disposal, have at their disposal the fulfilled forms of grammars that reflect, like literatures of the world, how we fulfil the underlying principles of text. We are all, as creators of literatures and speakers of languages, users and makers of the fulfilled and yet-to-be-fulfilled forms of grammars. A world, a language, a grammar, an interpretation, a reading — each is a metatext.

There is a latent world in the individual texts of language and literature. The principles suggested by this point of view are of manifold interest: a) the significances of syntax are only momentarily fixed; b) the experiences of a person, i.e. of that person's reading of the world, shape his or her interpretations; c) the explanation of true meaning in the world resides in the ability of the individual to confer meaning; d) the world as we know it, and individual worlds of experience that we come to know, embody a conceptual orientation that gives over endlessly to interpretation; e) writers discover more about themselves, their subject matter and their style for observation, description, and explanation as their writing takes place; the same is no less true for readers: a reader's sense of the world, and of self on a latent or conscious level, is fashioned during the reading experience; f) the study of text is the study of how ideation takes shape linguistically as it develops the species-specific self; g) literature as a context for studying the interpretation of text provides a further context for the study of understanding.

In reading the world, we construe reality as we confer meaning on our experiences, because the world as text engenders a peculiar mode of consciousness in us as onlookers. The grammar of that mode is expressed as some particular language; hence, the grammar of a language is indeed a theory of that language, as that language itself is a theory of the world. As each metatext is a theory of the other, in a generative chain of conferring meaning, there is no world of the human species without a language, no language without a grammar, no grammar without an interpretation of a particular world, no particular interpretation without a reading of a particular world, no particular reading without an interpretation of self, nor, finally, a self without the boundaries of self. In turn, each metatext is an implication of the other, where the world as we know it and the boundaries of self (the boundaries of knowing) interrelate language, grammar, interpretation, and reading.

For the linguist, interpretation induces the recategorization of grammatical relations and functions that make up the total of potential, true meaning. True meaning starts with the presence of self in the act of interpreting. An author, in writing about the world, writes about self, as all persons, in talking about worlds and others, project parts of self. "But isn't it true that an author can write only about himself?" asks Milan Kundera (1984: 221):

> I have known [certain specific] situations, experienced them myself, yet none of them has given rise to the person my curriculum vitae and I represent. The characters in my novels are my own unrealized possibilities ... Each one has crossed a border that I myself have circumvented ... [B]eyond that border begins the secret the novel asks about. The novel is not the author's confession; it is an investigation of human life.

The manifold character of texts rests on two features: they are composed and read. Writers wander through their texts, asking themselves questions about the developing text as they compose meaning by drawing on their conscious, subconscious, and supraconscious needs, interests, feelings, and on their intertextual knowledge of other texts, past readings, and prior experience. Natural readers wander through texts also, questioning what is unmarked and does not meet their expectations, drawing on the same human tendencies and traits to compose meaning as writers do. Alert writers and readers have strategies for looking into themselves and outside of themselves in order to make and use meaning. They construe reality and construct meaning.

Where literature is conceived of as the language, grammar, reading, and interpretation of interests and memories, it extends the aims of linguistics in that it offers, by merely being there, a study of human limitations and human consciousness. In taking up the challenge of the difficulty of literature, linguistics becomes a study of the categories, functions and relations of human consciousness. The abundant and creative permutations of all of them ought to be the data for a theory of human language.

Explaining moments of conflict in discourse

Christopher N. Candlin

1. Introduction

My particular concern in this paper[1] is to offer some explanation of how potential (or actual) conflicts between participants are resolved in discourse, how this is variably accomplished and how these ways of accomplishing are themselves informative of relativities among participants in how they perceive the encounters in which they are engaged. More ambitiously (and only to be adumbrated here), explanations of this variability may offer ways in which discourse analysis can reveal registerial conventions and suggest modes of typologising different underlying codes and their particular textual realisations.

My examples are chosen from two sources. The first from a police-witness interview originally transmitted as a piece of *cinéma vérité* by the BBC in a series to do with the work of the Thames Valley Police under the title of "A Complaint of Rape"; the second from a Family Planning Counselling Interview held at a welfare clinic in Honolulu, Hawaii, and recorded as part of a research group investigation into the discourse of a variety of asymmetrical encounters. My purpose is to show how conflict between the participants is variously managed: in the case of the police-witness data by what I will informally call a strategy of "concentrated effect" and in the case of the counselling data by, again informally, what I will call "cumulative effect".

2. Assumptions

A longer paper would allow acknowledgement of the extensive literature in critical discourse analysis on the relationships between language use and the reflection and reproduction of social formations, and, what is in turn required by this in given cases, namely a full discussion of how particular social institutions (here the Police, Family Planning Counselling) are variously constituted in the societies referred to. The following assumptions inform the analyses in this paper:

i. A concern for social interaction necessarily entails engagement with social theory (Habermas 1972).
ii. Social structure is not outside discourse but within it as "shared knowledge" (Berger & Luckman 1967).
iii. Strategic message construction is the key locus between language and society (Brown & Levinson 1978).
iv. Discourse cannot rely on generally shared conventions, but on those which are differentially distributed in accordance with social boundaries (Gumperz 1984).
v. There are ideological constraints on what is perceived by participants and what is attended to for interpretation.
vi. Understanding talk requires an understanding of goals, both linguistic and social, and the prototypical notions of what, say, "doing X" consists of, and the frames we "discover" do not have a separate existence from our own ideologies.
vii. That analyses of communication within institutions are not separable from an analysis of the institutions themselves. It is inadequate merely to analyse communication in terms of the conditions placed on communication by the institution. It is necessary to analyse the institution in terms of the conditions which determine it. These institution-determining conditions are realised through communication (Rehbein & Ehlich 1977).
viii. The forms of discourse which express ideology must be viewed, not only as socially and historically situated practices, but also as linguistic constructions which display an articulated structure: Discourse says something about something (Thompson 1984).

3. Texts and conflicts

Implicit in these assumptions is that particular instances of discourse will not be transparent in terms of revealing the forces and factors which constitute the social institutions which give rise to them and are reproduced by them. Indeed, it is the purpose of an explanatory mode of discourse analysis precisely to attempt to unpack what is naturalised and taken-for-granted in such discourse. More than this necessary general practice, however, is the need to question whether there are unitary ideologies which in part constitute the institutitions in question. There are always, potentially at very least, competing ideologies in respect of the purposes, practices, tenets, conventions and patterns of participation in any social institution. Now, if this is so, then as I have pointed out (Candlin 1983) and as Fairclough clearly advocates, one should be discriminating about the instances of discourse that one chooses to explain. If our purpose is to demonstrate this linkage between the macro level of analysis and the micro, then how these competing ideologies are textualised becomes of extreme interest.

Normally, in keeping with the naturalised-ness assumption, all textualisations are potentially significant for such work. Against this stands the major critique formulated by Jacob Mey that discourse analysis of the traditional kind has been uncritically eclectic in its selection of instances, an unprincipled collection of *objets trouvés*. It makes sense for us to be quite selective if we wish to point up the undemonstrated, as it were. Hence my call for a focus on interactional *cruces*; moments where normal conversational (as well as, of course, goal-oriented) cooperativeness either breaks down or requires major conversational work to be maintained. Moreover, as I hope to show, whether there is fracture or costly maintenance is itself of extreme significance for an understanding of the competing ideologies which are at work, both *across* participants and *within* them.

In short, moments of conflict are potentially more revelatory both of the linkages referred to and also of the discoursal and pragmatic resources of the participants. Furthermore, such moments of conflict are likely to offer examples of how texts are not unitary either. Fairclough (1986) criticises the Hallidayan concept of register and points to the frequency of what he terms "mixed register texts", texts where meanings from different codes are combined and more or less felicitously "resolve" contradictions at the level of the institution and the social formation. Given that it is precisely this conflict of ideologies which gives rise to the contradictions Fairclough refers to and which ought to be, in my view, the object of critical discourse analysis, it is at these moments of communicative crux, where contradictions are least felicitously textually resolved, that we ought to focus first our analytical attention. These will constitute *par excellence* cases of the mode of study we are proposing. Not that other less felicitously mixed register texts are not also appropriate objects; it is simply that they release their contradictoriness less easily, and require more explanatory "work". Their mixedness itself becomes conventionalized and taken-for-granted, and, of course, more insidious.

Examples (See Appendix)
I: A Complaint of Rape
(A) "Complaining" — Extract 1

Taking an interpretation of *ideology* to be a set of systems, concepts, values involved in explaining things, connecting events, placing events and objects in the context of patterns, structures and causes, and accepting Thompson's injunction about accompanying "conflict", in this extract what is significant is the alternative pragmatics of the verb *complain* for the Woman and for the Police. I would want to see the presence of the Woman from her perspective as:

(a) A "Doctor" Issue   i.e. the complaint of rape and the action to be taken
(b) A "Protection" Issue   i.e. her personal safety and the action to be taken.

Whereas, from the point of view of the Police, the Woman and the event in question are to be seen as:

(a) A Complaint of Rape   i.e. a legal issue where action by the Police is conditioned/constrained by general and particular knowledge, for example
 (i) Rape is a costly charge to investigate.
 (ii) The Woman in question is "known" to be a prostitute.
(b) A "Personal Safety" issue   i.e. something to be downplayed because it works against the constraints under (a).

I believe that the textualisations in the discourse of Extract 1 warrant this conflicting ideological interpretation. In particular, note the legal terminology employed by the Police, the markedly non-conversational tone of voice, the focus on "offender" and "offence", the special value adducing to "complain". Note also the contrast to the "common-sensical" argumentation of the Woman concerning adequate evidence for an investigation (the reference to the doctor) and the responsibilities of the Police to investigate when *they* believe a crime has been committed, not waiting on a citizen's complaint. Note especially the discoursal actions of the Police in seizing topic rights, dismissing (or at least minimising) the Woman's contribution, reformulating the topic and, in particular, their concerted talk whereby they cooperate in rejecting the challenge posed by the Woman.

(B) "Protecting" — Extract 2

The concerted action of the two policemen in rejecting the challenge of the Woman in respect of the grounds for complaint is further exemplified in this Extract, at the end of the taped interview, where (after an introductory extract included for clarification involving both policemen) the Woman is alone with the detective constable, Brian. The conflict remains that of the previous Extract; the Woman's perception of the need for proof and her ability to provide it, and the Police as protectors and preventers of crime versus the cost of rape investigations and the status of the complainant. What is especially significant here is the strategy of *concentrated effect* by means of which the powerful participant (in Giddens' sense of "using resources of whatever kind to secure outcomes"; cf. Giddens 1977: 347-349) "intervenes in a series of events to alter their course", by simultaneously marshalling linguistic resources of varying kinds to diminish and reject the challenge, viz.

i. Lexico-syntactic: foregrounding *Reading, 1980*; use of intensifier *bloody*; thematising *end up in the river*

ii. Phonological: intonational fall on *Hutch* and on *end up in the river* and, especially on *what's the matter with you*, signalling finality, not offering option of response

iii. Discoursal: interruption, turn seizure, dismissive reformulation, bald-on-recordness of FTA

iv. Pragmatic: revaluation of concepts, for example
   (i) Time Now (P) versus Time Then (W)
   (ii) Real world (P) versus TV world (W)
   (iii) Imputation of psychiatric disturbedness (P on W)

v. Kinesic/Proxemic: abrupt rising and leaving the event by P, dismissive arm/hand movements by P, aversion of eye contact by P

II: Modes of Counselling in Family Planning

In Extract 2 (see Appendix), there is no doubt that the moment of conflict is such as to fracture the encounter totally. The Woman is abandoned by her co-participant, left to present her case to the cameraman. Counselling, it would seem, presents the antithesis of such behaviour. Its main aim is to help the client explore and clarify feelings and courses of actions. To listen carefully, to resist intruding with interpretations and attitudes, to resist showing personal feelings, to respond in ways which encourage client's difficulties, all these are listed as key counsellor characteristics and are clearly directed at the avoidance of conflict. Family Planning Counselling (FPC) as one type, seems no less straightforward in its aims:

> The primary purpose of the FPC session is to assist the client (and partner, if included) in making informed decisions about fertility management. (Hale, Ho'ola Hou 1983)

Leaving aside the rich connotations of "fertility management", it quickly becomes apparent to some commentators that:

> ... the legitimation of family planning by no means lessens the fact that this is a highly value-laden arena for social work, perhaps as much as it is for those we seek to serve. (Haselkorn 1968)

Or, more directly:

> Any attempt to issue a flat directive in this intimate province (apart from legal considerations) not only may fail to convince the client to accept family planning but may reinforce suspicion that society, its institutions and especially its Department of Public Welfare seeks to impose denial of parenthood with the many other penalties of poverty. (Manisoff 1970)

What we have is a socially significant educational and informational activity, which by virtue of its intimacy and personal relevance cannot but be imbued by an awareness of client's needs for self-realization and self-determination but which is nonetheless subject to pressure from particular social policies. But, as Haselkorn (1968) identifies: "... the rub comes, as it always does, when one attempts to apply abstract values which collide with subsidiary, competing or conflicting instrumental values." This conflict is one which is characteristic of social work in general; what makes FPC especially problematic is that the issue of "individual freedom versus social responsibility" (itself very complex ideologically) is exacerbated by what are referred to in the FPC literature as "troublesome value dilemmas" surrounding the counsellor's and the public's views on sexual behaviour, the opinions of medical authorities concerning what are admissible modes of family planning for medically high-risk groups, and, not least, the conflicting views on what the counsellor is "there for" among counsellors and clients.

In keeping with the assumptions outlined at the beginning of this paper, we would both want to refer these contradictions and competing factors to ambiguities in the status and objectives of FPC within the social formations of contemporary societies at large and to be able to show how they "work down the line", as it were, to particular textualisations at the level of discourse. From the many examples in the data presented in Candlin and Lucas (1986), I want to highlight one such conflict and show how it is both revealed and worked out in an encounter between a family planning counsellor and her client.[2]

This example concerns a conflict *within* the counsellor, and relates specifically to the issue of "giving advice". From the foregoing it is, I hope, clear, that "advising" is explicitly excluded from the characteristic tenets of counselling. What if, however, the counsellor is faced with a client whose demands run counter to one of the more explicit foci for "value dilemmas" noted above, viz. that of admissible modes of family planning for the medically high-risk? Suppose also (which is true in this circumstance but not generally in the U.K. for instance) that the counsellor does not have the power to prohibit (or allow) prescription of a particular mode since that is the prerogative of the physician. In short, the counsellor's authority as a knowledgeable professional is constrained by two factors:

(i) Her lack of authority to make medically-related decisions.
(ii) Her awareness of the client's perception of her as an authority being in conflict with her desire to maintain a relationship with her client of solidarity and trust.

How can the counsellor manage that conflict? What effect does managing the conflict have upon her discourse? What strategies are open to her? What is the "cumulative effect" (see above) of her discoursal choices? How are the conflicts revealed?

As illustration, I draw upon data from the client JA who has come for the primary purpose of obtaining a fresh supply of birth-control pills. As CR (the counsellor) reviews her history she notes, among other medical contra-indications, that JA is 29, smokes heavily and comes from a family with a history of heart disease. In terms of her ascribed authority, CR cannot deny the pills. She can only prepare JA for that eventuality by the medical staff. Nonetheless, CR believes the pill to be dangerous in this case. Changing mode of family planning or quitting smoking are both preferable courses of action. For JA, however, both actions would be costly. Of course, there is no reason why both parties should view cost and benefit in the same terms. What is paramount for CR (personal communication) is to eschew overt authority and to maintain solidarity with the client:

> ... the only way you can have any kind of a good relationship in counselling ... is for the patient [sic] to feel she can trust you ... and if you come across as if you're really on a totally different level from what they are, it'll be really difficult for them to open up and let you know what their fears are or what questions they have.

In sum, managing the conflict involves CR in employing a range of strategies (see Appendix), the order of which appears significant in this encounter but which may not be so in other encounters, given the permutations possible among variables of topic, client type, client purpose, nature of client's responses to the counsellor etc. What follows is at best a hypothesis for more general (dis)confirmation.

Soon after the beginning of the consultation, CR employs Strategy (1), that of supplying the information relevant to the issue of smoking and the pill. She explains how the client's family history of both cancer and heart disease could make her a candidate for similar problems, if she takes the pill. She explains how the client's slightly abnormal blood pressure reading might contra-indicate her use of the pill. Insofar as this information is known already to the client, we have an instance here of a violation of Grice's (1967) maxim of Quantity. Even the giving of this information is mitigated, however:

1. CR: the reason im asking you these questions is because sometimes the birth control method you choose can affect your body in different ways and lets say circulation for the pill or hormonal for the pill . which if its family related . you could be more of a likely candidate for that problem . . so we like to know what your family history is . . we like you to be aware of that too

   \- \- \-

   CR: it looks like the left side is OK and . like I said . the bottom . this is not to alarm you its just to make you aware . . if its ninety or above there might be some contra-indication to the use of the pill or if next time you come back . and its like ten millimetres well want to discuss that since youre using the pill

Immediately following, CR refers to her client's smoking habit. Here, rather than explaining on-the-record the dangers of smoking and the pill, CR attempts to determine, via Strategy (2), how much JA already knows about the attendant risks. She then fills in the appropriate information.

2. CR: ok. the other thing that I see from your chart is that you do smoke cigarettes . . do you know about that and how it affects . how its affected with the use of the pill
    JA: yes I do
    CR: can you tell me what you know
    JA: huh
    CR: can you tell me what you know
    JA: about smoking and taking the pill
    CR: uh huh
    JA: mm . . . the risk of getting cancer is higher
    CR: ok . the risk of cancer with the pill might just be from a hormonal level like if you had cancer in your family . breast cancer for instance . but smoking . what it does is . it changes your circulation and it might be more chance . especially as you get older of strokes
    JA: oh

Strategy (3) involves CR telling JA that the Physician's Assistant will be talking to her about the problem. In this way, CR escapes the need to accept responsibility for the FTA by placing it on the higher authority.

3. CR: uh huh . so thats and you smoke quite a bit and youre twenty nine . so youre in a high risk group so shes definitely gonna talk to you about that today . . um . its up to the physicians assistant if the birth control method is dispensed or not . if its a prescribed method

Following this, CR begins a line of questioning focusing on the possibility of JA quitting smoking (A_1), her reasons for smoking, and possible alternatives to this "problem". Once again, however, CR's questions are heavily mitigated.

4. CR: have you ever thought about discontinuing smoking
    JA: uh . I thought about it (laughs)
    CR: do you think youd be able to do it
    JA: I dont know (laughs) I guess if I really wanted to . . Ive been smoking for a long time
    CR: are you under more stress now
    JA: um . I guess you could say so . yeah cause it was last year that I started smoking more .
    CR: do you think if you worked on those things you might be able to cut down
    JA: on the stress you mean
    CR: well . I dont know what the stress is and I dont know if youre open to talking

>   about that but . . from your facial expressions . it seems like youre really hesitant to make a decision to discontinuing smoke . I mean smoking . thats gonna have to be something up to you . . do you think if the stress was eliminated that maybe . .
>
> JA: I could cut down
>
> CR: or quit . . for you age its probably better for you to just quit altogether

CR mitigates even further, saying:

> CR: thats not necessarily a decision you have to make right this minute

CR once again refers to the Physician's Assistant, perhaps to justify her persistence in discussing the matter:

> CR: I know that B will be talking to you about that . and what we can do is maybe talk about some alternate birth control methods in case she really feels strongly that it wouldnt be real healthy for you to continue using the pill

With this, CR provides JA with a pamphlet on smoking and the pill, and then leaves the topic of smoking (A_1), steering the focus towards the topic of alternative methods of birth-control (A_2). In so doing she effectively approaches A_1 again, but by an indirect route. When JA mentions that she has heard about the IUD method, CR takes the opportunity not only to explain the method, but to suggest its particular appropriateness for JA.

> CR: um ... the iud might be an appropriate method for you to use since youve had two children . . two full term pregnancies . .

After explaining other available methods, CR appears to be moving toward ending the consultation by explaining the examination which is to follow, the hours of the Clinic etc. But before closing the consultation, she hedges, and using Strategy (5), returns to the topic of smoking (A_1), this time referring JA to the American Cancer Society for help in assisting her to quit smoking:

> 5. CR: I know this is kind of backtracking . um . as far as the cigarettes go . if you feel like you need help with that . theres the american cancer society . they have programs to help you with that .
>
> JA: to quit smoking
>
> CR: yeah . .

At this point CR introduces the possibility of her visiting the local mental health clinic, but immediately on performing this more on-record FTA, redresses with negative politeness:

CR: n . if you need a support group or if it gets down to that . and youre going to choose that over the pill or vice versa . or if you felt like whatever stress . youre having is out of control and you dont have insurance at your job . we dont offer that kind of counselling here . all our work is short term but there is a local mental health clinic
JA: mm mm
CR: according to where you live . . . from what im getting from you . you seem to be reasonably . a . everythings ok unless im not picking up .

The consultation continues, and CR makes use of Strategy (6), claiming common ground as an example of positive politeness, sharing her own experience with smoking and how she (CR) was able to quit:

6. CR: well . you know its not easy . cause everybody . well ive got my bad habits too . and its not easy . . I smoked for eight years too so I know its not easy.
   JA: did you quit
   CR: yeah .

CR's final strategy within the consultation proper is one which returns to the characteristic open-endedness of counselling. Strategy (7) places responsibility for the decision on the client. CR reminds her that, now that she is informed of the dangers, it is for the client to decide what is best for her. CR also mitigates again here, using phrases such as: "you cant maybe see . . but" and "that might make it easier . ."

7. CR: I got allergic to the smoke . so that made it easier I think . if theres some reason sometimes that you know its not good for you . I mean . I knew I could feel the allergy . the bumps on my tongue . . for you its the same way . its a little bit different you cant maybe see whats going on with the pill when youre smoking . but if you know from your knowledge has increased now . that might make it easier for you to make a decision about it

   ---

   CR: if you feel like you want to come back and talk to me again about alternate birth control . we can do that . . of course you can always go to another doctor and get pills . but its just a matter of deciding whats best for you . ok . cause thats kind of how we like to operate . . we like to be concerned with your total health care . ok . .

Nonetheless, the references to unseen processes, the possibility of exploring further alternate birth-control methods and the suggestion that non-Clinic doctors might prescribe where the Clinic would not seem, in my view, to shift CR towards advising in the negotiation of the pragmatic space between informing and directing action.

I suggest a final Strategy (8) which, strictly speaking, is not linked to any particular point within the consultation, nor to any specific utterances. I refer to the proportion of overall consultation time devoted to the twin topics of smoking and the pill. More than two-thirds of the total talking time was so devoted, which indicates its significance to CR (and, presumably to JA) especially in view of CR's acknowledged complaint that insufficient time was available for client counselling.

Throughout this consultation the Counsellor employs strategies which quite typically shift within the counselling frame along this "advising" continuum. Characteristic is CR's indirectness, evidenced by much mitigation and redressive action.

4. Intertextuality and typology

In the examples, I was at pains to indicate how ideological conflicts gave rise to contradictions within the discourse and how these could be managed in two distinct situations. In particular, one example emphasised conflicts which were interpersonal (between the Police and the Woman), the other intrapersonal (within the Counsellor herself). What I did not do there, was to highlight how the texts themselves also evidenced the intertextuality or "mixed registerness" that I referred to earlier.

It should be clear, however, that just such a conflict of textual source is more or less resolved in the texts in question. In the Police example, we see it infelicitously resolved in the final contribution from Brian where he adopts the dismissive mode of reference to the world of the Woman in terms of fantasy and television, at the end of a sequence which begins with the legal mode of "laying a complaint". Moreover, throughout the encounter the text shifts from the legalistic, cross-examinatory mode of talk, appropriate to a defendant under a charge (itself revealing ideologically in the case of a rape complainant) to the conversational, helping mode appropriate to the Police as guardian of citizens' rights. Such "hard" and "soft" modes of talk have even entered public consciousness in the wake of the Cyprus military spying interrogations. In the Counselling example, in a parallel but different way, CR has two registers to resolve in her text. One is oriented towards maintaining solidarity and the tenets of counselling as a non-directive non-judgemental process, much evidenced by indirectness and mitigation; the other is oriented towards prohibition because of the medically contra-indicated mix of factors in question, yet unable to be fully realised as such because of her own institutionalised lack of authority and sanction. In my view, the blend is more successfully managed in the Counselling example.

The question now arises whether we should indeed regard the "successful" and felicitous blend in the Counselling case as being an example of a well-managed conflict and, in contrast, the Police example as mismanaged. In one sense, of course, history has shown that this is in part justified. Practices in rape complaints have been drastically revised following the broadcasting of that particular programme. Women police officers are now regularly required to take initial depositions, medical evidence is sought at an early stage, to assist in the warranting of the complaint. Nonetheless, to argue that the Police example was a mismanaged ideological conflict begs the question as to whether the powerful party intended the conflict to be kept under textual control. Arguably the Police had a vested interest in fracture in the way that CR had a vested interest in conversational cooperativeness.

If that is so, then we may begin to suggest a way in which critical discourse analysis can not only contribute to an understanding of social institutions, and through them to social formations, but also to an understanding of the range of variably intertextual text types that are current at a given moment, and thus aid what is, after all, a prime descriptive linguistic task.

Appendix

Examples
1:   *A Complaint of Rape*
(A) "Complaining" — Extract 1

Brian (Detective Constable)	Woman	*Colin (Detective Sergeant)*
B	W	C
d you or d you not want to make a complaint of rape/		
	no I dont /	
cos as far as Im concerned if you dont its a complete and utter waste of time us three sittin in this room and talking about it . we might as well just pack up and let you get going /		
	well exactly /	

B	W	C
. oh theres two of us think the same thing then /		
	I dont wan//t to]	.. listen very carefully what Ive got to say /
		// listen] listen carefully what Ive got to say . my colleagues just asked you . if you wish to make a complaint rape /
	mm	
		and you said no /
	mm	
		if that is so . then we will take a statement off you to that effect /
	mm	
		alright? . now understand . we dont want you coming back in two or three days time .. and saying THAT .. I made a complaint of rape .. and .. I NOW .. want to . make that same complaint again /
	mm	
		not withdrawin it or changing my mind .. alright? /
	mm	
		Im very sceptical . I dont think it happened /
	[why dont you get a doctor in straight away ..	
		//we] were not satisfied at the moment that its happened . alright? thats why were talking . to you (2.0) we do not//
	//what if [what	
		// w]
	if someone doesnt want t'make a complaint but you believe there is a rape ../	
/we dont//[do any		
		//we cant do] a thing about it because . if you .. arent going to COMPLAIN . then

B	W	C
		. as far as were concerned weve got no offence/
because you cant have an offender for an offence that doesnt EXIST (2.5) much to OUR annoyance/		

(B) "Protecting" — Extract 2 (Introductory)

B	W	C
		are you prepared to make a statement and . if . we apprehend the offenders . are you willing to go to court and give evidence ../
	what . if if//	//if we catch them yeah
	if you get all three of them . yes/	if we catch one of them two of them or three of them /
	no if you catch one of them the other two are going to get me mate /	
		are you willing //[
// know that]		// are you willing . to make a statement . and attend court . and give evidence (3.0) thats what it boils down to //
// before a judge and jury ./		
	I dont want to go to court/	are you sure /
	yeah/	then thats your decision /
	mm	well take a statement off you . Im going to see my inspector now . and tell him whats happening /
	mm	and then well take a statement off you and then youre quite free to leave the police station /

B	W	C
	right/	
	mm (6.0) hhh .	alright/ (leaves)
whats that for /		
	I dont want to end up in the river thats all//	
//och this is Reading nineteen eighty . its not bloody Starsky and Hutch . end up in the river whats the matter with you (leaves) /		
	honestly (3.0) hh . they havent met some of the people I know .. you can see what people mean . by . you know . its easier not to say anything than go through this lark /	
(Cameraman) for sure /		
	you know what I mean (5.0) I was definitely RAPED (4.0) Ive got a stomach ache to PROVE it . I could prove it with the doctor as well .. if they got a doctor in and did it straight away I would it would be much easier .. why dont they do the physical first .. then you could prove it one way or the other . and then then Id prove it to them /	

These data derive from a BBC TV Documentary on the Thames Valley Police. The episode in question was entitled: *A Complaint of Rape*. The original discussions on the data took place in the context of a Departmental Working Group at Lancaster (U.K.) on *Unequal Encounters* involving my colleague Norman Fairclough and graduate students Jenny Thomas, Mike Makosch and Sue Spencer. These discussions have been followed up at Hawaii (U.S.A.) in the context of a graduate course on *The Discourse of Unequal Encounters*.

11: *Modes of Counselling in Family Planning*

Strategies
(1) Provide relevant information;
(2) Ascertain H's awareness of this information;
(3) Shift responsibility for overt FTA to higher authority;

(4) Focus on A_1 of H (i.e. giving up smoking), but indirectly with mitigation;
(5) Abandon focus on A_1 of H, focus on A_2 (i.e. issue of contraceptive pills), then resume focus on A_1;
(6) Claim common ground with H, emphathise;
(7) Place responsibility for choice on H, be indirect;
(8) Allocate disproportionate consultation time to addressing A_1 and A_2.

These data derive from a study of Family Planning Counselling (Candlin & Lucas 1986). The complete study is available as part of the Lancaster Linguistics Papers Series from the Department of Linguistics, University of Lancaster.

Notes

1. This paper owes a debt to the research group on Ideology and Discourse in the Department of Linguistics at the University of Lancaster and to student groups in the United States and at Lancaster concerned with the study of the discourse of Counselling, with various types of Counsellor and client. More directly, it owes a theoretical debt to Norman Fairclough (1986), whose discussion of the relationships between ideology and discourse and in particular the interdependence of the social formation, the social institution and social action broadly inform what is being said here.

2. Once again, I am aware that much that is needed is omitted here, in particular a more detailed social analysis (from counsellor's and client's perspective) of the ideologies surrounding family planning in welfare clinics for "the poor, the immigrant and the medically high-risk" in the U.S. in general and in Honolulu, Hawaii in particular. Some of that necessary information is contained in Candlin and Lucas (1986).

Is there a literary language?

Ronald A. Carter

1. Introduction

This paper explores the interface between language and literature. The question "Is there a literary language?" is consistently addressed throughout, but it is one which cannot be addressed in isolation either from questions concerning the nature of literature itself or from the institutional contexts in which literature and language are taught. It will be apparent, too, that linguistics can help supply some partial answers to the main question but it will be argued that it is within sociolinguistic theories and descriptions of discourse that these answers may be most successfully located.

In one sense, literary language is the language of literature; it is found in literary texts and is, for many literary critics, an unproblematic category. You know when you are in its company. Such a position cannot, however, be as unnegotiable as it seems to be, if only because the term literature itself is subject to constant change. In the history of English "literature", literature has meant different things at different times: from elevated treatment of dignified subjects (15th century) to simply writing in the broadest sense of the word (e.g. diaries; travelogues; historical and biographical accounts) (18th century) to the sense of creative, highly imaginative literature (with a hieratic upper-case "L") appropriated under the influence of Romantic theories of literature by Matthew Arnold and F.R. Leavis in the last one hundred years. For a fuller account of such semantic change in respect of literature, see Williams (1976) who also points out the semantic detritus of the eighteenth century sense of the word in its use to describe the "literature" of an academic subject, or in the collocations of insurance "literature" or travel agents' "literature". Literature is subject to constant change; it is not universally the same everywhere and is eminently negotiable. Definitions of literary language have to be part of the same process.

2. Literary language: a brief history of definitions

The history of definitions of literary language in this century is a long and battle-scarred one with various interest groups competing for power over the property(ies); and each definition has itself inevitably assumed a theory of literature whether explicitly recognised or admitted to be one or not. Two main camps can be discerned and these can be grouped, rather loosely, into *formalist* and *functionalist* though the division is by no means a clear cut one. We shall begin with formalist definitions because they are historically anterior but also because their influence is pervasive in the export of Russian Formalism into American New Criticism and its subsequent import into practical criticism in Britain.

2.1. Formalism

Formalist definitions, especially those of the Russian formalists, were predicated on a division between poetic and practical language and to this extent paralleled I.A. Richards' opposition in his writings in the 1920s between scientific and poetic discourse. The Russian Formalists shared the belief of the Symbolists at the turn of this century in the aesthetic autonomy and ahistorical ontological separateness of art and literature from other kinds of discourse, but were unhappy about the Symbolists' vague subjectivity and impressionism when it came to discussions of literature.

Paradoxically, they wanted to set up a *science*, a *poetics* of literature which would seek to define the literariness of literature, that is, isolate by rigorous scientific means the specifically literary forms and properties of texts. Since there is no literary content, they argued, poetics should evince a concern with the how rather than the what. Thus the early Formalists such as Shklovsky, Tynyanov, Eichenbaum and Jakobson gave special attention to the linguistic constituents of the literary medium — language — and drew on the new science of linguistics for their theoretical and descriptive apparatus. Their main theoretical position was that literary language is deviant language. It is a theory which has had considerable influence.

According to deviation theory literariness or poeticality inheres in the degrees to which language use departs or deviates from expected configurations and normal patterns of language and thus defamiliarises the reader.

Language use in literature is therefore different because it makes strange, disturbs, upsets our routinised normal view of things and thus generates new or renewed perceptions. For example, the phrase "a grief ago" would be poetic by virtue of its departure from semantic selection restrictions which state that only temporal nouns such as "week", "month" can occur in this sequence. As a result grief is perceived as a temporal process. Deviation theory represents a definition of literary language which contains interesting insights but which on close inspection is theoretically underpowered or at least underbuilt. For example:

i. If there is a deviation then this can only be measured if you state the norm from which the deviation occurs. What is the norm? Do we not mean norms? Is the norm the standard language, the internally constituted norms created within the single text, the norms of a particular genre, a particular writer's style, the norms created by a school of writers within a period? And so on. If it is the standard language norms then what level of language is involved? Grammar, phonology, discourse, semantics? This is an important question: because a deviation at one level may be norm adherence at another level. And there is a further problem in that our ability to measure and account accurately for deviations will depend on what levels of language linguists know most about. Since the greatest advances this century have been in grammar and phonology, formalist poetics has tended to discuss literariness, rather limitedly, in terms of grammatical and phonological deviations.

ii. What is defamiliarizing in 1912 may not be in 1922.

iii. There will be a tendency to discover literariness in the more maximally deviant forms — i.e. poetry rather than prose, *avant garde* rather than naturalist drama, in e.e. Cummings and Dylan Thomas rather than Wordsworth's Lucy poems or George Eliot's shorter fiction.

iv. It presupposes a *distinction* between poetic and practical language which is never demonstrated. It can easily be shown that deviation routinely occurs in everyday language and in discourses not usually associated with literature. Similarly, in some historical periods, literature was defined by adherence to, rather than deviation from, literary and linguistic norms. (See work by Halliday 1971, on the notion of "deflection" as opposed to deviation.)

Yet the idea of literary language as language which can result in renewal or in a new way of seeing the familiar cannot be as easily discounted as this. But it needs greater theoretical and linguistic precision for the definition to hold and it needs augmentation by complementary definitions.

2.2. Self-referentiality

Another influential Formalist definition is associated with Roman Jakobson. Originally connected with the Russian formalists, Jakobson subsequently moved to the United States and in a famous paper (Jakobson 1960) he articulated a theory of poetic language which stressed the *self-referentiality* of poetic language. In his account, literariness results when language draws attention to its own status as a sign and when as a result there is a focus on the message for its own sake. Jakobson's notion has been clearly explained by Easthope (1982):

> The poetic function gets into the syntagmatic axis something which normally would stay outside in the paradigmatic axis: it does so by operating a choice in favour of something that repeats what is already in the syntagmatic axis, thus reinforcing it.

Thus, in the examples:

I hate horrible Harry or *I like Ike*

the verbs *hate* and *like* are selected in favour of "loath" or "support" because they establish a reinforcing phonoaesthetic patterning. The examples cited (the latter is Jakobson's own) demonstrate that poeticality can inhere in such everyday language as political advertising slogans. This notion is developed more extensively below. But we should note here that Jakobson's definition is, like that of deviation theory, founded in an assumed distinction between "poetic" and "pragmatic" language. According to Jakobson, in non-literary discourse, the signifier is a mere vehicle for the signified. In literary discourse it is brought into a much more active reinforcing relationship serving, as it were, to symbolise or represent the signified as well as to refer to it. (See also Widdowson 1985: Ch. 11 for related discussion.)

This emphasis on patterning and on the self-referential and representational nature of literary discourse is valuable; but it should be pointed out that (i) Jakobson's criteria work rather better in respect of poetry than of prose; (ii) he supplies no clear criteria for determining the *degrees* of poeticality or "literariness" in his examples. He does not seem to want to answer his own question as to what exactly makes some messages more unequivocal examples of works of art than others (see also Waugh 1980); (iii) Jakobson stresses too much the *production* of effects, neglecting in the process the recognition and reception of such effects. The reader or receiver of the message and his or her sociolinguistic position tends to get left out of account.[1]

2.3. Speech acts and language functions

Accounts of literary language which attempt more boldly to underscore the role of the reader interacting in a sociolinguistic context with the sender of a verbal message are generally termed *speech act theories* of literary discourse. Where the work of Jakobson and others can be termed formalist, these theories are more functionalist in orientation, although one of their main proponents, Richard Ohmann, might be better described as a formalist disguised as a functionalist.

Ohmann's basic proposition is that in literature the kinds of conditions which normally attach to speech acts such as insulting, questioning and promising do not obtain. Instead we have quasi- or mimetic speech acts. As Ohmann (1971) puts it:

> A literary work is a discourse whose sentences lack the illocutionary forces that would normally attach to them ... specifically, a literary work purportedly imitates (or reports) a series of speech acts, which in fact have no other existence ... Since the quasi-speech acts of literature are not carrying on the world's business — describing, urging, contracting, etc., the reader may well attend to them in a non-pragmatic way and thus allow them to realize their emotive potential ...

Thus, the literary speech act is typically a different kind of speech act — one which involves (on the part of the reader) a suspension of the normal pragmatic functions words may have in order for the reader to regard them as in some way representing or displaying the actions they would normally perform.

The notion of a displayed, non-pragmatic fictional speech act certainly goes some way towards explaining why we do not read Blake's *Tyger* for information about a species of animal or Wordsworth's *Daffodils* because we are contemplating a career in horticulture. Or why we cannot be guilty of breach of promise when that promise is in a love poem rather than a love letter. (See Widdowson 1975.) It also explains to some extent why Gibbon's *Decline and Fall of the Roman Empire* is still widely read today or appears on literature syllabuses in numerous English Departments, when his statements about the Romans are, as history, either invalid or at least irrelevant.

Ohmann's theory suffers from an essentialist opposition between literary and non-literary which careful consideration does not really bear out. Pratt (1977), for example, has convincingly demonstrated that non-fictional, non-pragmatic, mimetic, disinterested, playful speech acts routinely occur outside what is called literature. Hypothesizing, telling white lies, pretending, playing devil's advocate, imagining, fantasizing, relating jokes or anecdotes, even using illustrations to underscore a point in scholarly argument, are then, by Ohmann's definition, literary. Ohmann's theory does not explain either the "literary" status of certain travel writings, or Orwell's essays on the Spanish Civil War (and he would have been extremely perturbed for people to read those essays as merely pretended speech acts); nor does it explain how Thomas Keneally's *Schindler's Ark*, a piece of non-fiction, a "novel" based on documentary research into real events and characters in a Second World War German concentration camp, won the Booker Prize for "Literature" in 1982. Neither does it explain why detective novels, science fiction or popular romances which are fictional are not literary; nor why the prose works of Milton or Donne, which are non-fictional, are literary. Indeed, as Leitch (1983) has also argued, the distinction between fiction and non-fiction is not an absolute one since truth itself is a convention determined institutionally and to which commitments differ in different contexts. Work by Hayden White in the field of historiography also raises the intriguing possibility that the writing of history is a kind of narrative in which our interpretation of the past, indeed the facilitating of historical thought, is often made by means of "literary" tropes. Work on metaphor by Lakoff and Johnson (1980) and others shows how so-called "literary features" of language routinely occur outside what are commonly called literary texts. And Moeran (1984) has demonstrated the existence in advertisements of such literary-linguistic elements as allusiveness, intertextuality, phonetic symbolism, ambiguity, represented language and so on.

2.4. Literariness in language

In the next section it will be argued that the opposition of literary to non-literary language is an unhelpful one and that the notion of literary language as a yes/no category should be replaced by one which sees literary language as a continuum, a cline of literariness in language use with some uses of language being marked as more literary than others. The argument will follow the one advanced in Carter and Nash (1983), and illustrative material will be provided by a range of thematically connected texts which describe different aspects of Malaysia. Although the most immediate focus is on text-intrinsic linguistic features, it will not be forgotten that whether the reader *chooses* to read a text in a literary way, as a literary text as it were, is one crucial determinant of its literariness. For example, Herrnstein-Smith (1978: 67) discusses[2] how the first line of a newspaper article on Hell's Angels can, when arranged in a particular lineation, be read and interpreted for all kinds of different literary meanings:

Most Angels are uneducated.
Only one
Angel in
ten
has
steady work.

3. Literature, literariness and discourse: some examples

In this section some criteria for specifying literariness in language are proposed. The criteria are based, as already indicated, on those proposed in Carter and Nash (1983), although these are extended and modified in a number of ways. Reference to the criteria will enable us to determine what is prototypical in conventional literary language use, as far as it is understood in its standard, modern average Western conception; in other words, they will assist in determining *degrees* of literariness thus providing a systematic basis for saying one text is more or less "literary" than another. The texts about Malaysia used in this discussion are labelled A - E. (See pp 928-931)

3.1. Medium dependence

The notion of medium dependence means that the more literary a text the less it will be dependent for its reading on another medium or media. In this respect Text B is dependent on a code or key to abbreviations used and on reference to a map or illustrations (e.g. *inc.*; *indep.*; *a.*; *p.*; *cst.*; *exp.*, *est.*). To a lesser extent Texts A and C could probably be said to be medium-dependent in that they are or are likely to be accompanied by a photograph or by some means of pictorial supplement. By contrast, Text D

Text A

Watch *"Little Asia"* come alive in Kuala Lumpur, then relive the historical past of nearby Malacca.

Kuala Lumpur. Malaysia's capital city with an endless maze of colourful images. The people, the food, the sights, the sounds. All an exotic mix of European and Asian cultures. A pulsating potpourri of Malays, Chinese and Indians.

And there's more. To the south is the historic town of *Malacca*. Here, 158km from *Kuala Lumpur*, you can step into history and relive the glorious past of this ancient port.

Fish, sail, swim or simply relax on the sandy, sun-kissed beaches of *Port Dickson*, only 100km away from *Kuala Lumpur*.

Or take a scenic drive from the capital city to one of several hill resorts, set in the midst of lush green tropical jungles.

And it's all here in Malaysia. The country where great cultures meet, where the diversity of its history, customs and traditions is reflected in the warm hospitality of gentle, friendly Malaysians.

Come share a holiday in this wonderful land. Come to Malaysia. We welcome you now and any time of the year.

IT'S ALL HERE IN MALAYSIA.

Text B

Malaysia, East, part of Federation of Malaysia: inc. Sarawak and Sabah (formerly Brit. N. Borneo); less developed than W. Malaysia; p. concentrated on cst.; hill tribes engaged in hunting in interior; oil major exp., exploration off cst.; separated from W. Malaysia by S. China Sea; a. 77,595 sq. m.; p. (1968) 1,582,000.

Malaysia, Federation of, indep. federation (1963), S.E. Asia; member of Brit. Commonwealth; inc. W. Malaysia (Malaya) and E. Malaysia (Borneo sts. of Sarawak and Sabah); cap. Kuala Lumpur; a. 129,000 sq. m.; p. (1968) 10,455,000.

Malaysia, West (Malaya), part of Federation of Malaysia; consists of wide peninsula, S. of Thailand; most developed in W.; world's leading producer of natural rubber, grown in plantations; oil palm and pineapples also grown; world's leading exporter of tin; nearly half p. Chinese; a. 50,806 sq. m.; p. (1968) 8,899,000.

Text C

Batu Ferringhi Beach, Penang

Take our Singapore and Malaysia holiday and enjoy a whole week in Kuantan free of charge – unbelievable but true!

The beautiful setting of the Hyatt Hotel, Kuantan

Singapore + Malaysia
Kuala Lumpur: 2 nights ● Singapore: 3 nights
Kuantan: 4 nights Plus 7 nights (optional) FREE

Day 1 Fri London/Kuala Lumpur
Evening departure from Heathrow by Malaysian Airlines scheduled flight to Kuala Lumpur.

Day 2 Sat and Day 3 Sun Kuala Lumpur
Arrive in the early evening and transfer to the beautiful Regent Hotel (see page 48). In this rapidly growing, predominantly Muslim city, futuristic development blends with old Moorish architecture – but there is still plenty of evidence of the old England' of former British colonial days, including the cricket matches which are regularly played at KL's distinguished Selangor Club.

Day 4 Mon Kuala Lumpur/Singapore
A short flight brings you to Singapore where you will be met and transferred to your hotel the Hyatt Regency (see page 48).

Day 5 Tue and Day 6 Wed Singapore
Two days to enjoy Singapore with its fascinating blend of east and west. Try dinner at Raffles, a harbour cruise or stroll through Chinatown – and at the Hyatt Regency in the heart of the city you are right on the doorstep of literally hundreds of fabulous shops.

Day 7 Thu Singapore/Kuantan
Fly by MAS scheduled service from Singapore to Kuantan and transfer to your hotel, the Hyatt.

Day 8 Fri to Day 10 Sun Kuantan
In Kuantan the atmosphere is still very local and unspoilt – ideal if you don't like crowds: long, deserted stretches of beautiful sandy beach and the clear blue waters of the South China Sea.

Sightseeing on Malaysia's east coast is very much a journey through local lifestyles with tours to local villages, 'kampongs' and fishing ports to observe cottage industries such as 'songket' weaving, batik printing, the moulding of silver and brass, to witness the popular pastimes of top spinning and kite flying and perhaps to visit a local market – a veritable riot of colours and aromas.

Day 11 Mon Kuantan/Kuala Lumpur/London
Last day in Kuantan before leaving for the short evening flight to KL and MAS scheduled connection to Heathrow, landing next morning.

FREE WEEK OFFER
If you wish to extend your stay in Kuantan, you can have a further 7 nights at the Hyatt ABSOLUTELY FREE (see KUONI Plus on page 48).

PENANG EXTENSION
3 or 7 nights
After Kuantan continue north-west to the island of Penang for a further 3 or 7 nights to laze on more of Malaysia's sun-drenched beaches.

Day 11 Mon Kuantan/Kuala Lumpur/Penang
Leave Kuantan for the morning MAS flight via KL to Penang and the Hotel Golden Sands.

Day 14 Thu or Day 18 Mon Penang/Kuala Lumpur/London
A last full day on Penang before the short flight to KL connecting with MAS to Heathrow, arriving the following morning.

Room at Hyatt Hotel, Kuantan
HYATT KUANTAN
Located on a beautiful white sand beach, the mood here is one of peace and tranquility. The Verandah, overlooking the sea is an ideal corner for a sundowner, there's a speciality restaurant for continental cuisine, and the Kampong café restaurant offers delicious local delicacies. You can saunter along to the Chukka Club disco and a converted sampan down on the beach provides a cosy rendezvous. There is a beautiful swimming pool and children's pool, three tennis courts, two squash courts, a sauna or herbal steam bath with a massage and the Marina Sports Centre offers windsurfing, waterskiing, sailing and sea fishing. All 185 rooms are furnished with elegant rattan furniture and subtle colours. Rooms have balconies, air-conditioning, bath and shower, television, radio, direct dial telephone, minibar, fridge, video-movies and have either seaview or mountain view (non seaview).
Regency Club rooms also available (see p. 55).
Opinion: An excellent first-class hotel, good sports facilities and generally less expensive than its equivalent in Penang.
N.B. The rains on the east coast of Malaysia (Kuantan) may be prolonged and heavy during the period November to January.

HOLIDAY PRICES PER PERSON IN £ ex London			24 Oct-09 Dec		10 Dec-28 Feb		01 Mar-30 Apr		01 May-15 Jun		16 Jun-09 Sep		Sgl. sup. per nt.
Ref. No.		No. of Nights in Resort	7	extra wk(s)	7	extra wk(s)	7	extra wk(s)	7	extra wk(s)	7	extra wk(s)	
	Singapore only												
SK 701	Hyatt Regency (standard)	EP	—	—	658	98	658	98	658	98	683	98	14
SK 702	Hyatt Regency (superior)	EP	—	—	747	182	747	182	747	182	772	182	26
SK 704	Singapore Bargain	EP	399	70	449	70	429	70	399	70	429	70	9
			9		9		9		9		9		Sgl. sup. per tour
SK 703	Singapore + Malaysia	EP	—	—	688	91*	688	91*	688	91*	688	91*	98
					3		3		3		3		Sgl. sup. per nt	
—	Penang Extension	EP	—	—	69		69		69		69		11

Supplements: Flight departures ex UK 15-31 December £52, also SK 703 only: 15 Jun-15 Aug £81. Holidays over 16 nights duration £21. Peak hotel supplement: See page 47 for Penang hotels. Upgrading to superior rooms: Hyatt Regency; £12 per night in twin, £24 in single, Hyatt Kuantan £14 in twin, £16 in single, Golden Sands £5 in twin, £7 in single. MAP supplements: Hyatt Kuantan £14 per night; Golden Sands £14 per night.
Departures: WEEKLY. From Heathrow every Friday via Kuala Lumpur.
Flying: (long haul sectors): **Singapore + Malaysia:** Malaysian Airline System 747. **Depart/Land Heathrow:** Friday p.m./Tuesday a.m. (or Friday a.m. 3 night Penang Extension).
Singapore Only: Singapore Airlines 747. **Depart/Land Heathrow:** Friday p.m./Sunday a.m.
Holiday duration: Holidays can be extended by multiples of one week. Simply add the cost of extra week for Singapore and Kuantan or on page 47 for Penang then add extension supplement (if applicable) shown above. *Denotes cost of extra week at Hyatt Kuantan; single supplement during extra week £28.
Meals included: EP – none; MAP – full breakfast and dinner. **'What the price includes'** – see page 160. **Representation:** KUONI rep in K.L., Singapore Penang and agent in Kuantan.

Text D

VICTOR CRABBE slept through the *bilal's bang* (inept Persian word for the faint unheeded call), would sleep till the *bangbang* (apt Javanese word) of the brontoid dawn brought him tea and bananas. He slept on the second floor of the old Residency, which overlooked the river.

The river Lanchap gives the state its name. It has its source in deep jungle, where it is a watering-place for a hundred or so little negroid people who worship thunder and can count only up to two. They share it with tigers, hamadryads, bootlace-snakes, leeches, pelandoks and the rest of the bewildering fauna of up-stream Malaya. As the Sungai Lanchap winds on, it encounters outposts of a more complex culture: Malay villages where the Koran is known, where the prophets jostle with nymphs and tree-gods in a pantheon of unimaginable variety. Here a little work in the paddy-fields suffices to maintain a heliotropic, pullulating subsistence. There are fish in the river, guarded, however, by crocodile-gods of fearful malignity; coconuts drop or are hurled down by trained monkeys called *beroks*; the durian sheds its rich fetid smell in the season of durians. Erotic pantuns and Hindu myths soothe away the depression of an occasional *accidia*. As the Lanchap approaches the coast a more progressive civilization appears: the two modern towns of Timah and Tahi Panas, made fat on tin and rubber, supporting large populations of Chinese, Malays, Indians, Eurasians, Arabs, Scots, Christian Brothers, and pale English administrators. The towns echo with trishaw-bells, the horns of smooth, smug American cars, radios blaring sentimental pentatonic Chinese tunes, the morning hawking and spitting of the *towkays*, the call of the East. Where the Lanchap meets the Sungai, Hantu is the royal town, dominated by an Istana designed by a Los Angeles architect, blessed by a mosque as bulbous as a clutch of onions, cursed by a lowering sky and high humidity. This is Kuala Hantu.

Victor Crabbe slept soundly, drawn into that dark world where history melts into myth.

Text E

Malacca belles greet Dr M

PRETTY lasses, representing Malacca's Portuguese community, welcoming Prime Minister Datuk Seri Dr Mahathir Mohamad who is on a two-day visit to the state.

Dr Mahathir launched on Thursday a Portuguese cultural centre, "Medan Portugis," costing $1.3 million at Hujung Pasir in Malacca Town.

He said the centre, an idea he mooted two years ago, would help the community fall back on their rich cultural heritage to supplement incomes.

Malacca, once an ancient thriving port on the west coast of the peninsula, is the home of Malaysia's Portuguese community, many of whom still live in a small seafront enclave and eke a living from fishing. There are about 3,000 Portuguese in Malacca.

Dr Mahathir urged the Malaysian Portuguese to drop their "hang-up" over history and resolve to look ahead.

He assured them that the government has no intention of maltreating any community in the country.

In August last year, the government announced that it was allowing Malaysian Portuguese to invest in the National Unit Trust, until then preserved for Bumiputras. — NST picture.

is dependent only on itself for its "reading". It generates a world of internal reference and relies only on its own capacity to project. This is not to suggest that it cannot be determined by external political or social or biographical influences. No text can be so entirely autonomous that it refers only to itself nor so rich that a reader's own experience of the Malaysia it refers to (though, paradoxically, none of the places actually exist. There is no Kuala Hantu, etc.) cannot extend the world it creates. But the text is sovereign. Its sovereignty is that, relative to the other writing about Malaysia, this text requires no necessary supplementation.

3.2. Re-registration

The notion of re-registration means that no single word or stylistic feature or register will be barred from admission to a literary context. Registers such as legal language or the language of instructions are recognised by the neat fit between language form and specific function; but any language at all can be deployed to literary effects by the process of re-registration. For example, Auden makes use of bureaucratic registers in his poem *The Unknown Citizen*; wide use of journalistic and historical discourse styles is made in novels such as Salmon Rushdie's *Midnight's Children* and *Shame* and in numerous novels by Norman Mailer. This is, of course, not to suggest that certain stylistic or lexical features are not appreciably more "literary" than others; but such items as *twain, eftsoons, azure, steed, verdure*, together with archaic syntactic forms and inversions, belong to a past literary domain. They are associated with what was considered to be appropriately elevated and decorous in poetic discourse and were automatically used as such, losing in the process any contact with a living, current idiom and becoming fossilized and restrictedly "literary" in the process. Re-registration recognises that the full unrestricted resources of the language are open to exploitation for literary ends. Text D, for example, exploits the language more normally connected with travel-brochure and geography book discourse but re-deploys or re-registers it for particularly subtle literary purposes. Here the guide book style is regularly subverted, an ironic undercutting serving to suggest that the conventional geographical or historical presentation of the state is comically inappropriate to a world which is much more heterogeneous and resistant to external ordering or classification.

3.3. Interaction of levels: semantic density

This is one of the most important of defining criterial categories. The notion here is that a text that is perceived as resulting from the additive interaction of several superimposed codes and levels is recognised as more literary than a text where there are fewer levels at work or where they are present but do not interact. There are different linguistic levels at work in Texts A, B and C but in D, I would argue, we have a degree of semantic density which is different from that in the other texts and which results from an interactive patterning at the levels of syntax, lexis, phonology and discourse. The most prominent of these patterns is *contrast* (contrasts exist between a simple syntax of, variably, subject, predicate, complement (*The river Lanchap gives the state its name. This is Kuala Hantu*) (both of which act as a kind of frame for the first two paragraphs), and a more complexly patterned syntax involving greater clausal complexity through participial and subordinate clauses, more embedding and simply longer sentences. There are contrasts, too, on the level of lexis between words of Greek and Anglo-Saxon derivation (*accidia, unimaginable, pantheon, dominated, brontoid, progressive* as opposed to *clutch, hurled, sheds, smug, fat*) which is simultaneously a contrast between mono- and polysyllabic, formal and informal lexical items. The contrast is carried further into semantic oppositions marked in the items *inept/apt, lowering sky/high humidity, blessed/cursed, soothe away/blare* and the opposition of East and West in "smug American cars"/"*Los Angeles* architect" and "call of the *East*" and "*pentatonic* tunes".

Grammar, lexis and semantics are further complemented by effects at the level of phonology. Here the plosive *b* and *p* are predominant patterns (overlapping notably with the more formal and "ancient" lexical items, for example *bulbous, pentatonic, pullulating, brontoid, pantheon, paddy-fields, pantuns, prophets*); but they exist in contrast with an almost equally predominant pattern of *s* sounds (*second, source, snakes, sleep, shave, tigers*, etc.). This interaction of levels, particularly in the form of contrasts, serves to symbolise or represent the unstated content of the passage. For example, one of the possible functions of these linguistic contrasts is to underscore the contrast between Victor Crabbe, an idealistic colonial teacher, and an alien ex-colonial territory; but between these contrasting worlds there also subsists a less clearly marked, more heterogeneous reality to which Crabbe is directly exposed.

Text D is, however, not the only passage in which an interactive patterning of different linguistic levels is foregrounded. Text A contains many such features from the phonetic symbolism of:

Fish, sail, swim or simply relax on the sandy, sun-kissed beaches of Port Dickson

or the metaphoric and phonetic constellation of:

A pulsating potpourri of Malays, Chinese and Indians

or the syntactic and graphological self-referential deviation of:

IT'S ALL HERE IN MALAYSIA

or the strategic semantic reiterations of:

relive the historical past
relive the glorious past

and the contrasts between past and present figured in the juxtaposition of present and past, Malacca and Kuala Lumpur, the past tense and the eternal present of moodless clauses (*The people, the food, the sights, the sounds*).

Across this spectrum of texts about Malaysia it is clear that where different levels of language multipally interact there is a potential reinforcement of meaning. More than one possible meaning is thereby represented or symbolised although any activation of meanings must be dependent on a reader whose literary competence permits "reasonable" correlations of linguistic forms and semantic functions. In this respect Text D can be demonstrated to have greater semantic density than Text B, for example. The interesting case is Text A which, as we have seen, contains an interaction of levels. The existence of these texts illustrates one aspect of a cline of relative "literariness" and enables us to begin to talk about one text being more or less literary than another.

3.4. Polysemy

The main point in this section is one which has been widely discussed: the existence of polysemy in literary texts. In terms of this criterion of literariness Text B, by being restrictively and necessarily monosemic, sacrifices any immediate claims to be literary. The monosemy of the text is closely connected with the need to convey clear, retrievable and unambiguous information. This end is served by a number of means: the formulaic code of the headings, for example *Malaysia, Federation of*; the many abbreviations employed; the geographical and numerical explicitness and the extreme economy of presentation (giving as much information in as little space as possible). There is no indication that the text should be read in more than one way although the compositional skills which go into entries such as this in encyclopaedias and geography text books should not be dismissed. Polysemy is a regular feature of advertisements although there are no particular examples of this in Text A, which is perhaps best referred to as *plurisignifying* rather than polysemic in that it shares the capacity of many advertisements to be memorable, to promote intertextual relations and to provide a verbal pleasure which can result in frequent citation and embedding in discourses other than that for which it was originally intended. (See Moeran 1984, especially his discussion of the Heineken beer advertisements.) Text D is, however, polysemic (in that individual lexical items carry more than one meaning) *and* plurisignifying. Polysemic lexical items in Text D can be: *call* of the East (actual "sound" and "longing for"); *smooth* ... American cars ("surface metal" and, by extension, "the personality of their owners") and *dark* world ("lack of light and mysterious", "uncivilised", etc.). And so on.

One characteristic of the polysemic text is then that its lexical items do not stop automatically at their first interpretant; denotations are always potentially available for transformation into connotations, contents are never received for their own sake but rather as a sign vehicle for something else.

3.5. *Displaced interaction*

The notion of displaced interaction serves to help differentiate the direct speech acts of Text C, in which readers will, if they take the advertised holiday, actually perform the actions described in the sequence depicted in the itinerary itself, from the more indirect or displaced speech acts transmitted in Text D. In D the reader is asked to perform no particular action except that of a kind of mental accompaniment to the text in the course of which he or she interprets or negotiates what the message means. The meaning may change on re-reading of course; but this is unlikely to be the case with Texts C or B, although in the case of Text A there is some scope for taking it in more than one way and this is a function of its potential literariness. Displaced interaction allows meanings to emerge indirectly and obliquely. What we conventionally regard as "literary" is likely to be a text in which the context-bound interaction between author and reader is more deeply embedded or displaced.

3.6. Discourse patterning

Criteria for literariness discussed so far have focused mostly on effects at sentence level. At the suprasentential level of discourse, effects can be located which can help us further to differentiate degrees of literariness. Space prohibits detailed analysis at this level so the point will have to be underlined with reference to one example.

In Text D patterning at the level of discourse occurs by virtue of repetition of the particulars of place, which is concentrated in the long second paragraph. Reference to the river and town is made as follows:

> *The river Lanchap gives the state its name.*
> *As the Sungai Lanchap winds on ...*
> *As the Lanchap approaches the coast ...*
> *Where the Lanchap meets the Sungai, Hantu is the royal town ...*
> *This is Kuala Hantu.*

The effects of cross sentential repetition here, reinforced by repeated syntactic patterns of clause and tense, is to enact the lingering presence and progress of the river and to provide for the appearance of the town as if the reader were actually engaged in a journey through the jungle towards the town. The short focusing sentence *This is Kuala Hantu* is thus discoursally interconnected with a number of related patterns out of which it grows organically and, in terms of the content of the passage, *actually* grows. Although there is a related patterning around the word *Malaysia* in other texts (e.g. A and B and especially A) the discourse patterning does not reinforce content to the same extent.[3]

3.7. Some conclusions

In Sections 3.0-3.6 the following main points have been argued:

i. Literary language is not special or different in that any formal feature termed "literary" can be found in other discourses.[4]

ii. Literary language *is* different from other language uses in that it functions differently. Some of the differences can be demarcated with reference to criteria such as: medium dependence; re-registration; semantic density produced by interaction of linguistic levels;

displaced interaction; polysemy; discourse patterning. What is prototypically literary will be a text which meets most of the above criteria; a less literary text will only meet some of the above criteria; an unequivocally non-literary text will be likely to meet none of these criteria; that is, it will be monosemic, medium-dependent, project a direct interaction, contain no re-registrations and so on.

iii. The worst excesses of paradox and the essentialist dichotomies of an absolute division into literary/non-literary or fictional/non-fictional can be avoided by positing a *cline* of literariness along which discourses can be arranged.

iv. The terms literary and non-literary might be best replaced by the more neutral terms *text* or *discourse*.

v. The sociolinguistic and socio-cultural context of the discourse is important. This point is developed below.

4. Literariness, society and ideology

This section stresses one further point about literariness and with particular reference to the notion of semantic density. In this connection it is worth examining Text E because it is a text which can be read as displaying some relatively dense semantic patterning at the intersection of language, society and ideology. The underscoring of these dense relations — as with Text D — is to a considerable extent dependent on readers' interests, on how interested the reader is — in several senses of the word "interest". The degree of attention brought to its reading may be dependent on your "interest" as a journalist, or a feminist interested in the presentation of women, or as a student of Malaysian history and of Portuguese colonialization, contemporary Malaysian politics or the place of minority groups in majority cultures. The density of patterning here involves, to this reader at least, less interaction between levels but a number of apparent contradictions in the passage can be interestingly analysed with reference to options taken at different linguistic levels. For example, the lexical items used to refer to the feminine "representatives" *belles* and *lasses* might be linked to questions of the extent to which they represent that community and to the items used of the community itself, that is *community* and *enclave*. The semantic contrasts in the items used to describe their activities *eke* out a living/*rich* heritage, *thriving* past/*fall back* on their heritage/*drop* their *hang up* over history, can be set against the patterning of past and continuous present tenses in the passage to frame the contradiction that this community appears to be being adjured simultaneously to "draw on its rich cultural past" and "drop its hang-up about history". Analysis might be extended to include the kinds of verbal process options used of Dr Mahathir, *launched, said, urged, mooted, assured*, which become progressively contradictory as a set of propositions or to include the stark contrasts in *time* between *ancient* and *a year ago* when the Portuguese were allowed to invest in national Unit trusts. The whole patterning of the passage can then be explored in terms of the ideology of the newspaper, the medium-dependence or non-dependence of the text on the photograph, the use of the headline, the lexical items *bumiputras*, the Malayanization *Medan Portugis* and so on.[5]

4.1. Reading texts: the interested reader

One legitimate and major objection to the nature of the above discussion is that both the role and the relative position of the reader *vis à vis* the text has been underplayed. This has been touched on in the previous subsection and will be developed a little here. One main problem is that of regular agent-deletion in discussions of the reading process and the discussion in this paper is not innocent of such practice. Use of syntax such as: *The text signals that ...* or *The text can be read as representing* or *The semantic patterning here reinforces* requires to be exposed, because it is readers (not texts) who are performing these activities. And it is important not to forget that all readers will be located in a particular social, political and historical environment.

The study of the reader and the reading process is now in the forefront of research in a number of disciplines. But a number of unanswered questions do need to be highlighted. For example: to what extent do all readers perform the same kinds of operation when they read?; are different competences required at different points in the reading process and do they differ from one to another and, if so, in what ways? (see here Bennett 1983); do the same processes apply to non-verbal media such as film, television, radio, etc.? (see MacCabe 1984); to what extent might the kind of attention readers bring to a text depend on the social, cultural or material functional position they adopt or are *taught* to adopt (often institutionally, that is in schools and colleges) when encountering such a text? The attention brought to bear on a text can, as I hope to have illustrated in Section 4.0, depend on the reader's own *interests* and this can be further underlined by the kind of interpretive *attention* brought to bear by "readers" on such texts as suicide notes, statements by politicians during elections or during times of crisis or even on the comment *No comment*. Such scrutiny can, of course, lead to overinterpretation and there is never a reliable way in which the intentions of the sender of a message can be "read". The point to underline here is that semantic densities and re-readings are activated by readers and that readers are interested parties willing, in certain sociolinguistic circumstances, to do interpretive work on all kinds of discourses if it appears contextually appropriate for them to do so.

This conclusion leads to the much-debated area of the ways in which "literature" and its interpretation exists ideologically, as it were, by courtesy of communities of socio-culturally and sociolinguistically situated readers with common interests (see Bennett 1983; Eagleton 1983; Fish 1980; Carter 1985) and to the question of the extent to which Barthes' statement that "Literature is what gets taught" (and, by extension, literary language is what gets taught as literary language) is appropriate or not. It certainly requires recognition of the ideology of the writer of this paper as middle-class, middle-aged, white, W. European, Anglo-Saxon, male, tenured University teacher writing in the 1980s but taught within the institutional boundaries of English studies in the 1960s. Differently positioned readers may well frame different answers to questions concerning the nature of literary language.

5. Integrating language and literature: pedagogical consequences

Discussion of the pedagogical consequences of the notion of clines of literariness in language requires a separate paper. But it can be briefly recorded here that studying texts along clines can serve to free texts from the kinds of institutional labels which can be all too frequently assigned to them and serve to release readers from the constraints of narrowly aesthetic consideration into more regular encounter with broader, discursive issues of moral, social and aesthetic import and with the role of language in the mediation of such issues.[6] This would be the beginning of a sociolinguistic theory of discourse which would have far-reaching consequences for literature and language study, both in contexts where no integration between these domains takes place and in contexts where the integration results in a narrowly "literary" stylistics based on canonical texts. In addition, reading and interpretation could become more inclusive operations and may even be sharpened by the resulting exposure to a range of juxtaposed discourses. Far from demeaning literature and reducing appreciation of literary language use, such a study would only lead to an enhanced understanding of and respect for the richness of language in its multiple uses.[7]

6. Conclusion

The questions addressed in this paper have resulted in the posing of further questions; and such questions can only begin to be answered by the integrated study of linguistics with other disciplines such as sociology, literary theory and reading theory in education. It is hoped, however, that a principled basis has been prepared for discussion and analysis of the notion of literariness and that it has been demonstrated that discussion of literary language cannot take place with reference only to text-intrinsic features. Literary language use has to be defined with reference to sociolinguistic theories of discourse and this paper does no more than take a small step in that direction. But in the world of English language and literary studies stylisticians have, for better or for worse, always been those prepared to argue for the need for one small step at a time.

Notes

1. For further discussion, see Werth (1976).
2. See also related discussion in Eagleton (1983: 1-17) and Fish (1980: Ch. 14).
3. For further discussion, see Hasan (1971), de Beaugrande and Dressler (1981: 154-161).
4. See also Fish (1973), Fowler (1982, 1984) and Halliday (1983).
5. Further analysis of this kind of semantic density is exemplified in Fowler *et al.* (1979).
6. See also Stubbs (1982) and Brazil (1983).
7. For further discussion of these issues and of the notion of a compositional and process stylistics based on re-writing by students of texts from one discourse into another, see essays in Brumfit and Carter (eds.) (1986) as well as Brazil (1983) and Fowler (1984).

Coherence in language and culture

Benjamin N. Colby

Halliday and Hasan (1976: 4) have used "cohesion" to refer to "relations of meaning that exist within the text, and that define it as a text". However, "cohesion" and the nearly synonymous term "coherence" have been used by others more broadly, extending beyond the notion of a text or even of interpersonal communication. Since the time of Durkheim, social scientists have used "cohesion" to indicate the unitary quality of a society or collectivity, or the attraction that a group has for its members. Recently, "coherence" has come into personality characterization as well. Aaron Antonovsky (1979) speaks of coherence as a sense or feeling that individuals have about themselves and their lives. Is there any connection between these instances of coherence and the cohesion of a well-formed text?

This question can be given a little more direction by considering the process of language acquisition. The child begins with a set of semantic systems or microparadigms associated with specific social contexts. In Halliday's view, these microparadigms, at first insulated from each other, combine and are reinterpreted and generalized as the child moves toward an adult language system. Clearly, there are cognitive predilections that guide the child along this path, not the least of which would certainly be some kind of demand for coherence. This would not be limited to grammatical or lexical coherence in texts but would necessarily extend to semantic coordinations with immediate wants and needs, including simply the wish to comment on the passing scene, to express oneself in such a way as to be understood and responded to by others. A child's utterances are but the observed tip of a submerged complex of cognitive systems. Along with verbal expression the child learns about the world (s)he lives in, the roles (s)he must understand, and the beliefs, values, and interpretations of those (s)he interacts with. It would not be surprising if these wider cultural processes became increasingly integrated in the course of maturation just as a child's microparadigms in language merge into adult linguistic systems. If, as seems clear, "coherence" is important for these processes, what does it involve? Can we develop a systematic approach to it that can be linked to the "cohesion" that exists at the level of texts?

We know now that people remember neither the syntax nor the semantics (narrowly conceived) of what they read or hear. Rather, what they retain is representations at some deeper level. While these representations are neither semantic in the sense of direct lexemic correspondences, nor representations of what precedes late lexicalizations (Watt 1973), they may be "semantic" in the sense used by Halliday and Hasan who say that a text as a semantic unit does not consist of sentences but is realized or encoded in sentences (1976: 2). Before being encoded in sentences, representations must be incorporated into some kind of cognitive schema that models or preforms the relationships and situation to be expressed. One way of examining how this might take place is to study how people use metaphors to model more abstract, hazy, or inchoate ideas. Another is to study how people conduct conversations. Yet another is to analyze extended discourse, particularly narrative. The predication or mapping of metaphors in linguistic expression, the maintenance of topics across turns in conversation, and the linking of topics across sequences of events in a narrative are all different ways of achieving coherence in communicative situations. Communicative coherence allows people to make assumptions, to interpret elliptical statements, to make implicatures, and to arrive at tacit understandings — in short, to predict and understand on the basis of shared experience. From these communicative processes seen at a deeper level it is but a small step to noncommunicative coherence, either social or personal. We can begin, then, by considering different kinds of communicative coherence where extensive analysis and discussion already exist. Then we can move on to consider broader and deeper kinds of cognitive integration.

The cohesion created when sentences are brought together in a text is of five basic kinds: reference, substitution, ellipsis, conjunction, and lexical (Halliday and Hasan 1976). These are what Halliday and Hasan call nonstructured text-forming relations. They do not include those aspects of coherence sometimes discussed at the level of paragraphs or larger segments of a text as topic relevance, effective arrangement of ideas, and inclusiveness. Nor do they include other kinds of text processing involving mnemonic devices, formulaic expressions, and hierarchical embedding that facilitate the production of oral discourse, as in epic singing (Lord 1965) or the forming of eidochronic sequences (the coded events generated by a story grammar, see Propp 1968 and Colby 1973). The kinds of cohesion that operate in these broader kinds of text processes can be seen as a series of ties. But in addition they relate to what might be called structural coherence as described by Lakoff and Johnson (1980: 81) for metaphoric predication and which might be extended to other semiotic processes as well. According to Lakoff and Johnson, a set of experiences is coherent by virtue of having a structure. For example, the concept of a two-party conversation has six structural dimensions: participants, parts, stages, linear sequence, causation, and purpose. A similar dimensional structure exists for war. To represent a conversation as an argument involves the superimposition of part of the structure of war upon the structure of conversation.

Yet another kind of communicative coherence is that of the text in relation to its context and audience. This includes the coherence of text with the register expected for the communication occasion. It also includes coherence of text perspective, which concerns the relationship between the producer, the content, and the audience. To what extent is the producer of a text involved in the events or ideas being expressed, what is the producer's purpose, and what assumptions are made about the audience's understanding of these events? If the purpose is to entertain or provide information rather than persuade, there is pressure to bring the text into harmony with the interests and understandings of the audience. This is illustrated by contrasting genres of history. A written text in the genre of Western history has a very different perspective from other histories, such as Southeast Asian court writings. Western histories attempt to persuade the reader that a particular theory or interpretation is correct. Events are seen as part of a causal chain, one event leading to another, and the author and reader are at a distance from them. This allows political generalities and theories of historical cause to be developed and considered. In Southeast Asian court writings (*hikayat*) Errington (1979) sees no argumentation. The court writings have a different purpose and may seem flat in contrast (Errington 1979). Here the purpose determining the perspective and content is shaped by the communicative occasion and the interests of the parties involved. Another exemplification of this latter type of text/audience coherence is in the epic songs celebrating historical events of ancient Mycenae. These relate battles and wars that grew out of competition for the slave market and trading privileges, but the pressure for text/audience coherence over many generations made the singers feature events that concerned romantic relationships and motivations such as the story of Helen of Troy.

Still part of communicative coherence is the kind of social cohesion that Greg Urban discusses in an analysis of ceremonial dialogues (1986). In ceremonial dialogues the speaker and respondent alternate in turns. The speech is characteristically more rhythmic and structured than casual conversation. Urban argues convincingly that a major function of the dialogue is to maintain or build social cohesion. The dialogues are metacommunicative models that concern one or more of three types of solidarity: shared tradition, exchange of material items and/or women, and balance of power. The last of these might be characterized as establishing or acknowledging relationships of social power or affirming the existing pecking order so as to reduce any anxiety and danger that may arise if threat of change in that order is perceived.

Beyond the social coherence of metacommunication is a realm in which the individual's quest for coherence, meaning, and relevance, moves into deep psychocultural relationships. Here coherence is a harmonious linkage of life goals to plans, agendas, and ideologies. As one moves from the communicative to this wider cultural realm, analytical understanding of cohesion becomes yet more elusive. However, one of the most interesting recent findings is the empirical one by Antonovsky (1979) relating a sense of coherence among individuals to physical well-being. Those who score high on Antonovsky's measure of sense of coherence tend to be physically healthier than those who have lower scores (Antonovsky 1979).

The sense of coherence in which Antonovsky is interested involves a view of the world as (1) comprehensible (ordered, consistent, clear, and, hence, predictable), (2) manageable, (3) meaningful, and (4) positive (problems and difficulties being seen as challenges rather than as burdens). A large part of this sense of coherence is of the same general order as that which people seek to derive from religion. Indeed, religion might be defined as an attempt to satisfy or give expression to the need for coherence.

Some of the ways in which coherence is effected in religion have been described by James Fernandez (1982) in an account of the Bwiti cult among the Fang of West Africa. This cult, which interdigitates new cultural patterns with traditional ones, makes it possible for members to revitalize and reconstruct their view of the world and of their place in it through ritual participation. In the words of a cult leader, Bwiti "ties the world together" (Fernandez 1982: 533). In their coordinated activities Bwiti members are exposed to organizing semiotics and cultural models that are sufficiently rich in meaning — multivocal — to allow each member to construct his or her own special version of a Bwiti system, a version nevertheless channelled by an overarching architectonic in coordination with the ritual sequence. As Fernandez explains it: "For many members there is a pleasure in the invention and handing about of symbols — various substances or objects that have a place in the religious interaction and, while fulfilling a function, bring into association other domains and levels of experience" (1982: 534).

The eating of manioc and peanuts at the morning meal exemplifies how these relationships are tied together. Manioc stands for the members' own bodies after being purified by water and the heat of worship; peanuts stand for the discarding of the external body that the Bwiti experience is supposed to allow its devotees. Among cultural models serving the same general purpose is the *ngombi* harp, which represents a female deity (the support post representing her backbone, the keys her ribs, the strings her sinews, and so on). But this model also represents the cult chapel. Further, it is carved out of two sacred trees. Trees, in turn, can be used to create a quality space involving different metaphoric domains and levels of experience. Thus objects of ritual interaction link and reconcile different domains and levels of experience in a "knitting together" (1982: 539).

Coherence is also built through the use in sermons of eleven recurrent themes that Fernandez calls "preoccupying problems or troubles". This effect is enhanced by a simple structure of movement in sermons from undesirable to desirable quality states. A well-formed sermon, according to Fernandez, addresses these thematic preoccupations, plays with elementary images in them, transforming them into more complex ones, and identifies the essential inchoate subjects of Bwiti ritual through metaphoric predictions which are then reconciled. Further, a well-formed sermon uses apt multivocal images that link or resonate with one of five planes or levels of experience: subsistence, family, sociopolitical, ritual, and physiological.

In sum, through the use of rituals, sermons, and other interactions, the Bwiti religion helps individuals shape a more coherent world view and self-image. This is a process of change or healing in a world that has been rent asunder by exploitive agents of the colonial world, witches, sorcerers, and the unsettling influences of modernity.

Our experiences are continually being compared and classified as structural arrangements in space and structured sequences through time. These arrangements and sequences recur with different degrees of variation. At one extreme, experience is coded into formulae and behaviours and rituals standardized as "scripts". Here coherence might be equated with predictability through habit or routine. At the other extreme are the variable arrangements and sequences that result from language use or creative activities and are generated from large combinatorial systems or grammars. Coherence here is more a matter of subjecting variation to a system. Again, the analogy here is with Halliday's theory of the child's progress from early discrete formulations of language systems to something like the highly interrelated systems used by adults. Somewhere in the middle of these two extremes — relatively invariant scripts at one end and infinite combinatorial sequences and arrangements at the other — is the kind of coherence that comes from metaphoric predication.

These various conceptions of coherence in culture and language point to two shared characteristics of coherence-building processes: (1) the establishment of continuity or sameness across conceptual boundaries (including those of sequence) and (2) explicit recognition (the indication) that conceptual boundaries are being crossed.

To describe and classify processes of coherence building, therefore requires a map of the kinds of domains, levels, and systems that are involved.

We can return to the recent work by Lakoff and Johnson (1980) on metaphor for the beginnings of such a map. Lakoff and Johnson (p.17) speak of basic or natural kinds of experience as being cognitively organized in gestalts that arise out of three areas of human concern: (1) our interactions with our physical environment (moving, manipulating objects, eating, etc.); (2) our interactions with other people within our culture (in terms of social, political, economic, and religious institutions); and (3) our bodies (perceptual and motor apparatus, mental capacities, emotional make-up, etc.). If the last of these areas of concern is seen as extending from sensory perception and movement through emotional responses and simple thought to general self-conceptualization and interpretive experience, Lakoff and Johnson's scheme corresponds to one derived from evolutionary theory for a theory of adaptive potential (Colby 1981, 1986, n.d.), in which the three broad areas of human concern are the ecological, the interpersonal, and the interpretive. These areas correspond, in turn, to Halliday's threefold classification of ideational, interpersonal, and textual systems.

There is something natural about these categories, which continually appear in a great variety of formulations, not the least fruitful of which is Malinowski's (1960) notion of three major developments in human evolution: the use of tools in human activities in the physical environment, the development of interpersonal relationships or bonds, and symbolism. Further, when categorizations of coded experience differ from this threefold classification, it is often possible to translate them into it. For example, when Fernandez describes coherence in well-formed sermons of the Bwiti cult, he speaks of five levels of experience running from the physiological through ritual, sociopolitical, family, and subsistence levels. Subsistence fits easily into the ecological category, family and sociopolitical into the interpersonal, and ritual and physiological categories into the interpretive.

If each of these three areas of human concern can be seen as containing levels or layers of abstraction from concrete, direct codings of experience to more abstract kinds of cognitive integration, one can speak of cohesions when these levels are crossed as they are in metaphoric predication. To develop the map further, the levels within the three areas of human concern can be described as constituted of domains of coded experience. Domains on the lower levels are more fundamental than others, being rooted more deeply in the foundational elements of the three areas as postulated by Lakoff and Johnson: our interactions with the material environment; our relations with others; and ourselves as experienced through our bodies.

It is possible, then, to sketch the dim outlines of a cognitive map that will enable us to describe and classify different kinds of coherence. At the lowest level of abstraction we have domains of coded experience that allow us to make metaphoric predications at other levels; Lakoff and Johnson call these natural domains. Then there is organization, still poorly understood, at higher levels of abstraction. Finally, all of this experience can be organized under the three broad areas of human concern, ecological, interpersonal, and interpretive, which map onto Halliday's ideational, interpersonal, and textual systems.

The ecological area has to do with the relationship between the individual and the material world, particularly in terms of procedural knowledge and action. This includes subsistence and work patterns, including the learning of skills that bring greater efficacy in important tasks. Csikszentmihalyi (1975) has shown that learning is ideally experienced as a "flow". If tasks are too difficult, the effort produces anxiety; if they are too easy, the result is boredom. Thus there needs to be a middle-range fit, or coherence, between external demands and internal capabilities.

In the interpersonal area the focus is on coherence of roles, one's own and those of others, in different spheres of life — at home, at work, and in the neighbourhood. First there is coherence among roles in the same general situation of circumstance. People working together or communicating must do so easily — ideally they "mesh" well and cooperate rather than conflict and work at cross- purposes. Second there is the matter of consistency in role behaviour from one time to another. Finally, there are the interpersonal modalities of role behaviour (Colby 1986) and the various ways that they can cohere in interaction.

In the interpretive area, the emphasis is to link views of the world to notions of the self through a set of values. Conflict here may dissipate energy that might otherwise be used to overcome obstacles, engage with problems, and even create new forms. Finally, a coherent view of the world and one's place in it — identifying with and accepting the world one lives in — maximizes the fit of an individual in his niche. This is the kind of coherence that Antonovsky sees correlating with physical health.

The higher the level of abstraction and the farther from a communicative situation one works in, the more elusive and problematic the notion of coherence becomes. Yet it is precisely in these more difficult regions of cognitive processing that we touch on matters of greatest importance, for example, matters of life and death as shaped by the kinds of lives we lead and the kinds of political systems and societies in which we participate.

Antonovsky suggests that coherence is independent of morality or ethics. What made the Nazi system work, for example, was the enthusiasm of the people for it, and this enthusiasm appears to have stemmed very largely from a sense of coherence brought to them by skilful, state-organized propaganda. Nazism brought in myths and rituals to create an emotional basis for a reinterpretation of the world in which racism played a central role. The spotlighted night rallies, the theatrics, the martial music, and the pseudo-religious ritualization and aestheticization of politics in Nazi Germany produced a sense of coherence and purpose in a great number of Germans. Riefenstahl's films, which portrayed the pomp and the enthusiasm of the crowds, highlighted Hitler's charisma and themselves contributed substantially to the process.

Nazi propaganda worked toward making individuals feel part of a superior race with a utopian future. Harmony was the goal, with everything in its functional place. Emphasis on the beauty of nature meant that the weak and ugly did not deserve to exist. According to Bernt Hagtvet, Nazi ritual became a means of deifying social structures, giving them a new legitimacy without requiring of them any fundamental change. Unlike the Marxians, who aimed at demystifying the world, the Nazis turned farmers into "blood nobility, the salvation of the nation" (Hagtvet 1984: 10). Each enthusiastic individual saw himself as having a meaningful place within the system. Everyone was incorporated into a hierarchical organic order with an aestheticized sense of community — in short, a highly coherent psychopolitical system.

The sense of coherence developed by the Nazis placed Jews and others beyond the pale; it applied only to what was described as the Aryan race. Social coherence, then, can be limited to a particular local setting, ethnic group, tribe, or nation. The wider the area bounded, the more diverse the cultural patterns that have to be included, and coherence in the face of diversity requires more cognitive effort. While Antonovsky may have been essentially correct about the amoral aspect of coherence, he spoke of coherence in the absence of scope. Once scope is included, coherence takes on a different aspect. Coherence across the boundaries of individual subcultures that go beyond tightly controlled political systems has profound moral significance. Among other things a more inclusive coherence would necessarily have a higher level of social perspective (Kohlberg 1983). Scope is thus a critical factor that should not be overlooked in analyses of coherence.

Another factor of special importance at this high level is the matter of cohesive *process*. The Quran, for example, may be seen as providing coherence to traditional Muslim cultural systems, but the emphasis has always been on rote learning, recitation, and literal, unambiguous truth, a far cry from the hermeneutic thinking that Geertz writes about (1983). The coherence provided by the Quran is not part of a constructed process for the individual as among the participants in Fernandez's Bwiti. It is absorbed lock, stock and barrel with little room for creative variation. From these considerations it looks as though coherence at more abstract levels of human concern must be considered in conjunction with creative processes as well as scope if it is to have useful consequences for a systemic understanding.

The notion of coherence, then, can be broadly applied. It would appear that its earliest expression is in the child's effort to master the language of his or her adult world. This can go beyond the quest for systemic competence to the most elemental linkage of microanalysis, that between the sign and what it signifies. It can also extend in the other direction to matters of ideology, politics, religion, and philosophy. At both micro- and macro-levels, the similarities of the coherence-building processes are such as to suggest the possibility of the same underlying motivations in both semiotics and non-communicative thought.

Semiotics of document design

Mary Ann Eiler

This paper represents research in progress that has resulted from working with statistically oriented texts, specifically texts of demographic data. It also represents inquiry into processes of genre development itself, where the primary field comprises arithmetic data and where the realization of that field in a secondary field or meta-text incorporates significant visualization through tabular and graphic design as well as written language — in short, through verbal and "visible" language. The attempt to study such texts (and genres) or to develop a theoretical construct for the properties of such genres in my research is based on the concept of register theory as delineated historically by Halliday (1964: 129-130) and Hasan (1973). The experiential, ideational, and textual components of Halliday's linguistic theory (e.g. field, tenor, and mode) are explored in the context of a semiotic that we might call *document design*, with parallels to be found in Halliday (1977).

Our research revolved around the major question of what constitutes the generic structure of a document of statistical data. Halliday understands generic structure as "the form that a text has as a property of its genre". As he explains, "the generic structure is outside the linguistic system; it is language as the projection of a higher-level semiotic structure. It is not simply a feature of literary genres; there is a generic structure in all discourse ..." (1977: 193). The structure of narrative genre has been widely studied from both literary and linguistic perspectives. In my own earlier research, as part of a larger study of student writers' responses to literature, I analyzed the generic structure of meta-texts where narrative fiction was the primary or informing field. The findings at several points suggested that, at least for developmental writing, the meta-language of literary analysis often accounted for the structure of the students' analytic essays (Eiler 1979).

That is to say, not only does narrative typology define the structure, let us say, of a short story, but in the study was also seen to direct choices within the processes of narrative analysis that students used to write about their short stories. With statistical texts, the relation of a meta-text to genre and the entailment of composing processes also requires the formulation of a specific text/genre-heuristic. This heuristic, however, may be derived from the types of inquiries Hasan (1984a) makes in the context of her preliminary work on the nursery tale as genre. As Hasan has later explained of her questions on the nursery tale "... my work has led me to conclude that they apply *mutatis mutandis* ... to text typology as a whole" (1984b: 96).

The application, then, of Hasan's inquiries to statistical data texts may be seen to include questions like the following: What counts as a statistical text? Is there a canonical form for statistical texts? What obligatory and optional properties adhere in a text of statistical data as an instance of statistical genre? To these inquiries might be added yet another: How do theories of document design contribute to determining the generic structure of statistical texts?

To address these questions systematically, this paper is divided into the four following discussions:
1. data, story, and texture in visible and verbal language;
2. contextual configuration for an instance of statistical text;
3. data reduction strategies, design, and sublanguage;
4. verbal and visible language and semiotic structure of situation.

These discussions are not intended as definitive but rather as background for the development of a formal theory that will study features of such texts through extensive empirical research. Such endeavours will need to include field testing of documents for levels of usability as well as draw upon related research not only in linguistics but in cognitive psychology, human pattern recognition, neuropsychology, and communication engineering (Kolers *et al.* 1980).

Data, story, and texture

"Texture" may be defined as the verbal and visual expression of data according to use in a context of situation. There are three separate but intersecting understandings of texture in a text of statistical data: (1) the texture of written text as verbal language; (2) the texture variation that derives from the characteristics and properties of the retinal variables in the graphics system; and (3) texture understood as pattern. The first is based on Halliday's understanding of text as a semantic unit defined by the textual component of the grammar — "the way the language hangs together, the 'texture' "(Halliday 1978: 223). The second derives from image theory in the graphics system. Bertin (1983) draws a rigorous distinction between this sense of texture (*grain* in French) and pattern (*texture* in French). Differences in texture understood as *grain* are not differences in elementary shapes. If elementary shapes are different, there exists, according to Bertin, a difference in pattern or *texture*. "Texture" in the sense used in this paper embraces (1) linguistic texture in the Halliday sense, (2) variations in retinal variables and (3) pattern. One might refer to a MACROTEXTURE realized through an integration of written text and graphics as exists in a text of statistical data.

When we relate the macro understanding of texture to register — variation according to use — we enter also the dimension of *story*. Hasan's (1984a) observation that "It is somewhat disturbing to find the term *story* equated with narrative", has implications for meanings implicit in the structure of numerical sets and subsets conceived as a dimension of register variety. Hasan (1984a) argues that the equating of story with narrative "is disturbing because, even without such an equation, the term *story* is wide enough to refer to a range of discourse types which differ markedly from each other in their structure". One of these discourse types might be seen to include numerical data as "story" as has been described in methodologies for choice of graphic design. White endorses an expansion of ideas inherent in statistics through forms that give them natural expression — "the shape should grow organically out of the story" (White 1984: 144).

The "texture" in a story of statistical data can be seen to exist in arrangements predicated on choices that include numbers and words: the first through the components of visible language — charts, graphs, diagrams, tables — and the second through verbal language at rank levels of word, group, sentence, paragraph, and discourse. Halliday's concept of linguistic texture in written text and the texture in graphic design discussed earlier represent the foundation for a basic heuristic to study statistical data texts. As such this heuristic can be tentatively charted in the following separate but related sets of inquiries:

Texture in Textual Display	what are the linguistic features of a text of statistical data?

| | . what governs choice of expression?
| | . what are the options in expression?
| | . what makes one set of expressions more acceptable? or superior to another?
| | . how can the stories implicit in numerical data be told?
| Texture in Visual Display | . how can data stories be optimally visualized and patterned?
| | . how can data be presented in meaningful summaries so as to tell "their" stories?
| | . how should theories of data graphics influence or govern choices of "visible" language?

Having asked these questions, one can begin to plot a theoretical construct as the first step in the development of a working heuristic for an instance of text in the register "statistical data story".

Contextual configuration for statistical text

Field, tenor, and mode as constituents of a generic context of situation are displayed in Figure 1. Field, tenor, and mode as specified for an instance of text in the register "statistical story" are presented in Figure 2. While Figure 1 schematizes a generic context of situation with general applicability for register theory with decisions proceeding from left to right but in the process of text creation occurring concurrently, Figure 2 looks at a specific register variety, that of a demographic statistical text. Figure 2 also explicitly contends that the components of the context of situation apply in decisions for both project and document design. That is to say, the design of the project itself significantly governs the design of the final text document. This point is one that is made over and over by statistical editors who confront researchers with statistical gaps, missing data, and other fragmented results often because the project plan was deficient in its anticipation of the final report.

Figure 1 asks the question: "How do data drive document design?" Data here might apply to any information source, as indicated above. In the case of the statistical demographic text, data explicitly relate to numbers and the implicit story structure in sets and subsets. For heuristic purposes, we might posit a rough analogue to linguistic syntax and discourse as is suggested in Figure 2 for field. That is to say, we might ask: "How can numbers be used 'like' words to tell a story?" If we also include mode, we can

SEMIOTICS OF DOCUMENT DESIGN 465

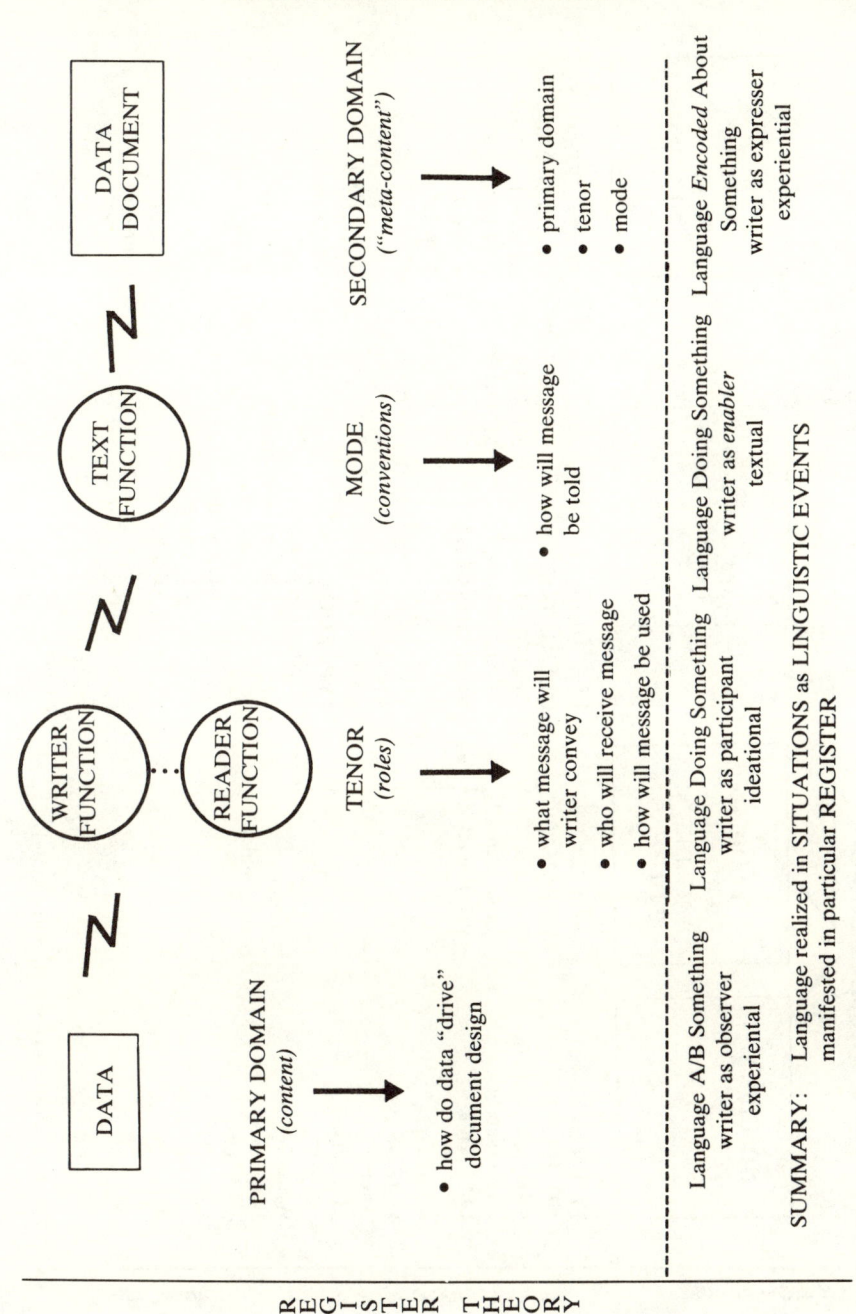

DATA	WRITER FUNCTION ···· READER FUNCTION	TEXT FUNCTION		DATA DOCUMENT
PRIMARY DOMAIN *(content)*	TENOR *(roles)*	MODE *(conventions)*	SECONDARY DOMAIN *("meta-content")*	
• how do data "drive" document design	• what message will writer convey • who will receive message • how will message be used	• how will message be told	• primary domain • tenor • mode	
Language A/B Something writer as observer experiential	Language Doing Something writer as participant ideational	Language Doing Something writer as enabler textual	Language *Encoded* About Something writer as expresser experiential	

SUMMARY: Language realized in SITUATIONS as LINGUISTIC EVENTS manifested in particular REGISTER

Figure 1. Context of situation

REGISTER THEORY

466 MARY ANN EILER

PROJECT DESIGN → **DOCUMENT DESIGN**

```
DOMAIN^(2)                    MODE =                      DOMAIN^(1)
TEXT OF        TENOR =        CONVENTIONS                 DATA =
STATISTICAL    WRITER =       X, Y, Z                     NUMBERS
DATA           READER =
               EDITOR =
```

MODE → DESIGN OF MESSAGE, MEDIUM

FEATURES: *FEATURES:*   *FEATURES:*
NUMBERS   FORMAL?   OBLIGATORY ⎫
• implicit structure,   DISTANT?   OPTIONAL   ⎬ REALIZED BY:
  sets, subsets   *authoritative?*   EVALUATIVE ⎭   RELATIONSHIPS,
LINEAR   *significant?*   **HIERARCHICAL** PATTERNS IN DATA
                                                                     • visual
ANALOG (?)   ANALOG (?)   • verbal
WORDS   NARRATIVE (?)
"syntax"   **TYPOLOGY** *EXPLICIT*
"discourse"   TONE — polemic   macro-structure
                                                         descriptive/analytic
                                                         explanatory   *ANALOG*
                                                         existential   *STORY*
                                                         heuristic
                                                         definitive

Writer as   writer as   writer as   story *as*
experiencer,   story-teller   enabler   written
observer

Figure 2. Context of situation (revisited)
```
R E G I S T E R
S T A T I S T I C A L
S T O R Y
```

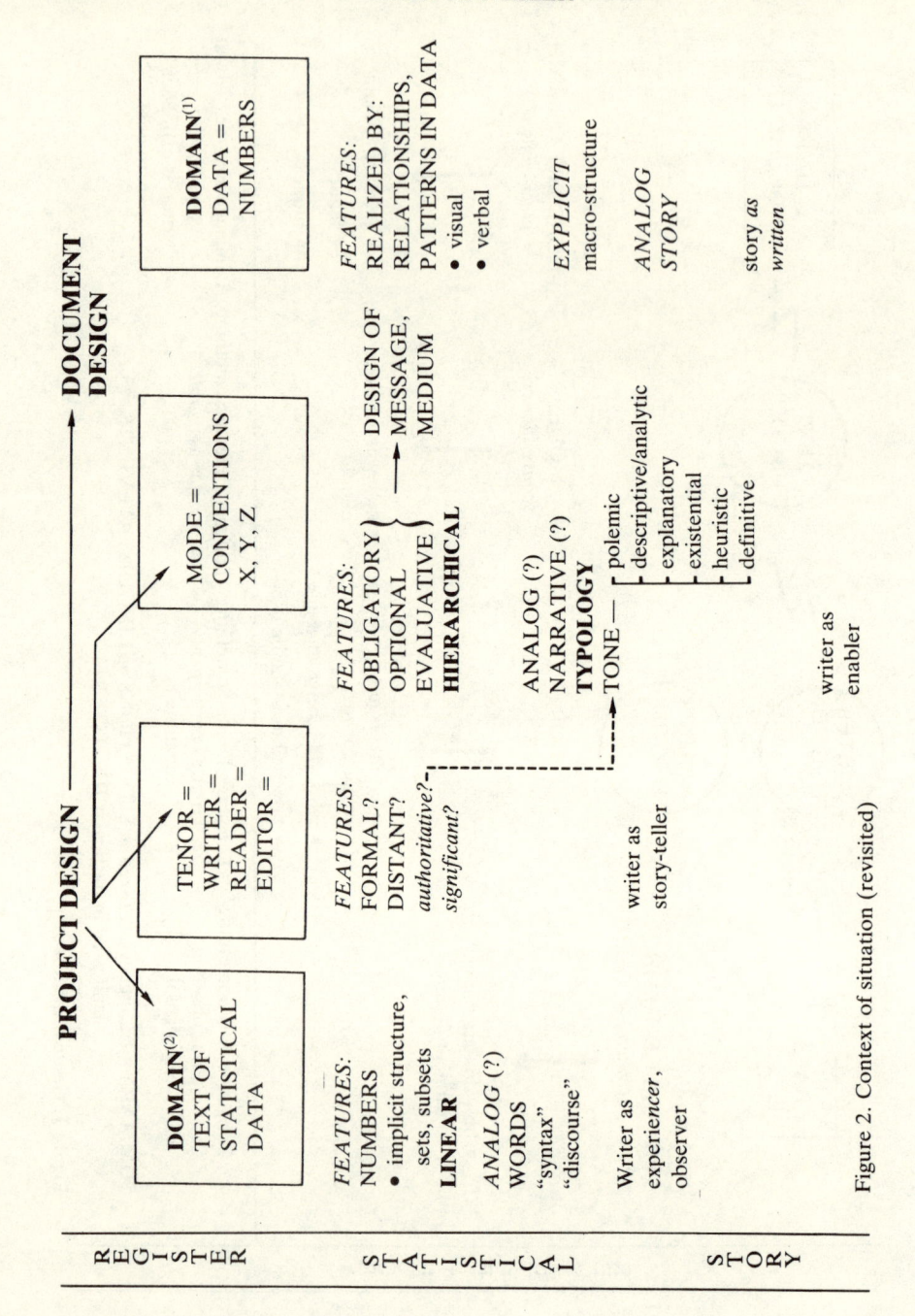

ask: "How can numbers be used with words to tell the story?" At the macro level we might further ask: "How do large quantities of statistical data affect both verbal and visible display of story?" and "What is the nature of the linguistic and non-linguistic configuration in the final document?"

The statistical story implicit in Figure 2 also represents a theoretical framework for a document on physical demographics (from the design of the project to the document itself). The document specifically referred to in this paper consisted of detailed, aggregated data tables on physician professional characteristics and distribution, written text, summary tabulations, and graphics. The primary field was mathematics itself, expressed in absolute counts and percentages and potentially in statistical formulae such as we might find in procedures to arrive at an arithmetic mean. Thus, the primary field may be viewed as constituting experientially implicit meaning in numerical sets and subsets while the secondary or meta-field may be viewed as giving explicit meaning to the primary field through the use of natural language and a variety of graphic displays. The interpersonal meaning may be viewed as tenor values, consisting of both personal and social communicative role relationships between participants in the discourse event.

The tenor values for the text on physician demographics may be further defined as adhering between in-house writers and editors and external audience comprised of physicians, policy analysts, and researchers. These values can be further described as *formal* rather than *informal*, the latter applying in a casual exchange between colleagues rather than in a scholarly document (Benson & Greaves 1973: 99-128). These values were also *functional* in that they corresponded specifically to the document's social end, namely to inform and provide a research base for further physician-related statistical studies.

Tenor relationships depicted in Figure 2 are multiple, with the writer/reader or audience relationship warranting further explication. This explication can be correlated to a series of inquiries modelled on those suggested in studies of document design (Felkner (ed.) 1980: 27):

- who is the audience (more than one?)?
- what does the audience(s) want to know?
- what does the audience already know?
- what does the audience need to know?
- what does the audience want to know first?
- how will the audience process the data message?

. how will the audience use the data and the data message?

The values of mode involve questions of canon, rhetorical conventions, and the purpose of the project plan itself. The "search" for a canon in turn relates to Hasan's observations of obligatory and optional properties of genres. A statistical text may be described as *necessarily* comprising relationships between and among numbers, words, syntax, and *optionally* including charts, tables, diagrams, maps, and other visible language markers. This is not to say, however, that a text with only obligatory features will be aesthetically pleasing or indicative of favourable levels of reader usability. Nor will a text that integrates the obligatory and optional features be deemed *de facto* a model instance of the genre. Text evaluation in the sense of an optimal representation includes the optional and obligatory in a mix whose features include validity, reliability, aestheticism, usability, among other properties. Another way of referring to this mix is to talk in terms of the explicit features of a document's macrostructure — the verbal and visual realization of patterns in the data.

To concretize the above discussion, we might recapture the "real-life" design decisions and considerations from project plan to document that characterized the recent publication on physician characteristics and demographics used as the case study in this paper. These decisions involved the writers, editors, and designers in a heuristic inventory that was conducted for each component of the contextual configuration displayed in Figures 1 and 2.

For mode, the writers asked: "What data stories do we want to tell?" "Will these stories be based on hypotheses, assumptions, issues in the health-care literature, or more simply on descriptive observations inherent in the raw data?" (e.g. women physicians show a percent increase of x,y,z percent). Additional questions included: (1) "What relationship should adhere between project design and final document?" (2) "How should the project be designed to 'best' tell the stories?" and (3) "What, if any, canons, conventions, or theories of design for this register variety are available and should be invoked?"

For primary field the major consideration concerned how type of data suggested or demanded the way in which the stories would be told. For secondary field, the project plan stage was none too early to begin visualizing the final document. The writers and designers asked themselves how they could visualize the document in terms of (1) obligatory features and optional features, (2) the integration of these features in text, and (3) the proportion and focus given to these features in the macrostructure of the final document. The writers also asked questions regarding the state of the art of document design research and how the final product should reflect this research.

For tenor, the inquiries tended to be generic as were those given earlier in this discussion. They included: (1) "What *prior knowledge* does the audience most likely have regarding this physician population?" and (2) "How will audience process the document?" Finally, design was predicated on (3) "How will the document be used?" That is to say, will the document constitute a reference source or is it more likely that it will be read "cover-to-cover"?

The writers determined that the project plan, and by extension, the secondary field (or final document) would focus on a DATA STORY involving the professional characteristics (specialty, activity, sex, age, etc.) and geographic distributions of foreign medical graduates in the U.S. The tone would be primarily descriptive and analytic (rather than polemic). Data would be presented in a hierarchically ordered text with obligatory and optional properties. Based on the tenor value regarding what the reader wants to know, text would address issues like (1) the proportionate increases and supply requirements of physicians in a time series, (2) the patterns of residency training, and (3) physician-population comparisons. The foreign medical graduate population would be more discretely defined by the citizenship variable into two major categories: foreign national foreign medical graduates and U.S. citizen foreign medical graduates. This latter decision was motivated by growing audience interest in the training and dispersion of U.S. citizen foreign medical graduates as was suggested in a variety of physician forums and in the literature. Thus, these decisions constituted the first of the design maxims: ISSUES GOVERN CHOICE OF DATA VARIABLES.

The second maxim, also issue-oriented, had even more direct design implications. Since the literature suggested a growing interest in the effect U.S. foreign medical graduates were or were not having on residency training programs, the writers decided to include selected variables (e.g. country of graduation) in cross-tabulations for foreign nationals, U.S. citizen foreign medical graduates, and graduates of U.S. medical schools so as to invite comparisons at even lower levels of delicacy in population categories, and to do so for given trend years. This decision motivated cross-tabulations in a time series that would yield data like state-of-residency by state-

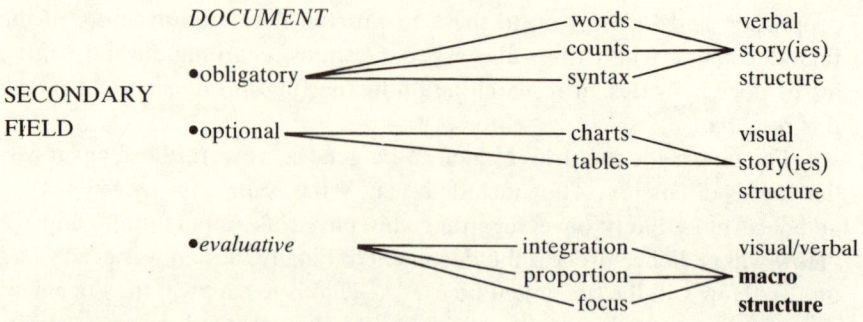

```
                          DOCUMENT         ┌── words ──┐     verbal
                                           ├── counts ─┼──▶ story(ies)
SECONDARY       •obligatory ──────────────┤── syntax ─┘     structure
FIELD
                •optional ─────────────────┬── charts ─┐     visual
                                           └── tables ─┴──▶ story(ies)
                                                            structure

                •evaluative ◀──────────────┬── integration ─┐  visual/verbal
                                           ├── proportion ──┼─▶ **macro**
                                           └── focus ───────┘  **structure**
```

Figure 3. Properties of statistical data texts

of-practice and country of graduation. This decision constituted the second design maxim: ISSUES GOVERN DESIGN OF DATA VARIABLES.

It was also determined that some data characteristics posed real constraints in display. For example, to plot a tabulation with over 100 countries of graduation by more than 80 specialty categories by 50 states would prove unwieldy and taxing for reader usability. Thus, further selection was warranted, which in turn underscored the third design maxim: DATA CHARACTERISTICS GOVERN DISPLAY. Conventions for statistical data reporting included absolute counts, row and column percentages in tabular designs, as well as percent changes, line graphs for time series, bar charts for population and other variable comparisons, and so forth. To summarize, the resulting document or secondary field would be constituted of the obligatory and optional as well as the evaluative properties suggested in Figure 3.

Figure 3 reveals the final and global design maxim: VISUAL AND VERBAL DISPLAY GOVERNS DOCUMENT MACROSTRUCTURE.

At the micro level were remaining texture considerations as they applied to text and graphics. These texture considerations are treated in the next section in the discussion of data reduction strategies, table and graphic design, and sublanguage features and constraints.

Data reduction, sublanguage, graphics

Texture at the level of graphics and tabular design incorporates what Wright calls "user-friendliness". The use of a table, Wright explains, involves processes like: (1) grasping the logical principles behind the organization of information; (2) locating required information in the table;

(3) interpreting the information once it has been found. Given that there is "no universal optimal table design", the realization of what we are calling tenor values should address, according to Wright, the following recognitions: (1) the reader's ability to specify the question/problem in a way that maps onto the organization of the table; (2) the designer's ability to anticipate the kinds of questions readers will ask; and (3) the designer's ability to select an appropriate format for the answer. As Wright explains, there is "No appropriate alternative to analyzing the user's requirements in detail". She seems also to speak in terms of what the contextual configuration in Figures 1 and 2 displays as field — "the range of meaningful design options will vary with the nature of information presented" (1982: 329).

The topic of table design both in Wright's work and in the literature is, of course, far more complex and much richer than this introductory paper on the semiotics of document design can demonstrate. Empirical research as indicated earlier would need to tap this complexity by considering areas like human memory, redundancy and cognitive processing, and what Wright (1982: 326) tells us is referred to in the research as a "natural" decision structure, for example categorized lists versus alphabetized sequences, and the like.

Although unable to engage in or conduct studies of such research while preparing the physician publication, the writers and designers did incorporate principles of user-friendliness in their tabular designs. One of these points of access was found in data reduction principles as presented by Ehrenberg (1978). Ehrenberg's strategies for analyzing and interpreting statistical data through meaningful summaries, explicit patterns, and conceptual focus correspond to mode values. Proceeding on the principle that "the need is to let the data speak", Ehrenberg (1978) addresses texture by teaching the reader to see patterns and relationships in numerical data and to reduce these patterns to summaries that can be interpreted, used, and communicated. Data handling strategies include initial visual scanning of rows and columns, basic layout, new data and prior knowledge relationships, and empirical generalization (Ehrenberg 1978: 3-56).

The following table designs represent time series displays for data by country of graduation and U.S. citizen status for physicians. For purposes of demonstration, counts are fabricated and countries are represented symbolically (e.g. A, B, C, etc.). Table 1 focuses on trend years while Table 2 focuses on a specific population under study, in this case native born U.S. citizens.

Table 1.

	1980		1985	
Country	NB	NT	NB	NT
A	11	144	15	175
B	166	1,777	243	1,999
C	559	1,633	1,666	1,777
D	6,777	8,888	7,003	9,987
E	44	566	50	635
F	21	38	41	48

	1990		1995	
Country	NB	NT	NB	NT
A	25	225	35	335
B	343	2,888	443	3,888
C	2,654	3,421	3,654	4,444
D	10,987	11,789	11,321	12,987
E	66	777	77	888
F	51	58	61	68

The numerical display in Table 1 obfuscates rather than clarifies patterns and data relationships. The data story in Table 1 is at best obscure, its "texture" lacks cohesion. Table 2, by contrast, illustrates some of Ehrenberg's data reduction principles. Through a rank order of countries responsible for highest absolute counts for the native born population, Table 2 patterns the data so that they are more visible and can be more readily interpreted.

Table 2.

Country	Native Born 1980	1985	1990	1995
D	6,777	7,003	10,987	11,321
C	559	1,666	2,654	3,654
B	166	243	343	443
E	44	50	66	77
A	11	15	25	35
F	21	41	51	61

Table 2, again following Ehrenberg, now makes possible further data reduction strategies so that the data can "tell" their story. Among the possibilities, row averages might be calculated across time for each country to give prominence to those years that fell below or were above the average. These procedures in turn suggest immediate analytic observations for the written "story" in text.

Like document design, the systematic study of sublanguages is in the early stages of development. The term itself is subject to sometimes delicate linguistic distinctions and has been defined in discussions of register. Zwicky and Zwicky view register as involving "an association between a set of linguistic features, the contexts in which these forms appear, and the uses to which the forms are put in these contexts" (1982: 6). For Zwicky and Zwicky, baby talk, newspaper headlines and recipes constitute registers. Recipes, however, in addition to being a register are also a sublanguage, for they, unlike the other varieties, have a corresponding well-defined semantic domain (Zwicky and Zwicky 1982: 6).

For Lehrberger, the properties "which help to characterize a sublanguage" include: (1) limited subject matter; (2) lexical, syntactic and semantic restrictions; (3) "deviant" rules of grammar; (4) high frequency of certain constructions; (5) text structure; and (6) use of special symbols (Lehrberger 1982: 102). The concepts of corresponding semantic domain (whether viewed as register or sublanguage) as well as properties of limited subject matter and high frequency of certain constructions are of particular interest in studying statistical and other texts for constraints in linguistic choice such features represent.

Hiż (1982) speaks to the concern of this paper in his study of the connections between specialized languages. Speaking of verbs like *doubt, suppose, think*, Hiż observes that "Verbs of this class ... are often used in metalanguage of a sublanguage. They do not occur in the theorems of a science (except, of course, in psychology). They indicate that the text is speaking at that moment about the science itself rather than about its subject matter ..." (1982: 209). He makes further distinctions between "rudimentary" and "meta-arithmetic" English sentences. Verbs like *exceeds, divides, results* are rudimentary-arithmetic while *seems* and *proves* are meta-arithmetic.

In writing statistical data texts that constitute a strictly descriptive meta-language, verbs often limit the scope of stylistic variation. Verb strings comprised of entries like *increased, demonstrated, accounted for, revealed*, *presents*, *provides*, *comprised*, as well as the existential BE verb dominate texts of the secondary field. As such they, as well as other properties, require further study and explication as descriptors of genre.

One such study, for example, which was based on a lecture-chapter on quantum behaviour (Eiler 1986) revealed a high incidence of the coordinator *and* in clause and sentence openings, where *and* signified multiple semantic relations, to include *sequence*, *contrast* and *comment* (Eiler 1986: 59). These occurrences were seen as typical of oral discourse and as such provided a heuristic for the lecture foundation of the text.

In the same study the distribution of *but* was interpreted as functionally advancing the progress of the lecture and the process of scientific inquiry as it tests expectations. Instances of *but* that contributed to the advancement of the lecture included examples like "We could, of course, continuously skirt away from the atomic effect *but* we shall instead interpose here a short circuit". The function of *but* contrasting expectations with observations serves well to illustrate procedures of scientific investigation as we see in "Newton thought that light was made up of particles *but* then it was discovered ... that it behaves like a wave" (Eiler 1986: 59). These findings among others in the chapter study corroborate the contention that writers select from among linguistic options given genre constraints of their work and that based on this contention we can make heuristic generalizations regarding text design that reflect writers' choices. Further, sublanguage variety (genre and aspect of genre) can be seen as specific incidents of linguistic choice that, in turn, are correlated with use and function given a context of situation like that delineated earlier in Figures 1 and 2.

As linguistic texture is realized in genre specific ways, graphics may be viewed as data specific in the selection of pattern or shape. Graphics can also contribute to optimal display of data if they focus on data variation rather than design variation (Tufte 1983: 61). To illustrate percent proportions by four world regions of graduation for U.S. citizen physicians over a 10-year period at five year intervals through four pie charts would constitute an essentially flawed design for these types of data. Although the physician universe would be proportionately represented in a pie at each interim (e.g. year 1, year 2, year 3, year 4) the relations between or among the data over time would be obscured. For the illustration of quantitative trends such data would be better illustrated or could more clearly tell their stories through a bar chart where the units (e.g. regions) would have direct visual relationships to each other.

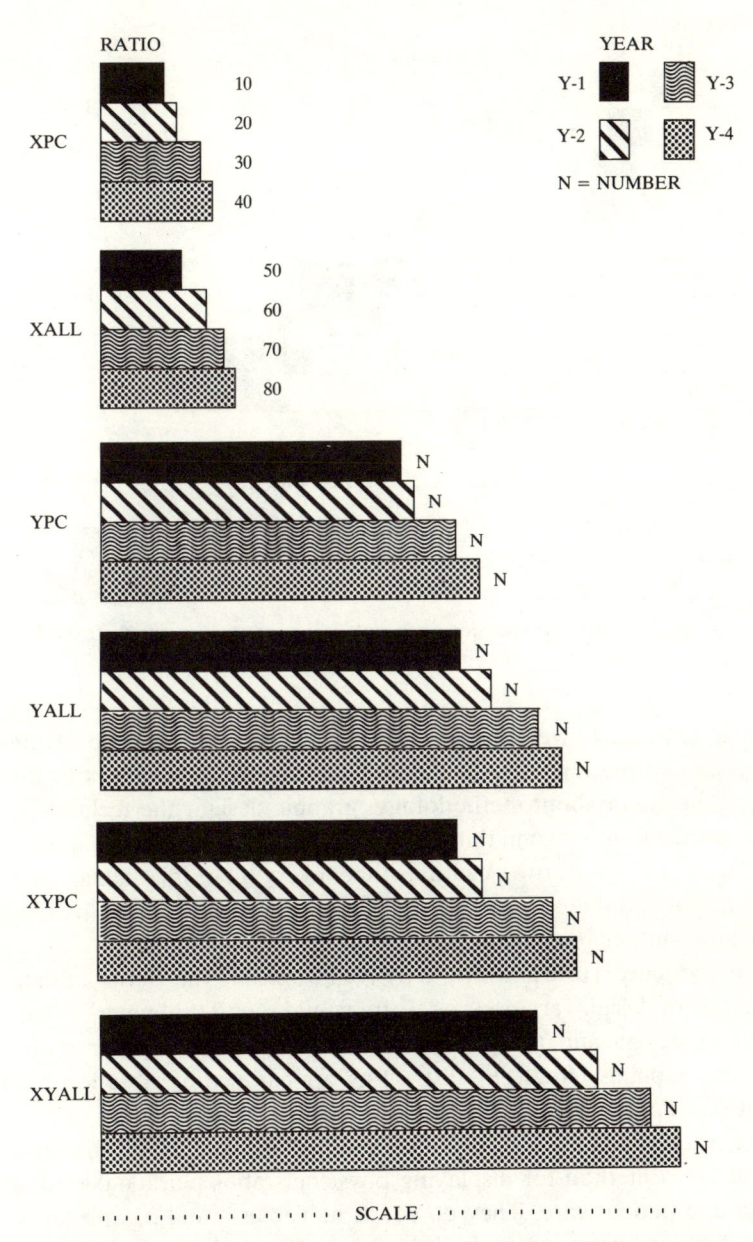

Figure 4. Note: Numerical propertions are not drawn to scale as figure exists for design only.

476   MARY ANN EILER

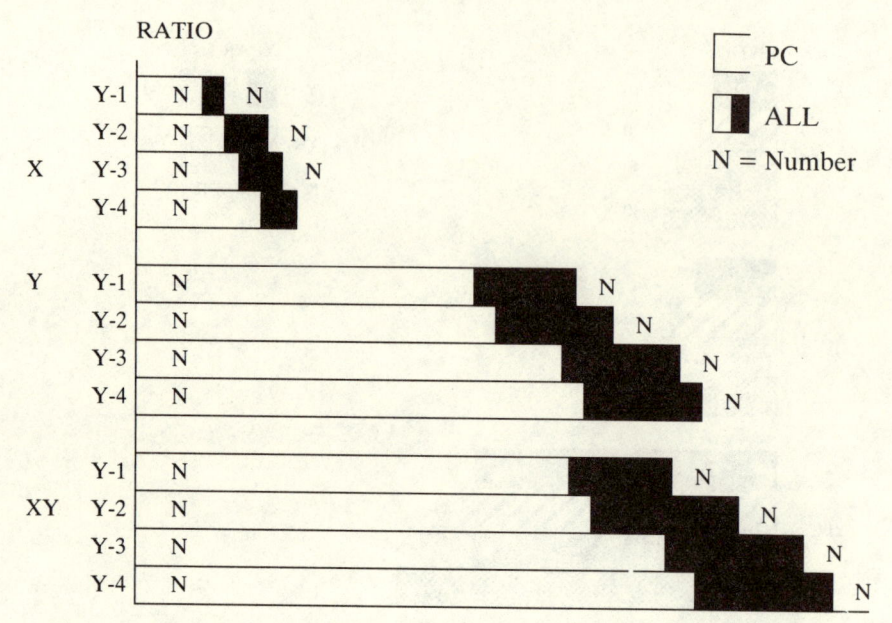

```
            RATIO
                                                  ▭ PC
      Y-1   N    N
      Y-2   N       N                             ▰ ALL
X     Y-3   N        N                            N = Number
      Y-4   N

      Y-1   N                      N
Y     Y-2   N                         N
      Y-3   N                            N
      Y-4   N                              N

      Y-1   N                         N
XY    Y-2   N                            N
      Y-3   N                               N
      Y-4   N                                  N
```

Figure 5. Note: Numerical proportions are not drawn to scale as figure exists for design only.

Graphic texture, however, is not limited to pattern or shape. Tufte (1983) argues that graphics should "induce the viewer to think about the substance rather than about methodology, graphic design, the technology of graphic production, or something else" (Tufte 1983: 13). In his discussion of data-ink ratio he further cautions that "every bit of ink on a graphic requires a reason. And nearly always that reason should be that the ink presents new information" (p.96).

Figure 4 violates Tufte's principle by compromising the clarity of data in the interests of design variation. As Tufte would say, it "shimmers". This interaction of design and the physiological tremor of the eye or moiré effects, Tufte explains, create a "distracting appearance of vibration and movement that makes for bad data graphics" (1983: 107-108).

Figure 5 alleviates these effects by showing the data. Both Figures 4 and 5 illustrate a method for displaying physician ratios per 100,000 total population and patient care. They do so, as in Tables 1 and 2, with fabricated data for demonstration purposes only. In Figure 4, the hypothetical physician group, let us say in patient care (e.g. XPC) is cited separately from the same group in all aspects of medical practice (e.g. XALL). Thus, using bogus counts and bogus groups, Figure 4 tells us that the physician group in patient care numbered 10 per 100,000 population in Year 1, 20 in Year 2, 30 in Year 3, and 40 in Year 4. Similarly, when the total cohort of X physicians are measured, the bogus ratios for each year are 50, 60, 70 and 80, and so on through the groups.

Figure 5 not only eliminates the distracting shimmer and communicative noise but is more economical and cohesive in graphic design and texture through its integration visually of the patient care ratio and that for total population in one bar for each year.

Verbal/visible language and semiotic structure of situation

Tabular and graphic design, as well as sublanguage, are topics of study in themselves beyond the scope and intent of this paper. What this paper proposes is that these topics are not only contributions to a potential theory of document design but that Halliday's linguistic theory can be seen as "accommodating" the linguistic scope of such a theory. Further, this paper suggests that the experiential, ideational, and textual components can, in extension, be seen to theoretically provide a framework for the integration of verbal and visible language. We are positing here the possibility of a grammar of document, a semantics of document. The extension, of course, is a heady matter and one that requires extensive research and formalization. The genre of statistical data texts is extremely complex and evolving, and visible language itself is in the early stage of development, as was discussed earlier. Yet, given these caveats, Halliday's position on the relation between text and environment and the semiotic structure of situation seems to address these dimensions. Halliday (1977), speaking of field, tenor, and mode as the semiotic construct of situation, explains that:

> The patterns of determination that we find between the context of situation and the text are a general characteristic of the whole complex that is formed by a text and its environment ...
> The principle is that each of these elements in the semiotic structure of the situation activates the corresponding component in the semantic system, creating in the process a semantic configuration, a grouping of favoured and foregrounded options from the total meaning potential that is typically associated with the situation type in question.

For Halliday, "This semantic configuration is what we understand by 'register'", while register is, in turn, "the necessary mediating concept that enables us to establish the continuity between a text and its sociosemiotic environment" (Halliday 1977: 203).

Thus, it would appear that when Wright (1980, 1982) lists as a criterion for designing written information such variables as reader characteristics

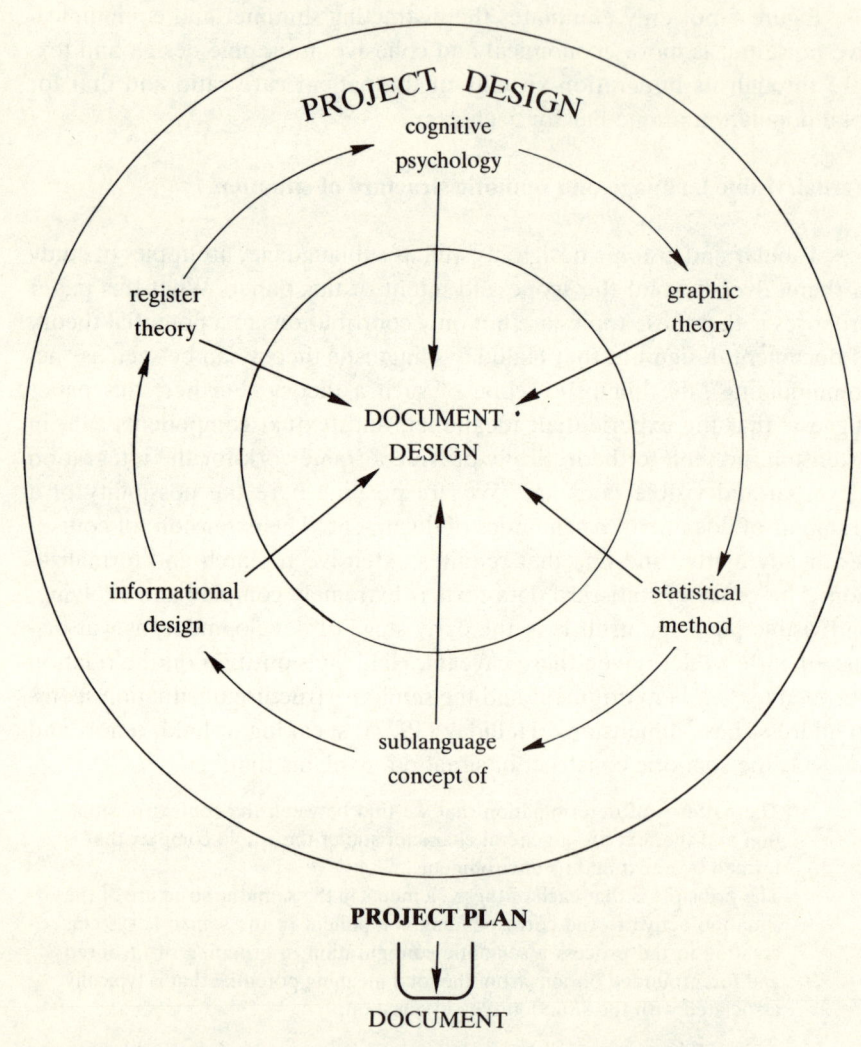

Figure 6. Disciplines contributing to a theory of document design

and purpose, task constraints, and characteristics of text, she is speaking of register in the Halliday sense, and when she observes that the problem is "how to incorporate such disparate factors within a conceptual framework which can be used to guide both design and research" she seemingly is addressing the concept of sociosemiotic environment (1980: 186).

Waller (1980) sounds a similar theme when he discusses typography as decorative and functional and observes that in the absence of formally codified rules "the state of typographic theory is relatively primitive" and that as a consequence, "there is no assurance that writers, or indeed typographers, use typographic options consistently" (1980: 242). What is needed, it appears, is a theory of document *both* as argument *and* as artefact at the same time.

The semiotics of document design require a coherent formal theory. As Wright contends, "The characterization of a text is not complete if only the linguistic structure is considered" (1980: 185). Layout, print type and quality, and other presentational factors must be included. By way of summary, Figure 6 presents the textual and visual display of data in a project design and document design matrix. Based on document design state of the art, Figure 6 recognizes the contribution of a variety of disciplines and reflects the contention that "document design is a multi-disciplinary, integrative undertaking" (Felkner (ed.) 1980: 5). Figure 6 also reflects the contention of this paper that the various disciplines should and must be integrated in the contextual configuration for project design, which in turn suggests the design of the final reporting document.

Notes on critical linguistics

Roger Fowler

When the deadline for this paper approached, I was faced with a dilemma of priority. On the one hand, I wanted to express my appreciation of Halliday's linguistics by writing the paper; on the other hand, I was at that time making swift progress with my book *Language in the News*, a project which Halliday had encouraged. The more substantial tribute would be the book, a work enabled by Halliday's sociosemantic model of language. I have resolved the dilemma by compromise: by writing, quickly and briefly, these notes on some general issues in critical linguistics which were in my mind during the writing of the book.

"Functional linguistics" is "functional" in two senses: it is based on the premise that the form of language responds to the functions of language use; and it assumes that linguistics, as well as language, has different functions, different jobs to do, so the form of linguistics responds to the functions of linguistics. The first paper in *Explorations in the Functions of Language* makes this point about requests for a definition of language: "In a sense the only satisfactory response is 'why do you want to know?', since unless we know what lies beneath the question we cannot hope to answer it in a way which will suit the questioner" (1973: 9). In the interview with Herman Parret, Halliday accepts that there may be an "instrumental linguistics ... the study of language for understanding something else" and that an instrumental linguistics will have characteristics relevant to the purpose for which it is to be used. In doing instrumental linguistics, though, one is also learning about the nature of Language as a whole phenomenon, so there is no conflict or contradiction with "autonomous linguistics" (1978: 36).

"Critical linguistics" emerged form the writing of *Language and Control* (Fowler, Hodge, Kress & Trew 1979) as an instrumental linguistics very much of that description. We formulated an analysis of public discourse, an analysis designed to get at the ideology coded implicitly behind the overt propositions, and to examine it particularly in the context of social formations. The tools for this analysis were an eclectic selection of descriptive categories suited to the purpose: especially those structures identified by Halliday as ideational and interpersonal, of course, but we also drew on other linguistic traditions, as for example when we needed to talk about speech acts or transformations. Our conception of instrumentality or purpose was quite complicated, and perhaps not fully enough discussed in the book. We were concerned to theorize language as a *social practice*, a "practice" in the sense that word has acquired in English adaptations of Althusser: an intervention in the social and economic order, and one which in this case works by the reproduction of (socially originating) ideology (Kress & Hodge 1979). In this way the book was intended as a contribution to a general understanding of language. But why "critical"? Here two models were relevant. It has to be said (and I hope this will not be regarded as a damaging admission) that our education and working context made us familiar with the hermeneutic side to literary criticism, and we, like the literary critics, were working on the interpretation of discourse — though equipped with a better tool-kit! Contemporary marxist, post-structuralist, and deconstructionist criticism is actually of more use to us than literary criticism (see Belsey 1980; Eagleton 1976; Harare 1979; Norris 1982) and more in line with the important influence of these frameworks was the sense of "critique" established in the social sciences under the influence of the Frankfurt School:

> "Critique" ... denotes reflection on a system of *constraints* which are humanly produced: distorting pressures to which individuals, or a group of individuals, or the human race as a whole, succumb in their process of self-formation.... Criticism ... is brought to bear on objects of experience whose "objectivity" is called into question; criticism supposes that there is a degree of inbuilt deformity which masquerades as reality. It seeks to remove this distortion and thereby to make possible the liberation of what has been distorted. Hence it entails a conception of emancipation. (Connerton 1976: 18, 20)

These definitions are worded somewhat negatively, or militantly; I will return to the question of negativity in criticism in a moment. Imagine them stripped of the negative implications, and it will emerge that they fit well with the concerns of critical linguistics. The first paragraph relates to the social determination of ideology, and the constraining role of language in socialization. The second paragraph relates to the central preoccupation of critical linguistics with the theory and practice of *representation*. Critical linguistics insists that all representation is mediated, moulded by the value-systems that are ingrained in the medium (language in this case) used for representation; it challenges common sense by pointing out that something could have been represented some other way, with a very different significance. This is not, in fact, simply a question of "distortion" or "bias": there is not necessarily any true reality that can be unveiled by critical practice, there are simply relatively varying representations.

Although the *theory* of critical linguistics is a value-free theory of representation, of "language as social semiotic", in *practice* the instrumentality of the model is reformative. The goals are parallel to those of "critical sociology", again admirably summarized by Connerton:

> Criticism ... aims at changing or even removing the conditions of what is considered to be a false or distorted consciousness ... Criticism ... renders transparent what had previously been hidden, and in doing so it initiates a process of self-reflection, in individuals or in groups, designed to achieve a liberation from the domination of past constraints. Here a change in practice is therefore a constitutive element of a change in theory. (1976:20)

The proponents of the linguistic model occupy a variety of socialist positions, and are concerned to use linguistic analysis to expose misrepresentation and discrimination in a variety of modes of public discourse: they offer critical readings of newspapers, political propaganda, official documents, regulations, formal genres such as the interview, etc. Topics examined include sexism, racism; inequality in education, employment, the courts and so on; war, nuclear weapons and nuclear power; political strategies; commercial practices. In relation to public discourse on such matters, the goals of the critical linguists are, in general terms, defamiliarization or consciousness-raising.

In terms of "autonomous linguistics" (e.g. transformational-generative grammar), critical linguistics is not linguistics at all, and it is certainly not fair play. In the more liberal world of functional linguistics, however, which allows both applications and the tailoring of the theory to the requirements of those applications, critical linguistics is a legitimate practice which does not need any special defence. So functional linguistics not only provides the theoretical underpinning for critical linguistics, it also offers a supportive intellectual and political climate for this work. This is a tolerance for which I am exceedingly grateful; one can imagine the difficulty of trying to make a career, get published, in circumstances which were less tolerant of pluralism and of comment.

It is not that critical linguistics is marginalized or embattled anyway. The model has attracted considerable interest and recognition in at least Great Britain and some other European academic circles (notably The Netherlands, West Germany and Spain) and of course Australia. Particular centres of interest would include the University of East Anglia, Lancaster, Warwick, Murdoch, Amsterdam, Utrecht. Papers inspired or provoked by the model appear regularly at diverse conferences, for example the Utrecht Summer School of Critical Theory in 1984, the Lancaster conference on Linguistics and Politics in 1986. The label "critical linguistics" and the book *Language and Control* are frequently used as reference points. (See for example, Chilton 1985: passim and especially p.215; Fairclough 1985: especially p.747). On the other hand, certain aspects of critical linguistics have been subjected to interesting critique (e.g. Pateman 1981; Chilton 1984). Recently, a kind of institutional recognition has been implied in my being invited to contribute a long entry on "critical linguistics" for *The Linguistic Encyclopaedia* (Mason forthcoming).

If linguistic criticism now enjoys a certain academic standing, that is not to say that it is completed as a theory of language or an instrumentality of linguistics — or even half-way satisfactory. Before 1979 the co-authors of *Language and Control* had dispersed to other continents, cities and employments, and this made even the final editing of the book very difficult, and of course prohibited further teamwork on the development of the model. My own work for the last five years has prevented sustained concentration on the theory and practice of critical linguistics. Returning to the subject in 1986, I find myself troubled by an awareness of difficulties, unclarities, and by the lack of a plan for further development. The original linguistic model, for all its loose ends, at least possessed a certain theoretical and methodological compactness, and I think it is important now to consolidate and develop this (essentially Hallidayan) model. If this is not done, the danger is that "critical linguistics" in the hands of practitioners of diverse intellectual persuasions will come to mean loosely any politically well-intentioned analytic work on language and ideology, regardless of method, technical grasp of linguistic theory, or historical validity of interpretations.

One is grateful, then, that in two excellent recent publications, Gunther Kress (1985a, 1985b) has both raised some radical questions about the state of the art, and valuably clarifies some central aspects of the theory which were not at all well elaborated in *Language and Control*. These papers take the model several stages on, without distorting the original intellectual base; but they do not raise all the problems which I feel ought to be considered.

Kress opens his contribution to the Chilton volume on nukespeak with a challenging question:

> There is now a significant and large body of work which enables us to see the operation of ideology in language and which provides at least a partial understanding of that operation. Some, perhaps the major, problems remain. I take these to be around the question "what now?" Having established that texts are everywhere and inescapably ideologically structured, and that the ideological structuring of both language and texts can be related readily enough to the social structures and processes of the origins of particular texts, where do we go from here? (1985a: 65)

The context makes it clear that the motives for posing this question are essentially strategic: how are we to go ahead and use this model as an instrument of social change? But clearing the way necessitates an improvement to the theory. The effectiveness of critical linguistics, if it could be measured, would be seen primarily in its capacity to equip readers for demystificatory readings of ideology-laden texts (thus the main activity of critical linguistics is inevitably *within the educational system*). But as Kress points out, the original theory — all traditional linguistic theory, it might be observed — privileges the *source* of texts, ascribing little power to the reader because the reader simply is not theorized. In response to this problem, Kress elucidates what might be called a "poststructuralist", more specifically "Foucaultian", position on the interrelated set of concepts *discourse, writer (author), reader*.

> Discourses are systematically-organised sets of statements which give expression to the meanings and values of an institution ... A discourse provides a set of possible statements about a given area, and organises and gives structure to the manner in which a particular topic, object, process is to be talked about. (1985b:6-7)

"Discourse" relates to the more recent Hallidayan formulation of *register* as "the configuration of semantic resources that the member of a culture typically associates with a situation type. It is the meaning potential that is accessible in a given social context" (Halliday1978:111). But its status is crucially different. Whereas a register is a variety of language, a discourse is a system of meanings within the culture, pre-existing language. Again, one speaks of a text as being "in" some register R_1, whereas several discourses $D_1 \ldots D_2$ maybe "in" a text.

Writers and readers are constituted by the discourses that are accessible to them. A writer can make texts only out of the available discourses, and so, *qua* writer, is socioculturally constituted. Authors are writers "who own their own texts" (Kress 1985b: 49), but this does not make them any less discursively constructed. Texts construct "reading positions" for readers, that is, they suggest what ideological formations it is appropriate for readers to bring to texts. But the reader, in this theory, is not the passive recipient of fixed meanings: the reader, remember, is discursively equipped prior to the encounter with the text, and reconstructs the text as a system of meanings which may be more or less congruent with the ideology which informs the text. In modern literary theory, this discursive activity of the reader is known as "productive consumption".

Intertextuality, dialogue and contradiction are some other important parts of this discursive view of communication, but it is not necessary to discuss these concepts here.

This more dynamic and egalitarian view of the processes of reading is a great advance over the original source-centred theory, and a distinct advantage for educational practice: by giving more power to the reader, it promotes the confidence that is needed for the production of readers (and interlocutors) who are not only communicatively competent, but also critically aware of the discursive formations and contradictions of texts, and able to enter into dialogue with their sources. The dialogue might be internal, for a reader, in which case (s)he will learn something about society and its values by becoming aware of alternative beliefs. For a speaker, the dialogue may be real, and manifest in interaction with an other, or internal, as, for example, when a lecturer or writer achieves consciousness of his or her relationship with the "other" values of the audience or readership (as I did here, in writing "(s)he" and "his or her"), acknowledging an ideological problematic to which I would have given no thought some years ago). In all these areas of communication, critical linguistics could give strategic guidance. No doubt the concept of *genre* of discourse (interview, sermon, etc.), which Kress also foregrounds, will be instructive in establishing appropriate strategies. These are pedagogic questions which I cannot take on board here, but they are important for the extension of critical linguistics, since practice can develop theory. Experiments with discourse strategies, for example, would almost certainly help refine the presently unclear definitions of discursive genres.

There is, however, the question of whether we are trying to run before we have learned to walk. I agree with Kress that major problems remain with critical linguistics, but I do not agree that these are principally at the level of strategic utilization. It seems to me that further work is needed on both theory and method, as well as application. It is one thing to demonstrate the general principle that ideology is omnipresent in texts. I agree with Kress that that principle has been demonstrated. But doing the analyses remains quite difficult, and those analyses that have been published are not as substantial as Kress implies. A small number of practitioners have become adept at uncovering ideology in texts; and a smaller number still (mainly the authors of *Language and Control* and their associates) employ anything approaching a standard, consistent apparatus. Although demonstrations have focused on a good range of types of texts, they tend to be fragmentary, exemplificatory, and they usually take too much for granted in the way of method and of context.

As for method, it has to be said that functional linguistics is a complicated subject not well provided with straightforward short textbooks. For the purposes of critical linguistics, Halliday's *Introduction to Functional Grammar* (1985) offers both more and less than is required. More, because critical linguists do not need all the detail: in practice, critical linguists get a very high mileage out of a small selection of linguistic concepts such as transitivity and nominalization. Yet these fundamental concepts are abstract and difficult, and need to be explained more clearly than they are in Halliday's own writings. Less, because certain methodological areas referred to by critical linguists are better covered in other models: for instance, speech-act theory and Gricean conversational analysis are important aids to understanding aspects of performative and pragmatic transactions. A comprehensive methodological guide, tailored to the needs of the discipline, on the lines of the last chapter of *Language and Control*, is needed, but of course more formal and more extensive than that early "check-list": a textbook specifically designed for the teaching of critical linguistics. Meanwhile, there is a need for published analyses to be more explicit, less allusive, about the tools they are employing. What I am saying is that we need to be more formal about method, both in order to improve the analytic technique, and to increase the population of competent practitioners. At the moment, students do not find the practice easy.

There is another substantial omission in the published literature, which I want to connect with the question of history and context. Apart from the nukespeak volume (Chilton 1985) — which is methodologically diverse — there is as yet no book-length study of one topic, or one mode of discourse, genre, or large corpus. A large study would allow the critical linguist to specify historical context in detail. The fragmentary analyses published so far have tended to sketch the background to the text, or assume the reader's prior knowledge of context and genre. This is in my view a dangerous economy because of the inevitable transience of the materials treated: who, in ten years' time, will remember the sacked Cabinet Ministers of the 1980s, or the leaders of CND, or the main protagonists in the "Miners' Strike" (what miners' strike?)? I think there is a great danger that the writings of critical linguistics will rapidly become opaque through historical supercession.

But the problem is more fundamental than the awkwardness of transience and consequential opacity. The theory of critical linguistics acknowledges that there is a lack of invariance between linguistic structures and their significances. This premise should be affirmed more clearly and insistently than has been the case. Significance (ideology) cannot simply be read off the linguistic forms that description has identified in the text, because the same form (nominalization, for example) has different significances in different contexts (scientific writing versus regulations, for example). This is the whole point of our insistence on the dialectical inseparability of two concepts, "language" and "society" that happen to be separately lexicalized in English (Kress 1985b: 1), and the reason for Halliday's use of portmanteau words such as "sociosemantic". One implication of this interdependence of language and context is a considerable procedural difficulty for students. They are likely to believe that the descriptive tools of linguistics provide some privilege of access to the interpretation of the text, but of course this is not so, and thus students find themselves not knowing where to start. By the theory of productive consumption, you can only understand the text if you can bring to it relevant experience of discourse and of context. Linguistic description comes at a later stage, as a means of getting some purchase on the significances that one has heuristically assigned to the text. Teachers often make the mistake of overestimating the discursive experience of young students, who turn out to have no intuitions about a particular text, and therefore cannot get started on the analysis. When teaching, it is necessary to be quite open about the fact that linguistics is *not* a discovery procedure, and also to specify context in some detail, indicating relevant historical, economic and institutional circumstances.

A healthy provocative way of generalizing about these problems would be to assert that critical linguistics is a form of history-writing or historiography. This characterization would suitably reflect the central interest of the subject, which is not Language as traditionally understood by linguists. As we have seen, critical linguistics is an "instrumental" linguistics looking beyond the formal structure of Language as an abstract system, towards the practical interaction of language and context. I link critical linguistics with history rather than, say, sociology (as disciplines devoted to what, from the traditional linguist's point of view, constitutes "context") because the broadest possible frame of reference is needed: there is no knowing what the critical linguist will be interested in next. But there are more specific connections of aim and method with history. Like the historian, the critical linguist aims to understand the values which underpin social, economic and political formations, and, diachronically, changes in values and changes in formations. As for method (one aspect at any rate), the critical linguist, like the historian, treats texts both as types of discursive practice (charters, letters, proclamations, acts of Parliament) and as documents (sources for the beliefs of institutions, for example). Like the historiographer, the critical linguist is crucially concerned with the ideological relativity of representation.

In passing it should be observed that critical linguistics is a useful tool for the historian (several students at the University of East Anglia have creatively combined the subjects), but that is not the main point. The important consideration is for the critical linguist to take a professionally responsible attitude towards the analysis of context. Up to now, the majority of the texts analyzed have been supposed to relate to a social context well known to both the analyst and to her or his readers: contemporary popular newspaper, advertisements, political speeches of the current scene, classroom discourse, etc. The plausibility of the ideological ascriptions has had to rest on intersubjective intuitions supposedly shared by writer and reader in a common discursive competence, backed up by informal accounts of relevant contexts and institutions. As was noted in my comments about young students' difficulties, this informal presentation cannot be relied on to prove the point. I think it is about time we stopped saying "lack of space prevents a full account ...". What are needed are, exactly, full descriptions of context and its implications for beliefs and relationships.

My final general query concerns the status of *ideology* as a theoretical concept in critical linguistics. In a sense it is not the definition of the term that is at fault or inadequate. Critical linguists have always been very careful to avoid the definition of ideology as "false consciousness" (it is a pity that Connerton's very serviceable definitions of "criticism" quoted above contain pejorative words like "distortion" and "deformity"), making it clear that they mean something more neutral: a society's implicit theory of what types of objects exist in their world (categorization); of the way that world works (causation); and of the values to be assigned to objects and processes (general propositions or paradigms). These implicit beliefs constitute "common sense", which provides a normative base to discourse. Just as it is not the basic definition that is at fault, so also the existing ideological analyses are adequately illuminating as far as they go. There have been some excellent demonstrations of the structuring power of ideology in the areas of categorization and of causation. (For example, Trew 1979: Chs. 6 and 7; Kress 1985b: Ch. 4, and several of his earlier writings.) My observation is that progress in the linguistic analysis of ideology has been greatest in those two areas where Halliday's *ideational* function has given the clearest methodological inspiration, namely *lexical classification* and *transitivity*. The question that urgently needs to be asked is whether the structural characteristics of the systemic-functional model of grammar have not unduly constrained the range of statements made about ideology in critical linguistics up to now. Function determines form, says the general premise, and I feel that critical interest so far has been largely centred on those ideological functions which are most clearly mapped by observable and well-described linguistic forms, namely vocabulary structure, and the structure of the clause. We need to take a more inclusive view of what constitutes ideology in language, and in particular, give consideration to those implicit meanings which do not have direct surface structure representation.

Numerous methodological and theoretical proposals exist; it is just a question of bringing them within the critical linguistics model, and submitting them to methodological development in the service of that model. I am thinking of the various proposals to the effect that the interpretation of discourse hinges on "shared knowledge" or "shared beliefs". In discourse analysis, there are the "general propositions" of Labov and Fanshel (1977), which are relevant beliefs, of a high level of generality, which participants bring to the activity of conversation. They may be equivalent to the "conventional implicatures" of Grice (1975), whose "conversational implicatures" are of course also relevant. (In this context it may be noted that the undoubted applicability of Sperber and Wilson's theory of "relevance" (1986) awaits detailed assessment.) If, following the proposals of Kress, we give the reader a more prominent role in our model, it will be appropriate to look to the various kinds of *schemata* (see Rumelhart 1980) which have been developed in cognitive psychology and artificial intelligence: "frames", "scripts" and "plans" (Minsky 1975; Schank & Abelson 1977). From cognitive semantics we might adopt the notion of "prototype" (Rosch 1975); from literary criticism, the concept of "metaphor" (cf. Kress 1985b: 70ff.).

Preliminary work on analysis of the more abstract dimensions of ideology already exists, including Kress on metaphor as just mentioned. Fowler and Marshall (1985) concentrate on underlying "paradigms", very abstract and unstated beliefs underpinning (in this case) pro-nuclear discourse. In the materials we studied, for example, there were persistent signs, traceable in metaphors, syntactic oppositions, and semantic contradictions, of general and normative paradigms used as referential bases: a dichotomous dissociation of politics and morality, and similarly of politics and domestic life; an association of power, war, technical expertise, and money. We argued that the discourse was about these matters as much as about nuclear armaments, and we predicted that these paradigms would be found to recur in other sections of the materials we were reading at that time — the financial, domestic and sports pages of the newspapers, for example. In a pioneering paper, Downes (1978) uses the apparatus of "frame" and "prototype" to analyse and present the underlying belief-systems in the practice of McCarthyism. This paper contains an excellent theoretical discussion of the kinds of semantic or pragmatic model which might be relevant for the analysis of beliefs in discourse, and is a useful starting-point for methodological development. Like Fowler and Marshall, Downes insists that we are talking about historically grounded processes. Fowler and Marshall deal with a delimited historical period (April 1983) for which they provide a Calendar and contextual notes; further documentation is recoverable from libraries. Downes concisely indicates the context of McCarthyism and indicates further reading. Ideology is of course both a medium and an instrument of historical processes.

I hope that these brief notes are sufficient to make the point that major development is possible in basic aspects of critical linguistics: in formulating a more inclusive concept of ideology-in-language, with an attendant analytic methodology; in regularizing the study of the historical or contextual dimension. Fundamental theoretical problems are at issue here. Other advances of a more pedagogic and methodological kind are indicated, and being explored in Kress's work; I would stress here not only the goals and techniques of classroom practice, but also the basic accessibility of the method to inexperienced students (particularly in view of limitations of discursive competence). *Standardization* of the method and its metalanguage particularly concerns me: nowadays it seems that anything can count as "discourse analysis", and if, as is happening, critical linguistics gets classified under that heading, there is a danger that the compactness of the original analytic methodology will dissipate in the presence of competing and uncontrolled methodologies drawn from a scatter of different models in the social sciences. The original model has the advantage of being based on the powerful and much-discussed linguistic theory of Halliday. I have argued that part of critical linguistics needs developing in its own terms, and supplementing with the insights of other models. There are opportunities for considerable progress with the augmented model. One motive for ensuring that this development occurs is the sharp realization of my colleagues and myself that in the present political and social climate, occasions for ideological critique are pressed upon our lives daily.

Grammar, society and the pronoun

Richard A. Hudson

1. Introduction

Readers familiar with Michael Halliday's work will recognise that the title of this paper derives from the title of the paper he gave as his inaugural lecture when he became the first Professor of Linguistics at University College London (1966): "Grammar, society and the noun". The basic message of the present paper also derives from Halliday's paper, namely that social structures ("society") are inextricably interwoven with linguistic structure ("grammar"). I shall exemplify this with reference (*inter alia*) to pronouns. As pronouns, a somewhat minor category, are to nouns, so the present paper is to Halliday's important, scholarly and well developed presentation.

Here I shall concern myself with the notion "speaker". This is a category of social structure, because it applies to the analysis of a type of social activity, namely speaking. It is clearly not in itself a linguistic category in the sense that, say, "subject" and "noun" are; these are categories used in the analysis of the patterns which are internal to speech. In other words, they refer to properties of linguistic *expressions*. Thus a linguistic expression may be a subject or a noun, but it could not be a speaker. Let us assume then that some category is a "linguistic category" only if its members, or instances, are linguistic expressions (words, phrases, sounds, etc.).

On the other hand, although "speaker" is not a linguistic category by this definition, it is clear that it is one of the categories to which grammars ought to be able to refer. Indeed, "speaker" is peculiarly close to being a "linguistic" category, because it is a relation category, and is always related to some linguistic expression. It is necessary in grammars because there are linguistic expressions (or classes of such expressions) to which rules apply which refer to the speaker of these expressions. To take an obvious example, the person referred to by the word *me* is the speaker of that word. We shall see that this is not the only example of an expression which is linked, by the grammar, to the category "speaker"; and of course "speaker" is not the only expression-related category to which the grammar must be able to refer.

These facts are self-evident but the curious fact is that linguistic theories generally provide no place for rules which refer to categories such as "speaker". This is because the theories are concerned only with relations among linguistic expressions, to the exclusion of relations between such expressions and the "outside world". This has been a characteristic of structural linguistics throughout this century, and reflects the assumption that language is an "autonomous system". As Newmeyer rightly says of Chomsky, he retained this "insight" that "at the heart of language lies a structured interrelationship of elements characterizable as an autonomous system. Such an insight is the essence of 'structuralism' ..." (Newmeyer 1986). The same could be said (by definition) of any linguist in the main stream of structural linguistics. The theoretical apparatus is developed to deal with relations among expressions (syntagmatic relations in the sentence, and paradigmatic relations in the grammar), on the assumption that such relations in fact exhaust the "linguistic system" (the contents of the grammar). A natural consequence of this approach is that non-linguistic categories such as "speaker" cannot be represented at all, or only in *ad hoc* ways, in these theories.

This exclusion of non-linguistic categories can be seen either as a virtue or as a vice, according to whether one believes that there is a significant difference between structures which are purely internal to language and those which link expressions to things outside language. I have argued elsewhere (Hudson 1984) that the boundary around language is an invention of linguistics, rather than a discovery. In the present paper I shall simply assume that there are facts which involve both expressions and non-linguistic categories, and that these can be expressed and formalised in just the same way as facts about inter-expression relations. I shall also assume that it is simply a matter of terminology whether we call these facts "grammatical". It seems to me perfectly reasonable to call them "grammatical", on the assumption that the grammar contains everything which a native speaker knows about expressions in his or her language.

Are there any linguistic theories to which the above remarks do not apply (apart from Word Grammar, a theory which I have been developing for some years — 1984, 1985a, 1985b, 1985c, 1985d, 1986)? The obvious candidate is Functional Systemic Grammar (Halliday 1985), which pays a good deal of attention to the non-linguistic structures within which language is embedded. However I suspect that it would be hard even in this theory to refer directly to the speaker of some expression, because all these non-linguistic structures — the "socio-semantics", as I understand it — are expressed in terms of paradigmatic classifications of situations. This seems to prevent one from referring formally to participants in those situations. There is naturally no problem in using terms like "speaker" informally, and this is done (Halliday 1985: 68). However, I doubt if one could easily express a relation between the speaker of some word and, say, the meaning of that word.

I hope to be able to show that it is rather easy to put together two fundamental tenets of systemic grammar and derive a way of referring in a satisfactory way to categories such as "speaker". The tenets concerned are:
   a. the view that participant roles should be related to process types;
   b. the view that speech should be analysed as a kind of social behaviour.

2. Participant roles

One of the most significant contributions that Halliday has made to theoretical and descriptive linguistics, in my opinion, is his analysis of participant roles. It is now widely accepted among linguists that semantic structures should include labelled relations, and Halliday was one of the first to develop this idea into a systematic classification of relations (1967). In contrast with the system which was independently being developed by Fillmore (1968) on the basis of work by Gruber (1965), Halliday suggested that "processes" (alias states-of-affairs) could be classified into a number of general types, and that each of these types of process would be associated with a different list of semantic relations (or participant roles) — actor and goal for material processes, phenomenon and senser for mental processes, and so on (I follow the terminology of Halliday 1985).

These categories — both the process types and the participant roles — are presented by Halliday as part of semantic structure. However he also recognises that language "enables human beings to build a mental picture of reality, to make sense of their experience of what goes on around them and inside them". It presumably follows from this that we may construct the same "mental picture of reality" for some scene that we are witnessing or imagining as we would for a clause that was used to describe it: we would classify the process concerned according to the same set of process types, and the various participants could be represented in terms of the same set of participant roles. For example, if the clause *Fred kicked the ball* evokes a mental representation whose structure is X, it is at least possible that X could also be evoked by seeing Fred kick the ball — though of course X is likely to be just a small part of the mental structures produced by this piece of experience. This is not to deny in any way that a given item of experience can be interpreted in different ways by different people, or by the same person under different circumstances. All I am suggesting is that "semantic structures" are part of general cognitive structure, and are distinctive only in that they are directly associated with linguistic expressions. Although by no means standard in linguistic circles, this view has recently been supported by a number of linguists (e.g. Jackendoff 1983: Chap. 6; Langacker 1985), and it seems compatible with Halliday's views as quoted above.

Let us assume, then, that we have the categories "material process" and "actor" available to us in our mental repertoire for use not only when we are assigning semantic structures to utterances but also when we are analysing our experience in general. In the terminology of Artificial Intelligence, "material process" is the name of a very general "script" (Schank & Abelson 1977), characterised among other things by the presence of an actor — the entity which can be characterised as "doing" something in the process (Halliday 1985: 103). Any particular instance of this script automatically "inherits" all its properties, including that of having an actor, unless these properties are already known. Thus as soon as we mentally classify some process as a material process we automatically gain access to the information that it has an actor (and, presumably, knowing that it has an actor leads automatically to the conclusion that it is a material process).

Alongside the three "major" process types — material, mental and relational — Halliday distinguishes three "minor" ones, one of which is called "verbal processes" (Halliday 1985: 129). The name is perhaps less than ideal as it is intended to cover "any kind of symbolic exchange of meaning", as represented by the meanings of all the following three example clauses:

> *I said it's noisy in here.*
> *My watch says it's half past ten.*
> *The notice tells you to keep quiet.*

Perhaps "communication" would have been a more helpful name, to make it clear that at least some of the processes in question are not "verbal" except by metaphor. The characteristic participant roles associated with such processes are the "sayer", the "target" and the "verbiage" (a role which is in fact a special case of "range" — Halliday 1985: 137). Thus once again, if we know that something is a communication, we can assume that it has all these participants. And once again by assumption we use these categories not only in the semantic structures of utterances, but also in processing our experience. So if I hear someone talking a language I cannot understand, at least I can register the event as an instance of a verbal process, whose speaker (and possibly target) I know.

An interesting question arises about straightforward cases like the sentence *He said "Good morning"*. The event to which this refers is clearly an instance of a communication, but it is surely *also* an instance of a material process, in which he is the actor. If we assume that an actor is "the one that does the deed" (Halliday 1985: 102) then he presumably counts as the actor of the "deed" of saying "Good morning". And if a process which contains an actor is a material process, then this too must be a material process. If this is so, then we have at least one example of a particular process (X saying Y) which shares the properties of two distinct general process types — material process and communication. The particular case inherits roles from both of these, so the actor inherited from the former must be mapped onto the "sayer" inherited from the latter; but the latter also contributes the role "target".

To summarise the argument so far, I have quoted Halliday's analysis of semantic structure in terms of process types and participant roles, and I have suggested two ways in which it might be extended. First, it can be extended to cognitive processing in general, instead of being restricted to the analysis of sentence meanings. Second, some overlap between the general process types can be allowed in order to permit actors to occur in communications.

3. Speech as action

The sentence *He said "Good morning"* might be called a "material communicative process". Now suppose someone uttered this sentence. How would we describe this event? In other words, how would an observer represent the event to himself or herself? There can be no doubt about the answer: this too is a material communicative process. This is not of course because it contains a bit of reported speech; the same would be true for an utterance of any sentence (e.g. *Snow is white*). Any utterance is a material communicative process.

This conclusion hardly counts as a major breakthrough in linguistics, because it simply restates the obvious fact that speech is a kind of action whose purpose is communication — something which nobody could possibly deny. It contrasts sharply, of course, with the fact that the other manifestation of language, namely writing, is in no sense an instance of "material process", or action. But then, we all know that speech and writing are fundamentally different. However, for all its lack of impact, I think it is worth restating the axiom that speech is a material communicative process, because its implications seem to have been ignored by those who design linguistic theories.

Let us examine a potential objection which runs as follows. Granted that speech is a kind of action, this is a fact about utterances, i.e. performance. But utterances are different from the sentences on which they are based. Sentences are abstract models directly generated by competence grammars, and do not occur, as such, in real time. So even if utterances are actions, sentences are not (or need not be). Thus if one of the characteristics of material processes is that they have actors, then speech has an actor, but sentences don't; and if sentences don't have actors, there is no reason for grammars to refer to actors either. At least the conclusion is very familiar, even if the arguments that lead to it are more often implicit than explicit.

This objection misses the point entirely. Take a completely non-linguistic example of a material process such as walking. How do we know an instance of walking when we see one? Surely it must be because we have a stored mental representation of the typical case against which we can compare the instance in question. If the two have enough properties in common, we say that one is an instance of the other. More generally, how do we know an instance of a material process when we see one? Surely, by the same procedure, which rests crucially on the existence of a stored mental representation (a mental model in the sense of Johnson-Laird 1983) of the category "material process".

Thus we can, and do, represent some kinds of material process to ourselves, in our permanent store of knowledge, as abstract concepts; and the same is (presumably) true for all types of process. It is also true of linguistic expressions. If I say X and X may be taken as an instance of *Hello*, then both *Hello* and X must have similar properties in my mind; if one is a material process, then so must the other be. In other words, there is no reason for thinking that the difference between perceived and stored expressions goes beyond the difference between the perceived and the stored. In particular we must not assume that they belong to conflicting ontological categories (e.g. "process" versus "abstract pattern").

We may assume, then, that if spoken expressions are material communicative processes then so are their representations in our internalised grammars. What follows from this? Recall that if some concept is an instance of a material communicative process, it must inherit the participant roles which are associated with such processes, namely actor-cum-sayer, target and "verbiage". This means that every expression or category of expression *as represented in the grammar* also has these participant roles associated with it. For example the lexical item *dog* has an actor-cum-sayer and so on; and the same is true for the category "noun". Of course, these participant roles need not be spelled out separately for each lexical item and category; the whole point of including general categories in an analysis is to allow some properties to be stated just once and then inherited by implication by instances of the general categories. Expressions inherit the participant roles simply by being classified as instances of material communicative processes.

What we have now achieved is to apply the same kind of analysis, in terms of process types and participant roles, to the *expressions themselves* as we applied earlier to their semantic structures. This step, which is not generally taken in linguistic theory, leads easily to a solution for our problem: how to make the category "speaker" available in grammar. The solution is obvious: the speaker is none other than the actor-cum-sayer of the expression concerned.

Precisely because this solution is so obvious, it is easy to miss its significance which lies in what is made explicit in the analysis. "Speaker" has been integrated, in a principled way, into the grammar. To summarise the analysis, expressions are now seen as part of a hierarchy of processes. I have adopted Halliday's terminology for the categories in this hierarchy, but other analyses also deserve consideration (e.g. I have tended to assume categories such as "event" and "action" in my earlier work — 1984, 1985a, 1985b). If we assume (as I do in Word Grammar) that the typical expression is a word, then we can continue the hierarchy down into the grammar, itself, as shown in the following system network:

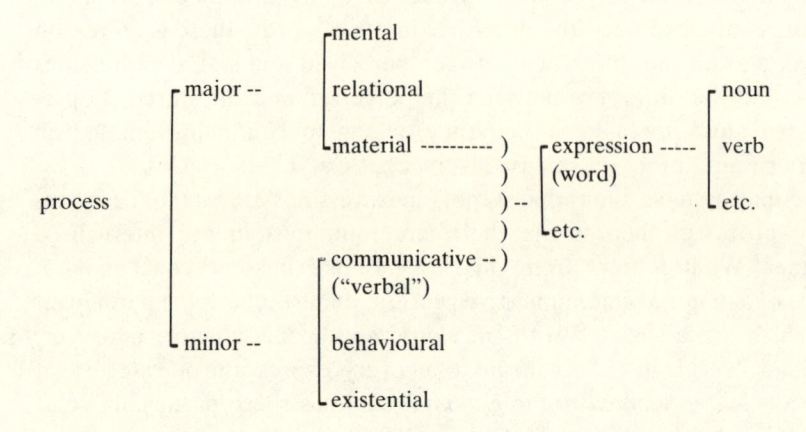

```
                    ┌─mental
         ┌─major──  │ relational
         │          └─material ────────)   ┌─expression ─────  ┌─noun
         │                              )  │ (word)            │ verb
process  │                              )──│                   └─etc.
         │                              )  └─etc.
         │          ┌─communicative ──)
         │          │ ("verbal")
         └─minor──  │ behavioural
                    └─existential
```

Moreover, this hierarchy guarantees that the general category "expression" — or any particular expression — will inherit all the properties of the categories "material (process)" and "communicative (process)", including the various participant roles which are associated with these categories. (The mechanism by which this takes place is precisely the same process of generalisation which guarantees that any particular noun will be able to occur with adjectives and so on.)

Thus once we take seriously the idea that speech is a kind of action, we can develop a theory which actually *predicts* that expressions have speakers. If it had actually been the case that expressions did not have speakers, then either we should have to radically revise the hierarchy, or we should have had to add a special statement to override the normal expectations. The grammar would thus be *more* complex if there had been *no* speakers. In contrast, for other theories a speaker-free grammar is clearly simpler than one that does make provision for speakers, because some extra arrangements (so far unspecified) would have to be added in order to allow for speakers.

4. The uses of speakers

We can now assume that a grammar may refer to the category "speaker of X", where X is the name of some expression, and that statements of this kind have precisely the same status, in terms of formal motivation and definition, as statements about for example "subject of X" or "meaning of X". What remains is to show that there is some work to be done by this category. Strictly speaking we should perhaps refer to it as "actor-cum-sayer", but for simplicity I shall use "speaker".

I have already hinted at one use of "speaker": in statements about deictic semantics. It is essential for the meaning of the first person singular personal pronouns: *I*, *me*, *my*, *mine*, *myself* (hence the term "pronoun" in the title of this paper). Assuming that all of these have the same meaning (with a slight modification for *my*), it can be stated as follows (using X as the name for the word concerned):

The referent of X is the speaker of X.

This statement translates directly into a formula of Word Grammar, but other theoretical frameworks could no doubt express it in their own notation. "Speaker" is also needed in defining the meanings of other pronouns: *we* refers to a group of people which does include the speaker, and *you* and the third person pronouns must not include the speaker. Thus "speaker" has an important part to play in *deictic semantics*.

Another area of grammar where "speaker" is relevant is in the domain of "power and solidarity" (Brown & Gilman 1960; Brown & Ford 1961). Here it is important to be able to refer to the social relations (in terms of perceived power and solidarity) between the speaker and the addressee in order to explain the choice between second-person pronouns in many European languages (e.g. French *tu* versus *vous*), the choice between alternative forms of personal name in some languages (e.g. English *Fred* versus *Mr Green* when addressing Fred Green) and many other alternative expressions which by now are well known (Hudson 1980: 125ff.). It is still not absolutely clear, even after extensive empirical investigation, precisely how the relevant rules should be formulated — in particular how the sometimes conflicting demands of power and of solidarity should be combined — but it is absolutely clear that they cannot be formulated without reference to "speaker". We might call this function of the category an "*interpersonal social*" function. It is hard to see any reason why such information should not be included in a grammar, because it is clearly part of the knowledge which is essential to a native speaker.

A third type of use for "speaker" is in the whole area of what we might call "*social identification*" contrasts, the miriad cases where a particular form of expression is associated with a particular kind of speaker. These cases range from the very particular (e.g. *ain't* versus *aren't*, *isn't*, *hasn't*, etc.) through general constructions (e.g. "double negatives", "double subjects") to categories as general as "language X". What these cases have in common is that by choosing to use some particular form of expression the speakers indicate something about their social identity in terms of categories such as sex, region of origin, socio-economic class, education, etc. The literature of sociolinguistics is full of such examples: *sidewalk* is used by Americans, *bags I* ... is used by (British) children, non-prevocalic /r/ is used in New York by the young and aspiring, etc.

It is beyond doubt that such choices are made on the basis of knowledge, because the same knowledge can be used in order to classify other speakers. Presumably the whole point of making these choices is precisely to exploit the knowledge that potential hearers have about the expressions concerned. Consequently it is again hard to see why the knowledge concerned should not be included in a grammar. To take a very simple example, a grammar should be able to express the following fact:

The speaker of *sidewalk* is an American.

However the fact is formalised, it cannot be expressed at all unless the category "speaker" is available.

In summary, I have shown that "speaker" is essential if the grammar is to make explicit at least three kinds of fact: about deictic semantics, about interpersonal social signalling, and about social identification. We can now generalise the discussion by making similar points in relation to some other participant roles which can be associated with expressions.

5. Other participant roles

One other participant role which has already been mentioned is what Halliday calls the "target" of a "verbal" process (our "communicative" process). This is what is more normally called the *addressee*, and I shall use the latter term. What uses can we find in a grammar for this category?

It is easy to find parallels with the first two uses of "speaker". In deictic semantics, "addressee" is needed for all the second person pronouns, because *you* obviously refers either to the addressee of *you*, or to a set which includes its addressee (but which excludes its speaker). In interpersonal social signalling, "addressee" is needed for precisely the same reasons as "speaker", namely because we need to be able to refer to the relationship between speaker and addressee.

It is also easy to find cases where the addressee is needed for purposes of social identification, i.e. expressions which are characteristically used only when speaking to certain types of addressee. However, for some reason nearly all the clear cases appear to involve sex. There are many languages in which certain forms are reserved for use to addressees of just one sex, though there are no clear cases of this in English. And there are languages in which certain special forms are used when speaking to a taboo relation, such as to a mother-in-law (the case most often quoted is the special sub-language parasitic on Dyirbal reported by Dixon 1972). What we do not find, however, is expressions for which there are restrictions on the addressee similar to those on the speaker — an expression which is for use only when speaking to Americans, for example. (We must obviously exclude here cases where the expression concerned actually refers to the addressee, for example for some people the word *Taffy* may be characteristically used when addressing a Welshman.) There is more discussion of these matters in Hudson (1985b), but I confess to having no explanation for this rather intriguing fact.

What other participant roles can we invoke, other than "speaker" and "addressee"? It all depends on what you mean by "participant roles", but I see no reason to draw the line at concrete discrete entities like people and objects. We could at least include any kind of entity which can be realised as a direct object in terms of linguistic structure. This is true of times and places (cf. *We chose Thursday/behind the gym for our party*), so it seems reasonable to include them in our list of potential participant roles. The question, then, is whether these new participant roles have a place in the grammar.

"*Time*" is needed in deictic semantics for the reference of words like *now*, *tomorrow* and *ago* (which are "deictically anchored" at the time when the word concerned is uttered). Most obviously, the referent of *now* is the time of *now*; but the other cases allow analyses which also refer to the notion "time of X", where X is the word concerned. Another deictic function of "time of X" is in relation to tense, since a past tense verb typically refers to a process whose time precedes the time of the verb itself: the time of the "referent" of a past-tense verb precedes the time of the past-tense verb. As far as deictic semantics is concerned, "time" has very much the same kind of status in a grammar as "speaker" or "addressee".

Similar points could be made in relation to "*place*". First we have words like *here* and *there* which refer to places defined in relation to the place in which they themselves are uttered. Thus, the referent of *here* is the place of *here*. Then there are all the other cases of words whose meanings contain a reference to deictic place, such as *come* and *go*. So there is no shortage of work for the category of "place" in a grammar.

It is less easy to find examples of expressions which are restricted in respect of time or place of utterance, without actually referring to the time or place. Could we include here greetings such as *Good morning*, or do they also refer in some sense to the time at which they are used? There are reports of societies in which certain words are not allowed to be used at certain times, and in some multilingual societies it is said that each language is used only in certain places; for example in parts of Nairobi society Kikuyu is used inside the home and Swahili outside it (Parkin 1977). Maybe there are genuine examples of temporal or locational restrictions on expressions, but it is certainly much harder to find them, compared with the rich array of restrictions on speakers.

Once we have allowed times and places to figure among the participant roles of an expression, it is but a short step to various other possibilities. For example, we might consider the *purpose* of the expression as another one, and use this as a hook on which to hang information about illocutionary force. A very simple example of this use is provided by the meaning of the imperative, which can be stated as follows: the process referred to by an imperative verb is the purpose of the imperative verb. Thus if I say *Come in!*, the process referred to is one in which you come in, and the purpose of the process is that you should come in.

One final candidate that we might consider is what Halliday calls the "verbiage", which is a special kind of "range". In a sentence like *He said "Hullo"*, the quoted wording is the verbiage, but is this in fact distinct from the process itself? As Halliday remarks (1985: 135):

> The Range may be not an entity at all but rather another name for the process. Consider *John and Mary were playing tennis*, where *tennis* is Range. Tennis is clearly not an entity; there is no such thing as tennis other than the act of playing it. Likewise with *sing a song*; if we look up *song* in the dictionary we are likely to find it defined as "act of singing", just as *game* is "act of playing".

This description seems to fit the "verbiage" kind of range precisely. If he says "Hullo", then the process is none other than the uttered expression "Hullo". In other words, the sentence *He said "Hullo"* is just a more precise way of describing the same situation that we could have described by means of *He spoke* — where no object is possible, and therefore there is less temptation to take the verbiage as a participant role. If we now transfer this conclusion to the analysis of expressions themselves, we shall find the same: the expression *is* the process. Indeed, this assumption underlies the whole of the preceding discussion, in which it has been crucial that expressions themselves are processes, so that they can fit into the hierarchy of processes. And after all, it is surely obvious that expressions are processes — for example *Hullo* is a process in which the speaker first pronounces /h/, and so on.

In conclusion, I have tried to show that Halliday's ideas about processes and participant roles have important implications which go well beyond the area of linguistics in which they have been applied so far, namely semantics. They make it possible to produce a theory of grammar in which social categories like "speaker" or "speaker who is an American" have a proper place alongside the more internal categories like "pronoun".

The structure of situations and the analysis of text

Bernard A. Mohan

Introduction

Halliday's view of language as social semiotic (Halliday 1978, 1985), in the tradition of Malinowski and Firth, has two key terms: text and situation. Every text, spoken or written, unfolds in some situation, or context of use. And just as a text is analysed according to categories of language and discourse, so a socio-cultural situation is analysed as a situation type according to categories of situation and, ultimately, culture. A situation type is a semiotic construct, a structure of meanings, shared by its various instances.

Because he considers situation as well as text, Halliday's approach has distinctive implications in a number of language areas, such as language learning. Many scholars view the interactions of the child or non-native speaker simply in terms of learning the language, not in terms of learning other things as well. Insofar as situation is taken into account, it is seen merely as a factor promoting or retarding language learning. But for Halliday, the child learns language and culture at the same time, and the dynamic inter-relationship between learning language and learning culture and subject matter continues throughout education. Language socialisation means not only socialisation in the ways of talk, but socialisation through language. Language is a major source for learning about and expressing what one must say, know, value and do in order to participate in the socio-cultural situations of society. And being an instrument of social reality, language is also a document of social reality.

To explore these insights we need to relate situation and text. This has always been a concern of the Firthian tradition in linguistics which has been "with the possible exception of tagmemics, the only influential school of thought to take the connection between linguistic and situational analysis to be a necessary part of its work" (Steiner 1985: 225). And Steiner clearly identifies the longstanding problem in this: "the concept of situation lacked both generality and a set of descriptive concepts permitting the analysis of linguistic and situational items in such a way as to relate them explicitly".

What is needed are general models of situation, explicitly related to text. This paper will address this problem. But there is another question here, seldom discussed: the dilemma of situational analysis. Who will provide a situational analysis? For many scholars, it is not the linguist's role to do so. Linguists analyse texts, not situations. Hence there is an apparently insuperable problem for any approach to linguistic and situational analysis: the linguist requires a sophisticated analysis of situation, but, as a linguist, cannot provide it. If only situations could be analysed with the linguistic sophistication that is applied to texts! Until this problem is resolved, progress is likely to be superficial. I will suggest a natural way out of this dilemma which has been foreshadowed in the Firthian tradition.

This paper will discuss situation types and instances, or the theory of a situation and its practice. It will contrast theory texts which explicate situation types with practical texts which operate instances of a situation. I will propose a model of the structure of situations and illustrate it with an analysis of theory texts. Then I will show how the study of situation and text can be transposed into the discourse analysis of the relation between a theory text and its practical texts.

The distinction between a situation type and instances of that situation is easily seen in sports and games: it is not difficult to distinguish between the game of football and football matches, the game of tennis and tennis matches, the game of bridge and bridge play. To use common terms, we can distinguish between the theory of a situation and its practice, that is, the occasions when it is in operation. Or, to follow some anthropologists, we can distinguish between a situation frame and the events it applies to (Hall 1976). This distinction relates to different kinds of text. Explanations of the rules of football, tennis or bridge are one kind of text; they explain the theory of the situation, the situation type or situation frame. The verbal interaction of participants during football, tennis and bridge matches is another kind: these practical texts guide a situation when it is in operation. This suggests a way out of our dilemma: we can analyse theory texts to find out about situations and we can then analyse practical texts to see how discourse "operates" a situation.

Situation type as a socio-cultural knowledge system

Situation is a poorly understood concept in much of linguistics, yet the notion of situation derives from a tradition of ethnography which continues to offer many actual analyses of situations. Malinowski is a key figure in this tradition of qualitative analysis, which regards socio-cultural situations as basic units of cultural meaning. Situations are "culture's building blocks" (Hall 1977: Ch. 9). Recent approaches to ethnographic research (Spradley 1980: 39ff.) have studied culture by analysing situations such as: family meal times, corporate board meetings, hospital operating rooms, and city gaols.

In "Coral Gardens and their Magic" (Malinowski 1935), Malinowski's aim is to describe the meaning of gardening from the standpoint of Trobriand cultivators. He outlines the distinctions they make with regard to land and gardens, crops, agricultural techniques, and the social, legal, economic and magical aspects of agriculture. Trobriand gardening, then, is both a theory, known to members of the culture and learned by children and cultural strangers like anthropologists, and a practice, embodied in actual work in gardens. Malinowski's description is of gardening as a situation type.

A major part of Malinowski's situational analysis of agriculture is his analysis of agricultural texts. He uses textual analysis to perform situational analysis. Ethnographers, qualitative researchers, and historians use language as social document, since language is a reflection of cultural members' social reality, though by no means a perfect reflection. Malinowski illustrates his account of gardening with documentary texts, and he chooses them from the discourse of theory rather than the discourse of practice.

He says little about his well-known category of the pragmatic function of speech in the context of action. As he points out, gardening seldom requires concerted teamwork, though where it does, conversation is about the progress of the work. That is, it is discourse dealing with the particular case, the discourse of practice rather than the discourse of theory. By contrast, Malinowski illustrates his analysis of Trobriand gardening mainly with definitions of technical terms elicited from his Trobriand informants. But "such definition texts are not merely answers elicited from informants, but are an intrinsic part of the native educational process" (Malinowski 1935: 4). He counters the objection that such texts are "merely artificial by-products of ethnographic fieldwork" and do not fit into "the normal context of tribal life" (Malinowski 1935: 50), replying that giving information to strangers and instructing children are frequent in Trobriand communities. The normal context for his fieldwork texts is when speech has an explanatory or educational function: "The most important aspects of native agricultural speech ... would be found in education" (1935: 61). In other words, educational texts — Malinowski means direct explanation and exposition — provide evidence for the meaning of situation types. They are a major kind of "discourse of theory". To explain a situation to someone is to explicate its meaning.

It has been a continuing concern in the Malinowski-Firth tradition to identify general categories of situational knowledge; to identify the structure of situational types, or cultural knowledge systems. In "A Scientific Theory of Culture", Malinowski (1944) claimed that traditional cultural knowledge systems are similar to the knowledge systems of modern science, in terms of certain structural features. This view of science as a natural outgrowth of traditional cultural knowledge is now a basis for work in the sociology of science and the study of science as a cultural process (Richter 1972):

> What assumptions have we to make concerning man's reasonable behaviour, the permanent incorporation of such behaviour in tradition, and the fidelity of each generation to the traditional knowledge inherited from their ancestors? One of the simplest and most fundamental primitive crafts is that of fire-making. In this, over and above the manual ability of the craftsman, we find a definite scientific theory embodied in each performance, and in the tribal tradition thereof. Such a tradition had to define in a general, that is, abstract manner, the material and form of the two types of wood used. The tradition also had to define the principles of performance, the type of muscular movement, its speed, the capture of the spark, and the nourishment of the flame. The tradition was kept alive not in books nor yet in explicit physical theories ... First and foremost, it was embodied in the manual skills of each generation, which, by example and precept, were handed over to the new growing members. (Malinowski 1944: 9)

And "primitive knowledge" has another factor, value, for "... their fidelity to the theoretical principles on which they work, and their technical accuracy are determined by the desired end of their activity. This end is a value in their culture" (Malinowski 1944: 9).

In this account of the structure of a situation as a cultural knowledge system, Malinowski distinguishes theory from performance or practice. He implies that theory will include types or classes, principles, and values. It will also include a procedural element ("... muscular movement ... the capture of the spark and the nourishment of the flame ..."). I think he is right. I suggest, then, that a situation type as a socio-cultural knowledge system is a mode of thought and conduct, a way of understanding and valuing the world and a way of acting on it. Ironically, Malinowski's analysis in "Coral Gardens" deals almost solely with types or classes, the taxonomy of Trobriand agricultural concepts and terms.

The structure of situation

Malinowski, like many ethnographers since, found evidence for a situation type by analysing educational texts. Linguists, as I will show, can find evidence for the *structure* of situation types, theories or frames by analysing the *structure* of theory texts. Clearly, this is a question of a different order, reflecting a difference in perspective between ethnographers and linguists.

My framework for the structure of situation is given in detail in Mohan (1986). Briefly, the hypothesis is that a situation type, frame or theory includes background knowledge and procedural or action knowledge. Background knowledge includes classes, principles and values. Action knowledge includes description (of circumstances or conditions), sequence (of actions and events), and choice (i.e. decision). Detailed logical and semantic analyses of each of these categories exist in the research literature but will not be examined here. The concern of this paper is to convey a sense of how together they form a cohesive whole, a coherent semiotic structure.

I will examine educational texts from four topic areas: gardening, in deference to Malinowski; and because it represents physical action, bridge, because the structure of games has been an important model for thought about situation since Wittgenstein; statistics because it represents academic, symbolic action; and parliamentary procedure, because it represents speech action. In this range of situations, the participant may act verbally or nonverbally, socially or individually, seriously or for pleasure, and act on physical things or symbols. The texts have been chosen because they provide fairly brief expositions of whole situations. With the exception of the parliamentary procedure text, they are part of books which explain many similar situations.

A. *Gardening* (*Roses*; Calkins 1979: 178-187)

Sequence. There are procedures for cultivating plants. The section of the text headed "Step-by-Step Guide to Rose Planting" includes the sub-headings "Preparing the roses before planting" (elaborated in a six-step process), "Shaping the hole to fit the roots", and "Planting bush roses at proper depth" (elaborated in a four-step process).

Description. Gardening requires an understanding of plant, soil and weather conditions. In the section headed "Creating the best conditions for roses", we are told that roses "do best in an open sunny location that has a fairly rich, slightly acid soil".

Choice. The gardener must make appropriate choices in the treatment of plants: "If bare-root plants arrive with dry, shrivelled stems, immerse them in water completely for a few hours. If they do not plump up, return them to the nursery for replacement".

Classes. Gardeners recognise different types of plants, soils, insecticides, fertilizers and so on. In the section labelled "The most popular classes of roses", sub-headings include "hybrid tea" ("more roses of the hybrid tea class are sold than of any other"), "tree or standard", and "shrub roses".

Principles. When growing plants or curbing pests, gardeners rely on causal principles. A table relating to plant disorders contains:

SYMPTOMS & SIGNS: Leaves are eaten and sometimes also rolled.
CAUSE: Caterpillars and sawfly larvae.
CONTROL: Spray with carbaryl ...

Values. Gardeners evaluate roses particularly on appearance, but not solely. We are told that rose varieties are evaluated by All-America Rose Selection judges according to a prescribed point system of evaluative criteria: "They are scored on vigor, hardiness, disease resistance, foliage, flower production, bud and flower form, opening and final color, fragrance, stem, and overall value and quality".

B. *Card games* (*Contract Bridge*; Moreshead & Mott-Smith 1958: 1-25)

Sequence. Card games have a procedure of play. The sequence of play is reflected in the section headings: "Preliminaries", "The deal", "The auction" and "The play".

Description. In card games a player must be able to "read" his/her hand. In bridge there are "systems" (e.g. the Goren system) for interpreting and scoring cards in order to bid appropriately, for instance, "Ace = 4 pts. King = 3 pts. Queen = 2 pts. Jack = 1 pt."

Choice. The "auction" presents the player with an obvious choice: "Beginning with the dealer, each player in turn may call (pass, bid, or double or redouble if appropriate) until any call has been followed by three passes".

Classes. Bridge players recognise different types of cards, "tricks", players, calls and bids, as in the following definitions: "SLAMS. A bid of six odd tricks is a little slam (or small slam); a bid of all seven odd tricks is a grand slam".

Principles. Games are governed by conventional rules, which are one type of principle. Thus there is a text section headed "Contract Bridge Laws", which includes, for example: "CHANGE OF CALL. A player may change a call without penalty if he does so without pause".

Value. In card games, players typically must evaluate cards and hands. In the bridge text, cards are assigned a rank order of value: "In each suit the cards rank: A (high), K, Q, J, 10, 9, 8, 7, 6, 5, 4, 3, 2. The suits rank: spades (high), hearts, diamonds, clubs; in bidding the rank is the same except that no-trump ranks highest, above spades".

C. *Statistics (Chi-Square*; Siegel 1956: 104-111)

Sequence. There are systematic procedures for applying statistical tests to research data. The application of the chi-square test is given in four steps in the section "Summary of procedure". It begins: "These are the steps in the use of the chi-square test for two independent samples. 1. Cast the observed frequencies in a k x r contingency table".

Description. The competent user of statistical tests must be able to recognise when a test is appropriate to the research data and the research problem. The use of the test depends on the description of the data: "When the data of research consist of frequencies in discrete categories, the chi-square test may be used ... The measurement involved may not be as weak as nominal scaling".

Choice. A researcher employs a statistical test to decide a research question, to decide about the research hypothesis, specifically to choose between the null hypothesis (H0) or the alternative hypothesis (H1). The final step of the chi-square procedure is: "4. ... If the probability given by Table C is equal to or smaller than alpha, reject H0 in favour of H1." The author labels this step "the decision" both for this test and for statistical tests generally (Siegel 1956: 14).

Classes. Statisticians recognise different types of tests, hypotheses, data and scales of measurement. At the beginning of the book, Siegel classifies non-parametric tests on the basis of the characteristics of the data to which they apply. Each chapter then discusses a different group of tests, for example: Chapter 4. The one-sample case. Chapter 5. The case of two related samples. Chapter 6. The case of two independent samples. The discussion of chi-square is a section of Chapter 6, so that it is grouped with tests for two independent samples.

Principles. Statistical tests use formulae expressing mathematical relationships, which constitute another type of principle. A brief example is: "The degrees of freedom for an r x k contingency table may be found by

$$df = (r-1)(k-1)$$

where r = number of classifications (rows), k = number of groups (columns)."

Values. The choice between tests depends on evaluative criteria of suitability:

> The choice among the tests ... is predicated on the strength of the measurement obtained, the size of the two samples and the relative power of the available tests. The chi-square test is suitable for data which are in nominal or stronger scales ... In many cases the chi-square test may not make efficient use of all the information in the data. If the population of scores is continuously distributed, we may choose ... the Wald-Wolfowitz Runs test in preference to the chi-square test.

D. *Parliamentary Procedure* (Bridge 1967)

Sequence. Formal meetings have a sequential order of business, usually reflected in a written agenda, and contain a repeated subsequence of proposal of motion, discussion, and vote on the motion or "question". The chapter on "Business meetings and conduct of business" includes the sections "Order of business", "Introducing business", "Discussion", "Putting the question".

Description. Members of meetings must know the appropriate conditions for motions, voting, and the transaction of business generally. Action in meetings depends on the description of the circumstances, such as the conditions for voting by general (or unanimous) consent. "This procedure cannot be used in the following cases: 1. When the question may possibly be controversial. 2. In any matter where there might be a minority opinion. 3. In any matter affecting the rights of absent members ..."

Choice. The chairman must make numerous choices about the conduct of a meeting and members must make choices about the business in hand. A chapter on "Motions and regulations pertaining to voting" states: "The chairman when he puts the question may, if he has a choice, require any one of three types of vote, a voice vote, a vote by show of hands, or a standing vote. He should, however, use good judgement". Even more obvious is the very notion of voting, where members exercise their choice for or against a motion.

Classes. Members of meetings recognise different types of motions, meetings, officers and committees. A complete classification of motions is given in a "Table of Motions", but the reader is cautioned: "the reader should not try to use the table of motions ... until he has studied the different kinds of motion — Main, Subsidiary, Privileged, Incidental, and Miscellaneous". Each of these has a separate chapter where usually the type of motion is defined and its subtypes enumerated.

Principles. The principles which apply to meetings are rules, the "rules of order":

> It is the duty of the chairman to see that the rules of order are observed. He shall not permit a motion that is contrary to the laws of the country, or to the rules governing the organisation, or to the fundamental principles of parliamentary procedure.

A central rule about Main Motions is:

> Only one main motion can be immediately pending (i.e. undecided, awaiting decision, undisposed of) at any one time. Any person who tries to make a main motion before a pending main motion is out of order.

Values. Parliamentary procedure incorporates values of efficiency and democracy. Parliamentary Law is "principles adopted voluntarily by free men for the purpose of transacting business cooperatively in an efficient, expeditious and democratic manner". A chapter on "Dilatory, Absurd or Frivolous Motions" reflects the value of efficiency: "Motions that are absurd or frivolous or that are obviously intended merely to obstruct the transaction of business are prohibited ..." and "the chairman should rule them out of order". Democratic respect for persons appears in the following rules of decorum in discussion:

> Any member who, in speaking from the floor, refers to another member in a discourteous, or disrespectful manner or impugns the motives of another or uses improper or offensive language or is disorderly in any way, should be ruled out of order.

"There are hundreds if not thousands of different situational frames in cultures as complex as our own" (Hall 1976: 129). The above examples give some hint of the variety of situation types, ranging from those requiring physical action to those requiring symbolic action. The analysis of the examples also gives some sense of the situation type or frame as a coherent unit of meaning. "The situational frame is the smallest viable unit of a culture that can be analysed, taught, transmitted, and handed down as a complete entity" (Hall 1976: 129).

This implies that the situation type or frame is an essential unit for the study of the learning of language and culture, both in informal socialisation and in formal education. There is a distinguished tradition in the philosophy of education which takes this holistic approach, using the term "activity" for situation (Dewey 1916; Peters 1966). Lack of a conceptual model for situation or activity (cf. Frankena 1965: 170) has meant that the insights of this approach have hardly been explored. Much more prominent has been the separatist approach taken by scholars such as Bloom (1956) where knowledge is divided into three distinct domains leading to three different types of learning: cognitive, affective (i.e. attitudes and values), and psychomotor (skilled action). This separation of knowledge, action and value overlooks the intimate connections between them evident in the situations we have examined, and overlooks situation as a coherent unit of meaning and learning.

For an ethnographer's purposes the approach I have taken would be limited and naive. It is limited to explicit statements of cultural knowledge, whereas much cultural knowledge is tacit, though complex, literate cultures produce an enormous body of explicit statement, written and spoken. It would be naive if it assumed that these texts give detailed situational knowledge which is a rigid map that people must follow in practice, rather than a set of principles to be negotiated interactively (see Spradley 1979: 7-9). But it is the linguist's role to analyse theory texts and to examine the structure of situations. This model of the structure of situation type does not depend on the specific details of situational knowledge, but on the general organisation of situational knowledge. It depends on the idea that plants, bids, statistical tests and motions are classified, in one way or another. It therefore allows for negotiation, and it applies not only to routinised situations with a relatively unchanging knowledge base, but also to developing situations with a dynamic knowledge base. For instance, when medical doctors recognise new classes of disease and develop new medical procedures, the knowledge base of medical practice changes, but there are still classes of disease and procedures of treatment. There is continuity in the organisation of situational knowledge, though not in its details. In education, recognition of the progressive obsolescence of information has led to an increasing awareness that learners must grasp the structure of knowledge as well as its specifics, a goal much easier to state than to achieve.

The model should itself be seen as a target for inquiry rather than a final pattern. Complex detail has been avoided with the aim of making some main lines of investigation clear. One complexity is recursiveness. Action procedures, for instance, often include sub-procedures which may invoke situation sub-types. Another complexity is the element of goal-directness. This is likely to play a large role in the overall coherence of situations and in the dynamic development of situations.

The model forms part of a linguistics of context and action. The research background of the concept of context and the theory of action has been excellently reviewed by Steiner (1985). Relating the model to Halliday's view, situation type is a semiotic construct which is structured in terms of three components: field (the activity or significant social action), tenor (the role relationships of the participants) and mode (the status that is assigned to text within the situation). The examples above deal with four different fields (gardening, bridge and so on), but have a similar structure. This structure, then, could be termed the structure of field. We have focused on the overall pattern of situation, not on the roles of participants or the status assigned to text. It is worth noting that in some cases above the structure of situation is directly reflected in discourse organisation. Classes may be reflected through the chapter headings of a book, or sequence may be shown in numbered steps. In other cases, such as values, situational structure is realised semantically but not foregrounded in discourse organisation.

This section has outlined a general model of situation and illustrated it by an analysis of theory texts. It therefore addresses the problem of finding general categories of situation. But it also addresses the dilemma of situational analysis because it uses a textual method to analyse situation.

Theory texts and practical texts

The texts analysed above are theory texts; they are about situation types; they are metasituational. They explain a situation type so that a learner can understand and participate in actual instances. Reading the rules of bridge helps one play bridge and reading about parliamentary procedure helps participation in meetings. Playing bridge and participating in a meeting produce different kinds of texts, practical texts.

The parliamentary procedure text contains a practical text, an instance of a "Model Business Meeting":

> Mr. M.: I move that the treasurer and the directors be instructed to refinance the mortgage.
> Mr. N.: I second the motion.
> President: You have heard the motion. Is there any discussion?
> Several: Question.
> President: All those in favour will say "aye". (They vote.)
> Those opposed will say "no". (They vote.) The motion is carried.

The parliamentary procedure text explains motions, meeting procedures and voting. The model meeting text embodies and enacts a motion, a procedure and a vote. The metasituational, theory text explains a situation type. The situational, practical text enacts a case of the situation. (This dimension of difference in texts, of course, covers a range, including explaining a meeting to learners and reporting a meeting, as in Hansard.)

Part of this difference is captured by Halliday's two meanings of field. Field can mean either the topic or subject matter of a text or the socio-cultural action participants are engaged in. "Formal meetings" are the subject of the parliamentary procedure text. "Formal meeting" is the socio-cultural action which the participants in the model meeting are engaged in. The theory text discusses its subject matter. The practical text enacts it. Notice, however, the importance of saying which "field" we are talking about. The meeting text enacts a meeting but is about an item of business, in this case a mortgage. The parliamentary procedure text is about meetings, but it can enact instruction for an interested reader. Most texts incorporate both aspects of field, talking about something and enacting something.

Another part of this difference relates to the contrast between situation type and situation instance:

(1) Motions that are absurd or frivolous ... are prohibited.
(2) The motion is carried.

(1) is taken from the parliamentary procedure text. It is a universal or generic, timeless proposition about the situation type. (2) is taken from the model meeting text. It is a singular proposition about an actual motion carried at a particular time in an instance of the situation. Generally we might expect texts of theory to be essentially universal and timeless and texts of practice to be essentially particular and "timed", with all that this implies about their semantic features, but matters are not straightforward. (3) could be a commentary on play but is actually from the bridge rules text:

(3) The dealer gives each player thirteen cards.

Minimally, theory texts appear not to presuppose that their instances exist.

The parliamentary procedure text is a metasituational text about meetings and thus about situational texts like the model meeting. In this sense it is a text about texts, but it should be obvious that it is not a metalinguistic text or a metacommunicative text. These apply different theories. Metalinguistic text describes text according to linguistic categories such as subject or verb. Metacommunicative text describes text according to categories such as message or turn. The parliamentary procedure text describes meetings according to categories such as motion or vote. Participants at a meeting may make metalinguistic comments, metacommunicative comments, or metasituational comments about instances, as when a motion is ruled out of order. Metasituational texts describe situations theoretically according to categories local to that situation.

The difference between theory texts and practical texts is not a difference between texts without nonverbal action and texts with nonverbal action. This may be the case for bridge rules and bridge play, but it is not so for parliamentary procedure and meetings. Nor is it a contrast between monologue versus dialogue, written versus spoken language, between "displaced" versus situated speech, or between communication which is face-to-face and communication which is not. Many of these distinctions have been conflated in current discussions of context-dependent versus context-reduced discourse. Bridge rules, for instance, do not have to appear only in written text. They can be discussed in conversation at the card table, in which case they appear as spoken dialogue, situated in their context of reference and face-to-face. Again, Halliday's analysis of the components of situation helps to express this difference. The difference lies within field, and is not essentially a difference of mode or tenor.

There are thus major differences between theory texts and practical texts, differences which any theory of text should recognise and account for. But we must also consider the relation between a theory text and its associated practical texts. The parliamentary procedure text relates to the meeting text in the following way: it specifies essential, general information which is needed to interpret the meeting text. This is centrally important for a linguistic tradition concerned with the relation of situational analysis and linguistic analysis.

In discourse theory there has been much discussion of the notion of frame or schema (Brown & Yule 1983: 235). Essentially a frame is background information required to interpret a text, for instance, the meeting text. While it is generally recognised that some of this background information may have been created by prior discourse, the full significance of this point does not seem to have been grasped.

It is clear that the parliamentary procedure text specifies essential elements of the frame for the meeting text. Or, to put it more accurately, since the notion of frame is vague and can include all background knowledge relevant to this particular meeting, it specifies the general situational frame for the meeting text, knowledge which is general to all meeting texts. The importance of this for future research on frames and schema should be obvious. Its importance for the Firthian tradition is this: the relation between situation and text has been transposed into the relation between a theory text and its practical texts. This means that the relation between situation and text can be studied by a *discourse* comparison between a theory text and a practical text.

To give one example of how this works: the parliamentary procedure text states a sequence of interaction — motion, discussion, vote; the meeting text enacts a corresponding sequence. We could say that the parliamentary procedure text, the situation type, specifies a discourse sequence rule and the meeting text follows it. But the underlying metaphor of syntactic rules is misleading. Discourse sequencing is not simply rule-governed action, it is also rational, strategic action, a point now well recognised (Stubbs 1983: 101). In a study of discourse sequence (Mohan 1974) I was able to demonstrate the weakness of the rules of metaphor by comparing the discourse sequence specified in the rule texts of a game with the actual discourse sequences of play. In a large number of cases they did not correspond, but there was no evidence that a rule had been violated. Thus evidence for the relation of situation type and text was provided by a discourse comparison of rule texts with "play" texts, of theory texts with practical texts.

The interplay between theory and practice is very noticeable in education. To quote examples from my fieldnotes, a lecture about biological theory is followed by practical work in the laboratory; the mathematics teacher explains certain principles of algebra and then works through an algebra problem with the students; the social studies teacher explains the aerial analysis of cities and the students analyse a map of their own city. I know of no work which analyses the theory-practice dimension of discourse in the classroom, yet such analysis would be of great value, not only for understanding the role of language in education, and the mutual learning of language and situation, but also for our understanding of the interplay of situation and text.

Conclusion

Pursuing the goal of relating situational analysis and linguistic analysis, I have described a general model of situation and illustrated a way out of the dilemma of situational analysis for the linguist. Given a model of the structure of situation, and a recognition that a theory text like parliamentary procedure explains a situation and a practical text like a meeting enacts and operates a situation, we can use textual methods to relate situational analysis and linguistic analysis.

The distinction between theory texts and practical texts follows from the concept of situation type and should be recognised by any theory of discourse. The general model of situation appears to fit within Halliday's concept of the field of situation. The application of this approach to the role of language in education is shown in detail in Mohan (1986). The research applications of the approach open up a wide field for the future analysis of discourse and situation. Because discourse in education and socialisation makes situations explicit for learners, the data of educational discourse and the theory of language and situation illuminate each other. The study of language and meaning depends on the theory of language and situation.

The place of socio-semiotics in contemporary thought

Gordon Bruce McKellar

1. Introduction

From its beginnings in roughly the second half of the last century, most markedly in the work of Comte, Dilthey, Lewes, Durkheim, Mead, Saussure, Schutz, Wittgenstein and John Hughlings Jackson,[1] there has been emerging a radical and far reaching transformation in the scientific conception of human nature, and with it new horizons of research in disciplines ranging from linguistics to neuropsychology, speech pathology and language disorders.

The thrust of this transformation, at once altering the face of human self perception and providing principles of unification for the human sciences, and of these with the natural sciences, consists in this: in the rejection of a static, autonomic and psychic mode of interpretation of human nature — one thus affecting interpretations of language and the external world as well — and its replacement by a dynamic, evolutionary and sociobiological mode.

Until the mid-nineteenth century, philosophical and scientific inquiries, building notions of the autonomy and independence of human nature into their core, conceived of men as distinct from other men (a social autonomy), man as distinct from other forms of life (a biological autonomy) and — first on supernatural and then on introspective grounds — man as a psychic "real self" (i.e. as a subjective self or "ego" and objective "mind" proper) distinct from the natural mechanisms of body (a psychic autonomy). This reductionism, clear in historical scientific perspective, generated libraries of disconnected, incomplete, often arbitrary theories and descriptive fragments, with man as a passive processor of a world independently existing "out there", and human language constituting a simple symbolic representational mechanism for the objects and reified abstractions of this external world passively perceived.

But the cumulative accomplishments of scientific inquiry since the seventeenth century, first in natural and physiological explanation, then in the grand generalization of evolutionary theory, and later in segments of sociological, anthropological, and linguistic research, has by our age produced a very different vision of human nature. Illusions of human autonomy — social, biological or psychic — inescapably constituting an harmonious link in the evolutionary chain, are no longer possible to maintain. Hence, as with all life, each human bodily structure, physiological, neurological, neuropsychological and neurobehavioural, is as it is because of the functions that it had evolved to serve. And these necessarily — uniquely and collectively — define man. But they cannot, in and of themselves, define *a man*, for the functions evolved reach beyond the individual organism to other like organisms. Here intersects another major force, the socio-interpersonal perspective, in the contemporary reconceptualization of human nature. And in this lie the contributions of sociology, linguistics and allied inquiries.

The human environment is a *dual* environment consisting of other men — of other biologically based "subjectivities" — as well as of physical objects and processes. Thus human nature is not simply biological, nor even evolutionary and biological, but rather evolutionarily socio-biological. And with this come critical consequences.

First, man is not at all a passive processor of a given external reality but rather an active creator of it. He is the creator, intersubjectively with others, of the meaning systems that constitute much of his social (or socio-semiotic) environmental context, as well as the context of much of his "internal" world, and the re-creator, again intersubjectively with others, of the social and cultural semiotic systems into which he was born. This casts the nature and function of human language in a radically different light from its analysis on a static, autonomic view.

Language here is itself a semiotic system — a complex system of meanings, codings and interrelations — constituting a dynamic, evolutionary and functional mechanism for the creative interpretation, control and adjustment of the external world (including the world of other men), and, through this, for the creative interpretation and control of the individual himself. Hence the paramount function of the nervous system in the evolution of complex systems by which to inter- and intra-subjectively "mean".

Moreover, both in the broad structural aspects and in the internal processing mechanisms of the evolutionary socio-biology, a necessarily "constructionalist" approach is emerging: wholes are not necessarily reduceable to the sum of their parts but rather often precede or are generated by the parts. Hence we speak of *constructive*, evolutionary socio-biology.

Today the full force of this transformation is being felt in virtually every branch of the human and biological sciences though there has yet to be formulated a coherent and scientifically rigorous theory of language and social man of sufficient scope to provide the degree of scientific unification and theoretical relativity experienced by the physical sciences.

In their epoch making book *Not in our Genes*, the evolutionary geneticist R.C. Lewontin, the neurobiologist Steven Rose and the psychologist Leon Kamin, have most clearly articulated and crystallized the necessity for the development of an integrated socio-biology in our age. They have rejected singular programs of cultural determinism, or of biological determinism, and have cogently detailed the dangers of reductionist thinking. Lewontin, Rose and Kamin, however, do not offer a blueprint for sociobiological theory. Their task, rather, is the exploration of a spectrum of issues in their respective fields. Joining the tradition begun by Comte, Dilthey and Lewes, though now with voices reflecting motivations stemming from considerations internal to science, Lewontin, Rose and Kamin (1984) thus restrict themselves to fundamental issues and generally aim:

> ... to *point the way* toward an integrated understanding of the relationship between the biological and social. We describe such an understanding as dialectical, in contrast to reductionist. Reductionist explanation attempts to derive the properties of wholes from intrinsic properties of parts, properties that exist apart from and before the parts are assembled into complex structures. (pp.10-11; my italics)

Dialectically the properties of parts and wholes *codetermine* each other; they are not abstracted from their association in wholes (i.e. in "coherent unities" p.11). Thus on dialectical grounds, the properties of individual human beings:

> ... do not exist in isolation but arise as a consequence of social life, yet the nature of that social life is a consequence of our being human. It follows, then, that dialectical explanation contrasts with cultural or dualistic modes of explanation that separate the world into different types of phenomena — culture and biology, mind and body — which are to be explained in quite different and nonoverlapping ways ... Wholes are composed of units whose properties may be described, but the interaction of these units in the

> construction of the wholes generates complexities that result in products qualitatively different from the component parts. Think, for example, of the baking of a cake: the taste of the product is the result of a complex interaction of components ... (p.11)

Thus the importance of *history* in a system of such complex developmental interactions: "Where and how an organism is now is not merely dependent upon its composition at this time, but upon a past that imposes contingencies on the present and future interaction of its components" (p.11). The interaction of nonhuman organisms and their environment is far more complex than the biological determinists would have it. How much more so must it be — and how much more wrong must the biological and cultural determinist be — in the case of man:

> All organisms bequeath to their successors when they die a slightly changed environment; we make our own history, though in circumstances not of our own choosing.
>
> It is precisely because of this that there are such profound difficulties with the concept of "human nature". To the biological determinists the old credo "You can't change human nature" is the alpha and omega of the explanation of the human condition. We are not concerned to deny that there *is* a "human nature", which is simultaneously biologically and socially constructed, though we find it an extraordinarily elusive concept to pin down ...
>
> All humans are born, most procreate, all die; yet the social meanings invested in any of these acts vary profoundly from culture to culture and from context to context within a culture.
>
> This is why about the only sensible thing to say about human nature is that it is "in" that nature to construct its own history. The consequence of the construction of that history is that one generation's limits to the nature of human nature becomes irrelevant to the next ... (pp.13-14)[2]

> At every instant the developing mind, which is a consequence of the sequence of past experiences and of internal biological conditions, is engaged in a *recreation* of the world with which it interacts. There is a *mental world*, the world of perceptions, to which the mind reacts, which at the same time is a *world created by the mind*. It is obvious to all of us that *our behavior is in reaction to our own interpretations of reality*, whatever that reality may be ... Any theory of psychic development must include not only how a given *biological individual* develops psychically in a given *sequence of environments*, but how the developing individual in turn *interpenetrates* with the *objective* and *subjective* worlds to recreate its own environments. (p.276; my italics)

With this, Lewontin, Rose and Kamin have brought the general structural foundations necessary for the construction of an evolutionary socio-biology to the doorstep of contemporary science. Such a socio-biology, if realized, would mirror the physical sciences and break the last remaining links of the human and biological sciences with the metaphysical speculations and disciplinary boundaries of the past. But though the work of Lewontin, Rose and Kamin and the socio-biological tradition that has been emerging in the last century have gone far in crystallizing the necessity of an evolutionary socio-biology, the construction of its mechanisms, systems, processes and structures has been left to others.[3]

If we are to take the construction of an evolutionary socio-biology seriously, the contributions of disciplines ranging from evolutionary genetics and evolutionary biology to clinical and theoretical neuropsychology, psychology and psychiatry, speech pathology, language disorders and neuropsychology, and sociology and anthropology must be given considerable weight. But as we are dealing with the inherent *evolutional* saturation of socially constructed *meaning*, of *semiotic systems*, represented throughout the socio-biological spectrum and defining not only the ground of our experience of an "external" and "internal" world, but also the essence of human nature itself, it is to the evolutionally based semiotician, and to a social, semiotic and evolutionary-functional theory of living language, that we must turn for the keys, for the core, of the system. Thus we require a linguistics that is broadly interdisciplinary.

From the late 1950s through much of the 1970s, the dominant linguistic paradigm in the United States, as abroad, had been the transformational generative grammar of Noam Chomsky in its interpretation both as: (1) a formal (and idealized) general theory of language; and (2) as a psychological (psycholinguistic) analogue characterizing the general theory as a rationalist theory of "language and mind" specifying (a) the linguistic competence — the "knowledge of his language" — of a neutral speaker-hearer, and (b) a rationalist theory of language acquisition where the speaker-hearer's grammar is chosen by the evaluation procedure from among potential grammars permitted by the theory.

Chomsky's work in general linguistic theory has, from a formal and generative point of view, been highly illuminating and challenging, and has constituted a positive influence on linguistics. However, the psychological analogue to the general theory — Chomsky's rationalist theory of language and mind, the theory of competence and the theory of language acquisition — has served only to obscure serious work relating to the nature of living language, its realization in broad and integrated socio-biological systems, and the social, semantic, and evolutionary-functional foundations of language. Thus a *rationalist* theory of *mind*, elucidated on the ideas of the Cartesians of the seventeenth and eighteenth centuries, who are seen as collectively producing a "coherent and fruitful development of a body of ideas and conclusions regarding language and mind" worthy of "rediscovery" (Chomsky 1966: 1) has taken precedence over later centuries of solid scientific progress, empirically based, in the human and natural sciences, and over the potentialities of the constructive socio-biology that has been emerging over the last century. Hence also the idea that a formal, disciplinary linguistic theory in, of, and by itself could be "explanatory" of human language processes, psychologically interpreted.

The assumptions and projections of transformational psycholinguistics have not only obscured the larger socio-biological context, and the necessity of seeing living language in its socio-functional identity as the object of linguistic inquiry, but they have also served to obscure the contributions of a linguist who has, in many essential aspects, provided an outline of the core linguistic component (the linguistic system) of a constructional and evolutionary-functional socio-biology. This is the socio-semiotic and systemic-functional grammar of Michael Halliday. Though Halliday's work is generally seen in the contexts of applied linguistics, text analysis, education and child language studies, history will judge his contributions to human knowledge far more broadly as providing major contributions to the emerging reinterpretation of human nature — hence to our understanding of a myriad of issues in the sciences of man.

2. Halliday's contributions to an emerging socio-biology

Contrasting markedly with Chomsky's view of the autonomy and self-containedness of linguistics and linguistic theory, Halliday's work assumes the inverse view: the necessity of invoking non-formal foundational elements and criteria of relevance taken from the fruits of *scientific inquiry external* to linguistics as the basis for a *principled* and *descriptive* linguistic theory sufficient to the needs of various disciplinary "consumers".[4] Formal linguistic mechanisms are, for Halliday, simply representational devices with no intended psychological, neuropsychological, philosophical or metaphysical status.

The foundational elements of Halliday's socio-semiotic theory are divisible into two groups: (1) *primary foundational elements*, including Halliday's focus upon the evolutionary-functional analysis of structure (reduceable to biology),[5] the social (interpersonal, interactional) interpretation of man as developing and acting within a social and a physical environment (reduceable to sociology and anthropology), the primacy of intersubjective, semiotic, meaning systems — and hence the primacy of "meaning" itself — as definitive of human nature and social man (reduceable to semiotics and — broadly — to sociology), the mechanisms of cultural transmission (reduceable to education theory and sociology), and the importance of spoken, living language texts as basic to the construction of linguistic theory (reduceable to anthropology and sociology); and (2) *secondary foundational elements* ranging from the unconscious nature of spoken language (and its relationship to "conscious" written language), to the biological basis of socio-semiotic ("sociolinguistic") facts and, by implication, to the construction of an evolutionary socio-biology.

2.1. Primary foundations: the socio-semiotic and evolutionary-functional basis of human nature

A. The socio-semiotic, intersubjective basis[6]

Compatible with the requirements for a constructional, evolutionary socio-biology, the major premise of Halliday's general linguistic theory is the necessity for the return of language and man to their social (interpersonal) environment: man as "social man" and language as a living, spoken and intersubjective social semiotic. Halliday is clear in his view that the most important change in linguistic inquiry in the past decade and a half has been:

> ... that man has come back into the centre of the picture. As a species, of course, he was always there: his brain, so the argument ran, has evolved in a certain way — *ergo* he can talk. But truly speaking man does not talk: *men* talk. People talk to each other ...
>
> Linguistics is necessarily part of the study of people in their environment, and their environment consists, first and foremost, of other people. Man's ecology is primarily a social ecology, one which defines him as "social man"; and we cannot understand about social man if we do not understand about language ... [What is needed is an] integrated picture of the relation of language to other social phenomena, a general framework expressing the social meaning of language ... the terminal direction of which will be towards integration — towards eliminating boundaries rather

than imposing them, and towards a unifying conception of language as a form of social semiotic. (Halliday 1975: 17-46)

The notion of "social man" reflects for Halliday "not simply man in relation to an abstract entity like 'society as a whole' but man in relation to other men" (1971: 165). It is a perspective which "shifts the emphasis from the physical on to the human environment" (1974: 8) and in which the individual is seen as "the focus of a complex of human relationships which collectively define the context of his social behaviour" (1971: 165). But most important, it provides a perspective on language. An essential part of the behaviour of human beings in relation to the social environment is that it is "linguistic behaviour". Thus the study of social man "presupposes the study of language and social man" (1971: 165).

These are most important presuppositions. They imply the pre-eminence of spoken language, meaning and intersubjectivity as among the primary constructs and processes underlying linguistic theory.

First we note the subordination of "intersubjectivity" to the socio-semiotic model. Halliday is clear, in his acceptance of a dynamic model of human nature, that intersubjectivity plays a central role. This is reflected in several places in his writings, most clearly in his discussion of the child's construction of language (though applicable throughout the life of man). Though various sociolinguistic theories in recent years have sought to place the developing child in a social context, and thereby have replaced the traditional nativist/environmentalist perspective with an "interactionist" approach, Halliday writes:

> But learning to mean cannot be reduced to a matter of learning how to behave [linguistically] in the contexts in which meanings are exchanged ... The theory fails to account for the dynamics of dialogue, the ongoing exchange of speech roles through which conversation becomes a reality generating process ...
> We need to interpret language development more in terms of a conception of social or intersubjective creativity. Learning to mean is a process of creation whereby a child [or adult] constructs, in interaction with those around, a semiotic ["meaning"] potential that gives access to the edifice of meanings that constitute social reality ... (Halliday 1978: 90; my brackets)

The effect of this social, semiotic intersubjectivity is twofold. First there is the pre-eminence of *meaning* in the system; and secondly there is the consequence of the *social construction* of reality. Taken together, these further imply that man is not bounded by his skin. Rather, "society creates mind, mind creates society, and language stands as the mediator and metaphor for both ... Social man is effectively 'sociosemantic man' as a repository for social meanings" (1977a: 31). In Firth's words (1957: 199), we are in the world and the world is in us. This is to say that though the language construction process is usually looked upon from the static point of view of the individual and fixed external reality as represented by language, its construction is in fact an intersubjective, dialectical process, "at once a part and a means of the construction of reality" and Halliday continues:

> ... It is natural to western thinking to view both these processes [the "part" and "means" processes] largely from the standpoint of the individual. In either case he is seen as serving as the external locus of external process [reflecting] a tendency to think of a child as acquiring language and the rest of reality from somewhere "out there" — as if he was a pre-existing individual who, by the process of learning the rules, achieves in conformity with a pre-existing scheme ...
> [Rather, it is] in these intersubjective processes that lie the foundations of the construction of reality. Reality is created through the exchange of meanings — in other words through conversation ... An act of meaning is inherently an intersubjective act, one which makes possible the exchange of meanings and hence the construction of reality ... The organizing concept is that of shared meanings — a meaning potential, a semantic system, that is shared between himself and significant others. (Halliday 1978: 89-90, 95; my brackets)

Here we are returned to the pre-eminence of meaning as the leading, primary and primitive element of the system; meaning as intersubjectively developed in contextualized situational settings and unfolding as a "meaning potential" or "semantic system" in the life of an individual.[7] From the point of view of language, this systemic semantic potential is then *realizable*, in Halliday's terms, through (learned) lexicogrammatical or phonological systems (or "potentials") which constitute the lower two strata of the tristratal language system. Hence Halliday's reversal of the general linguistic perspective which has treated language as systems of forms with meanings attached: here, rather, a language "is treated as a system of meanings with forms attached to express them; not grammatical paradigms with their interpretation, but semantic paradigms with their realization" (1983: 13).

Meaning — and meaningfulness — is not, however, restricted to the semantic strata, or even to language alone. With respect to the language system, meaning is carried as well by the grammatical and phonological systems, though here as developing on a different evolutionary-functional basis than the semantic system. Firth's comments (1957: 191-192) that "It is part of the meaning of an American to sound like one" or that "... voice quality is part of the mode of meaning of an English boy" (1957: 250-251), provide striking examples of how symbolic all aspects of the language system are. "The term 'meaning' in its lay use", Halliday writes:

> ... usually suggests experiential or "content" meaning; but if the implication is that other areas of syntactic choice are not meaningful, it may be desirable to emancipate technical usage from everyday terminology. (Halliday 1968: 209; my brackets)

Even prior to the beginning of the development of the mother tongue by the child — in the "doing functions" of protolanguage — Halliday finds, again in the broad sense of the term, "meaning" (1969: 35). In fact, it is "... precisely in relation to the child's conception of language that it is most vital for us to redefine our notion of meaning, not restricting it to the narrow limits of representational [i.e. "content"] meanings, but including within it all the functions that language has as purposive, non-random, contextualized activity" (1969: 35).

But the tapestry of meanings in the life of the human being is not, and cannot be, restricted to the language system; it is not even language alone that is created by intersubjective, semiotic "conversation". All human institutions, all human creations, and the entire human environmental context in and through time — essentially the *Geisteswissenschaften* as described under various names by various thinkers — are constituted of meaningful semiotic systems. Man as "socio-semiotic man" is, in Pribram's words,[8] the only animal who must, and does, make the entire spectrum of his experience meaningful, and as such he is the only animal who has created and who is suspended in systems of society and culture.

Thus, reaching "beyond" language to the culture itself as the highest order semiotic system — containing the language system as one component in its total organization — Halliday defines "culture" compatibly as:

> A meaning potential of many modes ... comprising many semiotic systems ranging from kinship systems and modes of commodity exchange through dance and music, modes of adornment and display, architecture and art forms, imaginative literature, mythology and folklore — these are the symbolic resources with which people discover, create and exchange meanings. (1977b: 47)

And one could certainly include between the linguistic system and the culture, as Halliday does, the semiotic structure of the contexts of situation within which social men interact.

Thus the pervasiveness of meaning throughout the symbolic and meaning laden spectrum of language, situation, society and culture, and thus the corresponding evolution, on the shoulders of Saussure and Pierce,[9] of the field of semiotics. It has been with the development of semiotics, and with the maturation of the semiotician, that the fundamental nature of meaning in the life of man has been taken up as a whole. As a result of this work, the semiotic core of human nature is being greatly clarified[10] and such inquiry clearly has much to say to the emerging socio-biology.

But it is the further recasting of the *linguist* as a sociosemiotician, and of linguistics as socio-semiotics, that has shown the greatest promise for the inter-related understanding of the nature of language and the nature of (social) man. And in this lies the heart of Halliday's work. "A distinctive feature of the present decade", he writes:

> ... has been the development of semiotics as a mode of thinking, not just about language, but about all aspects of culture. From the semiotic standpoint culture is ... "a body of knowledge which members use to interpret experience and to structure behaviour ..."
>
> Semiotics is not a discipline defined by subject matter. It is a way of interpreting things. In Pyatygorsky's words, "when I analyze anything from the point of view of what it means, this is a 'semiotic situation' ..."
>
> Once the semiotic perspective develops an intellectual stance, it can, so to speak, turn back on [the system of] language, so that language is thought of as one among many semiotic systems [a social semiotic] that constitutes the culture ... (1977b: 47; my brackets)

Thus the essence of Halliday's socio-semiotic inquiry will be the investigation, though focusing on language, of the interrelations between *systems of meaning*.

In its linguistic focus, this is to interpret the entirety of the linguistic system as constituting a system of heterogeneous mechanisms of meaning: (1) stratal systems of semantic meaning, lexicogrammatical (lexical and grammatical) meaning, and phonological meaning; (2) structural meaning; (3) functional meaning (for example the categories of actor, theme, past, given, and so on which define the functional meaning of lexical items, etc., in grammatical use); and (4) an underlying, so to speak, macrofunctional meaning axis of ideational[11] (experiential and logical), interpersonal and textual semantic organization (1977a: 26; 1970: 144). And these, together constituting the linguistic system as a whole, in turn realize the other semiotic systems of the culture (1977a: 25; 1977b: 47), the behavioural or sociosemantics of the social system, and the semiotic structure of contexts of situation (1978: 183-192).

Such heterogeneous mechanisms of meaning, however, do not arise arbitrarily, randomly or by chance. If the analysis is to be scientifically viable, they must arise on a *principled basis* yielding *principled and motivated criteria*, and in Halliday's thinking they do. They arise on a *functional* — ultimately *evolutionary* — basis, and with the introduction of this axis we simultaneously put forward the second of Halliday's primary foundations.

B. *Language and evolution: the functional basis of language structure*

Thus far we have emphasized meaning, in its multivarious and heterogeneous mechanisms, and in its broadest semiotic sense, as the most general and most pervasive function of language and (social) man. Here we must be more specific.

Just as meaning is here conceived as the most general and most pervasive *function* in the human life *context* — one carried by a number of heterogeneous structures and mechanisms — so too do these structures function in respective contexts. This is not by chance for it is a fundamental law of biology that all structures, whatever their nature, are as they are because of the functions that they evolved, in specific environmental contexts, to serve. Thus, as with the first of his primary foundations, Halliday has again rooted his general theory in a scientific construct — with an independent origin and with independent confirmation — external to linguistics: the theory of evolution — the "greatest unifying theory in all biology" (Mayr 1963) — and the "dynamic relationship between structure and function" (Curtis 1968: 9) that this implies. As principled bases of wide scope, such external criteria of relevance thus serve as a means of insuring a far reaching interdisciplinary validity.

In part, support for the evolutionary-functional view of language has been cited earlier in our discussion of the general and pervasive distribution of meaning, through varied and heterogeneous socio-semiotic mechanisms in the language and in the life of man. Here we move still further into the essence of human nature by placing these socio-semiotic mechanisms themselves, and meaning itself as the most general of human functions, within the wider — causal — mechanisms of biological evolution. Halliday's question, and his answer, are crucial here:

> Why is language as it is? The nature of language is closely related to the demands that we make of it, the functions it has to serve. In the most con-

crete terms, these functions are specific to a culture ... But underlying such specific instances of language use, are more general functions which are common to all cultures. We do not all go on fishing expeditions; however, we all use language as a means of organizing other people, and directing their behaviour ... The particular form taken by the grammatical system of language is closely related to the social and personal needs that language is required to serve. But in order to bring this out it is necessary to look at both the system of language and its functions at the same time; otherwise we will lack any theoretical basis for generalizations about how language is used. (1970: 141)

Halliday's point is that if we consider what language is required to *do* in the life of man, what *functions* it must fulfil in all human cultures regardless of differences in the physical environment, then we have a basis for understanding *why* language is as it is (1974: 19). "There is", Halliday notes, "no *a priori* reason why human language should have taken just the evolutionary path that it has and no other", and that, were it not for a set of universal demands made upon language by the social intersubjective environment of man during the course of his evolution, "our brains could have produced a symbolic system of quite a different kind" (1974: 19).

For linguistics this is a critical step, and for socio-biology, particularly for neuropsychology, it is equally so. In one giant step we have moved well beyond the static associationistic view of language and localization put forward in the last century toward a principled dynamic process model, one now related to (social) environmental demands and through this to the structure of *living* language, of complex, emergent, and evolutionary-functional neuropsychological systems much more compatible with the conclusions of Jackson, Lashley and Luria.[12]

As outlined by Halliday, the general functions that language has had to evolve to serve in the life of social man are three. (See Halliday 1968: 209; 1974: 19-20).

First, language has to *interpret* the whole of our *experience*, and reduce in the process the indefinitely varied phenomena of the world around us, and of the world inside us, to a manageable number of classes of phenomena representing types of processes, events and actions, classes of objects, persons, institutions, qualities, states, abstractions and so on. Additionally language must represent basic logical relations like "and", "or" and "if" as well as those relations that are themselves created by language as "namely", "says" and "means". Together the mechanisms of the experiential and logical functions constitute the ideational component of the linguistic system.[13]

Secondly, language has to express the speaker's participation in the speech situation in the form of the roles that the speaker assumes and those that (s)he imposes on others, as well as the speaker's expression of his/her feelings, attitudes and judgements. In this we find the categories and systems of the interpersonal component of the linguistic system. These define speech functions like statement, question and answer, command and exclamation, the speaker's comment on probabilities, degree of relevance, etc., of the message, and his/her attitude about it as, for example, confirmation, reservation and contradiction.

Lastly, language must provide mechanisms for the creation of "texture" in human language by which text is distinguishable from non-text. This is the function of the textual component of language and in this we find the categories and systems of theme, information and cohesion which organize the clause as a message in and through time.

"It is the demands posed by the service of these functions", Halliday thus writes, "which:

> ... have moulded the shape of language and fixed the course of its evolution. These functions are built into the semantic system of language, and they form the basis of the grammatical organization, since the task of grammar is to encode the meanings deriving from these various functions into articulated structures. Not only are these functions served by all languages, at least in their adult form; they have also determined the way human language has evolved. (1974: 20)

But it is not only the ideational, interpersonal and textual mechanisms of language that have evolved in service of the demands made upon intersubjective semiotic exchange. All parts of the linguistic system have similarly evolved from the demands made by widely varying environmental contexts. For example, of the evolution of the tri-stratal system, its nature and its organization, Halliday cites the adaptive "problem of reduction",[14] and its intersection with the general functions of social and personal need just discussed as simultaneously having to be faced by language in its stratal evolution.[15]

Moreover, Halliday writes of the evolution of language "in conditions which relate it to the creation and maintenance of the social system" (1977a: 25), and even of the determination of the pattern of language varieties or registers by the evolution of the social functions (in the broadest sense) of language so that the register range, or linguistic repertoire of a community or of an individual is derived from the range of uses that language is put to in that particular culture or subculture (1978: 22).

Similar evolutionary-functional conclusions can be drawn for the other mechanisms of meaning of the linguistic and extra-linguistic systems for they are all, underlyingly, the result of the evolutionary relationship between environmental (contextual) demand, function and biological mechanism. It is abundantly clear that the aspect of meaning characterized by the locution "meaning is function in context" and the biological law that "evolution creates function in context" are not just parallel by chance.

2.2. Secondary foundations: the socio-biological and neuropsychological assumptions

A. *The embedding of social facts in a biological view: neuropsychology and evolutionary socio-biology*

It follows from the primary foundations — from the socio-semiotic and evolutionary-functional basis of language and human nature — that there is an an implicit socio-biological organization underlying Halliday's linguistic work. But there are other, more explicit, avenues of approach as well.

Throughout his writings from the 1960s on, Halliday has contrasted his "inter-organism" perspective on language (i.e. language as (social) behaviour — a perspective leading to sociology), with the "intra-organism" perspective dominant in linguistic and psycholinguistic studies throughout this period (i.e. language as knowledge — an inquiry leading to psychology and biology).

The first perspective, regarding the individual as a single entity — an "integral whole" — and looking at him/her from the "outside" (1974: 8), arises from the assumption that expressive and receptive speech demands the linguistic interaction of at least two individuals; the second, focusing on the "parts" and looking "inside" (1974: 8) arises because it is also possible to investigate language from the perspective of the internal mechanisms of the individual, that is "the brain structure and cerebral processes that are involved in speaking and understanding, as well as learning to speak and understand" (1974: 5). Halliday has tended to view these two — the social and the biological perspective — as "*complementary*, though with *shifts of emphasis* between them" (1974: 5; my italics). Thus Halliday's explicit acceptance in principle of the socio-biological frame[16] and his rejection in principle of cultural and biological determinism.[17]

Some caution must be exercised here, for a superficial reading of Halliday's papers might yield the impression that it is a psychological rather than a biological (neuropsychological, etc.) basis that he has in mind for the internal mechanisms of the individual. Halliday's writings sometimes do tend to blur the line between a psychological or psycholinguistic basis (i.e. language as "knowledge") and one more biological (i.e. a more mechanistic view of language where notions like knowledge are of little relevance),[18] but this is more an artefact of the contexts in which he is writing[19] than a commitment to psychological explanation. Taken on balance, however, there is little question of Halliday's evolutionary, biological foundations.

Continuing his discussion of the complementarity of the social and the biological perspectives, Halliday goes yet farther and notes the possibility of embedding one inside the other. "We can", Halliday writes, "look at social fact from a biological point of view, or at biological facts from a social point of view ... The inseparability holds in both directions" (1974: 8-9). Consequently:

> It is true that the individual's potential for linguistic interaction with others implies certain things about the internal make-up of the individual himself. But the converse is also true. The fact that the brain has the capacity to store language and use it for effective communication implies that communication takes place: that the individual has a "behaviour potential" which characterizes his interaction with other individuals of his species.
>
> Since no doubt the human brain evolved in its present form through the process of human beings communicating with one another, the latter perspective is likely to be highly significant from an evolutionary point of view. But that is not our main point of departure here. There is a more immediate sense in which the individual, considered as one who can speak and understand and read and write, who has a "mother tongue", needs to be seen in a social perspective. (Halliday 1974: 9)

Hence there is an explicit dialectical relationship between the social and the biological components underlying Halliday's thinking. Analytically, however, it is, as was implicit in the evolutionary-functional parts of his writing, the functional study of the social and semiotic phenomena of man — not just the pathological, physiological and so on — that can shed much light upon the biological phenomena. In Halliday's words:

> The ability to speak and understand, and the development of this ability in the child, are essential ingredients in the life of social man. To approach these from the outside, as inter-organism phenomena, is to take a functional view of language. The social aspect of language becomes the refer-

ence point for the biological aspect, rather than the other way around. (Halliday 1974: 12)

Halliday's dialectical, evolutionary and socio-biological assumptions (heavily influenced by Firth and Mead) are again made clear in his writing of the central role of language in the construction, from "biological specimens" (1974: 8) of identities (reflecting social roles) and of personalities (social role complexes). This is carried through in his conclusions regarding child language development. The process is "environmental with a biological foundation ... Biological conditions must be met, the level of maturation must have been reached ... but given this I would look for environmental causes in the social system" (Parrett 1974: 109). Halliday would, assuming a biological base, focus his attention on the side of the structure of the socio-situational environment within which the child learns, on the nature of the structure of the language input to the child, on the nature of the shaping of the child's environment by the culture, and of course on the functions that language serves in the life of the child (see Halliday 1974: 21).

But there is yet another area reflective of Halliday's underlyingly socio-biological perspective, one that in a sense brings us full circle to a central presupposition of his general linguistic theory: Halliday's focus on *spoken* and *living* language in its relationship to unconscious process, and writing in relation to conscious process.

B. *Language and neuropsychological process: intra-organism implications of spoken and written modes of meaning*

A central assumption of Halliday's work has been the importance of spoken, natural language as the foundation of linguistic analysis, and in the preceding pages we have discussed, in the context of his evolutionary-functional and socio-semiotic theory, a number of its consequences. All, however, have been cast within the "intra-organism" perspective. Here, with Halliday, we move briefly to the "inter-organism" perspective and to three interrelated conclusions that are illuminated in this domain: the respective natures of spoken and written language, their relationship by form and if possible by underlying mechanism; the ineffability of the grammatical categories of language; and the implications of the distinction, implicit throughout, of spoken language as "process" and written language as "product".

Prior to the appearance of the tape recorder in the 1950s, it was difficult to record significant stretches of spoken discourse. Thus written language, as much by default as by unwarranted assumption, became the model of language and the object of systematic study. In the early 1960s, in the context of teaching English intonation to foreign students, Halliday began to notice and to record unexpected phenomena concerning spoken language.[20]

Particularly Halliday noticed that individuals were often *unconscious* of the kinds of grammatical forms that they themselves were producing (Halliday forthcoming b: 1). Most striking was the remarkable complexity of many of their utterances, a complexity reflecting: (1) patterns of parataxis and hypotaxis between clauses running to considerable length and depth; and (2) given this, an unexpected well-formedness where, although the speaker seemed to be running through a maze, "he did not get lost, but fluently emerged at the end with all brackets closed and all structural promises fulfilled" (Halliday forthcoming b: 3-5). Halliday did not find in speech, in its normal, spontaneous and unselfconscious form, the kinds of false starts, hesitations, anacolutha and slips of the tongue that he had expected. And these observations about speakers led to yet another: that listeners assimilated these complex passages easily and quite unconsciously, though they were difficult to follow in writing.

Taken together, these conclusions seem to reflect something essential about the unconscious mechanism of speech itself — a mechanism which, as Halliday had noted, Boas had already discussed:

> Although over a half century earlier, Boas stressed the unconscious character of language, unique (as he saw it) among the phenomena of culture ... the lack of conscious awareness of the underlying system, and the difficulty that people have in bringing it to consciousness, are things which language shares with other semiotic systems; what is unusual about language is the extent to which the manifestation of the system, the actual processes of meaning, remains hidden from observation by performer and receiver alike. In this respect, talking is more like dancing or running than chess. (Halliday forthcoming b: 2-3)

These observations led Halliday to compare textual variants of language samples, specifically texts in the form of written language (typically considered as consciously produced) and spoken ("unconscious") language. Hence two axes.

The results of the (grammatical) analyses were striking. First, though common opinion would have written language as more complex than spoken language, complexity itself turned out to be a complex notion. Though writing was more complex in terms of measures of lexical density,[21] spoken language was more complex in "grammatical intricacy".[22] Conversely, while written language tended to be grammatically simple (a complement to lexical density), spoken language tended to be lexically sparse (a complement to "grammatical intricacy").

Secondly, introducing a "continuum" from the most spontaneous, unconscious language to the most self-monitored, attention-directed and conscious language, Halliday confirmed the former as *usually* spoken, achieving its ends grammatically,[23] and the latter as *usually* written, achieving its ends lexically. Thus the identification of the two modal points as "spoken" and "written" respectively. But discourse in either medium could be reversed, with spoken language as conscious and self-monitored (as much political discourse, lecturing, etc.) and written language as coding unconscious spontaneous language. Thus two quite distinct (though connected) neuropsychological mechanisms with characteristic processes that produce preferred — though variable — lexicogrammatical patterns and characteristic patterns of fluency and disfluency.[24]

Turning further to the unconscious side, Halliday found other "curious facts". For example, though speakers and listeners were aware that a speaker was speaking and "meaning", they were not *conscious* of what (s)he was *saying* — i.e. were not conscious of the *wording* — and a request for repetition of either party would be met with a paraphrase (from the conceptual level of meaning) and not a proper repetition (from the memory level of wording).

Another aspect of this unconscious mechanism was of great significance for Halliday: not only were the productive and receptive process mechanisms hidden from speaker and listener, so too was the nature (the "meaning") of the grammatical categories underlying language (i.e. subject, actor, theme, new, definite, present, finite, mass, habitual, locative, etc.) in their identity as linguistic categories representing — existing as — unconscious rather than conscious slices of meaning (1983: 13; 1985: xxv). This Halliday noted as an essential problem for grammatical theory, once again underscoring his rejection of the possibility of an individual's knowledge of his language. Knowledge is a function of "conscious" thought. Hence the *ineffability* of grammatical categories. Thus the existence of grammatical categories that we cannot *know* the meaning of — "That is, to which [we] could give no adequate gloss which would relate them to the categories of [our] conscious experience ... They have evolved in order to say something that cannot be said in any other way" (1983: 11). There can, that is, be no exact paraphrase of Subject, or Actor, or Theme "because there is no language-independent clustering of phenomena in our experience to which they correspond. If there was, we should not need the linguistic category to create one" (1983: 11).

And this brings us full circle to the bedrock of Halliday's general linguistic theory with which we began — for *meaning*, in turn, is:

> ... formed in action; people create meaning, by exchanging symbols in shared contexts of situation. The symbols evolve along with the meanings: there is just one process taking place here, not two, though we have to interpret it as if it was two ... [When the child] moves into the adult mode of language [he] takes over the mother tongue with its ready made grammatical categories. The symbols of the mother tongue, which have been around him from the start, now become his reality, at once a part of, and a key to, the complex phenomena of his experience. Language and culture are constructed as one. (1983: 11)[25]

In closing this section, we make one final point. Halliday has discussed the textual effects of conscious and unconscious processes as typically (respectively) producing written and spoken language, and insisted upon the primacy of spoken language for linguistic theory. Spoken language as *process* requires a different form of grammar from written language, traditionally the dominant model of language, represented as *product*. "The natural tendency", Halliday writes, "is to think of a text as a thing — a product — which is presented to us as a piece of writing ... Even 'spoken text' is turned into an object in order to attend to it" (1985: xxii).[26]

C. *Relations and realization: theoretical relativity and interdisciplinary inquiry in socio-semiotic research*

In his discussion of Saussurean semiotic theory, Jonathan Culler recounts Ernst Cassirer's assessment of the most crucial and revolutionary aspect of modern linguistics as "Saussure's insistence on the primacy of relations and systems of relations" (Culler 1976: 115).

Critical and revolutionary, that is, not only insofar as they have illuminated the field of linguistics, but more, in the sense that Saussure's methodological assumptions and conceptual foundations constitute a striking example of the means by which a number of disciplines — most notably physics — have become modern. There has been, Culler writes, an interdisciplinary "shift in the focus from objects to relations", reflecting a deeper shift in human scientific understanding that, "it is relationships that create and define objects", not objects that create and define relationships. "The misconception which has haunted philosophic literature throughout the centuries", Culler quotes Whitehead as saying:

> ... is the notion of "independent existences". There is no such mode of existence; every entity is to be understood in terms of the way it is interwoven with the rest of the universe. (Culler 1976: 115)

It would be hard to find a more appropriate characterization of Halliday's deep philosophical and scientific commitments than these. In his analysis of the underlying paradigmatic systems of potential of the linguistic system, or in his systemic analyses of socio-semiotic systems, situation and culture, Halliday has transcended Saussure, moving yet more deeply into linguistic relativity and still more decisively toward an interdisciplinary interweaving of scientific foundations.

But what of the principle of realization? Here Halliday's thinking again projects beyond disciplinary boundaries and again connects with the scientific community at large.[27] Though in Halliday's early thinking the principle of realization had a decidedly deterministic cast of irreversibility to it,[28] the influence of his strongly Whorfian base, and of a number of readings external to linguistics (e.g. Bohm 1980), convinced Halliday that the principle of realization could not be seen in simplistic cause and effect terms. Though still feeling far from satisfied with his conceptualization of the nature of this principle, Halliday is now certain that it is "something much deeper than I have thought — something underlying human systems, natural systems, and biological systems, and it is is something to which modern developments in science are coming closer". Thus again a principle confronted by Halliday in linguistics is conceived as an interprinciple reflecting fundamental unities in scientific understanding.

As Saussurean linguistics provided science with a manageable principle which, on analysis, reflected fundamental insights compatible with the conclusions of other sciences, so too in Halliday's eyes does the principle of realization — and this for related reasons. But here Halliday sees linguistics as taking the lead. While, in the past, linguistics has tended to lag behind other sciences (as in evolutionary linguistic studies following Darwin's work), Halliday sees a possible reversal here with human systems — specifically language systems — becoming the model for systems of nature. Particularly, Halliday, believes, if the linguist can understand the principle of realization properly, generalizable feedback from linguistics to natural science, meeting and connecting with compatible principles emerging from their enquiries, might be possible.

Given Halliday's strongly interdisciplinary leanings, leanings realized in *all* facets of socio-semiotic theory, it is fitting to highlight perhaps his most important message — one directed to the health of future science: the critical need for interdisciplinary research as the lifeblood of progress and through which alone the potential of contemporary scholarship can be realized. Taking aim at his own field, Halliday has in the past characterized linguistics as "overspecialized", "underapplied" and, most importantly, as "assuming that the human being is bounded by his skin" (1977a: 20). And this, Halliday notes further, is related to a question that has exercised philosophically minded linguists from Saussure onwards: " 'Where is' language — 'in here' or 'out there'?" (1977a: 20). Of course the answer is "neither" — or "both" — as you like. It is the boundaries that must be reset.[29] If this is true for linguistics, even for as broad a linguistics as Halliday's, how much more so for the investigation of a far reaching, and encompassing, socio-biology?

3. MATRIX: the multimodal analytic theory and research instrument of a constructional and evolutionary socio-biology

Lewontin, Rose and Kamin, following and reinforcing a tradition now a century old, have cogently articulated and crystallized the importance of an integrated and principled socio-biological theory for our age. Scientifically and historically the time is right, through interdisciplinary research, to lay out the blueprint by which it, along with the modifications, additions and reinforcements definitive of scientific progress, can be constructed.

Socio-semiotics is not this, nor — even — can it stand as its foundation. Socio-biology, as a representation of human nature and of the biological, neuropsychological, socio-semiotic and neurolinguistic mechanisms that have evolved in its realization, demands independent foundations and independent initiatives. But Halliday's work — contacting and interpenetrating socio-biological theory *through the mediation of common, fundamental and embracing scientific principles* of the scope and generality of evolutionary theory and the derivative functional analysis, the primacy of meaning and the centrality of semiotics in the life of man, the socio-interpersonal perspective of language and human nature, and the deep methodological necessity of constructionalism and of relational systems as theoretical givens — constitutes a major contribution and promising component of this inquiry.

Though the most general principles of constructive socio-biological theory — evolution, function, semiotics, meaning, and social interaction — pervade and underlie all components of the socio-biological system, it is the mechanism and profound significance of the notion of "relational system" that provides the structure. As a socio-biological construction, the human being (as an individual and as a species) constitutes the final common path of interpenetrating socio-semiotic and neuropsychological-neurolinguistic *systems*. Said in another way, man is constituted of a *socio-semiotic matrix* interpenetrating and interpenetrated by a *neuropsychological-neurolinguistic matrix*:[30] process and system, not object and product.

From the point of view of the research effort in contemporary science, a system of three interpenetrating systems, and thus three interpenetrating though self-contained theories, is at issue here: $MATRIX_1$, the general theory of a constructional, evolutionary socio-biology as constituted of the interpenetration of $MATRIX_2$, the general theory of socio-semiotics — that is of language and social man roughly in the form outlined by Halliday,[31] and $MATRIX_3$, the general theory of neuropsychology-neurolinguistics in the form that it is currently evolving at Casa Colina Hospital for Rehabilitation Medicine, Pomona (California).[32]

Thus, through the complex system constituting the general socio-biology — one as well capturing the essence of a human nature in a way that sets its boundary beyond the skin of the individual — we are able to shift the focus of our inquiry and view the system through the lens, and from the vantage point of either socio-semiotics or neuropsychology.

Earlier Lewontin *et al.* wrote of the profound difficulties inherent in the notion of a human nature at once biologically and socially constituted, and of the difficulty of pinning down such an extraordinarily elusive concept. After centuries of supernaturalism, metaphysics and individualism, and thus with relatively little historical precedent upon which to draw, this is no surprise. Socio-biology as the science of social man is a science of *our* age, and one for which considerable ground-breaking thus remains. But this notwithstanding, MATRIX would seem to be a step in the right direction.

Notes

1. Cf. Books I and II of my *Social Man: The grand synthesis. On the foundations of a contemporary neurolinguistics* (unpublished) for the development and particulars of this tradition.

2. Lewontin, Rose and Kamin note further that no human behaviour is built into our genes in such a way that it cannot be modified and shaped by social conditioning: "Even biological features such as eating, sleeping and sex are greatly modified by control and social conditioning ... The sexual urge in particular may be abolished, transformed, or heightened by life history events" (p.267). But human beings cannot either be "simple mirrors of social circumstance; if that were the case there could be no social evolution" (p.267).

3. "We are at a severe disadvantage, for unlike biological and cultural determinists who have simple, even simplistic views of the bases and forms of human existence, we do not pretend to know what is a correct description of all human societies, nor can we explain all criminal behavior, wars, family organization and property relations as a manifestation of one simple mechanism" (Lewontin *et al.* 1984: 266). Historically speaking, discoveries in science simply happen in their own time. Though George Henry Lewes, following Comte and the impact of evolutionary theory on his own age would call for the constitution of a socio-biology as early as the 1870s, the synthesis could not proceed without greater progress being made in allied sciences. For example, though the centrality of evolution and of language — that is of *meaning* or *semiotic* systems — have been the cornerstones of what we here call the "socio-biological tradition", linguistics was far from the necessary interpretation of language in semantic, evolutionary and socio-functional (and hence biologically compatible) terms. Questions of historical change, then questions of static language structure, would occupy the linguist through the first half of the twentieth century. Only then did an appropriate linguistic theory emerge.

4. This characterization is taken from Halliday's "Syntax and the Consumer" (1964).

5. Halliday himself does not reduce his work to, or discuss his work in biological terms.

6. More descriptively: "Language and Text as Intersubjective, Sociosemiotic Behavior: the functional primacy of meaning, socially constructed".

7. There is some ambiguity in the notions of "meaning potential" and "semantic system" in Halliday's work. These, and other technical terms, are employed differently in different contexts. Though the present paper should provide some clarification, an explanatory digression is impossible here.

8. Pribram, K., *What Makes Man Human* (1971).

9. Semiotics, though recent as a formal field of inquiry, has its origins in early Greek thought. Saussure — and Hjelmslev's Saussurean distinction between the "expression plane" and the "content plane" — and not Pierce, constitutes the basis of Halliday's semiotic thinking.

10. Umberto Eco in *Semiotics and the Philosophy of Language* (1984) concludes that: "Certainly, the categories posited by a general semiotics can prove their power insofar as they provide a satisfactory working hypothesis to specific semiotics. However, they can also allow one to look at the whole of human activity from a coherent point of view. To see

human beings as signifying animals — even outside the practice of verbal language — and to see that their ability to produce and to interpret signs, as well as their ability to draw inferences, is rooted in the same cognitive structures, represent a way to give form to our experiences. There are obviously other philosophical approaches, but I think that this one deserves some effort". See also John Sturrock's review of this book (1985).

11. These are the "content" or "representational" meanings discussed earlier along with the logical meanings.

12. Thus we move toward a functional, evolutionary process model of the brain acknowledging though subsuming the localizationist, associationist model within a wider, all encompassing one.

13. Halliday (1968: 209) notes further that: "The three terms 'semantic', 'representational' and 'logical' refer to different aspects of this combined function: 'semantic' suggests its place in the total linguistic system, 'representational' emphasizes its relation to extralinguistic factors, while 'logical' implies an underlying structure that is independent of syntax and may be opposed merely to 'grammatical' as meaning to 'form'"

14. The "problem of reduction" is that a large number of complex meanings must be encoded in a small number of simple sounds, and this can only be achieved by the evolution of intervening levels of grammar and phonology.

15. "But this stratal structure has evolved in the context of the demands that are made on language, and the nature and organization of these intermediate levels ... reflect the role of language in the life of man" (Halliday 1974: 50-51).

16. Note also: "When we talk of 'social man' the contrast we are making is not that of social versus individual; the contrast is rather that of the social versus the psychophysiological" (Halliday 1974: 8).

17. Though in the course of his work often assuming much more cultural influence than this more balanced view might imply. For a more extended statement, see Parrett 1974: 108-110.

18. This blurring is the consequence of Halliday's trying to do two things at once in his characterization of the intra-organism perspective: he is trying to place the inter-organism perspective relative to contemporary psycholinguistic inquiry, saying that *in principle* the two could be mediated by the same underlying theory and hence are complementary (without necessarily subscribing to psychological explanation himself), and, at the same time, he is characterizing his preference, following Firth, of biological — hence neuropsychological or neurolinguistic — explanation rather than that of the psycholinguist. Hence the lumping together of the psycho-philosophical "language as knowledge/language as rule" view with the neuropsychological view in his discussion of the intra-organism perspective. The two, however, should be kept rigorously separate.

19. Specifically the Chomskian polemics of the 1960s and 1970s.

20. See Halliday's "Patterns in Words," *The Listener* (January 13, 1986: 53-55).

21. Lexical density is measured in various ways as the proportion of lexical items (content words) to the total discourse, reflecting the "solidarity among its parts such that each equally prehends and is prehended by all the others" (Halliday forthcoming b: 6, 13).

22. Grammatical intricacy refers to complex patterns of the organization of the clause complex reflecting a flow of "dynamic mobility" whereby "each figure provides a context for

the next one, not only defining its point of departure but also setting the conventions by reference to which it is to be interpreted" (Halliday forthcoming b: 12-13).

23. See Halliday (1985: xxiv).

24. Halliday conjectures that the fluidity of unconscious processes in language is necessitated by its relationship to the changing aspects of context within which it is functioning. Specifically, it is because spoken language *does* respond continually to even the most subtle shifts in its environment that a corresponding fluidity and mobility is necessary. Hence, not only does spoken language exhibit rich semantic patterning and grammatical variation not found in writing, but there are severe semantic demands placed as well upon systems which vary the form of the message (e.g. theme and information), upon tense and modality, and so on.

25. Under these circumstances, Halliday points out, the *only* available linguistic option is "the displaying of the categories at work, in paradigmatic contexts, so as to highlight the semantic distinctions they are enshrining" (1983: 11).

26. Here, reflecting the roots of his work, Halliday turns to the importance of Hjelmslev for the foundations of a compatible linguistic theory (see Halliday 1985: xxii-xxiii).

27. The following discussion is the result of numerous personal communications from Professor Halliday.

28. This Halliday has referred to as his "first period". See Halliday (1977a: 110).

29. See Halliday (1977a: 21 and 1985: xxii-xxiii).

30. This theoretical framework was begun at the ·University of Illinois, Chicago Circle, as early as 1974 with my (unpublished) paper entitled "Language, Process and Reality: Toward a socio-biological theory". This work was continued at Stanford University both in the Department of Linguistics and under Professor Karl Pribram, and later at the University of Sydney under M.A.K. Halliday in the Department of Linguistics and with Anne Deane at Lidcombe Hospital, Lidcombe, N.S.W. I am indebted to all who have been so kind to me.

31. There remain, however, some significant problems to be worked out in this theory. As Halliday himself has stated (personal communication) only the broad outlines of the theory are coherent; the details are not. For a good summary of Halliday's socio-semiotic theory, see Halliday (1974: 17-46).

32. See "Casa Colina Hospital Research Memorandum No. 2" (1985, unpublished).

Changing the subject[1]

Terry Threadgold

1. Introduction

In 1978 when he published *Language as Social Semiotic* Michael Halliday sketched out an extraordinarily rich proposal (for, in Hallidayan terms, it was clearly not yet a proposition) for a social theory of language and for a theory of language as a reality-constructing and reality-changing semiotic process. This is what I take a "social semiotic" to be — a probabilistic, never entirely predictable system for making meanings (and thus always a process) which at once constructs and changes, and is constructed and changed by, social processes and social realities.

The details of this sketch, rich as they are, have never been fully developed by a linguistics which is always struggling to break down the walls of the "inside" constructed on the Saussurean predication of an "inside" and an "outside" to linguistics and on the exclusion of the "outside" (ethnography, the social world, history, the speaking subject and the culture) from the "inside" (Saussure 1974: 15-30).

Thus Halliday's important inclusion of the ideas of Whorf and Bernstein in his sketch of language as social semiotic — ideas which, like Halliday's own, challenge this position (Derrida 1974) — has been, until fairly recently, systematically and tactically ignored by most of those working within the major linguistic paradigms. Hasan (e.g. 1984) and Martin (1986) are notable exceptions. To take up those ideas would involve "changing the subject", acknowledging what Michael Gregory called twenty years ago "the absence, with some notable exceptions (...) of development of a contextual and situational statement ... due to what might well be called a remarkable failure of nerve ..." (Gregory 1967: 178), and recognising that linguistics itself is "inside" this contextual problematic or rather that the latter is not "outside" linguistics.

The consequence of this would be to acknowledge that Michael Halliday's ideas about language, like language itself, do not stand apart from other important theories of social meaning, that they have intellectual contexts/intertexts which far exceed the usually attested Firthian/Malinowski and even Prague School backgrounds (Halliday 1984), and that these include the work of Bakhtin/Vološinov (1973, 1981, 1973), Michel Foucault (1972) and Umberto Eco (1976) — to name but a few. These contexts/intertexts are important for they locate Hallidayan linguistics "outside" mainstream linguistics, in ways that explain its "otherness" in that context, but give it a far wider intellectual validity in a larger socio-historical framework.

To acknowledge this would change the subject of linguistics and the linguistic subject by making some effort to put into practice theoretically, in the business of text analysis, Halliday's own insight that:

> In order to understand language ... we have to understand many other things besides and hence a linguistic theory has to be a means of inter-semiotic translation, interfacing with other theories of social meaning and so facilitating the input of findings from elsewhere. (1978: 7)

The analysis of Pope's early eighteenth century "imitation" of Chaucer's fourteenth century *House of Fame* which follows will explore some of the enormously complex consequences of this insight: but I want to suggest at the outset that there is no way of dealing with the different constructions of reality and subjectivity in these texts, with the historical, social, and cultural "changing of the subject" that they realise and instantiate, without changing the subject of linguistics and the linguistic subject in the directions outlined by Halliday (1978). The consequences of such new directions are, as Fowler (1987) has pointed out, a critical linguistics often characterised by linguists as "not linguistics".

2. The subject of history in space and time: a linguistic analysis of Pope's version of Chaucer's *House of Fame*

What I propose to do in this paper involves giving an account of a detailed systemic-functional analysis of two passages, one from Chaucer's *House of Fame* and the other from Pope's eighteenth century imitation of it, *The Temple of Fame*. This analysis reveals a number of interesting differences in the "choices" in meaning that are actually made, and that can be made within the historically defined discursive formations of which the poems are a part.

The narrative structures of the poems, which realise these meanings *and* instantiate systematically, in a metagrammatical[2] way the characteristic ways of meaning in two cultures, belong to two different historical modes of narration, and are situated within two different sets of perceptual (Lowe 1982) or discursive/intertextual semantic fields.[3] My argument will be that the choices in meaning which structure the two poems constitute two quite different grammars and that these stage a metagrammatical argument (Halliday 1980) about differences in perception, about the subject of history in time and space, about the question of subjectivity as discursively and historically constrained and produced, and about social meaning making practices.

The differences in the two texts can be related to what Lowe (1982) calls a perceptual field constituted of an oral-chirographic culture, a hierarchy of sensing (touch, sight, smell etc.) and an epistemic order of anagogy in which concepts of space and time were inexact: and a seventeenth/eighteenth century perceptual field constituted of a typographic culture, the primacy of the sense of sight and an epistemic order of representation in space based on identity and difference.

This particular view of the relationship or difference between the late medieval and seventeenth-eighteenth century discursive formations or "perceptual fields" owes much to Foucault's early work (1972, 1973) and to Bakhtin's account of the medieval world of Rabelais and Carnival (1970). It is a view which has been elaborated in a number of other accounts of the systems of knowledge and belief which are instantiated systemically in texts as the characteristic ways of meaning in these periods.

I am thinking of Ong's work on Ramus and the decay of dialogue (1958), and on the media (1967) which traces, in the rhetorics and topical logics of the early fifteenth to the mid-seventeenth century, the development of "method" (scientific method) as spatial, visual representation and dichotomy: of Slaughter's (1982) work on Universal languages and Scientific taxonomy in the seventeenth century which explores the development of "method", and of these spatial, visual and dichotomising tendencies in philosophy and "natural" science: and of work like that of Gouldner (1976), Colish (1968) and Cohen (1977) which traces these same concepts in relation to ideas about language, reality and mind in the medieval and seventeenth/eighteenth century periods respectively. All of these studies deal with the "epistemic" disjunctions between the periods in various ways, and provide considerable empirical evidence for the existence of the structures of perception and the epistemes[4] of Lowe's account across a wide range of texts and situation-types in both periods and cultures.

The purpose of my systemic analysis of Pope's and Chaucer's poetry is to explore the relationship between text and context (Halliday & Hasan 1985), between language as social semiotic and other socially constructed and constructing semiotic systems, in order to try to understand the "what" and the "how" and the "why" of the construction of social realities in and through texts. This involves exploring, extending and stretching Halliday's (1978) systemic-functional account of language as social semiotic. Practice (textual analysis) inevitably strains at the limits of theories. Its function is precisely to question the autonomy of theories and to extend them by forcing them to participate in those social processes which involve the exchange (and change) of meanings.

In all of the texts mentioned above as dealing with medieval and seventeenth century "fashions of speaking" (Whorf 1956) what is actually being described is the discursive construction of the speaking/knowing subject of twentieth century science, and of the distancing and separation of that subject from his/her object of enquiry. In this process consciousness becomes centred in an autonomous subject who is seen as distinct from and thus able to *observe* the perceived truth and unity of the social "*real*", in ways that are constructed as unproblematic and unmediated by the processes of semiosis. That is, the subject and the social are here conceived as "natural", not semiotically "constructed" phenomena.

It is precisely the historical semiotic construction of this contemporary and historically determined view of the subject and the social world which is foregrounded by a systemic analysis of Pope's and Chaucer's poems. (See Foucault 1972, 1973; Kristeva 1980: Ch. 5; Barthes 1977; Bakhtin 1970; Wilden 1980; Eco 1976 for other accounts of this process).

As Eco put it: "In every century the way artistic forms are *structured* reflects the way in which science or contemporary culture views reality" (1981: 57; my italics).

However the problems of how this happens — the analysis of discourses, genres, subjectivity and narrative, of their historical and ideological determinations, and of the kinds of systems of knowledge and belief which they presuppose and reproduce, has hardly been explored at all in literary semiotics in any systematic way. Apart from the seminal and suggestive work of Foucault and Bakhtin and more recently the work of for example Reiss (1982), Sharratt (1982), Patey (1984), Wellbury (1984), Easthope (1983) and Thibault (1985), specific textual studies which attempt to explore these issues are remarkably scarce.[6]

This paper then, will explore in specific contexts and in specific instances the linguistic/semiotic structure of texts and contexts and the functioning of textual and contextualising processes.

3. Text and context: constructing a social semiotic theory

My systemic-functional analysis of Chaucer (Text A) and Pope (Text B) will attempt to make meanings, to re-read Chaucer's and Pope's texts, by way of an elaboration of Halliday's (1978) account of the relations between text and context; an elaboration which attempts to build into Halliday's (1978: 69) metaphorical graphic model of textual production an account of reading codes and practices, the work of Lemke (1983, 1984), Martin (1984) and Thibault (1985) within systemic-functional linguistics, and of Foucault (1972), Eco (1976, 1981), Bakhtin (1970, 1973, 1981), Whorf (1956) and Bernstein (1971, 1982) in a wider framework.

The theory aims to *make possible* metagrammatical readings[2] of the linguistic/semiotic structure of texts, that is, of their characteristic ways of meaning, and of the relations texts have with other texts. Systems of knowledge and belief, social relations, actions and events and fields of "content" are produced, re-produced and changed only *through* this intertextual process and *in* texts which are the product of specific conditions of production and reception.

In any given period there are clusters of globally shared meanings which are instantiated in different forms in everyday talk and in various institutionalised discourses. These constitute part of the discursive practices (Halliday's (1978) higher order social semiotic), what Foucault called the *episteme* and Whorf (1956) and Eco (1976) identify as recurrent patterns of semantic choice in a culture, its characteristic "ways of meaning" (Hasan 1984) determined by cultural pertinence.

Foucault in "History of Systems of Thought"[7] describes discursive practices and the sets of "discursive regularities" which he later (1973) called the episteme as follows:

> (...) it is usually the case that a discursive practice assembles a number of diverse disciplines or sciences or that it crosses a certain number among

them and regroups many of their individual characteristics into a new and occasionally unexpected unity.

Discursive practices are not purely and simply ways of producing discourse. They are embodied in technical processes, in institutions, in patterns for general behavior, in forms for transmission and diffusion, and in pedagogical forms which, at once, impose and maintain them.

One of the functions of dominant discursive practices (the episteme) as a partial instantiation of the higher order social semiotic appears to be that they serve to suppress or background all the other meanings potentially available within the semiotic systems where they are realised, and thus naturalise existing disjunctions between systems and contradictions within them.[8]

In this respect the "discursive regularities", the "characteristic ways of meaning" which constitute an episteme also function, as part of a larger field of power and practice, in ways that are akin to the functioning of what Bernstein (1982) has called the principles of framing and classification which constitute context. Thus:

> We can see that power relations can accomplish their reproduction by establishing a principle of classification which suppresses its own contradictions and dilemmas through the insulations it creates, maintains and legitimates. (p.315)
>
> ... Variations or changes in framing produce variations or changes in the rules regulating what counts as legitimate communication/discourse and its possible texts. (p.325)
>
> Every culture specialises principles for the creation of a specific reality through its distinctive classificatory principles and, in so doing, necessarily constructs a set of procedures, practices and relations from a range of such sets. As a consequence each modality can be regarded as an arbitrary angling of a potential reality. (p.319)

Context then (the social semiotic) can be described in terms of the "messages" (practices) and "voices" (categories) which are the realisations of the strong or weak principles of framing and classification which *are* coding orientations (Bernstein 1982:329).

What is clear is that this "social semiotic" in each case encodes many more "voices" than the dominant episteme articulates. These are the "other voices" of which Bakhtin (1981: 43, 327) speaks in his accounts of textual polyphony and social heteroglossia (1973, 1981: 263, 428):

> (...) all utterances are heteroglot in that they are functions of a matrix of forces practically impossible to recoup, and therefore impossible to

> resolve. Heteroglossia is as close a conceptualisation as possible of that locus where centripetal and centrifugal forces collide; as such, it is that which a systematic linguistics must always suppress. (Holquist 1981:428)

Heteroglossia is also that entropy in the system which constitutes the very possibility of change[10] and it thus has affinities with Bernstein's "yet to be voiced":

> Modality *within* culture ... has its source ... in a specific distribution of power which creates, maintains, reproduces and legitimates a specific syntax of generation of meaning. We shall assert that, in its tacit acquisition, not only are dominating and dominated "voices" produced, but equally an oppositional "yet to be voiced", whose syntax is constituted by *insulations* created by the classificatory principle ... the latter are a source of change in "voice" ... but they can only be a source of change ... if they are already a feature of that "voice". (Bernstein 1982: 320-321; see also Foucault 1972: Ch. 3, "Contradictions").

The problematising of meaning then, the many-voicedness, the conflict which is the potential for change is where the subject enters the picture. This heterogeneity positions the subject at the intersection of the cultural coding processes I have already described and the labour of producing texts from a position within discourse and the social: for it is human labour which transforms social meanings and values into texts as objects or as social discourse. Eco (1976) and Lemke (1983) both stress this role of human labour in sign and meaning production and reading. Whether the text is object, commodity (closed system) or social discourse (praxis, open) is a historically and ideologically constrained choice which the subject is positioned to make. It depends as much on genres of reading and writing (practices) and thus on subject positioning, as it does on the nature of the text.

What positions and constrains the subject is located by Eco (1981:61) and Halliday (1987) in "a way of looking at the world", what Hasan has called "a congruence between verbal and non-verbal behaviour, both of which are informed by the same set of beliefs, values and attitudes" (Hasan 1984: 106), what Whorf called "fashions of speaking" (1956), Foucault (1973) located in epistemology, and Bernstein (1971, 1982) thought of as coding orientations. All of them were identifying the "discursive regularities" which Eco (1981:61) and Foucault identified as contradictory epistemological situations.

Such discursive regularities constrain in very real ways the meanings that can be made, the stories that can be told, and the cultural and social construction of realities and subjectivities. They are the "stuff" which genres fashion to transmit and reproduce the situation and text-types of a culture, the corners of the language around which it is not impossible, but certainly difficult, to see (Reddy 1979; Silverstein 1979). Eco's (1981) account, like all those mentioned above, assumes that the episteme as a world-view does not preclude a view of cultural conflict or heteroglossia. Indeed the notion of world-view, episteme, presupposes a view of culture with conflict.

4. Subjectivity and the social semiotic codes

Such a view of culture assumes the discursive and socio-historical determination as well as the freedom of the labouring subject of semiosis (Eco 1978:2:14).

This requires elaboration in relation to the social semiotic codes of Halliday's (1978) account of language as social semiotic. These social semiotic codes are the "orientations towards meaning", described in Bernstein's work in the crucial socialising contexts of the family (Bernstein 1973: 40-41) and the school (1982, 1986). In Halliday's theory they provide a way of accounting for the fact that, while each language provides a very wide range of meaning potential, certain sub-groups of its speakers characteristically "*select* only a particular sub-set of the options permitted by the overall system" (Hasan 1984: 107).

These coding orientations then provide another way of accounting for social heteroglossia in terms of the differential access subjects have to the genres and discourses that construct and maintain relations of power and knowledge at the highest level of the discursive and social formation. In Bernstein's work coding orientations are related to the central concept of role-system which is basic to his theory of social structure and cultural transmission. They provide a hypothesis as to why certain forms of behaviour are likely under certain specifiable social conditions (Bernstein 1982: 336; Hasan 1973: 285). The term "code" itself is used as follows:

> Code refers to a specific cultural regulation of the realisation of commonly shared competencies. Code refers to specific semiotic grammars regulated by specialised distributions of power and principles of control. Such grammars, will have amongst other realisations, specific linguistic realisations. (Bernstein 1982: 337)

Bernstein's (1971, 1973) account of the codes recognised two fundamental varieties, which he called elaborated and restricted. Hasan (1984) has subsequently called them explicit and implicit semiotic styles respectively. It is the distinction between what are called communalized and individuated types of role-systems which is pertinent to code variation in these accounts (Hasan 1984: 282-283), and what is most important about this is that it foregrounds the issue of social class and raises questions of ideology which cannot be avoided in any critical account of the way meanings are made in social systems.

Thus, despite criticisms of Bernstein's work[11] as being overly deterministic and based on too narrow a functionalist view of social class (Henriques *et al*. 1984: 271; Cameron 1985: 159), his basic recognition of the fact that various styles of meaning and speaking are socially constructed phenomena, which reinforce established power structures, and that the peculiarities of semiotic or semantic styles must be explained in terms of the peculiarities of social structure is of fundamental importance.

This is relevant not only to the synchronic study of semiotic styles *within* a culture, but as Hasan (1984) has shown, to the study of the semiotic/semantic distance *between* cultures,[12] and as Bernstein (1984: 336) suggested and I shall demonstrate here, to the semiotic/semantic distance between epistemically distinct and diachronically different texts in the same culture. The semiotic differences between language varieties of these kinds are created by differences in characteristic ways of meaning which can be related to cultural differences between the two communities involved. Central to this relationship is the subject who labours to produce meanings (Eco 1978), whose subjectivity is constantly produced and reproduced in and through language: for meaning "styles" are the realisations of subjects' differential positioning in relation to power, knowledge and compliance, and this always involves differential access to the practices and activities, the social discourse roles, the systems of information and the processes of production and consumption that constitute the culture and the social. This account of subjectivity borrows much from Foucault, Bernstein and Lacan and from the useful synthesising work of Henriques *et al*. (1984): but the question of semiotic styles has often been explored in the literature in quite different contexts.

What Bernstein and Hasan identify as implicit/explicit coding orientations is not unrelated to Eco's (1976: 135) undercoding/overcoding categories, which he in turn correlates with Lotman's (1975) distinction between text-oriented/grammar-oriented societies. These distinctions are comparable to Wilden's (1972: 164-165, 192-194) distinction between analog and digital modes of communication.

Bakhtin's (1981: 411, 84) monologic/dialogic styles and chronotope categories also parallel aspects of the implicit/explicit semiotic distinction. The monologic correlates with "modes of control which utilise strong boundary control" (Hasan 1984), that is strong framing/classification. The dialogic corresponds with weak framing and classification (Bernstein 1982). The question of "context dependency" as a characteristic of "implicit" codes (Hasan 1984: 283-284) is relevant to the realisation of particular "chronotopes" and impinges on the speech/writing distinction and the whole question of the different dialectics between texts and contexts that speech and writing involve.

Speech and writing as technological constraints on semiotic coding orientations, are systematically related to the monologic/dialogic difference. Thus speech/writing related questions of grammatical intricacy/lexical density and of differences in experiential (congruence or incongruence) and interpersonal (affect, status etc.) *distance* (Martin 1986; Halliday 1979, 1985), which are to some extent an effect of the different technologies and posibilities of the spoken and written modes, are also systematically related to "semiotic styles".

Table 1 sets out some of the oppositions in "semantic styles" which the work outlined above has recognised. In each case the labels (and their implicit binarism) seem to point to the recognition of apparently opposite kinds of "discursive regularities", or regular patternings of lexicogrammatical "choices". The labels are "metagrammatical" readings of systemic choices which convey meanings in what Halliday (1980) has called a metag-

TABLE 1. SEMANTIC STYLES/SEMIOTIC CODING ORIENTATIONS

Restricted	Elaborated
Implicit	Explicit
Speech	Writing
Grammatical intricacy (hypotaxis)	Grammatical simplicity (parataxis)
No lexical density (congruence)	Lexical density (incongruence)
Chronotype — subjective/synchronic	Chronotype — objective/diachronic
Dialogic	monologic
Undercoding	Overcoding
Text-oriented	Grammar-Oriented
Analog	Digital
(Subject/object not disjoined)	(subject/object disjoined)
(Subjectivity — multiple)	(Subjectivity — unified)

rammatical way. They point to the implicit recognition in all this work of what Bernstain called "specific semiotic grammars regulated by specialised distributions of power and principles of control" (1982: 337).

Again, in Bernstein's (1982) terms, one could characterise the two kinds of semiotic codes that seem to be involved here in terms of weak or strong framing and classification. In fact, as will be apparent in the outline of the juridico-political, informational and technological semiotics (see Table 2) which position the subjects of the Chaucer and Pope texts and are themselves constructed in and through them, the situation is extremely ambiguous, even at the most superficial level. For the medieval subject the contextual configuration is variously very strongly *and* very weakly *classified* (with respect to social roles, relationships and so on) while the discursive situation (with respect to disjunctions between scientific discourses etc.) is very weakly *framed*. For the eighteenth century subject both framing and classification are strong. A subject with access to/positioned in and by this kind of "certainty"/"truth" has apparently far greater access to power and knowledge than one whose position with respect to power constantly fluctuates and whose access to knowledge is both of a different order (a different set of available resources) and more a matter of "undercoding" (constructing new meanings) than of "overcoding" (mapping already culturally coded meanings onto cultural products). But that is already a historically contingent reading.

What is extraordinarily interesting is that the respective semiotic styles of Chaucer's and Pope's texts which I shall examine in the next section are realisations of this basic difference in coding orientation, and that what appears to be realised in Pope's early eighteenth century text is precisely the emergence of that middle-class "explicit" style identified by Hasan (1984).

Yet this in itself is an indication of the dangers of locating significance in the systemic choices or lexicogrammatical patterns *themselves*. For it is very clear that if, as Bernstein has argued, the "institutional availability, distribution and realisation of elaborated codes is established through the modality of education" (1982: 312) then *both* the Chaucer and Pope texts represent "elaborated" codes. But an "elaborated" code cannot, for example, be "context-independent" in a pre-typographic age (Febvre & Martin 1984); nor can it have the same value in a period when education and religion are not yet disjoined, *insulated* (Bernstein 1982: 313) categories. Nor can the "knowledge" it articulates be, in the same way, bound up with "writing", which, as Derrida (1974) has pointed out in another context, is a condition for a Pope's kind of "knowing". Chaucer's truth/knowing *must* still have more to do with speech, or at least with the speaking of writing (in a manuscript technology) than Pope's can have. And thus the oppositions attested to in Table 1 no doubt exist as realisations/systemic choices in texts but they have no *intrinsic* significance as implicit/explicit, elaborated/restricted and so on, until they are contextualised and read in metagrammatical ways which locate them in and recognise them as constructing part of the social semiotic itself.

Genres, specific texts and situation types, are the sites for and the processes which instantiate the episteme with which we began, either as reified textual object or as open social discourse. This paradoxical return of/to the episteme by way of the instantiations of the intertextual processes by which it is produced explains the production of text both as unity characterised by systemic closure, and as always polyphonic, dialogic in Bakhtin's sense, characterised by its "many voicedness". It explains the contradictory voices in monologic texts which aim to suppress all but the episteme, and the reification of contradiction/polysemy/openness in texts that are dialogically oriented: and it allows us to see how social meaning making practices and reading codes can re-produce these structures or change them through the negotiation of intertextual meanings. This foregrounds the need to look closely *both* at textual structure and at intertextual relationships *and* at the necessary positioning of the subject at the intersection of these discursive practices. This as we shall see places this theory's metaphor or allegory of social meaning making practices and reading codes much closer to Chaucer's than to Pope's.

5. The texts

TEXT A: Chaucer *The House of Fame*

The Dream.

Whan I was fro thys egle goon, 1110
I gan beholde upon this place.
And certein, or I ferther pace,
I wol yow al the shap devyse
Of hous and site, and al the wyse
How I gan to thys place aproche 1115
That stood upon so hygh a roche,
Hier stant ther non in Spayne.

But up I clomb with alle payne,
And though to clymbe it greved me,
Yit I ententyf was to see, 1120
And for to powren wonder lowe,
Yf I koude any weyes knowe
What maner stoon this roche was.
For hyt was lyk alum de glas,
But that hyt shoon ful more clere; 1125

But of what congeled matere
Hyt was, I nyste redely.
But at the laste aspied I,
And found that hit was every del
A roche of yse, and not of stel. 1130
Thoughte I, "By seynt Thomas of Kent!
This were a feble fundament
To bilden on a place hye.
He ought him lytel glorifye
That hereon bilt, God so me save!" 1135
　Tho sawgh I al the half ygrave
With famous folkes names fele,
That had iben in mochel wele,
And her fames wide yblowe.
But wel unnethes koude I knowe 1140
Any lettres for to rede
Hir names by; for, out of drede,
They were almost ofthowed so
That of the lettres oon or two
Was molte away of every name, 1145
So unfamous was woxe hir fame.
But men seyn, "What may ever laste?"
　Thoo gan I in myn herte caste
That they were molte awey with hete,
And not awey with stormes bete. 1150
For on that other syde I say
Of this hil, that northward lay,
How hit was writen ful of names
Of folkes that hadden grete fames
Of olde tyme, and yet they were 1155
As fressh as men had writen hem here
The selve day ryght, or that houre
That I upon hem gan to poure.
But wel I wiste what yt made;
Hyt was conserved with the shade 1160
Of a castel that stood on high —
Al this writynge that I sigh —
And stood eke on so cold a place
That hete myghte hit not deface.
Thoo gan I up the hil to goon, 1165
And fond upon the cop a woon,
That al the men that ben on lyve
Ne han the kunnynge to descrive
The beaute of that ylke place,
Ne coude casten no compace 1170
Swich another for to make,
That myght of beaute ben hys make,
Ne so wonderlych ywrought;
That hit astonyeth yit my thought,
And maketh al my wyt to swynke, 1175
On this castel to bethynke,
So that the grete craft, beaute,
The cast, the curiosite
Ne kan I not to yow devyse;
My wit ne may me not suffise. 1180
　But natheles al the substance
I have yit in my remembrance;
For whi me thoughte, be seynt Gyle!
Al was of ston of beryle,
Bothe the castel and the tour, 1185
And eke the halle and every bour,
Wythouten peces or joynynges.
But many subtil compassinges,
Babewynnes and pynacles,
Ymageries and tabernacles, 1190
I say; and ful eke of wyndowes,
As flakes falle in grete snowes.
And eke in ech of the pynacles
Weren sondry habitacles,
In which stoden, al withoute — 1195
Ful the castel, al aboute —
Of alle maner of mynstralles,
And gestiours, that tellen tales
Both of wepinge and of game,
Of al that longeth unto Fame. 1200
　Ther herde I pleyen on an harpe
That sowned bothe wel and sharpe,
Orpheus ful craftely,
And on his syde, faste by,
Sat the harper Orion, 1205
And Eacides Chiron,
And other harpers many oon,
And the Bret Glascurion;
And smale harpers with her glees
Sate under hem in dyvers sees, 1210
And gunne on hem upward to gape,
And countrefete hem as an ape,
Or as craft countrefeteth kynde.
　Tho saugh I stonden hem behynde,
Afer fro hem, al be hemselve, 1215
Many thousand tymes twelve,
That maden lowde mynstralcies
In cornemuse and shalemyes,
And many other maner pipe,
That craftely begunne to pipe, 1220
Bothe in doucet and in rede,
That ben at festes with the brede;
And many flowte and liltyng horn,
And pipes made of grene corn,
As han thise lytel herde-gromes, 1225
That kepen bestis in the bromes.
Ther saugh I than Atiteris,
And of Athenes daun Pseustis,
And Marcia that loste her skyn,
Bothe in face, body, and chyn, 1230
For that she wolde envien, loo!
To pipen bet than Appolloo.
Ther saugh I famous, olde and yonge,
Pipers of the Duche tonge,
To lerne love-daunces, sprynges, 1235
Reyes, and these straunge thynges.
Tho saugh I in an other place
Stonden in a large space,
Of hem that maken blody soun
In trumpe, beme, and claryoun; 1240
For in fight and blod-shedynge
Ys used gladly clarionynge.
Ther herde I trumpen Messenus,
Of whom that speketh Virgilius.
There herde I trumpe Joab also, 1245

Theodomas, and other mo;
And alle that used clarion
In Cataloigne and Aragon,
That in her tyme famous were
To lerne, saugh I trumpe there. 1250
There saugh I sitte in other seës,
Pleyinge upon sondry gleës,
Whiche that I kan not nevene,
Moo than sterres ben in hevene,
Of whiche I nyl as now not ryme, 1255
For ese of yow, and los of tyme.
For tyme ylost, this knowen ye,
Be no way may recovered be.
Ther saugh I pleye jugelours,
Magiciens, and tregetours, 1260
And Phitonesses, charmeresses,
Olde wicches, sorceresses,
That use exorsisacions,
And eke these fumygacions;
And clerkes eke, which konne wel 1265
Al this magik naturel,
That craftely doon her ententes
To make, in certeyn ascendentes,
Ymages, lo, thrugh which magik
To make a man ben hool or syk. 1270
Ther saugh I the, quene Medea,
And Circes eke, and Calipsa;
Ther saugh I Hermes Ballenus,
Limote, and eke Symon Magus.
There saugh I, and knew hem by name, 1275
That by such art don men han fame.

Ther saugh I Colle tregetour
Upon a table of sycamour
Pleye an uncouth thyng to telle;
Y saugh him carien a wynd-melle 1280
Under a walsh-note shale.
What shuld I make lenger tale
Of alle the pepil y ther say,
Fro hennes into domes day?
Whan I had al this folk beholde, 1285
And fond me lous, and nought yholde,
And eft imused longe while
Upon these walles of berile,
That shoone ful lyghter than a glas
And made wel more than hit was 1290
To semen every thing, ywis,
As kynde thyng of Fames is,
I gan forth romen til I fond
The castel-yate on my ryght hond,
Which that so wel corven was 1295
That never such another nas;
And yit it was be aventure
Iwrought, as often as be cure.
Hyt nedeth noght yow more to tellen,
To make yow to longe duellen, 1300
Of this yates florisshinges,
Ne of compasses, ne of kervynges,
Ne how they hatte in masoneries,
As corbetz, ful of ymageries.
But, Lord! so fair yt was to shewe, 1305
For hit was al with gold behewe.
But in I wente, and that anoon.

(From *The Complete Works of Geoffry Chaucer*, edited by F.N. Robinson. 2nd ed. 1974)

TEXT B: Pope *The Temple of Fame*

A Train of Phantoms in wild Order rose,
And, join'd, this Intellectual Scene compose. 10

  O'er the wide Prospect as I gaz'd around,
Sudden I heard a wild promiscuous Sound,
Like broken Thunders that at distance roar,
Or Billows murm'ring on the hollow Shoar:
Then gazing up, a glorious Pile beheld, 25
Whose tow'ring Summit ambient Clouds conceal'd.
High on a Rock of Ice the Structure lay,
Steep its Ascent, and slipp'ry was the Way;
The wond'rous Rock like *Parian* Marble shone,
And seem'd to distant Sight of solid Stone. 30
Inscriptions here of various Names I view'd,
The greater Part by hostile Time subdu'd;
Yet wide was spread their Fame in Ages past,
And Poets once had promis'd they should last.
Some fresh ingrav'd appear'd of Wits renown'd; 35
I look'd again, nor cou'd their Trace be found.
Criticks I saw, that other Names deface,
And fix their own with Labour in their place:
Their own like others soon their Place resign'd,
Or disappear'd, and left the first behind. 40

Nor was the Work impair'd by Storms alone,
But felt th'Approaches of too warm a Sun;
For Fame, impatient of Extreams, decays
Not more by Envy than Excess of Praise.
Yet Part no Injuries of Heav'n cou'd feel,   45
Like Crystal faithful to the graving Steel:
The Rock's high Summit, in the Temple's Shade,
Nor Heat could melt, nor beating Storm invade.
There Names inscrib'd unnumber'd Ages past
From Time's first Birth, with Time it self shall last;   50
These ever new, nor subject to Decays,
Spread, and grow brighter with the Length of Days.
    So *Zembla*'s Rocks (the beauteous Work of Frost)
Rise white in Air, and glitter o'er the Coast;
Pale Suns, unfelt, at distance roll away,   55
And on th' impassive Ice the Lightnings play:
Eternal Snows the growing Mass supply,
Till the bright Mountains prop th' incumbent Sky:
As *Atlas* fix'd, each hoary Pile appears,
The gather'd Winter of a thousand Years.   60
    On this Foundation *Fame*'s high Temple stands;
Stupendous Pile! not rear'd by mortal Hands.
Whate'er proud *Rome*, or artful *Greece* beheld,
Or elder *Babylon*, its Frame excell'd.
Four Faces had the Dome, and ev'ry Face   65
Of various Structure, but of equal Grace:
Four brazen Gates, on Columns lifted high,
Salute the diff'rent Quarters of the Sky.
Here fabled Chiefs in darker Ages born,
Or Worthys old, whom Arms or Arts adorn,   70
Who Cities rais'd, or tam'd a monstrous Race;
The Walls in venerable Order grace:
Heroes in animated Marble frown,
And Legislators seem to think in Stone.

(From *The Poems of Alexander Pope*, edited by John Butt, 1963)

Pope's rewriting (Text B) of Chaucer's medieval dream-vision (Text A) "in a manner entirely my own" is "imitation" in Dryden's sense (Atkins 1951: 127), an original fully adapted so that if the author were "living, and an Englishman, the result would be much as he would probably have written". This apparently simple statement expresses an extraordinary complexity of historical and discursive intertextual relationships which I shall now begin to explore.

Pope's poem is a neo-classical restructuring of the incomplete Chaucerian original, in which notions of correctness, order and unity play no small part. Pope uses only Book III of Chaucer's poem and one or two short passages from Chaucer's Book II. The omissions and rearrangements in the Pope text are extraordinarily interesting and have to do with coding orientations and possible meanings. There is only space to illustrate this from the two passages which are Pope's and Chaucer's descriptions of the House of Fame and represent choices in meaning which are characteristic of the poems as a whole.

Both poems are about social meaning making practices and reading codes in that they instantiate in their structures as narrative and representation their own conditions of production and reception. They both deal with the question of what it is to write and read, with the fate of texts in the social world and with the world of literature and knowledge as they know it. Inevitably then the poems deal with the question of what knowledge is and how meanings are made. Pope's

> A train of phantoms in wild order rose,
> And join'd, this intellectual scene compose,

is a clear statement of his poetic method, and of the way his poem is to be read, and bears the mark of the episteme of his age. The disorder of the dream-world (or of reality) is to be reduced to order by a process of "joining", juxtaposition of words, couplets, images, addition of one meaning to the next; and this is to be done visually (*scene*), by observation, and intertextually, by processes of comparison and contrast and addition. Here is Hobbes' ordering judgement and Locke's emphasis on the visual and observation; the structure recalls the arrangement of objects/names in space of the Ramist logics and the scientific taxonomies of the seventeenth century, all of which bear the marks of the same episteme that persists in the neo-classical literary theory itself — the emphasis on method (Descartes) and order. "Nature methodis'd" is how Pope describes poetry. Moreover the typographic technology, the book as writing, its conditions of production and consumption, require that the text be produced as commodity, as product. This encourages the "viewing" of the text as "object"/"product", and makes possible its autonomy as *aesthetic* object. In terms of reception/reading however, we do not yet have the passive consumer of the later "realist" text/capitalist society. The reader's role is conceived of as productive/reproductive, its function is that of making the connections (pre-given in the object) that will construct the object for the viewer. Lessing's Aesthetic theories (Wellbury 1984) give a particularly active role to the reader, as do the philosophical nominalisms of Hobbes and Locke, the pedagogic theories of Comenius and so on.

The dominant episteme is that of order, the visual, and the mind whose function is to connect and relate the linearly arranged objects of its observation. "What is is right" — the natural order — is given, it precedes man's observation, and the perception/understanding of its inherent order/arrangement guarantees knowledge and truth.

Chaucer's narrator, on the other hand, doesn't know, can't understand, won't explain. His text, as Boitano (1983) has shown, is *labyrinthine*, like Borges' (1970) or Eco's (1983) library, or the structure of a late Gothic Cathedral (Panofsky 1957; Boitano 1983), without clear divisions, or distinct images, a continuous, elaborated structure that moves from order to disorder, from knowledge to confusion, from completeness (unity) to incompleteness.... An early exercise in narrative deconstruction, or rather in the construction of a very different kind of narrative.

The narrator's activities are an allegory of processes of textual production and of reading practices. In Book I he reads and re-produces an ordered, unified text, Book I of the *Aeneid*. In Book II, disavowing any attempt at order, he produces a fragmented account of the fourteenth century literary and scientific world — the world of the dialogue between dreamer and eagle about the physics of sound — the world of Bakhtin's carnival. The "matters" which constitute literature are a "confusioun" of "olde gestes". These cannot be *read* visually — they are oral/heard — and they can only be known through interrogation — "How do I make sense of this?" In the *enounced* (the clauses projected from his own sayings/enunciations) (Benveniste 1971), the narrator is constantly moving about, doing, saying, thinking and questioning. He negotiates the meanings of the discursive formation and its social heteroglossia, trying to make sense of its contradictions.

In Book III literature is de-constructed into the human labour and meanings of which it is made. The whirling House of Rumour is the original model of the dynamic system and of the grammar of projection. Here is reality as reported, told. The messangers and pilgrims who produce and reproduce "the tydinges" in the labyrinth of this house are those who labour to construct the social semiotic. Here are the oral origins of narrative and the problematic of words, truth and reality. It is here in *speche* that meaning and knowledge originate — but the text ends, incomplete, before any *final* meaning, any closure is possible — the man of authority doesn't in the end speak. Meaning is a noisy, oral, uncertain business in Chaucer, a silent and certain, visually perceived, arrangement of things in space in Pope.

The oral-chirographic representation systems have not yet produced the text as commodity/fixed "product" and cannot yet produce representational writing or reading practices or the reader as silent maker of visually perceived aesthetic objects. Yet the very incompleteness, the lack of closure in the text reifies the anagogic episteme, reproduces the limits imposed on the knowing of the subject by the absolute authority of God as final cause. The emphasis on speech and dialogue as the origin of meaning, and on dialogic interaction and interrogation as the way to knowledge is a realisation and reproduction in the text of the intertexts of scholastic logic/rhetoric/grammar and of the epistemic hierarchy of senses these discourses encode. There is also the intertext of the inherent scepticism built into the oral traditions of disputation and into medieval theories of knowledge. This is the episteme encoded in the structure of disputation in scholastic logic itself and in the theories of meaning in the speculative grammars of the thirteenth century Modistae and William of Ockham's nominalism. This is the discursive formation and the episteme which places the "I" narrator and his sceptical dialogism firmly at the centre of Chaucer's text.

The different semiotic grammars of the two texts, their characteristic "fashions of speaking" and ways of constructing social reality and subjectivity can be illustrated in visual texts which instantiate the same discursive regularities in a different semiotic medium where it is structured by different generic constraints. Texts C, D and E are reprinted from Walter T. Ong (1958) *Ramus and the Decay of Dialogue*. Text C illustrates the medieval view of logic as geometry/labyrinth, a specific way of "knowing", Text D is a visual allegory of the disputing/scholastic subject whose body and senses and speaking voice are not yet excluded from the representation. Text E is a Ramist dichotomised table. The subject is absent, the graphic representation is to be *seen* (in silent observation), and knowledge is ordered and arranged in space and constructed as dichotomies.

These are the very differences the semiotic grammars of Chaucer's and Pope's texts also construct and reproduce.

6. Context as semiotic construct

An outline of the social, discursive and technological semiotics referred to above as involved in the discursive production and reproduction of subjects, texts and social realities in the fourteenth and early eighteenth centuries in England is provided in Table 2.

What I am arguing here is that socio-political positioning and available technologies of representation give speakers access to and investments in

CHANGING THE SUBJECT 567

Text D

Murner's Outline of Logic (1509)

Text C

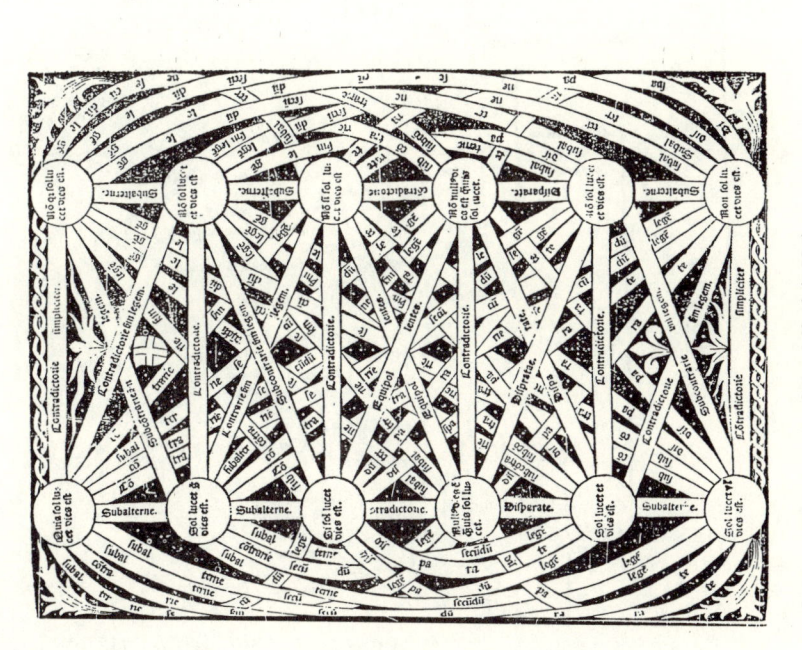

Celaya's Geometry of the Mind (1525)

Text E

P. RAMI DIALECTICA.
TABVLA GENERALIS.

```
Logicæ                  ┌ Primum ─┬ Simplex ─┬ Côsentá- ─┬ Absolutè ─┬ Caufa.
partes                  │         │          │  neum.    │           ├ Effectus.
duæ         ┌ Artifi-   │         │          │           └ Modo quodam ┬ Subiectum.
sunt        │  ciale.   │         │          │                          └ Adiunctum.
            │           │         │          └ Diffenta- ┬ Diuerfa.
            │           │         │            neum.     └ Oppofi- ┬ Difparata.
            │           │         │                        ta.     └ Contraria ┬ Affirmata ┬ Relata.
            │           │         │                                            │           └ Aduersa.
            │           │         │                                            └ Negata ┬ Priuantia.
            │           │         │                                                     └ Contradicentia.
            │           │         └ Compa- ┬ Quâtita- ┬ Paria.
            │           │           ratum. │   tis.   └ Imparia ┬ Maiora.
            │           │                  │                    └ Minora.
            │           │                  └ Qualitatis ┬ Similia.
            │           │                               └ Difsimilia.
            │           └ A' primo or- ┬ 1. Nomen ┬ Coniugata.
            │             tum.         │          └ Notatio.
            │                          └ 2. ┬ Diftributio ┬ Partitio.
            │                               │             └ Diuifio.
            │                               └ Definitio.
INVEN-      └ Inartificiale, ut Teftimonium.
TIO ar-
gum'nto-
rum. Eft
autem ar-
gumentū
aut
            ┌ Axiomaticum in ┬ 1. Partes ┬ Anteceden.
            │ Enunciato: in  │           └ Confequen.
            │ quo confider.  │
            │                │           ┌ 1. ┬ Affirmatio.
            │                │           │    └ Negatio. ─ Hinc contradictio.
            │                └ 2. Affe- ─┤
            │                  ctio-     │    ┌ Contingens, cuius iudicium Opinio.
            │                  nes.      └ 2. ┼ Verum ─┤
            │                                 │        └ Necessarium cuius iudicium Scientia.
            │                                 └ Falfum Impofsibile oppofitum neceffario.
            │                                                    ┌ Generale.
            │                             ┌ Simplex ┬ Speciale ┬ Infinitum feu particulare.
            │                             │         └          └ Proprium.
            │                ┌ Species ───┤                    ┌ Copulatum.
IVDICIVM,   │                             │         ┌ Côgregatiuum ┼ Connexum.
quod eft aut│                             └ Compofiti ┤             
            │                                        └ Segrega- ┬ D fcretum.
            │                                          tiuum.   └ Difiunctum.
            │                                                    ┌ Propofitio.
            │                          ┌ 1. Partes ┬ Anteceden ─┴ Affumptio.
            │           ┌ Syllogi- ────┤           └ Confequens.
            │           │   fmo:       │
            │           │              └ 2. Affectio, u, v'ÿ ít.
            │           │                         ┌ Simplex ┬ Contractus.
            └ Dianoeiæ ─┤              ┌ Species ─┤         └ Explicatus.
              cum in    │              │          │         ┌ Connexus.
                        │              │          └ Compofitus ┴ Difiunctus.
                        │
                        └ Methodo. ┬ Perfecta.
                                   └ Imperfecta, ucpūtiuxí.
```

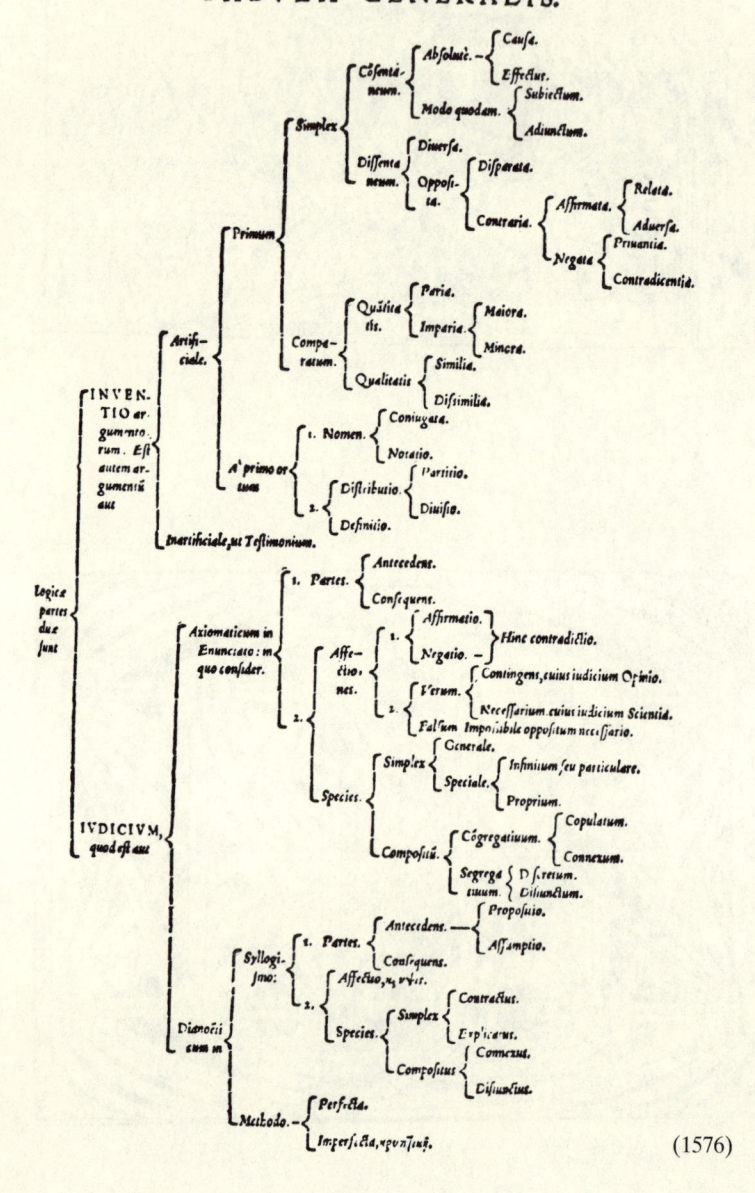

(1576)

TABLE 2. CONTEXT

{ Discursive practices { Framing (discourses)	{ Discursive positioning { Classification (categories, social roles)
Chaucer weak/strong classification (variable) weak/strong framing (variable)	*Pope* strong classification strong framing

1. Juridico-political

God: absolute power	*God*: nominally absolute power → withdrawing
Government: fragmented, King, church, estates, merchants, etc. Social disorder: fragmentation of powers, questioning of authority. Social order in question.	*Government*: central — (Locke — social contract). Social order pre-given.
Law: King, church, estates. Class difference: private property guaranteed by primogeniture, etc.	*Law*: guarantees private property. Central.
Subject: independence vs. dependency at all levels — not yet patriarchal, autonomous (subject/object not yet distinct).	*Subject*: sovereign rights of individual — patriarchal, autonomous (subject/object split).
Church: great power (in question)	*Church*: less control, less questioning.
Education: church	*Education*: secular
Bourgeoisie: not a separate class at end 14th century/socio-economic dependence on upper classes.	*Bourgeoisie*: independence from upper classes (new socio-economic status).
Family — Marriage: lack of privacy, affect low.	*Family — Marriage*: privacy, affect high.
Career: literature/politics/science/commerce — not yet disjoined (role of poet — teacher, populariser).	*Career*: literature/politics/science disjunction (role of poet — elitist, intellectual).
Language (as political semiotic — i.e. power/knowledge)	*Language* (as political semiotic — i.e. power/knowledge)

(Social heteroglossia: social conflict)

Latin, French English, [high, middle, low rhetorical "styles"]	Latin, French, English, [high, middle, rhetorical styles]
Latin — religion, education, philosophy.	Latin — religion, education, philosophy, literature, law, government.
French — law, government, literature.	

Table 2. (Cont.)

Vernacular — science, popular culture (romance), politics, bureaucracy, trade, commerce, literature (Still clear disjunctions/insulation between Latin, French, vernacular functions. *But* relatively weak framing)	Vernacular — "new" science, popular culture (e.g. Romance, broadsheets, ballads, etc.), politics, bureaucracy, trade, commerce, education, religion (Protestantism/Puritanism), philosophy, literature, translation (from Latin etc.). (strong framing between latin and vernacular. Literary (aesthetic) vs. ordinary language split — already strong framing; relatively weakly framed institutional boundaries and thus weakly framed discursive practices in the vernacular).

2. Discursive practices
(i.e. discursive regularities/intertextual semantic fields)
Discourse-conflict between co-existing discourses — discursive/cultural "capital" — systems for the exchange of information)

Rhetoric/Logic/Grammar

Aristotle, scholastic logic disputation. Rhetorics — Latin grammars.	Ramus, topical logics/scholasticism, Rhetorics — Latin grammars.

Natural Science/Philosophy

Aristotle, Modistae, Ockham. science/alchemy	Aristotle/Hobbes, Locke (nominalism) Royal Society (Plain English) universal languages (representation).

Education

Latin/French	→ Vernacular movement

History

Bible/history, narrative — not disjoined.	Bible/history, narrative — disjunction.

Literature

Classics, Bible, contemporary literature (high and low), aesthetic code: not articulated → many different genres, text types (Lotman: text-oriented).	Classics, contemporary literature (high) aesthetic code: neo-classicism. Clearly articulated genres. (Lotman: grammar-oriented)

Language
(Knowledge about language)

Latin, French, English	Latin, French, English

Table 2. (Cont.)

Vernacular — "language of lewed men." Language of science, move away from Latin, French towards vernacular.	Vernacular — inferior, move towards → elitist intellectual style (imitating Latin, French models).

3. Representation
(Reproductive technologies)
Speech/Writing

Speech, manuscript tradition, early printing.	Writing, typographic tradition, books. Commerical printing.

Art/Architecture/Music etc.

Gothic	Classical

Genres of reading/Writing practices etc.

Text as performance. Written MSS/oral performance, aural/visual reception	Text as product. Reader as Maker-recogniser of connectedness/harmony of text as aesthetic object.

Notes to Table 2

In Table 2 the juridico-political and representation outlines are, I think, self-explanatory. The Discursive Formations outline requires a little more explanation. For the late fourteenth and early eighteenth century, there are many and contradictory elements in the discursive practices which provide the potential for meaning within this area of the social semiotic. Those differences which are relevant have to do with changes between the periods that involve extensions in the field of knowledge and more precise classifications or shifts in register disjunctions in the later period, which produce different possibilities of meaning, and the foregrounding of different epistemic choices. The discourses involved are outlined in Table 2. A single illustration will demonstrate the multiple "readings" available for any realisation of such discourses in the texts.

The texts share the discursive systems of classical rhetoric and logic, the scholastic inheritance, and the doctrine of the figures and tropes, and of the topics are shared. However the Ramist discourse with its conflation of rhetoric and logic, of scientific and probable truth, and its emphasis on dichotomy, method, and the visual, spatial and taxonomic arrangement of knowledge (as truth) in tables which exclude the speaking voice and the subject provides a new development which counters the tradition of scholastic logic and disputation with its emphasis on questioning, and the speaking subject (see above, Texts D, E). The Ramist development parallels that of the Agricolan topical logic, with its emphasis on place, and the disposition of arguments in linear space. These in turn anticipate the seventeenth century Baconian and Cartesian concern with method in natural science and philosophy (Ong 1958) re-producing the same taxonomic, classificatory tendencies in these areas (Slaughter 1982). This happens despite the fact that philosophy and science, for most of the seventeenth century are based on a medieval Aristotelian framework of knowledge (the Great Chain of Being). The two discourses then, the Ramist and the Aristotelian coincide for a time but always involve potential conflict and contradiction.

(that is, coding orientations towards) reproducing or not certain text-types and their systematic relations to the discursive capital of the community. The text-types I am dealing with here are the specific literary genres that are institutionally valued and may be invested with the reproduction or subversion of power relations and ideologies.

In following the post-structuralist emphasis on the production of subjectivity through social apparatuses, I am focusing on the ways in which language is implicated in the production of particular regimes of truth, associated with the regulation of specific social practices, such as the practices of the family, the education system, the world of knowledge/science and so on. Implicit in this kind of view is the claim that the production of particular discourses is associated with the production of particular kinds of Rationality, for example "the knowing subject" of scientific thinking.

I am therefore not suggesting a simple determination from the sociocultural downwards and I am explicitly rejecting the assumption of a pre-given individual subject as a point of origin which merely interacts with or is affected by a context which is outside it. I also reject the reification implicit in a representation of juridico-political systems, discursive practices and systems of representation as if they were realities which pre-existed the individual or the individual's construction of them or the text. In social semiotic terms the subject and the higher order social semiotic are involved in a mutual and intertextual process of production, in which both are discursively, behaviourally constructed only in texts as social discourse.

7. Genres

Within literature as institution in these periods, there is a highly elaborated set of genres in the classical traditions which frame the production of texts (as literary proscriptions and intertextual resources in other texts) and provide both the potential for choice, and constraints on possible meanings (see Table 3). The differences in contextual framing and classification produce a far greater adherence to the generic rules and to generic consistency in Pope than in Chaucer who mixes genres, blurs their boundaries and produces a text which in the end defies generic classification in the terms of the genres with which it begins.

Generic choices then also mean systematically and metagrammatically — realising the implicit/explicit difference and the differential access to power and knowledge. They effect almost all further differences in meaning

TABLE 3. GENRE

(The interface between discursive practices, reproductive technologies, and juridico-political categories, that is between context and text.)

Genres structure discursive practices from Institutional sites within the categories of the juridico-political and under the constraint of available reproductive technologies. As cultural "capital" genres do not all have the same value.

Genres are socially ratified text-types which function to reproduce hegemony, social conflict, social categories and to maintain and transmit the culture.

The relative strength of framing and classification within the contextual processes make it possible for the discursively constructed individual with access to particular genres, to comply with or resist their regulating influences. Compliance ensures the stability of the existing order, resistance, always subversive, produces new genres and new meanings.

A weakening of framing and/or classification (Bernstein 1982) seems to be a necessary co-requisite in the dialectic between genre/text/context that produces change.

So also are the systematic relations between genres and discursive practices which ensure that only certain discourses are possible in particular genres but also allow for considerable entropy — the disorder and incompatibility of discourses, evident in the general structuring of the processes of cultural conflict that produces textual dialogism/heteroglossia. This is always potentially the source for new discourses and new genres.

Chaucer	Pope
Dream-Vision	Dream-Vision
Allegory	Allegory
1st person narrative express self/address other "exchange of meanings"	*1st person narrative* express self only *3rd person narrative* representation of "real". Tell/know.
Quest Narrative quest (chivalric Romance) Socratic quest Travel literature (journey to other world	
Satire: humour, irony	Satire: heroic genre/didactic purpose.
Open text: i.e. not "goal-oriented"	Closed text: i.e. "gaol-oriented".

Notes to Table 3

The fact that Pope's poem is an imitation of Chaucer's involves the sharing of the Dream-Vision schema, the allegorical figures of Fame and Rumour and their Houses, and the satire and allegory of the suppliants to Fame.

The "questing" genres are not present in Pope's poem and the journey genre is excluded from it. The knowing subject has no need to "quest", the uncertainty of the "other world" is excluded, in favour of the visible and knowable reality of "this one", and the dialogism of a split narrative voice is replaced by Pope's monologism. The controlling narrative voice of Pope's genre is a single absent voice, what we call the voice of the "third person", and has a consistency which is absent from the many generic voices that debate within Chaucer's poem.

The dream-vision genre in Chaucer affects choices in field, tenor and mode in Chaucer and the omission of several elements of it affect these choices in Pope. This genre requires certain choices from the topics of Rhetoric, particularly those topics which derive from Demonstrative oratory's topics/codes for the praise of places. Pope's use of these codes is much more evident than Chaucer's. Pope includes the *locus amoenus*, whereas Chaucer does not and Pope then chooses the topics of history, appearance and comparison to elaborate the choice (11. 1-20).

On the other hand the inclusion of the "quest" in various generic forms in Chaucer, constrains the choice of speech/dialogue which becomes a feature of the dream vision genre, and then inevitably produces a mixture of styles from the available rhetorical types (here high and middle). This introduces social heteroglossia into the text. So that Chaucer's text is dialogic throughout; its voices and its speech always multi-valued.

The exclusion of dialogue of this kind from Pope's text results from its monologism. Only one voice speaks in this text. This voice controls the representation from the position of absence ("outside" the text) constituted by third person narrative. The language used is the high style appropriate to the heroic status of satire and allegory (Dryden, in Atkins 1951: 117ff.), a style which consciously alludes to Milton, Virgil, Ovid and the native tradition (and thus introduces other voices) but the voices are incorporated into the monologic elitist, intellectual and upper class voice of the text, naturalised, their social diversity eliminated.

The generic differences constrain different choices from the logical and grammatical codes and construct different reading and writing practices.

Logically (syntactically), Chaucer's poem is labyrinthine in structure and follows the scholastic pattern of disputation (*videtur quod - sed contra respondeo dicendum*), a constant dialogue with self (Plato's thought), directed at the listener, which is continually establishing a position and then retreating from it, undermining its own ability to know or learn, but going on speaking. The text and the syntax is continuous, hypotactic, the relations between parts often implicit, and it has to be broken down into its parts to be read.

Pope's text on the other hand, despite the conscious debt to Aristotle in neo-classicism, realises the orientation toward order and control through the Ramist, topical logical episteme of ordered representation in space. The parts of the text, at every level, are distinct units, to be juxtaposed and connected according to their similarity and difference. The style is predominantly paratactic and explicit. The reading process involves adding, building up the whole from its parts.

The same coding tendencies are present in the figurative and tropic choices. Chaucer's generic positioning constrains *detractio*, and Pope's *compar* as the dominant figurative mode. From these follow the choices in Chaucer of *aposiopeses* (interruptions/abrupt changes), *praeteritio* (announcement of omission), *diminutio* (I can't or won't describe it). The detractive method is an implicit one, which constantly leaves out information necessary to the interpretation. It involves a recurrent alternation between affirmation and negation, reticence and allusion, and produces ambiguity and multiple meanings. It is a construction of the subject's uncertainty and produces uncertainty as a textual object.

In Pope the choice of *compar*, or comparison as the primary choice, produces the dominance of the figures of *contentio* and *synonymia* (similarity and difference) and the focus on *amplificatio* by means of juxtaposed images (comparison). The extensive use of the tropes of metaphor and metonymy is another realisation of the comparative tendency. It is an explicit mode of representation where all the elements necessary to meaning are ordered and juxtaposed and reified for ease of comparison.

---

at the micro-level of lexico-grammatical realisation.

Generically the telling/knowing semiotic subjects, uncertain and certain, implicit and explicit in their orientations are already constrained to focus on enunciation/*discours* or enounced/*histoire* (Benveniste 1971). They are positioned as the linguistic "I" of the enunciation, as overtly present in or implicitly absent from their linguistic representations, and as teller, perceiver and so on. They are already positioned in subjective or objective relation to knowledge as pre-coded (generic) possible authorial positions: and in the same way the generic/discourse tie-up specifies that one of the discourses in each text will be neo-classicism or medieval realism respectively.

8. "Systemic choice instantiating metagrammatical meanings" — notes on reading the grammar

The analysis of the lexico-grammatical patterns that constitute the Chaucer and Pope texts is provided in detail in the Appendix and "read" below. These patterns instantiate the "semiotic styles" (Table 1), and thus the contexts, the discourses, the technologies (Table 2) and the genres (Table 3) and subjectivities I have been discussing in this paper. These texts, as "fashions of speaking" are both constituted by and constitutive of the two very different social worlds and subjectivities that are involved.

Field

Choices in field are realised through the experiential and logical functions (after Halliday 1985). The choices in the two texts — despite the shared fields — are different at almost every point.

Transitivity and logical structure

Chaucer's "I" (Appendix 1.iii.4) is the subject of verbal, mental and material processes. He is a dynamic speaking and thinking subject who acts as thinker teller (in the enunciation) and as doer, thinker, teller in the static dream-world projected from his verbal and mental processes. The dream world of the projected clauses (the enounced) is represented by way of relational processes — "x is at y", "x is y" —, for example *The house is on a hill - then fame was molte away*. But the dreamer is extraordinarily active.

The whole text is a projection of ideas and indirect reports, usually questions — in clauses projected from the narrator's verbal and mental processes and these processes are negated and modalised realising the impossibility of knowing, the inability to find out, and so on.

The dream world and the "I" who is "other" — the dreamer — is a projection of the narrator's mind and voice. *There is no separation between subject and object*. The subject tells, tries to know this world from a position within it.

At the same time the subject "I" is split between the enunciation — the narrative context of the quoting clauses — and the enounced, the projected context of the quoted clauses where the "I" is dreamer. The "I" is also split by the dialogic mode in which it operates — the other "voices" (registers) which speak the "I" at various points.

The Pope text (Appendix 1.1; 1.4) reverses these choices. Pope's "I" is the subject of perceptual processes (I *saw/gazed*, once *viewed* etc.: *heard*). What he sees is *never* projected; the transitivity pattern is senser/mental/phenomenon, with the phenomenon coded as nominal group. The "I" never addresses the other, *you*. Subjectivity, as indexed by first/second person pronominal reference is absent from the representation of the object. The subject "I" of the enunciation (*I saw*) is already distanced — in the past tense — from the narrative moment of utterance.

Where there is no verb of perception, the text is "third person narrative":

> On this foundation Fame's High Temple stands
> Stupendous pile! not reared by mortal hands.

An ostensibly objective representation in Benveniste's sense of *histoire* — from which the subject as teller has withdrawn.

The subject as distanced perceiver/understander however observes an object world which is extraordinarily dynamic. There are some relational processes but in general the object (fame's House) is dynamic — poets think, critics deface other's names, gates salute the skies and so on. The object world, as image, art object, lives and speaks to the viewer (the aesthetic intertext: see Wellbury 1984). A great deal of this involves metaphor: the personification of inanimate objects in Virgilian terms, an overcoded latinate style, a way of coding relational process and circumstance ("x is at y") as actor /material process/ goal (Appendix 1.4, a-e). This dynamic representation is the re-enactment of the Latin past as visually perceived object overcoded with the values of universal truth.

The separation of the perceiving subject from the object is very clear here in the transitivity patterns and the logical structure: but this subject — monologic, and distanced from the object is now also unitary — the absent empirical subject who maintains his identity in withdrawal — and thus cannot be split between contexts and registers like Chaucer's "I".

Time and space (Spanning choices in field, tenor and mode — Appendix 1.3)

The differences between the medieval and seventeenth/eighteenth century constructions of space and time are realised in the texts in a number of ways.

The major difference is that in the Pope text all temporal categories are spatialised and made visible in the text: and there is nothing to parallel this in the Chaucer.

Lexis

Time An elaborated lexical set (cohesive (textual) and circumstantial (ideational)) in which time is quantified, *eternal, unnumbered, thousand length*, classified, *ages, days, years*: and spatialised as *past* or *new* or *continuous, eternal, length* and so on.

Nothing corresponds with this in Chaucer.

Space There are locative expressions in both texts. In the Chaucer, they locate the narrator in the narrating clauses and in the dream world of the projected/narrated clauses. (See Appendix 1.3(a)).

In the Pope, in the narrating clauses, the place circumstances specify the narrator's *viewing* point or perspective at a distance from the object: "O'er the wide *prospect* as I gaz'd around / *gazing up*" (see appendix 1.3(b)).

In the narrated clauses — *the locatives*, both deictics and circumstances — relate parts of the object, the visual images that make up the description of fame's Temple to one another (see 1.4 (d) for examples) *or* they relate the object to the absent subject by way of grammatical metaphor:

appear'd to distant sight of solid stone. (See Appendix 1.4 (e))

that is, interpersonal meanings are coded as ideational and re-insert the absent subject in the representation of the object. (See Appendix 1.4 (d) and (e)).

Tense operates in ways that are quite different in the two texts.

In Chaucer, tense is primarily deictic, foregrounding the here and now of telling in the present, and projecting the dream world into the past in relation to that present.

In Pope, tense functions deictically *and* modally (Kress 1977) and becomes a spatialising/ordering category. The narrative *I saw* clauses — are all past tense. The nominalisations and third person narrative are present, past and future.

(1) Tense functions to spatialise, locate and separate images of aesthetic objects in time and in relation to one another: viz. Zembla's rock (ll. 53-60) and the four-sided Temple in ll. 61-74 Text A.

(2) Tense functions modally to maintain social distance. The past of *I saw I view'd*, directed towards no explicit addressee, referring to a past distanced from the moment of enunciation, functions as a modality of certainty. As the subject withdraws from the object generic statements in the present tense (of certainty and knowledge) — "That is how it is", "this is universal truth" — become a possibility. In Pope the "I" is no longer free in time and space: he has a position, a perspective, a point of view from which as viewer he can know and control and order the object.

In Chaucer, the narrator is *in* the object. He has no control over it. The eagle puts him in it and takes him out of it at will. He can do and tell and wonder, but he has no control over the spatio-temporal co-ordinates of his telling. The absence of nominalisation and spatialisation of time categories, in Chaucer, is paralleled in that text by the continuity of the hypotactic structure, the enjambement in the octosyllabic poetic line, and the absence of spatial or temporal ordering at all levels.

The presence of the spatialisation of time in Pope and the different uses of these is paralleled by the predominance of parataxis, and the rigidly observed spatial limits of the couplet — the syntactic unit always coinciding with the end-stopped line.

Notes on mode/field/tenor interaction

Lexis (See Appendix 1.1; 1.2)

Despite the fact that the two passages share a common "field" — the narration/description of Fame's House — and therefore share a number of lexical sets indexing "semantic" fields and sub-fields — there are enormous differences between the lexical patternings in the two texts.

The Pope text is lexically much denser than the Chaucer (see Halliday 1985a). This obviously instantiates a systemic patterning that is constrained by the speech/writing nexus and by that as related to textual modes of production (technology) (see Goody 1986). However it also has very specific secondary effects in relation to textual features like cohesion and grammatical metaphor which are then also very different in the two texts: and the speech/writing nexus is not enough to account for what happens. There is a simultaneous re-structuring of semantic fields going on (Eco 1976), a process of obsolescence and semogenesis (Halliday 1985b) which makes sense only in relation to other aesthetic discourses (medieval realism vs. eighteenth century neo-classicism) and generic norms and functions (Virgilian "poetic" diction vs. "ordinary"/*lewed* language) and the everyday construction of social realities like that of the architectural norms of a society (see Appendix 1.1: 1-3) — none of which is unrelated to the speech/writing question.

Chaucer's collocational sets tend to consist of fewer items, and to involve the repetition of the same *one* or *two* lexical words. Pope's corresponding sets consist of up to twice as many actual items, and since these are elaborated (by rhetorical constraints at other levels) as synonyms or antonyms — there are many more individual items as well —

e.g. Chaucer: *ofthowed*   cf. Pope: 13 different material process
            molte away   verbs
            molte away   (See Appendix 1.2)
            deface

Architecture/aesthetics

In *three* cases in these two passages the most lexically dense cohesive sets in one or other text are simply not in the other one. Pope leaves out *and* replaces the most lexically elaborated architectural sets in the Chaucer passage (see Appendix 1.2: (1) and (2)) and replaces these with a carefully ordered, symmetrical verbal object, constructed of symmetry and dichotomies — *four sides/four gates, chiefs* vs. *heroes, artists* vs. *legis-*

lators and etc. (1.2: (3)).

The Gothic barbarity of Chaucer's building is simply not a possible meaning for Pope; the Gothic lexis is obsolete, no longer part of the synchronic "field". But it is also excluded by the aesthetics of neo-classicism — its ideals of symmetry, coherence and ordered arrangement — and the new field this constructs.

Associated with these are two sub-fields, one to do with "order", the other "confusion" — the first in Pope, the second in Chaucer. Confusion is edited out of Pope's text (see Appendix 1.3: (a)).

The power/knowledge axis

The single most lexically dense set in Chaucer is that to do with mental processes of *knowing, understanding* etc. + negation and modality (see Appendix 1.1: (b)). These are frequently metaphorical (*maketh al my wyt to swynke*). This systemic pattern instantiates the generic meaning of *detractio*, the rhetorical position of "not knowing", and thus the metagrammatical meanings of implicit/uncertain/ — power (with respect to knowledge) in the text.

"Not knowing" is not a possible meaning in Pope. The corresponding set in the Pope text consists of ten simple processes of visual perception (e.g. 6 x *I saw*). The difference in the grammatical area of elaboration is interesting. Chaucer elaborates meaning in the verbal group, and in groups where the narrator is subject. It is the doing and the being and the saying and the feeling and the subject's involvement in these that matters. All Pope's elaboration is in the representation of *things*, in nominal groups. The subject is no longer *in* its own representations, except in non-congruent, grammatically metaphorical ways (Halliday 1985b; see Appendix 1.4: 2; 1.2: Pope (i) and (j)).

Chaucer's nominal groups involve many pronoun heads (*I/you*). The nominal heads are almost all congruent (things coded as things) (only 5/81 examples are exceptions). There is practically no pre-modification and therefore no epithets to code interpersonal meaning in the nominal group. In the eight examples of post-modification (See Appendix 1.5):

e.g. [*that al the men (**that ben on lyve**); he han the kunnynge (**to descryve the beaute of that ylke place**)*]

there are many non-finite clauses of mental process involving the knowing of the narrating subject. They are often proposals not propositions: so that "knowing" is again instantiated here systemically as a problematic issue.

In Pope, there are 6/88 nominal groups with pronominal heads (*I* only). There is extensive pre-modification involving process — (or circumstance —) related epithets and interpersonal meanings (attitude/belief). Postmodification is extensive, and involves prepositional phrases and finite material process clauses, propositions, dealing with the actions of persons/events in the representation. For example:

> Four brazen gates, *on columns lifted high*.
> Or Worthys old, *whom arms or arts adown*,
> *Who Cities rais'd*, or *tam'd a monstrous race*.

Hypotaxis/parataxis (See Appendix 1.5)

Pope's text is more lexically dense and characterised by extensive nominalisation and grammatical metaphor. All the grammatical complexity therefore exists at group rank and the logical structure is predominantly paratactic, involving elaboration of meaning by the juxtaposition (addition and alternation; Halliday 1985b) of nominal groups.

Chaucer's text has few elaborated nominal groups, and therefore little grammatical metaphor. All the grammatical complexity is at clause rank and the logical structure is hypotactic involving a continuous chain of dependent and recursive structures.

This is exactly the set of oppositions one would expect the spoken/written production of the texts to instantiate, but in these texts it is a conjunction of features which raises a number of questions. One of these is that of the multi-functionality and simultaneity of choices in meaning realised in single wordings — which I raised at the outset — and the need to recognise simultaneous access to instantiation of several systems at once. Apart from the multiple mapping of discursive and generic meanings outlined above, there is another choice involved here which positions the speaking subject/narrator in other discourses: that is, the "choice" of undercoded vernacular style in Chaucer and overcoded (after Eco 1976) Latinate style in Pope.

Both poets had access to both styles: the choice has political and ideological implications in both cases: the Latin, French, vernacular discourses in both periods have clear social values.

Chaucer's choice is a didactic position, the role of teacher/populariser. The choice is undercoded, implicit — because there is no model for this kind of vernacular style in literature at the time: the choice itself may, in terms of the historical state of the language, constrain the absence of elaborated nominalisation and the lack of lexical density.

Pope's positioning within the neo-classical discourse is one of political withdrawal to an elitist, intellectual and aesthetic position, which is a rejection of the "plain language" of science, and instantiates systemically the disjunction between science and humanism and the assumption of an apolitical aesthetic discourse — a problem humanism has been struggling with ever since.

What happens here is that the Latinate discourse has become itself multifunctional — realising and instantiating metagrammatically two different discourses — the literary Virgilian Latinate one *and* the order/taxonomy discourse of "science" (knowledge) and rhetoric.

Pope's text encodes both discourses simultaneously, maintaining the nominalisation, juxtaposition, connection/order of science *and* constraining the re-insertion of the distanced subject in the objective representation both in accord with current aesthetic codes and as a necessary consequence of the subjective distancing involved in the construction of the object as "other". The Virgilian discourse constrains grammatical metaphor, coding interpersonal meanings of modality and attitude within nominal groups as attributes of things. The other scientific/logical function of the Latinate discourse constrains the *Ideational* coding of interpersonal meanings — more metaphor — once the subject is withdrawn. (See Appendix 1.4: 2). This makes a fiction of the notion of linguistic transparency (Barthes 1977; Kristeva 1981) and of the absent subject. As the subject withdraws from the phenomenon observed, congruence becomes impossible. Nominalisation and grammatical metaphor follow — the subject remains as a modal presence in the representation, the unitary monologic subject split between the positions it occupies at the intersection of the multiple voices that emanate from the many centres of the culture, and the autonomous object, are almost but not quite constructed in this textual semantics: but crucially could *only* have been constructed in a *written* text, which is why Derrida (1974) and Goody (1986) were right about the essentially ideological relationship between writing and science (knowing) — at least as science is presently constructed.

Tenor

I have already discussed several aspects of tenor and mode in connection with field. The differences in tenor involve further instantiations of the metagrammatical meanings I have been calling different semiotic grammars.

There is considerably more interpersonal mood interaction in

Chaucer's text than in Pope's, coding through systemic "choice" the speech/writing, implicit/explicit differences in orientation within the interpersonal function. The interesting differences are in the coding of modality, comment and affect as these relate to the position and constitution of subjectivity, to the distance between semiotic subject and language as object, and to the distance between language as object and the reality it codes (the question of congruence) — which is the point at which mode and tenor become difficult to keep apart.

Chaucer's modality choices are all to do with his own ability (or lack of it) as narrator to perceive, know or understand. In Pope the modality is consistently coded as ideational, as part of the representation of reality, ad thus as grammatical metaphor (Appendix 1.4: 2). For example, *no trace could be found* distances the object from the subject (who is absent; neither *I* nor any agent is expressed) and represents possibility as an attribute of *trace* when it means person and ability (*I could not find any trace*). In this way interpersonal meanings are coded as ideational.

Comment works in a similar way. Chaucer comments overtly in the first person, quotes himself in indirect speech or direct speech, or quotes "men's" opinions as words. This introduces other voices and heteroglossia (the dialogic code). In direct *speche* he can resort to low style (oaths), and humorous comment, step out of his narrator role and comment in another voice on the impossibility of his mental projections (11. 1131-1135) or allow other voices to comment (1. 1147). The dialogism that results produces polysemy which directly involves the reader in the interpretation of implicit meanings. Chaucer reports "words", meanings, other voices, the voice of the other, without attempting to control, make explicit the relationships between them.

In Pope the comment is all in the form of a kind of free indirect speech (as signs of subjectivity and possible *only* in writing) coded as part of the representation of the object. This means that we have not "words", quotes of a voice speaking or projections of meanings, but interpersonal meanings of attitude and belief already re-processed and re-coded by a monologic knowing subject as part of a linguistic structure of representation. These are the speaker's "words" at one remove, so to speak: and the coding is explicit — one meaning, one belief, made manifest in the representation of the object. Thus:

> Their names first inscrib'd *unnumber'd* ages past
> From time's first birth, with time itself *shall* last.

codes as an epithet and a modal/future auxiliary within the representation the subject's proposal/prediction of a future event and his inability to count the ages. These are the kinds of choices which make the subject immanent in Pope's text, not quite the subject of later bourgeois realism, a distanced subjectivity returning to deny the transparency of language.

The choices in attitude and emphasis reflect differences in subjectivity very clearly. Attitude is foregrounded in Chaucer primarily through the rhetoric of *detractio*, which is negative in terms of the subject's position, his access to power and knowledge (coded as implicit/uncertain), and focuses always on the self in a negative way, excluding that subject from access to the high rhetoric (discourse of power) of Pope's poem, but choosing another vernacular discourse as a language of learning and a means of communicating knowledge.

Attitude and position in Pope are both explicit and objectified. The focus is entirely on the object where the expression of attitude is in the lexical items of the representation as nominal groups. Position is coded in the process of comparison, and explicit relationships which instantiate the subject's right to knowledge, and his control over the object, but also in his need to make all relationships explicit within his text. Overt interpersonal relationships which would allow implicit meanings are excluded.

Mode

As discussed above (under hypotaxis/parataxis) Chaucer's text is a continuous, recursive, self-reflexive (*detractio*) structure, where the spatial limits of the line are rarely observed (*enjambement*) and the temporal/spatial extension of the clause complex lasts for up to 8 or 10 lines or more. Pope's text, on the other hand, is a discontinuous structure, built up on the principle of the juxtaposition of similarities and differences (rhetorical *compar*/figures of synonymy and difference and metaphor), where spatial limits are rigidly observed — the syntactic unit always coinciding with the end-stopped line, the temporal extension of the sentence limited by the structure of the couplet, which is the space within which units can be arranged. (See Appendix 1.5.) It is at this point, of course, that logical structure operates as both a field and mode category. It structures realities (field) and texts (mode) and metagrammatically instantiates the complexity of the speech-writing cline within mode.

There is a foregrounding of connection in the Chaucerian text in the number of conjunctive and structural *themes*. Pope's *themes* are predominantly ideational, nominal, and consist of the noun groups, which are the dominant units in the juxtapositional structure. (Appendix 1.6: (a)). Pope's distinct linear and syntactic units are juxtaposed and depend on *lexical* cohesion, that is the recognition of similarity and difference as the primary mode of semantic connection. Chaucer's continuous, recursive structures rely on syntactic cohesion and the semantics of logical hypotaxis. (See Appendix 1.5; 1.6: (b)). Again the one is juxtapositional, paradigmatic, vertical: the other continuous, syntagmatic, horizontal.

The choices enact metagrammatically the implicit/explicit and ± the power coding orientations in a number of interesting ways. Despite the surface emphasis on connection in Chaucer, the meaning conveyed by that connection is a continuity, which is the lack of order, arrangement, clear distinctions and so on. This is reflected also in the fact that Chaucer's adverbial clauses are primarily of hypothesis and concession (implicit meanings) whereas Pope's (there are only 6 to Chaucer's 14) all involve time or explicit comparison ("this is like this", "this was then"). (See Appednix 1.3: (c)). Chaucer can tell his reality, but it is a projection of himself: he cannot or will not order it — his discursive positioning does not provide him with the power or the knowledge or the will to order it. Pope, the knowing subject, controls the object he constructs, contains his meanings within a spatio-temporal structure whose carefully arranged parts control chance, polysemy and ambiguity. The viewing subject and the episteme of order, visually perceived, become a model of political stability and clear power relations in the narrative just as Chaucer's narrative world reflects a political instability and an ambiguity of power relationships.

9. Conclusion

We can then argue that the choices in meaning which structure these two poems constitute two quite different semiotic grammars: that these grammars are discursively and intertextually produced in the process of making social meanings within historically defined discursive formations and that they stage a metagrammatical argument about the constitution and positioning of the speaking subject in time and space, about his positioning and construction at the intersection of the representational discourses of speech and writing, and about the kinds of "knowing"/meaning and structures of knowledge/meaning that are possible for such a subject in such a position. The subject is *he* deliberately, for these different grammars articulate the positioning of the patriarchal subject of knowing, at the intersection of the suppression of the body as hierarchy of senses, the suppression of the feminine as "other" and the construction of the object as separate, observable, visual phenomenon.

Notes

1. The title of this paper is a quotation from the book by the same name by Henriques *et al.* (1984).
2. Halliday (1980: 44) defines "metagrammatical readings" as follows:

   The linguistic analysis of text is a necessary step in the interpretation of how meanings are exchanged.

   A clause, while it realizes directly only a very small unit of text (sometimes referred to as a "message unit"), stands also as the realization of a text as a whole, or some structurally significant portion of it, in the indirect, metaphorical sense that these examples suggest. The former is its automatic function, as determined by the system of the language. The latter is what Mukarovsky recognized as "deautomatization": still, of course, part of the potential of the linguistic system, but deployed in a metagrammatical way, conveying meaning by the act of systemic choice instead of (in fact always as well as) by the act of realization.
3. I am using "discourse" and "discursive formations" here in a Foucauldian sense (Foucault 1972). Elsewhere I have extended the systemic term "field" using it to describe "intertextual semantic fields", to characterise the same phenomenon. "Intertextual semantic fields" (Threadgold forthcoming) can also be seen as similar to Eco's (1976) sememe, a representation of the cultural coding of systematic patterns of meaning in the texts of the/a culture. The crucial point is that none of these is intended to define an abstract system which somehow "lies behind" cultural production. The systematicity is productive of and produced by cultural processes. See also Lemke (1983).
4. Lowe borrows the term *episteme* from M. Foucault and defines it as Foucault does:

   By *episteme*, we mean ... the total set of relations that unite, at a given period, the discursive practices that give rise to epistemological figures, sciences, and possibly formalised systems ... The episteme is not a form of knowledge (*connaissance*) or type of rationality which, crossing the boundaries of the most varied sciences, manifests the sovereign unity of a subject, a spirit or a period; it is the totality of relations that can be discovered, for a given period, between the sciences when one analyses them at the level of discursive regularities. (Foucault 1972: 191)
5. See, for example, two recently published works, which adopt these aspects of current semiotics to deal with educational transmission and reproduction, Michael W. Apple, ed., 1982, *Cultural and Economic Reproduction in Education* (RKP: London & Boston) and the problem of feminine subjectivity Henriques *et al.*, 1984, *Changing the Subject*.
6. Other accounts which attempt to tackle this problem include Anthony Wilden's (1972: 213) account of the *cogito ergo sum* as the philosophical paradigm for the Galilean revolution in

science, Eco's (1981: 57) account of the relationship between the structure of artistic forms and the way contemporary science or culture views reality, and Hasan's (1984: 133) concluding remarks on the specificity of "semantic styles" in English and Urdu.

7. The course description of Foucault's first year at the College de France (1977: 199-201).

8. Tzvetan Todorov has described the similar co-existence of philological and patristic exegesis and the historically determined dominance of one or the other (1983: 163-165). Slaughter (1982) and Kress & Hodge (1979: 42ff.) have described the co-existence and conflict between medieval taxonomies and experimental/ hypothetical discourses in Seventheenth Century Science.

9. These represent an expansion of Halliday's higher order or social semiotic categories, social structure, culture and linguistic system in his 1978 version of language as social semiotic.

10. Dreyfus and Rabinow (1982: 200) provide a pragmatic, less metaphorical account fo the way the relationship between epistemic modalities and heteroglossia co-exist within social formations:

> But, of course, in any given society at any given time, there will be different groups with different shared senses of the state of things. Thus, for example, although almost all of the intellectuals in France have felt, since the revolution, that society is in a major crisis which puts it in peril, there is presumably a consensus among administrators, expressed within memos and to each other, that things are basically in hand and that the general welfare and productivity of the population is constantly improving.

11. These have often been quite misguided and based on confusion. See Halliday's (1973) Introduction to *Class, Codes and Control*, Vol. II.

12. See Wilden's similar account of Ancient Chinese versus modern western epistemology in terms of analog and digital coding orientations (Wilden 1972: 166 n.7).

Appendix

1. FIELD

1.1. LEXICAL COHESION (some comparisons)

Processes (subject "I")

a. **Pope** *Perception: visual/behavioural processes* (place: from narrator's "point of view")
I gazed around — o'er the wide prospect
I heard
  gazing up — at distance
  beheld — on the hollow shore
I view'd — on a rock of ice
I look'd again — to distant sight
I saw

b. **Chaucer** *material* (place: direction)
    I   was goon   fro' this eagle
    I   pace   upon this place
    I   gan approche   to this place
        upon so high a roche
    I   clombe up   on a place hye
        to climbe
    I   gan to goon

    perception: cognition   *verbal: projecting*
    I   gan beholde   I will yow devyse
        to see   (men) seyn
        to powren   I say
        aspied   to descryve
        found   devyse
    I   sigh
        found
    I   saw
        gan to poure

    mental processes: projecting
    it   greved me
    I   ententif was
if I   could knowe (modality:
        ability hypothetical)
    I   nyste (negated)
    I   thoughte
    I   could knowe   well unnethes (negative: modality/ability)
    I   wel wyste
    hit   astonyth yet my thought
        maketh al my wit to swynke   *detractio/diminutio*
        (negative
    I   ne kan not to yow devyse   modality/ability)
        me wit ne may me not suffise
        he han the kunnynge to
        descryve ne coulde casten
        no compace

1.2. *SOME OTHER LEXICAL SETS* (note: in each case the set marked with the same alphabetical letter is the equivalent set in the other text).

Chaucer
(a) ygrave   (b) famous   (c) names
    was written   fames   names
    had written   fame   name
    al this writing   fames   names

(d) ofthowed   (e) fresh
    was molte away   conserved
    were molte away   not deface

				(f)	roche	(g)	house	(h) stood
					ston		site	stant
					roche		castel	lay
					roch		woon	stood
(i)	grete craft	(j)	beaute				castel	stood
	cast		beauty					
	curiosite		beaute					

Pope

(a) inscriptions
    engrav'd
    trace
    place
    graving
    inscribed

(e) fresh
    appear'd
    fix
    should last
    shall last
    nor subject to decays

(b) fame
    renown'd
    Fame
    Fame

(c) names
    other names
    their own (names)
    their names

(d) subdued
    nor could be found
    deface
    resign'd
    disappear'd
    decays
    impair'd
    melt

(i) & (j) glorious
    towering
    high
    high

    wondrous
    Parian
    solid

- pile (f) & (g)
- summit
- summit
- structure
  rock
- rock
- marble
- stone
  crystal

(h) growing
    supply
    prop
    fix'd
    rear'd
    lifted
    salute

    Zembla's
    beauteous
    growing
    hoary
    stupendous
    beauteous

  rock
- Rock
- work
- mass
- pile
- pile
- work of frost

Architecture

Chaucer

1. ll. 1181-1196 - description of the castle (omitted from Pope)

ston of beryle	castel	peces	
	tour	foyninges	
	halle	compassings	subtel
	bour	halewynnes	
		halewynnes	
		pynacles	
		ymageries	
		tabernacles	
		wyndowes	
		pynacles	
		habitailes	

aller maner of mynstralles — stoden al about — in ech of the pynacles.

2. 11. 1301-1306 description of castle gates (this set omitted from Pope)
   this Castel-Gate
   this gates florisshinges
               compasses
               kervynges   with gold behewe
               masoneries
               corbetz
               ymageries

3. **Pope**: replaces (1) and (2) with a symmetrical, four-sided structure, on which classical heroes, instead of mynstrels, are depicted:

fabled	- chiefs	- frown	*four*	brazen	gates
old	- worthies	- think			columns
	heroes				
	legislators		Fame's	high	temple
proud	- Rome				frame
artful	- Greece				dome
elder	- Babylon		*four*		faces
			every		face

   The different *quarters*   of the sky.

1.3. TIME/PLACE/ORDER

(a) **Pope**: *Time and order sets* (not in Chaucer)
   Time

by	- hostile	Time			in ages past
from	-	Time's	- first bi rth		once
		Time	- itself	unnumber'd	- ages past
with	-	the length	- of days		
					in darker ages
of	-	a thousand	- years	eternal	

Compare: *Time* (Chaucer)

   1155 - of alde tyme
          the selve day ryght,
          or that houre that I upon hem gan to poure
   1284 - Fro hennes into domesday

These are the only lexicalisations of time in the Chaucer text. They lack the quantification and spatialisation of the Pope set and they all refer specifically, deictically to the immediate context of the enunciation, except *of olde tyme* which contrasts with it.

Order (distinct parts) - not in Chaucer   *Confusion* (Undifferentiated mass) not in
In venerable order -   various   Pope
                        of various structure   Compare: withouten peces or joynynges
                                               alle maner of mynstralles ... be aventure
                        the different quarters ywrought, as often as be cure

(b) *Place*

Pope (from narrator's distanced "point of view)
 o'er the wide prospect

 at distance
 on the hollow shore
 on a rock of ice
 to distant sight

Chaucer (direction, location — of narrator's activities)
 fro' this eagle
 upon this place
 to this place
 upon so high a roche
 on a place of hye

(c) *Enhancement*

Pope
 Time
  as I gazed around
  Then gazing up
  Till the bright mountains
  prop the incumbent sky

 Comparison
  like broken thunders etc.
  like Parian marble shone
  As Atlas fix'd

Chaucer
 Time
  Whan I was fro this eagle goon
  Or I ferther pace

 Concession
  though to climbe it greved me
  but that it shone full more clear

 Result
  that of the lettres oon or two
  was molte away of every name
  that hete might hit not deface
  that hit astonyth yet my thought

 Comparison
  As if men had written it there today.

1.4. TRANSITIVITY

Pope (examples of experiential meanings)

1. Enunciating Clauses: first person narrative

Behaver	*Behavioural*		*Phenomenon*
			(complex nominal groups)
I	heard	-	a wild promiscuous sound
			Comparison
	like		broken thunders that at distance roar
	or		Billows murm'ring on the hollows shore
I	beheld	-	a glorious pile
			whose Towering summit
			ambient clouds conceal'd
I	view'd	-	inscriptions here of various names, the greater part by hostile time subdu'd.

2. "Third person" narrative (representation of the object)
(a) *Relational*

Carrier	Process	Attribute/circumstance
The structure	lay	high on a rock of ice
its ascent	(was)	steep
The way	was	slippery
The wond'rous rock	shone	like Parian marble
	seem'd	of solid stone
Some (names) of wits renown'd	appear'd	fresh engrav'd

(b) *Material*

Agent/actor	Process	Goal
heat	could melt	The rock's high summit
beating storm	could invade	
by storms	was impair'd	the work

(c) *Mental/behavioural*

Senser/behaver	Process	Phenomenon
the work	felt	the approaches of too warm a sun
part	could feel	no injuries of heav'n
proud Rome, Greece, Babylon	beheld	whate'er

Note: (b) and (c) are metaphorical and involve personification of inanimate subjects as actors, sensers etc.

The examples in (d) below involve the same kind of personification, but are also grammatical metaphors in which material processes constantly code relational meanings.

(d)

Actor	Material	Circumstances/attribute
Zembla's rocks, the beauteous work of frost	rise	white in air
	glitter	o'er the coast (circ.)
metaphor:	{ are + high / are + shining }	
pale suns	roll	away, at distance
the lightnings	play	on the impassive ice (circ.)
metaphor:	{ are + round / are + playful }	
eternal snows	supply	the growing mass
the bright mountains	prop	the incumbent sky
metaphor:	{ be + in addition to / be + under }	
its frame	excelled	whate'er proud Rome or artful Greece or Elder Babylon beheld
metaphor:	(be + better than)	
Fame's High Temple	stands	on this foundation (circ.)

                each hoary pile,
                the gather'd winter of
                    1000 years   appears   as Atlas fix'd
metaphor: { be + there }
                                                 { be + like }

(e) The experientialisation of interpersonal meanings — grammatical metaphor
         Actor/Carrier   *Material/Relational*   *Circumstance/Attribute*
  (i)   the rock   shone   like Parian marble
  (ii)   seem'd   of solid stone
  (iii)   "   to distant sight
  (iv)   Some   appear'd   fresh engraved
  (v)   their trace   could not be found

In all these cases visual perception, personal opinion or ability is coded as a relational representation, involving comparison (i) and (ii), phase: reality (ii) and (iii), nominalisation of visual process (iii), negative polarity and modality: coding ability as possibility (v) or the same material/relational metaphor as in (d) above ((i) and (v)).

Chaucer (some examples of Experiential Meanings)

3. (a) Projection: ideas/facts from mental processes
       Projecting Process   *Projection* (indirect thought)
       to see, to powren   - if I could any weyes knowe
                                         what maner stoon this roche was
            knowe   - what maner stoon this roche was
       aspied I and found   - that it was every del
                                         a roche of yse and not of stel
            I nyste   - of what congeled matere it was
       gan I caste   - that they were molte away with hete
                                         and not away with stormes bete
            I say (= "saw")   - How hit was writen full of names
                                         of folkes that hadden grete fames etc.
                                         Projection (direct thought)
       thoughte I   - "By Saint Thomas of Kent!
                                         This were a feble fundament
                                         to bilden on a place hye.
                                         He ought him lytel glorifye
                                         than hereon bilt, God so me save!"

   (b) Projection: meanings/wordings from verbal processes
       Projecting Process   *Projection* (indirect speech)
       I wol yow devyse   - how I gan to this place aproche
                                         that stood upon so hygh a roche,
                                         Heer stant there none in Spain
                                         Projection (direct speech)
       men seyn   - "What may ever I aske?"

4) Experiential meanings in projected clauses:
(a) *Relational*
    Carrier   Process   *Circumstance/Attribute*
    this place   (that) stood   upon so hygh a roche
    hit   was   lyk alum de glas

594   TERRY THREADGOLD

hit	shoon	ful more clere
hit	was	every del a roche of yse
al	was	of ston of beryl

(b) *Material*

Actor	Process (passive)	Goal	Circumstance/agent
-	ygrave	al the half of the lettres oon or two of every name	with famous folkes names fele
-	was molte awey		
-	were molte awey	- they -	with hete
-	was writen	- hit -	full of names of folke
-	was conserved	- hyt -	with the shade of a castel

See Appendix 1.1 (b) (above) for mental/verbal/material processes in the enunciation/ enounced with subject *I*.

1.5. HYPOTAXIS/PARATAXIS

Chaucer

The predominant pattern in clause complexes is of projection from mental and verbal processes (see 1.4 (3)).

There is considerable use of hypotactic enhancing clauses of concession, result, reason (see Appendix 1.3 (c)) instantiating the metagrammatical meaning of disputation/ uncertainty:

11. 1165-1180 (a typical example of clause complex in first person narrative):

			Conjunction
1	Thoo gan I up the hil to goon,	α	-
2+	And fond upon the cop a woon,	↓	explicit
	That al the men (that ben on lyve)	embedding$^{=\beta}$ x (result)	explicit
	Ne han the kunnynge (to descryve		NE implicit
1	the beaute of that ylke place),	embedding^x (purpose)	-
2+	Ne coulde casten no compace	α	implicit
	(Swich another for to make)	(purpose)	implicit
1	(that might of beaute ben his make,	embedding$^+$	explicit
2+	[Ne so wonderlych ywrought]) included clause- $^{\alpha x}$ (reason)		implicit
1	that hit astonyth yit my thought,	γx	explicit
2+	and maketh al my wyt to swynke,	(result)	explicit
	[On this castel to bethynke,] — {nominal clause — subject}		-
	So that the grete craft, beaute, {process as Head}		explicit
	the cast, the curiosite	γx	-
	Ne kan I not to yow devyse.	(result)	-

+ - addition   1 2 etc - parataxis
= - alternative   etc - hypotaxis
x - enhancing

(after Halliday 1985b, but the coding here is intended only to give some graphic indication of the complexity involved).

Note: that this logical structure involves *implicit* coding at a number of levels. Much of the conjunction is implicit. Most of the enhancing elaborations realise the rhetorical figures of *detractio*, *diminutio*. That is, this castle is so beautiful *that it cannot be described*. Its beauty remains implicit.

The hypotactic dependency structure and the embedding in nominal groups results in constant *enjambement and* recursion within the logical structure, instantiating continuity and circularity as metagrammatical meaning.

Pope

The predominant pattern in Pope's text within the clause complex is parataxis. The grammatical intricacy occurs at group rank, within the nominal group, and is associated with the rhetorical figures of *synonymia, contentio, metaphor, personification*. These figures are all aspects of *compar*, comparison, an *explicit* code which provides (in the form of epithets, classifiers and postmodifiers within the nominal group) all details necessary to the description. It is a code which depends on explicit lexical cohesion.

There is some hypotactic enhancement (see Appendix 1.3 (c)) frequently involving time (see Appendix 1.3 (a)) and thus reinforcing the foregrounding of time in the text. But the predominant semantics of the logical structure is addition $^+$ alternative $^=$ — as indicated graphically below — instantiating elaboration of represented objects.

The paratactic structure produces predominantly end-stopped lines, and a syntactic unit which is restricted to the two-line space of the heroic couplet, instantiating discontinuity, order and arrangement as metagrammatical meaning.

Examples:
(1) ll. 21-26

			O'er the wide prospect as I gazed around	β^x (Time)
			Sudden I heard [*a wild promiscuous sound*	
nominal	embedding$^=$	1	(like broken thunders that at distance roar)] - embedding$^+$	α
group		2$^=$	Or Billows (murm'ring on the hollow shore)] - embedding$^+$	
nominal		2+	Then gazing up, [*a glorious Pile* beheld	β^x (time) α
group			(Whose tow'ring summit ambient clouds	
			conceal'd)]	- embedding$_+$

figures: *synonymia*, parallelism.

(2) ll. 36-38
All the grammatical intricacy is in the nominal group:
Criticks I saw, [that other names deface,
and fix their own with labour in their place]:

Head	Postmodifier		
Criticks	1	that other names deface ⎫	embedding$^+$
	2+	and fix their own etc. ⎭	

Figures: *synonymia, parallelism*
(3) ll. 51-52   1   2+
nominal   [These (*ever new, nor subject to decays*)] - embedding$^+$
group   *Spread, and grow brighter* with the length of days.
                           1   2+

Figures: *synonymia, parallelism*

1.6. THEME

(a) Pope

Textual Structural	Conjunctive	Interpersonal finite/polarity	Ideational	
			Adj.	o'er the wide prospect
			Adj.	Sudden
				broken thunders billows
	then		Compl.	<<gazing up>> a glorious pile
				(Fronted) high, steep, slippery
			Compl.	The wondrous rock
			Compl.	inscriptions
	yet		Compl.	wide
and				poets
				Some
				I
nor		could		
			Compl.	Critics
		-		their own
nor		was		
	for			Fame
	yet			part
			Compl.	the rock's high summit
				their names
				these evernew
	So			Zembla's rocks
				pale suns
				eternal snows
			Adj.	As Atlas fix'd
			Adj.	on *this* foundation
		Interrog		stupendous pile
		Whate'er		Whate'er
				four faces
				four brazen gates
			Adj.	Here
			-	
				Heroes
				legislators

(b) Chaucer

Textual Structural	Conjunctive	Interpersonal finite/polarity	Ideational	
			Adj.	Whan I was fro this eagle gon.
And		certein	Adj.	or I ferther pace
But			Adj.	up
	Yit			I
if				I
	for			hyt

But					
But					of what congeled matere
					it was
					I
But				Adj.	at the laste
				Pred.	thoughte I
					This
					He
	Tho			Pred.	sawgh I
But				Adj.	wel unnethes
	for		out of drede		*they*
But					men
	Thoo	gan			I
	for			Adj.	on that other side
and	yet				they
But				Adj.	wel I
					Hyt
And				Compl.	al this wrytinge
				Pred.	stood
	thoo	gan			I
that					al the men that ben on lyve
			ne coude		
that				Compl.	hyt
so that					the great craft, beaute
					the caste, the curiosite.

# 4. An Interview with Michael Halliday

An Interview with Michael Halliday

Paul J. Thibault

Introduction

   Michael Halliday is the founder and principal architect of the systemic-functional school of linguistics, which has its historical basis in the earlier work of Malinowski, Firth, Hjelmslev, and Whorf. However, the present interview does not attempt to trace in any detail the "origins" and historical developments of Halliday's work. An excellent sketch of this is to be found in the Introduction to Kress (1976). It is also inappropriate to suggest that systemic-functional linguistics embodies a single, necessarily coherent epistemology through which its theoretical practices can be assessed. Indeed, the theoretical practices of systemic-functional linguistics produce a number of theoretically constructed and defined "objects" which range from the critical, materialist sociolinguistics of Hodge and Kress (1979), to Fawcett's (1980) cognitive model of a "communicating mind", Mann's (1985) non-finalistic teleological interpretation of the metaphor of "choice" in terms of "intentionality", and Halliday's own "social semiotic" and "functional" emphasis on the relations between the "internal" paradigmatic functional organization of the linguistic system and the patterns of social use of its linguistic resources.
   The present interview thematizes the systemic, the functional, and the social semiotic bases of Halliday's work. It attempts to explore and clarify the epistemological and theoretical criteria on which these are based. This involves some re-exploring of the development of the conceptual basis of the model. However, it also provides the opportunity to situate Halliday's thinking in relation to other contemporary theoretical positions in linguistics and semiotics. A further aspect of this interview concerns recent developments of the systemic-functional model, which are taking place in

Sydney and elsewhere.

It is now some ten years since the first appearance of the previous interview with Herman Parret (1974). Michael Halliday's contribution to linguistic and semiotic studies has long been recognized as a leading and central one. Further, it seems to the present interviewer that Michael Halliday has always refused a kuhnian positivistic conception of a linguistic science, whereby scientific activity is analogous to the increasingly specialized study of specific problems seen independently of their social and cultural contexts. The present interview attempts to give "voice" to the social conditions and epistemological foundations in which the specialist knowledges and techniques of systemic-functional linguistics are now being recognized as playing a key role in the so-called New Dialogue between the humanities, the social sciences and the biological and life sciences. This is now beginning to be "voiced" as a unified theory and praxis of human social meaning making. This is witnessed, for example, by the success of the first two International Systemic Workshops to be held in North America: at Glendon College, York University (Toronto) in August 1982 and at the University of Michigan, Ann Arbor in August 1985. Not to mention the course "A Social-Semiotic of Grammar" which Michael Halliday taught in June 1985 at the International Summer Institute for Semiotic and Structural Studies at Indiana University, Bloomington.

This interview took place in the Department of Linguistics in the University of Sydney (Australia) on 4th September, 1985. Paul J. Thibault completed his Ph.D. thesis under Michael Halliday's supervision in the Department of Linguistics at the University of Sydney in 1984.

P.J. THIBAULT: You relate your work quite explicitly to the principal European functional schools of linguistics: the Prague school, the French functionalists, the London and Copenhagen schools. How would you describe the relations of your work to these various schools of linguistics?

M.A.K. HALLIDAY: I would see my work as falling clearly within this tradition. As you know, I was taught by Firth, and so the Malinowski-Firth or the so-called "London school" is the closest, and I accept a lot of the basic concepts that come from there. But in two aspects in particular I've taken ideas from other European functional schools: from Hjelmslev, or the "Copenhagen school", a particular theoretical orientation, especially in relation to system and text — Hjelmslev's interpretation of the Saussurean position, which I find most helpful; and then from the Prague school, their interest in what we would call register variation, in the text as an object, and, of course, in the theory of verbal art.

P.J.T.: Anything about the French in particular?

M.A.K.H.: I'm less aware of this as a specific component, but I would of course regard it as a central element in European functionalism.

P.J.T.: The focus of much of your work has been on the relations between system and text — or system and process in Hjelmslev's terms. What does this distinction mean in the systemic-functional perspective?

M.A.K.H.: I think the notion of system and process in Hjelmslev's sense is a good starting point. I would see text as instantiation of the system; the two must be mutually determining. Hjelmslev says that you could, in principle, have a system without process — a system without it generating any text, but you couldn't have the process without the system; he presents it as a one-way determination. I prefer to think of these as a single complex phenomenon: the system only "exists" as a potential for the process, and the process is the actualization of that potential. Since this is a *language* potential, the "process" takes the form of what we call text.

P.J.T.: The Saussurean discussion of this relation has tended to disjoin system from text so that the ontological status of the system is privileged. The systemic-functional model, as well as the earlier work of Firth and Hjelmslev, has quite a different view of this relation. The systemic-functional model is oriented to both "meaning" and "text". Can you explain this relation?

M.A.K.H.: I've always felt it was rather a distraction in Saussure that he defined linguistics as the study of *la langue*, with *parole* being simply the evidence that you use and then throw away. I don't see it that way. Firth, of course, was at the other end of the scale, in that for him the phenomenon was the text. He wasn't interested in the potential, but rather, as I think I put it in one of my papers, in the generalized actual, so that it was the typical texts that he was interested in. Firth tended to privilege the text as against the system. I don't want to privilege either.

P.J.T.: Actually, that's new to me — the notion of "generalized actual". Is that, perhaps, where the notion of register comes from — i.e. the typical semantic choices made in social situation-types.

M.A.K.H.: Yes, I think it is. Firth himself had the concept, as you know, of restricted languages, and this derived from his concern with "typical texts in their contexts of situation", to use his own wording.

P.J.T.: The systemic aspect of the theory, like Saussure's, is defined relationally in terms of the oppositional values among the terms in a given system, i.e. that these relations are neither contingent nor external, but are defined only by internal criteria. How do you account for the work — i.e. the formal and institutional conditions — which must be performed on the system to produce text?

M.A.K.H.: Can we put it this way? You have to express the system in some form of discourse which is obviously going to be metaphorical, and I tend to use the notion of "choice". That does raise problems of possible misunderstanding. As you know, the way that I think of this is that the system at any one level is a set of interrelated options and the selection of any one option at any one point becomes the environment for a further set of selections. So if, in the situation where you have options x, y, and z, you choose x, this means that, in turn, you are in a position where you choose in another set of options a/b; and so forth. Remember that it is a synoptic representation: the "movement" is in delicacy, or progressive approximation, not in time. That's something which you can think of in various ways. You can think of it as something which you switch on and operate randomly; and there are some forms of pathological discourse which could be modelled in that way, as being random passes through the system. In most discourse, the operation of the system is part of a total activity set: the selections are motivated in some way, from a higher level semiotic.

P.J.T.: Is it an abstract potential then, or is it something more concrete?

M.A.K.H.: No, it is an abstract potential. Let's say human beings engage in social processes, in various social activities; and we can represent any of these in terms of general semiotic concepts. These are the systems which represent the meaning potential of the culture as a whole, and some of these are activated through language. That's Hjelmslev's sense of the connotative semiotic — language as being the semiotic system which is the expression plane of other semiotic systems, which are not language. This means it is an abstract potential, but one which is called upon as a form of social action. Language is not only a *part* of the social process — it is also an *expression* of it; and that is why it is organized in a way which makes it a *metaphor* for social processes at the same time. In that sense, there's a concrete aspect to the system: language as a form of social activity.

P.J.T.: You make a careful theoretical distinction between system and structure (Halliday 1981), calling structure the output or instantiation of some pathway through the system networks. Does this mean that "structure" is a transformation of the systemic "meaning potential" into something which is necessarily complete?

M.A.K.H.: Well, obviously, the basis of this is the original Saussurean-Hjelmslevian paradigmatic-syntagmatic generalization, which will apply to any semiotic systems, any systematic form of behaviour. Firth made a clear distinction between system and structure as the organizing concepts for these two axes respectively: system is the organizing concept for interpreting relations on the paradigmatic axis, and structure that for interpreting those on the syntagmatic axis. His interpretation of text was as the interplay of these two, so that typically the structure — if you like, the deep syntagm — defined environments within which then the systems — i.e. the deep paradigms — were operating. The environment for any system was a specific place in the structure.

Now, I found it helpful in the work that I was doing to re-order this system-structure distinction so that I could represent the whole system (in the Hjelmslevian sense) entirely in paradigmatic terms as a series of system networks, which are formally equivalent to one huge system network. That meant that the structure became the output of the network; it became the work that you had to do in order to translate a path through the network into an actualization. The structure then becomes the way in which systemic choices are realized. Whether the structure is always "complete" depends on how you are using the network — and on how you define "complete", of course.

P.J.T.: Is there, perhaps, a non-finalistic teleology implicit in your notion of structure as the output of a pathway through a system network?

M.A.K.H.: If I understand what you mean by that, then I think the answer is "no", because there is no implicit teleology at all. Let's start from the notion of exponence, or realization: the "output" is simply what you do in realizing a particular choice. This is talking about the network as a generative device; if we think of "parsing" then of course the direction is reversed. The thing itself is entirely neutral; but there is no way of talking about it that is neutral — no metalanguage that detaches it from some particular way of using the network. The system-structure model says nothing at all about any decision-making process, or any intentionality on the part of speakers or listeners. We model a semiotic system as a set of sets of alternatives; and a structure is simply the realization of some choice among these alternatives — of a "selection expression", as we call it. The notion of structure as output is also neutral as between a propositional form, which says "the selection of option a is realized by structure $x + y + z$", and an instructional form, where you say "in order to select option a, then perform operations $p + q + r$". But remember that it's the system network, not the structure, that embodies the theoretical interpretation; so if you want to build any teleological implications they would relate to the notion of system rather than to that of structure.

P.J.T.: I should like to explore your use of the notion of "function". You claim (Halliday 1970) that language structure is as it is because of the social functions it serves. This seems quite close to Durkheim's notion of "function" as the correspondence between social structure and its needs (*besoins*) or "necessary conditions of existence" in Radcliffe-Brown's later modification of this term. Isn't there the risk of a tautological connection between the two? Does this presume a necessary functional unity of the social system?

M.A.K.H.: Yes, I take this point. There is a risk of this being seen in terms of some rather naive social functionalism. What I would say here is that it does seem to me we're looking for explanations of the nature of language — why it is as it is. I do not believe that representing something as a formal system is in itself any explanation of it. An explanation is something which shows correspondences with other things we know about human cultures, about human societies. If you observe language in contexts of situation, especially in what Bernstein (1975) called "critical socializing contexts", where language is being worked hard to construe the social system (unconsciously, of course), you can make generalisations from this, and the most important single generalisation you can make is that language is being used, in the Lévi-Straussian sense, both to act with and to think with. Now, when you come to interpret the grammar — and this was part of my own personal history, because I had never thought of grammar in this way at first — when you start representing the grammar of an actual language in these systemic (paradigmatic) terms, then you find these clusters in its organization; one tightly organized network of options here, and another one here, but with relatively sparse interconnections between them. So you say, well, what are these clusters doing? Are these purely arbitrary features of the syntax? Clearly they're not. It turns out that there's a dense grouping of options which relate to language as reflection — language to think with — and these are centred around the transitivity systems; and another group that relates to language as action, with the mood systems at the heart of it.

P.J.T.: These are the metafunctions.

M.A.K.H.: Yes, these are the metafunctions, exactly. Now, the notion of metafunction is simply an attempt to capture this relationship between the internal forms of the language and its use in contexts of social action.

P.J.T.: You have suggested (Halliday 1977: 19-31; esp. p.25) that a means-end, goal-oriented conception of the speaker helps to explain the functional "choices" which are made. Doesn't this suggest an empirical, rationalist conception of the speaking subject in your theory?

M.A.K.H.: Have I? What do you see as the alternative to this? What are you opposing the empirical, rationalist conception of the speaking subject to?

P.J.T.: What I'm thinking of really goes back to this issue in relation to the notion of "choice", which, of course, we move on to later on. What does it imply epistemologically? What kind of speaker — is it one who makes ready-made rational choices, rational decisions, or not? I see the possible danger that the rational, goal-oriented subject is seen as the starting point for rational choices and so on. Personally, I don't think so.

M.A.K.H.: Not if you put it that way; that's why I was asking you how far you are pushing this. I think of the speaker-listener — the semiotic "subject", the one who engages in acts of meaning — as an active participant in social processes. But semiotic actions, especially those that are central to the subject's construal of reality (including himself) are largely unconscious. Especially acts of language: I agree with Boas, if we may go back that far, that language is unique among cultural processes in the extent to which it remains below the level of consciousness. If you want to understand the nature of semiotic acts, and particularly semantic acts — the linguistic ones, you have to pay attention to the most unconscious uses of language. It is there, interestingly enough, where you see not only language at work, but also language *expanding*, both within the individual and also within the culture, phylogenetically and ontogenetically. The frontier of language, where new meanings are created, is located in its most unconscious uses.

P.J.T.: Systemic theory is said to be functional in much more than the sense that items in structure are functionally related. This would be a structural account of linguistic function. In what other senses is the theory a functional one?

M.A.K.H.: I see it as three interrelated senses. One is in the technical, grammatical sense: a grammar is interpreted in terms of functions rather than classes. There's a reason for that, of course: it has to be a *functional* grammar to get you from the system to the text. So there we're talking about the low-level sense of grammatical functions; using notions like Theme, Actor, Medium, and so on. That in turn relates to the second sense of function, which is the metafunctional one. What this means is that the whole paradigmatic organization of the grammar is functional, as seen in the way the systems are interrelated: they fall into the broad metafunctional categories of what I call the ideational, the interpersonal, and the textual. That is what relates language to what is outside language, to other semiotic systems.

P.J.T.: So, the metafunctional level is the interface between language and the outside.

M.A.K.H.: Exactly. There's been a lot of confusion about this, and I suspect I'm responsible! Let me say clearly that I see the metafunctional organization as belonging to that interface which is what we mean by semantics. But for that very reason it also determines the form of the grammar. The relation between the grammar and the semantics is non-arbitrary. People have said to me: sometimes you say the metafunctions are in the semantics, sometimes you say they're in the grammar; where are they? They're in both. The metafunctions are the theoretical concepts that enable us to understand the interface between language and what is outside language — and it is this interfacing that has shaped the form of the grammar. Then there is the third sense of function, again related to these two, but which is more like a commonsense use of the term, where function equals use. This is the sense in which you have the traditional non-linguistic functional theories of language, like those of Malinowski, and Bühler, which were taken up by the linguists and built into their own systems: Malinowski by the London school, Bühler by the Prague school. Jakobson is on the fringe here. You remember the arguments that the Prague linguists had over the years about whether the functions were functions of the utterance or functions of the system, and they never got fully built into the system.

P.J.T.: Yes, and that seems to me to be a flaw in Jakobson's theory.

M.A.K.H.: I agree.

P.J.T.: What distinguishes a systemic-functional interpretation of language from other, more syntagmatically based functional interpretations?

M.A.K.H.: Well, I think you've given what I would give as the answer: it's the paradigmatic basis of systemic grammar which I think is the distinguishing factor between this and other functional grammars. Now, I don't believe in an all-purpose grammar; I have in mind, rather, a grammar for the sort of purposes that I have been interested in, and those people that I have worked with. Grammars vary in their delicacy of focus. You may need for certain purposes a very dedicated grammar, one that's only going to do one job, and that job will totally determine the form of the grammar that you choose. At the other end of the scale, you have the notion — as is traditional in linguistics — of an all-purpose grammar, one which is the best for every job, which I really don't believe in. I've tried to move in at a midpoint on this scale — aiming at a grammar that will do a number of different jobs. It won't be totally dedicated, but nor will it be the reverse: it's not designed to do all possible jobs. So for the sort of questions that I have been interested in, this paradigmatic orientation has helped, in a number of different ways of which I'll just mention one. When you write a grammar this way, then the question "what is the description (or — I prefer — the interpretation) of this item, this clause, or whatever you're looking at?" and the question "how is this item related to other items?" become one question and not two. In other words, if you have a syntagmatic grammar, then the question "what is the nature of phenomenon a?" and the question "how does phenomenon a relate to phenomenon b?" are discrete questions. In a paradigmatic grammar they're not. They're the same question; you can't ask one without the other.

P.J.T.: This question relates, in part, to the third aspect of functionalism, which we talked about before. The systemic-functional approach adopts a functional interpretation of the internal, paradigmatic (systemic) organization of meaning relations. But what are its wider implications — in relating the linguistic system to the social system, for instance? How does systemic-functional theory interpret this relation?

M.A.K.H.: This is one direction we're trying to explore. One of the ways that I see the two relating is probabilistically. Jay Lemke (1984) put this very clearly in his discussion of the need for intermediate level generalizations between the macro- and the micro- that you're familiar with (except that it shouldn't be represented as size: it should be "meta-" rather than "macro-"). Let's discuss these in terms of Malinowski's notion of the context of situation. The context of situation is a generalized semiotic construct deriving from the culture — something that is recognized by the members as a form of social activity that they engage in. Now any given instance of a situation-type can be defined in terms of three factors that we call the field, tenor, and mode: what's going on, who's taking part, and what part the particular semiotic system (in this case language) is playing. What happens is that the interactants in any given situation access certain aspects of their semiotic potential: they get them ready so they can be brought into play. What is the nature of this operation? As I see it, it is not a cutting off device. It is not that I switch on this bit and switch off that bit. It is, rather, that I re-order the probabilities among them. So I think you must see language as a probabilistic system. I would represent language in terms of a global set of probabilities. There's good evidence that speakers of a language are sensitive to relative frequency — to this being more, or less, frequent than that. Register variation is analogous in many ways to dialect variation; but it is functionally based and it can be interpreted, therefore, as a re-alignment of the probabilities in relation to the particular contextual configuration — in particular, the context of situation. We're trying to find ways of modelling this at the moment.

P.J.T.: Register, it seems to me then, is another interface notion; in this case, between the semantics and the social situation.

M.A.K.H.: I welcome the opportunity to clarify this, because I know I've often been misunderstood — again, it's my own fault. I would see the notion of "register" as being *at* the semantic level, not above it. Shifting in register means re-ordering the probabilities at the semantic level ...

P.J.T.: ... which way they're skewed in that situation-type.

M.A.K.H.: ... whereas the categories of field, mode, and tenor belong one level up. These are the features of the context of situation; and this *is* an interface. But the register itself I see as being linguistic; it is a setting of probabilities in the semantics.

P.J.T.: Speech act theory proposes an autonomous "pragmatic" component to account for language use. You make no such distinction between the "pragmatic" and "semantic" dimensions of meaning. Why?

M.A.K.H.: I've never seen that it's necessary. It seems to me that in the grammar — that is, at the lexicogrammatical level — we don't need to make a distinction between the *system* and its instantiation in *text*. Our theory of "grammar" is at one and the same time an interpretation of the system and an interpretation of the texts that are engendered by that system. Now, it seems to me that pragmatics is simply the name of the semantics of the text. I'm not just making a terminological point. It seems to me that a theory of semantics must encompass both the system and the process in exactly the same way that the grammar encompasses both the system and the process. We don't want a separate thing called pragmatics.

P.J.T.: In any case, it seems to me that most of so-called linguistic pragmatics has a very impoverished view of grammar.

M.A.K.H.: I couldn't agree more.

P.J.T.: You say that the organizing principle of meaning is its internal, paradigmatic organization. Can you explain this? How does this relate to the grammar of the clause, for instance?

M.A.K.H.: The clause, I think, is the gateway, the main gateway between the semantics and the grammar, just as the syllable is the main gateway between the content and the expression. The clause is where the meanings are all organized together. So I see the clause as being the primary grammatical unit in the sense that it is there that the options relating to the different kinds of meaning — the different metafunctions — are brought together so that they get mapped on to one another into this single output. I sometimes use the metaphor of polyphonic music: that, in a sense, you have one unfolding melodic line from the experiential, another melodic line from the interpersonal, and another from the textual component. These operate through three major systems at the clause rank: the transitivity, the mood, and the theme.

P.J.T.: Systemic-functional theory proposes, as we have just seen, that at the grammatical level of the clause, meanings are organised into three simultaneous sets of options. These relate to distinct kinds of metafunctional components in the semantic organization of the language. What is the relation between the semantics and the grammar in a "metafunctional" account? What do you consider to be its principal advantages over other accounts of language structure?

M.A.K.H.: It's a hypothesis, obviously; but one which can be tested. Not simply; we won't get a formal test — but then the problem in the human sciences is that anything that can be subjected to formal tests of the kind that we have available at the moment tends to be rather trivial, so that doesn't worry me very much. But over the longer term it's something that can be inspected and tested.

The hypothesis — as embodied in the term "metafunction" — is that there is this relationship between the form of the grammar and the semiotic construction of the culture as instantiated in particular situations. I don't think any other linguistic theory has suggested an interface organization of this kind. This leads to a further hypothesis, which is that these different metafunctions are typically represented by different *kinds* of grammatical organization. Specifically: (1) experiential meaning is typically represented in constituent-like, particulate structures. Most people who've worked on language have been largely taken up with experiential meaning; and this means that they view language in terms of constituency, which is a very partial consideration. (2) Interpersonal meanings are typically prosodic, with field-like manifestations. (3) Textual meanings typically give you the periodic movement which is so characteristic of discourse at all levels; everything from the very smallest waves to the very large ones. In other words, there is a hierarchy of periodicity, and that comes from the textual metafunction. So not only can you build this bridge systematically between the language and the situation, but you can also say that the different patterns of realization taken by the linguistic system relate to these metafunctional distinctions.

P.J.T.: The distinction between the ideational and interpersonal metafunctions helps to overcome the classical dichotomy in the western cultural tradition between language as "thought" and language as "action". Wittgenstein's notion of "language-game" is one attempt to integrate both language and the social actions it performs into an integral whole. How do you conceive of the relationship between language and social action?

M.A.K.H.: If I can say this without it sounding as if it's just a clever slogan: language is both a part of and a metaphor for social action. Actually there is a threefold relationship. First, language is the *realization* of social action:

in other words, it stands to social action in the same way that, within language, the phonology stands to the grammar. That's Hjelmslev's connotative semiotic. Secondly, language is a *part* of social action: one component of any instance of social action is the verbal action that takes place within it. In some types of situation the two are very closely interrelated — instructions, games, and things of this kind; in others there is more distance. Thirdly, language is also a *metaphor* for social action: the forms of the language itself give us a metaphoric representation of the forms of social action. This can be seen, for example, in the facts of register variation and dialect variation, which represent metaphorically variation in social processes, on the one hand, and in the social structure on the other.

P.J.T.: What kind of distinction would you make between text and discourse in this regard?

M.A.K.H.: I've not been consistent in making any clearcut distinction between the two. I started with the term "text" because it's the traditional term in linguistics; certainly among the functional schools. So I was simply adopting their terminological practice. In contemporary usage I think we can talk about either discourse analysis or text analysis — it doesn't make much difference. But it has become useful in recent work to have "discourse" as a separate term in order to be able to use it to refer to heteroglossic notions (Bakhtin 1981) — the "discourse of" something or other; and also (as you use it yourself) to the way in which text functions to embody or enact an ideology. We're accustomed now to using the term "discourse" to focus on these aspects, and "text" to focus on the more linguistic aspects.

P.J.T.: Is it perhaps discourse in the sense of the social practices in which texts are embedded and which, in some sense, they are the realization of (viz. the first of the three kinds of relationships between language and social action)?

M.A.K.H.: Yes, right.

P.J.T.: The systemic-functional model assumes a tri-stratal organization of language, consisting of a phonology, a lexicogrammar, and a semantics. What particular assumptions concerning meaning are made in this model?

M.A.K.H.: Maybe two things. One is that the tri-stratal model embodies, initially, the Saussurean line of arbitrariness, at the frontier between lexicogrammar and phonology. Of course, one has tended to exaggerate the extent to which this line is solid: there are a great many non-arbitrary aspects of the relation between the expression and the content (though that's a separate point, I think it is a very interesting and important one). So the first cut, if you like, is that between the content plane and the expression plane; and you see that kind of bi-stratal organization in children's protolanguage (Halliday 1975). As you know, I think the ontogenesis of language shows very clearly the beginning of language as a bi-stratal system, which then evolves into a tri-stratal one. Presumably that's how language evolved in the human race. It makes it sound very concrete if I put it this way, but it has to be read in the light of everything we said before: what happens is that in moving from the protolanguage to the mother tongue the child slots in a grammar in between the meaning and the expression, so that the content plane now splits into two and becomes a semantics and a grammar. We can see both how it happens and why it happens. The new interstratal line that is created in this process, however, is definitely non-arbitrary; this is important. I'm not sure to what extent Saussure was also referring to that stratal boundary; Ruqaiya Hasan certainly thinks that his discussion encompasses that line as well as the other one. Anyway, there is a different relationship between the semantics and the lexicogrammar, which is non-arbitrary, from the one between that "content" block and the phonology, which is basically arbitrary. Now the second point is this: as you know, Firth always insisted that each level is itself meaning-creating, and he didn't like the term "meaning" to be siphoned off to refer only to what I am calling semantic patterns.

P.J.T.: Indeed, because you can have foregrounded patternings on any given level.

M.A.K.H.: Exactly — I agree with that. Jim Martin has pulled me up for obscuring that aspect and making too close a tie-up between "meaning" and this notion of a specifically "semantic" level. I admit I have done that, and I think it's wrong; the whole system is meaning-creating. Meaning is the product of the interrelations among the parts. This is well brought out by the foregrounding you referred to: the kind of "de-automatization" whereby meaning is being created at the phonological level, and at the grammatical level, as well as in the "automatized" process of the realization of semantic features.

P.J.T.: More recent developments in the Department of Linguistics here of the tri-stratal model propose a stronger orientation to discourse. Here the concern is with the relations among the levels of discourse, lexicogrammar, and phonology. Why has this shift in emphasis taken place?

M.A.K.H.: This is a part of the discussion with Jim Martin (1983). He is making two points. One is that moving above the lexicogrammar essentially has to be a move on the "size" scale as well. In other words, what he's locating there are conjunctive relations and so on which enable the grammatical system to be used for the construction of larger units. This he sees as a necessary step in order to get from the grammar, through this interface, to the register and the genre, and eventually up to the ideological system. Secondly, he's not convinced that you need to have a separate semantic representation of all the features that are there in the grammar. He considers that you don't need a semantic cycle for the transitivity system over and above the transitivity system itself as represented in the grammar. I think you do.

P.J.T.: Does he say then that that cycle in the transitivity system is its own semantics?

M.A.K.H.: Yes. He's saying that you can handle the whole thing in terms of transitivity itself.

P.J.T.: ... when in fact it's easier in the case of the interpersonal component to put above that role relations and so on.

M.A.K.H.: He sees the need for a semantics of the interpersonal component, but not for a general semantic stratum. I think that one phenomenon we've been working on a lot lately, that of grammatical metaphor, demonstrates that we do need this.

P.J.T.: Your theory is also described as a "social semiotic" one (Halliday 1978). What is the relation between the social semiotic and the linguistic system? How do you position your use of the term "social semiotic" in relation to the principal European schools of semiotics — the Greimasians in Paris, Eco in Bologna, for instance?

M.A.K.H.: When I used the term "social semiotic" in the first place what I was trying to say was something like this. We need an interpretation of language which does not treat language as a thing in itself, but as part of a wider set of phenomena which we call the social system (or the culture, in American parlance). It doesn't make sense to me to try and interpret language except in a context of this kind. That was the "social" part. I wanted to say, furthermore, that we can represent the culture as a whole as an assembly of semiotic systems, of which language is one. It was those two things that I was trying to say in one move. I think it was Greimas, in fact, who used that same term in the International Days of Sociolinguistics Conference in Rome in the late 1960s (Greimas 1969). I wasn't there, but I think it was in Greimas's paper that you find the term "social semiotic".

P.J.T.: Yes, I've seen the term even in more recent work of his as well (Greimas 1983).

M.A.K.H.: It seemed to me we were talking about the same thing and that what I was trying to say fell naturally within the scope of European semiotics. I see certain points of difference; one difference would be that I am still working as a linguist — a grammarian, in fact. What I'm seeking to do is primarily to interpret language, rather than using language to interpret other things, which is the perspective of most semioticians. But to make sense of grammar you had to relate it to society.

P.J.T.: Greimas is a linguist with a Hjelmslevian basis, which can be traced right back to his earlier work (Greimas 1966).

M.A.K.H.: Right; I would also differ in that I'm trying to interpret language in relation to other processes (for example, those of learning), rather than by attempting a formal representation of semiotic systems — as, say, Eco does.

P.J.T.: What is the status of "grammar" in both the systemic-functional and social semiotic perspectives?

M.A.K.H.: I gave a course in Bloomington this year called "Grammar and Daily Life" (Halliday 1985) and there I was saying two things. First, insofar as language plays a part in the total array of social semiotics, the central processing unit of language is grammar. We have to understand that, in order to get any kind of sensible interpretation of the whole. Secondly, referring back to the foregrounding notion we mentioned earlier, the grammatical system takes on a life of its own — as symbolic systems always can do. We see this at work in a lot of spheres of social action. Now, when we focus on the grammar in its relation to various aspects of daily life, we can see how the grammar itself — the grammatical system — in addition to functioning as the automatized realization of the semantics, and through that of the context of situation, is also functioning directly as a form of social action in its own right.

P.J.T.: There is a Whorfian dimension to your theory, which seems relevant here. Much confusion has been created — not by Whorf, but by others — concerning Whorf's conception of the relation between "grammar" and so-called "world view" or "metaphysic". Could you comment on this in relation to your own theory?

M.A.K.H.: Yes, there has been a lot of confusion here. People are still disproving Whorf; there's been another round just recently, and yet he pops up again because he's not been disproved at all. These efforts have very little to do with what he was on about. I think that the great merit of Whorf was to point out the essential dialectic relationship between language and the social semiotic systems within which language functions as a realization. In other words, there is no one-way determinism. Now Whorf concerned himself only with the system; but what he was saying applies both to the system and to the text. Text creates the situation as well as the situation creating the text; just as the linguistic system creates the other semiotic systems of the culture as well as their creating it. But Whorf did not go over to the other extreme. He didn't replace one form of determinism by the other. He insisted on this rather complex form of dialectic: that between a symbol and what it symbolizes — between the two sides of the sign, if you like. This has an enormous importance, for example, in the process by which a child grows up as a member of a culture — being given, in Whorf's terms, a "recept". Children are given this through the linguistic system, and that becomes the grid, to use Sapir's old metaphor, through which they interpret their experience. But what Whorf was able to show is, I think, a necessary part of our explanations of how we, in turn, can use semiotic systems in order to change the things that generated them in the first place. This is a major factor which people who "reject" Whorf totally fail to explain — how by working on the language you can have such an influence on the other systems in the culture.

P.J.T.: Yes, indeed. The Chomskyan concept of "creativity", which is not set within any notion of either linguistic or social practice, is just so badly off the mark, in my opinion. What you're saying there really embodies a much richer, more effective notion of creativity itself.

M.A.K.H.: Yes, that is an important sense of creativity. I agree with that. At one end of the scale, there's the interesting case of the highly valued text — the great poem or whatever — through which an individual, or the discourse of an individual, can actually innovate: the writer as creator of new meanings. These are rare, but they're not non-existent. And then there is the more general sense, which is that whereby the social processes as a whole — people engaging in these forms of activity — create, bring about change: change at every level of semiosis.

P.J.T.: Transformational-generative approaches to grammar are primarily concerned with form — form relations. Systemic-functional theory is concerned with the relations between grammatical forms and their patterns of social use. How would you characterize this relation?

M.A.K.H.: I'm not sure that I want to say much more than what has already been said; except perhaps just one small point, since you refer here to grammatical forms. As you know, I don't argue at all from the form of the grammar to the structure of the human brain or to any kind of psychological processes. I think that we can, however, use some of our insights into the forms of the grammar to help us towards an understanding of how people construct social realities; and an obvious example would be transitivity. It seems to me that transitivity systems in all languages — I think this is a universal feature — embody a tension between the ergative and the transitive modes of interpretation. Now, these are not, to my mind, simply formal alternatives. I think they represent different, complementary ways of interpreting experience. They're complementary because they're mutually contradictory. That's what enables the tension between them to create this very vital, unstable interpretation which we live with: we see our processes both in terms of an ergative-type, cause and effect model and in terms of a transitive-type, mechanical transmission model. I think that by looking at the grammar — by understanding the nature of the system — we can get quite a lot of insight into our social construction of reality.

P.J.T.: Yes, expressed more metaphorically or, perhaps, more accurately, in terms of the contemporary epistemological confrontation between dynamics and thermodynamics in the physical and life sciences, we can say that in our social construction of reality there's a constant tension between the mechanistic and deterministic Newtonian model, which is seen as embodying a fundamental level of description and, hence, of reality, and there is the dynamic quantum model which introduces both instability and probabilistic features into our interpretations.

M.A.K.H.: I see these as embodied in every clause in English, and no doubt in every other natural language. But taking your formulation seriously; this is where it gets more complicated. I don't think Newton's picture *was* mechanistic, though it's been interpreted that way (Hill 1974). What the grammar provides is the two sides, two complementary components, of Newton's universe: the technological (transitive: process as the *transmission* of force) and the scientific (ergative: process as the *explanation* of force). The dynamic, quantum model is represented, I think, not by either one of these, nor by some third interpretation — I don't see any third interpretation in the grammar; but rather by the tension between the two. This is an aspect of its nature as a dynamic open system, as Lemke has shown it to be.

P.J.T.: That's very encouraging, for most linguistics is still at the Newtonian stage in its epistemology. We have to get both.

Register theory is one of the intermediate levels of analysis proposed for cutting up the social semiotic system into different social situation-types. How do you define the social situation?

M.A.K.H.: I find it useful to talk in terms of the three concepts of field, tenor, and mode. As you know, I started many years ago trying to re-interpret the Malinowski-Firth concept of the context of situation, and arrived at these notions from above, so to speak. It was only later on that I saw them to be motivated also from below — from the grammar, in the form of the metafunctional hypothesis. That seemed to suggest an independent reason for using this kind of model: it shows just *how* the context of situation "redounds with" (construes and is construed by) the semantic system.

P.J.T.: The concept of "register" relates typical co-patternings of discourse and lexicogrammatical options to their social situation-types. As we have seen, it is an intermediate level of analysis, which can relate texts to the social formations which produce and re-produce them. How do you see "register" as a possible analytic construct for relating texts to social institutions as sites for the production of particular kinds of social meanings?

M.A.K.H.: As I was saying earlier, I see the "register" as essentially the clustering of semantic probabilities: it's a linguistic category. The context of situation is "above" the register. The context of situation is what is modelled in terms of field, mode, and tenor. Just to add one point: Jim Martin (forthcoming) and Ruqaiya Hasan (1980) are both working in this area, asking how one can refine this notion and get more insight into it. Jim is operating with the notion of a stratal distinction between register and genre. He feels it's necessary to have another level above the register, a level which in a sense is a development out of field, and which specifies the nature of the activity, but in terms of purpose or intentionality. He says this is what engenders the structure of a particular genre, and this higher level construct is then represented through the register. So he has two levels here. Ruqaiya does it in a single level, using what she calls the "contextual configuration", the specific values of the context of situation in terms of the variables of field, mode, and tenor. It is this contextual configuration which determines the structure *potential* for the text.

P.J.T.: In the systemic-functional model, "structure" is the realization of a configuration of systemic choices, which are then mapped on to the resulting syntagm. In what sense do you intend the notion of "choice"? Does it perhaps imply individual voluntary actions in the sense of the early Parsons, or something more like his later notion of functional requisites or functional imperatives?

M.A.K.H.: No, certainly not — I've not guarded enough, I realize, against that sort of interpretation. What it implies is simply an OR relationship, a set of alternatives. We can define the "system" as a set of alternatives with an entry condition. Now there are instances where the activation of a system of that kind can be seen to involve a conscious choice. But those are special cases. There is no suggestion of intentionality — voluntary action — or of functional imperatives, in the theoretical concept of a system, or system network.

P.J.T.: The concept of register itself suggests a constrained skewing of the probabilities of the meaning system, as we saw before, according to the situation-type. Is there a danger that this overemphasises the normative or consensus basis of social power relations? How would you characterize differences of power among discourse interactants?

M.A.K.H.: I wouldn't see it as normative. I would interpret the power relations in a particular situation, when we represent that situation in terms of field, tenor, and mode, by building in to our representation the fact that the situation may be different things for different interactants. The total picture is obviously going to bring in all angles; but in any typical context of situation in which there is a power relationship of inequality, then the configuration embodied in that situation is different from the way it is seen from either end. This means, of course, that the register that is being operated by the interactants will be bifurcated, although we may choose to characterize the register of the situation as a whole by building in both strands. I wouldn't call this normative, if that implies, as you say, a kind of consensus basis.

P.J.T.: ... which is the structural-functionalist model in a sociological interpretation of, for example, Talcott Parsons (1964).

M.A.K.H.: But again with that view you would not be able to explain the way that the interactants can manipulate this in order to try and change the power relations. Often they don't, and they may not succeed when they try; but it is a permeable frontier.

P.J.T.: The interpersonal metafunction, which is concerned in part with the social role relations among interactants, suggests the principle of exchange structuralism in the sense that a given society is maintained by the reciprocal exchange of information and goods-and-services, i.e. by a general norm of reciprocity, which helps to explain social behaviour. Is the emphasis here on the structured patterns of social relations or on the processes of social interaction?

M.A.K.H.: You can set up — we haven't dealt with this — a kind of system-structure cycle at this level also. If you do this, then what you're emphasising, as the underlying representation, is processes of social interaction, and these can also be seen as interrelated sets of alternatives. Then the patterns of social relations are set up as the manifestation of these social processes via the statuses and roles of the interactants.

P.J.T.: Could the role notion which is built into the interpersonal component help to bridge that gap?

M.A.K.H.: Yes, I think it could. I think that it can be a link in the total interpretative chain. How much part it would play I don't know. I think Jim Martin might say that there would be a danger of reifying it, where his view of the interpersonal tenor relationships is rather in terms of power and distance — as relations rather than as terms in the relations. I think one can avoid that danger if one keeps both perspectives in mind.

P.J.T.: Most linguistic theory is speaker oriented. Do you have a corresponding conception of the hearer?

M.A.K.H.: You're right, of course; most linguistic theory is speaker-oriented. I would accept this has also been true of my own work, although I try to emphasise the notion of speaker-listener — this is why I prefer the term "listener" to "hearer", because the listener is the active role. The text, the discourse itself, is a creation of both speaker and listener; I see this as a single unity, the speaker-listener complex, if you like.

P.J.T.: I think you've called it an "interact" (Halliday 1977).

M.A.K.H.: Yes, an interact. And similarly with constructions that the text creates in its turn. This is very important in child language: in the protolanguage stage, there is a sense in which the speaker is privileged, because the parents don't speak the protolanguage — only the child does. But one has to look behind that and recognize that even there the protolanguage is very clearly the creation of child and parents together. The parents, or other caregivers, have to be creating the language along with the child. The fact that they are speaking English or some other adult language, not the child's protolanguage — may distract attention from the fact that they are, as listeners, also creating the protolanguage. Even here the text is very much the creation of listener and speaker together.

P.J.T.: You have written (Halliday 1975) an extensive and important body of work on the process of language development in the first years of a child's life. This involves the process of inserting the child into a symbolic order of the socio-cultural meanings of a given community. How would you characterize in general terms the model of "man" and "woman" which informs this thinking?

M.A.K.H.: You could start from a kind of socialization model, in which "man" and "woman" are the human being who has been through this kind of process — through the stages of child language and all the other "socializing" processes of the culture. But that seems to me to imply a rather too deterministic approach. It's as if there is something given "out there" and in some sense this reality moulds the human being to fit itself. There is an element of this in the process, but I think it's one-sided, put like that. This relates perhaps to what I was saying before; that the child, in the process of becoming "man" or "woman", is taking part in the creation of that socio-cultural reality. The language is as much a means whereby the child construes the culture as it is a means whereby the culture constructs the child.

P.J.T.: How would you position systemic-functional linguistics in relation to contemporary social theory?

M.A.K.H.: It seems to me that social theories tend to have a big hole in the middle where language should be and I would hope to see systemic-functional linguistics as, in a sense, filling the hole. That's the context in which I've always thought of it. As you know, one of the reasons why I was always interested in Bernstein's work is that he seemed to me to be unique among social theorists in not merely paying lip service to language, as everyone does — saying yes, of course, language is important — but actually building it into his interpretative framework and seeing it as an essential part of the process of cultural transmissions. In linguistics we've now had a generation of work that has been called "sociolinguistics", stemming mainly from Labov and Fishman, which has been significant for the theory of language (variation theory, for example). This makes explicit that there is a social context to language; but it hasn't aroused much interest among social theorists because it has still been largely a theory of language: of language in its social context, yes; but not really a theory of language in society. Excepting the later work of Dell Hymes, it lacks the conception of a social semiotic. Language and society haven't really met yet, but I would like to think that systemic-functional linguistics could have something to say about that.

P.J.T.: Does a specific social programme inform your work? If so, how would you describe this?

M.A.K.H.: I've always been interested in applications of linguistics, and never seen any real gap between theory and practice, or theory and application. On the other hand, I've been interested in a number of different applications of linguistic theory, ranging from research applications, at least what are in the immediate sense research applications like the study of literature, to more immediately practical ones particularly in education. I suppose the context in which I myself have worked most — and I think this is probably true of people working in systemic theory generally — has been educational. Not in the specific sense of language pedagogy, although there often are implications for what a teacher would do in a classroom, but more in the broader sense of language as the main resource through which the human being develops and gains knowledge. So I do see linguistics as part of a programme which is concerned with the development of human beings in the social context, with language and language development as the primary resource.

P.J.T.: Most of Western linguistics is founded on a narrow range of culturally and ideologically dominant notions concerning language, society, and the individual. You have had extensive experience throughout your career with non-Western linguistic and cultural traditions. What can these offer to a Western social science of language?

M.A.K.H.: I'd have to answer on two levels. One, in the specific sense of non-Western traditions in the study of language itself, I think there is a great deal to be learnt from these. Linguists are now familiar, of course, with the Indian tradition, which was in many ways more fruitful than the Western one in that it was clearer about the nature of language as a phenomenon. It was able to objectify — to identify language as object — in the way the Western tradition found extremely hard.[1] Then from the Chinese tradition, I think there's a great deal to be learnt towards prosodic interpretations of language; both directly at the phonological level — Chinese phonology was very Firthian in its prosodic approach — but also in its implications for other levels of language, which can be seen as not being constituent-like. The Chinese, who were of course highly theoretical thinkers, were able to create a totally abstract model of phonology — the only people who did. That's at the more specific, technical linguistic level. If you then move on to, as you put it, a "Western social science of language", then I don't know enough about other aspects of these major traditions to be able to say whether or not there was a relationship set up there between language and society — language and the social order — in the way that we need. I'm not aware of it, but that doesn't mean it wasn't there. Of course if we move up to other aspects of these traditions, I mean Chinese thought as a whole, clearly we have another way in to the whole question; but not through language. I'm not aware how far language was linked with society in those traditions.

P.J.T.: The social semiotic orientation of your work assumes no specific psychological or biological models of language. Yet, cognitive and psychological theories of language have frequently dominated Western linguistic theory. Why have you so consistently refused such a position?

M.A.K.H.: Partly, I suppose, that I am just obstinate. If everyone does a thing one way, I tend to think it ought to be done the other way, if only to redress the balance. But also partly my own personal inclinations. I tend to believe in social explanations for phenomena where I find it hard to believe in psychological ones. But this is because I can't see the sort of psychological explanations we are familiar with as a basis for modes of action. Do you see what I mean? — as something you can use when you're facing particular problems in an educational context. Educational practice has tended to be dominated by the theoretical stance that has come in from psychology, and it has tended to neglect both the sociological and the linguistic. At a deeper level this has to be explained as Bruce McKellar has done, in terms of the history of ideas in the West, especially the constant conviction of a separate order of existence called "mind", or "soul". In recent centuries — I've said this often enough — this has led to our Western obsession with the individual. Using cognitive instead of semantic interpretations — talking about "thought" instead of about "meaning" — is another way of elevating the individual at the expense of the collective.

P.J.T.: Systemic-functional linguistics is currently involved in computer models of text-generation; in particular, the NIGEL Project at the Information Sciences Institute in the University of Southern California. Does the human-computer interface underscore any major shift in the predominantly humanistic epistemological assumptions in linguistics concerning the production of meaning and of knowledge itself?

M.A.K.H.: I hope not; I certainly don't see it that way. Let me say first that I have been in and out of computational linguistics twice in my life before this; first back in the 1950s, in the early days of machine translation (Halliday 1960), and then again in the mid-sixties when we were doing our research in London in the scientific English project (Huddleston, Hudson, Winter & Henrici 1968). In those early stages the technology simply hadn't caught up; there was no way that you could do computational research on language. (You could build dictionaries, and so forth, which was important, but didn't address the questions that I was interested in.) When we came into the second round, we were able to get as far as using the computer to form a paradigm from a system network, to test simple forms of output and so on (Henrici 1981). I was surprised, then, to find myself back in again a third time in 1980; but the reason is that in the meantime the technology has changed so drastically that we are now learning fundamental things about language by modelling it in the computer, for example through text-generation projects (Mann & Matthiessen 1983). It used to be linguistically trivial — it was a purely internal housekeeping matter — what form the system had to take in the computer. We didn't learn anything from it. Now we're beginning to learn something from the way in which grammars have to be written — how they are represented in the text-generation or parsing process. But the most important point is that, in the study of a language like

English, which has been reasonably well worked over — we're about to pass from pre-history to history in the linguistics of English, and the interpretation of the grammar has now got to the point where you can no longer test it manually: it's just too big. You have to put it in a computer in order to be able to test it. That's looking at the question from the point of view of the contribution to our understanding of language. There are, secondly, a number of applications of this work, which will be important for human life. Going back to the early days, the reason I got interested in machine translation in the first place was because I was convinced of the value of people being educated in the mother tongue. Now, people can't be educated in the mother tongue if there aren't any textbooks. There are not enough human translators; but maybe a machine could do the job. Thirdly, then, we come to the question of the effect of the man-machine dialogue on forms of meaning and of knowledge. This is a huge question, which we haven't time for here. I see three levels at which the impact is taking place, those of the channel (new forms of text), the register (new semantic patterns) and the ideology. The last is where we will see linguistics developing as the new "science of sciences", replacing physics, to cope with the interpretation of the universe in terms of exchange of information, rather than of cause and effect.

P.J.T.: How would you define the role of the academic discipline of linguistics in relation to the current historical phase of technological, mass consumer, and increasingly information based capitalist society?

M.A.K.H.: I think that anything which increases our understanding of ourselves as human beings, and of the nature of human social processes, is valuable. It has a practical value in helping to protect the consumer from the massive pressures of high tech selling, whether what is being sold is goods-and-services or information. And like any other scientific knowledge it can be used and it can be abused. You can use linguistics to help you sell information, or goods-and-services, to people just as much as you can use linguistics to protect people against having these things sold to them. This is the familiar ethical dilemma of the sciences and I think it's very clear that linguistics is a science in this sense. It is capable of being used in all kinds of ways. I hope, of course, that we're constructing a kind of linguistics which is able to be used in the ways that I would see as humanistic, progressive, forward looking — such as defending the individual against the excesses of this kind of society. Let's take our notion of grammatical metaphor as a case in point. I think the sort of work that we're trying to do in this area is enabling us to see much more clearly the linguistic processes and, therefore, the underlying semiotic processes that are going into mass consumer discourse, or bureaucratic (Hardaker 1982) or political or militaristic discourse. Grammar is the most powerful tool we have for understanding and therefore for controlling these things. It shouldn't be seen just as a form of defence, though. With a grammar derived from a social semiotic it should be possible to *shape* the kind of technological, information-based society you're talking about, to ensure that it is not dehumanized in the ways we see happening today. By "grammar" here of course I mean a theory of grammar — it is a curse of English to use the same term both for a phenomenon and for the study of that phenomenon. Would you let me coin the term "grammatics" to refer to grammar in this second sense? We need a grammatics to account for, and hence enable us to control, the languages that are now construing this information-based society (and the information-based universe of the physicists that I was referring to just now, since we model nature on ourselves). I hope our systemic linguistics can make some contribution to that.

Note

1. Halliday makes the distinction between language as "object" and language as "instrument". In the first perspective, the focus is on the nature of the linguistic phenomenon itself, that is language as object. The second perspective is concerned with using language to ask questions about something else as is the case in speech act theory or propositional analysis. See Halliday and Martin (1981: 15-16) for further discussion of this. The Indian tradition referred to here is exemplified, for example, by Panini's Sanskrit grammar of around the fifth century B.C.

List of references

Adams, A. 1985. "Language, Schooling, and Society, 1964-2004". *Language, Schooling, and Society* ed. by S.N. Tchudi. Upper Montclair, N.J.: Boynton-Cook.
Adams, K.L. & N.F. Conklin. 1973. "Towards a Natural Theory of Classification". *CLS* 9. 1-11.
Aers, D. 1980. *Chaucer, Langland and the Creative Imagination*. London: Routledge & Kegan Paul.
Aitchison, J. 1983-4. "The Mental Representation of Prefixes". *Osmania Papers in Linguistics* 9-10. 61-72.
Aitchison, J. 1987. *Words in the Mind: The mental lexicon*. Oxford: Blackwells.
Aitchison, J. & M. Straf. 1981. "Lexical Storage and Retrieval: A developing skill?" *Linguistics* 19. 751-795. Also in *Slips of the Tongue and Language Production* ed. by A. Cutler, 197-241. The Hague: Mouton, 1982.
Akmajian, A. & A. Lehrer. 1976. "NP-Like Quantifiers and the Problem of Determining the Head of an NP". *Linguistic Analysis* 2. 395-413.
Albrow, K.H. 1981. "The Kazan School and the London School". *Towards a History of Phonetics* ed. by R.E. Asher & E.A.J. Henderson, 9-18. Edinburgh: Edinburgh University Press.
Allan, K. 1977a. *Singularity and Plurality in English Noun Phrases: A study in grammar and pragmatics*. Unpublished Ph.D. Dissertation, University of Edinburgh.
Allan, K. 1977b. "Classifiers". *Language* 53. 281-311.
Allan, K. 1980. "Nouns and Countability". *Language* 56. 54-67.
Allen, H.B. 1964. *Readings in Applied Linguistics*, 2nd ed. New York: Appleton-Century-Crofts.
Allen, M.R. 1978. *Morphological Investigations*. Unpublished Ph.D. Dissertation, University of Connecticut.
Allen, W.S. 1953. "Relationship in Comparative Linguistics". *Transactions of the Philological Society* 52-108.
Allerton, D.J. 1982. *Valency and the English Verb*. London: Academic

Press.

Allerton, D.J. & A. Cruttenden. 1974. "English Sentence Adverbials: Their syntax and their intonation in British English". *Lingua* 27. 1-29.

American Institutes for Research. 1980. *Document Design: A review of the relevant research* ed. by D.B. Felkner. Washington: American Institutes for Research.

American Institutes for Research. 1981. *Guidelines for Document Designers*. Washington: American Institutes for Research.

Anderson, J.M. 1965. *A Grammar of the Verb Phrase in English*. Dissertation for the Diploma in General Linguistics, University of Edinburgh.

Anderson, J.M. 1971. *The Grammar of Case: Towards a localistic theory*. Cambridge: Cambridge University Press.

Anderson, J.M. 1976. *On Serialisation in English Syntax*. (= *Ludwigsburg Studies in Language and Linguistics* 1.)

Anderson, J.M. 1977. *On Case Grammar: Prolegomena to a theory of grammatical relations*. London: Croom Helm.

Anderson, J.M. 1980. "Towards Dependency Morphology: The structure of the Basque verb". *Studies in Dependency Phonology* ed. by J.M. Anderson & C.J. Ewen, 225-286. (*Ludwigsburg Studies in Linguistics* 4.)

Anderson, J.M. 1982. "Analysis and Levels of Linguistic Description". *La Lingua Inglese nell'Universita* ed. by E. Siciliani, R. Barone & G. Aston, 3-26. Bari: Adriatica Editrice.

Anderson, J.M. 1984. *Case Grammar and the Lexicon*. (= *Occasional Papers in Linguistics and Language Learning* 10.) Coleraine: University of Ulster.

Anderson, J.M. 1985. "Structural Analogy and Dependency Phonology". *Acta Linguistic Hafniensia*. Revised version in *Explorations in Dependency* ed. by J.M. Anderson & J.M. Durand, forthcoming. Dordrecht: Foris.

Anderson, J.M. 1986. "Suprasegmental Dependencies". *Dependency and Non-Linear Phonology* ed. by J.M. Durand, 55-133. London: Croom Helm.

Anderson, J.M. Forthcoming a. *Structural Analogy and Case Grammar*.

Anderson, J.M. Forthcoming b. *Against Arbitrary Syntax*.

Anderson, J.M. & J.M. Durand. 1986. "Dependency Phonology". *Dependency and Non-Linear Phonology* ed. by J.M. Durand, 1-54. London: Croom Helm.

Anderson, J.M. & J.M. Durand. eds. Forthcoming. *Explorations in Dependency Phonology*. Dordrecht: Foris.

Anderson, J.M. & C.J. Ewen. eds. 1980. *Studies in Dependency Phonology*. (*Ludwigsburg Studies in Linguistics* 4.)
Anderson, J.M. & C.J. Ewen. Forthcoming. *Principles of Dependency Phonology*. Cambridge: Cambridge University Press.
Anderson, J.M., C.J. Ewen & J. Staun. 1985. "Phonological Structure: Segmental, suprasegmental and extrasegmental". *Phonology Yearbook* 2. 203-224.
Anderson, J.M. & C. Jones. 1974. "Three Theses Concerning Phonological Representations". *Journal of Linguistics* 10. 1-26.
Anderson, J.M. & C. Jones. 1977. *Phonological Structure and the History of English*. Amsterdam: North-Holland.
Anderson, S. 1982. "Where's Morphology?" *Linguistic Inquiry* 13. 571-612.
Anderson, S. Forthcoming. *Inflection*. Milwaukee.
Andrejčin, L., N. Kostov & E. Nikolov. 1947. *Bǎlgarska Gramatika*. Sofia.
Antonovsky, A. 1979. *Health, Stress and Coping*. San Francisco: Jossey-Bass.
Apple, M.W. ed. 1982. *Cultural and Economic Reproduction in Education: Essays on class, ideology and the state*. London: Routledge & Kegan Paul.
Aranoff, M. 1976. *Word Formation in Generative Grammar*. Cambridge, Mass.: MIT Press.
Asenova, P. 1977. "La notion de l'interférence et l'union linguistique balkanique". *Linguistique Balkanique* 20. 23-32.
Atkins, M.W.H. 1951. *English Literary Criticism: Seventeenth and eighteenth centuries*. London: Methuen.
Atkinson, P. 1985. *Language, Structure and Reproduction*. London: Methuen.
Bailey, R.W. 1976. "Maxwell's Demon and the Muse". *Dispositio* 1. 293-301.
Bailey, R.W. 1983. "Literacy in English: An international perspective". *Literacy for Life: The demand for reading and writing* ed. by R.W. Bailey & R.M. Fosheim, 30-44. New York: The Modern Language Association.
Bain, B. ed. 1983. *The Sociogenesis of Language and Human Conduct*. New York: Plenum Press.
Baker, C.L. 1978. *Introduction to Generative Transformational Syntax*. Englewood Cliffs, N.J.: Prentice Hall.
Baker, R.J. & J.A. Nelder. 1978. *The GLIM System Release 3 Manual*.

Distributed by the Numerical Algorithms Group, 7 Banbury Road, Oxford OX2 6NN.

Bakhtin, M.M. 1970. *L'Oeuvre de Francois Rabelais et la culture populaire au Moyen Age et sous la Renaissance.* Paris: Editions Gallimard.

Bakhtin, M.M. 1973. *Problems of Dostoevsky's Poetics* transl. by R.W. Rotsel. Ann Arbor: Ardis.

Bakhtin, M.M. 1981a. *The Dialogic Imagination: Four essays* ed. by M. Holquist. Austin: University of Texas Press.

Bakhtin, M.M. 1981b. "Discourse in the Novel". *The Dialogic Imagination: Four essays* ed. and transl. by C. Emerson & M. Holquist, 259-422. Austin: University of Texas Press.

Bardell, E. 1978. "Does Style Influence Credibility and Esteem?" *The Communicator* 35. 4-7.

Barthes, R. 1975. *The Pleasure of the Text* transl. by R. Miller. New York: Hill & Wang.

Barthes, R. 1977. "Introduction to the Structural Analysis of Narratives". *Image-Music-Text*, essays selected & transl. by S. Heath. Fontana/Collins.

Baxter, L. & M. Cummings. 1983. "Computerized Analysis of Systemic Tree Diagrams in Old English". *The Ninth LACUS Forum 1982* ed. by J. Morreall, 540-548. Columbia, S.C.: Hornbeam Press.

Bazell, C.E., J.C. Catford & M.A.K. Halliday. 1966. *In Memory of J.R. Firth.* London: Longman.

Beaugrande de, R. & W. Dressler. 1981. *Introduction to Text Linguistics.* London: Longman.

Becker, A.L. 1967. *A Generative Description of the English Subject Tagmeme.* Ph.D. Dissertation, University of Michigan.

Beekman, J. & J. Callow. 1974. *Translating the Word of God.* Grand Rapids, MI: Zondervan Publishing House.

Beekman, J., J. Callow & M. Kopesec. 1981. *The Semantic Structure of Written Communication.* Dallas: Summer Institute of Linguistics.

Belsey, C. 1980. *Critical Practice.* London: Methuen.

Bennett, T. 1983. "Texts, Readers, Reading Formations". *Literature and History* 9. 2. 214-227.

Benson, J.D., B. Brainerd & W.S. Greaves. 1986. "A Quantificational Approach to Field of Discourse". *Actes du Colloque ALLC de Nice*, ed. by E. Brunet & M. Juillard. Geneva: Slatkine.

Benson, J.D. & W.S. Greaves. 1973. *The Language People Really Use.*

REFERENCES

Agincourt: Book Society of Canada.
Benveniste, E. 1971. *Problems in General Linguistics*. University of Miami Press.
Berger, P.L. & T. Luckman. 1966. *The Social Construction of Reality: A treatise in the sociology of knowledge*. New York: Doubleday.
Berman, H. 1982. "A Supplement to Robins's Yurok-English Lexicon". *International Journal of American Linguistics* 48. 197-222.
Bernstein, B. 1971. *Class, Codes and Control*. Vol. 1: *Theoretical Studies Towards a Sociology of Language* (2nd rev. edn. 1974). London: Routledge & Kegan Paul.
Bernstein, B. 1975. *Class, Codes and Control*. Vol. 3: *Towards a Theory of Educational Transmission* (2nd rev. edn.). London: Routledge & Kegan Paul.
Bernstein, B. 1982. "Codes, Modalities and the Process of Cultural Reproduction: A model". *Cultural and Economic Reproduction in Education: Essays on class ideology and the state* ed. by M.W. Apple, 304-355. London: Routledge & Kegan Paul.
Bernstein, B. 1986. "On Pedagogic Discourse". *Handbook for Theory and Research in Sociology of Education* ed. by J. Richardson. Connecticut: Greenwood Press.
Berry, M. 1975. *An Introduction to Systemic Linguistics: 1. Structures and Systems*. London: B.T. Batsford.
Berry, M. 1982. "Review of Halliday 1978". *Nottingham Linguistics Circular 11*. 64-94.
Bertin, J. 1983. *Semiology of Graphics: Diagrams, Networks, Maps*, transl. W.J. Berg. Madison: University of Wisconsin Press.
Bickerton, D. 1969. "Prolegomena to a Linguistic Theory of Metaphor". *Foundations of Language* 5. 34-52.
Birnbaum, H. 1970. *Problems of Typological and Genetic Linguistics Viewed in a Generative Framework*. The Hague: Mouton.
Bliss, J., M. Monk & J. Ogborn. 1983. *Qualitative Data Analysis for Educational Research: A guide to uses of systemic networks*. London: Croom Helm.
Bloom, B.S. ed. 1956. *Taxonomy of Educational Objectives. Handbook I: Cognitive Domain*. New York: McKay.
Bloom, H. 1979. "The Breaking of Form". *Deconstruction and Criticism* ed. by H. Bloom *et al.*, 1-37. New York: The Seabury Press.
Bloomfield, L. 1933. *Language*. New York: Holt.

Bohm, D. 1980. *Wholeness and the Implicit Order*. London: Routledge & Kegan Paul.

Boitani, P. 1983. "Chaucer's Labyrinth: Fourteenth-century literature and language". *The Chaucer Review* 17. 3. 198-220.

Bolinger, D.L. 1972. *Degree Words*. The Hague: Mouton.

Bolinger, D.L. 1979. "*Couple* an English Dual". *Studies in English Linguistics* ed. by S. Greenbaum, G. Leech & J. Svartvik. London & New York: Longmans.

Booij, G. 1985. "Coordination Reduction in Complex Words". *Advances in Nonlinear Phonology* ed. by H. van der Hulst & N. Smith, 143-160. Dordrecht: Foris.

Borges, J.L. 1970. *Labyrinths*. Harmondsworth: Penguin.

Botha, R. 1981. "A Base Rule Theory of Afrikaans Synthetic Compounding". *The Scope of Lexical Rules* ed. by M. Moortgat & T. Hoekstra, 1-77. Dordrecht: Foris.

Bouchard, D. 1982. *On the Content of Empty Categories*. Ph.D. Dissertation, MIT.

Bray de, R. 1951. *Guide to the Slavonic Languages*. London: Dent.

Brazil, D.C. 1983. "Kinds of English, Spoken, Written and Literary". *Readings on Language, Schools and Classroom* ed. by M.W. Stubbs & H. Hillier, 149-166. London: Methuen.

Brazil, D.C. 1985. *The Communicative Value of Intonation in English*. Birmingham: English Language Research.

Brekle, H. 1975. "Zur Stellung der Wortbildung in der Grammatik". *Flexion und Wortbildung* ed. by H. Rix, 26-39. Wiesbaden: Reichert.

Bridge, L.W. 1967. *Parliamentary Procedure*. New York: Funk & Wagnalls.

Briggs, E. 1961. *Mitla Zapotec Grammar*. Mexico, D.F.: Instituto Lingüístico de Verano.

Browman, C. 1978. "Tip of the Tongue and Slip of the Ear: Implications for language processing". *UCLA Working Papers in Phonetics* 42.

Brown, G. & G. Yule. 1983. *Discourse Analysis*. Cambridge: Cambridge University Press.

Brown, P. & S. Levinson. 1978. "Universals in Language Usage: Politeness phenomena". *Questions and Politeness: Strategies in Social Interaction* ed. by E. Goody. Cambridge: Cambridge University Press.

Brown, R. & M. Ford 1961. "Address in American English". *Journal of Abnormal and Social Psychology* 62. 375-385.

Brown, R. & A. Gilman. 1960. "The Pronouns of Power and Solidarity". *Style in Language* ed. by T.A. Sebeok, 253-276. Cambridge, Mass: MIT Press.

Brown, R. & D. McNeill. 1966. "The 'Tip of the Tongue' Phenomenon". *Journal of Verbal Learning and Verbal Behavior* 5, 325-337.

Browne, W. 1974. "On the Typology of Anaphoric Peninsulas". *Linguistic Inquiry* 5. 619-620.

Brumfit, C.J. & R.A. Carter. eds. 1986. *Literature and Language Teaching*. Oxford: Oxford University Press.

Bühler, K. 1934. *Sprachtheorie*. Jena: Fischer.

Burchfield, R.W. ed. 1976. *A Supplement to the Oxford English Dictionary*, Vols. II-III.

Butler, C.S. 1985. *Systemic Linguistics: Theory and applications*. London: Batsford Academic and Educational Publishers.

Butler, I.M. 1976. "Verb Classification in Yatzachi Zapotec". *SIL — Mexico Workpapers* 2. 74-84.

Butler, I.M. 1980. *Gramática Zapoteca (Zapoteco de Yatzachi el Bajo)*. Mexico, D.F.: Instituto Lingüístico de Verano.

Butterworth, B. 1983. "Lexical Representation". *Language Production*, Vol. 2 ed. by B. Butterworth, 257-294. London: Academic Press.

Bybee, J.L. & D.I. Slobin. 1982. "Rules and Schemas in the Development and Use of the English Past". *Language* 58. 265-289.

Calkins, C.C. ed. 1979. *Illustrated Guide to Gardening in Canada*. Montreal: Reader's Digest Association.

Candlin, C.N. 1983. "Beyond Description to Explanation in Cross-Cultural Discourse". Paper presented at the *Conference on English as an International Language: Discourse patterns across cultures*. Honolulu, Hawaii: East-West Center; reprinted in *Discourse Across Cultures* ed. by L. Smith. London: Prentice-Hall, 1987.

Candlin, C.N. & J. Lucas. 1986. "Modes of Advising in Family Planning". *Discourse in Public Life* ed. by T. Ensink *et al*. Dordrecht: Foris.

Carlson, A.M. 1978. "A Diachronic Treatment of English Quantifiers". *Lingua* 46. 295-328.

Carter, R.A. ed. 1982a. *Language and Literature: An introductory reader in stylistics*. London: Allen & Unwin.

Carter, R.A. ed. 1982b. *Linguistics and the Teacher*. London: Routledge & Kegan Paul.

Carter, R.A. 1985. "A Question of Interpretation". *Linguistic Contribu-*

tions to Literature ed. by Theo D'haen, 7-25. Amsterdam: Rodopi.
Carter, R.A. & W. Nash. 1983. "Language and Literariness". *Prose Studies* 6. 2. 123-141.
"Casa Colina Hospital Research Memorandum No. 2". 1985 (unpublished).
Chafe, W. 1984. "How People Use Adverbial Clauses". *Proceedings of the Tenth Annual Meeting of the Berkeley Linguistics Society*. Berkeley: Berkeley Linguistics Society.
Chen, F.R. *et al.* 1983. "Speaking Clearly: Acoustic characteristics and intelligibility of stop consonants". *Speech Communication Group Working Papers*, MIT RLE Vol. 2. 1-8.
Cheshire, J. 1982. *Variation in an English Dialect: A sociolinguistic study*. Cambridge: Cambridge University Press.
Chilton, P. 1984. "Orwell, Language and Linguistics". *Language and Communication* 4. 2. 129-146.
Chilton, P. ed. 1985. *Language and the Nuclear Arms Debate: Nukespeak Today*. London & Dover, N.H.: Frances Pinter.
Chomsky, N. 1957. *Syntactic Structures*. The Hague: Mouton.
Chomsky, N. 1965. *Aspects of the Theory of Syntax*. Cambridge, Mass.: MIT Press.
Chomsky, N. 1966. *Cartesian Linguistics: A chapter in the History of Rationalist Thought*. New York: Harper & Row.
Chomsky, N. 1981. *Lectures on Government and Binding: The Pisa Lectures*. Dordrecht: Foris.
Chomsky, N. & M. Halle. 1968. *The Sound Pattern of English*. New York: Harper & Row.
Chomsky, N. & H. Laznik. 1977. "Filters and Control". *Linguistic Inquiry* 8. 425-504.
Clanchy, M.T. 1983. "Looking Back from the Invention of Printing". *Literacy in Historical Perspective* ed. by D.P. Resnick, 7-22. Washington, D.C.: Library of Congress.
Clark, E.V. & B.F. Hecht. 1982. "Learning to Coin Agent and Instrument Nouns". *Cognition* 12. 1-24.
Clocksin, W.F. & C.S. Mellish. 1984. *Programming in PROLOG*, 2nd edn. New York: Springer Verlag.
COBUILD. A project in lexical computing at the University of Birmingham, financed by Collins, Publishers.
Cohen, L.J. & M. Avishai. 1972. "The Role of Inductive Reasoning in the Interpretation of Metaphor". *Semantics of Natural Language* ed. by D.

Davidson & G. Harman. Dordrecht/Holland: D. Reidel.
Cohen, M. 1977. *Sensible Words: Linguistic practice in England 1640-1785*. Baltimore: Johns Hopkins University Press.
Colby, B.N. 1973. "A Partial Grammar of Eskimo Folktales". *American Anthropologist* 75. 3. 645-662.
Colby, B.N. 1981. "A Cultural Theory". *Social Science Research Reports* 9.
Colby, B.N. 1986. "Toward a Systemic Anthropology". *Functional Perspectives on Discourse: Selected Papers from the 12th International Systemic Workshop* ed. by. J.D. Benson & W.S. Greaves. Norwood, N.J.: Ablex Publishing Co.
Colby, B.N. Manuscript. *Anthropological Well-Being: A Theoretical Program*.
Collins English Dictionary. 1979. ed. by P.W. Hanks. London: Collins.
Comrie, B. 1976. *Aspect*. Cambridge: Cambridge University Press.
The Concise Oxford Dictionary. 7th. edn. 1982. London.
Connerton, P. ed. 1976. *Critical Sociology*. Harmondsworth: Penguin.
Coombs, P.H. 1985. *The World Crisis in Education: The view from the eighties*. New York: Oxford University Press.
Corum, C. 1973. "Anaphoric Peninsulas". *PCLS* 9. 89-97.
Couture, B. 1986. "Effective Ideation in Written Text: A functional approach to clarity and exigence". *Functional Approaches to Writing: Research perspectives* ed. by B. Couture, 69-92. London: Frances Pinter.
Crabbe, G. 1834. *The Poetical Works of the Rev. George Crabbe ... by his Son*, 8 vols. London: John Murray.
Crawford, J.C. 1963. *Totonpec Mixe Phonotagmemics*. Santa Ana: Summer Institute of Linguistics.
Cressy, D. 1980. *Literacy and the Social Order*. Cambridge: Cambridge University Press.
Crothers, E. 1979. *Paragraph Structure Inference*. Norwood, N.J.: Ablex.
Cruse, D.A. 1986. *Lexical Semantics*. Cambridge: Cambridge University Press.
Crystal, D. 1969. *Prosodic Systems and Intonation in English*. Cambridge: Cambridge University Press.
Csikszentmihalyi, M. 1975. *Beyond Boredom and Anxiety*. San Francisco: Jossey-Bass.
Culicover, P. 1982. *Syntax*. New York: Academic Press.
Culler, J. 1976. *Saussure*. Fontana Modern Masters Series. Glasgow: Collins.

Cummings, M. Forthcoming. "Simulating Linguistic Networks with List Processing". *Mélange à la mémoire de John Brückmann* ed. by A. Bardot. Toronto: Éditions du GREF.

Cummings, M. & A. Regina. 1985. "A PROLOG Parser-Generator for Systemic Analysis of Old English Nominal Groups". *Systemic Perspectives on Discourse: Selected applied papers from the 9th International Systemic Workshop* ed. by J.D. Benson & W.S. Greaves, 88-101. Norwood, N.J.: Ablex.

Curtis, H. 1968. *Biology*. New York: Worth Publishers.

Cutler, A. 1980. "Productivity in Word Formation". *Papers from the Sixteenth Regional Meeting, Chicago Linguistic Society*, 45-51.

Cutler, A., J.A. Hawkins & G. Gilligan. 1985. "The Suffixing Preference: A processing explanation". *Linguistics* 23. 689-706.

Denny, J.P. 1976. "What are Noun Classifiers Good for?" *CLS* 12. 122-132.

Denny, J.P. 1979. "The 'Extendedness' Variable in Classifier Semantics: Universal features and cultural variation". *Ethnolinguistics: Boas, Sapir, and Whorf Revisited* ed. by M. Mathiot, 99-119. The Hague: Mouton.

Derrida, J. 1974. *Of Grammatology*. Baltimore, Md.: Johns Hopkins University Press.

Dewey, J. 1916. *Democracy and Education*. New York: Macmillan.

Dixon, R.M.W. 1972. *The Dyirbal Language of North Queensland*. Cambridge: Cambridge University Press.

Downes, W. 1978. "Language, Belief and Verbal Action in an Historical Process". *UEA Papers in Linguistics* 8. 1-43.

Dressler, W.U. 1981. "General Principles of Poetic Licence in Word Formation". *Logos Semantikos, Fs. Coseriu II* ed. by H. Weydt, 423-431. Berlin: de Gruyter.

Dressler, W.U. 1985a. *Morphonology*. Ann Arbor: Karoma Press.

Dressler, W.U. 1985b. "On the Predictiveness of Natural Morphology". *JL* 21. 321-337.

Dressler, W.U. 1985c. "Typological Aspects of Natural Morphology". *WLG* 35-36. 3-26.

Dressler, W.U. Forthcoming. *Preferences vs. Strict Universals in Morphology: Word based rules*. Milwaukee.

Dressler, W.U., W. Mayerhaler, O. Panagl & W.U. Wurzel. Forthcoming. *Leitmotifs in Natural Morphology*. Amsterdam: Benjamins.

Dressler, W.U. & L. Merlini. Forthcoming. "Interradical Interfixes". *Festschrift, R. Filipović*.

Durand, J.M. ed. 1986. *Dependency and Non-Linear Phonology*. London: Croom Helm.
Eagleton, T. 1976. *Criticism and Ideology*. London: New Left Books.
Eagleton, T. 1983. *Literary Theory: An introduction*. Minneapolis: The University of Minnesota.
Easthope, A. 1982. "Literature, History and the Materiality of the Text". *Literature and History* 9. 1. 28-37.
Eco, U. 1976. *A Theory of Semiotics*. Bloomington: Indiana University Press.
Eco, U. 1981. *The Role of the Reader: Explorations in the semiotics of texts*. London: Hutchinson.
Eco, U. 1983. *The Name of the Rose*. New York & London: Harcourt, Brace, Jovanovich.
Eco, U. 1984. *Semiotics and the Philosophy of Language*. Bloomington: Indiana University Press.
Ehrenberg, A.S.C. 1978. *Data Reduction: Analyzing and interpreting statistical data*. Chichester, England: Wiley.
Eiler, M.A. 1980. *Meaning and Choice in Writing about Literature: A study of cohesion in the expository texts of ninth graders*. Dissertation, Illinois Institute of Technology. Ann Arbor: UMI. 1980. 80-03647.
Eiler, M.A. 1983. "Meaning and Choice in Writing about Literature". *Advances in Discourse Processes 10* ed. by R. Freedle & J. Fine, 169-223. Norwood, N.J.: Ablex.
Eiler, M.A. 1986. "Thematic Distribution as a Heuristic for Written Discourse Function". *Functional Approaches to Writing: Research perspectives* ed. by B. Couture, 49-68. London: Pinter.
Ellis, J. 1952. "Affinité grammaticale". *Proceedings of the Seventh International Congress of Linguists*, 125. London.
Ellis, J. 1966a. *Towards a General Comparative Linguistics*. The Hague: Mouton.
Ellis, J. 1966b. "Review of Lyons, J. (1963) *Structural Semantics*". *Linguistics* 24. 85-115.
Ellis, J. 1966c. "On Contextual Meaning". *In Memory of J.R. Firth* ed. by C.E. Bazell *et al.*, 79-95. London: Longman.
Ellis, J. 1967. "Some Remarks on the Place of Balkan Linguistics in General Linguistic Theory". *Linguistique Balkanique* 12. 37-44.
Ellis, J. 1971a. "The Definite Article in Translation between English and Twi". *Actes du huitième Congrès de la Société Linguistique de l'Afrique*

Occidentale ed. by M. Houis, 367-380. Abidjan: Abidjan University Press.

Ellis, J. 1971b. "Some Dimensions of being in John, Chapter 1 (a 'Transfer' Presentation of Descriptive Comparison)". *Journal of African Languages* 10, pt. 3. 18-33.

Ellis, J. 1978. "Identification and Grammatical Structure in Akan and Welsh". *Approaches to Language* ed. by S. Wurm & W. McCormack, 297-305. The Hague: Mouton.

Ellis, J. 1979. "Describing Balkan Languages". Paper read to 1979 Systemic Workshop, Cardiff.

Ellis, J. 1984. "Some Speculations on Language Contact in a Wider Setting". *The Semiotics of Culture and Language* ed. by R.P. Fawcett *et al.*, Vol. 1, 81-104. London: Pinter.

Enkvist, N.E. 1981. "Experiential Iconicism in Text Strategy". *Text* 1. 1. 97-111.

Enkvist, N.E. 1985. "A Parametric View of Word Order". *Text Connexity, Text Coherence. Aspects, Methods, Results* ed. by Emel Sözer, 320-336 (= *Papiere zur Textlinguistik*, Band 49). Hamburg: Helmut Buske Verlag.

Enkvist, N.E. Forthcoming a. "Textualization as Conflict and Conspiracy". *Linking in Text* (= *Linguistic Calculation*, Vol. 2), F. Kiefer (ed.). Dordrecht: D. Reidel Publishing Company.

Enkvist, N.E. Forthcoming b. "Styles as Parameters in Text Strategy". *Stylistics as Social Practice*, W. van Peer (ed.). London: Routledge & Kegan Paul.

Errington, S. Forthcoming. *Transcending Politics in a Southeast Asian Realm*. Princeton: Princeton University Press.

Fairclough, N.L. 1985. "Critical and Descriptive Goals in Discourse Analysis". *Journal of Pragmatics* 9. 739-763.

Fairclough, N.L. 1986. "Critical and Descriptive Goals in Discourse Analysis". *Journal of Pragmatics* 9. 1.

Fawcett, R.P. 1980. *Cognitive Linguistics and Social Interaction: Towards an Integrated Model of a Systemic Functional Grammar and the Other Components of a Communicating Mind*. Heidelberg: Groos & Exeter University.

Fawcett, R.P. Forthcoming. "What Makes a 'Good' System Network Good?" *Systemic Functional Approaches to Discourse: Selected Papers from the 12th International Systemic Workshop* ed. by J.D. Benson & W.S. Greaves. Norwood, N.J.: Ablex.

Fay, D. & A. Cutler. 1977. "Malapropisms and the Structure of the Mental Lexicon". *Linguistic Inquiry* 8. 505-520.

Febvre, L. & H.-J. Martin. 1984. *The Coming of the Book. The Impact of Printing 1450-1800*, transl. by D. Gerard, ed. by G. Nowell-Smith & D. Wootton. Verso Editions.

Fernandez, J.W. 1982. *Bwiti; An Ethnography of the Religious Imagination in Africa*. Princeton: Princeton University Press.

Fiedler, W. 1966. "Zu einigen Problemen des Admirativs in den Balkansprachen". *Actes Balkaniques 1966*. 367-369.

Fienberg, S.E. 1978. *The Analysis of Cross-Classified Categorical Data*. Cambridge, Mass.: MIT Press.

Fillmore, C.J. 1968. "The Case for Case". *Universals in Linguistic Theory* ed. by E. Bach & R. Harms, 1-88. New York: Holt, Rinehart & Winston.

Fillmore, L.W. Forthcoming. "The Role and Function of Formulaic Speech in Conversation". *What's Going on Here? Complementary Studies of Professional Talk* ed. by A.D. Grimshaw *et al*. Norwood, N.J.: Ablex.

Firth, J.R. 1935. "The Technique of Semantics". *Transactions of the Philological Society*. (Reprinted in Firth. 1957a. 7-33.)

Firth, J.R. 1950. "Personality and Language in Society". *The Sociological Review* 43. 2. (Reprinted in Firth. 1957. 177-189.)

Firth, J.R. 1951. "Modes of Meaning". *The English Association: Essays and studies* ed. by John Murray. (Reprinted in Firth. 1957.)

Firth, J.R. 1957a. *Papers in Linguistics 1934-1951*. Oxford: Oxford University Press.

Firth, J.R. 1957b. "A Synopsis of Linguistic Theory: 1930-1955". *Selected Papers of J.R. Firth: 1952-59*, ed. by F.R. Palmer, 168-205. Bloomington: Indiana University Press.

Fish, S.E. 1973. "How Ordinary is Ordinary Language?" *New Literary History* 5. 41-54.

Fish, S.E. 1980. *Is There a Text in this Class?* Cambridge, Mass.: Harvard University Press.

Fish, S.E. 1981. "What is Stylistics and why are they Saying such Bad Things about it?" *Essays in Modern Stylistics* ed. by D.C. Freeman, 53-78. New York: Methuen.

Ford, C. & S.A. Thompson. 1985. "Conditionals in Discourse: A text-based study from English". *On Conditionals* ed. by Traugott, ter Meulen & Reilly. Cambridge: Cambridge University Press.

Foucault, M. 1972. *The Archaeology of Knowledge*, transl. by A.M. Sheridan Smith. London: Tavistock.

Foucault, M. 1973. *The Order of Things: An archaeology of the human sciences*. New York: Random House.

Foucault, M. 1977. "History of Systems of Thought". Course Description of Foucault's first year at the Collège de France.

Fowler, R. 1981. *Literature as Social Discourse: The Practice of Linguistic Criticism*. London: Batsford.

Fowler, R. 1984. "Studying Literature as Language". *Dutch Quarterly Review of Anglo-American Letters* 14. 171-184.

Fowler, R. Forthcoming. "Critical Linguistics". *The Linguistic Encyclopoedia* ed. by K. Malmkjaer. London: Routledge & Kegan Paul.

Fowler, R., R. Hodge, G. Kress & T. Trew. 1979. *Language and Control*. London: Routledge & Kegan Paul.

Fowler, R. & T. Marshall. 1985. "The War Against Peacemongering: Language and Ideology". *Language and the Nuclear Arms Debate: Nukespeak Today* ed. by P. Chilton, 3-22. London & Dover, N.H.: Frances Pinter.

Frankena, W.K. 1965. *Three Historical Philosophies of Education*. Chicago: Scott, Foresman.

Frei, H. 1929a. *Linguistic Analysis*. Oxford: Blackwell.

Frei, H. 1929b. *La Grammaire des Fautes*. Paris: Geuthner.

Freire, P. 1980. "Letters for a Young Nation". *The UNESCO Courier* June.

Friedman, V. 1979. "Tense and Status in Albanian, Balkan Slavic and Turkish: The Category of Admirativity vs. Admirative Usage". *Fourth International Congress of Balkanistics*, Ankara.

Friedrich, P. 1974. *On Aspect Theory and Homeric Aspect* (IJAL 40, Memoir 28). Chicago: University of Chicago Press.

Fries, C. 1952. *The Structure of English*. New York: Harcourt, Brace, & World.

Gáldi, L. 1966. "Le Système des Articles Balkaniques". *Actes Balkaniques* 1966. 593-598.

Geertz, C. 1983. *Local Knowledge; Further essays in interpretive anthropology*. New York: Basic Books.

Genette, G. 1972. *Figures III*. Paris: Éditions du Seuil.
Giddens, A. 1977. *Studies in Social and Political Theory*. London: Hutchinson.
Giroux, H.A. 1983. "Theories of Reproduction and Resistance in the New Sociology of Education: A critical analysis". *Harvard Educational Review* 53. 3. 257-293.
Givón, T. 1982. "Tense-Aspect-Modality: The Crole prototype and beyond". *Tense-Aspect* ed. by P.J. Hopper, 115-163. Amsterdam: John Benjamins.
Gleason, H.A. 1965. *Linguistics and English Grammar*. New York: Holt, Rinehart & Winston.
Goffman, E. 1967. *Interaction Ritual: Essays on face-to-face behavior*. Garden City: Doubleday (Anchor).
Goffman, E. 1974. *Frame Analysis: An essay on the organization of experience*. New York: Harper (Colophon).
Goffman, E. 1981. *Forms of Talk*. Philadelphia: University of Pennsylvania Press.
Goodwin, W.W. 1912. *Syntax of the Moods and Tenses of the Greek Verb*. London: Macmillan.
Goody, J. 1968. "Introduction" to *Literacy in Traditional Societies*. Cambridge: Cambridge University Press.
Goody, J. 1986. *The Logic of Writing and the Organisation of Society. Studies in Literacy, Family, Culture and the State*. Cambridge: Cambridge University Press.
Goody, J. & I. Watt. 1968. "The Consequences of Literacy". *Literacy in Traditional Societies* ed. by J. Goody. Cambridge: Cambridge University Press.
Gordon-Salant, S. 1986. "Recognition of Natural and Time/Intensity Altered CVs by Young and Elderly Subjects with Normal Hearing". *Journal of the Acoustical Society America* 80. 1599-1607.
Gove, P.B. 1964. "Lexicography and the Teacher of English". *College English* XXV. 344-357.
Gove, P.B. ed. 1966. *Webster's Third International Dictionary of the English Language Unabridged*. Springfield.
Granger, G.-G. 1983. *Formal Thought and the Sciences of Man*. (*Boston Studies in the Philosophy of Science* 75.) Boston: D. Reidel.
Greenbaum, S. 1969. *Studies in English Adverbial Usage*. London: Longman.

Greenberg, J. 1972. "Numeral Classifiers and Substantival Number: Problems in the genesis of a linguistic type". *Working Papers in Language Universals* 9. 1-39.
Gregory, M. 1967. "Aspects of Varieties Differentiation". *Journal of Linguistics* 3. 177-198.
Greimas, A.J. 1966. *Sémantique Structurale*. Paris: Larousse.
Greimas, A.J. 1969. "Des modèles théoriques en socio-linguistique". International Days of Socio-Linguistics Conference, Instituto Luigi Sturzo, Rome. Reprinted in A.J. Greimas. *Sémiotique et Sciences Sociales* 61-76. Paris: du Seuil.
Greimas, A.J. 1983. *Du Sens II. Essais sémiotiques*. Paris: du Seuil.
Grice, H.P. 1967. "Logic and Conversation" (mimeo); also 1975. reprinted in *Syntax and Semantics 3: Speech Acts* ed. by P. Cole & J.L. Morgan, 41-58. New York: Academic Press.
Grimes, J.E. 1975. *The Thread of Discourse*. The Hague: Mouton.
Grimshaw, A.D. 1980. "Mishearings, Misunderstandings and Other Non-successes in Talk: A plea for redress of speaker-oriented bias". *Sociological Inquiry* 40. 31-74.
Grimshaw, A.D. 1982. "Comprehensive Discourse Analysis: An instance of professional peer interaction". *Language in Society* 11. 15-47.
Grimshaw, A.D. 1987. "Disambiguating Discourse: Members' skill and analysts' problem". *Social Psychology Quarterly* 50.
Grimshaw, A.D. Forthcoming a. *Collegial Discourse: Professional conversation among peers*. Norwood, N.J.: Ablex.
Grimshaw, A.D. Forthcoming b. *What's Going on Here? Complementary studies of professional talk*. Norwood, N.J.: Ablex.
Grize, F. 1981. *BARBARA: Analyse de Données Informelles à l'aide de Reseaux Systémiques*. Ph.D. Dissertation, University of Neuchatel.
Gruber, J. 1965. *Studies in Lexical Relations*. Ph.D. Dissertation, MIT.
Guethner, F. 1975. "On the Semantics of Metaphor". *Poetics* 4. 14/15. 199-220.
Guiraud, P. 1966. "Le Système relatif en Français populaire". *Langages* 3. 40-48.
Gumperz, J. 1982. *Language and Social Identity*. Cambridge: Cambridge University Press.
Gunther, R.T. 1930. *Early Science in Oxford*. Vol. VI: *The Life and Work of Robert Hooke* (Part 1). Oxford: Oxford University Press.
Habermas, J. 1972. "Towards a Theory of Communicative Competence".

Recent Sociology II ed. by F. Dreitzel. London: Macmillan.
Habermas, J. 1984. *The Theory of Communicative Action*. Vol. 1: *Reason and the Rationalization of Society* transl. by T. McCarthy. Boston: Beacon Press.
Hagtvet, B. 1984. "Skjonnheten som grusomhytens folgesvenn (Beauty and the Beast)". *Nytt Norsk Tideskuft* 2. (English translation in MS.)
Hale, Ho'ola Hou. 1983. Kaliki-Palama Health Clinic Annual Report.
Hall, E.T. 1977. *Beyond Culture*. New York: Anchor Books.
Halliday, M.A.K. 1957. "Some Aspects of Systematic Description and Comparison in Grammatical Analysis". *Studies in Linguistic Analysis* (Special Volume of the Philological Society). Oxford: Blackwell, 54-67.
Halliday, M.A.K. 1961. "Categories of the Theory of Grammar". *Word* 17. 3. 241-292.
Halliday, M.A.K. 1962. "Linguistics and Machine Translation". Reprinted in *Patterns of Language. Papers in General, Descriptive and Applied Linguistics* ed. by Angus McIntosh & M.A.K. Halliday, 134-150. London: Longman.
Halliday, M.A.K. 1964. "Syntax and the Consumer". *Monograph Series in Languages and Linguistics* 17, ed by C.I.J.M. Stuart, 11-24. Washington, D.C.: Georgetown University Press.
Halliday, M.A.K. 1966a. "The Concept of Rank: A reply". *Journal of Linguistics* 2. 1. 110-118.
Halliday, M.A.K. 1966b. "Lexis as a Linguistic Level". *In Memory of J.R. Firth* ed. by C.E. Bazell, J.C. Catford, M.A.K. Halliday & R.H. Robins. London: Longman.
Halliday, M.A.K. 1966c. "Some Notes on 'Deep' Grammar". *Journal of Linguistics* 2. 1. 57-67.
Halliday, M.A.K. 1966d. "Typology and the Exotic". *Patterns of Language* ed. by A. McIntosh & M.A.K. Halliday, 165-182. London: Longman.
Halliday, M.A.K. 1967a. *Grammar, Society and the Noun*. London: H.K. Lewis (for University College London).
Halliday, M.A.K. 1967b. *Intonation and Grammar in British English*. The Hague: Mouton.
Halliday, M.A.K. 1967/68. "Notes on Transitivity and Theme in English" (Parts 1-3). *Journal of Linguistics* 3.1.1967. 37-81, 3.2.1967. 199-244. 4.2.1968. 179-215.
Halliday, M.A.K. 1969. "Relevant Models of Language". *The State of Language*. (*Educational Review* 22.1). University of Birmingham, 26-37.

Halliday, M.A.K. 1970. "Language Structure and Language Function". *New Horizons in Linguistics* ed. by J. Lyons, 140-165. New York: Penguin.
Halliday, M.A.K. 1971. "Language in a Social Perspective". *The Context of Language.* (*Educational Review* 23.3). University of Birmingham, 165-188.
Halliday, M.A.K. 1971. "Linguistic Function and Literary Style: An inquiry into the language of William Golding's "*The Inheritors*". *Literary Style: A Symposium* ed. by S. Chatman. London: Oxford University Press.
Halliday, M.A.K. 1972. "Options and Functions in the English Clause". *Syntactic Theory I* ed. by F.W. Householder, 248-257. Harmondsworth: Penguin.
Halliday, M.A.K. 1973a. "Towards a Sociological Semantics". *Explorations in the Functions of Language* ed. by M.A.K. Halliday, 72-101. London: Edward Arnold.
Halliday, M.A.K. 1973b. Foreword to *Class, Codes and Control.* Vol. 2: *Applied Studies Towards a Sociology of Language* ed. by Basil Bernstein. London: Routledge & Kegan Paul.
Halliday, M.A.K. 1974a. *Language and Social Man.* London: Longman (Schools Council Programme in Linguistics and English Teaching: Papers, Series II, Vol. 3.)
Halliday, M.A.K. 1974b. "Language as Social Semiotic: Towards a general sociolinguistic theory". *The First LACUS Forum* ed. by A. Makkai & V.B. Makkai, 17-46. Columbia, S.C.: Hornbeam Press.
Halliday, M.A.K. 1974c. "The Place of 'Functional Sentence Perspective' in the System of Linguistic Description". *Papers on Functional Sentence Perspective* ed. by F. Daneš, 42-53. The Hague: Mouton.
Halliday, M.A.K. 1975. *Learning How to Mean. Explorations in the development of language.* London: Edward Arnold.
Halliday, M.A.K. 1976. "The English Verbal Group". *Halliday: System and function in language* (Selected papers) ed. by G. Kress, 136-158. London: Oxford University Press.
Halliday, M.A.K. 1977a. "The Context of Linguistics". *Aims and Perspectives in Linguistics*, Occasional Papers 1 (Applied Linguistics Association of Australia), 19-31.
Halliday, M.A.K. 1977b. "Text as Semantic Choice in Social Contexts". *Grammars and Descriptions* ed. by J.S. Petöfi & T. van Dijk. Berlin: De

Gruyter.

Halliday, M.A.K. 1978a. "An Interpretation of the Functional Relationship between Language and Social Structure". *Language as Social Semiotic* ed. by M.A.K. Halliday, 183-192. London: Edward Arnold.

Halliday, M.A.K. 1978b. *Language as Social Semiotic. The social interpretation of language and meaning.* London: Edward Arnold.

Halliday, M.A.K. 1978c. "Meaning and the Construction of Reality in Early Childhood". *Modes of Perceiving and Processing Information* ed. by H.L. Pick & E. Saltzman, 67-96. Hillsdale, N.J.: Lawrence Erlbaum & Associates.

Halliday, M.A.K. 1979. "Systemic Theory Seminar". Department of Linguistics, University of Sydney.

Halliday, M.A.K. 1981a. "Structure". *Readings in Systemic Linguistics* ed. by M.A.K. Halliday & J.R. Martin, 122-131. London: Batsford.

Halliday, M.A.K. 1981b. "Text Semantics and Clause Grammar: Some patterns of realisation". *The Seventh LACUS Forum* ed. by James E. Copeland & Philip W. Davis, 31-59. Columbia, S.C.: Hornbeam Press.

Halliday, M.A.K. 1983a. "On the Ineffability of Grammatical Categories" *The Tenth LACUS Forum* ed. by A. Manning, P. Martin & K. McCulla, 3-17. Columbia, S.C.: Hornbeam Press.

Halliday, 1983b. Introduction to *The Language of Literature* ed. by M. Cummings & R. Simmons, vii-xvii. Oxford: Pergamon.

Halliday, M.A.K. 1984. "Systemic Background". *Systemic Perspectives on Discourse.* Vol. 1: *Selected Theoretical Papers from the Ninth International Systemic Workship* ed. by J.D. Benson & W.S. Greaves, 1-15. Norwood, N.J.: Ablex.

Halliday, M.A.K. 1985a. *An Introduction to Functional Grammar.* London: Edward Arnold.

Halliday, M.A.K. 1985b. "The Social-Semiotic of Grammar". Course presented at the International Summer Institute for Semiotic and Structural Studies, Indiana University, Bloomington, May-June 1985. To appear as *Grammar and Daily Life.* Bloomington: Indiana University Press.

Halliday, M.A.K. 1985c. *Spoken and Written Language.* Geelong, Vic.: Deakin University Press.

Halliday, M.A.K. 1986. "Patterns in Words". *The Listener*, January 13. 53-55.

Halliday, M.A.K. Forthcoming a. "Language and the Order of Nature". *The Linguistics of Writing* ed. by D. Attridge, A. Durant, N. Fabb & C.

MacCabe. Manchester: Manchester University Press.

Halliday, M.A.K. Forthcoming b. "Spoken and Written Modes of Meaning". *Comprehending Oral and Written Language* ed. by R. Horowitz & J. Samuels. New York: Academic Press.

Halliday, M.A.K. & R. Hasan. 1976. *Cohesion in English*. London: Longman.

Halliday, M.A.K. & R. Hasan. 1985. *Language, Context, and Text: Aspects of language in a social-semiotic perspective*. Geelong, Vic.: Deakin University Press.

Halliday, M.A.K. & J.R. Martin. eds. 1981. *Readings in Systemic Linguistics*. London: Batsford.

Halliday, M.A.K., A. McIntosh & P. Strevens. 1964. *The Linguistic Sciences and Language Teaching*. London: Longman.

Harare, J.V. ed. 1979. *Textual Strategies: Perspectives in post-structuralist criticism*. Ithaca: Cornell University Press.

Hardaker, D. 1982. *Language in a Regulative Context*. Honours Thesis, Department of Linguistics, University of Sydney.

Hartman, G. 1985. "Critical Practice and Literary Theory. An interview by V. Mishra". *Southern Review: Literary and Interdisciplinary Essays* 18. 2. 188-199.

Hasan, R. 1971. "Rime and Reason in Literature". *Literary Style: A Symposium* ed. by S. Chatman, 299-329. London: Oxford University Press.

Hasan, R. 1973. "Code, Register, and Social Dialect". *Class, Codes and Control: Applied Studies Towards a Sociology of Language* Vol. 2, ed. by B. Bernstein, 253-292. London: Routledge.

Hasan, R. 1975. "The Place of Stylistics in the Study of Verbal Art". *Style and Text* ed. by H. Ringbom, 49-61. Stockholm: Abo.

Hasan, R. 1980. "The Identity of a Text". *Text and Context: Aspects of language in a social-semiotic perspective* ed. by M.A.K. Halliday & R. Hasan, 75-91. Tokyo: Sophia Linguistica.

Hasan, R. 1984a. "The Nursery Tale as a Genre". In manuscript.

Hasan, R. 1984b. "The Structure of the Nursery Tale: An essay in text typology". *Linguistica Textuale* ed. by Lorenzo Coveri, 95-114. Rome: Bulzoni.

Hasan, R. 1984c. "Ways of Saying: Ways of Meaning". *The Semiotics of Culture and Language*, Vol. I, ed. by R.P. Fawcett, M.A.K. Halliday, S.M. Lamb & A. Makkai. London: Frances Pinter.

Haselkorn, F. 1968. *Family Planning: The role of social work*. Adelphi Uni-

versity School of Social Work.
Haugen, E. 1954. "Problems of Bilingual Description". *Report of the Fifth Annual Round Table Meeting on Linguistics and Language Teaching* ed. by H.J. Mueller, 9-19. Washington, D.C.: Georgetown University Press.
Haugen, E. 1979. "The Stigmata of Bilingualism". *Sociolinguistic Aspects of Language Learning and Teaching* ed. by J.B. Pride, 72-85. London: Oxford University Press.
Henrici, A. 1981. "Some Notes on the Systemic Generation of a Paradigm of the English Clause". *Readings in Systemic Linguistics* ed. by M.A.K. Halliday & J.R. Martin, 74-98. London: Batsford.
Henriques, J., W. Hollway, C. Unwin, C. Venn & V. Walkerdine. 1984. *Changing the Subject: Psychology, social regulation and subjectivity.* London and New York: Methuen.
Hetzer, A. 1978. *Lehrbuch der vereinheitlichten albanischen Schriftsprache.* Hamburg: Buske.
Hill, C. 1974. *Change and Continuity in Seventeenth Century England.* London: Weidenfeld & Nicolson.
Hiz, H. 1982. "Specialized Languages of Biology, Medicine, and Science and Connections between them". *Sublanguage: Studies of Language in Restricted Semantic Domains* ed. by R. Kittredge & J. Lehrberger, 206-212. Berlin: de Gruyter.
Hjelmslev, L. 1937. "La syllabation en slave". *Mélanges Aleksander Belic.* 315-324. Belgrade.
Hjelmslev, L. 1938. "Essai d'une théorie des morphèmes". *Actes du quatrième congrès international de linguistes*, 140-145. Copenhagen.
Hjelmslev, L. 1939. "The Syllable as a Structural Unit". *Proceedings of the Third International Congress of Phonetic Sciences*, 266-272. Ghent.
Hjelmslev, L. 1947. *Prolegomena to a Theory of Language*, transl. by F.J. Whitfield. Madison: Wisconsin University Press. Orig. publ. 1943, Copenhagen: Munksgaard.
Hjelmslev, L. 1959. *Essais linguistiques* (= *Travaux du cercle linguistique de Copenhague* XII).
Hobbs, J.R. 1979. "Coherence and Coreference". *Cognitive Science* 3. 67-90.
Hobbs, J. & D. Evans. 1980. "Conversation as Planned Behavior". *Cognitive Science* 4. 349-377.
Hofmann, J.B. 1965. *Lateinische Syntax und Stilistik.* Munich: Beck.

Hopper, P.J. & S.A. Thompson. 1980. "Transitivity in Grammar and Discourse". *Language* 56. 251-299.

Hopper, P.J. & S.A. Thompson. eds. 1982. *Studies in Transitivity* (Syntax and Semantics 15). New York: Academic Press.

Hopper, P.J. & S.A. Thompson. 1984. "The Discourse Basis for Lexical Categories in Universal Grammar". *Language* 60. 703-752.

Horvath, B. 1985. *Variation in Australian English: The sociolects of Sydney* (= *Cambridge Studies in Linguistics* 45). London: Cambridge University Press.

Householder, F. 1966. "Phonological Theory: A brief comment". *Journal of Linguistics* 2. 99-100.

Hoyles, M. ed. 1977. *The Politics of Literacy*. London: Writers and Readers Publishing Cooperative.

Huddleson, R.D. 1984. *Introduction to the Grammar of English*. Cambridge: Cambridge University Press.

Huddleston, R.D., R.A. Hudson, E.O. Winter & A. Henrici. 1968. *Sentence and Clause in Scientific English*. London: Communication Research Centre, University College London (Final Report of D.S.I.R./O.S.T.I. Programme in the Linguistic Properties of Scientific English).

Hudson, R.A. 1973. "An 'Item-&-Paradigm' Approach to Beja Syntax and Morphology". *Foundations of Language* 9. 504-548.

Hudson, R.A. 1984. *Word Grammar*. Oxford: Blackwell.

Hudson, R.A. 1985a. "A Psychologically and Socially Plausible Theory of Language Structure". *Meaning, Form and Use in Context: Linguistic applications* ed. by D. Schiffrin, 150-159. Washington, D.C.: Georgetown University Press.

Hudson, R.A. 1985b. "Sociolinguistics in Grammar". *Sheffield Working Papers in Language and Linguistics* 2. 1-30.

Hudson, R.A. 1985c. "The Limits of Subcategorisation". *Linguistic Analysis* 15. 233-255.

Hudson, R.A. 1985d. "Some Basic Assumptions about Linguistic and Non-Linguistic Knowledge". *Quaderni di Semantica* 6. 284-287.

Hudson, R.A. 1986. "Frame Semantics, Frame Linguistics, Frame ...". *Quaderni di Semantica* 7. 95-111.

Humboldt, W. von. 1836. *Über die Verschiedenheit des menschlichen Sprachbaues*. Reprinted 1949, Darmstadt: Claassen & Roether.

Hunnicutt, S. 1985. "Intelligibility versus Redundancy — Conditions of dependence". *Language and Speech* 28. 47-56.

Hymes, D. 1974. *Foundations in Sociolinguistics*. Philadelphia: University of Pennsylvania Press.
Illich, I. 1983. "Vernacular Values and Education". *The Sociogenesis of Language and Human Conduct* ed. by B. Bain, 462-496. New York & London: Plenum Press.
Jackendoff, R. 1977. *X̄ Syntax: A study in phrase structure*. Cambridge, Mass.: MIT Press.
Jackendoff, R. 1983. *Semantics and Cognition*. Cambridge, Mass.: MIT Press.
Jakobson, R. 1932. "Zur Struktur des russischen Verbums". *Charisteria G. Mathesio* 74-84. Prague: Cercle Linguistique de Prague.
Jakobson, R. 1936. "Beitrag zur allgemeinen Kasuslehre: Gesamtbedeutungen der russischen Kasus". *Travaux du cercle linguistique de Prague* 6. 240-283.
Jakobson, R. 1960. "Closing Statement: Linguistics and poetics". *Style in Language* ed. by T. Sebeok, 350-377. Cambridge, Mass.: MIT Press.
Jarvella, R.J. & G. Meijers. 1983. "Recognizing Morphemes in Spoken Words: Some evidence for a stem organized mental lexicon". *The Process of Language Understanding* ed. by G.B. Flores d'Arcais & R.J. Jarvella, 81-112. New York: John Wiley & Sons.
Jefferson, G. 1973. "A Case of Precision Timing in Ordinary Conversation". *Semiotica* 9. 47-96.
Jeziorski, J. 1983. *Substantivische Nominalkomposita des Deutschen und ihre polnischen Entsprechungen*. Wrocław: Ossolineum.
Johns, T.F. 1980. "The Text and its Message: Organising coherence". *Leserverstehen im Fremdensprachenunterricht* ed. by H. Eichheim & A. Maley, 147-170. Munich: Goethe Institut.
Johnson, S. 1970. *The Plan of a Dictionary 1747*. Menston: The Scolar Press.
Johnson-Laird, P.N. 1983. *Mental Models*. Cambridge: Cambridge University Press.
Jones, D. 1958. *English Pronouncing Dictionary*, 11th edn. London: Dent.
Jones, D. 1962. *The Phoneme*, 2nd edn. Cambridge: Heffer.
Jones, D. 1973. "The History and Meaning of the Term 'Phoneme' ". *Phonetics in Linguistics, A book of readings*, ed. by W.E. Jones & J. Laver, 187-204. London: Longman.
Jones, J. 1566. *A Dial for All Agues*. London: William Seres.
Jones, L.K. & R.E. Longacre. eds. 1979. *Discourse Studies in Mesoameri-*

can Languages, 2 vols. (SIL Publications in Linguistics, no. 58.) Arlington, Texas: SIL and the University of Texas.

Jones, S. & J.McH. Sinclair. 1974. "English Lexical Collocations". *Cahiers de lexicologie* 24. 15-61.

Joos, M. 1962. "The Five Clocks". *International Journal of American Linguistics* 28. 2.

Jordan, M.P. 1984. *Prose Structures in Everyday English Texts*. London: George Allen & Unwin.

Källgren, G. 1979. *Innehåll i Text*. Lund: Studentlitteratur.

Kalmár, I. 1982. "Transitivity in a Czech Folk Tale". *Studies in Transitivity* ed. by P.J. Hopper & S.A. Thompson, 241-260. New York: Academic Press.

Kato, K. 1986. "Gradable Gradability". *English Studies* 67. 174-180.

Katz, J.J. 1972. *Semantic Theory*. New York: Harper & Row.

Katz, J.J. & P.M. Postal. 1964. *An Integrated Theory of Linguistic Description*. Cambridge, Mass.: MIT Press.

Keil, H. ed. 1855. *Grammatici latini* Vol. 2. Leipzig: Teubner.

Key, M.R. 1975. *Male/Female Language*. Metuchen, N.J.: The Scarecrow Press.

Klein, W. & N. Dittmar. 1979. *Developing Grammars*. Berlin, Heidelberg & New York: Springer-Verlag.

Kohlberg, L. 1983. *The Psychology of Moral Development: Essays on moral development*, Vol. 2. New York: Harper & Row.

Kolers, P.A., M.E. Wrolstad & H. Bouma. eds. 1980. *Processing of Visible Language*, Vol. 2. New York: Plenum Press.

Kolln, M. 1986. Review of D.C. Freeman, *Essays in Modern Stylistics*. *College Composition and Communication* 37. 1. 109-111.

Koneski, B. 1965. *Istorija na makedonskiot jazik*. Skopje.

Koneski, B., B. Vidoeski & O. Jašar-Nasteva. 1966. *Distribution des balkanismes en macédonien*. Skopje: Skopje University Press.

Kress, G. ed. 1976. *Halliday: System and function in language*. Selected Papers. Oxford: Oxford University Press.

Kress, G. 1977. "Tense as Modality". *UEA Papers in Linguistics* 5. 40-52.

Kress, G. 1980. "Usability: The criterion for designing written information". *Processing of Visible Language* ed. by P.A. Kolers, M.E. Wrolstad & H. Bouma, Vol. 2, 183-205. New York: Plenum.

Kress, G. 1985a. "Discourse, Texts, Readers and the Pro-Nuclear Arguments". *Language and the Nuclear Arms Debate: Nukespeak Today* ed.

by P. Chilton, 65-87. London & Dover, N.H.: Frances Pinter.

Kress, G. 1985b. *Linguistic Processes in Sociocultural Practice.* Geelong, Vic.: Deakin University Press.

Kress, G. & R.I.V. Hodge. 1979. *Language as Ideology.* London & Boston: Routledge & Kegan Paul.

Kristeva, J. 1980. *Desire in Language.* Oxford: Oxford University Press.

Kuhn, T.S. 1962. "The Structure of Scientific Revolutions". *Encyclopedia of Unified Science*, Vol. 2, no. 2. Chicago: The University of Chicago Press.

Kuiper, A. & W.R. Merrifield. 1975. "Diuxi Mixtec Verbs of Motion and Arrival". *International Journal of American Linguistics* 41. 32-45.

Kundera, M. 1984. *The Unbearable Lightness of Being*, transl. by M.H. Heim. New York: Harper & Row.

Kuryłowicz, J. 1948a. "Contribution à la théorie de la syllabe". *Bulletin de la société polonaise de linguistique* 8. 80-114.

Kuryłowicz, J. 1948b. "Les structures fondamentales de la langue: groupe et proposition". *Studia Philosophica* 3. 203-209.

Kuryłowicz, J. 1949. "La notion de l'isomorphisme". *Recherches structurales* 48-60. (= *Travaux du cercle linguistique de Copenhague* V.)

Labov, W. 1963. "The Social Motivation of a Sound Change". *Word* 19. 273-309.

Labov, W. 1966. *The Social Stratification of English in New York City.* Washington, D.C.: Center for Applied Linguistics.

Labov, W. 1969. "Contraction, Deletion, and Inherent Variability of the English Copula". *Language* 45: 715-762.

Labov, W. 1972. "The Transformation of Experience in Narrative Syntax" (= Ch. 9). *Language in the Inner City: Studies in the Black English Vernacular.* Philadelphia: University of Philadelphia Press.

Labov, W. 1978. "Where Does the Linguistic Variable Stop? A response to Beatriz Lavandera". *Sociolinguistic Working Paper* 44. Austin, Texas: Southwest Educational Development Laboratory.

Labov, W. & D. Fanshel. 1977. *Therapeutic Discourse: Psychotherapy as conversation.* New York: Academic Press.

Labov, W. & T. Labov. 1977. "Learning the Syntax of Questions". *Recent Advances in the Psychology of Language* ed. by R. Campbell & P. Smith. New York: Plenum Press.

Lakoff, G. & M. Johnson. 1980. *Metaphors We Live By.* Chicago: Chicago University Press.

Lakoff, G. & J. Ross. 1972. "A Note on Anaphoric Islands and Causatives". *Linguistic Inquiry* 3. 121-125.
Lamb, S.M. 1966. *Outline of Stratificational Grammar*. Washington, D.C.: Georgetown University Press.
Lamb, S.M. 1980. "Discussion: Louis Hjelmslev's position in genetic and typological linguistics". *Typology and Genetics of Language: Proceedings of the Rask-Hjelmslev Symposium* (= *Travaux du cercle linguistique de Copenhague* XX) ed. by T. Thrane, V. Winge, L. Mackenzie, U. Canger & N. Ege, 49-63.
Langacker, R.W. 1985. *An Overview of Cognitive Grammar*. Mimeo.
Laudan, L. 1984. *Science and Values: The aims of science and their role in scientific debate*. Berkeley: University of California Press.
Lavandera, B. 1978. "Where Does the Sociolinguistic Variable Stop?" *Language in Society* 7. 171-183.
Lehrberger, J. 1982. "Automatic Translation and the Concept of Sublanguage". *Sublanguage: Studies of language in restricted semantic domains* ed. by R. Kittredge & J. Lehrberger, 81-106. Berlin: Gruyter.
Lehrer, A. 1986. "English Classifier Expressions". *Lingua* 68. 228-264.
Lemke, J.L. 1983. "Thematic Analysis: Systems, structures and strategies". *RS/SI* 3. 159-187.
Lemke, J.L. 1984a. "Ideology, Intertextuality and The Notion of Register". *Systemic Perspectives on Discourse: Selected papers from the 9th International Systemic Workshop* ed. by W.S. Greaves & J.D. Benson. Norwood, N.J.: Ablex.
Lemke, J.L. 1984b. "Textual Politics: Heteroglossia, discourse analysis, and social dynamics". School of Education, City University of New York, Brooklyn College. Mimeo.
Lerner, G. 1986. "Collaborative Turn Sequences: A study of sentence construction and social action". Ph.D. Dissertation, University of California, Irvine (in preparation).
Levenston, E. & J. Ellis. 1964. "A Transfer Grammar Development of System-Reduction Quantification Method". *Zeitschrift für Phonetik* 17. 449-452.
Lévi-Strauss, C. 1974. *Tristes Tropiques*, transl. by J. & D. Weightman. New York: Atheneum.
Levin, S.R. 1977. *The Semantics of Metaphor*. Baltimore, Md.: The Johns Hopkins University Press.
Levinson, S.C. 1983. *Pragmatics*. Cambridge: Cambridge University Press.

Lewis, G.L. 1953. *Teach Yourself Turkish*. London: Edinburgh University Press.
Lewis, G.L. 1967. *Turkish Grammar*. Oxford: Clarendon Press.
Lewontin, R.C., S. Rose & L.J. Kamin. 1984. *Not in our Genes: Biology, Ideology and Human Nature*. New York: Pantheon Books.
Liberman, M. & A. Prince. 1977. "On Stress and Linguistic Rhythm". *Linguistic Inquiry* 8. 249-336.
Lieber, R. 1984. "Grammatical and Sublexical Elements". *Parasession on Lexical Semantics* ed. by D. Testen *et al.*, 187-199. Chicago: CLS.
Lieberman, P. 1963. "Some Effects of Semantic and Grammatical Context on the Production and Perception of Speech". *Language and Speech* 6. 172-187.
Lightfoot, D. 1979. *Principles of Diachronic Syntax*. Cambridge: Cambridge University Press.
Lindblom, B. 1983a. "Economy of Speech Gestures". *The Production of Speech* ed. by P.F. MacNeilage. Springer-Verlag.
Lindblom, B. 1983b. "On the Teleological Nature of Speech Processes". *Journal of Speech Communication* 2. 155-158.
Lindblom, B. & R. Lindgren. 1986. "Speaker-Listener Interaction and Phonetic Variation". *Perilus*, 77-85.
Logicware. 1984a. *MPROLOG Language Reference: Release 1.5*. Toronto: Logicware, Inc.
Logicware. 1984b. *Logic-Lab Reference: Release 1.5*. Toronto: Logicware, Inc.
Longacre, R.E. 1976. *An Anatomy of Speech Notions*. Lisse: The Peter de Ridder Press.
Longacre, R.E. 1983. *The Grammar of Discourse: Notional and surface structures*. New York: Plenum Press.
Longacre, R.E. & S.A. Thompson. 1985. "Adverbial Clauses". *Language Typology and Syntactic Description* ed. by T. Shopen. Cambridge: Cambridge University Press.
Lord, A. 1965. *The Singer of Tales*. New York: Atheneum.
Lowe, D.M. 1982. *History of Bourgeois Perception*. Harvester Press.
Lunt, H.G. 1952. *Grammar of the Macedonian Literary Language*. Skopje.
Lyman, L. 1964. "Verb Syntagmemes of Choapan Zapotec". *Linguistics* 7. 16-41.
Lyons, J. 1966. "Towards a 'Notional' Theory of the 'Parts of Speech'. *Journal of Linguistics* 2. 209-236.

Lyons, J. ed. 1970. *New Horizons in Linguistics*. Harmondsworth: Penguin.
Lyons, J. 1977. *Semantics*, Vol. 2. Cambridge: Cambridge University Press.
MacCabe, C. 1984. "Towards a Modern Trivium — English Studies Today". *Critical Quarterly* 26. 1/2, 69-82.
Maling, J. 1983. "Transitive Adjectives: A case of categorical reanalysis". *Linguistic Categories: Auxiliaries and related puzzles*, Vol. 1, ed. by F. Heny & B. Richards, 253-289. Dordrecht: Reidel.
Malinowski, B. 1923. "The Problem of Meaning in Primitive Languages". Supplement to *The Meaning of Meaning* ed. by C.K. Ogden & I.A. Richards. London: Routledge & Kegan Paul.
Malinowski, B. 1935. *Coral Gardens and their Magic*. Vol. II: *The Language of Magic and Gardening*. London: George Allen & Unwin.
Malinowski, B. 1960. *A Scientific Theory of Culture; and Other Essays*. New York: Oxford University Press.
Manisoff, M. 1970. *Family Planning Training for Social Service*. Planned Parenthood Federation of America Inc.
Mann, S.E. 1977. *An Albanian Historical Grammar*. Hamburg: Buske.
Mann, W.C. 1984a. "A Linguistic Overview of the Nigel Text Generation Grammar". *The Tenth LACUS Forum 1983* ed. by A. Manning, P. Martin & K. McCalla, 255-265. Columbia, S.C.: Hornbeam Press.
Mann, W.C. 1984b. *Discourse Structures for Text Generation*. USC/Information Sciences Institute, Technical Report RR-84-127, February 1984. Also appeared in the Proceedings of the 1984 Coling/ACL Conference, July 1984.
Mann, W.C. & C. Matthiessen. 1983. *Nigel: A systemic grammar for text generation*. Marina del Rey, Cal.: Information Sciences Institute, University of Southern California.
Mann, W.C. & S.A. Thompson. 1985. "Assertions from Discourse Structure". *Proceedings of the Eleventh Annual Meeting of the Berkeley Linguistics Society*. Berkeley: Linguistic Society.
Mann, W.C. & S.A. Thompson. 1986. "Relational Propositions in Discourse". *Discourse Processes*, 57-90.
Mann, W.C. & S.A. Thompson. 1987. "Rhetorical Structure Theory: A theory of text organization". *Discourse Structure* ed. by L. Polanyi. Norwood, N.J.: Ablex.
Marks, D. 1980. "Morphophonemics of the Guevea de Humboldt Zapotec Verb". *SIL-Mexico Workpapers* 4. 43-84.
Martin, J.R. 1983. "Conjunction: The logic of English text". *Macro and*

Micro Connexity of Speech ed. by J.S. Petöfi & E. Sozer, 1-72. Hamburg: Helmut Buske (Papers in Textlinguistics 45).

Martin, J.R. 1983. "The Development of Register". *Developmental Issues in Discourse* (= *Advances in Discourse Processes* X) ed. by J. Fine & R.O. Freedle. Norwood, N.J.: Ablex.

Martin, J.R. 1984. "Functional Components in a Grammar: A review of deployable recognition criteria". *Nottingham Linguistics Circular* 13. 35-71.

Martin, J.R. 1986. "Politicalising Ecology: The politics of baby seals and kangaroos". *Semiotics, Ideology, Language* ed. by T. Threadgold *et al*. Sydney: The Pathfinder Press.

Martin, J.R. Forthcoming. "Process and Text: Two aspects of human semiosis". *Systemic Perspectives on Discourse: Selected theoretical papers from the Ninth International Systemic Workshop* ed. by W.S. Greaves & J.D. Benson. Norwood, N.J.: Ablex.

Martin, J.R. & J. Rothery. 1981. "Writing Project Report No. 2". *Working Papers in Linguistics* 2. Department of Linguistics, University of Sydney.

Mason, K. Forthcoming. *The Linguistic Encyclopaedia*. London: Routledge & Kegan Paul.

Matthews, P.H. 1970. "Recent Developments in Morphology". *New Horizons in Linguistics* ed. by J. Lyons, 96-114. Harmondsworth: Penguin.

Matthews, P.H. 1972. *Inflectional Morphology: A theoretical study based on aspects of Latin verb conjugation*. Cambridge: Cambridge University Press.

Matthews, P.H. 1974. *Morphology: An introduction to the theory of word structure*. Cambridge: Cambridge University Press.

Matthiessen, C. 1984a. "How to Make Grammatical Choices in Text Generation". *The Tenth LACUS Forum 1983* ed. by A. Manning, P. Martin & K. McCalla, 266-284. Columbia, S.C.: Hornbeam Press.

Matthiessen, C. 1984b. *Logic-Lab Reference: Release 1.5*. Toronto: Logicware, Inc.

Matthiessen, C. Forthcoming. "Semantics for a Systemic Grammar: The chooser and inquiry framework". *Linguistics in a Systemic Perspective* ed. by J. Benson, M. Cummings & W. Greaves. Amsterdam: John Benjamins.

Matthiessen, C. & S.A. Thompson. Forthcoming. "The Structure of Discourse and 'Subordination'". *Clause Combining in Grammar and Dis-*

course ed. by Haiman & S.A. Thompson. Amsterdam: John Benjamins.
Mayerthaler, W. 1981. *Morphologische Natürlichkeit*. Wiesbaden: Athenaion.
Mayr, E. 1963. *Animal Species and Evolution*. Cambridge, Mass.: Harvard University Press.
The McBride Report. 1980. *Many Voices, One World: Towards a new more just and more efficient world information and communication order*. London: Kogan Page.
McIntosh, A. 1966. "Patterns and Ranges". *Patterns of Language* ed. by A. McIntosh & M.A.K. Halliday, 183-199. London: Longman.
McKellar, G.B. Unpublished. *Social Man: The grand synthesis. On the foundations of a contemporary neurolinguistics*, Books II & III.
Melville, H. *Moby Dick*. Text based on the Hendricks House edn. of *Moby Dick*, prepared by Professor E.F. Irey, University of Colorado.
Meyer, B.J.F. 1982. "Signalling the Structure of Text". *The Technology of Text* ed. by J. Assen. Englewood Cliffs, N.J.: Educational Technology Publications.
Milroy, J. 1984. "The History of English in the British Isles". *Language in the British Isles* ed. by P. Trudgill, 5-31. Cambridge: Cambridge University Press.
Minsky, M.L. 1975. "A Framework for Representing Knowledge". *The Psychology of Computer Vision* ed. by P.H. Winston. New York: McGraw-Hill.
Mithun, M. 1984. "How to Avoid Subordination". *Proceedings of the Tenth Annual Meeting*. Berkeley: Berkeley Linguistics Society.
Mittelberger, H. 1966. "Genitiv und Adjektiv in den altanatolischen Sprachen". *Kratylos* 11. 99-106.
Mock, C.C. 1983a. *A Comparative View of Zapotecan Tense-Aspect*. Paper presented at the 22nd Conference on American Indian Languages, American Anthropological Association.
Mock, C.C. 1983b. *Temporal Orientation Without Tenses; The deixis of Time in Isthmus Zapotec*. Paper presented at the Linguistic Society of America.
Mock, C.C. 1983c. "Tone Sandhi in Isthmus Zapotec: An autosegmental account". *Linguistic Analysis* 12. 91-139.
Mock, C.C. 1984a. "La alternancia tonal en el Zapoteco del Istmo". *Language in the Americas* ed. by D.F. Solá, 268-311. Ithaca: Latin American Studies Program, Cornell University.

Mock, C.C. 1984b. *Moving on: Conversational strategies for 'changing the subject in' Isthmus Zapotec*. Paper presented at the Linguistic Symposium of the University of Missouri, Columbia.
Moeran, B. 1984. "Advertising Sounds as Cultural Discourse". *Language and Communication* 4. 2. 147-158.
Mohan, B.A. 1986. *Language and Content*. Reading, Mass.: Addison-Wesley.
Morehead, A.H. & G. Mott-Smith. 1958. *Hoyle's Rules of Games*. New York: New American Library.
Moulton, W.G. 1962. *The Sounds of English and German*. Chicago: Chicago University Press.
Muirhead, L.R. 1956. *Rome and Central Italy* (The Blue Guides). London: Ernest Benn Limited.
Munro, P. 1982. "On the Transitivity of 'Say' Verbs". *Studies in Transitivity* ed. by P.J. Hopper & S.A. Thompson, 301-318. New York: Academic Press.
Newmeyer, F.J. 1986. "Has there been a 'Chomskyan Revolution' in Linguistics?" *Language* 62. 1-18.
Nixon, G. 1976. Contribution on Phonology to Conference on The Teaching of Linguistics in Higher Education. Middlesex: Polytechnic.
Novák, P. 1958. "K zdvojování předmětu v albánštině". *Sborník slavistických prací věnovaných. IV: mezinárodnímu sjezdů slavistu v Moskvě* ed. by. K. Horálek & J. Kurz, 27-32. Prague: Universita Karlova. Státní Pedagogické Nakladatelství.
Norris, C. 1982. *Deconstruction: Theory and practice*. London: Methuen.
Oehrle, R. 1984. "Toward an Adequate Theory of Tag Questions". Manuscript.
Ohmann, R. 1964. "Generative Grammars and the Concept of Literary Style". *Word* 20. 423-439.
Ohmann, R. 1971. "Speech, Action and Style". *Literary Style: A Symposium* ed. by S. Chatman, 241-259. London: Oxford University Press.
Ong, N.J. 1958. *Ramus, Method and the Decay of Dialogue*. New York: Octagon Books.
Palmer, F.R. 1958. "Linguistic Hierarchy". *Lingua* 7. 225-241.
Panagl, O. 1976. "Sprachhistorisch-komparatistische Oberlegungen zur 'lexikalistischen Hypothese' in der Wortbildungstheorie". *Wortbildung synchron-diachron* ed. by O. Panagl, 25-55. Innsbruck.
Panagl, O. 1980. "Die verbale Rektion deverbaler Substantiva im Lichte

der neueren Wortbildungstheorie. *Symmicta Philologica Salisburgensia* ed. by J. Dafen *et al.*, 293-307. Rome: Ateneo.

Panofsky, E. 1957. *Gothic Architecture and Scholasticism*. New York: World Publishing Co.

Parkin, D. 1977. "Emergent and Stabilized Multilingualism: Polyethnic peer groups in urban Kenya". *Language, Ethnicity and Intergroup Relations* ed. by H. Giles, 185-210. London: Academic Press.

Parret, H. ed. 1974. "Discussion with M.A.K. Halliday". *Discussing Language*, 81-120. The Hague: Mouton.

Parsons, Talcott. 1964. *Social Structure and Personality*. Chicago: Free Press.

Partee, B.H. 1973. "Syntax and Semantics of Quotation". *A Festschrift for Morris Halle* ed. by S. Anderson & P. Kiparsky. New York: Holt, Rinehart & Winston.

Pateman, T. 1981. "Linguistics as a Branch of Critical Theory". *UEA Papers in Linguistics* 14-15. 1-29.

Patey, D.L. 1984. *Probability and Literary Form: Philosophic theory and literary practice in the Augustan age*. Cambridge: Cambridge University Press.

Peng, F.C.C. ed. 1981. *Nihongo no Danjo Sa* (Male/Female Differences in Japanese). Tokyo: The East-West Sign Language Association.

Peng, F.C.C. 1986a. "Language and Cross-Cultural Communication". *Cross-cultural Communication: East and West* ed. by John H. Koo & N. St. Clair, 13-42. Seoul: Samji Publishing Company.

Peng, F.C.C. 1986b. "On the Context of Situation". *International Journal of the Sociology of Language* 58. 91-106.

Perlmutter, D.M. 1970. "On the Article in English". *Progress in Linguistics* ed. by M. Bierwisch & C. Heidolph, 233-248. The Hague: Mouton.

Peters, R.S. 1966. *Ethics and Education*. London: George Allen & Unwin.

Picheny, M.A. *et al.* 1985. "Speaking Clearly for the Hard of Hearing, I: Intelligibility differences between clear and conversational speech". *Journal of Speech and Hearing Research* 28. 96-103.

Picheny, M.A. *et al.* 1986. "Speaking Clearly for the Hard of Hearing, II: Acoustic Characteristics of Clear and Conversational Speech". *Journal of Speech and Hearing Research*, 434-445.

Pickett, V.B. 1955. "Isthmus Zapotec Verb Analysis II". *International Journal of American Linguistics* 21. 217-232.

Pickett, V.B. 1967. "Isthmus Zapotec". *Handbook of Middle American*

Indians, Vol. 5, ed. by N.A. McQuown, 291-310. Austin, Texas: University of Texas Press.

Pickett, V.B. 1976. "Further Comments on Zapotec Motion Verbs". *International Journal of American Linguistics* 42. 162-164.

Pike, K.L. 1967. *Language in Relation to a Unified Theory of the Structure of Human Behavior*. The Hague: Mouton.

Pike, K.L. 1974. "Agreement Types Dispersed into a Nine-Cell Spectrum". *Language, Culture, and Religion: In honor of Eugene A. Nida*, ed. M. Black & W.A. Smalley, 175-186. The Hague: Mouton.

Pike, K.L. 1976. "Toward the Development of Tagmemic Postulates". *Tagmemics 2: Theoretical Discussion* (= *Trends in Linguistics, Studies and Monographs* 2) ed. by R.M. Brend & K.L. Pike, 91-127. The Hague: Mouton.

Pike, K.L. & E.G. Pike. 1947. "Immediate Constituents of Mazateco Syllables". *International Journal of American Linguistics* 13. 78-91.

Pike, K.L. & E.G. Pike. 1977. *Grammatical Analysis*. Dallas: Summer Institute of Linguistics.

Pike, K.L. & E.G. Pike. 1983. *Text and Tagmeme*. London: Frances Pinter.

Plank, F. 1981. *Morphologische (Ir)regularitäten*. Tübingen: Narr.

Plank, F. 1984. "Romance Disagreements: Phonology Interfering with Syntax". *Journal of Linguistics* 20. 329-349.

Plum, G. 1985. "Field in Contextual Theory: A proposal for its systemic representation". Unpublished paper, Department of Linguistics, University of Sydney.

Poe, E.A. 1903. "The Fall of the House of Usher". Text based on the Collier edition of "The Fall of the House of Usher".

Porat, M.U. 1977. *The Information Economy: Definition and measurement*. Washington, D.C.: Office of Telecommunications, U.S. Department of Commerce.

Porat, M.U. 1978. "Communication Policy in an Information Society". *Communications for Tomorrow* ed. by G.O. Robinson. New York: Prager.

Posner, R. 1976. "Poetic Communication v. Literary Language, or: The linguistic fallacy in poetics". *Poetics and the Theory of Literature* 1. 1-10.

Posner, R. 1985. "Non-Agreement of Romance Disagreements". *Journal of Linguistics* 21. 437-451.

Posner, R. *Poetry as Rational Discourse*. The Hague: Mouton.

Postal, P. 1969. "Anaphoric Islands". *PCLS* 5. 205-239.
Pratt, M.L. 1977. *Towards a Speech Act Theory of Literary Discourse*. Bloomington: Indiana University Press.
Pribram, J. 1971. *What Makes Man Human*. Thirty-Ninth James Arthur Lecture on the Evolution of the Human Brain. New York: American Museum of Natural History.
Propp, V. 1968. *Morphology of the Folktale*, 2nd rev. edn., ed. by L.A. Wagner. Austin, Texas: University of Texas Press.
Quinn, C.J. Jr. 1982. "'Literary' Language: Is it different?" *University of Michigan Papers in Linguistics* 10. 1. 29-56.
Quirk, R., S. Greenbaum, G. Leech & J. Svartvik. 1972. *A Grammar of Contemporary English*. London: Seminar Press.
Quirk, R., S. Greenbaum, G. Leech & J. Svartvik. 1985. *A Comprehensive Grammar of the English Language*. London: Longman.
Reddy, M.J. 1979. "The Conduit Metaphor. A case of frame conflict in our language about language". *Metaphor and Thought* ed. by A. Ortony, 284-324. Cambridge: Cambridge University Press.
Reed, A. 1977. "CLOC: A collocation package". *ALLC Bulletin* 5. 168-173.
Rehbein, J. & K. Ehlich. 1977. "Wissen, kommunikatives Handeln und die Schule". *Sprachverhalten im Unterricht* ed. by H. Goeppert. Munich: Fink.
Reiss, T.J. 1982. *The Discourse of Modernism*. Ithaca & London: Cornell University Press.
Revoile, S.G. et al. 1986a. "Some Rehabilitative Considerations for Future Speech-Processing Hearing Aids". *Journal of Rehabilitation Research* 23. 1. 94-98.
Revoile, S.G. et al. 1986b. "Speech Cue Enhancement for the Hearing-Impaired. I: Altered Vowel Durations for Perception of Final Fricative Voicing". *Journal of Speech and Hearing Research* 29. 240-255.
Richter, M.N. 1972. *Science as a Cultural Process*. Cambridge, Mass.: Schenkman Publishing.
Riddle, E.M. 1984. "The English Possessive as Topic-Focus Structures". Paper read at the LSA Winter Meeting, December, 1984. Baltimore, Maryland.
Riffaterre, M. 1985. "Text, Textuality, and Interpretation. An interview by Vijay Mishra". *Southern Review: Literary and Interdisciplinary Essays* 18. 1. 109-119.

Robins, R.H. 1958. *The Yurok Language*. Berkeley: University of California Press.
Robins, R.H. 1959. "In Defence of WP". *Transactions of the Philological Society* 116-144.
Robinson, F.N. ed. 1957. *The Works of Geoffrey Chaucer*, 2nd edn. Boston: Houghton Mifflin.
Rohrer, C. 1974. "Some Problems of Word Formation". *Actes du Colloque Franco-Allemand de Grammaire Transformationelle* ed. by N. Ruwet & C. Rohrer, 113-123. Tübingen: Niemeyer.
Romaine, S. 1981. "On the Problem of Syntactic Variation: A reply to Beatriz Lavandera & William Labov". *Sociolinguistic Working Paper* 82. Austin, Texas: Southwest Educational Development Laboratory.
Rosch, E. 1975. "Cognitive Representation of Semantic Categories". *Journal of Experimental Psychology* 104. 192-233.
Rosén, H. 1983. "The Mechanisms of Latin Nominalization and Conceptualization in Historical View". *Aufstieg und Niedergang der Römischen Welt II* ed. by H. Temporini & W. Haase, 178-211. Berlin: de Gruyter.
Rumelhart, D.E. 1980. "Schemata: The building blocks of cognition". *Theoretical Issues in Reading Comprehension* ed. by R.J. Spiro, B.C. Bruce & W.F. Brewer. Hillsdale: Erlbaum.
Russell, B. 1946. *History of Western Philosophy*. London: Allen & Unwin.
Sacks, H. 1967. Unpublished lectures.
Sacks, H., E.A. Schegloff & G. Jefferson. 1974. "A Simplest Systematics for the Organization of Turn-Taking in Conversation". *Language* 50. 696-735.
Sadiku, Z. 1975. "Rreth opozicionit perfekt/aorist në gjuhën shqipe". *Gjurmime Albanologjike. Seria e Shkencave Historike*. Prishtina: Instituti Albanologjik 5. 51-59.
Sadock, J.M. 1985. "Autolexical Syntax". *Natural Language and Linguistic Theory* 3. 379-439.
Sadock, J.M. 1986. "Some Notes on Noun Incorporation". *Language* 62. 19-31.
Sampson, G. 1980. *Schools of Linguistics*. Stanford: Stanford University Press.
Sandell, L. 1982. *English Language in Sudan*. London: Ithaca Press.
Sanfeld, K. 1930. *Linguistique Balkanique. Problèmes et résultats*. Paris: Société de Linguistique.
Sankoff, D. 1973. "Above and Beyond Phonology in Variable Rules". *New*

Ways of Analyzing Variation in English ed. by C.-J. Bailey & R. Shuy, 44-62. Washington, D.C.: Georgetown University Press.

Sankoff, D. 1978. "Probability and Linguistic Variation". *Synthèse* 37. 217-238.

Sankoff, D. Forthcoming. "Sociolinguistics and Syntactic Variation". *Linguistics: The Cambridge Survey* ed. by F. Newmeyer. London: Cambridge University Press.

Sankoff, D. & Labov, W. 1979. "On the Uses of Variable Rules". *Language in Society* 8. 189-223.

Saussure, F. de 1974. *Course in General Linguistics*. London: Peter Owen.

Savini, M. 1984. "Phrasal Compounds in Afrikaans". *SPIL* 12. 37-114.

Scalise, S. 1984. *Generative Morphology*. Dordrecht: Foris.

Schank, R. & R. Abelson. 1977. *Scripts, Plans, Goals and Understanding. An inquiry into human knowledge structures*. Hillsdale, N.J.: Erlbaum.

Scheflen, A.E. 1973. *Communication Structure: Analysis of a Psychotherapy Transaction*. Bloomington: Indiana University Press.

Schegloff, E.A. & H. Sacks. 1973. "Opening up Closings". *Semiotica* 8. 289-327.

Schiffrin, D. 1981. "Tense Variation in Narrative". *Language* 57. 1. 45-62.

Schiller, H.I. 1981. *Who Knows: Information in the age of the Fortune 500*. Norwood, N.J.: Ablex.

Schmaus, A. 1966. "Beobachtungen zu Bedeutung und Gebrauch des albanischen Admirative". *Beiträge zur Südosteuropa-Forschung*, 103-124. Munich.

Schwartz, L. 1978. "On the Island Status of Lexical Clitics". *Parasession on the Lexicon* (*CLS* 1978), 326-335.

Schwartz, M. 1984. "Response to Writing: A college-wide perspective". *College English* 46. 1. 55-62.

Scribner, S. & M. Cole. 1981. *The Psychology of Literacy*. Cambridge, Mass.: Harvard University Press.

Searle, J. 1975. "The Logical Status of Fictional Discourse". *New Literary History* 6. 319-332.

Selkirk, L. 1982. *The Syntax of Words*. Cambridge, Mass.: MIT Press.

Short, M.L. & C. Candlin. 1986. "Literature, Language Study and the Teaching of Literature". *Literature and Language Teaching* ed. by C.J. Brumfit & R.A. Carter, 89-109. Oxford: Oxford University Press.

Siegel, S. 1956. *Nonparametric Statistics*. New York: McGraw-Hill.

Siertsema, B. 1965. *A Study of Glossematics*. The Hague: Martinus Nijhoff.

REFERENCES

Sigurd, B. 1974. *Experiment med Text (PILUS* 34). Stockholm: University of Stockholm, Department of Linguistics.

Sigurd, B. 1977. *Om textens dynamik (PILUS* 34). Stockholm: University of Stockholm, Department of Linguistics.

Silverstein, M. 1979. "Language structure and linguistic ideology". *The Elements: A parasession on linguistic units and levels* ed. by P.R. Clyne, W.F. Hanks & C.L. Hofbauer. Chicago: Chicago Linguistic Society.

Sinclair, J.McH. 1966. "Beginning the Study of Lexis". *In Memory of J.R. Firth* ed. by C.E. Bazell, J.C. Catford & M.A.K. Halliday. London: Longman.

Slaughter, M.M. 1982. *Universal Languages and Scientific Taxonomy in the Seventeenth Century*. Cambridge: Cambridge University Press.

Sola Pool, I. de 1983. "Tracking the Flow of Information". *Science* 221.

Speck, C.H. & V.B. Pickett. 1976. "Some Properties of the Texmelucan Zapotec Verbs *Go, Come,* and *Arrive*". *International Journal of American Linguistics* 42. 58-64.

Sperber, D. & D. Wilson. 1986. *Relevance: Communication and cognition*. Oxford: Basil Blackwell.

Spradley, J.P. 1979. *The Ethnographic Interview*. New York: Holt, Rinehart & Winston.

Spradley, J.P. 1980. *Participant Observation*. New York: Holt, Rinehart & Winston.

Sproat, R.W. 1985. *On Deriving the Lexicon*. Ph.D. Dissertation, MIT.

Sproat, R.W. Forthcoming. *On Anaphoric Islandhood*. Milwaukee.

Stachowiak, F.-J. 1978. "Some Universal Aspects of Naming as a Language Activity". *Language Universals* ed. by H. Seiler, 207-228. Tübingen: Narr.

Steiner, E. 1985. "The Concept of Context and the Theory of Action". *Language and the Nuclear Arms Debate: Nukespeak Today* ed. by P. Chilton. London & Dover, N.H.: Frances Pinter.

Steiner, G. 1976. *Extraterritorial: Papers on literature and the language revolution*. New York: Atheneum.

Steiner, G. 1978. "The Distribution of Discourse". *On Difficulty and Other Essays*, 61-94. New York: Oxford University Press.

Stemberger, J. & B. MacWhinney. Forthcoming. *Are Inflecting Forms Stored in the Lexicon?* Milwaukee.

Stölting, W. 1966. "Das Artikelsystem im Albanischen und Rumänischen". *Beiträge zur Südosteuropa-Forschung*, 40-78. Munich.

Strassmann, P.A. 1983. "Information Systems and Literacy". *Literacy for Life: The demand for reading and writing* ed. by R.W. Bailey & R.M. Fosheim. New York: The Modern Language Association.

Tadros, A. 1985. *Prediction in Text.* Birmingham: English Language Research.

Thomason, R.H. 1972. "A Semantic Theory of Sortal Incorrectness". *Journal of Philosophical Logic* 1. 209-258.

Thompson, S.A. 1985. " 'Subordination' in Formal and Informal Discourse". *Meaning, Form, and Use in Context: Linguistic Applications* ed. by D. Schiffrin. Washington, D.C.: Georgetown University Press.

Thompson, S.A. 1985. "Grammar and Written Discourse: Initial vs. final clauses". *Text* 5. 1. 55-84.

Thrane, T., V. Winge, L. Mackenzie, U. Canger & N. Ege. eds. 1980. *Typology and Genetics of Language: Proceedings of the Rask-Hjelmslev Symposium* (= *Travaux du cercle linguistique de Copenhague* XX).

Threadgold, T. 1986. "Semiotics-Ideology-Language". *Semiotics, Ideology, Language* ed. by T. Threadgold *et al.*. Sydney: Sydney Association for Studies in Society and Culture.

Threadgold, T. 1987. "The Semiotics of Halliday, Vološinov and Eco". *American Journal of Semiotics* 4. 3-4. 107-141.

Threadgold, T. Forthcoming. "Stories of Race and Gender: An unbounded discourse". *The Functions of Style* ed. by L.M. O'Toole & D. Birch. London: Frances Pinter.

Thürmer, R. & U. Thürmer. 1985. "Textparameter als Instrument zum Vergleich von Texten". *Linguistische Arbeitsberichte* 50. 81-92. Leipzig: Karl-Marx-Universität.

Timberlake, A. 1982. "Invariance and the Syntax of Russian Aspect". *Tense-Aspect* ed. by P.J. Hopper, 305-331. Amsterdam: John Benjamins.

Todorov, T. 1983. *Theories of the Symbol*, transl. by C. Porter. Oxford: Basil Blackwell.

Togeby, K. 1951. *Structure immanente de la langue française* (= *Travaux du cercle linguistique de Copenhague* VI).

Toklas, A.B. 1961. *The Alice B. Toklas Cook Book*. Harmondsworth: Penguin Books Ltd.

Tolhurst, G.C. 1954. "The Effect of Intelligibility Scores on Specific Instructions Regarding Talking". Joint Project NM001 064.01 Report 35. Ohio State University Research Foundation and U.S. Naval School

of Aviation Medicine.
Toman, J. 1978. "A Gloss of Pronominalization in Idioms". *Papiere zur Linguistik* 19. 78-82.
Toman, J. 1985. "A Discussion of Coordination and Word-Syntax". *Studies in German Grammar* ed. by J. Toman, 407-432. Dordrecht: Foris.
Trudgill, P. ed. 1984. *Language in the British Isles*. Cambridge: Cambridge University Press.
Tsunoda, T. 1985. "Remarks on Transitivity". *Journal of Linguistics* 21. 385-396.
Tufte, E.R. 1983. *The Visual Display of Quantitative Information*. Cheshire, Conn.: Graphics Press.
Turk, C. 1978. "Do you Write Impressively?" *Bulletin of the British Ecological Society* 9. 5-10.
UNESCO. 1980. *Literacy 1972-1976: Progress achieved in literacy throughout the world*. Paris: UNESCO.
Urban, G. 1986. "Ceremonial Dialogues in South America". *American Anthropologist* 88. 2. 371-386.
Van der Auwera, J. "Relative *That*- A centennial dispute." *Journal of Linguistics* 21. 1. 149-181.
Van Dijk, T.A. & W. Kintsch. 1983. *Strategies of Discourse Comprehension*. New York: Academic Press.
Vennemann, T. 1983. "Theories of Linguistic Preferences as a Basis for Linguistic Explanations". *FLH* 4. 5-26.
Vološinov, V.N. 1973. *Marxism and the Philosophy of Language*, transl. by L. Matejka & I.R. Titunik. New York: Seminar Press.
Vu, My T. 1983. *Short-Term Population Projection, 1980-2020, and Long-Term Projection, 2000 to Stationary Stage, by Age and Sex for All Countries of the World*. Washington, D.C.: Population, Health & Nutrition Department, World Bank.
Wallace, S. 1982. "Figure and Ground: The interrelationship of linguistic categories". *Tense-Aspect* ed. by P.J. Hopper, 201-223. Amsterdam: John Benjamins.
Waller, R.H.W. 1980. "Graphic Aspects of Complex Texts: Typography as macro-punctuation". *Processing of Visible Language* ed. by P.A. Kolers, M.E. Wrolstad & H. Bouma, Vol. 2, 241-253. New York: Plenum.
Watt, W.C. 1973. "Late Lexicalizations". *Approaches to Natural Language* ed. by Hintikka *et al*, 457-489. Dordrecht-Holland: D. Reidel Publishing Co.

Waugh, L.R. 1980. "The Poetic Function and the Nature of Language". *Poetics Today* 2. 1. 57-82.

Weber, M. 1958. "The Chinese Literati". *Essays in Sociology* ed. by H.H. Gerth & C. Wright Mills, 416-420. New York: Oxford University Press.

Weiner, E.J. & W. Labov. 1983. "Constraints on the Agentless Passive". *Journal of Linguistics* 19. 29-58. (= W. Labov & E. J. Weiner. 1977. Paper given to the LSA Summer Meeting, Honolulu.)

Weinreich, U. 1953. *Languages in Contact*. New York: Linguistic Circle.

Weinreich, U. 1966. "Explorations in Semantic Theory". *Current Trends in Linguistics* 3, ed. by T.A. Sebeok. The Hague: Mouton.

Wellbury, D.E. 1984. *Lessing's Laocoon: Semiotics and aesthetics in the age of reason*. Anglia Germanica Series 2. Cambridge: Cambridge University Press.

Wells, R.A. 1973. *Dictionaries and the Authoritarian Tradition*. The Hague: Mouton.

Werth, P. 1976. "Roman Jakobson's Verbal Analysis of Poetry". *Journal of Linguistics* 12. 21-74.

White, H. 1973. *Metahistory: The historical imagination in nineteenth century Europe*. Baltimore: Johns Hopkins University Press.

White, J.V. 1984. *Using Charts and Graphs*. New York: Boker.

Whorf, B.L. 1956. *Language, Thought, and Reality: Selected writings of Benjamin Lee Whorf*, ed. & introd. by J.B. Carroll. Cambridge, Mass.: MIT Press.

Widdowson, H.G. 1972. "On the Deviance of Literary Discourse". *Style* 6. 294-306.

Widdowson, H.G. 1975. *Stylistics and the Teaching of Literature*. London: Longman.

Widdowson, H.G. 1985. *Explorations in Applied Linguistics*, Vol. 2. London: Oxford University Press.

Wilden, A. 1980. *System and Structure: Essays in communication and exchange*. Suffolk: Richard Clay Ltd.

Williams, E.S. 1981. "On the Notions 'Lexically Related' and 'Head of a Word' ". *Linguistic Inquiry* 12. 245-274.

Williams, R. 1976. *Keywords*. London: Fontana/Croom Helm.

Winograd, T. 1972. *Understanding Natural Language*. Edinburgh: Edinburgh University Press.

Winograd, T. 1983. *Language as a Cognitive Process*, Vol. 1: *Syntax*. Reading, Mass.: Addison-Wesley.

Winter, E. 1982. *Towards a Contextual Grammar of English*. London: George Allen & Unwin.
Wise, M.R. 1971. *Identification of Participants in Discourse: A study of form and meaning in Nomatsiguenga*. Santa Ana: Summer Institute of Linguistics.
Wolfson, N. 1979. "The Conversational Historical Present Alternation". *Language* 55. 1. 168-182.
Wright, L.B. 1935. *Middle-Class Culture in Elizabethan England*. North Carolina: University of North Carolina Press.
Wright, P. 1982. "A User-Oriented Approach to the Design of Tables and Flowcharts". *The Technology of Text: Principles for structuring, designing, and displaying text* ed. by D.H. Jonassen, 317-340. Englewood Cliffs, N.J.: Educational Technology Publications.
Wurzel, W.U. 1984. *Flexionsmorphologie und Naturlichkeit*. Berlin: Studia Grammatica 21.
Zwicky, A.M. 1969. "Phonological Constraints in Syntactic Description". *Papers in Linguistics* 1. 411-463.
Zwicky, A.M. 1973. "The Analytic Leap: From 'some Xs are Ys' to 'all Xs are Ys'". *PCLS* 9. 700-709.
Zwicky, A.M. 1985a. "Heads". *Journal of Linguistics* 21. 1-29.
Zwicky, A.M. 1985b. "Rules of Allomorphy and Phonology-syntax Interaction". *Journal of Linguistics* 21. 431-436.
Zwicky, A.M. & A.D. Zwicky. 1982. "Register as a Dimension of Linguistic Variation". *Sublanguage: Studies in language in restricted semantic domains* ed. by R. Kittredge & J. Lehrberger, 213-218. Berlin: Gruyter.